The Baker
COMPACT
BIBLE
Dictionary

The Baker COMPACT BIBLE Dictionary

Tremper Longman III
General Editor

Peter Enns
Old Testament Editor

Mark Strauss
New Testament Editor

a division of Baker Publishing Group
Grand Rapids, Michigan

Condensed from *The Baker Illustrated Bible Dictionary*

Published by Baker Books
a division of Baker Publishing Group
P.O. Box 6287, Grand Rapids, MI 49516-6287
www.bakerbooks.com

Printed in the United States of America

Library of Congress Cataloging-in-Publication Data

The Baker compact Bible dictionary / Tremper Longman III, general editor ; Peter Enns, Old Testament editor ; Mark Strauss, New Testament editor.

pages cm

Condensed from The Baker illustrated Bible dictionary.

ISBN 978-0-8010-1544-1 (paper)

1. Bible—Dictionaries. I. Longman, Tremper, editor of compilation.

BS440.B255 2014

220.3—dc23 2013036470

14 15 16 17 18 19 20 7 6 5 4 3 2 1

Contents

Preface

Christians read the Bible because the triune God has revealed himself to us through these pages. We worship God, not the Bible, but we learn about who God is and what pleases him through these divinely inspired words. We not only learn about God, but also about ourselves and, using the language of Jesus' parable of the sower (Mark 4:1–20), the word of God, like a seed, if planted in the rich soil of a receptive heart and mind, will transform the lives of those who read it.

The main message of the Bible is clear and easy to understand. God created everything, including us, but we rebelled against him. We need a savior, and that savior is Jesus Christ. That said, though the main message is clear, the Bible is not always easy to understand. We encounter many strange names, places, customs, and concepts. *The Baker Compact Bible Dictionary* is a handy tool that can help the interested reader gain the knowledge necessary to read the Bible with clarity of understanding.

The *Compact Bible Dictionary* is a shorter version composed of the most important entries from the much larger *Baker Illustrated Bible Dictionary*. Thus, the same team that produced the *BIBD* is to be thanked for the work that led to the *Compact Dictionary*. I served as the general editor and made the choices of which articles to include in the *Compact Dictionary* and also helped make them, well, more compact. Mark Strauss and Peter Enns were the New Testament and Old Testament editors of the *BIBD* respectively. Well over one hundred contributors wrote the articles that compose both these reference works and I thank them heartily for their labors.

I also want to express my appreciation to Baker Publishing Group. Jack Kuhatschek, my longtime friend, initiated the project by inviting me to be editor. I also want to thank Brian Vos and James Korsmo for their work on this project. The latter in particular was extremely helpful in his close reading of the text that helped us avoid many mistakes. That said, as general editor, any remaining errors are my responsibility.

My sincere prayer and hope is that this tool will help you, its user, to read the Bible with understanding so that you may come to know God even better.

Tremper Longman III
Editor

Contributors

Stephen J. Andrews, PhD, Professor of Old Testament, Hebrew, and Archaeology, Midwestern Baptist Theological Seminary, Kansas City, MO

Sarah-Jane Austin, ThM from Westminster Theological Seminary, Glenside, PA

Karelynne Gerber Ayayo, ThD, Assistant Dean of the School of Ministry and Associate Professor of Biblical Studies, Palm Beach Atlantic University, West Palm Beach, FL

Deron Biles, PhD, Dean of Extension Education and Associate Professor of Old Testament, Southwestern Baptist Theological Seminary, Fort Worth, TX

Michael F. Bird, PhD, Lecturer in Theology and Bible, Crossway College, Queensland, Australia

Tony Bird, PhD, Lecturer in Biblical Studies, Presbyterian Theological College, Melbourne, Australia

Dave L. Bland, PhD, Professor of Homiletics and DMin Director, Harding School of Theology, Memphis, TN

Art Boulet, graduate student at Columbia University, New York, NY

Norah Caudill, PhD, Adjunct Assistant Professor of Old Testament, Fuller Theological Seminary, Pasadena, CA, and Faculty Associate of Old Testament, Bethel Seminary, San Diego, CA

Rosalind S. Clarke, PhD student at Highland Theological College, Dingwall, Scotland

Bill Coe, MATS, Adjunct Professor of Music at Southwestern College, Chula Vista, CA

Rob Dalrymple, PhD, Academic Dean, Koinonia Graduate School of Theology, Livermore, CA

John A. Davies, PhD, Principal Emeritus, Presbyterian Theological Centre, Sydney, Australia

John C. DelHousaye, PhD, Associate Professor of New Testament, Phoenix Seminary, Phoenix, AZ

Joseph R. Dodson, PhD, Assistant Professor of Biblical Studies, Ouachita Baptist University, Arkadelphia, AR

Jason Driesbach, PhD student at Hebrew University of Jerusalem, Israel

Ben C. Dunson, PhD, Sessional Assistant Professor of Religion and Theology, Redeemer University College, Ancaster, Ontario, Canada

J. Scott Duvall, PhD, Professor of New Testament and J. C. and Mae Fuller Chair of Biblical Studies, Ouachita Baptist University, Arkadelphia, AR

Seth Ehorn, PhD candidate at University of Edinburgh, New College, Edinburgh, Scotland

Peter Enns, PhD from Harvard University, Cambridge, MA; Biblical Scholar and Author, Lansdale, PA

Paul S. Evans, PhD, Assistant Professor of Old Testament, McMaster Divinity College, Hamilton, Ontario, Canada

Charles Farhadian, PhD, Associate Professor of World Religions and Christian Mission, Westmont College, Santa Barbara, CA

Jerad File, MTh student at Southwestern Baptist Theological Seminary, Fort Worth, TX

David Firth, PhD, Director of Extension Studies, St. Johns College, Nottingham, England

Daniel Fletcher, PhD from Westminster Theological Seminary, Glenside, PA; Instructor, Eastern University, St. Davids, PA

Douglas Geringer, PhD candidate, Associate Professor of New Testament Language and Literature, Associate Dean of Talbot School of Theology, Biola University, La Mirada, CA

Greg Goswell, PhD, Biblical Studies Lecturer, Presbyterian Theological College, Melbourne, Australia

Scott Gray, DMin student at Southwestern Baptist Theological Seminary, Fort Worth, TX; Pastor, Sycamore Baptist Church, Decatur, TX

Brad Gregory, PhD, Assistant Professor of Scripture, University of Scranton, Scranton, PA

David P. Griffin, PhD student at University of Virginia, Charlottesville, VA

Norris Grubbs, PhD, Associate Professor of New Testament and Greek, Senior Associate Dean of Extension Center System, New Orleans Baptist Theological Seminary, New Orleans, LA

Joel Hamme, PhD candidate, Fuller Theological Seminary, Pasadena, CA; Assistant Professor at William Carey International University

Micah Haney, PhD candidate, Adjunct Professor of Old Testament, Azusa Pacific University, Azusa, CA

Matthew S. Harmon, PhD, Professor of New Testament Studies, Grace College and Theological Seminary, Winona Lake, IN

J. Daniel Hays, PhD, Professor of Biblical Studies and Dean of Pruet School of Christian Studies, Ouachita Baptist University, Arkadelphia, AR

N. Blake Hearson, PhD, Assistant Professor of Old Testament and Hebrew, Midwestern Baptist Theological Seminary, Kansas City, MO

Tim Henderson, PhD candidate, Adjunct Professor of New Testament, Bethel Seminary, St. Paul, MN

Renate Viveen Hood, PhD, Associate Professor of Christian Studies, University of Mary Hardin-Baylor, Belton, TX

Douglas S. Huffman, PhD, Professor and Associate Dean of Biblical and Theological Studies, Talbot School of Theology, La Mirada, CA

Scott Hummel, PhD, Vice President for Institutional Advancement and Church Relations and Professor of Religion, William Carey University, Hattiesburg, MS

David Jackson, PhD, Head of Biblical Studies, William Carey Christian School, Prestons, NSW, Australia, and Honorary Associate, School of Historical and Philosophical Inquiry, University of Sydney, Sydney, Australia

Scott Jackson, PhD, Associate Professor of Christian Ministries, Ouachita Baptist University, Arkadelphia, AR

Joshua T. James, PhD candidate at Fuller Theological Seminary, Pasadena, CA

Stephen Janssen, PhD candidate, Adjunct Professor of Biblical Education, Cedarville University, Cedarville, OH

Joanne J. Jung, PhD, Associate Professor of Biblical Studies and Theology, Talbot School of Theology, La Mirada, CA

Thomas Keene, PhD, Lecturer in New Testament, Westminster Theological Seminary, Glenside, PA

Shane B. Kelly, BA from Westmont College, Santa Barbara, CA

Dongsu Kim, PhD, Professor of Bible and Theology, Nyack College, New York, NY

JinKyu Kim, PhD, Professor of Old Testament, Baekseok University, Cheonan, South Korea

Koowon Kim, PhD, Faculty, Reformed Theological Seminary, Seoul, South Korea

Yoon-Hee Kim, PhD, Associate Professor of Old Testament, Torch Trinity Graduate School of Theology, Seoul, South Korea

John F. Klem, ThD, Senior Pastor, Brookdale Baptist Church, Moorhead, MN

Sheri Klouda, PhD, Associate Professor of Biblical Studies, Taylor University, Upland, IN

Will J. Kynes, PhD, Departmental Lecturer in Old Testament Studies, St. Peter's College, Oxford

Brian Labosier, PhD, Professor of Biblical Studies, Bethel Seminary, St. Paul, MN

David T. Lamb, DPhil, Associate Professor of Old Testament, Biblical Seminary, Hatfield, PA

Bernon Lee, PhD, Professor of Hebrew Scriptures, Bethel University, St. Paul, MN

Peter Y. Lee, PhD, Assistant Professor of Old Testament, Reformed Theological Seminary, Washington, DC

Michelle Lee-Barnewall, PhD, Associate Professor of Biblical and Theological Studies, Biola University, La Mirada, CA

Thomas G. Lengyel, MDiv student at Bethel Seminary, San Diego, CA

Stephen J. Lennox, PhD, Professor of Bible, Indiana Wesleyan University, Marion, IN

Darian Lockett, PhD, Associate Professor of Biblical and Theological Studies, Talbot School of Theology, La Mirada, CA

Tremper Longman III, PhD, Robert H. Gundry Professor of Biblical Studies, Westmont College, Santa Barbara, CA

Nathan Patrick Love, PhD, Associate Professor of Old Testament, Ambrose Seminary, Calgary, Alberta, Canada

Melinda G. Loyd, MA, Southwestern Baptist Theological Seminary, Fort Worth, TX

Sun Myong Lyu, PhD, Senior Pastor, Korean Presbyterian Church of Ann Arbor, Ann Arbor, MI

Robert G. Maccini, PhD from the University of Aberdeen, Aberdeen, Scotland

Thor Madsen, PhD, Dean of the College, Midwestern Baptist College, Kansas City, MO

Steven Thatcher Mann, PhD, Adjunct Professor, Azusa Pacific University, Azusa, CA

Steven Mason, PhD, Provost and Dean of Faculty for Academic Affairs and Associate Professor of Biblical Studies, LeTourneau University, Longview, TX

Nathan Mastnjak, graduate student at University of Chicago, Chicago, IL

Andrew Mbuvi, PhD, Associate Professor of Biblical Studies and Hermeneutics, Shaw University Divinity School, High Point, NC

Walter McConnell, PhD, Pastor, Belfast Chinese Christian Church, Belfast, Ireland

Susan Michaelson, MDiv from Westminster Theological Seminary, Glenside, PA; Adjunct Professor of Theology, St. Joseph's University, Philadelphia, PA

Eric A. Mitchell, PhD, Associate Professor of Old Testament and Archaeology, Southwestern Baptist Theological Seminary, Fort Worth, TX

James Mohler (deceased), PhD, Former Associate Professor of Biblical Studies and Chair of Biblical and Theological Studies, Talbot School of Theology, La Mirada, CA

Jeffrey Monk, PhD candidate and Teaching Fellow in Hermeneutics and Biblical Interpretation, Westminster Theological Seminary, Glenside, PA

Erika Moore, PhD, Associate Professor of Old Testament and Hebrew, Trinity School for Ministry, Ambridge, PA

Kathleen Murray, ThM student at Fuller Theological Seminary, Pasadena, CA

Neil Newman, MDiv from Westminster Theological Seminary, Glenside, PA

Steven M. Ortiz, PhD, Associate Professor of Archaeology and Biblical Backgrounds and Director of the Tandy Archaeology Museum, Southwestern Baptist Theological Seminary, Fort Worth, TX

Dukjoon Park, PhD candidate at Westminster Theological Seminary, Glenside, PA

C. Marvin Pate, PhD, Chair of the Department of Christian Theology and Elma Cobb Professor of Christian Theology, Ouachita Baptist University, Arkadelphia, AR

Elaine Phillips, PhD, Professor of Biblical Studies, Gordon College, Wenham, MA

Leong Cheng Michael Phua, PhD, Associate Professor of Old Testament, Singapore Bible College, Singapore

Bill Pickut, PhD student at University of Chicago, Chicago, IL

Timothy Pierce, PhD, Pastor, Woodland Heights Baptist Church, Bedford, TX, and Resident Fellow, B. H. Carroll Theological Institute, Arlington, TX

Jesse Rainbow, PhD candidate at Harvard University, Cambridge, MA

Hulisani Ramantswana, PhD, Faculty, Heidelberg Theological Seminary, Pretoria, South Africa

Melissa D. Ramos, PhD candidate at University of California Los Angeles, Los Angeles, CA

Cristian Rata, PhD, Assistant Professor of Old Testament, Torch Trinity Graduate School of Theology, Seoul, South Korea

Tiberius G. Rata, PhD, Professor of Old Testament Studies and Chair of Department of Biblical Studies, Grace College and Theological Seminary, Winona Lake, IN

David Redelings, PhD, Faculty Associate, Bethel Seminary, San Diego, CA

Rodney Reeves, PhD, Professor of Biblical Studies and Dean of the Courts, Redford

College of Theology and Ministry, Southwest Baptist University, Bolivar, MO

Randy Richards, PhD, Professor of Biblical Studies and Dean of the School of Ministry, Palm Beach Atlantic University, West Palm Beach, FL

Andrew J. Schmutzer, PhD, Professor of Bible, Moody Bible Institute, Chicago, IL

George Schwab, PhD, Professor of Old Testament, Erskine Theological Seminary, Due West, SC

Timothy Senapatiratne, PhD, Reference Librarian, Bethel Seminary, St. Paul, MN

Boyd V. Seevers, PhD, Professor of Old Testament Studies, Northwestern College, St. Paul, MN

Jerry Shepherd, PhD, Associate Professor of Old Testament, Taylor Seminary, Edmonton, Alberta, Canada

Martin Shields, PhD, Honorary Research Associate, Department of Hebrew, Biblical and Jewish Studies, University of Syndey, Sydney, Australia

Benjamin C. Shin, DMin, Associate Professor of Bible Exposition, Talbot School of Theology, La Mirada, CA

Ian Smith, PhD, Principal, Presbyterian Theological Centre, Sydney, Australia

Robert S. Snow, PhD, Assistant Professor in New Testament, Ambrose University College, Calgary, Alberta, Canada

Bradley J. Spencer, PhD candidate at Harvard University, Cambridge, MA

John Michael Stanley, MDiv from Phoenix Seminary, Phoenix, AZ; Pastor, Grace Brethren Church, Columbus, OH

Mark L. Strauss, PhD, Professor of New Testament, Bethel Seminary, San Diego, CA

Brian Tabb, PhD candidate, Assistant Professor of Biblical Studies, Bethlehem College and Seminary, Minneapolis, MN

Dieudonne Tamfu, PhD student at Southern Baptist Theological Seminary, Louisville, KY; Associate Professor of Biblical Theology, Cameroon Baptist Theological Seminary, Ndu, Cameroon

W. Franklin Thomason II, PhD student at Southwestern Baptist Theological Seminary, Fort Worth, TX; Adjunct Professor of History of Religion, Navarro College, Corsicana, TX

Karyn Traphagen, PhD student at University of Stellenbosch, South Africa

Cephas Tushima, PhD, Adjunct Professor, Eastern University, St. Davids, PA, and Lecturer, ECWA Theological Seminary, Jos, Plateau State, Nigeria

Preben Vang, PhD, Professor of Biblical and Theological Studies, Palm Beach Atlantic University, West Palm Beach, FL

Andrew E. Walton, PhD student at Harvard University, Cambridge, MA

Daniel R. Watson, PhD, Associate Professor of Old Testament, Midwestern Baptist Theological Seminary, Kansas City, MO

Ken Way, PhD, Associate Professor of Bible Exposition, Talbot School of Theology, La Mirada, CA

Brian L. Webster, PhD, Associate Professor of Old Testament Studies, Dallas Theological Seminary, Dallas, TX

Paul D. Wegner, PhD, Professor of Old Testament, Phoenix Seminary, Phoenix, AZ

Forrest Weiland, PhD, Adjunct Professor, Bethel Seminary, San Diego, CA, and North American Coordinator, Zaporozhye Bible College and Seminary, Zaporozhye, Ukraine

Joshua Williams, PhD, Assistant Professor of Old Testament, Southwestern Baptist Theological Seminary, Fort Worth, TX

Daniel Willson, student at Fuller Theological Seminary, Pasadena, CA

Michael Woodcock, PhD, Pastor, First Baptist Church, North Hollywood, CA

Michael Yankoski, MCS from Regent College, Vancouver, Canada

Stephen Young, PhD candidate at Brown University, Providence, RI

Jason Zan, MA candidate at Southwestern Baptist Theological Seminary, Fort Worth, TX

Abbreviations

General

//	parallels
Aram.	Aramaic
c.	circa
cf.	confer
chap(s).	chapter(s)
DSS	Dead Sea Scrolls
e.g.	for example
esp.	especially
Gk.	Greek
Heb.	Hebrew
i.e.	that is
Lat.	Latin
lit.	literally
LXX	Septuagint
mg.	margin
MT	Masoretic Text
NT	New Testament
OT	Old Testament
par(s).	parallel(s)
r.	reigned

Bible Versions

ESV	English Standard Version
HCSB	Holman Christian Standard Bible
KJV	King James Version
MSG	*The Message*
NAB	New American Bible
NASB	New American Standard Bible
NET	New English Translation
NIV	New International Version
NJB	New Jerusalem Bible
NKJV	New King James Version
NLT	New Living Translation
NRSV	New Revised Standard Version
REB	Revised English Bible
RSV	Revised Standard Version

Apocrypha and Septuagint

Jdt.	Judith
1–4 Macc.	1–4 Maccabees
Sir.	Sirach
Tob.	Tobit

Old Testament Pseudepigrapha

Let. Aris.	*Letter of Aristeas*
Pss. Sol.	*Psalms of Solomon*
Sib. Or.	*Sybilline Oracles*
T. Levi	*Testament of Levi*

Dead Sea Scrolls

11Q13	*11QMelchizedek*

Rabbinic Tractates

m.	*Mishnah*
Roš. Haš.	*Rosh HaShanah*

Apostolic Fathers

1–2 Clem.	*1–2 Clement*
Did.	*Didache*
Mart. Pol.	*Martyrdom of Polycarp*

Greek and Latin Works

Herodotus

Hist.	*Historiae (Histories)*

Josephus

Ant.	*Jewish Antiquities*
J.W.	*Jewish War*

Ovid

Metam.	*Metamorphoses*

Philo

Embassy	*On the Embassy to Gaius*

Pliny the Elder

Nat.	*Naturalis historia (Natural History)*

A

Aaron–Aaron was Moses' older brother and his close associate during the days when God used both of them to establish his people Israel as a nation. Aaron's particular importance came when God selected him to be the first high priest of Israel.

Aaron plays a supportive role in the Exodus account of the plagues and the departure from Egypt. He was at Moses' side. As previously arranged, Aaron was the spokesperson, acting as a prophet to Moses, who was "like God to Pharaoh" (Exod. 7:1).

The event of greatest significance involving Aaron in the wilderness was his appointment as high priest. The divine mandate for his installation is recorded in Exod. 28. Aaron did not fare well on the one occasion when he acted independently from Moses. While Moses was on Mount Sinai receiving the two tablets of the law from the hand of God, Aaron gave in to the people's request to make a calf idol out of golden earrings that they gave him.

In spite of Aaron's sin, God did not remove him from his priestly responsibilities (thanks to the prayers of Moses [Deut. 9:20]), the height of which was to preside over the annual Day of Atonement (Lev. 16). The incident of the golden calf was not the only occasion when Aaron tried God's patience. According to Num. 12, Aaron and his sister, Miriam, contested Moses' leadership. Using his marriage to a Cushite woman as a pretext, Moses' siblings asserted their equality. God, however, put them in their place, affirming Moses' primacy.

Other tribal leaders questioned Aaron's priestly leadership, according to Num. 17. Moses told all the tribal leaders to place their walking staffs along with Aaron's before God at the tent of testimony. God showed his favor toward Aaron by causing his staff to bud.

Both Moses and Aaron forfeited their right to enter the land of promise when they usurped the Lord's authority as they brought water from the rock in the wilderness (Num. 20:1–13). Sick and tired of the people's complaining, Moses wrongly ascribed the ability to make water come from the rock to himself and Aaron, and rather than speaking to the rock, he struck it twice. For this, God told them that they would die in the wilderness. Aaron's death is reported soon after this occasion (Num. 20:22–27).

In the NT, the most significant use of Aaron is in comparison to Jesus Christ, the ultimate high priest. Interestingly, the book of Hebrews argues that Jesus far surpassed the priestly authority of Aaron by connecting his priesthood to Melchizedek, a mysterious non-Israelite priest who blesses God and Abram in Gen. 14 (see Heb. 7:1–14).

Aaron's Rod–Aaron's rod is his wooden walking stick, which had a significant role in the accounts of the plagues of Egypt. In Moses and Aaron's first confrontation with Pharaoh, Aaron threw his rod to the ground, and it turned into a snake. Although the Egyptian magicians could mimic this act, Aaron's snake swallowed the snakes produced by their rods, thus showing the superiority of Aaron's God over their false gods (Exod. 7:8–13). Aaron used his rod by either extending it or striking the ground in order to initiate other plagues as well. Interestingly, Aaron's rod was featured in the early plagues, whereas Moses used his rod in some of the later and more powerful plagues as well as in the crossing of the Red Sea, perhaps showing Moses' prominence (9:23 [hail], 10:13 [locusts], 14:16 [Red Sea]).

The rod was not a magical wand but rather a symbol of the presence of God. It is best to

A

understand the rod as related to a tree that stands for God's presence. It is a portable tree.

Abaddon–A transliteration of the Hebrew word for "destruction," signifying the grave or the underworld (Rev. 9:11).

Abana–A river in the region of Damascus mentioned by the Syrian general Naaman as surpassing the Jordan River (2 Kings 5:12).

Abba–An Aramaic term for "father," used three times in the NT (Mark 14:36; Rom. 8:5; Gal. 4:6), always coupled with its Greek equivalent, *patēr*. A term of endearment used to refer to God, it demonstrates that the speaker has an intimate, loving relationship with God.

Abednego–The Babylonian name given to Azariah, one of Daniel's three friends, by Nebuchadnezzar's chief official, Ashpenaz, as part of an attempt to turn him into a Babylonian official (Dan. 1:7).

Abel–The name of Cain's brother. As Adam and Eve's second son, he is mentioned in Gen. 4:2–9 (also v. 25) as the murdered brother of Cain, who slew him out of anger at his being more favored by God for offering a better sacrifice. He is not mentioned again until the Gospels (Matt. 23:35; Luke 11:51), where he is cast as the first representative of the "righteous blood" shed on earth. In Heb. 11:4 an explanation is given for why Abel's sacrifice was favored over Cain's: it was offered in faith. In Heb. 12:24 Abel's blood is contrasted with Christ's. The nature of the contrast is not made explicit, but the context suggests that whereas both Christ and Abel were innocent, it is Christ's shed blood that is efficacious to mediate the new covenant.

Abiathar–A high priest, son of Ahimelek, first mentioned in 1 Sam. 22:20, when he escaped Saul's slaughter of the priests of Nob. He took refuge with David in the cave of Adullam and, having escaped with the ephod (1 Sam. 23:6–12), became the high priest after David's reign was established. When Absalom rebelled against David, Abiathar remained supportive (2 Sam. 15). Later, however, he supported Adonijah rather than Solomon as David's successor, which led to his banishment to his hometown, Anathoth, by Solomon, thus fulfilling Eli's prophecy (1 Sam. 2:30–35; 1 Kings 2:26–27). He is mentioned once in the NT, Mark 2:26, where Jesus recounts when David took the showbread to feed his men "in the days of Abiathar the high priest."

Abigail–The wife of Nabal, a wealthy man from Carmel (1 Sam. 25). While David was hiding from Saul in the desert, he sent a word of greeting to Nabal to ask for some food. This would have been a gesture of good faith on Nabal's part, since his servants had been treated well by David and his men (vv. 7, 15–16). Nabal treated David's request and his ten messengers with disrespect, so David intended to retaliate, even swearing that not a male would be left alive among Nabal's people (vv. 21–22). Thinking quickly, and without telling Nabal, Abigail prepared food and brought it to David. She pleaded with David not to shed any blood, which would be to act like the foolish Nabal ("Nabal" in Hebrew means "fool" [v. 25]). She asked for forgiveness on Nabal's behalf, spoke of the Lord's favor on David's "lasting dynasty" (v. 28), and said that she wished to be remembered when David's current status was behind him and his rule was established (v. 31). David was persuaded by her words. Abigail then returned home and reported to Nabal what she had done. Upon hearing the news, his heart failed and he became "like a stone" for ten days, and then God struck him dead (vv. 37–38). David rejoiced at hearing the news and then made Abigail his wife.

Abihu–The second of Aaron's four sons (Exod. 6:23). He and his older brother, Nadab, were allowed to approach the Lord on Mount Sinai with Moses, Aaron, and the seventy elders (Exod. 24:1, 9). He and his three brothers (the younger two were Eleazar and Ithamar) were made Israel's first priests (Exod. 28:1). He and Nadab "offered unauthorized fire before the Lord, contrary to his command," so they were consumed by fire (Lev. 10:1–2; cf. Num. 3:4; 26:61; 1 Chron. 24:2).

Abijah–**(1)** Samuel's second son, who, along with his older brother Joel, served as judge in Beersheba, but whose corruption drove Israel's elders to ask Samuel to appoint a king (1 Sam. 8:2–5). **(2)** Son of Jeroboam, the first king of the northern kingdom (930–909 BC). He died as a boy, in accordance with Ahijah's prophecy, because of Jeroboam's idolatry (1 Kings 14:1–18). **(3)** Son of Rehoboam, called "Abijam" in 1 Kings 15:1–8. He was the second king of the southern kingdom (913–910 BC).

Abijam–*See* Abijah.

Abilene–A region in Syria named after its chief town, Abila, located about eighteen miles northwest of Damascus. Luke reports that at the beginning of John the Baptist's ministry the region was governed by Lysanias II (Luke 3:1) as one of four rulers in the Judea province (with Pontius Pilate, Herod Antipas, and Philip).

Abimelek–**(1)** The king of Gerar who took Sarah into his house, deceived by Abraham into thinking that she was Abraham's sister. God warned Abimelek of this in a dream, so he released her and made restitution to Abraham and Sarah. He is likely the same person mentioned in Gen. 21:22–24 as one who made a treaty with Abraham at Beersheba.

(2) The king of Gerar during Isaac's lifetime (Gen. 26:1–35) and likely a son or grandson of the Abimelek mentioned in 20:1–18. As in the earlier incident with Abraham and Sarah, Isaac passed his wife, Rebekah, off as his sister, causing Abimelek great concern when he found out the truth. Abimelek ordered his people to cause no harm to the couple.

(3) Son of Gideon and his concubine (Judg. 8:31). After Gideon's death he murdered his seventy brothers in an effort to consolidate power under himself in Shechem. The youngest of the brothers, Jotham, escaped and spoke a parable against the citizens of Shechem. Three years later they rebelled against Abimelek under Gaal, but Abimelek was successful in capturing Shechem and killing many of its residents. When he attacked Thebez, he was killed by women who dropped a millstone on his head. That incident is mentioned later in 2 Sam. 11:21 by Joab as he is preparing his messenger for possible criticism by David for his strategy in besieging Rabbah.

(4) The man before whom David pretended to be insane, according to the superscription to Ps. 34. If the incident of 1 Sam. 21:10–15 is in view, where Achish the king of Gath is named, then it is possible that "Ahimelek" is a title for Philistine kings.

Abinadab–**(1)** The man in whose house the ark of the covenant rested for twenty years after it was returned by the Philistines (1 Sam. 7:1; 1 Chron. 13:7). **(2)** Son of Jesse and older brother of David who was passed over by Samuel when choosing a king (1 Sam. 16:8; 17:13; see also 1 Chron. 2:13).

Abishag–A young Shunammite woman brought to David's bed in his old age to keep him warm (1 Kings 1:3, 15). After David's death, his son Adonijah asked to marry her (1 Kings 2:17), which was a declaration of his continued attempt to secure the throne (see 1 Kings 1), for which Solomon put him to death (1 Kings 2:23–25).

Abishai–Son of Zeruiah, David's sister, and brother of Joab, David's general (1 Sam. 26:6; 1 Chron. 2:16), he was an accomplished soldier in David's army.

Abner–Son of King Saul's uncle, Ner (1 Sam. 14:50–51). Abner was Saul's military commander. He maintained loyalty to the house of Saul during Saul's struggle with David. Upon Saul's death, Abner made Saul's son Ish-Bosheth king over the northern kingdom. In battle with David's forces, Abner killed Asahel, the brother of David's military commander, Joab (2 Sam. 2:17–23). Abner rallied support for David's kingship after Ish-Bosheth accused Abner of sleeping with Saul's concubine (2 Sam. 3:7–13). Joab later murdered Abner to avenge his brother Asahel's death (3:22–27).

Abomination, Abomination of Desolation–Abomination is used of idols (e.g., 2 Kings 23:13, 24; Jer. 7:30; cf. Ezek. 8:10), forbidden practices (e.g., 2 Kings 23:24), and generally anything contrary to the true worship of Israel's God (e.g., 2 Chron. 15:8; Isa. 66:3; Jer. 4:1; cf. forbidden foods [Lev. 11:10, 13, 42] and ceremonial defilement [Lev. 7:21]). The term also includes the prohibition of idol worship (Deut. 7:25; 27:15; 32:16) but can more widely apply to immorality (e.g., Lev. 18:22, 26–27), prophecy that leads to paganism (Deut. 13:13–14), blemished animals offered in sacrifice to Yahweh (Deut. 17:1), and heathen divination (Deut. 18:9, 12).

The "abomination of desolation" (NIV: "abomination that causes desolation"), or "desolating sacrifice," refers to the desecration of the Jerusalem temple. The description occurs or is alluded to in Dan. 8:11; 9:27; 11:31; 12:11; Matt. 24:15; Mark 13:14; Luke 21:20; 2 Thess. 2:4, as well as 1 Macc. 1:54–64. These texts seem to attest to two or three stages of fulfillment of the prophecy.

Abraham–Abram is a well-known biblical character whose life is detailed in Gen.

11:25–25:11. Abram's name (which means "exalted father") is changed in Gen. 17:5 to "Abraham," meaning "father of many nations."

The narrative account in Genesis details one hundred years of Abraham's life and moves quickly through the first seventy-five years of events. In just a few verses (11:26–31) we learn that Abram was the son of Terah, the brother of Haran and Nahor, the husband of the barren Sarai (later Sarah), and the uncle of Lot, the son of Haran, who died in Ur of the Chaldees. The plot line marks significant events in Abraham's life chronologically. He left Harran at the age of 75 (12:4), was 86 when Hagar gave birth to Ishmael (16:16), 99 when the Lord appeared to him (17:17) and when he was circumcised (17:24), 100 when Sarah gave birth to Isaac (21:5), and 175 when he died (25:7). In summary, the biblical narrator paces the reader quickly through the story in such a way as to highlight a twenty-five-year period of Abraham's life between the ages of 75 and 100.

The NT features Abraham in several significant ways. The intimate connection between God and Abraham is noted in the identification of God as "the God of Abraham" in Acts 7:32 (cf. Exod. 3:6). The NT also celebrates the character of Abraham as a man of faith who received the promise (Gal. 3:9; Heb. 6:15). Abraham is most importantly an example of how one is justified by faith (Rom. 4:1, 12) and an illustration of what it means to walk by faith (James 2:21, 23).

Those who exercise faith in the living God, as did Abraham, are referred to as "children of Abraham" (Gal. 3:7). Regarding the covenant promises made to Abraham in the OT, the NT writers highlight the promises of seed and blessing. According to Paul, the seed of Abraham is ultimately fulfilled in Christ, and those who believe in Christ are the seed of Abraham (Gal. 3:16, 29). In a similar way, those who have Abraham-like faith are blessed (3:9). The blessing imparted to Abraham comes to the Gentiles through the redemption of Christ and is associated with the impartation of the Spirit (3:14).

ABRAM–*See* Abraham.

ABSALOM–The third of David's sons, born in Hebron while David was king of Judah alone. He plays a prominent role in the violence that overtook David following his murder of Uriah (2 Sam. 11). Absalom's sister Tamar was raped by his older half brother Amnon (13:1–19), and two years later he ordered his men to murder Amnon (13:23–33) before fleeing to Geshur. Joab convinced David to restore him (14:1–21). David snubbed him on his return, and he later rebelled against David, coming close to toppling him before being killed by Joab in the forest of Ephraim after his hair became caught in a tree (18:9–15).

ABYSS–In the NT, "abyss" refers to the world of the dead (Rom. 10:7; KJV, NIV: "deep") and especially the subterranean prison of disobedient spirits (fallen angels?; Luke 8:31; Rev. 9:1–2, 11; 11:7; 17:8; 20:1–3).

ACHAIA–Achaia is a region along the northern coast of the Peloponnesus, the southern peninsula of Greece. Paul's letters to the Corinthians were sent to this region (1 Cor. 16:15; 2 Cor. 1:1). In the NT, the term also has a broader meaning, so that the phrase "Macedonia and Achaia" refers inclusively to all of Greece (Acts 19:21; Rom. 15:26; 1 Thess. 1:7–8).

ACHAN–A Judahite who disobeyed Joshua and kept for himself some of the plunder from Jericho (Josh. 7:1, 21). Achan's sin was discovered after the Israelite army was defeated by the men of Ai (7:4–21). He was stoned and burned along with his family and possessions (7:25–26). The place where he was killed was known as the Valley of Achor, the valley of "trouble" (Josh. 7:26).

ACHISH–A Philistine, king of Gath. When David sought sanctuary at Gath by pretending to be insane, Achish turned him away (1 Sam. 21:10–15). When Saul continued to persecute David, David and his men allied themselves with Achish, who gave David the city of Ziklag (27:1–6).

ACHOR–A valley in northern Judea (Josh. 15:7). Achor was the place where judgment was rendered to Achan after he stole plunder from Jericho (Josh. 7:24–26). The prophets envision the transformation of Achor into a verdant area (Isa. 65:10; Hos. 2:15).

ACROPOLIS–An acropolis (lit., "high city") is the elevated portion of an ancient city, typically containing temples, palaces, or other public architecture. The most famous acropolis in the Greco-Roman world was that of Athens, where the Parthenon stands. Paul preached within sight of the Athenian acropolis, already ancient by his time, on the nearby Areopagus during his visit to the city (Acts 17:19–34).

Acts of the Apostles–This book, commonly referred to simply as Acts, is the sequel to the Gospel of Luke and records the exciting history of the first three decades of the early church. The book begins with the ascension of Jesus, followed by his sending of the Holy Spirit, and ends with the gospel message being proclaimed by Paul as a prisoner in the capital city of the Roman Empire. In the pages in between, the reader is introduced to the key people, places, and events of this strategic and crucial time of Christian history.

In terms of authorship, the book technically is anonymous; however, there are good reasons for holding to church history's traditional view that its author is Luke.The specific recipient of Acts is Theophilus (1:1). Theophilus could be characterized as a relatively new believer of high social status, a person educated in Greco-Roman rhetoric and history, and one who possessed the financial means to promote and publish Luke's work (both the Gospel of Luke and Acts).

Witnesses in Jerusalem (Acts 1:1–8:3). Immediately following his ascension, Jesus tells his followers to return to Jerusalem and wait for the coming of the Holy Spirit. They promptly obey, and after ten days of waiting, the disciples are dramatically filled with the Holy Spirit and begin to share the gospel with those around them. This event occurs at the Jewish Pentecost festival, which was attended by Jews and Jewish proselytes from throughout the Roman Empire. After the Spirit comes at Pentecost, Peter boldly preaches to the crowds, and over three thousand people respond with saving faith (2:41).

Luke next provides a summary of the Spirit-led life within the early church. This life is characterized by the early believers' participation together in the sharing of worship activities, material possessions, and spiritual blessings (2:42–47). This summary is followed by several dramatic healing miracles accomplished through Peter and the subsequent arrest of Christian leaders by Jewish religious authorities. Instead of squelching the Christian movement, however, these arrests only enhance the spiritual revival and its accompanying miracles. This revival is characterized by extreme generosity and unity within the early church (4:32–37).

The revival joy, however, is marred by the deceitful actions of Ananias and Sapphira, who lie to the church and to the Holy Spirit and are judged by God with immediate death (5:1–11). This story proves that God will go to extreme lengths to protect the unity of his church. Following more persecution and miracles, the disciples choose seven men to oversee distribution of food to Hellenistic widows who have been neglected in daily food distributions (6:1–7). One of these leaders, Stephen, is arrested and brought before the Sanhedrin. Stephen testifies boldly before the Jewish leaders and is promptly executed by stoning (chap. 7). This execution is endorsed by Saul, a zealous Pharisee who begins to lead fierce persecution against the church in Jerusalem (8:1–3).

Witnesses in Judea and Samaria (Acts 8:4–12:25). Saul's persecution forces many of the early church believers to leave Jerusalem. These believers scatter throughout the surrounding areas of Judea and Samaria. As they scatter, however, they continue to preach the gospel (8:4). Philip preaches in Samaria and performs many miraculous signs, producing a spiritual revival in the region. Hearing about this, the apostles send Peter and John to Samaria to minister to the Samaritans (8:18–25), thus confirming the cross-cultural nature of the gospel (Samaritans traditionally were hated by the Jews). Next Luke tells of Philip's evangelizing of an Ethiopian eunuch (8:26–40).

Following the Ethiopian's belief in Jesus, the narrative tells of Saul's dramatic conversion while traveling to Damascus to persecute Christians there (9:1–19). Saul's turnaround is met with suspicion by the other disciples, but eventually he is accepted by the believers with the help of Barnabas (9:27–30). Next Peter travels to the Judean countryside and heals the paralytic Aeneas and raises Dorcas from the dead (9:32–42). These miracles produce a spiritual revival in the region. Following this, God gives Peter a vision to go to the coastal city of Caesarea in order to minister to Cornelius, a Roman army officer. Cornelius is a God-fearer, and through Peter's witness he responds to the gospel message and receives the Holy Spirit (chap. 10). Peter explains his actions with Cornelius to his concerned Jewish companions and verifies that God has indeed included the Gentiles in his plan of salvation (11:1–18).

A

This verification is followed by the report of what is happening in the church at Antioch, where Jews begin to share the gospel with larger groups of Gentiles (11:19–21). This cross-cultural evangelism produces a spiritual revival in Antioch, causing the Jerusalem church to send Barnabas to the large Syrian city to investigate (11:22–30). Barnabas confirms that God is indeed at work in Antioch and invites Saul to come and help him disciple the new Gentile believers (11:25–26). Next Luke reports more persecution breaking out against Christians in Jerusalem, resulting in the arrest of James and Peter by King Herod. James is executed, but Peter miraculously escapes from prison with the help of an angel (12:1–19), and the church continues to increase, spreading throughout the Roman Empire.

Witnesses to the ends of the earth (Acts 13:1–28:31). Starting with chapter 13, the narrative shifts its focus from the ministry of Peter to that of Paul (formerly Saul). The church at Antioch begins to take center stage over the church at Jerusalem. This church commissions Paul and Barnabas and sends them off on their first missionary journey, accompanied by Barnabas's cousin John Mark. The missionaries first sail to Cyprus, where they preach in synagogues and encounter a Jewish sorcerer, Bar-Jesus. Next they sail to Pamphylia, thus crossing into Asia Minor, and preach the gospel in Pisidian Antioch, Iconium, Lystra, and Derbe (this area was known as part of the region of Galatia). In these cities, God provides numerous miracles, and the missionaries experience a great response to the gospel as well as much persecution because of the gospel. On one occasion, Paul is actually stoned and left for dead (14:19–20).

Unfazed, Paul and his team boldly continue their mission. Eventually, they retrace their steps, strengthen the churches that they have started, and sail back to Syrian Antioch, where they give an exciting report to the church (14:26–28). Following this report, Luke tells of an important meeting of church leaders in Jerusalem (the Apostolic or Jerusalem Council). The subject of the meeting involves whether or not the new Gentile Christians should be required to follow the Jewish laws and customs. After debating the issue, the leaders side with Paul, determining that the Gentiles should not be burdened with Jewish laws and traditions, but simply must live moral lives and not eat food that has been sacrificed to idols (chap. 15).

Following this meeting, Paul and Barnabas decide to make a second missionary journey. Unfortunately, the two missionaries get into a dispute over whether to take John Mark with them again. The argument is such that the missionaries decide to separate, and Paul chooses a new partner, Silas. They travel by land back to Galatia. Barnabas takes John Mark and sails to Cyprus. Paul and Silas return to Derbe and Lystra and then make their way to Macedonia and Greece. They spend significant time in Philippi, Thessalonica, and Corinth before returning to Caesarea and Antioch (chaps. 16–18). Following his return, Paul makes a third missionary journey, revisiting churches in Galatia and Phrygia and staying in Ephesus for three years before visiting Macedonia and Greece for a second time.

Paul concludes his third missionary journey with a trip to Jerusalem, where he is falsely accused of bringing a Gentile into the temple. This accusation creates a riot, and Paul is rescued by Roman soldiers, who arrest him and transfer him to a prison in Caesarea, where he spends two years awaiting trial under the rule of Felix and Festus (23:34–25:22). Paul eventually exercises his right as a Roman citizen to have his case heard by the emperor. He is sent to Rome by boat and is shipwrecked on the island of Malta. Eventually he makes his way to the capital city, where he is placed under house arrest. While in Rome, Paul maintains a rented house and is free to receive visitors and write letters. In fact, it is thought that Paul penned his "prison letters" during this time of house arrest (Ephesians, Philippians, Colossians, Philemon). The narrative of Acts ends with Paul ministering boldly in Rome while awaiting his trial.

Adam–*See* Adam and Eve.

Adam, Town of–A town on the western bank of the Jordan River near Zarethan, just below where the Jabbok River empties into the Jordan. It was here that the waters of the Jordan stopped so that the Israelites under the leadership of Joshua could cross into Canaan further to the south, opposite Jericho (Josh. 3:14–17).

Adam and Eve–The first human beings. According to Gen. 2, God created Adam (whose name means "humanity" and is related to the word for "ground") from the dust of the ground and his own breath, showing that humankind is a part of creation but has a special relationship with God. God placed Adam in a garden in Eden (a name that means "delight" or "abundance"). Even so, God, noting that it was not good for Adam to be alone, created Eve (whose name means "living"), his female counterpart. She was created from Adam's side (or rib), signifying their equality. She was to be his "helper," a word that does not denote subordination. Eve was Adam's wife, and God pronounced that future marriage will be characterized by leaving one's parents, being joined as a couple, and consummating the relationship with sexual intercourse (Gen. 2:24).

Adam and Eve were to tend the garden of Eden. They were permitted to eat the fruit of all the trees of the garden except for the tree of the knowledge of good and evil. Eating the fruit of this tree, against God's express prohibition, would be an assertion of moral independence that would meet with God's punishment.

In Gen. 3 the serpent convinced Eve that it would be good to eat the fruit of the forbidden tree. Adam was present with her as the serpent spoke, but he remained silent. After eating the fruit, Eve gave some to Adam, and he ate without protest. Both Adam and Eve were therefore guilty of the first sin. The results were immediate, including the alienation of Adam and Eve, signaled by the fact that they could no longer stand naked before each other without shame.

Adam and Eve were punished for their rebellion. Eve was punished in her most intimate relationships. She would now experience increased pain when giving birth, and her relationship with her husband would become a power struggle as her desire to control him would be met with his attempt to dominate her (Gen. 3:16). Adam felt the consequences of his action in his work, which now would be tinged with frustration (3:17–19). In addition, although they did not die immediately, they were removed from the garden and access to the tree of life, so death would be their ultimate end.

After Adam and Eve departed from the garden, they had children. We know of Cain and Abel, whose conflict is well known from Gen. 4. After the death of Abel, Eve gave birth to Seth.

In the NT, Adam is mentioned in the Lukan genealogy of Jesus (Luke 3:38) and in Rom. 5:12–21; 1 Cor. 15; 1 Tim. 2:13–14; Jude 14. In Romans, Paul associates Adam with the entry of sin and death into the world. Paul contrasts Adam with Christ. Whereas Adam's act introduced sin and death, Christ's act brought reconciliation with God and life. Paul makes essentially the same point in 1 Cor. 15 (see esp. vv. 22, 45). Christians thus read Gen. 3 through the commentary supplied by Paul and believe that it supports the notion of original sin, that all humans are sinners from birth.

Eve is mentioned twice in the NT. In 1 Tim. 2:11–15 Paul argues that women should learn quietly and not teach or have authority over men because Eve was created after Adam and was the one deceived by the serpent. Debate surrounds the issue whether Paul here addresses a local situation or is citing a universal principle. Paul again mentions the deception of Eve in 2 Cor. 11:3, but here he applies it to men and women who are in danger of being deceived by false teachers.

Adoni-Bezek–The leader of Bezek who was defeated by men of the tribes of Judah and Simeon early in the conquest of Canaan.

Adonijah–David's fourth son, a rival to Solomon for the succession to David's throne. When David became old, Adonijah strengthened his claim on the throne greatly by garnering the support of Joab and Abiathar (1 Kings 1:7), whose support Absalom had failed to win in his earlier rebellion. When David heard of Adonijah's actions, he instructed his leaders to install Solomon as king in Gihon, which they did so loudly that Adonijah and his supporters were able to hear the commotion at their own feast (1:33–41). Solomon mercifully chose not to kill Adonijah for his treason (1:50–53). The peace between Solomon and Adonijah quickly came to an end when Adonijah requested that Abishag the Shunammite, a virgin attendant of David, be given to him as a wife. Solomon then ordered Benaiah to kill Adonijah.

Adoni-Zedek–The Amorite king of Jerusalem who organized a five-city coalition to attack the city of Gibeon after its capitulation to Joshua (Josh. 10:1–3).

Adoption–The voluntary process of granting the rights, privileges, responsibilities, and status of child or heir to an individual or group that was not originally born to the adopter. While birth occurs naturally, adoption occurs only through the exertion of will. Two significant figures in the OT were adopted, Moses (Exod. 2:10) and Esther (Esther 2:7).

Although adoption is fairly uncommon in the OT, God's adoption of Israel is of the utmost importance. It demonstrates God's willingness to initiate relationship with humankind, a truth that later culminated in Jesus Christ. God chooses to adopt the nation of Israel as his child (Deut. 7:6; Isa. 1:2; Hos. 11:1) and more significantly as his firstborn son (Exod. 4:22; Jer. 31:9).

The concept of adoption is more prevalent in the NT, primarily in the apostle Paul's writings. Based on the belief that Israel's exclusive position as the adopted firstborn son of God the Father is no longer deserved, the NT includes those who believe in Jesus Christ as adopted children of God's eternal family (John 1:12; 11:52; Gal. 4:5; Eph. 1:5; Phil. 2:15; 1 John 3:1). The adopted children of God enjoy all the rights of a natural-born child, including the opportunity to call God "Father," as Jesus did (e.g., Matt. 5:16; Luke 12:32). Paul in particular uses adoption to describe the Christian's new relationship with God through the atoning sacrifice of Jesus Christ (Rom. 8:15–16, 21–23; 9:25–26).

Adrammelek–**(1)** A god of the people of Sepharvaim. After the exile of the northern kingdom, the king of Assyria transplanted people from all over his empire into the territory that he had taken from the Israelites. Each of these people groups "made its own gods in the several towns where they settled" (2 Kings 17:29). Those people who had been transplanted from Sepharvaim established worship of Adrammelek and Anammelek in former Israelite territory by sacrificing their own children in fire (2 Kings 17:31).

(2) One of the sons of the Assyrian emperor Sennacherib who, along with his brother Sharezer, assassinated his father in the temple of Nisrok and escaped to the land of Ararat.

Adramyttium–*See* Asia Minor, Cities of.

Adriatic Sea–The Adriatic Sea is a portion of the Mediterranean Sea that separates Italy from Greece. It was in these waters that Paul found himself adrift for fourteen days during his trip to Rome to plead his case before Caesar (Acts 27:27).

Adullam–A city in the western foothills of Judah, located about fifteen miles southwest of Jerusalem (Josh. 15:35). Prior to the conquest of Canaan, the patriarch Judah lived for some time in Adullam (Gen. 38:1–5). The Israelites conquered the city several hundred years later under Joshua (Josh. 12:15), and Rehoboam fortified the city after the division of Israel (2 Chron. 11:7). Adullam became a refuge for David both before and after his enthronement (1 Sam. 22:1–2; 2 Sam. 23:13–17).

Micah warned the people of Adullam and several nearby cities that disaster was imminent (Mic. 1:10–15); this materialized when Sennacherib captured all the fortified cities of Judah (Isa. 36:1). The Bible does not mention Adullam again until Nehemiah's returnees from exile reestablish an Israelite presence in the city during the time of Artaxerxes (Neh. 11:30).

Adultery–One of the sins forbidden in the Ten Commandments (Exod. 20:14; Deut. 5:18). Narrowly interpreted, the prohibition forbids extramarital relations with a married woman (Lev. 20:10), but it is applied more broadly in Lev. 20 and Deut. 22–24 to cover a variety of sexual offenses.

Adversary–A human or heavenly opponent. Adversaries include David's soldiers (2 Sam. 19:22), David (1 Sam. 29:4), and God (Num. 22:22). God both raises up (1 Kings 11:14) and delivers one from (Ps. 107:2) adversaries. In Job, the adversary (Heb. *satan*) works for God (Job 1:7–12).

Advocate–In John 14:16, 26; 15:26; 16:7 the term *paraklētos* (lit., "called alongside" [NRSV, NIV: "Advocate"; RSV: "Counselor"]) refers to the Holy Spirit, sent as the Spirit of truth. The advocacy roles of the Spirit are to remain with God's people; to teach, remind, and testify about Jesus; to convict the world of guilt regarding sin; and to guide into all truth. In 1 John 2:1 Jesus is the *paraklētos* who speaks in defense of his children.

Agabus–The only church-era prophet whose spoken words are recorded in Scripture. Agabus was one of a company of prophets who traveled from Jerusalem to the fledgling church at Antioch (Acts 11:27–28).

Agag–A title used for the king of the Amalekites. When Balak king of Moab hired Balaam to curse the Israelites, Balaam blessed Israel in an oracle, including a prophecy that Israel's king would "be greater than Agag" (Num. 24:7).

Agagite–Haman, the opponent of Mordecai, is identified as an Agagite (Esther 3:1, 10; 8:3, 5; 9:24). Given Mordecai's descent from Kish, father of Saul (2:5), the term is intended to recall the Amalekite king (Agag) whom Saul spared (1 Sam. 15). *See also* Agag.

Agriculture–For the biblical Israelites and their ancestors, agriculture was one of the primary expressions of subsistence in their economy and life. The priority of agricultural pursuits for Israel's worldview is indicated in the fact that it was among the first mandates given by God to man in the garden (Gen. 1:28–29).

The primary produce of the biblical farmer included cereals (wheat, barley, millet), legumes (beans, peas), olives, and grapes. Less predominant crops included nuts (almonds, walnuts, pistachios), herbs (cumin, coriander, sesame), and vegetables (cucumbers, onions, greens). The production of the various crops was largely limited to certain geographic regions of Israel (such as the coastal plain or the plains of Moab) because much of the land was ill suited for agriculture, being rocky and arid.

The actual craft of agriculture involved the three steps of sowing, reaping, and threshing/production. The fields typically were plowed following the first autumn rains, and sowing lasted about two months. Harvest season lasted seven months in all. Cereal products went through the process of threshing, whereas fruits were immediately produced into wine or dried. The practice of threshing the grains mostly took place on threshing floors located adjacent to the fields. The threshing floors were designed as a circle, generally twenty-five to forty feet in diameter. Typically animals such as donkeys or oxen were driven around the floor as the grains were fed into their paths and subsequently crushed. The resulting broken husks were then thrown into the air, allowing the wind to carry away the chaff and producing a separated grain that could then be cleaned and processed for home use.

Besides playing a significant role in the practical matters of life, agricultural practices found numerous applications in the images and ideals of the biblical writers (Judg. 8:2; 9:8–15; Ezek. 17:6–10). The medium could be used to express both blessings and curses. Several texts point to the cursing of agricultural endeavors as a punishment from God. Ceremonial defilement was a possibility if proper methodology in sowing seeds was not followed (Lev. 19:19; Deut. 22:9). Similarly, Yahweh's assessment of Israel's failure to uphold the covenant commitments could lead to disease, locust attacks, crop failure, and total loss of the land (Deut. 28:40; Joel 1:4; Amos 7:1). Conversely, agricultural bounty and blessings were also a part of covenant stipulations. Indeed, many of the offerings themselves were centered on agriculture (Lev. 2; Num. 18:8–32). Even the Sabbath rest itself was extended to matters of agriculture and care for the land (Lev. 25:1–7). Finally, the covenant saw some of the greatest benefits of life before Yahweh as being blessed through agricultural bounty (Deut. 28:22; Amos 9:13). In a few cases, agricultural imagery cut both ways. For instance, the vine was an image that could express judgment, care, and restoration in both Judaism and Christianity (Isa. 5:1–8; John 15:1–11). Despite the link between agricultural realities and the covenant, the Scriptures are very careful to distinguish Israel from the fertility cults of its Canaanite neighbors (1 Kings 18:17–40; Hos. 2:8–9). This distinction also seems to have found expression in certain NT texts (1 Cor. 6:15–20).

Agrippa–*See* Herod.

Agur–The son of Jakeh whose oracle is recorded in Prov. 30. Agur directs his oracle to Ithiel and Ukal (Prov. 30:1; see NIV mg.).

Ahab–**(1)** Son of Omri, king of Israel, whom he succeeded, reigning for twenty-two years (871–852 BC). The summary of Ahab's reign in 1 Kings 16:29–33 serves as a prologue to the Elijah narrative, identifying the issue that Elijah addressed: Ahab's patronage of Baal at the instigation of his foreign wife, Jezebel. Ahab is condemned by the writer of 1 Kings in superlative terms (16:33).

(2) Son of Kolaiah, Ahab was a false prophet whom Jeremiah condemned in his letter to the exiles (Jer. 29:21–23).

Ahasuerus–*See* Xerxes.

Ahava–A place in Babylonia to which a canal flowed (Ezra 8:15). Ezra's camp on the Ahava Canal served as the launching point for his expedition to Jerusalem during the reign of the Persian king Artaxerxes (Ezra 8:31).

A

Ahaz–Son of Jotham, king of Judah, and father of Hezekiah. His reign is described in 2 Kings 16 and 2 Chron. 28, and his confrontation by the prophet Isaiah in Isa. 7:1–17. Ahaz reigned for sixteen years (743–727 BC). He followed the syncretistic pagan practices of the Israelite kings. When besieged by the Syrian and Israelite kings, with the aim of replacing him with a puppet ruler (734 BC), he sent a massive tribute to elicit Assyrian protection (2 Kings 16:5–9). This resulted in pro-Assyrian religious compromise (16:10–18). The goal of Isaiah's embassy to the fearful Ahaz was to encourage a response of faith (Isa. 7:9). Though Isaiah offered him any sign of his choosing, Ahaz masked his refusal in a facade of piety about not testing God (Isa. 7:10–12; cf. Deut. 6:16). The hypocritical Ahaz did not want a sign because he had no intention of trusting God in this national crisis. The exasperated prophet responded by announcing the sign of Immanuel.

Ahaziah–**(1)** Ahaziah became the eighth king over the northern kingdom of Israel after his father, Ahab, died in battle (1 Kings 22:40). He reigned for only two years (852–851 BC) and he served and worshiped Baal (22:51–53).

(2) Ahaziah the son of Jehoram became the sixth king of Judah around 843 BC. During his one-year reign he "did evil in the eyes of the Lord" (2 Kings 8:27). He became an ally of King Jehoram (Joram) of Israel against King Hazael of Aram, but both were killed in Jehu's revolt (8:28–29; 9:16–29).

Ahijah–The prophet from Shiloh who superintended the division of Solomon's united kingdom (928 BC). He predicted to Jeroboam that he would tear away ten tribes from the Davidic house (1 Kings 11:29–39). This prediction was fulfilled after Solomon's death (1 Kings 12:15; 2 Chron. 10:15). Certain events in Solomon's reign were written up in "the prophecy of Ahijah the Shilonite" (2 Chron. 9:29). Later, Jeroboam's wife went in disguise to Ahijah to inquire about her sick son. Ahijah predicted the death of the child and the destruction of Jeroboam's entire house as a punishment for idolatry (1 Kings 14:1–16). Both predictions came true (1 Kings 14:17–18; 15:29).

Ahikam–One of King Josiah's royal advisers, Ahikam was part of the delegation that Josiah sent to the prophetess Huldah to inquire about the future of the kingdom of Judah in light of its wickedness before the Lord (2 Kings 22:12–14). Ahikam supported Jeremiah during the reign of Jehoiakim; this support saved Jeremiah from being put to death by the people of Judah (Jer. 26:24). Nebuchadnezzar appointed Ahikam's son Gedaliah as governor over the remnant in Judah after the Babylonian deportation (Jer. 40:5).

Ahimaaz–Son of Zadok the priest. As David fled from Jerusalem during his son Absalom's conspiracy, he told Zadok and Abiathar, also a priest, to return with their sons to Jerusalem and to bring him information about Absalom's military plans (2 Sam. 15:27–29). When Zadok and Abiathar learned of Absalom's plans, they informed Ahimaaz and Abiathar's son Jonathan. Ahimaaz and Jonathan had to flee to Bahurim and hide in a well when Absalom's men learned of their presence in nearby En Rogel. After their pursuers could not find them, the two men delivered the news to David (17:15–22). Ahimaaz was eager to inform David of his son Absalom's defeat and became the first to tell David of his victory by outrunning another messenger. However, Ahimaaz concealed the news of Absalom's death (18:19–33).

Ahithophel–From the town of Giloh, he was originally King David's most respected and wise adviser (2 Sam. 15:12; 16:23). Ahithophel allied himself with King David's son Absalom during Absalom's rebellion. Ahithophel committed suicide in Giloh, presumably anticipating the defeat of Absalom and David's reprisal for his treason (2 Sam. 17:23).

Ai–The Hebrew term behind Ai means "the ruin." Biblical Ai was situated east of Bethel in the highlands of Ephraim overlooking the Jordan Valley.

In the Bible, Ai first appears as a landmark in Abram's travels (Gen. 12:8; 13:3). In the book of Joshua, it figures prominently as a lesser city in the initial conquest of Canaan (7:3; 10:2; but see 8:25). Following Israel's initial defeat (7:4–5), Joshua proscribes Ai according to Yahweh's instruction (8:2), slaying its inhabitants and hanging its king, then reducing the settlement to a ruin (8:25–28). This strikes fear into the neighboring populations (9:3–4; 10:1–2). The disproportionate attention given to its capture sets the conquest within a theological framework: victory depends on obedience to Yahweh.

Aijalon–The Aijalon Valley provided access from the northern Philistine Plain on the Mediterranean Sea through the foothills to the hill country. The city of Aijalon was near the eastern end of the valley. During Israel's conquest of Canaan, a confederation of Canaanite cities attacked the Gibeonites, who had made an alliance with the Israelites (Josh. 9–10). The Israelites defeated the confederation forces at Gibeon and pursued them west through the Aijalon Valley. Some centuries later, after Jonathan and his armor bearer attacked the Philistine outpost at Mikmash in the hill country, the Israelites struck them down from Mikmash to Aijalon in the valley (1 Sam. 14:31).

Akeldama–The place where Judas Iscariot met his demise after betraying Jesus. According to the book of Acts, with the money he received for betraying Jesus to the chief priests, he bought a field, where "he fell headlong, his body burst open and all his intestines spilled out"; the inhabitants of Jerusalem called the field "Akeldama," an Aramaic name meaning "field of blood" (Acts 1:18–19). According to Matt. 27:7–8, the field was purchased by the chief priests and subsequently used as a burial place for foreigners.

Aksah–The daughter of Caleb who was given as a wife to Othniel when he captured the city of Debir (Josh. 15:16–17; Judg. 1:12–13).

Alexander the Great–Alexander, born in 356 BC, was the son of Philip, king of Macedon. The amazing, swift conquests of Alexander are alluded to in Daniel. Daniel 8:5–8 (cf. 2:40–43; 7:19–24) portrays Greece as the "goat" from the west, with a notable horn between its eyes (representing Alexander), which defeats the ram (the Medo-Persian army). This prophecy was fulfilled when Alexander led the Greek armies across the Hellespont into Asia Minor in 334 BC and defeated the Persian forces at the river Granicus. Alexander again met and quickly defeated the Persians at Issus ("without touching the ground" [Dan. 8:5]). Alexander then turned south, moving down the Syrian coast and conquering Egypt without a blow. He then moved eastward, again defeating Darius the Persian for the last time, east of the Tigris River. Babylon, Susa, and Persepolis (the last two were capitals of Persia) all fell to the young warrior king. Alexander marched his armies as far eastward as the Hydaspes River in India and won a decisive battle there. Because his armies refused to go any further, however, Alexander was forced to return to Persepolis and then to Babylon. There he died in 323 BC at the age of thirty-three.

Alexandria–Alexandria was a Greek city founded in Egypt in 331 BC by Alexander the Great. It soon became the capital of Egypt. In the Bible, Alexandria is mentioned only in the book of Acts: the home of some of the Jews who opposed Stephen (6:9); the home of Apollos (18:24); the source of ships that helped carry Paul to Rome (27:6; 28:11).

Alms–Provision for the extremely needy. Alms provide what is essential to human survival: food, clothing, and shelter (1 Tim. 6:8).

Alpha and Omega–The first and last letters of the Greek alphabet. The book of Revelation uses "the Alpha and the Omega" for God or Christ (1:8; 21:6; 22:13) and closely connects it with "First and Last" and "the Beginning and the End" (1:17; 2:8; 21:6; 22:13) to declare God's sovereign control of history.

Altar–Altars were places of sacrifice and worship constructed of various materials. They could be either temporary or permanent. Some altars were in the open air; others were set apart in a holy place. They could symbolize either God's presence and protection or false worship that would lead to God's judgment.

Amalek, Amalekites–The Amalekites inhabited the Negev territory south of Judah (Num. 13:29). The OT represents the Amalekites as descended from Esau and thus related to the Edomites (Gen. 36:12, 16).

The history of relations between the Amalekites and the Israelites is one of perpetual hostility. The Amalekites attacked the Israelites shortly after the Red Sea crossing. The outcome of the battle included a declaration of perpetual war between the Amalekites and the God of Israel (Exod. 17:8–16; Deut. 25:17–19). There were several subsequent conflicts (Num. 14:45; Judg. 3:13; 6:3, 33; 7:12; 10:12), continuing in the campaigns of Saul (1 Sam. 15:1–9) and David (1 Sam. 27:8; 30:16–20).

The final chapter in the historic struggle between Israel and the Amalekites is Mordecai and Esther's confrontation with Haman, who

A

is identified as an "Agagite"—that is, a descendant of Agag, the Amalekite king spared by Saul (Esther 3:1; cf. 1 Sam. 15:8).

AMANA–A mountain mentioned in Song 4:8, associated with the more commonly known Hermon. *See* Hermon, Mount.

AMASA–A relative of David (2 Sam. 19:13). Absalom, during the rebellion against David his father, appointed Amasa as the leader of his army. Following Absalom's defeat, which included his death, David requested that Amasa continue to serve as the military commander (2 Sam. 19:13). Upon his arrival in Jerusalem, David ordered Amasa to summon the men of Judah due to an uprising incited by the Benjamite Sheba and to return before the king within three days. Amasa arrived late; as a result, David sent men out under the command of Abishai to pursue Sheba. When Amasa finally met up with the men, he was greeted by Joab, who killed him with a dagger. Once Amasa's body was removed from the road, the men followed Joab in pursuit of Sheba (2 Sam. 20:1–13).

AMAZIAH–**(1)** The son of King Joash of Judah who succeeded him on the throne after the murder of his father (2 Kings 12:21). His reign is narrated in 2 Kings 14:1–22; 2 Chron. 25. Amaziah was twenty-five years of age when he became king, and he reigned twenty-nine years (798–769 BC). He was one of the better kings of Judah, though not measuring up to David's high standard (2 Kings 14:3).

(2) "The priest of Bethel" (Amos 7:10), which may signal that Amaziah was head priest of this northern shrine, a position also suggested by the authoritative way in which he rebuked and tried to silence Amos. In instructing Amos not to prophesy, Amaziah directly contradicted God's words (7:15–16). Amaziah's opposition earned him an oracle personally directed at him and his priestly family (7:17), the only oracle of Amos against an individual. Amaziah would die "in an unclean country" (NIV mg.), preventing him from exercising priestly functions.

AMMI–This name occurs only in Hosea as a symbolic name for one of Hosea's children (see 2:1). It means "my people." The term is used particularly of Israel, especially to express the covenant relationship between God and his people. Its negation (1:9) and subsequent affirmation (2:23) seem to make a powerful statement about God's judgment and also his restoration of his unfaithful people.

AMMINADIB–This word occurs only in Song 6:12 (KJV). If it is a proper name (so LXX, KJV), the identity of the person is unknown (NIV mg.: "Amminadab"). The expression seems to mean "my people is princely" or something similar. English Bibles vary widely in their translations, though most seem to take the expression as a reference to magnificent chariots fit for a bridal party. A good translation might be: "Before I knew it, my desire placed me (among) the noble chariots of my people" (cf. NIV).

AMMON, AMMONITES–Ben-Ammi was the son of Abraham's nephew Lot and the younger of Lot's two daughters (Gen. 19:36–38). He is represented as the ancestor of the Ammonites, a Transjordanian people who were a perennial threat to Israel from the wilderness period through to David's reign.

The nation of Ammon was located east of the Jordan, just north of the Dead Sea. Its capital was Rabbah, and it bordered Gad to the west, the half-tribe of Manasseh to the northwest, and Moab to the south (see also Deut. 3:16). Much of the source of their contention was over the fertile land of Gilead, which encompassed the Jordan River and bordered Ephraim, the western tribe of Manasseh, Benjamin, and Judah.

AMNON–The firstborn son of King David (2 Sam. 3:2). He became infatuated with the beauty of his half-sister Tamar. Then he listened to counsel to deceive her and David. When she brought him a meal, he raped her. Afterward, he despised her. Tamar's brother Absalom cared for her and later deceived Amnon and David by inviting Amnon to a feast. There Absalom had Amnon killed (2 Sam. 13). David is portrayed as an ineffective leader throughout.

AMON–The fourteenth king of Judah (641–640 BC) and the son of Manasseh, he continued unrepentant in idolatrous worship. He was assassinated by his officials in his second year as king (2 Kings 21:19–26; 2 Chron. 33:21–25; Zeph. 1:4; 3:4, 11).

AMORITES–One of the nations that occupied part of Canaan and the Transjordan (by the Jordan River) before Israel's conquest. They appear in lists of the peoples occupying Canaan (e.g., Gen. 15:21). According to the Table of Nations (Gen. 10), they are descendants of Canaan, one of the sons of Ham. This territory was conquered by Abram and his forces (Gen. 14), and in fact Abram was living "near the great trees of Mamre the Amorite" (14:13). Later the Israelites remain enslaved for four generations because the sin of the Amorites has not reached its full measure (15:16).

The Amorites were constantly in conflict with the Israelites. They were to be driven out of Canaan, along with the other Canaanite peoples (Exod. 23:23; 33:2). In Num. 21:21 the Amorites are mentioned as one nation through which Israel would need to go in order to reach Canaan. King Sihon refused, a war ensued, and the Israelites were victorious and settled in the land of the Amorites (Num. 21:31).

Amos–*See* Amos, Book of.

Amos, Book of–Amos is largely concerned with judgment oracles against the nations, particularly Judah and Israel.

Amos has a message of divine judgment against God's people, particularly those in the northern kingdom. God is sovereign and will see to the appropriate punishment. God controls the nations, so he can raise up an enemy to bring destruction on Israel as well as other offending nations. Although the nations are the tool of his anger, there should be no mistake that it is God himself who is behind their punishment (1:4; 3:2, 14; 9:4).

The punishment is for idolatry and ethical violations, particularly social injustice. God's people worshiped false gods (2:8; 5:5, 26; 7:9–13; 8:14). Also, the wealthy classes indulged in sins and oppressed the lower classes (2:7–8; 5:12; 8:6).

Amos is also well known as the first to use the language of the "day of the Lord" (5:18–20). Although this appears to be the first mention of this day in Scripture, the way Amos refers to it indicates that it was already known in his society. The people thought that the day of the Lord would be good for them, but Amos says that because of their sins, it will be horrible. The day of the Lord is the day of God's coming as a warrior to judge sinners.

Amram–Grandson of Levi, son of Kohath (Exod. 6:16–18; 1 Chron. 6:1–2), and the father of Aaron, Moses, and Miriam (Exod. 6:20; 1 Chron. 6:3).

Amraphel–A member of a coalition of four kings who raided Canaan during Abraham's lifetime (Gen. 14:1, 9). They defeated five local kings, plundered the area, and kidnapped Lot along with some other people. Abraham set out and defeated these kings, recovered the plunder, and rescued Lot and the other captives. Amraphel was king of Shinar (i.e., Babylon).

Anakites–The descendants of Anak, the Anakites (NRSV: "Anakim"), known for their height (Deut. 2:10, 21; 9:2), inhabited the Judean hill country when Israelite spies entered the land (Num. 13:21–33; Deut. 1:28). The spies viewed them as Nephilim (Num. 13:33; cf. Gen. 6:4). Arba, a hero among the Anakites, gave his name to Kiriath Arba (Josh. 14:15), later Hebron (Josh. 15:13–14; Judg. 1:20).

Ananias–**(1)** A member of the Jerusalem church whose death was followed by that of his wife, Sapphira, as a result of holding back part of their possessions (Acts 5:1–11). **(2)** A disciple at Damascus who helped restore Saul's eyesight and baptized him in accordance with the Lord's direction in a vision (Acts 9). **(3)** A high priest in Jerusalem during AD 47–58. He presided over the interrogation of Paul at the Sanhedrin of Jerusalem (Acts 23:1–10) and testified against Paul before Felix (24:1).

Anath–The father of Shamgar the judge (Judg. 3:31; 5:6). This name is also associated with a Canaanite war goddess and with Egyptian and Syrian goddesses as well.

Anathema–A transliterated Greek word meaning "curse." *See* Blessing and Cursing.

Anathoth–Anathoth was just a few miles northeast of Jerusalem in the tribal allotment given to Benjamin. This village was assigned to the Levites (Josh. 21:18; 1 Chron. 6:60). The city's most famous resident was the prophet Jeremiah (Jer. 1:1).

Ancient of Days–A title for the sovereign God seated on his heavenly throne in Daniel's vision of Dan. 7:9, 13, 22. A passage relevant to the Ancient of Days in Dan. 7 is Rev. 1:14–16, where John sees a heavenly figure in whom is combined the features of the heavenly Son of Man and the Ancient of Days. Imagery characterizing the latter figure (white hair, fiery presence) is now applied to Jesus, indicating that the Son of Man is equal to the Ancient of Days in glory and authority.

Andrew–One of the twelve apostles and brother of Peter. Andrew came from Bethsaida in Galilee (John 1:44), though he lived and worked with Peter in Capernaum as a fisherman (Matt. 4:18). At first a disciple of John the Baptist, he, with an unnamed disciple (possibly John), transferred allegiance to Jesus (John 1:35–40). His first recorded act was to bring his brother to Jesus (John 1:41–42). Subsequently, he was called by Jesus to become a permanent follower (Matt. 4:19) and later was appointed as an apostle (Matt. 10:2).

Angel–The English word "angel" refers to nonhuman spirits, usually good. The biblical words usually translated "angel" mean "messenger" and can refer to one sent by God or by human beings. A messenger must be utterly loyal, reliable, and able to act confidentially (Prov. 13:17). The messenger speaks and acts in the name of the sender (Gen. 24).

Messengers sent by God are not always angels. Yahweh's prophets were his messengers (Hag. 1:13), as were priests (Mal. 2:7).

Anger–*See* Wrath; Wrath of God.

Anna–An elderly Jewish prophetess at the time of Jesus' birth. Anna is the daughter of Penuel, and she is from the tribe of Asher (Luke 2:36). She was married for only seven years and then remained a widow for many years. Anna was present when the baby Jesus was dedicated, and she responded in worship of God and spoke prophetically about the child (2:38).

Annals of the Kings–In 1–2 Kings there are eighteen references to the "book of the annals of the kings of Israel" (e.g., 1 Kings 14:19; 15:31) and fifteen to the "book of the annals of the kings of Judah" (e.g., 1 Kings 14:29; 15:7). These (now lost) works may identify sources from which information was extracted or at least where further information about a king may be obtained.

Annas–An influential high priest who played a part in the trial and death of Jesus (John 18:12–24). Annas served as high priest in AD 6–15 and continued as high priest emeritus while his son-in-law Caiaphas held that position in an official capacity. Immediately after Jesus was arrested (and before being sent to Caiaphas), he was brought to Annas, who questioned him about his disciples and teaching. His name heads the list of important members of the Sanhedrin when Peter and John were arrested (Acts 4:6), suggesting that he was a dominant figure of the high-priestly party.

Anoint, Anointed–*See* Messiah.

Antediluvians–These were the people who lived before the worldwide flood in Noah's time. They were divided between two ancestral lines, those of Cain (Gen. 4:17–24) and Seth (Gen. 5). Although it is common to speak of the Cainites and Sethites, the second line is depicted as starting with Adam, not Seth (5:3).

Anthropomorphism–A special type of figure of speech that is quite common in the Bible. Anthropomorphism is a figure of speech in which God is represented with human features or human characteristics. Anthropomorphisms abound in Scripture. Isaiah 59:1, for example, states: "Surely the arm of the Lord is not too short to save, nor his ear too dull to hear." Likewise, note the colorful anthropomorphic description of God in Ps. 104:2–3: "The Lord wraps himself in light as with a garment; he stretches out the heavens like a tent and lays the beams of his upper chambers on their waters. He makes the clouds his chariot and rides on the wings of the wind."

Antichrist–The term "antichrist" is used only four times in the Bible (1 John 2:18, 22; 4:3; 2 John 7). John defines the antichrist as the one who denies that God has come in the flesh in the person of Jesus Christ (1 John 2:22; 4:3; 2 John 7).

Antioch–***Antioch of Pisidia.*** *See* Asia Minor, Cities of (Pisidian Antioch).

Antioch of Syria. The most important Antioch mentioned in the NT was the capital city of the Roman province of Syria. Syrian Antioch was an important political, economic, and religious center during the Roman period.

Antioch's diverse population made for a great diversity of religions connected to the city. Its suburb of Daphne was a major worship site for paganism, and the city maintained a large Jewish population throughout its history. Additionally, it was to Antioch that many Jerusalem Christians fled during the early persecution of the church. Here, for the first time, the Jewish Christians began to intentionally focus on sharing the gospel with Gentiles (Acts 11:19–21). The result was a large, multicultural, and vibrant church. The church at Antioch was known for its ethnic and cultural diversity, its generosity (sending an offering to Jerusalem during a famine [see 11:27–30]), and its heart for missions (serving as Paul's headquarters for his three missionary journeys). Not surprisingly, it was at Antioch that Christ followers were first called "Christians" (11:26).

Antiochus (Epiphanes)–Antiochus IV Epiphanes (r. 175–164 BC) was the younger son of Antiochus III, ruler of the Seleucid Empire. The name "Epiphanes" means "manifest," implying "manifest as a god." Daniel 8:11; 9:27; 11:31; 12:11; 1 Macc. 1:54–64 speak of his desecration of the Jerusalem temple in 167 BC.

Antipas–**(1)** One of the sons of Herod the Great who ruled as tetrarch ("ruler of a fourth [part]") of Galilee and Perea (Luke 3:1). He was responsible for the imprisonment and subsequent beheading of John the Baptist (Matt. 14:1–12). He interviewed Jesus at length following his arrest without getting a response (Luke 23:6–12). (*See also* Herod.) **(2)** A faithful witness to the gospel who was martyred at Pergamum during a period of intense persecution when believers in that city were under pressure to renounce their faith in Christ (Rev. 2:13).

Antipatris–A city built by Herod the Great to honor his father, Antipater, in 9 BC. The city was built on the site of the ancient city of Aphek. Roman soldiers took Paul to Antipatris from Jerusalem by night to avoid a plot on his life, and cavalry took him on to Caesarea the next day (Acts 23:31–33). The city was forty miles from Jerusalem and twenty-five miles from Caesarea on the Via Maris.

Antonia, Tower of–The primary military fortification of Jerusalem near the Herodian temple, also called the Antonia Fortress. The tower may have served as an official residence for the Roman procurator. Thus, the tower's courtyard has traditionally been considered the site of Jesus' trial before Pilate (John 18:28; 19:13). However, Herod's palace may have been used for the procurator and as a residence of the governor. The fortress was destroyed during Titus's siege of Jerusalem in AD 70.

Antonia Fortress–*See* Antonia, Tower of.

Aphek–The most significant Aphek in the Bible is about seven miles east of Tel Aviv. Traffic on the international coastal route passing through Israel was forced between the foothills to the east and the river, making this a strategic location. During the transition to the monarchy, the Philistines were at Aphek when the Israelites attacked them from Ebenezer (1 Sam. 4:1) just east in the foothills. The Philistines won the battle, captured the ark, and continued Philistine control of the international coastal highway. At the end of Saul's life, the Philistines mustered their troops at this northern "boundary" of the Philistine plain before setting off to challenge Israel for control of the Jezreel Valley (1 Sam. 29:1).

Apis–A sacred bull worshiped in Egypt, apparently a representation of the Egyptian god Ptah. Jeremiah may mention the bull in his ridicule of the people's idolatry in his taunt "Why has Apis fled?" (Jer. 46:15 NRSV).

Apocalypse–*See* Revelation, Book of.

Apocalyptic–The word "apocalypse" means "revelation." Scholars have identified those texts that resemble the form of the book of Revelation as "apocalyptic literature," including the visions of Isaiah, Ezekiel, Daniel, and Zechariah.

Apocrypha, New Testament–The word "apocrypha" is derived from a Greek word meaning "secret" or "hidden" and refers to texts regarded by some Jews and Christians as religiously valuable but not meeting the criteria of canonicity. The more specific title "New Testament Apocrypha" distinguishes certain writings from those commonly referred to as "the Apocrypha," a collection of works written by Jews (with later Christian editing in places) between approximately 200 BC and AD 90, recognized as Scripture by Roman Catholic and Orthodox Churches but generally rejected by Protestants.

Apocrypha, Old Testament–The Greek word *apokrypha* means "hidden" or "secret," and later it came to refer to religious books considered to be of inferior quality to the OT and the NT. During the third century, several church fathers (e.g., Origen [d. 253], Irenaeus [d. 202], Tertullian [d. 220]) used this term to distinguish these works from canonical works. Currently, the phrase "Old Testament Apocrypha" refers to Jewish literary works written between approximately 200 BC and AD 90 that were included in the earliest Greek codices of the LXX.

Since the time of Luther, Protestants have rejected the canonicity of the Apocrypha. However, the Roman Catholic Church has argued that thirteen apocryphal works are part of their authoritative Scriptures (Wisdom of Solomon, Sirach [or Ecclesiasticus], Tobit, Judith, 1 Esdras [or 3 Ezra], 1 Maccabees, 2 Maccabees, Baruch, Epistle of Jeremiah, Additions to Esther, Susanna, Bel and the Dragon, and Prayer of Azariah and Song of the Three Young Men). In the past, two other books have been included (2 Esdras [or 4 Ezra, Apocalypse of Ezra] and Prayer of Manasseh). The Greek Orthodox Church includes two additional works (3 Maccabees; Psalm 151) in its authoritative canon.

Apollos–Apollos was born in Alexandria (Acts 18:24) and probably educated there. He came to Ephesus, perhaps on business, after Paul had left the city during his second missionary journey. In addition to his knowledge of the OT, Apollos had been instructed in the way of the Lord and was teaching accurately his knowledge of Jesus. He knew only the baptism of John—that is, the baptism of repentance. When Priscilla and Aquila "explained to him the way of God more adequately" (18:26), this probably entailed an explanation of the atoning significance of Jesus' death, God's vindication of Jesus in the resurrection, and the personal experience of the Holy Spirit for all believers. After ministering in Ephesus (18:24), he went to Corinth (19:1; cf. 1 Cor. 3), where he was able to overwhelm the Jews in argument that Jesus was the Christ (Acts 18:28). Apollos returned to Ephesus sometime thereafter and was present in that city when Paul wrote 1 Corinthians (1 Cor. 16:8). Apollos probably remained a faithful member of the Pauline missionary band, for he is mentioned later in Paul's letter to Titus and was probably a courier of that letter with Zenas (Titus 3:13).

Apollyon–The Greek name, meaning "destroyer," for the angel of the Abyss, the bottomless pit. The Hebrew form is "Abaddon" (Rev. 9:11). The name may derive from Apollo, an important Greek god.

Apostasy–In the Bible this term is used specifically to describe rebellion against God. While there is a sense in which every human being has consciously and deliberately sinned and fallen short of God's standards (Rom. 3:23), apostasy is normally used only in reference to those who have flagrantly and highhandedly known the truth, turned their back on it, and rejected God.

Apostle–*See* Offices in the New Testament.

Apostolic Council–*See* Acts of the Apostles.

Aqaba, Gulf of–*See* Red Sea, Reed Sea.

Aqueduct–A conduit used to transport water from one place to another. It could be either a trough cut into rock or soil, or pipes made from stone or other materials. Aqueducts were used in OT times to transport water into cities from nearby springs. The "aqueduct of the Upper Pool" in Jerusalem is mentioned in 2 Kings 18:17; Isa. 7:3; 36:2. Its location is uncertain, though it is said to be "on the road to the Washerman's Field." Hezekiah's tunnel was an underground aqueduct that took water from the Gihon spring to the Pool of Siloam (2 Kings 20:20).

Aquila and Priscilla–Aquila and Priscilla were important coworkers with the apostle Paul in his missionary effort. They joined Paul in cooperative efforts and also worked in relative independence. They were Christian workers in what came to be important centers of early Christianity: Corinth, Ephesus, and Rome. Mentioned in the NT as a pair (Acts 18:18, 19, 26; Rom. 16:3; 1 Cor. 16:19; 2 Tim. 4:19), four of these list Priscilla first, probably indicating her wealth, social status, or prominence in the Christian community.

Arabah–One of several major topographical features of Israel (Deut. 1:7; Josh. 11:16). The Arabah corresponds to the Great Rift Valley running north to south through the land. Situated within it is the Jordan River Valley, which extends southward from the Sea of

Galilee (Kinnereth) sixty-five miles to the Dead Sea (Sea of the Arabah). The Dead Sea and its surroundings are also part of it, as is the desert region to the south, which extends 103 miles to the Gulf of Aqaba. "The way of the Arabah" (*derek ha'arabah*) occurs five times, once indicating a road leading from the Gulf of Aqaba (Deut. 2:8), possibly the King's Highway (see Num. 20:17, 21).

Arabia–A large peninsula lying between the Red Sea on the west and the Persian Gulf on the east. In the Bible the term is actually seldom used (2 Chron. 9:14; Isa. 21:13; Jer. 25:24; Ezek. 27:21; 30:5; Gal. 1:17; 4:25), and when it is, it refers more to the general area than to any specific group of people or geographic location. It seems to stand as a designation for that expanse of land that lies to the south and east of Canaan and the Transjordan peoples. On several occasions the term "Arabs" is used to designate the people from those regions (2 Chron. 17:11; 21:16; 22:1; 26:7; Neh. 4:7; Acts 2:11). Elsewhere they are referred to as "eastern peoples" (Gen. 29:1; Judg. 6:3, 33; 7:12; 8:10) or "people of the East" (1 Kings 4:30; Job 1:3; Jer. 49:28; Ezek. 25:4, 10). In Gen. 25:6 Arabia is referred to as the "land of the east," and in Isa. 2:6 simply as "the East" (although this may refer simply to Syria and Mesopotamia).

In the NT, Arabs were among those present at Pentecost (Acts 2:11). After his conversion Paul journeyed to Arabia (Gal. 1:17), by which is meant the Nabatean kingdom, stretching from the Transjordan southwest toward the Sinai Peninsula. Interestingly, Paul's reference to Mount Sinai as being in Arabia (Gal. 4:25) may suggest a location other than the traditional one of the Sinai Peninsula—for example, across the Gulf of Aqaba (the eastern arm of the Red Sea) in or near Midian (see Exod. 2:11–3:3)—although there is no consensus on this matter.

Arad–A Canaanite city located in the Negev Desert, approximately eighteen miles northeast of Beersheba. This was the site of the defeat by the king of Arad when the Israelites attempted a southern entrance into Canaan, the result of which was the capture of several of their own people (Num. 21:1; 33:40). Later, the king of Arad is listed among the conquered kings of Canaan (Josh. 12:14). The city was destroyed and renamed "Hormah" (Num. 21:2–3). The area is also mentioned as a reference point for the land of the Kenites, the descendants of Moses' father-in-law (Judg. 1:16).

Aramaic–Aramaic comprises one of the two main branches of the northwest Semitic language group. The language most closely related to Aramaic is Hebrew, although Akkadian and Arabic also show considerable similarities in terms of morphology, grammar, and lexical content. There is considerable extrabiblical literature dating from around 1500 BC through the biblical period and beyond that is written in Aramaic, some of which is important for the study of the Bible. Also, considerable portions of the books of Ezra and Daniel are written in Aramaic.

Arameans–Descendants of Shem (Gen. 10:22) and Nahor (Gen. 22:21) identified in the LXX and English translations as "Syrians." According to the patriarchal narratives in Genesis, Arameans originated from Upper Mesopotamia in the early second millennium. Abraham is referred to as a "wandering Aramean" (Deut. 26:5), which suggests that the Hebrews descended from Arameans.

Their expansion to the west impacted ancient Israel as early as the days of Saul (1 Sam. 14:47). David defeated the alliance of the Ammonites with the Aramean king Hadadezer (2 Sam. 8:3–8; 10–12). King Asa of Judah made a treaty with an Aramean king in his war against Baasha of Israel (1 Kings 15:16–22). King Ahab was defeated and killed in his battles with the Arameans (1 Kings 22:1–38). Later, God provided a "deliverer" (possibly an Assyrian king or officer), which relieved Aramean pressures upon Israel (2 Kings 13:3–5). This allowed Jehoash of Israel to defeat the Arameans and regain previously lost territories. In the eighth century BC the Aramean king Rezin, in alliance with Israel and Tyre, attempted to force Ahaz of Judah into their league to oppose the growing Assyrian threat (2 Kings 16:5–9; Isa. 7:1–9). By the end of the eighth century, all Aramean territories had become provinces in the Assyrian Empire.

Aram Naharaim–Literally, "Aram of the Two Rivers." This is a region of the northern Euphrates above the point where it is joined by the River Harbor in the west of what is now Syria, and thus northwest of Mesopotamia proper. Associated with the patriarchs, its proximity to Israel also made it a place from which opposition might come. Genesis 24:10 notes that it was here that Abraham's servant came to the city of Nahor and met Rebekah at the well, while Deut. 23:4 indicates that this was Balaam's home region. Cushan-Rishathaim, Israel's first foreign oppressor in Judges, came from here (Judg. 3:8), while both 1 Chron. 19:6 and the title of Ps. 60 indicate that the Ammonites hired mercenaries from the region when engaged in war against David.

Aram Zobah–A minor state in the Anti-Lebanon among a group of Syrian states that attacked Israel after David's message of sympathy to the Ammonites was misconstrued (1 Chron. 19:6), but which he ultimately defeated (2 Sam. 8:3; cf. Ps. 60:1).

Ararat–Ararat refers to a mountainous region in eastern Asia Minor. The best-known reference to Ararat is as the location where Noah's ark comes to rest after the flood. Genesis 8:4 actually speaks of the "mountains of Ararat," not one particular mountain. In Gen. 8:2–14 the perspective is of the rain stopping and the floodwaters slowly receding in an extended process during which the ark is deposited on the Ararat mountain range. Tradition has favored Agri Dag, an extinct volcano rising 16,916 feet on the northeastern border of Turkey, as a viable site for Ararat.

Araunah–A Jebusite (called "Ornan" in Chronicles) who sold David a threshing floor on which the king constructed an altar (2 Sam. 24:16–25; 1 Chron. 21:15–27). This story legitimized the locale for the construction of the Solomonic temple (1 Chron. 22:1; 2 Chron. 3:1) by asserting that it was the place where the sacrifice of David averted the destroying angel of pestilence (2 Sam. 24:16, 25).

Arba–Arba was the leader of the Anakites, a tribe of giants (Deut. 2:10, 21; 9:2) that lived near Hebron. The town was originally called Kiriath Arba ("city of Arba"; Josh. 14:15; 15:13; 21:11).

Arbitrator–*See* Mediator.

Archangel–A chief or first angel. *See also* Angel.

Archelaus–The son of Herod the Great who, following his father's death and by permission from the Roman emperor Augustus, ruled over Judea, Samaria, and Idumea (Edom) from 4 BC to AD 6. Archelaus is mentioned once in the NT (Matt. 2:22). Joseph, warned by an angel of the Lord, had taken Jesus and Mary to Egypt to escape the murderous intentions of Herod the Great. After the death of Herod, Joseph was told to return to Israel, but on arriving he discovered that Archelaus now governed Judea. Being afraid of him and warned in a dream, he settled in Nazareth in the district of Galilee, an area ruled by another of Herod's sons, Antipas.

Archippus–A Christian whom Paul encouraged to complete "the ministry you have received in the Lord" (Col. 4:17). Paul described him as a "fellow soldier" (Philem. 2), which probably indicates a position of leadership. The nature of the ministry received from the Lord that Paul refers to in Col. 4:17 is not specified.

Areopagus–An ancient and prestigious council of Athenians that met on Mars Hill and in former days exercised judicial and legislative authority. Paul was invited to address the Areopagus and explain his teaching about Jesus and the resurrection. Among the converts from this occasion, two are named: Dionysius, himself a council member, and Damaris, a woman about whom nothing else is said (Acts 17:16–34).

Aretas–The name of several Arabian kings. Paul mentions Aretas (2 Cor. 11:32), king of Arabia Petraea and father-in-law of Herod Antipas, who divorced his daughter to marry Herodias, his brother's wife (see Mark 6:17 pars.). This led to war and the subsequent destruction of Antipas's army, which the people blamed on his murder of John the Baptist (Josephus, *Ant.* 8.116). Following the death of Emperor Tiberius (AD 37), Aretas apparently had gained control of Damascus, where Paul, being pursued by the king's ethnarch, escaped in a basket through a window in the wall (Acts 9:25; 2 Cor. 11:32–33).

Arimathea–A town of Judea whose exact location is uncertain. It is mentioned in all four Gospels, only in connection with Joseph, a rich man and member of the Sanhedrin, in whose tomb Jesus was laid (Matt. 27:57; Mark 15:43; Luke 23:51; John 19:38).

Arioch–**(1)** The king of Ellasar who joined a coalition against five kings of the Dead Sea region (Gen. 14:1, 9). Abram was swept up in this conflict because his nephew Lot was captured in Sodom (14:12). **(2)** The captain of the guard in the court of Nebuchadnezzar who was commanded to kill the wise men of Babylon, including Daniel (Dan. 2:14–15). Arioch protected Daniel by warning him of the king's order and then securing an audience for Daniel with the king (2:24–25).

Aristarchus–A native of Thessalonica who was a close companion of Paul. Associated with Paul's Gentile mission, he and Gaius were seized by a mob and brought to the theater in Ephesus (Acts 19:29). Later he journeyed to Jerusalem (possibly as one of the delegates of the Macedonian churches) accompanying the collection for poor relief (Acts 20:4). When Paul appealed for his case to be heard by Caesar, Aristarchus sailed with him to Rome (Acts 27:2). Writing from prison in Rome, Paul commends him as a Jewish coworker (along with Mark and Justus) and fellow prisoner (Col. 4:10, 11; Philem. 24).

Aristobulus–The head of a household greeted by Paul (Rom. 16:10). According to church tradition, he was the brother of Barnabas and one of the seventy disciples, who eventually became a missionary to Britain. Others have suggested that he was the son of Aristobulus, grandson of Herod the Great and brother of Agrippa I.

Ark–God announced to Noah that he was going to destroy all the inhabitants of the earth and commanded him to build an "ark" (Heb. *tebah*; Gen. 6:14–16). Apart from the Genesis flood narrative, Exod. 2:3–5 is the only other passage in the Bible where this word is used, there for the ark of bulrushes in which the infant Moses was placed. Both arks were made waterproof by a coating of pitch (tar). An ark is something built to save people from drowning. It is not the name of a kind of boat as such (e.g., yacht), but rather a geometric boxlike shape. The ark was without rudder, sail, or any navigational aid. The NT refers to Noah's construction of the ark (Heb. 11:7; 1 Pet. 3:20) and his entering it (Matt. 24:38; Luke 17:27).

Ark of the Covenant–A sacred cultic object, in the shape of a box, that represented the presence of God among the Israelites. The ark, constructed in wood, measured forty-five inches long, twenty-seven inches wide, and twenty-seven inches high (Exod. 25:10), and it was transported by means of two poles inserted on either side of the ark. The most important aspects of the ark were the cover and the cherubim attached to the ark cover. Blood was ritually sprinkled on the cover, which was the designated place of atonement. In the earliest accounts, the ark became the place of atonement, meeting, and revelation between God and Israel.

Armageddon–Commonly believed to be the place of the final, cataclysmic battle that climaxes in the visible return of Christ (Rev. 16:16). The literal rendering "mount of Megiddo" is somewhat problematic, for there is no Mount of Megiddo. The apocalyptic indications relate Zech. 12:11 (the only apocalyptic reference to Megiddo, although there it is the "plain of Megiddo") with Ezek. 38–39 (where the final battle in history takes place on the "mountains of Israel"). At the least, Armageddon represents the place where the kings of the world will gather for the final battle before God judges the world. The choice of Megiddo may result from the fact that it was the place where the righteous Israelites repeatedly fought off attacks by wicked nations (cf. 2 Kings 23:29).

Army–The army of Israel was primarily a volunteer military force directed by God and his word. Deuteronomy 20 establishes the guidelines for warfare, Num. 1 describes organization, and Num. 2:17 highlights God's strategic position as commander in the sacred event of war. Israelite warriors were men twenty years and older from the nation's tribes, clans, and families. The Levites were appointed tabernacle caretakers and not counted in the census for military duties. The priest was responsible for addressing the nation prior to a battle and then leading the battle procession in connection with the ark of the covenant.

The Israelite army structure is not overly developed in the biblical material. Under God as commander in chief was the king, who then worked in connection with his commanders and officers to execute God's will by means of a tribal confederation. Prior to the monarchy, God worked through Moses and Joshua to rally the men for battle. Samuel warned the nation that the king would abuse the volunteerism of the army and take their sons and make them render military service with his chariots and horses (1 Sam. 8:11–12). This warning was realized under the leadership of Solomon and Rehoboam. Army divisions included a list of family heads, commanders of thousands, commanders of hundreds, and their officers. In addition, a period of their service was noted (1 Chron. 27).

Army size was not a matter of importance for success in battle. God as divine warrior led the nation in battle and determined the outcome in keeping with his sovereign purposes. Only a few Israelites were necessary to defeat thousands (Lev. 26:8; Deut. 32:8). The defeat of Pharaoh and his army in the exodus and the conquest provides the most dramatic premonarchy illustrations of God's defiance of the numbers. During the monarchy, God orchestrated the defeat of the vast Aramean army with a smaller Israelite army (1 Kings 20:27). On the other hand, when the Israelites were disobedient to the covenant, they would be put to flight (Josh. 7).

Arnon–The wadi and gorge that runs into the east side of the Dead Sea opposite En Gedi. It formed the northern boundary of Moab (Num. 22:36; Judg. 11:18) and southern boundary of the kingdom of Sihon the Amorite (Deut. 2:24, 36). Its first mention in the OT is as a campsite of the migrating Israelites (Num. 21:13–36). The Israelites captured all the territory of the Transjordan north of the Arnon River (Deut. 3:8–17; 4:48; Josh. 12:1–2). In the days of Jephthah, the Ammonite king attempted unsuccessfully to regain the territory from the Arnon to the Jabbok Rivers (Judg. 11). During Jehu's reign, the Syrian king Hazael captured from Israel the Transjordan territory as far south as the Arnon Gorge (2 Kings 10:32–33).

Aroer–A settlement on the northern rim of a deep gorge along the Arnon River, east of the Dead Sea. Because the gorge served as a natural border for surrounding territories, Aroer was a strategically attractive stronghold. Aroer was controlled by Sihon the Amorite until Moses defeated him (Deut. 2:36; 4:48; Josh. 12:2) and incorporated the settlement within Reuben's territory (Deut. 3:12; Josh. 13:9, 16), although Gad was involved in rebuilding it (Num. 32:34). Later, the settlement likely marked the starting point for David's census (2 Sam. 24:5). Still later, Hazael of Syria gained dominance over the Transjordan as far south as Aroer (2 Kings 10:33; cf. Isa. 17:2). By Jeremiah's time, Aroer had once again come under Moab's control (Jer. 48:19).

Artaxerxes–Artaxerxes I was the fourth king of the Persian Empire (464–424 BC). It was an appeal by provincial officials to Artaxerxes at the beginning of his reign that brought a halt to an early attempt to repair the walls of Jerusalem (Ezra 4:7–23). Ezra went up to Jerusalem in the seventh year of his reign (458 BC; Ezra 7:7). The appearance of beneficence in Artaxerxes' decree (7:11–26) was spoiled by the revelation of the self-serving political motivation behind its apparent generosity (7:23). Ezra's nonuse of the sweeping powers given to him by Artaxerxes further suggests that Persian royal assistance might not be the kind of help really needed by God's people. Nehemiah returned to Jerusalem in the twentieth year of Artaxerxes' reign (445 BC; Neh. 1:1). The positive impression made on the reader by Artaxerxes' personal favoritism toward Nehemiah, allowing him to return to rebuild the walls of his native city, Jerusalem (2:3, 5), is undercut by Nehemiah's disparagement of his royal master (1:11: "this man"). Nehemiah's second mission took place sometime later than the thirty-second year of Artaxerxes' reign (5:14; 13:6) but before the king's death.

Artemis–The goddess Artemis was known as the protector, nurturer, and overseer of Ephesus. The only mention of Artemis in the Bible is in Acts 19:23–41, the incident of the Ephesian riot and demonstration in the amphitheater. This was instigated by Demetrius the silversmith over his concerns that Paul's ministry was creating an economic hazard for him and his tradesmen, who made silver shrines of Artemis. They also feared that the temple and Artemis herself would suffer a decline in stature. The intercession of the city clerk eventually quieted the mob, but not until they had spent two hours chanting, "Great is Artemis of the Ephesians!"

Asa–The third king of Judah (1 Kings 15:8–24; 2 Chron. 14:1–16:14), succeeding his father, Abijah, and reigning for forty-one years (908–867 BC). Early in his life, Asa was a good king, obeying God and removing the worship of foreign gods from the land. He even removed an idolatrous object that his own grandmother Maakah had set up and removed her from leadership in the land. As a result, God blessed him, even providing a tremendous military victory over Zerah, an Ethiopian leader who had attacked Judah with a million-man army (2 Chron. 14:9–15). Later in life, however, he showed a lack of confidence in God when he enlisted the king of Aram to help him against the encroachment of Baasha, the king of Israel, even paying him with gold and silver objects from the temple. Although Baasha withdrew, Asa's actions caught up with him when he developed a serious foot disease, from which he died.

Asahel–One of the three sons of Zeruiah. He and his brothers, Joab and Abishai, were nephews of David who served prominently in his army. Asahel was noted as a swift runner (2 Sam. 2:18). His speed and persistence cost him his life at the hands of Abner and led to a division between David and Joab. Abner had been King Saul's general. After Saul was killed by the Philistines, Abner sided with Saul's son Ish-Bosheth for two years. Most of Israel followed Ish-Bosheth, while Judah followed David. In one battle, Abner and the men of Israel were put to flight (2:17). The swift Asahel decided to chase Abner down. Abner warned him off, but Asahel refused to relent, so when he caught up, Abner killed him. When a rift developed between Ish-Bosheth and Abner, Abner determined to bring the loyalty of Israel over to David. He met peaceably with David toward that end. But when Joab heard, he was upset. He tricked Abner into a meeting without David's knowledge and killed him in revenge for Asahel's death.

Asaph–One of the Levites appointed by David to lead in worship. Asaph was part of the procession to bring the ark of the covenant to Jerusalem. Along with Heman and Ethan, also mentioned in the Psalter, he was appointed by the Levites to the bronze cymbals (1 Chron. 15:19). Subsequently, David assigned Asaph continuing duties (16:7, 37). He served further under Solomon at the dedication of the temple (2 Chron. 5:11–14). Asaph is described as singer (1 Chron. 15:17), the chief (15:19), who played cymbals (15:19), gave thanks to God (16:7), ministered before the ark (16:37), prophesied under direction of the king (25:2); and gave direction to his sons (25:2). The sons of Asaph served under his direction (25:2); prophesied and sang with lyres, harps, and cymbals (25:1, 6); and served as gatekeepers (26:1). The descendants of Asaph continued these duties after the exile (Ezra 2:41; 3:10; Neh. 11:22; 12:46). Twelve psalms are associated with Asaph (Pss. 50; 73–83). They reflect his prophetic ministry by including sections of prophecy or of God speaking. God's covenant and justice are frequent topics of these psalms.

Ascension–The visible and bodily ascent of Jesus from earth to heaven concluding his earthly ministry, which then continued through the promised Holy Spirit, given at Pentecost.

A detailed historical account of the ascension is given only by Luke (Luke 24:51; Acts 1:4–11 [cf. Mark 16:19, in the longer ending to Mark's Gospel]). The event, however, was anticipated in John's Gospel (John 6:62; 20:17).

The ascension is frequently implied throughout the NT by reference to the complex of events that began with the death of Jesus and ended with his session at the right hand of God in glory. Paul writes of the divine-human Christ's ascent to the heavenly realms as the beginning of his supreme cosmic reign in power (Eph. 1:20–23) and as the basis for holy living (Col. 3:1–4; 1 Tim. 3:16). In Hebrews, the ascension is a crucial stage that marks off the completed work of Jesus on earth, in which he offered himself as the perfect and final sacrifice for sin (9:24–26), from his continuing work in heaven as our great high priest, which is described in terms of sympathy (4:14–16) and intercession (7:25). Peter makes the most direct reference to the ascension, explaining that Jesus, who suffered, is resurrected and "has gone into heaven" (1 Pet. 3:22). Therefore, just as Jesus, the righteous sufferer, was vindicated by God, so too will his people, who suffer for doing good.

Ascents, Song of–The titles, or superscriptions, of fifteen psalms include the designation "a song of ascents," also called "a song of degrees." The notion of ascending, or going up, has influenced the understanding of these psalms. The "going up" has been seen as going up to Jerusalem for a holy day, going up to Jerusalem as part of the return from the exile, going up the fifteen steps at the courts of the temple (a Jewish tradition in the Mishnah), or an aspect of their poetic style. These psalms occur together as a group, Pss. 120–34.

Asenath–The daughter of Potiphera, priest of On in Egypt, she was given as wife to Joseph and became the mother of Manasseh and Ephraim (Gen. 41:45, 50–52; 46:20).

A

Ashdod–One of five principal cities of the Philistines (Josh. 13:3). Ashdod was situated in the coastal plane of Canaan, roughly two and one-half miles inland from the Mediterranean Sea, near the main coastal route sometimes called the "Way of the Philistines."

Ashdod is mentioned in relation to both the overall success of the Israelite conquest of Canaan (Josh. 11:22; the feared Anakim remained only in Philistine territory [see Num. 13:28]) and its unfinished nature (Josh. 13:3). Joshua 15:46–47 lists Ashdod in the territory allotted to Judah. That this territory remained largely unconquered by Israel features prominently in the narrative of Judges and Samuel.

When the ark of the covenant was captured by the Philistines (1 Sam. 4), it was taken to Dagon's temple at Ashdod (5:1–2). Excavation of Tel Ashdod has yet to identify this cult site, although an incense stand portraying a procession of musicians may pertain to Dagon's cult (see 1 Sam. 10:5). First Macc. 10:84 reports Jonathan's burning of Azotus (Ashdod) and destruction of Dagon's temple during the Hellenistic period.

Among the prophets, oracles portend the destruction of Ashdod and the other Philistine cities (Amos 1:6–8; Zeph. 2:4; Zech. 9:5–6). Jeremiah 25:20 mentions "the people left at Ashdod," possibly alluding to Psamtik I's destruction of the city. Conspicuously absent is any mention of Gath, which by this time had been subjugated or destroyed (1 Chron. 1:18; 2 Chron. 26:6; also 2 Kings 12:17).

Asher–The name of a person (the eighth son of Jacob [Gen. 30:12–13]), a tribe of Israel (*see* Asher, Tribe of), and possibly a city (Josh. 17:7).

Asher, Tribe of–One of the twelve tribes, descended from the eighth son of Jacob, born to Jacob by Zilpah, Leah's handmaid (Gen. 30:12–13). The tribe of Asher is specifically recorded as participating in the enslavement in Egypt (Exod. 1:4), the rescue from Egypt and the failure to enter the land of promise (Num. 1:40–41; 13:13; 26:44–47), the conquest of the land (Josh. 19:24–31), and the failure to drive out the Canaanites as God had commanded (Judg. 1:31–32). The tribal allotment afforded Asher included the western hills of Galilee and the Phoenician coast north of the Carmel range and south of Sidon. In the NT, Asher is listed as the tribe of Anna, the prophetess who blessed the infant Jesus (Luke 2:36–38). Asher is also included among Revelation's listing of the tribes sealed for protection (Rev. 7:6).

Asherah–A cult object as well as a goddess attested throughout the Levant.

In the OT, Asherah refers primarily to a wooden cult object (see Deut. 16:21). That these were objects and not trees is evident from descriptions of their (NIV: "Asherah poles") being "made" (1 Kings 14:15) and "set up" (14:23).

The Israelites were instructed to destroy the Asherah poles upon entering Canaan (Exod. 34:13; also Deut. 7:5; 12:3). Instead, they fashioned their own (1 Kings 14:15, 23), assimilating them into worship of Yahweh (2 Kings 23:6). Later efforts at removing the poles were sporadic and temporary (cf. 2 Kings 18:4 with 21:3, 7). Despite the apparent pervasiveness of these cult objects, archaeologists have yet to retrieve one.

In a handful of instances, "Asherah" denotes a deity. In Judg. 3:7 "the Asherahs" (here indicating "goddesses") is grammatically parallel to "the Baals"; likewise "Asherah" corresponds to Baal and "the starry hosts," designating a specific deity (2 Kings 23:4). In 1 Kings 18:19 Elijah speaks of the "prophets of Asherah," who presumably spoke in the goddess's name.

Ashkelon–One of five principal cities of the Philistines (Josh. 13:3). It was situated approximately midway between Ashdod (north) and Gaza (south) on the shore of the Mediterranean Sea.

Ashkelon was listed among the territory still to be conquered at the end of Joshua's life (Josh. 13:3). Judah took the city but ultimately was unable to keep it (Judg. 1:18–19). The OT subsequently reckoned Ashkelon as part of Philistine territory, beginning with Judg. 14:19, which recounts one of Samson's exploits.

Ashkelon shared in the affliction visited on the Philistines for taking the ark of the covenant, which they attempted to forestall by reparations or "sympathetic magic" (1 Sam. 6:17 [the "gold tumors" were likely meant to bear away the source of the Philistines' suffering]). Ashkelon and Gath represent the Philistines overall as David anticipates their response to news of Saul's and Jonathan's deaths (2 Sam. 1:20).

The remaining references occur in the prophets, who portended the destruction of

Ashkelon and the other Philistine cities at various times (Jer. 25:20; 47:5, 7; Amos 1:8; Zeph. 2:4, 7; Zech. 9:5). Notably, Zeph. 2:7 expected that Judah would finally take possession of Ashkelon.

Ashpenaz–The chief eunuch in the court of King Nebuchadnezzar (Dan. 1:3), whom the king charged with the task of bringing in and training some young Israelite men to serve in his court. Ashpenaz changed the names of Daniel and his three friends to Babylonian names. Following the king's orders, he refused to let the four young men follow a strict diet of vegetables and water, but Daniel found a way to avoid the diet required by Nebuchadnezzar.

Ashtaroth–**(1)** A goddess attested in Syro-Phoenicia, Palestine, and Egypt. In the Bible, "Ashtaroth" is generally regarded as the plural form of the deity's name (NIV: "the Ashtoreths"; NRSV: "the Astartes"; NET: "the Ashtars"). It occurs all but once in conjunction with other deities, most often Baal or "the Baals" (Judg. 2:13; 1 Sam. 12:10), but also with the gods of neighboring peoples (Judg. 10:6) or "foreign gods" (1 Sam. 7:3). "Ashtaroth" broadly designates goddesses whom Israel pursued rather than the true God, Yahweh. In 1 Sam. 31:10 is mentioned a Philistine temple devoted to "the Ashtoreths." *See also* Asherah.

(2) A city associated with Og, king of Bashan (Deut. 1:4). "Ashtaroth" designates an Amorite city captured by the Israelites en route to the plains of Moab (Num. 21:33–35). The region was allotted to the half-tribe of Manasseh (Josh. 12:30–31), and the city to the Levites (1 Chron. 6:71).

Ashurbanipal–In 668 BC Ashurbanipal (Osnapper [Asnapper] is the Aramaic equivalent; Ezra 4:10) succeeded his father, Esarhaddon, in Assyria, while his brother Shamash-shum-ukin became the ruler of Babylon. Esarhaddon had made his vassals swear loyalty to the two sons before his death. They were able to rule peacefully alongside each other for seventeen years, with Ashurbanipal as the superior. Then a civil war broke out between them in 651 BC, which Ashurbanipal won, though at great cost. Less is known of him after this victory, and perhaps the decline of Assyria begins at that point.

Early in his reign he conquered Egypt as far south as Thebes, while to the east he defeated the Medes, which helped pave the way for the rise of the Persians. He may be the king who captured Manasseh (2 Chron. 33:11–12).

A

Asia–A Roman province in western Asia Minor, not to be confused with the modern designation for the larger continent. The exact boundaries are difficult to determine, but the region, formed in 133–130 BC, and since the time of Augustus ruled by proconsuls, included the older kingdoms of Mysia, Lydia, Caria, and part of Phrygia, as well as several islands. Paul and his companions enjoyed an especially successful mission in Asia (Acts 19:10, 22, 26–27; Rom. 16:5). He later wrote letters to Christians in Colossae and Ephesus (Ephesians; 1 Timothy). Inscriptions attest to the wealth of many Ephesians. Through Timothy, Paul warns those pursuing wealth in the city (1 Tim. 6:9–10; cf. Rev. 3:17). The apostle John eventually settled in Ephesus and later was exiled to the island of Patmos, where he wrote to the seven churches of Asia (Rev. 1:4–3:22).

Asia Minor, Cities of–Asia Minor, the land area of modern-day Turkey, was initially settled by the Hatti people between 2500 and 2000 BC. Toward the end of that period, the Indo-European Hittites, drawn to the mild climate, began a slow settlement alongside the indigenous Hattis, mixing peaceably with them. By 1750 BC, the Hittites had become the dominant people group.

In the twelfth century BC the Hittites fell to the Sea Peoples. They developed coastal cities along the Aegean, which by the eighth century were conquered by the Greeks. The Lydian king Croesus came to power in 560 BC in Sardis and subdued the Greeks, only to fall in 546 BC to Cyrus of Persia. In 334–333 BC Alexander the Great defeated the Persians in two key battles and won Asia Minor. After Alexander's death, one of his generals, Seleucus, took over. Then, in 190 BC the Romans defeated the Seleucids and assumed control. This inaugurated an extended period of peace, during which time Jewish communities of the Diaspora settled throughout the region.

The missionary journeys of the apostle Paul (Saul of Tarsus) took him into and around much of Asia Minor, and directly or indirectly he was responsible for the establishment of most of the first-century churches there. The following cities of Asia Minor are mentioned in the NT.

Eastern Mediterranean

Tarsus. The birthplace of the apostle Paul (Acts 9:11; 21:39; 22:3), Tarsus is located on the Mediterranean coast, nine miles northeast of modern-day Mersin. Tarsus became the capital of the Roman province of Cilicia in 67 BC. Cleopatra and Mark Antony met and built their fleet in this grand city. When his life was threatened after his conversion, Paul was sent to Tarsus from Jerusalem (9:30).

Antioch. Antioch (Antakya) is located just inland from the Mediterranean coast, on the east bank of the Orontes River. Jewish and Gentile believers who fled Jerusalem after the death of Stephen planted a church here, where followers of Jesus were first called "Christians." Barnabas brought Saul from Tarsus to Antioch, where they labored together for a year, teaching the church, prior to setting off on their first missionary journey (Acts 11:19–30). Paul later returned, along with Silas, bearing the requirements for Gentile believers from the Jerusalem council (15:22–35).

Southern Ports

Seleucia. Known today as Samandağ, Seleucia was Antioch's port, the place from which Saul, Barnabas, and John Mark embarked on their first missionary journey in AD 47 (Acts 13:4).

Perga in Pamphylia. Perga is just east of Antalya on the southern Mediterranean coast. Archimedes' student Apollonius the mathematician lived here in the late third century BC. On their first missionary journey, Paul and Barnabas disembarked in Perga for destinations in southwestern Asia Minor, while John Mark left them to return to Jerusalem (Acts 13:13–14). On their return trip of the same journey, Paul and Barnabas stopped in Perga again, this time preaching before heading to Attalia (14:25).

Galatia

The following cities became part of the politically defined Roman province of Galatia in 25 BC. They are to be distinguished from ethnic Galatia, which is a region farther north, around modern-day Ankara.

Pisidian Antioch. Modern Yalvaç, or Pisidian Antioch, is northeast of Isparta in the lake region. On their first missionary journey, Paul and Barnabas preached in the synagogue here and generated enormous interest in the gospel (Acts 13:14–43). The following Sabbath, nearly the entire city came out to listen to them. Jealous Jewish leaders incited a persecution, causing Paul and Barnabas to reorient their ministry to Gentiles and then leave the region for Iconium (13:26–51). They returned on their way back to Antioch to strengthen the disciples and appoint elders (14:21–23).

Iconium. Iconium, today called Konya, is about sixty-five miles southeast of Pisidian Antioch. It is one of the most ancient settlements of the region, dating to the third millennium BC. Paul and Barnabas preached in the synagogue here on their first missionary journey, initially winning Jewish and Gentile converts but angering other Jews. Paul and Barnabas eventually feared for their safety and escaped to Lystra and Derbe (Acts 14:1–6). However, they came back on the return trip to Antioch (14:21–23).

Lystra. Frequently mentioned with Derbe (Acts 14:6; 16:1), Lystra (modern Hatunsaray) is nineteen miles south of Iconium. Paul and Barnabas fled here from Iconium and preached. Paul healed a lame man, and as a result he and Barnabas were presumed by the enthusiastic crowd to be Zeus and Hermes. At the instigation of Paul's Jewish opponents, the crowd's sentiments turned, and Paul was nearly stoned to death. He and Barnabas left for Derbe the following day (14:6–20), but they came back on their return trip (14:21–23). Paul returned on his second missionary journey, where he met his protégé, Timothy (16:1–2).

Derbe. About fifty miles southeast of Lystra and slightly north of present-day Karaman is Derbe. Paul and Barnabas fled here after Paul's stoning in Lystra on their first missionary journey, preached the gospel, made many disciples, and appointed elders (Acts 14:21–23). Among the disciples likely was Gaius, who later accompanied Paul during his third missionary journey (20:4).

Western Aegean Ports

Troas. Troas was a major northwest seaport located about twelve miles southwest of Troy. On his second missionary journey, Paul, traveling with Silas and Timothy, was prevented from entering Bithynia by the Spirit of Christ and went instead to Troas. Here he had a vision beckoning him to Macedonia, which he promptly obeyed (Acts 16:6–11). Because this is the first of the so-called "we" passages in Acts, Luke may have joined the group here (16:10). Paul also stopped at Troas on the return to Jerusalem from his third missionary journey.

There he raised Eutychus after the latter's traumatic fall (20:4–12). Troas is mentioned twice more, suggesting that Paul spent time here in addition to the above visits (2 Cor. 2:12–13; 2 Tim. 4:13).

Adramyttium. A few miles south of Troas was the port of Adramyttium. It was the origin of the ship that transported Paul from Caesarea to Myra around AD 60 en route to Rome (Acts 27:2).

Assos. Assos is an acropolis sitting 774 feet above sea level, up from the village of Behramkale. It overlooks the Bay of Edremit and has a splendid view of Lesbos. Doric columns from the seventh-century BC temple of Athena are prominent at the site. According to Acts 20:13–14, on his return from his third missionary journey, Paul went overland from Troas to Assos, and there he joined his traveling companions on their ship. From here on the way to Miletus, they made several nearby island stops off the coast of Asia Minor: Mitylene on Lesbos, Chios, and Samos (20:14–16).

Miletus. Located about twenty miles south of Ephesus, at the point where the Meander River met the Gulf of Latmus (now silted over), was the important southwestern seaport of Miletus. The city was significant in the NT era for its four harbors. A center for commerce, scholarship, geometry, and science, it was also the prototype for principles of city planning later applied throughout the Roman Empire. On his third missionary journey, Paul's farewell to the Ephesian elders took place here (Acts 20:15–38). Later he left the ill Trophimus in Miletus (2 Tim. 4:20).

Southwestern Ports

Patara. Sitting on the Mediterranean coast at the mouth of the Xanthus River, about forty miles west of present-day Demre, Patara was a flourishing harbor and commercial center in antiquity. Paul changed ships here as he returned to Jerusalem from his third missionary journey, after island stops in Kos and Rhodes (Acts 21:1–2).

Myra. Myra is a coastal ruin due south of present-day Demre. In the NT era, the seaport featured a Roman theater, Roman baths, and two rock-cut necropolises. Here, Paul changed ships around AD 60 on his way to Rome while in the custody of a centurion (Acts 27:5).

Cnidus. At the tip of the long, narrow Datca peninsula on the extreme southwestern corner of Asia Minor lies Cnidus. Founded around 360 BC, the acropolis rises one thousand feet above sea level. The port included two harbors and four theaters but was most famous for its fourth-century BC statue of Aphrodite, carved by the Athenian sculptor Praxiteles. Around AD 60 the ship carrying Paul to Rome stopped here because of slow winds and changed course (Acts 27:7).

Seven Churches of Revelation; Lycus Valley

The seven churches of Rev. 1–3 lay along a north-south elliptical route in western Asia Minor. Laodicea, the seventh, forms a tight geographic triangle with Hierapolis and Colossae in the Lycus Valley.

Ephesus. Known today as Selçuk, ancient Ephesus is located on the Aegean coast of Asia Minor at the mouth of the Cayster River. It was founded in the eleventh century BC by the Ionians and later ruled successively by the Athenians, Spartans, Persians, and Greeks. Roman governance began in 190 BC. Later, Ephesus became the capital of the province of Asia, as well as its most important commercial center. During the NT era, the Artemision (*see* Artemis) was an important pilgrimage site.

Paul stopped in Ephesus briefly on his second missionary journey, leaving Priscilla and Aquila. They later encountered and mentored Apollos there (Acts 18:19–26). On his third journey, Paul remained in Ephesus for three years, teaching, performing miracles, and healing the sick (19:1–22) until the riot incited by Demetrius the silversmith (20:1). He wrote 1 Corinthians in Ephesus (1 Cor. 16:8) and later wrote to the Ephesians from his Roman prison cell (Eph. 3:1) as well as to Timothy in Ephesus (1 Tim. 1:3).

In Rev. 2:1–7 the Ephesian church is commended for its perseverance but chastised for having lost its first love.

Smyrna. Smyrna (modern İzmir) is located about thirty-five miles north along the coast from Ephesus. In 195 BC it became the first city in Asia Minor to erect a temple for the imperial cult, and by the next century it was known as "the ornament of Asia." In its letter, which mentions no negatives, the church is encouraged to be faithful in its suffering (Rev. 2:8–11).

Pergamum. About seventy miles north of Smyrna is Pergamum (modern Bergama). The dazzling acropolis sits one thousand feet high and about sixteen miles inland from the Aegean. The Attalids, who ruled 263–133 BC, allied Pergamum with Rome and built it into a major religious and intellectual center, constructing the great altar to Zeus Soter, the temple to Athena Nicephorus, and the large complex dedicated to Asclepius Soter. They also established a ruler cult and built a library containing two hundred thousand volumes, which at its peak was second only to the library at Alexandria.

The letter to the church (Rev. 2:12–17) references Satan's throne, which many believe to be a reference to the altar to Zeus. The church is commended for its faithfulness and yet is admonished for tolerating those advocating pagan practices within the community.

Thyatira. Thyatira (now called Akhisar) is about thirty-five miles southeast of Pergamum. It was mainly noted as having a significant concentration of trade guilds, especially those connected with textiles. Lydia, Paul's disciple and host in Philippi, was a dealer in purple cloth from Thyatira (Acts 16:14). The church is commended for its good deeds but criticized for tolerating the false teacher Jezebel (Rev. 2:18–29).

Sardis. Forty-five miles east of Smyrna, on the banks of the Pactolus, is Sardis, where Croesus, the sixth-century BC Lydian king, was said to have panned for gold. He also built an impressive Ionic temple to Artemis here. The letter to Sardis is a stern warning to wake up, highlighting the church's incomplete deeds and impurity (Rev. 3:1–6).

Philadelphia. Philadelphia (modern Alaşehir) is twenty-six miles southwest of Sardis on the Cogamis River. The city was noted for its wine production, and it was nicknamed "Little Athens" during the Roman era. Its letter is thoroughly positive; the church is commended for its deeds and faithfulness (Rev. 3:7–13).

Laodicea. Laodicea is located about a hundred miles east of Ephesus, in a valley where the Lycus River joins the Meander; Hierapolis is just to the north, and Colossae just to the east. Laodicea was founded in the third century BC by the Seleucid king Antiochus II, who named it after his wife. Cicero served as proconsul there in 51 BC.

Laodicea was a prosperous city, a center for banking, eye salve ("Phrygian powder"), and wool production. Its water was supplied via aqueducts from Hierapolis's hot springs, but it arrived lukewarm and heavy with mineral impurities—no match for either its hot source or Colossae's cold springs. The Laodicean letter employs all of this background in its harsh message to the church, which it describes as tepid, poor, blind, and naked (Rev. 3:14–22).

Hierapolis. Eight miles to the north of Laodicea, Hierapolis sits atop dramatic white cliffs created by its hot springs (Col. 4:13). The city was home to the reputed entrance to the underworld, the Plutonium, and had an enormous necropolis.

Colossae. Colossae, ten miles east of Laodicea, was a center for dyed red wool. Although wealthy in the late fourth century BC, it was later eclipsed by Laodicea.

The churches in Laodicea, Hierapolis, and Colossae (the oldest of the three cities) were begun by Epaphras and shared letters, including Paul's letter to the Colossians (Col. 4:13–16). The slave Onesimus carried it, along with the Letter to Philemon, to Colossae, where Philemon hosted the house church (Col. 4:9; Philem. 10–12).

Assassins–*See* Jewish Parties (Zealots).

Assyria–The geographic center of Assyria consisted of a triangle between the Kurdish mountains, the Tigris River, and the Upper Zab River (which flows into the Tigris). This triangle sits within the modern-day country of Iraq and for the most part contained the four most important cities in the history of ancient Assyria: Ashur, Nineveh, Arbela, and Calah. At the height of its power, the Assyrian Empire stretched far beyond this geographical region, but this heartland served as the political and social base throughout its history.

Though Assyria had a significant history beforehand, this survey begins with the neo-Assyrian period since that is when interaction with Israel and the biblical record begins.

After the death of Tiglath-pileser, Assyria entered another period of decline due to the absence of a sufficient administrative structure to rule the enormous territory of the empire as well as the increasing pressure by the Arameans. However, Assyria again gained stability under Ashur-dan II (c. 934–912 BC). He began to renew military campaigns to recover lands previously held and fortified the capital city of Ashur. His two successors, Adad-nirari II (911–891 BC) and Tukulti-Ninurta II (890–884 BC), continued the successful military campaigns and ambitious building projects. This revival of the Assyrian Empire under Ashur-dan II marks the beginning of what historians call the Neo-Assyrian

Empire, an era of power that would last for three hundred years and grow to supersede the accomplishments of all prior Assyrian reigns.

In 883 BC Ashurnasirpal II came to power. Under him the Assyrian army became better organized and thus more efficient and engaged in military campaigns regularly instead of sporadically. There was also an increase in the brutality exercised by the Assyrian army in order to dissuade smaller states from attempting to resist Assyria's expansion. Ashurnasirpal II also built the small town of Calah into a major city and relocated the capital of Assyria there.

Shortly after inheriting the Assyrian empire in 858 BC, Ashurnasirpal II's son Shalmaneser III turned his attention to the north and the west and began moving to assert Assyrian control over those territories. In 853 BC he dismantled a northern alliance and then proceeded southward. At Qarqar Shalmaneser's forces clashed with the Damascus coalition, which consisted of a number of nations, including Israel under King Ahab, that had banded together to resist the Assyrian encroachment. This battle is not mentioned in the Bible, but the lopsided nature of the victory claimed by the Assyrians seems overstated, since Shalmaneser continued to fight against the Damascus coalition over the next decade. By 841 BC, Israel (under King Jehu), Tyre, and Sidon had voluntarily submitted to Assyrian control. As Shalmaneser grew old, he delegated more and more authority to those under him, creating friction among his subordinates and sons over the direction of the monarchy. Even though Shalmaneser's son Shamshi-Adad V (823–811 BC) emerged as the monarch after his father's death, instability within the kingdom and the rapidly increasing external threat of the Urartian Empire to the north resulted in a weakening of the Assyrian Empire that would last for almost a century until the rise of Tiglath-pileser III in 744 BC.

With the ascension of Tiglath-pileser III (744–727 BC) to the throne, the empire entered a hundred-year period that would be the golden age of Assyrian rule in the ancient Near East. In addition to reclaiming lands lost in the previous century to Urartu, he reasserted Assyrian control over Damascus, Hamath, Byblos, Tyre, and Samaria. Shortly afterward, King Pekah of Israel and King Rezin of Damascus banded together to resist Assyrian hegemony in what is called the "Syro-Ephraimite coalition." When they tried to force King Ahaz of Judah to join them, he appealed to Tiglath-pileser for help in exchange for fealty, against the counsel of Isaiah (see 2 Kings 16; 2 Chron. 28; Isa. 7). In 734 BC Tiglath-pileser crushed the coalition, captured Gaza, and developed it into a trade center between Assyria and Egypt. In addition to improving the military and restructuring the administration of the empire, Tiglath-pileser instituted the policy of deporting and exiling subjects who rebelled against him, a policy that his successors would continue.

The next king over Assyria, Shalmaneser V, ruled for only about four years (726–722 BC). His chief importance is that he conquered Samaria, the capital of the northern kingdom of Israel (see 2 Kings 17–18), though he was killed around the same time. The next king, Sargon II (721–705 BC), exiled the northern Israelites and settled in their place peoples from Syria and Babylonia. Sargon also built an entirely new capital, Dur-Sharrukin, just a few miles north of Nineveh.

In 704 BC Sargon's son Sennacherib came to the throne and established the Assyrian capital at Nineveh. The kingdom of Judah and its capital, Jerusalem, became a top priority for Sennacherib because Judah was not only refusing submission to Assyria but also allying itself with Egypt and Ethiopia against Assyria. In 701 BC Sennacherib invaded Palestine, and at Eltekeh the Assyrian forces clashed with a coalition of Egyptian and Ethiopian forces that had come to the aid of Hezekiah, king of Judah. After defeating these forces, Sennacherib marched toward Jerusalem. Along the way he laid waste to the Judean countryside and exiled the inhabitants. The brunt of the damage was done in the Shephelah region, especially the city of Lachish. Although Sennacherib is not named explicitly, these are the circumstances that seem to be reflected in Mic. 1:8–16. When Sennacherib's army reached Jerusalem, it laid siege to the capital city. Although Sennacherib had gone to Libnah, he sent his Rabshakeh (a senior official in the Assyrian army) to press his claims. The account of the ensuing standoff between Hezekiah and the Rabshakeh is given in three places in the Bible: 2 Kings 18–19; 2 Chron. 32; and Isa. 36–37. According to the Bible, the angel of the Lord slaughtered much of the Assyrian army, forcing the survivors to retreat and thus delivering Jerusalem. Variant accounts are given by Josephus (*Ant.* 10.1.4–5) and Herodotus (*Hist.* 2.141).

A

After the death of Sennacherib in 681 BC, his son Esarhaddon took control of the Assyrian Empire until 669 BC. During his reign Assyria gained superficial control of Egypt. Before his death he appointed Ashurbanipal as his heir over Assyria (668–612 BC), but he made Shamash-shuma-ukin the king over Babylonia. This fateful move eventually led to the downfall of Assyria because it resulted in civil war. With its resources already depleted by the vast empire, Assyria crumbled in the late seventh century BC to a coalition of Babylonian, Median, and Scythian forces. The end came quickly, and in 612 BC Nineveh was sacked (see the book of Nahum) and the Neo-Babylonian Empire was born.

Astrologer–A person who studies the stars and their supposed effect on human personality and history. Such individuals were well known in both Mesopotamia and Egypt, though the former is more represented in the biblical texts.

In several places the OT prophets either ridicule or attack astrologers and their practice (Isa. 47:13; Dan. 2:27; 4:7; 5:7, 11; Amos 5:26), and the practice is strictly forbidden in the law codes (Deut. 4:19). Although there are several texts that may apply to astrology in the NT, the only explicit mentions of the practice are in connection with the magi (Matt. 2) and Simon, Bar-jesus, and Elymas (Acts 8:9; 13:6, 8). However, in light of admonitions against astrology and the fact that it is an affront to faith in God, the birth narrative of Jesus should not be read as an approval of the practice but rather as an extraordinary event in which the heavens themselves proclaim the coming of the one born "king of the Jews" (Matt. 2:2).

Athaliah–Daughter of Ahab and Jezebel, later the wife of the Judean king Jehoram and the mother of the succeeding short-lived king, Ahaziah (2 Kings 8:25–27; 2 Chron. 22:2). On first introduction to the Bible reader, she is ominously described as "a granddaughter of Omri king of Israel," a dynasty that profoundly damaged the spiritual life of the northern kingdom. Through her, this infection entered the southern kingdom. She encouraged her son Ahaziah to follow "the ways of the house of Ahab," promoting the false worship of Baal in Jerusalem (2 Chron. 22:3). On the death of her son at the hands of Jehu, she exterminated the royal family of Judah and reigned over the land (2 Kings 11). Only Joash, the infant son of Ahaziah, escaped the purge and remained hidden for six years. In the seventh year of her reign (836 BC) Jehoiada the priest brought Joash out of hiding and organized a palace coup against Athaliah, and she was executed. The destruction of the paraphernalia of Baal worship and slaying of the priest of Baal followed immediately on her death.

Athens–Athens is located five miles northeast of the port of Piraeus on the Saronic Gulf. It was the chief city of the ancient Greek province of Attica (2 Macc. 9:15; Acts 17:15–18; 18:1; 1 Thess. 3:1) and is the capital of modern Greece.

Paul visited this city on his second missionary journey. His debate with the Greek philosophers in the agora (the marketplace) brought him before the city council of Athens, the Areopagus, where religious matters were settled (Acts 17:16–34). Traditionally, the site is identified as Mars Hill, located on the west side of the Acropolis. Interestingly, Paul founded no church in Athens.

Atonement–The English word "atonement" comes from an Anglo-Saxon word, "onement," with the preposition "at"; thus "at-onement," or "at unity." In some ways this word has more in common with the idea of reconciliation than our modern concept of atonement, which, while having "oneness" as its result, emphasizes rather the idea of how that unity is achieved, by someone "atone-ing" for a wrong or wrongs done. Atonement, in Christian theology, concerns how Christ achieved this "onement" between God and sinful humanity.

The need for atonement comes from the separation that has come about between God and humanity because of sin. In both Testaments there is the understanding that God has distanced himself from his creatures on account of their rebellion. Isaiah tells the people of Judah, "Your iniquities have separated you from your God" (59:2). And Paul talks about how we were "God's enemies" (Rom. 5:10). So atonement is the means provided by God to effect reconciliation. The atonement is required on account of God's holiness and justice.

Atonement, Day of–*See* Festivals.

Atonement Cover–*See* Mercy Seat.

A

Augustan Cohort–An auxiliary unit in the Roman army made up of non-Roman citizens who could gain citizenship through their service. This particular unit was stationed in Syria and held some level of favor as related to its association with the famed emperor. The centurions of this cohort escorted Paul on his journey from Caesarea to Rome (Acts 27:1 [NIV: "Imperial Regiment"]).

Augustus–*See* Rome, Roman Empire.

Avenger–The term "avenger" occurs sixteen times in the NIV, usually in the phrase "avenger of blood." The Hebrew word may be translated "redeemer," "avenger," or "near relative" and referred to a kinsman who acted on behalf of a close relative. The term was used of one who avenged (repaid) the death of a murdered relative (Num. 35:12), received restitution for crimes against a deceased relative (Num. 5:7–8), bought back family property that had been sold (Lev. 25:25), purchased a relative who had been sold into slavery (Lev. 25:48–49), or married a relative's widow in order to raise up heirs for her deceased husband (levirate marriage) (Deut. 25:5–10). The "avenger of blood" refers specifically to the first of these functions, a murder victim's near relative who would exact justice by executing the murderer. This was in line with the OT principle of "eye for an eye" and "tooth for a tooth" (Exod. 21:24; Lev. 24:20; Deut. 19:21). Punishment was to be in proportion to the degree and severity of a crime. In the NT, this role of justice is assigned to government authorities (Rom. 13:4).

This procedure for justice for the avenger of blood is found in Num. 35:9–27; Deut. 19:11–13; Josh. 20. If a person was found guilty of intentional murder on the testimony of two or three witnesses (Deut. 17:6; 19:15), the avenger of blood served as executioner.

In cases of accidental manslaughter, the accused could flee to one of six cities of refuge, where the city assembly would judge the case and provide protection from the avenger of blood (Num. 35:6–34; Deut. 4:41–43; 19:1–14; Josh. 20:1–9). Numbers 35:12 designates that "they will be places of refuge from the avenger, so that anyone accused of murder may not die before they stand trial before the assembly" (cf. Josh. 20:9). Deuteronomy 19:4–7 explains the necessity of this protection: the avenger may be filled with rage and take revenge without concern for whether the death was accidental or intentional. If the accused left the city of refuge, the avenger of blood could take his life (Num. 35:27). This held true until the death of the high priest, at which time the accused could leave the city without fear of reprisal. The primary purpose of the laws related to the avenger of blood was to provide consistent justice and so reduce blood feuds and continued cycles of retaliation and revenge.

Awel-Marduk–The son and successor of Nebuchadnezzar of Babylon. In Hebrew tradition, he is known by the name "Evil-Merodach." Reigning in the years 562/561–560 BC, he pardoned King Jehoiachin of Judah, who had been imprisoned by Nebuchadnezzar. Thereafter, Jehoiachin dined at the king's table (2 Kings 25:27–30; Jer. 52:31–34; confirmed by Babylonian records).

Azariah–*See* Uzziah.

Azazel–Azazel appears only in Lev. 16 (NIV: "scapegoat"), instructions for the Day of Atonement, on which lots were cast over two goats, one for God and the other for Azazel. After sacrificing the first goat, the high priest confessed the Israelites' wickedness over the second goat and sent it into the desert.

There are multiple interpretations of the Hebrew word *'aza'zel*, one of which is "the goat [*'ez*] of removal." The term "scapegoat" (originally "escapegoat") comes from this interpretation. Nevertheless, a goat "for the goat of escape" is redundant. Instead, "Azazel" is likely the name of a demon of the wilderness.

Azekah–Between the protected hill country of Judah and the open coastal plain lies a range of low rolling hills cut through by significant valleys. Toward the western end of the Elah Valley, Azekah stands guard. Because of its strategic location, it played an important role in critical conflicts between Israel and its enemies.

As Joshua and the Israelites routed the Jerusalem confederation (Josh. 10), the enemies of Israel fled westward from the central Benjamin plateau, through the Aijalon Valley, and south beyond Azekah. Some centuries later, the major threat to Israel was the Philistine presence on the coast. The Philistines sought to expand their control into the hill country and camped on the south side of the Elah Valley between Sokoh and Azekah; the Israelites were on the opposite side of the valley. David challenged and killed the Philistine champion, Goliath, and the Philistines fled west past Azekah toward Ekron, one of their own cities (1 Sam. 17).

After Solomon's death, Rehoboam fortified a ring of cities to protect the southern kingdom. Among them was Azekah (2 Chron. 11:5–12), southwest of Jerusalem. At the end of the Judean monarchy, the Babylonians attacked Jerusalem and the other cities that were still holding out. Lachish and Azekah were the only fortified cities left in Judah (Jer. 34:6–7). A poignant letter discovered in the gate area of Lachish reads, "We were watching for the smoke signals of Lachish . . . because we do not see Azekah" (Lachish Letter 4).

B

Baal–A West Semitic weather and warrior deity. There is evidence that "Baal," meaning "lord," was a proper name for a deity as early as the third millennium BC and may have been identified with the god Hadad.

Second millennium texts from the ancient city of Ugarit depict Baal as a god of weather and storm whose provision of precipitation ensures the seasonal cycles of crops. The Baal Cycle from Ugarit also depicts him defeating Yamm, the god of the sea, and Mot, the god of death. Some of these associations shed light on polemics against Baal in the OT. Yahweh's withholding rain at Elijah's request (1 Kings 17:1), for example, undermines Baal's claim to control the weather. Further, descriptions of Yahweh as a storm god, such as Ps. 29, may be understood as polemical statements that Yahweh, not Baal, is the one who really controls the storm.

The worship of Baal alongside Yahweh received official sponsorship in Israel under Ahab (1 Kings 16:31–33) and in Judah under Manasseh (2 Kings 10:18–27). The worship of this deity was grounds for the exile of Israel (2 Kings 17:16).

Baalbek–*See* Heliopolis.

Baal-Berith–Meaning "Baal/Lord of the covenant," this was Shechem's local manifestation of the Canaanite deity Baal (Judg. 8:33; 9:4, 27, 46). *See also* Baal.

Baal Hermon–Also known as Seir, Mount Hermon, and Mount Baal Hermon, this is part of the territory of the half-tribe of Manasseh east of the Jordan (1 Chron. 5:23; cf. Josh. 13:11), which was taken by the Israelites under Moses from Og, king of Bashan (Deut. 3:8–9). Located northeast of Dan, it is the highest mountain in the traditional territory of Israel. According to Judg. 3:3, the Hivites remained in this region following the conquest.

Baali–A Hebrew name (meaning either "my husband/lord" or "my Baal") that occurs only in Hos. 2:16. Apparently, Israelites had been using this name for Yahweh. On the one hand, since *ba'al* can mean "lord" or "husband," this can be construed as an appropriate name for God. Since "Baal," however, is also the name of one of the Canaanite deities whose worship plagued the history of both Israel and Judah, Hosea saw this name as inappropriate for the God of Israel.

Baalis–The king of Ammon at the beginning of the exile of Judah. He conspired with Ishmael to assassinate Gedaliah, the governor of Judah installed by the Babylonians after the destruction of Jerusalem (Jer. 40:14).

Baal-Zebub–A deity of the Philistine city Ekron who appears only in 2 Kings 1:2, 3, 6, 16. "Baal-Zebub" probably means "Baal/Lord of the flies," but it is possible that the original name of this deity was "Baal-Zebul," perhaps meaning "Baal the prince." This possibility finds support in the appearance of a similar name for a god in Ugaritic texts and in the NT references to *Beelzeboul* as the name of a demon or prince of the demons (Matt. 10:25; 12:24, 27; Mark 3:22; Luke 11:15, 18–19).

Baasha–A king of Israel (906–883 BC) who gained ascendancy to the throne by means of a violent takeover, resulting in the death of his predecessor, Nadab (1 Kings 15:27–28).

Babel–The Hebrew name for Babylon. In standard English translations this name is consistently translated as "Babel" only in Gen. 11:9 and sometimes in 10:10 (NRSV, NET). Although all its other occurrences are translated as "Babylon," there is no distinction in the Hebrew. In the Babylonian language (Akkadian) the name means "Gate of God"; in Gen. 11:9 the Hebrew author connects the name "Babel" (*babel*) to the similar-sounding Hebrew word for "confused" (*balal*). This connection is best understood as a wordplay rather than an actual etymology. *See also* Babylon, Babylonia.

B

BABYLON, BABYLONIA–Babylon (Babel) was the capital city of Babylonia, an ancient kingdom located in Mesopotamia, the region between the Tigris and the Euphrates rivers, an area now in the modern country of Iraq. The city of Babylon was located on the banks of the Euphrates River, about fifty-five miles from the modern city of Baghdad. Babylon plays a major role in the Bible, especially during the time of the OT prophets. Babylon or the Babylonians are mentioned in the books of 2 Kings, 1–2 Chronicles, Ezra, Nehemiah, Esther, Psalms, Isaiah, Jeremiah, Ezekiel, Daniel, Micah, Habakkuk, and Zechariah. Babylon also appears at the very beginning of the biblical story (Gen. 10–11) as well as at the very end (Rev. 14; 16–18; cf. 1 Pet. 5:13).

Old Testament. Genesis 10:10 states that Babylon was one of the first centers of the kingdom of the mighty warrior Nimrod, but the puzzling nature of Nimrod and the difficulties encountered in interpreting Gen. 10 make it difficult to state much about this reference with certainty.

The better-known incident in Genesis regarding Babylon is the story about the tower of Babel (Gen. 11:1–9). Note that in Gen. 9:1–7 God commands Noah and his family to scatter over the earth and replenish its population. The builders of the tower of Babel are doing just the opposite of the divine injunction, trying to stop the scattering.

Thus, the city of Babel/Babylon carried negative connotations from the very beginning of the biblical story. Genesis 11 introduces Babel as a symbol of human arrogance and rebellion against God. Later in Israel's history the city of Babylon will continue to have negative associations, and once again it becomes a powerful symbol of human arrogance and rebellion against God.

The books of 1–2 Kings tell the tragic story of how Israel and Judah turn away from God to worship idols, ignoring the warnings that God gives them through the prophets. As foretold, the northern kingdom, Israel, is thus destroyed by the Assyrians in 722 BC. However, the southern kingdom, Judah, also fails to take heed and continues to worship pagan gods in spite of repeated warnings and calls to repentance from the prophets. Prophets such as Jeremiah repeatedly proclaim that if Judah and Jerusalem do not repent and turn from their idolatry and acts of injustice, then God will send the Babylonians to destroy them (see esp. Jer. 20–39). Jeremiah refers to the Babylonians 198 times, and the prophet personally experiences the terrible Babylonian siege and destruction of Jerusalem. Jeremiah 39 and 52 describe the actual fall of Jerusalem to Nebuchadnezzar and his Babylonian army. This same tragic story is recounted in 2 Kings 24–25. Thus, in 586 BC Nebuchadnezzar and his army completely destroy Jerusalem, burning the city and the temple to the ground and carrying off most of the population into exile in Babylonia.

Babylon appears in the OT prophetic literature in another context as well. Because of the apostasy of Israel and Judah, the prophets preach judgment on them. But the prophets also preach judgment on the enemies of Israel and Judah for exploiting or attacking and destroying God's people. Jeremiah, for example, prophesies against numerous nations and cities (Jer. 46–49), but he focuses especially upon Babylon (Jer. 50:1–51:58).

New Testament. Babylon appears again at the end of the biblical story. In Rev. 17–18 John describes the enemy of God's kingdom as a harlot dressed in scarlet and riding on a beast. One of the titles written on her head is "Babylon the Great" (17:5). Many scholars maintain that the harlot of Rev. 17–18 symbolizes ancient Rome, not a modern rebuilt Babylon. They argue that the term "Babylon" is used symbolically in Revelation. Supporting this view is the apostle Peter's apparent use of the term "Babylon" to refer to Rome in 1 Pet. 5:13 ("she who is in Babylon . . . sends you her greetings"). Most NT scholars conclude that in this verse "she" is a reference to the church and that "Babylon" is a coded or symbolic reference to Rome.

BAKA, VALLEY OF–A valley mentioned in Ps. 84:6. Worshipers are said to pass through this valley on the way to worship in Zion. The Hebrew word *baka'* may mean "balsam tree," thus "Valley of the Balsam." The word *baka'* also is similar to the Hebrew word for "weeping," thus "Valley of Weeping." Perhaps the name of the valley alludes to both words.

Bakers' Street–Street in Jerusalem during the time of King Zedekiah (Jer. 37:21; NIV: "street of the bakers"). This street is most likely where the majority of the bakers were located in Jerusalem.

Balaam–Toward the end of the forty years of wandering in the wilderness, Moses led the people of Israel to the plains of Moab, across the Jordan from Jericho (Num. 22:1). From this place, Israel would soon cross into the promised land. However, Israel had just defeated Sihon and Og (Num. 21:21–35), two Transjordanian kings, putting fear in the minds of the Moabites and their king, Balak.

To counteract the threat, Balak tried to enlist the aid of a well-known diviner, Balaam, who lived in Pethor, a site in northwest Mesopotamia (Num. 22:5). The king wanted to weaken Israel by having Balaam curse the Israelites. However, God made it clear to Balaam that he would not endorse any action against his people. Balaam at first refused to go with the Moabite messengers, but after being enticed by an even bigger payment, he left for Moab. God allowed him to go, but with a warning that Balaam could do only what God himself commanded him to do. God emphasized this last point by famously putting an invisible angel in the path of Balaam's donkey so that it could not pass. In frustration, Balaam whipped the donkey until God gave the animal voice to object to the beating, and then the Lord opened the diviner's eyes to the angel's presence. The episode puts Balaam in a negative light, having his donkey alert him, the diviner, to the angel's presence.

Nonetheless, Balaam continues on his journey, but due to God's command, he could only bless and not curse Israel. At Balak's urging, he tries to curse Israel four times, but each time he delivers an oracle of blessing. The final oracle directed to Israel (Num. 23:15–19) contains the most memorable words of Balaam as he predicts, "A star will come out of Jacob; a scepter will rise out of Israel" (24:17), which comes to fulfillment in the rise of the Davidic dynasty.

Thus, Balak of Moab's attempt to thwart Israel by prophetic curse fails. However, Num. 25 reports that a different tactic does succeed in bringing harm, though not utter ruin, to the people of God. Some Israelites start sleeping with women of Moab and Midian and worshiping their gods. The damage is stopped by the swift action of Phinehas the priest. Although Balaam is not named in this chapter, Num. 31:16 reports that he was the one who originated the plot. Apparently, Balaam was determined to get the payment. Later Scripture holds him up as a negative example of a false teacher who cares only about money (Judg. 11; 2 Pet. 2:15; Rev. 2:14). The Israelites kill him along with many other Midianites (Num. 31:8).

Balak–The Moabite king who, after witnessing the Israelite destruction of the Amorites, sent for Balaam the prophet to curse the Israelites (Num. 22:1–24:25). Balak's actions are recalled throughout the Bible (Josh. 24:9; Judg. 11:25; Mic. 6:5; Rev. 2:14).

Banner–A flag, streamer, emblem, or carved object raised on a pole. On the ancient battlefield, raised banners and blown trumpets served as the primary tools for mass communication. They could indicate troop movements and serve as rallying points (Isa. 18:3). Once the battle was won, banners proclaimed victory. Cloth banners usually were colored and carried symbols to represent a particular group, whether it was a military unit, clan, tribe, or nation (Num. 2:2; Ps. 60:4).

When Moses placed the bronze serpent on a pole, he raised it as a banner for the Israelites to look upon it and be healed (Num. 21:8). Jesus drew a parallel between the raised serpent and the raising up of the Son of Man (John 3:14). Metaphorically, Jesus was a banner lifted up to proclaim salvation for the world.

Banquet–A banquet is a joyful celebration, usually involving wine, abundant food, music, and dancing. Banquets celebrated special occasions such as the forging of a relationship (Gen. 26:26–30), the coronation of a king (1 Chron. 12:28–40), the completion of the temple (2 Chron. 7:8), victory over one's enemies (Gen. 14:18–19; Ps. 23:5), weddings (Gen. 29:22; John 2:1–11; Rev. 19:9), birthdays of royals (Mark 6:21), and the reunion of estranged relatives (Luke 15:23–24). Banquets also symbolized one's status, since they were by invitation only. One's seating arrangement corresponded to one's social status in the group, since there were "higher" and "lower" positions (Luke 14:8–9). During the meal, people reclined on bedlike seats.

Jesus uses the banquet as a metaphor for the presence of the kingdom (cf. Matt. 9:14–17). He tells a parable of a king who has planned a wedding banquet for his son. Those who were invited have refused to attend (i.e., the Jewish leaders), so the king commands his servants to go out into the streets and gather as many people as they can find, both good and bad (Matt. 22:1–10).

Jesus also uses the imagery of a banquet to describe the final future manifestation of the kingdom. He exhorts his disciples to be prepared for the unexpected return of the bridegroom, lest they be excluded from the wedding banquet (Matt. 25:1–13). At the Last Supper, he commands the disciples to continue the practice of sharing bread and wine after his departure, to remember his atoning death and to anticipate his future coming (Matt. 26:26–29). This future banquet will celebrate Christ's final union with his bride, the church (Rev. 19:6–9).

Baptism–The initiatory ritual of Christianity. This rite is of great significance in connecting the individual both to Christ and to the greater community of believers. Baptism carries an equal measure of symbolism and tradition, evoking a connection between OT covenantal circumcision and ritual cleansing and NT regeneration and redemption.

The immediate precursor of Christian baptism was the baptism of John the Baptist (Mark 1:4 pars.), a baptism of repentance for the forgiveness of sins, preparing the hearts of the people for the coming Messiah. But when Jesus himself was baptized by John to "fulfill all righteousness" (Matt. 3:15) and to allow Jesus to identify with sinful humanity, he became the firstfruits of the new covenant. John emphasized that his baptism with water was inferior to the baptism "with the Holy Spirit and fire" that Jesus would bring (Matt. 3:11). Jesus' disciples continued John's baptism during his earthly ministry (John 4:1–2).

Baptism was immediately important in the early church. Jesus commanded the disciples to "make disciples . . . , baptizing them" (Matt. 28:19). The disciples replaced Judas from among those "who have been with us the whole time . . . from John's baptism" (Acts 1:21–22). Peter's first sermon proclaims, "Repent and be baptized" (2:38). The apostles baptized new believers in Christ immediately (8:12–13, 38; 9:18; 10:48; 16:15, 33; 18:8; 19:5; 22:16).

For the apostle Paul, baptism represents a participation in the crucifixion and resurrection of Jesus Christ. Paul writes, "Don't you know that all of us who were baptized into Christ Jesus were baptized into his death? We were therefore buried with him through baptism into death" (Rom. 6:3–4); "In him you were . . . buried with him in baptism, in which you were also raised with him through your faith in the working of God, who raised him from the dead" (Col. 2:11–12).

Baptism in/with the Spirit–The outpouring of the Spirit that was prophesied in the OT to take place in the last days, in connection with the arrival of the Messiah.

The OT prophets had spoken of both the Spirit of God coming upon the Messiah (e.g., Isa. 11:2; 42:1; 61:1) and a giving or pouring out of the Spirit in the last days (e.g., Isa. 32:15; 44:3; Ezek. 36:27; 37:14; 39:29; Joel 2:28). Peter connects the giving of the Spirit with Jesus' being received by the Father and being granted messianic authority (Acts 2:33–38). The experience of Cornelius in particular associates the pouring out of the Spirit (Acts 10:45) with a baptism with the Spirit (11:16).

Seven passages in the NT directly speak of someone being baptized in/with the Spirit. Four of these passages refer to John the Baptist's prediction that Jesus will baptize people in/with the Spirit in contrast to his own water baptism (Matt. 3:11; Mark 1:8; Luke 3:16; John 1:33). In Matthew and Luke, Jesus' baptism is referred to as a baptism with the Holy Spirit and with fire. Two passages refer to Jesus' prediction that the disciples would receive Spirit baptism, which occurred at Pentecost. As recorded in Acts 2, tongues of fire came to rest on each of them, they were filled with the Holy Spirit, and they began to speak in other tongues. As the disciples spoke to the Jews who had gathered in Jerusalem for the festival, three thousand were converted. Acts 1:5 contains Jesus' prediction of this baptism with the Spirit, which Peter recounts in 11:16.

The final reference occurs in 1 Cor. 12:13, where Paul says, "For we were all baptized by one Spirit so as to form one body—whether Jews or Gentiles, slave or free—and we were all given the one Spirit to drink." Thus, Christians form one body through their common experience of immersion in the one Spirit.

Barabbas–A prisoner mentioned in all four Gospels. Barabbas is a prisoner of particular note according to Matthew (27:16), an insurrectionist and murderer according to Mark (15:7) and Luke (23:19), and a rebel according to John (18:40). Barabbas was being held in prison when the Jewish chief priests and elders brought Jesus before Pilate following Judas's betrayal in the garden of Gethsemane. After witnessing Jesus' silence before those who were accusing him, Pilate asked the crowd whether they would rather he release to them Barabbas or Jesus. The practice of releasing a prisoner is described as either Pilate's custom (Mark 15:8) or a Jewish Passover custom (John 18:39). Persuaded by the chief priests and elders, the crowd demanded the release of Barabbas and the crucifixion of Jesus.

Barak–A military commander of Israel during the time of the judges, commanded by God through the prophetess Deborah to lead an army in battle against Sisera, commander of the Canaanite forces. Barak agrees on the condition that Deborah accompany him, which she does, but only after passing the honor of killing Sisera from Barak to a woman, the wife of Heber the Kenite (Judg. 4:6–24). Deborah praises the victory (5:19–22). Barak is listed as a hero in 1 Sam. 12:11; Heb. 11:32.

Bar-Jesus–A Jewish sorcerer in the service of the proconsul of Paphos. As Paul predicted, Bar-Jesus became blind as a consequence of his opposition to Paul and Barnabas as they proclaimed the gospel to the proconsul (Acts 13:6).

Bar-Jonah–The surname of Simon Peter, identifying his father as Jonah (Matt. 16:17) or John (John 1:42).

Barnabas–A name given by the apostles to Joseph, a Levite from Cyprus, missionary companion of Paul, and cousin of John Mark (Acts 4:36). Luke interprets the name "Barnabas" to mean (in Aramaic) "son of encouragement."

Barnabas first appears in the book of Acts as a model of generosity for the Jerusalem church when he sells a piece of property to support the poor in the church (4:36–37). Barnabas next appears as the member of the Jerusalem church courageous enough to bring Saul, the former persecutor, to the leaders of the Jerusalem church (9:26–27). Later, when reports of Gentile conversions in Antioch were received in Jerusalem, Barnabas was sent to Antioch to supervise the work there. Barnabas went to Tarsus and brought Saul with him to Antioch (11:22–26). There they ministered together, at one point delivering famine relief to Jerusalem (11:30).

The church in Antioch received a revelation from the Holy Spirit to send Barnabas and Saul on the first missionary outreach (Acts 13:2). Accompanied by Barnabas's cousin John Mark, they traveled to Barnabas's home island of Cyprus and then to the Roman province of Galatia. Mark deserted the group in Perga and returned to Jerusalem, but Paul and Barnabas established churches in Pisidian Antioch, Iconium, Lystra, and Derbe (Acts 13–14). After returning to Antioch, Barnabas accompanied Paul to the Jerusalem council to settle the Judaizing controversy concerning whether Gentiles must keep the law and be circumcised to be saved (Acts 15).

Upon returning to Antioch, Paul suggested a return to the churches in Galatia. Barnabas proposed taking John Mark, but Paul refused, and the ensuing conflict resulted in Paul's departure to Galatia with Silas, with Barnabas taking John Mark to Cyprus (Acts 15:36–41). This is the last we hear of Barnabas in Acts.

Paul mentions Barnabas five times in his letters (1 Cor. 9:6; Gal. 2:1, 9, 13; Col. 4:10). He refers to Mark as Barnabas's cousin (Col. 4:10), speaks of their Jerusalem famine visit (Gal. 2:1, 9), and relates an episode of apparent hypocrisy when Barnabas withdrew from Gentile table fellowship under pressure from Jewish Christians (Gal. 2:13).

Barren, Barrenness–A barren woman is one who is infertile and without children. The biblical world placed great value on the blessing of having children. Being without children brought despair. This can be seen in Rachel's despondent plea (Gen. 30:1) and in the fact that wives would offer a servant in their place to bear a child (16:3; 30:3, 9).

In most of the stories about women and infertility, God reversed their circumstances: Sarah (Gen. 11:30), Rebekah (25:21), Rachel (30:22), Samson's mother (Judg. 13:2–3), Hannah (1 Sam. 1:2), the Shunammite (2 Kings 4:16), Elizabeth (Luke 1:7). For Michal, barrenness appears as a punishment (2 Sam. 6:23).

Caring for the barren is part of God's praiseworthy caring for the needy (Ps. 113:5–9).

B

Barsabbas–The family name of two men: **(1)** Joseph (Acts 1:23), having the necessary qualifications, was the unsuccessful candidate when lots were cast to replace Judas Iscariot as one of the twelve apostles (Acts 1:21–26). **(2)** Judas, a leading Christian and prophet (Acts 15:32), was commissioned along with Silas to convey to the newly planted churches (13:1–14:28) the decision of the Jerusalem council not to require circumcision of Gentile believers (15:22).

Bartholomew–A disciple of Jesus, and one of the twelve apostles. His name appears in the Synoptic lists of apostles (Matt. 10:2–4; Mark 3:16–19; Luke 6:13–16) and as a witness to Jesus' ascension (Acts 1:13).

Bartimaeus–Mark 10:46–52 tells of this blind beggar who properly identifies Jesus as the "Son of David" (cf. Matt. 20:29–34; Luke 18:35–43). Seeing and believing, Bartimaeus is cast as an ideal disciple, "following" Jesus (Mark 10:52).

Baruch–The secretary of Jeremiah the prophet. He recorded a deed of purchase that was central to a message about return after exile (Jer. 32:12). He recorded Jeremiah's dictated messages (36:18). Baruch also read Jeremiah's words of warning to officials and to the people at the temple on a fasting day, when visitors would be coming to Jerusalem (36:10, 14). For this service he had to go into temporary hiding with Jeremiah (36:19, 36). Baruch was also blamed as the supposed source of Jeremiah's oracle telling Judah not to go to Egypt (43:1–3). When he became discontent, he was rebuked but promised basic safety (45:1–5).

Barzillai–An old man from Rogelim in Gilead who was one of a group of wealthy men from the Transjordan who provided David and his troops with food and equipment when they reached Mahanaim while fleeing from Absalom (2 Sam. 17:27–29). Barzillai's loyalty was recognized when David invited him to join him in Jerusalem on his return, though this was tactfully declined on the grounds of advanced age but with the request that David take his son Kimham instead (19:31–39). This loyalty was further recognized when David instructed Solomon to deal loyally with Barzillai's descendants (1 Kings 2:7).

Bashan–Bashan lay in the Transjordan, to the east and northeast of the Sea of Galilee, and north of Gilead. It was a high plateau (Ps. 68:15), proverbial for oak forests (Isa. 2:13; 33:9; Ezek. 27:6; Zech. 11:2) and fat livestock (Deut. 32:14; Ps. 22:12; Ezek. 39:18; Amos 4:1). After Israel's defeat of King Og of Bashan (Num. 21:31–35; Deut. 3:1–11), Bashan was allocated to Manasseh (Num. 32:33). Israel retained Bashan until Solomon's time (1 Kings 4:13), but later it became disputed territory (2 Kings 10:32–33). The prophets longed for a permanent return to its pasturelands (Ps. 68:22; Jer. 5:19; Mic. 7:14).

Bath–*See* Weights and Measures.

Bath Rabbim–Song of Songs 7:4 compares the female protagonist's eyes to "the pools of Heshbon by the gate of Bath Rabbim." Heshbon was a Transjordanian site in traditionally Moabite territory. Presumably, the gate of Bath Rabbim was a prominent landmark, of comparable fame and beauty to the otherwise unknown "tower of Lebanon" (Song 7:4).

Bathsheba–Originally the wife of one of David's senior soldiers, Uriah the Hittite (2 Sam. 11:3), she married David after they committed adultery and he arranged for Uriah's murder (11:6–27). Bathsheba had become pregnant by David, but the sin's punishment included the child's death (12:10). After this, she bore Solomon to David (12:24). In David's latter days she played a part in Solomon's succession (1 Kings 1:11–27) and Adonijah's demise (2:13–25). She is listed in Jesus' genealogy (Matt. 1:6).

Bear–In the Bible, the bear is often paired with the lion (1 Sam. 17:34–37; Prov. 28:15; Lam. 3:10; Hos. 13:8; Amos 5:19) and is thought to be dangerous especially when bereft of its cubs (2 Sam. 17:8; Prov. 17:12; Hos. 13:8). "Bear" imagery is also employed in apocalyptic visions (Dan. 7:5; Rev. 13:2) and in descriptions of God himself (Lam. 3:10–11; Hos. 13:8; cf. Amos 5:19). The bear is also ironically paired with the cow in Isa. 11:7, and it functions as an agent of divine judgment in 2 Kings 2:24.

Beard–Israelite men, like most of their ancient Near Eastern neighbors, wore full beards, as is plain from casual references to bearded faces (e.g., 1 Sam. 21:13; 2 Sam. 20:9; Ps.

133:2; Jer. 41:5). A way of shaming a man was to forcibly shave him (e.g., 2 Sam. 10:4–5), and Isaiah's threat of an Assyrian invasion of Judah comes in the form of the imagery of shaving the head and pubic hair (lit., "the hair of your legs"; Isa. 7:20).

Beatitudes–The Beatitudes are a series of "blessings" announced by Jesus in Matthew's Sermon on the Mount (Matt. 5:3–10) and Luke's parallel Sermon on the Plain (Luke 6:20–22). Matthew's version contains eight beatitudes, with a ninth (5:11–12) expanding on the eighth. Luke has four beatitudes but balances these with "woes" against the rich and powerful. Each beatitude has two parts. The first begins with a statement of blessing followed by the identity of the one being blessed (e.g., "blessed are the poor in spirit"). The second part explains why the person is blessed (e.g., "for theirs is the kingdom of heaven"). In Matthew, the phrase "for theirs is the kingdom of heaven" appears in verses 3, 10, serving as an inclusio for the central message of the Beatitudes: the kingdom of heaven is present and powerful to those who are in relationship with Jesus.

The Beatitudes introduce a new reality to those who respond to the kingdom offered by Jesus. They present a radical reversal for the downtrodden: the poor in spirit, those who mourn, the meek, and the persecuted. From society's perspective, they are weak and disadvantaged, but Jesus calls them "blessed." The beatitudes in Matt. 5:6–10 reveal attitudes and actions that are pleasing to God: "those who hunger and thirst for righteousness" (v. 6), "the merciful" (v. 7), "the pure in heart" (v. 8), and "the peacemakers" (v. 9).

Beautiful Gate–A gate of Herod's temple where John and Peter healed a lame man (Acts 3:2, 10; NIV: "gate called Beautiful").

Bed–A surface to recline on for the purpose of sleep, convalescence, contemplation, and sexual activity. Construction ranged from a portable straw mat (Mark 6:55; Acts 9:34) to raised frames crafted of wood, metal, or stone inlaid with precious metals and jewels (Deut. 3:11; Amos 6:4) and topped with luxurious coverings (Prov. 7:16, 17; 31:22). The mats of poor people might be rolled up and stowed away during the day to save space when they slept in a common room (Luke 11:7). The rich reclined on permanent structures in rooms designated for sleeping (Exod. 8:3; 2 Kings 6:12), but people of more modest means also had bedrooms (2 Kings 4:10).

The most commonly cited use of a bed is not for sleeping (Ps. 132:3; Luke 11:7) but for convalescing (Gen. 48:2; Exod. 21:18; 2 Sam. 13:5; Ps. 41:3; Matt. 8:14; Acts 28:8) or dying (Gen. 49:33; 2 Kings 1:4, 6, 16). Elijah restores life to a boy after placing him on a bed (1 Kings 17:19; cf. Elisha in 2 Kings 4:21, 34, 35). Murder is attempted (1 Sam. 19:13, 15, 16) or accomplished (2 Sam. 4:7, 11; 2 Chron. 24:25) in bed.

The bed is for sexual activity, whether honorable (Song 1:16; Heb. 13:4) or not (Gen. 39:7, 10, 12; 49:4; 2 Sam. 13:11). People mope and mourn on beds (1 Kings 21:4; Ps. 6:6; Song 3:1; Hos. 7:14), loaf (Prov. 26:14), plot evil (Ps. 36:4; Mic. 2:1), meditate and rejoice (Pss. 4:4; 63:6; 149:5), and experience visions (Dan. 2:28; 4:5; 7:1). The bed is a metaphor for the grave (Job 7:13; 17:13; Ezek. 32:25).

Bedan–A judge listed in a speech by Samuel in a catalog of judges sent by God to deliver Israel (1 Sam. 12:11).

Beer Lahai Roi–A place in the Negev whose exact location and meaning are uncertain. It appears first in the narrative of Gen. 16, where Hagar is fleeing from Sarai, her mistress. After the death of Abraham, Beer Lahai Roi becomes the residence of Isaac (Gen. 24:62; 25:11). All three narratives that speak of this place support a location toward the Egyptian border (between Kadesh and Bered). The water source that gave rise to the name was located on the way to Shur (Gen. 16:7). The most likely translation is "well of the Living One who sees me."

Beersheba–Located in the biblical Negev, this city was significant for the patriarchs and continued as the recognized southern boundary of the political entity of Israel. Because the Negev receives between eight and twelve inches of rainfall per year, water is a critical issue.

Beersheba means both "well of the seven" and "well of the oath." The encounters between Abraham and the Philistine leaders Abimelek and Phicol had to do with water rights (Gen. 21:22–32). When Abimelek's servants seized a well that Abraham had dug, he, in order to demonstrate that his own claim on the well was valid, offered seven lambs to Abimelek, and the two made a treaty. The narrative incorporates both meanings of *sheba'*. Although Abraham was a formidable presence in the region, it is evident that it was under Philistine control at this time (Gen. 21:33–34). Abraham remained there for a long time, returning to Beersheba after the test on Mount Moriah (Gen. 22:19). These same elements and names recur in the interactions between Isaac and the Philistine leaders (Gen. 26:12–33). Beersheba continued to be a center for the seminomadic patriarchs. Isaac lived there with his family; after Jacob tricked Esau out of Isaac's blessing, Jacob left Beersheba and headed for Harran (Gen. 28:10). Near the end of his life, as he set out for Egypt to rejoin Joseph, Jacob stopped in Beersheba to offer sacrifices to God (Gen. 46:1–5). Much later, as Elijah fled from Jezebel and made his way back to Horeb, the source of the covenant, he stopped at Beersheba (1 Kings 19:1–8).

From the period of the judges until the end of the united monarchy, the expression "from Dan to Beersheba" indicated the extent from north to south of Israel (e.g., Judg. 20:1; 1 Sam. 3:23; 2 Sam. 3:10). After the secession and demise of the northern kingdom, Beersheba still indicated the southern boundary (e.g., 2 Chron. 19:4; 30:5). In the postexilic period the people of Judah inhabited territory from Beersheba to the Hinnom Valley (Neh. 11:27–30).

Behemoth–Found only in Job 40:15, "Behemoth" is a transliteration of the Hebrew plural word *behemot* (lit., "beasts"), meaning "the Beast" par excellence. The failure to identify the creature with any known animal species is deliberate. Some scholars suggest that it is possibly the hippopotamus or the elephant, but such mundane alternatives domesticate what is meant to be a mysterious, larger-than-life creature of fearsome strength, "which I [God] made along with you [Job]." Job complained that God had treated him like a monster who needed to be guarded (7:12). The poem implies that God can tame both Behemoth and Job.

Beka–*See* Weights and Measures.

Bel–Marduk, the chief god of Babylon, became the chief god of the pantheon, and he was given the title "Bel." Consequently, the term became interchangeable with his name. Bel occurs three times in the Bible, all of them within the context of the prophetic condemnation of the Neo-Babylonian Empire (Isa. 46:1; Jer. 50:2; 51:44). Thus, in Scripture Bel stands as a representative of Babylon and its rulers. *See also* Baal.

Belial–Occurring in the Bible only once (2 Cor. 6:15), it has a mythological connotation in the OT associated with Sheol, chaos, and death (2 Sam. 22:5; Ps. 18:4; cf. Ps. 41:8); it could also mean "worthlessness," "ruin," or "wickedness" (1 Sam. 25:25). Paul employs this conviction to show that the eschatological conflict is between Christ, who is the light, and Belial, who is the darkness (2 Cor. 6:15; cf. 2 Cor. 4:4).

Beloved Disciple–*See* John the Apostle.

Belshazzar–The regent of Babylon under his father, Nabonidus, during Babylon's final years (?–539 BC). Because the first three successors of Nebuchadnezzar were short-lived, and because Nabonidus left Babylon to stay in the Arabian city of Teima for a decade, Belshazzar may be considered the first significant acting king after Nebuchadnezzar. This is probably why Nebuchadnezzar is called Belshazzar's "father" in Dan. 5:2, 18. A prophecy of the doom of Babylon came as "the handwriting on the wall" at a banquet hosted by Belshazzar. Belshazzar was indicted for not having learned to be humble before the Most High God.

Belteshazzar–The name assigned to Daniel by King Nebuchadnezzar's chief official, Ashpenaz, when he brought Daniel to Babylon to train and mold him for government service (Dan. 1:6–7). The name may mean "May the lord protect his life."

Benaiah–Son of Jehoiada, and one of David's famed mighty men (1 Chron. 27:34 reverses the names of father and son). He was in command of David's personal guards, known as the Kerethites and the Pelethites. His great feats earned him a reputation like one of David's mightiest three (2 Sam. 20:23; 23:22–23). He was at Solomon's coronation (1 Kings 1). He killed Joab at Solomon's order and became his general (1 Kings 2:25–46).

Ben-Ammi–The son born of the incestuous union of Lot with his younger daughter (Gen. 19:38), he is the eponymous ancestor of the Ammonites, longtime enemy of Israel.

Benediction–Literally the "good word" that activates for its recipients such divine benefits as keeping, favor, grace, and peace (Num. 6:24–27).

Ben-Hadad–Several kings of Aram Damascus had the name "Ben-Hadad." The name means "son of Hadad," Aram's national god, and it could be taken by any king of Aram.

(1) Ben-Hadad I, son of Tabrimmon, was bribed with a large amount of silver and gold by King Asa of Judah to break his treaty with King Baasha of Israel, thus providing relief for the embattled Judah. Ben-Hadad I attacked the towns of Israel, successfully conquering several of them as well as the territory of Naphtali (1 Kings 15:16–22).

(2) Ben-Hadad II (but possibly the same person as Ben-Hadad I) attacked Samaria during the reign of King Ahab, who defeated him at Aphek. Ben-Hadad II begged for his life, and Ahab spared him, in the process regaining the cities that Ben-Hadad I had taken from Ahab's father, Omri, and obtaining market rights in Damascus (1 Kings 20). Ben-Hadad II later laid siege to Samaria again (2 Kings 6:24), but a miraculous intervention by God caused his forces to abandon their camp and flee (7:5–7). Later, Ben-Hadad II fell ill and, as prophesied by Elisha, did not recover, since one of his officers, Hazael, suffocated him and seized his throne (8:7–15). Ben-Hadad II is perhaps the king of Aram who sent Naaman to Elisha, via King Joram of Israel, to be cured of his leprosy (5:1–6).

(3) Ben-Hadad III was the son of King Hazael (2 Kings 13:24), who had gained the throne by murdering Ben-Hadad II. As prophesied by Elisha, King Jehoash defeated Ben-Hadad III three times and repossessed several cities that had been taken from his father, King Jehoahaz (13:14–25). Ben-Hadad III's oppressive actions made him the subject of prophetic condemnation (Jer. 49:27; Amos 1:4).

Ben Hinnom–A valley on the southern slopes of Jerusalem, variously referred to as "Valley of Hinnom," "Valley of Ben Hinnom" (lit., "son of Hinnom"), "Valley of the Sons of Hinnom," or even just "the Valley" (e.g., Jer. 2:23). At least two kings of Judah, Ahaz (2 Chron. 28:3) and Manasseh (33:6), sacrificed their own sons in the fire at the Topheth, a site in the valley. The practice, which certainly extended beyond just royalty, was condemned by the prophets, Jeremiah in particular (Jer. 7:31–32; 32:35). King Josiah, as part of his reform movement, defiled the Topheth to prevent further child sacrifice (2 Kings 23:10). "Valley of Hinnom" becomes in Greek "Gehenna," which in all its occurrences in the NT refers to hell.

Benjamin–The youngest son of Jacob and Rachel. Rachel died en route to Ephrath (Bethlehem) while giving birth to Benjamin (Gen. 35:18). Before she died, Rachel named her son "Ben-Oni," meaning "son of my sorrow." Jacob later renamed him "Benjamin," meaning "son of my right hand." Benjamin is the youngest of Joseph's eleven brothers (35:22–26), and Joseph specifically requested to see him when the other brothers journeyed without him to Egypt to buy grain during a famine (42:1–16). *See also* Benjamin, Tribe of.

Benjamin, Tribe of–After Genesis, almost every scriptural reference to "Benjamin" is to the tribe of Benjamin, named after the youngest son of Jacob. Jacob's blessing "Benjamin is a ravenous wolf" (Gen. 49:27) was prophetic, as the tribe of Benjamin came to be known for its prowess in warfare (Judg. 3:15; 1 Chron. 8:40; 2 Sam. 1:22). The land allotted for the tribe of Benjamin was "between the tribes of Judah and Joseph" (Josh. 18:11–20). Although the tribe of Benjamin was the second smallest during the exodus (Num. 1:36–37; Ps. 68:27), several prominent biblical figures are descended from it, including King Saul (1 Sam. 9:1), Queen Esther (Esther 2:5), and the apostle Paul (Rom. 11:1).

Benjamin Gate–*See* Gates of Jerusalem and the Temple.

Ben-Oni–*See* Benjamin.

Bera–The king of Sodom who, along with four other kings, rebelled against Kedorlaomer, king of Elam, in the valley of Siddim (Gen. 14:2). In their defeat, Abraham's nephew Lot was taken captive by the survivors, who fled to the hill country.

Berea–A city (NRSV: "Beroea") in southern Macedonia (modern Veria) forty-five miles southwest of Thessalonica. After fleeing Thessalonica, Paul and Silas preached there to receptive Jews who "examined the Scriptures every day" to confirm Paul's message (Acts

17:11). Sopater of Berea accompanied Paul (Acts 20:4).

Bernice, Berenice–Daughter of Agrippa I, great-granddaughter of Herod the Great, sister of Agrippa II and Drusilla. Bernice was married to her uncle Herod, king of Chalcis, who died in AD 48. In Acts 25–26 she appears as the queen consort of her brother King Agrippa II, who was in Caesarea visiting Festus, the Roman governor of Judea (AD 59–62). During their stay, Bernice witnessed Paul's imprisonment defense prior to his being sent to Rome for appeal to Caesar. Later, Bernice was briefly married to Polemo, king of Cilicia. She then resumed her significant role in Agrippa's reign. In AD 75 she went to Rome as the lover of Titus Vespasian, ten years her junior, until he dismissed her as politically untenable.

Bethany–**(1)** A village about two miles east of Jerusalem on the way to Jericho (John 11:18). It is mentioned twice in Matthew (21:17; 26:6), four times in Mark (11:1, 11, 12; 14:3), twice in Luke (19:29; 24:50), and three times in John (11:1, 18; 12:1). Bethany is identified as a place where Jesus lodged several times, primarily because his friends Lazarus, Mary, and Martha lived there (John 11:1; 12:1). It was here that Jesus raised Lazarus from the dead and dined at the house of Simon the leper. Simon's house in Bethany is where Mary anointed Jesus' body before his death and resurrection (Matt. 26:6–13; John 12:1–2).

(2) John the Baptist ministered in a place called "Bethany" beyond/across the Jordan (John 1:28). It was here on the east side of the Jordan that Jesus called his first disciples (John 1:35–42). The modern town of El-'Aziriyeh is traditionally associated with first-century Bethany.

Beth Aven–A village close to Ai and Bethel (Josh. 7:2). The wilderness of Beth Aven also served as a boundary marker for the tribe of Benjamin (18:12). This place, whose name is translated as "house of wickedness" or "house of iniquity," is mentioned three times by the eighth-century BC prophet Hosea (4:15; 5:8; 10:5).

Bethel–Bethel's situation and importance are explained by its copious springs and its location at the intersection of major ancient highways, the north-south mountain road and the east-west road from Jericho to the coastal plain.

The first mention of Bethel in the Bible is in Gen. 12:8, where Abram camped "east of Bethel" on his first entry into the promised land. He camped there again on his return from a stay in Egypt (13:3). On the first occasion Abram erected "an altar to the LORD." When Abram returned to that spot, he "called on the name of the LORD."

It was Jacob who gave it the name "Bethel," meaning "house of God," due to the dream he received in that location. In the dream he saw a ladder reaching to heaven, and God spoke to him (28:10–19). Its former name was Luz. God later appeared in Mesopotamia and spoke to Jacob, identifying himself as "the God of Bethel," instructing him to return to his native land. The title taken by God implied that God would be faithful to his earlier promise to bring Jacob back to his land (31:13). Later God specifically instructed Jacob to settle in Bethel (35:1–6). Deborah, Rebekah's nurse, died in Bethel and was buried there (35:8). God appeared to Jacob a second time in Bethel and spoke to him, reiterating the promise to give him the land of Canaan (35:9–15; cf. 28:13). All God's dealings with Jacob are connected to the theophanies and divine promises associated with Bethel.

Bethel is mentioned a number of times in the account of Joshua's capture of Ai, a city that lay to the east of Bethel (Josh. 7). The king of Bethel is listed among the kings defeated by Joshua (12:16). Under Joshua, the city was apportioned to Benjamin (18:13, 22), but the Canaanites repopulated it after the near extinction of the tribe of Benjamin (Judg. 20–21). Bethel was reconquered by the house of Joseph and incorporated into Ephraimite territory (Judg. 1:22–25; 1 Chron. 7:28), and later it became a fortress on its southern tribal border. Deborah held court between Ramah and Bethel (Judg. 4:5). Under the judgeship of Samuel, Bethel was one of his regular stops in his yearly circuit (1 Sam. 7:16). It continued throughout this period to be a sanctuary where offerings were made (see 1 Sam. 10:3).

This long-term cultic association explains the choice of Bethel as one of the two chief sanctuaries of the northern kingdom, the other center being in Dan. Jeroboam I built a royal shrine at Bethel to rival Jerusalem and to prevent the Israelites from drifting back to the Davidic dynasty (1 Kings 12:26–33). The prophet Ahijah's criticism of Jeroboam's actions were not due to Ahijah's commitment to a central sanctuary at Jerusalem (14:1–16) but rather arose from the use of bull images (golden calves). This was not an innocent move by Jeroboam, returning to pre-Jerusalem and more ancient cultic symbols. This became known as the chief sin of Jeroboam son of Nebat. It tainted the northern kingdom (see 2 Kings 10:29) and eventually led to that kingdom's judgment by God at the hands of the Assyrians (2 Kings 17:21–23).

The southern king Abijah captured Bethel from Israel in the latter part of Jeroboam's reign (2 Chron. 13:19), but then it later returned to northern control. The unnamed "man of God" in 1 Kings 13 predicted the later destruction of the Bethel altar by King Josiah (1 Kings 13:1–3), a prediction subsequently fulfilled (2 Kings 23:4, 15–18). Bethel was visited by Elijah before his translation to heaven (2 Kings 2:2–4), and a company of prophets dwelt there. Elisha revisited Bethel after his master's translation and cursed the forty-two youths who insulted him (2 Kings 2:23–25).

Hosea condemned the great wickedness of Bethel, presumably because of the false worship that went on there (Hos. 10:15), but more positively, he recalled that this was the location where God had talked with the patriarch Jacob (12:4). Jeremiah also explained the sad fate of Israel to be a result of their trust in Bethel (Jer. 48:13). Amos, in his condemnation of the worship system of the northern kingdom, ironically called to the people, "Go to Bethel and sin" (Amos 4:4). Later he dropped the irony and spoke plainly: "Do not seek Bethel" (5:5), predicting its destruction (5:6; cf. 3:14). It was in Bethel that Amos was criticized by the head priest Amaziah (7:10–17) and was told to no longer prophesy there because it was "the king's sanctuary."

The city was destroyed by the Assyrians about the time of their capture of Samaria (722 BC), but the shrine was revived in the form of a syncretistic cult at the close of the Assyrian period by the foreign peoples deported to the area (2 Kings 17:24–41). Some descendants of the inhabitants of Bethel were among those who returned from Babylonian exile in the first great caravan (Ezra 2:28; Neh. 7:32), and these Benjamite returnees resettled in their hometown (Neh. 11:31). Bethel prospered in the Hellenistic and Roman periods.

BETHESDA–A pool in Jerusalem where Jesus healed a man who had been sick for thirty-eight years (John 5:2). Other names for the pool, including "Bethzatha" and "Bethsaida," appear in various manuscripts. Eusebius also calls it the "sheep pool." The name means "house of mercy," and the pool is associated with the cleansing of the sheep for the temple sacrifice. Some manuscripts of John 5 report that the pool was stirred by angels, which allowed for the healing of whoever entered it first at that time.

BETH HORON–A city allotted by Joshua to the Levites (Josh. 21:22). The city was divided into two parts, Lower Beth Horon and Upper Beth Horon. The twin city of Beth Horon, first mentioned in Josh. 10:10–11, is located in the mountains of Judah in the valley of Aijalon. During the Israelite conquest of the land, many Amorites were killed at Gibeon and others pursued as far as Beth Horon. In the distribution of the land, Lower Beth Horon was allotted to Ephraim, while Upper Beth Horon was on the border between Ephraim and Benjamin (16:3, 5; 18:13–14). During Solomon's reign, Beth Horon was rebuilt after being burned by the Egyptians during one of their northern incursions (1 Kings 9:15–17).

The Chronicler reveals that the city was built by Sheerah, granddaughter of Ephraim (1 Chron. 7:24). Lower and Upper Beth Horon are described as "fortified cities, with walls and with gates and bars" (2 Chron. 8:5). The last mention of Beth Horon is made in conjunction with some Israelite troops who killed three thousand Judeans from Samaria to Beth Horon (2 Chron. 25:13).

BETHLEHEM–The well-known town about four miles south of Jerusalem in Judah, situated on a couple of hills about 2,300 feet above sea level. The ancient name was "Ephrath" or "Ephrathah" (Gen. 35:16, 19; 48:7; Ruth 4:11; Ps. 136:2; Mic. 5:2; *see also* Bethlehem Ephrathah).

Bethlehem first enters biblical history when Jacob's wife Rachel dies there while giving birth to Benjamin (Gen. 35:16–19). After the conquest, the town was inhabited by Ephrathites descended from Caleb, one of whom was called "father of Bethlehem" (in the sense of civic leader; 1 Chron. 2:51; 4:4; cf. 2:54). Judges mentions two Levites passing though, one who moved from Bethlehem to Ephraim (Judg. 17:7–9), and another who lived in Ephraim but took a concubine from Bethlehem (19:1). The most important references to Bethlehem from this era, however, are in Ruth. It was from Bethlehem that Elimelek's family set out for Moab (Ruth 1:1), and to Bethlehem that Ruth and Naomi returned (1:22). Two generations later, it was into this same Bethlemite family that the future king David was born (Ruth 4:18–22; 1 Sam. 16:1).

Bethlehem is mentioned frequently as David's hometown (e.g., 1 Sam. 17:12, 58; 20:6). Several of the mighty men on whom David depended so much were from there, including the brothers Joab, Abishai, and Asahel (2 Sam. 2:18, 32) and Elhanan (2 Sam. 23:24). At one point, when Bethlehem was temporarily garrisoned by Philistines, some of the mighty men risked their lives to fetch David water from the town well (2 Sam. 23:14–17; 2 Chron. 11:16–26). Bethlehem was later fortified by David's grandson Rehoboam (2 Chron. 11:6).

In the eighth century the prophet Micah promised that although Judah's defeat was inevitable, a new king would arise from this otherwise insignificant town to save the whole of Israel (Mic. 5:2). Both the place and the clan retained their identity through the exile, and 123 men of Bethlehem returned to Judah (Ezra 2:21; see also Neh. 7:26).

Luke stresses that Jesus was born in David's city (Luke 2:4; cf. 2 Sam. 7:12–16); Joseph had taken Mary to his ancestral home, Bethlehem, for a Roman census. The angels announced Jesus' birth to some shepherds in the vicinity of town (Luke 2:1–20). Matthew makes a more specific connection to Micah's prophecy; indeed, it was on the basis of this prophecy that Herod decided where to send the magi (Matt. 2:1–8) and where to slaughter the baby boys (2:16). Matthew sees in this slaughter a fulfillment of Jeremiah's prophecy that Rachel, who died at Bethlehem, would mourn her children (Matt. 2:18; Jer. 31:15). Ironically, some Jews rejected Jesus because they thought that he came from Galilee (John 7:42).

Bethlehem Ephrathah–"Ephrathah" or "Ephrath" distinguishes Bethlehem in Judah (Gen. 35:16, 19; 48:7, 19; Ruth 4:11; Mic. 5:2) from Bethlehem in Zebulun (Josh. 19:15). Some Ephrathites lived in Bethlehem (Ruth 1:2; 1 Sam. 17:12), but the clan may have been more widespread. *See also* Bethlehem.

Beth Millo–*See* Millo.

Beth Peor–A Transjordanian town located just east of the northern end of the Dead Sea. It was part of the holdings of King Sihon of the Amorites until the Israelite invasion as they passed by on their way to enter Canaan (Deut. 4:46). It is also from the valley near Beth Peor that Moses delivered his speeches in Deuteronomy. Already in Deut. 4:3 Moses refers to the sin of the Israelites in Num. 25:1–9 concerning Baal Peor, whose worship certainly was located in Beth Peor (i.e., "house of Peor"). That incident is referred to again in Hos. 9:10 as the incident that turned Yahweh against his people. Moses was buried in the valley opposite Beth Peor, although "to this day no one knows where his grave is" (Deut. 34:6).

Bethphage–A location near Jerusalem where Jesus sent his disciples to find a donkey for the triumphal entry (Matt. 21:1; Mark 11:1; Luke 19:29). Later Jewish sources believe it to be a suburb of Jerusalem that was located outside the city wall and surrounded by its own wall. It was located about a mile east of the summit of the Mount of Olives. Frescoes found at that location show two disciples untying both a donkey and a colt (cf. Matt. 21:2).

Bethsaida–A town located on the northern shore of the Sea of Galilee, near the Jordan River, about five miles east of Capernaum, although the precise location is disputed.

Bethsaida is the third-most-mentioned town in the Gospels, and it was at the heart of Jesus' ministry. It was the birthplace of Peter and Andrew and the home of Philip (John 1:44; 12:21). Jesus performed several miracles at or near the town. Near Bethsaida Jesus walked on water (Mark 6:45–52) and fed the five thousand (6:30–44). In Bethsaida Jesus healed a blind man (8:22–26). Unfortunately, the miracles do not seem to have had much effect on the inhabitants, and in Matt. 11:21 // Luke 10:13 Jesus denounces the city along with Chorazin for its lack of repentance.

Beth Shan–Known as Scythopolis at the time of Jesus, Beth Shan is a town located at the junction of the plain of Jezreel and the Jordan Valley, west of the Jordan River. This strategic site, with fertile lands and abundant water, overlooks major roads running west toward the Mediterranean and north and south through the Jordan Valley. The name also designates the district surrounding the town.

Beth Shan is first mentioned in the Bible in connection with Joshua's division of the land among the twelve tribes of Israel. Although located within the territory of Issachar, it was portioned to the tribe of Manasseh (Josh. 17:11) but remained under the control of the Canaanite inhabitants because they possessed iron chariots. When the Israelites gained strength, they put the Canaanites to forced labor but did not drive them out (Josh. 17:12–13, 16; Judg. 1:27).

During the period of the monarchy, after the Israelites were defeated in battle on Mount Gilboa, the Philistines fastened the bodies of Saul and his three sons to the wall of Beth Shan and placed Saul's weapons in the temple of Ashtaroth. When news of this atrocity spread, men from Jabesh Gilead retrieved the bodies and buried them (1 Sam. 31:7–13). David later retrieved the bones of Saul and his sons and reburied them in Zela (2 Sam. 21:14). Although Beth Shan had been under the control of the Philistines during Saul's reign, it is listed within one of Solomon's administrative districts (1 Kings 4:12).

Beth Shemesh–The name "Beth Shemesh" means "house of the sun," which suggests the presence of a temple to a sun god at that location. A city allocated to the tribe of Dan, in Josh. 19:41 it is called "Ir Shemesh," which means "City of Shemesh." It is also described as being located on the northern boundary of Judah (Josh. 15:10), as one of the cities that Judah allotted to the Levites (Josh. 21:16), and as being "in Judah" (2 Kings 14:11).

Beth Shemesh is best known for its role in the story of the Philistine capture of the ark of the covenant. After keeping the ark with disastrous consequences for seven months, the Philistines returned it to the border town of Beth Shemesh. The ark's safe arrival was a joyous occasion for the town until some of the residents looked inside the ark and were struck down by God (1 Sam. 6).

Beth Shemesh belonged to the second administrative district of Solomon (1 Kings 4:9) and was the location where King Jehoash (Joash) of Israel engaged King Amaziah of Judah in battle. The victorious Jehoash then marched on to Jerusalem and plundered the temple (2 Kings 14:11–14; 2 Chron. 25:21–24). During the reign of King Ahaz, the Philistines seized many towns in the lowlands of Judah, including Beth Shemesh (2 Chron. 28:18).

Beth Togarmah–A place mentioned twice in Ezekiel. First, Beth Togarmah appears as one of several trading partners of the Phoenician city of Tyre (27:14); Beth Togarmah's goods were "work horses, war horses, and mules." Second, Beth Togarmah, "from the far north," is named as one of the military allies of Gog of Magog (38:6). Scholars generally identify Beth Togarmah with Armenia. Togarmah, who settled in the area subsequently known as Beth Togarmah, was a son of Gomer and a great-grandson of Noah (Gen. 10:3; 1 Chron. 1:6).

Betrothal–Betrothal is a commitment designed to lead to marriage, comparable to being engaged today. There are a number of instructions in the OT law regarding proper conduct involving a woman who is betrothed or engaged (Exod. 22:16; Deut. 20:7). There are also references to Mary being betrothed to Joseph prior to Jesus' birth (Matt. 1:18; Luke 1:27; 2:5). However, the most significant references are the figurative descriptions of God betrothing himself to his people: "I will betroth you to me forever; I will betroth you in righteousness and justice, in love and compassion. I will betroth you in faithfulness, and you will acknowledge the Lord" (Hos. 2:19–20). Hosea's experience with his unfaithful betrothed and then wife, Gomer, is a classic picture of God's faithfulness to his unfaithful people. On one occasion, Paul uses the imagery of betrothal to picture his commitment to the churches he served: "I am jealous for you with a godly jealousy. I promised you to one husband, to Christ, so that I might present you as a pure virgin to him" (2 Cor. 11:2).

Beulah–This is a symbolic name promised to the personified Zion (Isa. 62:4). The new names in Isa. 62:4 signify the restoration of the relationship between God and Zion, as husband and wife (cf. 54:1–8), which was lost due to her sons' iniquities (cf. 50:1). The restoration of Zion's status is also highlighted with her marriage to her sons (62:5).

Beyond the River–In Josh. 24 "beyond the River" (NRSV; NIV: "beyond the Euphrates River") refers to the land of Abraham's birth, east of the Euphrates. Because Israel's ancestors worshiped other gods there, and God took Abraham from there to bring him to Canaan, it signified a threshold in redemptive history. Joshua invoked this place and memory when he called Israel to renew the covenant.

Israel under David defeated Aramean troops from there (2 Sam. 10:16–19; 1 Chron. 19:16–19). Since prophets later said Israel would be exiled there (1 Kings 14:15), and Judah's punishment would come from there (Isa. 7:20), the place name came to imply threat.

In 522 BC Darius I reorganized the vast Persian Empire into twenty satrapies, each composed of provinces (Esther 1:1; 8:9). The satrapy of "Beyond the River" (Ezra 4:10–11 NRSV; NIV: "Trans-Euphrates") extended from the Euphrates to the Mediterranean, and Yehud (Judah) was one of its provinces. In the mid-fifth century Persia built a network of fortresses there to maintain imperial control of local affairs and curtail rebellion.

Bezalel–Grandson of Uri and son of Hur, of the tribe of Judah, who was equipped by God's Spirit with skill to engage in all types of craftsmanship needed for the construction of the tabernacle, its furnishings, and the making of the sacred garments of the priests, the anointing oil, and fragrant incense (Exod. 31:1–11; 35:30–35; 36:1–5; 37:1; 38:22). He was given Oholiab as an assistant, and they had artisans to train and work under them.

Bible Texts and Versions–The NT and the OT have considerably different but partially overlapping textual histories. For clarity, it is best to begin with a survey of the NT manuscripts and versions.

New Testament

Greek texts. Although no autographs of the NT books survive, there exist more than five thousand Greek texts covering anywhere from a portion of a few verses up to the complete NT. Traditionally, these texts have been classified into five groups: papyri, uncials, minuscules, lectionaries, and quotations in patristic texts.

The earliest texts of the NT are those written on papyrus. Ninety-eight of these manuscripts have been identified. The second category of manuscripts is the uncials, which usually were written on parchment and span the fourth through the tenth centuries. About 270 uncials are known, and they range from a few verses up to complete copies of the NT or even the entire Bible. The third category of NT manuscripts is minuscules. These texts date from the ninth century and later and comprise approximately 2,800 manuscripts, which are denoted by a number not beginning with zero.

Versions. With the spread of Christianity during the time of the Roman Empire, the NT was translated into the language of the native peoples. These versions of the NT are important both for textual criticism of the NT and for the interpretive decisions that are reflected in how the text was rendered into a new language. Among the most important early versions of the NT are the following.

As Latin began to displace Greek as the dominant language of the empire, there was a need for a Latin version of the Bible. The earliest translation, known as the Old Latin or Itala, was made probably in the late second century, though the oldest manuscript (Codex Vercellensis) is from the fourth century. With the proliferation of Latin texts a standardized Latin translation became desirable, and in AD 382 Jerome was commissioned by Pope Damasus to provide a new translation known as the Vulgate.

Another family of NT versions is the Syriac texts. Around the late second century the four Gospels were translated into a version known as the Old Syriac. It is extant in two incomplete manuscripts that are probably fifth century. The translation that became the standard Syriac text is the Peshitta, which was produced in the early fifth century. It does not contain 2 Peter, 2–3 John, Jude, or Revelation because these were not considered canonical among the Syriac churches.

Other important versions of the NT from antiquity are the Coptic, Armenian, Georgian, and Ethiopic translations.

Old Testament

Hebrew texts. The text that has served as the basis for most modern editions and translations of the Hebrew OT is the Masoretic Text (MT), named after the Masoretes, the Jewish scribes who transmitted the text and added vocalization, accentuation, and notes to the consonantal text. The most important Masoretic manuscripts date from the end of the ninth century to the early eleventh century. Notable among these is the Leningrad Codex (AD 1008), denoted as L, which is the earliest Masoretic manuscript of the entire OT. Also important are the Aleppo Codex (c. AD 925), denoted as A, which preserves all of the OT except for most of the Pentateuch; the British Museum MS Oriental 4445 (c. AD 925), denoted as B, which contains most of the

Pentateuch; and the Cairo Codex (c. AD 896), denoted C, which contains Joshua through Kings and also the Prophets.

Although these manuscripts are much later than the biblical period, their reliability was largely confirmed with the discovery of the DSS beginning in 1947. Among the Qumran library are many manuscripts of biblical books as well as biblical commentaries, apocryphal and pseudepigraphal works, and sectarian literature. All the OT books are represented among the scrolls that were found except Esther and Nehemiah, though the latter is usually presumed to have been at the end of Ezra but has not survived. The books with the most manuscripts are, in order, Psalms, Deuteronomy, and Isaiah. One of the striking characteristics of these scrolls is that they reflect a diversity of text types. For example, there is a copy of Jeremiah that is close to the Masoretic version, but also a manuscript of Jeremiah similar to the much shorter version found in the Septuagint (the Greek translation of the OT).

Another Hebrew text of the OT is that of the Samaritan Pentateuch, which is the text transmitted by the Samaritans. It is similar to the MT in some respects but also has differences that reflect theological interests. The main manuscripts for the Samaritan Pentateuch are from the twelfth century.

Versions. Between the third and first centuries BC, the entire OT was translated into Greek. This version, known as the Septuagint (designated by the abbreviation LXX), became the main version of the OT used by the early church. Due to its adoption by the church, the LXX has been preserved in numerous manuscripts, including Sinaiticus, Alexandrinus, and Vaticanus. By the late first century BC or early first century AD, there were two revisions of the Greek text: the Proto-Lucianic version and the Kaige recension. The latter aimed to revise the Greek toward closer conformity with the Hebrew text and derives its name from its peculiar tendency to translate the Hebrew word *gam* ("also") with the Greek work *kaige*. In the second century AD three other Greek translations were made by Aquila, Theodotion, and Symmachus, all of which revised the Kaige recension back toward the MT.

Another important early version of the OT consists of the Targumim, which are Aramaic translations or paraphrases (and sometimes extensive elaborations) of OT books. The official Targumim for Judaism are Targum Onqelos for the Pentateuch (c. second century AD), which is quite literal, and Targum Pseudo-Jonathan for the Prophets (sometime before the fourth century AD), which ranges from being quite literal to somewhat paraphrastic. Unofficial Targumim for the Pentateuch include Targum Neofiti and Targum Pseudo-Jonathan. There are also various unofficial Targumim for the Writings section of the OT, except for Daniel and Ezra-Nehemiah (which are already written partly in Aramaic).

Besides the Greek and Aramaic translations, there are other important versions of the OT. Sometime in either the third or fourth century AD, the Peshitta of the OT was produced, though there is evidence that there were earlier Syriac translations of some books already circulating. Also important is a group of Latin translations known collectively as the Old Latin. These versions were produced sometime during the second century AD and were primarily made from already existing Greek translations rather than Hebrew texts. As with the NT, a later Latin translation was made by Jerome for the Vulgate.

BIBLE TRANSLATION–***The history of translation.*** Bible translation began long before the Bible as we know it was complete. In the fifth century BC the Israelites who returned from exile spoke Aramaic. Thus, they needed the Levites to translate the Hebrew law for them (Neh. 8:8). This Levitical teaching was probably an early example of a Targum, a translation into Aramaic with interpretation and expansion. We do not know exactly when the Targumim began to be written down, but some of the earliest fragments that have been found are among the DSS.

By about the third century BC the dominant languages of Palestine were Greek and Aramaic. Many NT quotations from the OT use an established Greek translation of the OT. This was known as the Septuagint (LXX), after the legend that it was translated by seventy-two men, six from each tribe of Israel, on the orders of Ptolemy Philadelphus of Egypt (285–247 BC). The NT was written in similar "common" (*koinē*) Greek, but in some places the Gospels and Acts translate words that Jesus and Paul originally spoke in Aramaic (Mark 5:41; 15:34; Acts 21:40; 22:2; 26:14; see also John 5:2; 19:13, 17, 20; 20:16).

Until Pentecost, God's revelation was translated only into the languages spoken by the Jewish people in their everyday life. At

Pentecost, however, the coming of the Holy Spirit was marked by a display of miraculous linguistic gifts, and a new era of Bible translation had begun (Acts 2). As Christians obeyed Christ's command to take the word of God into all the world, they began to translate it into all the languages used by the growing church.

Within three centuries, Scripture was translated from the original Hebrew, Aramaic, and Greek into Syriac, Coptic, and Latin. The earliest translations into these languages were then revised and improved in the subsequent centuries until some, such as Jerome's Latin Vulgate and the Syriac Peshitta, emerged as acknowledged standards. Other early translations included Ethiopic, Armenian, Georgian, and Old Slavonic. Many of these languages were already written, but as missionaries ventured farther, they sometimes had to start by reducing spoken languages to writing. Ulfilas, missionary to the Goths, was the first to do this.

All of the thirty-three translations prior to the Reformation had to be copied out by hand, and almost all were "secondary translations" made from the Latin. Moreover, despite the efforts of early reformers such as John Wycliffe (AD 1330–84), the Catholic Church continued to use the Latin text itself, which was accessible only to the educated. In the sixteenth century, however, the printing press was invented, Renaissance scholars rediscovered the value of consulting texts in the original Hebrew and Greek, and Protestants realized that believers need the Bible in their mother tongue.

The most influential sixteenth-century translator into English was William Tyndale (AD 1494–1536). His work on the NT and parts of the OT was gradually expanded and revised by other scholars, culminating in the 1611 King James Version, which is still widely used. Meanwhile, other European translations were produced in German (by Martin Luther), Spanish, Hungarian, Portuguese, and French.

The Reformation also gave new momentum to mission outside Europe, and by the end of the eighteenth century the number of languages having the Bible had roughly doubled. A much greater global achievement, however, began in the nineteenth century, when the newly formed Bible societies, with other mission agencies, were instrumental in the translation and publication of portions of Scripture in over four hundred languages. Famous translators from this century include William Carey in India, John Robert Morrison in China, Henry Martyn in Persia, and Adoniram Judson in Burma. About five hundred more translations were added in the first half of the twentieth century. Progress was, nevertheless, slow. Many languages were difficult to analyze, and it was particularly hard to produce translations that read smoothly, using the genres and idioms that a native speaker would use.

Since the 1950s, linguistic science has revolutionized the way that translation is carried out, and organizations such as Wycliffe Bible Translators have set themselves the task of giving every person in the world the Scriptures in their everyday language. Increasingly, translation is carried out by linguistically trained native speakers of the target languages, working wherever possible from the original Hebrew and Greek. Translators understand better than before how extended discourses are constructed at levels above the sentence, and how social and pragmatic factors affect meaning. The combination of linguistics and technology has also greatly increased the speed with which translations can be produced; sometimes a first draft in a new language can be generated from a closely related language using a computer program.

Types of translation. All translators aim for both accuracy and acceptability, but the work of translation constantly involves compromise between these two factors. There are, broadly speaking, two types of translation: formal correspondence and functional equivalence.

In a formal correspondence translation (also called "literal"), the translator, as far as possible, preserves the word order and structure of the original text and translates each word the same way every time it occurs, even if the result is slightly wooden. This is helpful for word studies, and it preserves patterns of repetition that give structure to the text. There is always a danger, however, that the closest formal match to the original actually conveys a meaning different from the original in a particular context. Literalness is not the same as accuracy. Pushed to its extreme, formal correspondence produces the kind of semitranslation found in interlinear texts (where the English is reproduced word for word below a line of Hebrew, Aramaic, or Greek); it is not grammatically acceptable, cannot be used on its own for public or private reading, and loses many of the nuances of the original. However, formal correspondence translations that avoid such extremes are important for detailed Bible study.

In a functional equivalence translation (also called "dynamic," "idiomatic equivalence," or "meaning-based"), the translator aims to produce the same response in a modern reader as the original text would have done in an ancient reader. To achieve this, the syntactic structures and figures of speech of Greek and Hebrew are replaced by their equivalents in the target language. A word may be translated many different ways in different contexts, even when it has a single basic meaning in the original. While this preserves some nuances, it loses others, obscuring structure and the deliberate echo of one verse in another. In this case there is always a danger that the translator has misunderstood the original meaning and the response that it would have produced. Pushed to its extreme, this type shades into paraphrase, and it may be overly subjective or jeopardize the historical particularity of the text. However, dynamic equivalence translations that avoid such pitfalls are valuable for evangelism, new readers, and public and devotional reading.

In practice most translations sit somewhere on the spectrum between these two extremes. Some intermediate translations are a deliberate compromise, aiming to keep as close as possible to the original while communicating its meaning clearly in a common language that is accessible to all. The NIV is a widely used example. One problem in using such a translation is knowing when form has been preserved at the expense of meaning, and when meaning has been preserved at the expense of form. For serious study, therefore, it is useful to compare intermediate translations with translations of the other two types, and to learn from the introductory material what translation principles have been used.

Biblical Hermeneutics–Hermeneutics is the science and practice of interpretation. It can refer more generally to the philosophy of human understanding, or more specifically to the tools and methods used for interpreting communicative acts.

The Bible is not exempt from this process of communication. The Scriptures are meant to be read, understood, and put into practice (Luke 8:4–15; James 1:18), a task that requires effort and study on the part of its readers (Acts 17:11; 2 Tim. 2:15). Everyone who reads the Bible is involved in this interpretative process, though readers will vary in their hermeneutical self-consciousness and skill. Thus, although readers are able to understand and appropriate much of the Bible without any special training in hermeneutical principles, such training is appropriate and helpful, both in attaining self-consciousness in interpretation and in acquiring new skills and insights in the effort to become a better reader.

Biblical Theology–Biblical theology has been defined in various ways: (1) theology based upon Scripture (or theology derived primarily from a study of Scripture), as opposed to theology based upon confessional statements or philosophy; (2) theology in harmony with Scripture; (3) theology that is descriptive of the Bible's contents; (4) a study of the theology found in the Bible; (5) the study of the main themes of the Bible; (6) the formulation of the theology of the entire Bible (in distinction from the theology of the OT, the theology of the NT, or the theology of the various books of the Bible, such as the theology of Isaiah or of Matthew); and (7) the ways the Bible has been studied throughout the history of the church.

One of the major weaknesses with these definitions is that they can function primarily as a way of distinguishing those theologies that are preferred from those that are dismissed. Although they may differ from one another, every Christian theologian formulates theology in reference to the Bible. Biblical theologies have a direct correlation to both the text of Scripture and the ways in which the authors of Scripture thought.

Bildad–Bildad is the second of Job's friends introduced in Job 2:11, where he is said to come from an otherwise unknown place, Shuah. Bildad's speeches (Job 8; 18; 25) reflect his staunch conviction that God deals with people (including Job) exclusively through the principle of retributive justice: God punishes sin and rewards good.

Binding and Loosing–Binding can mean physically restraining a person or people (Judg. 15:13; 2 Kings 25:7; Job 16:8; Pss. 119:61; 149:8); mending, as with a wound (Isa. 61:1; Ezek. 34:16; Hos. 6:1); or taking a legally constraining oath (1 Sam. 14:27–30; Neh. 10:29; Jer. 50:5). The opposite of binding is loosing or setting free, which can describe literally being freed from bonds (e.g., Acts 16:26) or the release from something that is binding.

The law, a binding covenant between Israel and God, is to be literally bound on one's forehead as a reminder (Deut. 6:8; 11:18). Non-Israelites who wish to identify with the God of Israel can bind themselves to his laws (Isa. 56:6). In Num. 30:6, 9, 13, an oath taken by a young woman still in her father's house will be binding only if the father is not against it. If he is against it, it is not binding and she is loosed from it (30:5). This is the same in the case of a married woman, whose approval has to come from the husband. However, for widows or divorced women, all pledges they make are binding since there are no men in their lives to void the pledges (30:9).

While contracts were binding, some had time limits. For example, the seventh year and the fiftieth year (Jubilee) allowed for cancellation of such binding contracts as slavery or land ownership (Lev. 25:10–54; 27:24).

The binding of Isaac (Gen. 22), traditionally known as the Akedah, has theological significance for both Christians and Jews. It is interpreted as a form of resurrection, a coming from the dead for Isaac after Yahweh had instructed his father, Abraham, to sacrifice him (Heb. 11:17–19). God inquires of Job whether he can "bind the chains of the Pleiades" or "loosen Orion's belt" (Job 38:31).

Introducing his ministry in Luke 4:18, Jesus quotes Isa. 61:1, which talks of binding up the brokenhearted, a reference to his healing ministry. Further, binding and loosing are found in Jesus' commissioning of his disciples (Matt. 16:19; 18:18; cf. John 20:23), where it may be referring to the binding of demons and loosing of demoniacs bound or oppressed by demons (cf. Mark 3:14–16; 6:7; Luke 13:6). Since Jesus has the power to bind and loose (John 8:36), he chooses to empower his followers to do the same. Binding Satan is the subject of the ultimate eschatological battle in Jewish lore (*T. Levi* 18:11–12) and becomes central in Christianity. Jesus encounters satanic forces embodied in humans and looses such people from the chains of Satan (Mark 5:3; Luke 13:12, 16). Ultimately, Satan is to be bound for a millennium and loosed only for eternal damnation (Rev. 20:1–3).

Birds–The OT employs thirty-five different words for birds (both wild and domestic), but the identification of these words with known species has proved to be very difficult. Like other words for animals, terminology for birds often is employed in personal names (e.g., Jonah, Oreb, Zippor, Zipporah). There is significant evidence for fowling practices in ancient Israel, usually by means of nets and snares (Pss. 124:7; 140:5; Prov. 6:5; 7:23; Lam. 3:52; Hos. 7:12; Amos 3:5). Small birds and chickens are occasionally even depicted on Iron Age II (1000–586 BC) seals and vessels from sites such as el-Jib (Gibeon) and Tell en-Nasbeh (Mizpah).

Like other animals in the Bible, birds are depicted as agents of God. Divine agency is especially evident in instances such as the ravens feeding Elijah (1 Kings 17:4–6) and the dove bringing an olive leaf to Noah (Gen. 8:11). The Bible also employs bird-related imagery such as in descriptions of divine judgment (Prov. 30:17; Jer. 12:9). Birds may also serve as ominous signs of impending judgment (Hos. 8:1). God's "wings" can offer both healing (Mal. 4:2 KJV, RSV) and protection (Ruth 2:12; Pss. 17:8; 36:7; 57:1; 61:4; 63:7; 91:4). The metaphor of the soul or spirit as a bird is referenced in the description of the Holy Spirit descending like a dove (Matt. 3:16; Mark 1:10; Luke 3:22; John 1:32). The observation that birds "do not sow or reap" is employed as an image of worry-free living (Luke 12:24; cf. Job 38:41; Ps. 147:9). Jesus' reference to "when the rooster crows" (Mark 13:35) is not strictly literal but rather refers to a watch of the night: the quarter of the night after midnight.

The prominence of sacrificial birds (especially doves and pigeons) in ritual literature indicates that they were likely raised for such purposes in ancient Israel. All birds could be eaten except those listed as unclean in Lev. 11:13–19 (twenty species) and Deut. 14:12–18 (twenty-one species). Generally speaking, birds of prey and those that feed on carrion or fish were considered unclean. Birds often served as food for the poor (Matt. 10:29–31; Luke 12:6–7). Poor people could offer birds as a substitute for expensive livestock (Lev. 5:7; 12:8; 14:21–22; cf. Luke 2:24), while the poorest of the poor were permitted to bring grain (Lev. 5:11). Finally, in one purgation ritual a live bird is used to carry away impurities (Lev. 14:52–53; cf. 16:22).

Birsha–King of Gomorrah, he was part of a five-king alliance that rebelled against Kedorlaomer king of Elam (Gen. 14:1–16). Kedorlaomer defeated Birsha and his allies and plundered the cities of Sodom and Gomorrah, but Abram recovered the plunder and captives.

Birth–Births in the ancient world were the domain of women. The women who bore children were often assisted in the birthing process by midwives (Gen. 35:17; 38:28; Exod. 1:15–20).

Many women utilized a birthing stool (Exod. 1:16). Upon birth, the newborn often was washed with water, rubbed with salt, and wrapped in cloths (Ezek. 16:4; Luke 2:7, 12). The OT required women to undergo a rite of purification following childbirth (Exod. 13:2, 20; 34:20; Lev. 12:6–8; Luke 2:22–24). This purification lasted forty days after the birth of a son and eighty days after the birth of a daughter and concluded with the sacrifice of both a burnt offering and a sin offering.

Birthing was valued, and women who were considered to be infertile often faced great shame (1 Sam. 1:10–11; Luke 1:25). Pain in childbirth was associated with the sin of Eve (Gen. 3:16), and conversely, absence of pain was interpreted as a sign that a woman was particularly righteous. According to Josephus, Moses was born with no pain to his mother, and the *Protevangelium of James* indicates the same about Mary's labor with Jesus.

The Bible sometimes employs the language of birth as a spiritual metaphor. In John 3:3–6 Jesus instructs Nicodemus about the need for spiritual birth by explaining that he must be born again. In Rom. 8:22 Paul describes the whole of creation as experiencing the pain of childbirth as it awaits redemption, and in Gal. 4:19 he says that he is in labor for a second time with the Galatians as he desires the formation of Christ in them.

Birthright–The birthright consists of the material blessings of a father being passed on to his sons. By right, the oldest son received a double portion of the inheritance received by the children (Gen. 25:29–34; Deut. 21:15–17; Luke 15:11–32). The birthright is often connected to, but needs to be distinguished from, the blessing. The blessing generally involved more of a focus on a spiritual allotment, but it crossed paths with the birthright with respect to future leadership and authority of the person (Gen. 27; 49). Royal succession was also a birthright, though God could countermand this privilege (1 Kings 2:15; 2 Chron. 21:3).

In the NT, Jesus' birthright includes the throne of David, a position of honor as God's unique Son, and creation itself (Rom. 8:29; Col. 1:18; Heb. 1:4–6). The low regard with which Esau viewed his birthright is also used as a warning in Hebrews to encourage Christians not to take their spiritual inheritance lightly (Heb. 12:16–17).

Birthstool–*See* Birth.

Bishop–*See* Offices in the New Testament.

Bithynia–A region in northern Asia Minor bordering the Black Sea that, along with Pontus, was ruled as one province by the Romans. Paul and his missionary companions desired to enter Bithynia during his second missionary journey but were prevented from doing so by the Holy Spirit, so they traveled to Macedonia instead (Acts 16:7). The Christians in Bithynia received greetings from Peter (1 Pet. 1:1).

Bitter Herbs–A food eaten with lamb and unleavened bread at the Passover meal. The herbs often consisted of whatever bitter greens were available. Though not specifically identified, they included lettuce, endive, parsley, watercress, cucumber, and horseradish, all of which were plentiful in areas of the Sinai Peninsula, Palestine, and Egypt. The bitter herbs recalled the misery of slavery in Egypt (Exod. 12:8; Num. 9:11). In John 13:26–27 Jesus, instead of dipping a "piece of bread" (Gk. *psōmion*), probably dipped bitter herbs, sharing them with Judas Iscariot (cf., in the Greek texts, Mark 14:20, where Jesus does not specify what is being dipped; Matt. 26:23, where Jesus talks about dipping a hand).

Bitter Water–Numbers 5:11–31 describes a judicial ordeal for determining whether a wife has been unfaithful. In the course of the ritual, the wife suspected of wrongdoing is to drink water mixed with dirt from the floor of the tabernacle, thus made "bitter," and in which a scroll containing curses has been washed (so that the water also contains the ink of the scroll). In the event that the woman was guilty of unfaithfulness, this concoction was intended to transfer to her body the curses against her. Deuteronomy 21:1–9 may represent a second judicial ordeal involving water, though bitterness is not involved.

Shortly after crossing the Red Sea, the Israelites came to Marah ("bitterness"), where the waters were bitter and not potable. Moses was divinely instructed to throw a piece of wood in the water, rendering it sweet and drinkable (Exod. 15:23–25), the first of several divine provisions of drinking water in the desert.

Revelation 8:11 depicts apocalyptic divine judgment in terms of bitter or poisoned water. In both of these passages, bitterness is effected or removed by the combination of wood and water: "wormwood" (Gk. *apsinthos*, a bitter substance derived from the wood of a particular shrub). The image of Rev. 8:11 recalls a similar divine threat in Jer. 9:15; 23:15.

B

Bitumen–A tarlike substance used as mortar for setting bricks, as in Gen. 11:3 (NIV: "tar") with the building of a ziggurat. It was also used, along with pitch, as a waterproofing agent for Noah's ark (Gen. 6:14) and for the reed basket in which Moses was placed as an infant (Exod. 2:3).

Blasphemy–Any contemptuous expression that rejects God's authority and questions his nature. Blasphemers include wicked enemies who mock God (Pss. 10:3, 13; 74:18), and God's people who reject the authority of his word (Isa. 1:4; 5:24).

This provides the foundation for the NT material. When the Pharisees wrongfully attributed Jesus' power to drive out demons to Beelzebul, Jesus declared that every sin and blasphemy would be forgiven, even speaking a word against the Son of Man, but not blaspheming or speaking against the Holy Spirit (Matt. 12:22–32). The Spirit's work was evident in the powerful demonstration they had seen. To attribute Jesus' work to Satan was a complete affront to the majesty of God.

Stephen was accused of speaking words of blasphemy against Moses and God (Acts 6:11), and Saul of Tarsus, in his vendetta against Christians, went from one synagogue to another trying to force early Christians to blaspheme (Acts 26:11). Later, knowing that he was "the worst of sinners," he acknowledged that he was a "blasphemer and a persecutor and a violent man" (1 Tim. 1:13–16). Knowing the seriousness of the offense, Paul declared that he handed Hymenaeus and Alexander over to Satan so they would be taught not to blaspheme (1 Tim. 1:20).

The source of all blasphemy will make its appearance in the final eschatological confrontation: on the heads of the beast will be a blasphemous name (Rev. 13:1; cf. 17:3), and it will utter blasphemy against God, his temple, and his people (13:5, 6). Paul describes this same scenario in 2 Thess. 2:3–4, where "the man of lawlessness" sets himself up in God's temple, proclaiming himself to be God. Finally, when the bowls of wrath are poured out on the earth, those who refuse to repent will curse God (Rev. 16:9, 11, 21), the final blasphemy.

Blastus–A personal servant of Herod Agrippa I mentioned in Acts 12:20. He was likely the chamberlain in charge of Herod's bed quarters. The citizens of Tyre and Sidon persuaded him to help them make peace with Herod regarding an issue with the supply of food.

Blemish–The physical defect on a sacrificial animal that makes it an unacceptable offering to the Lord (Lev. 22:17–25), or the physical defect on a priest that disqualifies him from performing certain priestly functions (Lev. 21:17–24). In the NT, Christ is the once-for-all sacrificial lamb without blemish or defect. In Christ, Christians are presented to God as holy and without blemish (Eph. 5:27; Col. 1:22; Heb. 9:14; 1 Pet. 1:19).

Blessing and Cursing–The blessings and curses of Scripture are grounded in a worldview that understands the sovereign God to be the ultimate dispenser of each. God is the giver of blessing and ultimately the final judge who determines withdrawal or ban. He is the source of every good gift (James 1:17) and the one who gives power and strength to prosper (Deut. 8:17).

Old Testament. The sovereign God sometimes employs agents of blessing in his creation. The blessing extends to the nations through Abraham (Gen. 12:3), to Jacob through Isaac (Gen. 26–27), and to the people through the priests (Num. 6:24–26).

The theme of blessing/curse is used to structure Deut. 27–28 and Lev. 26 (cf. Josh. 8:34) in the overall covenant format of these books. Scholars have observed that the object of this format is not symmetry or logical unity but fullness. From this perspective, the blessing/curse structure functions to enforce obedience for the purpose of ensuring a relationship. The blessing of Deuteronomy also includes the benefits of prosperity, power, and fertility. The curse, on the other hand, is the lack or withdrawal of benefits associated with the relationship.

The creation narratives are marked with the theme and terminology of blessing (Gen. 1:22, 28; 2:3; cf. 5:2; 9:1). The objects of blessing in Gen. 1:22, 28 (cf. 5:2; 9:1) are the living creatures and human beings created in the image of

God. As the revelation progresses, the blessing of God is particularized in the lives of Noah (Gen. 6–8), Abraham (Gen. 12–25) and his descendants, and the nation of Israel and its leadership (Gen. 26–50). In these contexts, the blessing is intended to engender offspring and to prosper recipients in material and physical ways (compare a similar NT emphasis in Acts 17:25; cf. Matt. 5:45; 6:25–33; Acts 14:17).

The blessing of God is also extended to inanimate objects that enhance and prosper one's quality of life. The seventh day of creation is the object of blessing (Gen. 2:7; Exod. 20:11), perhaps giving it a sense of well-being and health. Objects and activities of life such as baskets and kneading troughs (Deut. 28:5), barns (Deut. 28:8), and work (Job 1:10; Ps. 90:17) are blessed.

God promises to bless those who fear him (Ps. 128:1). Blessing is designed for those who, out of a deep sense of awe of God's character, love and trust him. The God-fearer confidently embraces God's promises, obediently serves, and takes seriously God's warnings. The blessings itemized in Ps. 128 are comparable to those detailed in Deut. 28 relating to productivity and fruitfulness (cf. Ps. 128:2 with Deut. 28:12; Ps. 128:3 with Deut. 28:4, 11). The Deuteronomic concept of blessing and curse is questioned when God-fearers undergo a period of suffering or experience God's apparent absence (e.g., Joseph, Job; cf. Jesus).

New Testament. In the NT, blessings are not exclusively spiritual. God gives both food and joy (Acts 14:17) and provides the necessities of life (Matt. 6:25–33). The NT does connect blessing with Christ, and it focuses attention on the spiritual quality of the gift that originates from Christ himself and its intended benefit for spiritual individuals.

Regarding curse, the NT explains that Christ bore the curse of the law to free us from its deadening effect (Gal. 3:10–13). Revelation 22:3 anticipates a time when the curse associated with sin will be completely removed and the blessing associated with creation will prevail. "Anathema" is a transliteration of a Greek word that means "curse" (see NIV). Paul invokes it for those who pervert or reject the gospel of God's free grace (1 Cor. 16:22; Gal. 1:8–9).

Blindness–Blindness was a common ailment in the ancient world. Some causes included old age (Gen. 27:1), trauma, or divine punishment (John 9:2). Israel was given special instructions to care for the blind (Lev. 19:14). True love helped the blind (Job 29:15), and misleading them was a serious violation (Deut. 27:18).

In figurative language, the Bible frequently describes the spiritual condition of people in terms of blindness. Isaiah capitalizes on the metaphor of blindness to describe the rebellious and apostate groups: prophets, priests, and rulers who were divinely afflicted with blindness (Isa. 43:8; 56:10; 59:10; cf. Zeph. 1:17).

Jesus highlighted the onset of the messianic age by fulfilling Isaiah's promise to proclaim "recovery of sight to the blind" (Luke 4:18). Forty-six of fifty-two references to blindness in the NT are Gospel stories of Jesus' healing. Because Jesus' ministry was one of opening blind eyes (cf. Isa. 42:7, 16, 18), calling the Pharisees "blind guides" was a sharp description (Matt. 15:14; 23:16, 24). But on others, Jesus would impose blindness, the very reverse of his mission (John 9:39–41), since he came as the "light of the world" (8:12). Spiritual blindness as applied to unbelievers could be used to describe the failure or hard-heartedness of some to accept the true identity of Jesus Christ. Using similar language, Paul describes the pagan unbelievers: "The god of this age has blinded the minds of unbelievers, so that they cannot see the light of the gospel that displays the glory of Christ" (2 Cor. 4:4).

Nearsightedness and blindness can also be used to describe believers who have grown dull to the truth (2 Pet. 1:9) or tepid in their faith (Rev. 3:17). Believers are blind when they fail to grasp their true spiritual condition.

Blood–The word for "blood" in the Bible is used both literally and metaphorically. "Blood" is a significant biblical term for understanding purity boundaries and theological concepts. Blood is a dominant ritual symbol in biblical literature. Blood was used in sacrifices and purification rites, and it was inherently connected to menstruation, animal slaughter, and legal culpability. Among the physical properties of blood are the ability to coagulate, the liquid state of the substance (Rev. 16:3–4), and the ability to stain (Rev. 19:13). Blood can symbolize moral order in terms of cult, law, and power.

The usage of blood in the OT is predominantly negative. The first direct mention of blood in the biblical text involves a homicide (Gen. 4:10). Henceforward, the shedding of human blood is a main concern (Gen. 9:6). Other concerns pertaining to blood include dietary prohibitions of blood (Lev. 17:10–12), purity issues such as the flow of blood as in menstrual blood (Lev. 15:19–24), and blood as a part of religious rites such as circumcision (Gen. 17:10–11; Exod. 4:24–26).

Leviticus 17:11 contains a central statement in the OT concerning the significant role of blood in the sacrificial system: "The life of a creature is in the blood." Blood was collected from all animal sacrifices, and blood was poured onto the altar (Lev. 1:5).

The covenant with Abraham was sealed with a covenantal ritual (Gen. 15:10–21). Moses sealed the covenant between the Israelites and God with a blood ritual during which young Israelite men offered young bulls among other sacrifices as fellowship offerings (Exod. 24:5). Moses read the words of the Book of the Covenant and sprinkled the blood of the bulls on the people, saying, "This is the blood of the covenant that the LORD has made with you in accordance with all these words" (Exod. 24:7–8).

During the Passover observance at the time of the exodus, blood was placed on the sides and tops of the doorframes of the Hebrews (Exod. 12:7). Not only altars were sprinkled and thus consecrated with blood, but priests were as well. Aaron and his sons were consecrated by the application of blood to their right earlobe, thumb, and big toe, and the sprinkling of blood and oil on their garments (Exod. 29:20). On the Day of Atonement, the high priest entered the holy of holies and sprinkled blood on the mercy seat to seek atonement for the sins of the people (Lev. 16:15).

Many events in the passion of Christ include references to blood. During the Last Supper, Jesus redefined the last Passover cup: "This is my blood of the covenant, which is poured out for many for the forgiveness of sins" (Matt. 26:28). Judas betrayed "innocent blood" (Matt. 27:4), and the money he received for his betrayal was referred to as "blood money" (Matt. 27:6). At Jesus' trial, Pilate washed his hands and declared, "I am innocent of this man's blood" (Matt. 27:24).

The apostle Paul wrote that believers are justified by the blood of Christ (Rom. 5:9). This justification or righteous standing with God was effected through Christ's blood sacrifice (Rom. 3:25–26; 5:8). The writer of Hebrews stressed the instrumental role of blood in bringing about forgiveness (Heb. 9:22). In the picture of the ideal community of Christ, the martyrs in the book of Revelation are situated closest to the throne of God because "they triumphed over him [Satan] by the blood of the Lamb and by the word of their testimony; they did not love their lives so much as to shrink from death" (Rev. 12:11). The blood of the Lamb, Christ, is the effective agent here and throughout the NT, bringing about the indirect contact between sinner and God.

BLOOD, FIELD OF–*See* Akeldama.

BLOODGUILT–The guilt that results from the shedding of innocent blood, the taking of an innocent life. The person who incurred bloodguilt was considered not only morally but also ritually impure; this impurity attached not just to the person, for the land was made ritually impure as well. The only way this impurity could be removed was by the execution of the guilty individual (Num. 35:29–34). The person responsible for carrying out the sentence was referred to as the "avenger of blood" (Num. 35:19–27; Deut. 19:6–13 [*see also* Avenger]). This responsibility fell to the slain person's nearest kin. For those whose taking of innocent life was accidental (manslaughter), there were cities of refuge established to which the accused could flee from the avenger, and a judicial process was set up to determine innocence or guilt (*see also* Cities of Refuge).

BOANERGES–A nickname, meaning "sons of thunder," given by Jesus to the brothers James and John when he appointed them as apostles (Mark 3:17). Mark does not explain the significance of the name, but it may refer to their fiery temperament (cf. Mark 9:38; Luke 9:54). Alternatively, if meant in a positive way, it could signify their future role as thunderous witnesses to the gospel.

BOAZ–**(1)** One of two bronze pillars erected by Solomon at the portico of the temple (1 Kings 7:15–22). Its name means "in him [is] strength." Together with the other pillar, Jakin, the names form a prayer: "May he [the LORD] establish strength in him [Solomon]." The pillars were broken up at the Babylonian conquest of Jerusalem (2 Kings 25:13). **(2)** A man of Bethlehem who married Ruth the Moabite during the time of the judges. Boaz was an older, wealthy landowner who honored God in his words (Ruth 2:4, 12; 3:10) and deeds. He honored the Mosaic custom of allowing the disadvantaged to glean in his fields, but he went beyond this in providing for Naomi and Ruth. He also extended the custom of levirate marriage (see Deut. 25:5–10) to accord Ruth's son to her deceased husband, although his own name appears in all the genealogies of David.

Bohan, Stone of–A boundary marker on the south boundary of the territory of the tribe of Benjamin and on the northern border of the territory of the tribe of Judah (Josh. 15:6; 18:17). The exact location of the stone is unknown, although it was most likely west of the Jordan River because the boundary between the tribes of Judah and Benjamin ran west from the Jordan River and the Dead Sea.

Boils–A skin disease caused by inflammation of hair follicles. Boils are the sixth plague sent by God upon the Egyptians (Exod. 9:8–12), described as the "festering boils" causing pain. These boils, along with the other plagues, show Yahweh's power so that his name is declared in all the earth (6:1–7; 9:16). As a contracted skin disease, boils are examined by a priest in order to determine if someone who has them is ritually clean or unclean (Lev. 13:18–23). In one case, God hears King Hezekiah's prayers and heals the boil that has afflicted him (2 Kings 20:7; Isa. 38:21). Boils are employed as one of the covenant curses for disobedience (Deut. 28:27, 35).

Bokim–A place near Gilgal where the angel of the Lord rebuked Israel for not tearing down the altars to foreign gods and proclaimed that the Lord would not drive out all the inhabitants of the land (Judg. 2:1–5). Thereupon the people wept, made sacrifices, and named the place "Bokim," which means "weeping ones."

Bond–A bond typically represents a close relationship in Scripture. It can carry positive or negative connotations, as do related words such as "bondage." In the sense of "chains," bonds literally hold a slave to the master or a prisoner to the jail. God's exiled people are likewise said to be held in bonds, from which he will rescue them (Jer. 30:8). Spiritually speaking, "bond" may describe the firm covenant relationship between God and his people (Jer. 2:20; 5:5; Ezek. 20:37). In the new covenant, believers are freed from bondage to sin and become Christ's bondspeople (Rom. 6:16–22). This relationship with Christ in turn joins Christians to one another; in Ephesians this unity is called "the bond of peace" (4:3).

Bondage, Bondman, Bondmaid, Bondservant–*See* Slave, Servant.

Bones–Of the 206 bones that compose the adult skeletal structure, the Bible mentions only a few: rib (Gen. 1:21–22), hip (Gen. 32:25), skull (Judg. 9:53), jaw (Isa. 30:28), and legs (John 19:31–33). Nevertheless, while bones could be isolated, anatomical description tended more toward a holistic sense so that bones could refer to physical and psychological collapse in laments (Jer. 23:9) or to the entire person as a corpse (Gen. 50:25; 1 Sam. 31:13).

Overwhelmingly, however, anatomical "units" are used metaphorically for human emotions or attitudes: shame becomes "decay in [the] bones" (Prov. 12:4), fear makes "bones shake" (Job 4:14), and a sad spirit "dries up the bones" (Prov. 17:22). The phrase "bone of my bones" is an idiom, a kinship formula used to describe unity and close relatives (Gen. 2:23; cf. 2 Sam. 5:1).

Book of Life–The phrase "book of life" occurs eight times in the Bible (Ps. 69:28; Phil. 4:3; Rev. 3:5; 13:8; 17:8; 20:12, 15; 21:27). The image may originate from the practice of keeping genealogical records or a registry of citizens in which the names of individuals were recorded. Some have suggested that it is a figurative record of all the living, from which the unsaved are eventually erased. But more likely the phrase metaphorically expresses the omniscience of God, who knows all those whom he has predestined to eternal life.

Books–The Bible refers to a large number of distinct books that existed at various times and places. Unfortunately, these extrabiblical books did not survive, but the authors of Scripture knew about them and may have quoted them or employed them in writing biblical history. Below is a list of nonbiblical literary works mentioned in the Bible.

- The Book of the Covenant (Exod. 24:7; 2 Kings 23:2, 21; 2 Chron. 34:30).
- The Book of the Law (Deut. 30:10; 31:26; Josh. 1:8; 8:34; 2 Kings 22:8; Gal. 3:10). This is also called the Book of the Law of Moses (Josh. 23:6; cf. Mark 12:26) and the Book of the Law of God (Josh. 24:26).

- The Book of the Wars of the LORD (Num. 21:14). Quotations from this source may include Num. 21:14b–15, 17–18, 27–30.
- The Book of Jashar (Josh. 10:13; 2 Sam. 1:18). This text contained David's lament for Saul and Jonathan (2 Sam. 1:19–27) and most likely Joshua's statement (Josh. 10:12).
- The scroll of Joshua (Josh. 18:9).
- The book of the annals of Solomon (1 Kings 11:41).
- The book of the annals of the kings of Israel (1 Kings 14:19). This source is mentioned eighteen times in 1–2 Kings.
- The book of the annals of the kings of Judah (1 Kings 14:29). This scroll is mentioned fifteen times in 1–2 Kings.
- Genealogical records from the reigns of Jotham king of Judah and Jeroboam king of Israel (1 Chron. 5:17).
- The book of the kings of Israel and Judah (1 Chron. 9:1; 2 Chron. 27:7).
- The book of the kings of Israel, which includes the annals of Jehu son of Hanani (2 Chron. 20:34). This may be the same as the book of the kings of Israel and Judah in 1 Chron. 9:1 (see ESV, NRSV).
- The book of the annals of King David (1 Chron. 27:24).
- The records of Samuel the seer (1 Chron. 29:29).
- The records of Nathan the prophet (1 Chron. 29:29; 2 Chron. 9:29).
- The records of Gad the seer (1 Chron. 29:29).
- The prophecy of Ahijah the Shilonite (2 Chron. 9:29).
- The visions of Iddo the seer (2 Chron. 9:29).
- The records of Shemaiah the prophet and of Iddo the seer (2 Chron. 12:15).
- The annotations of the prophet Iddo (2 Chron. 13:22).
- The book of the kings of Judah and Israel (2 Chron. 16:11). This includes information on Hezekiah's reign in the vision of the prophet Isaiah son of Amoz (2 Chron. 32:32).
- The annotations on the book of the kings (2 Chron. 24:27).
- The annals of the kings of Israel (2 Chron. 33:18).
- The records of the seers (2 Chron. 33:19).
- The genealogical record of those who had been the first to return (Neh. 7:5).
- The book of the annals (Neh. 12:23). This contained genealogical data and possibly other historical material on the returning exiles.
- The book of the annals of the kings of Media and Persia (Esther 10:2; cf. Esther 2:23; 6:1; Ezra 4:15).
- The book of life (Ps. 69:28; Phil. 4:3; Rev. 3:5; 13:8; 17:8; 20:12, 15; 21:27; cf. Exod. 32:32–33; Ps. 139:16).
- The Book of Truth (Dan. 10:21).
- The scroll of remembrance (Mal. 3:16).

BOOTH–A hut made with branches from a tree. Jacob lived in a booth (NIV: "shelter") on his journey to Sukkoth, a place named after booths (Heb. *sukkot* [Gen. 33:17]). The Feast of Booths, or Festival of Tabernacles (Lev. 23:33–43; Deut. 16:13–17)—known in Hebrew as Sukkoth—takes place on the fifteenth of Tishri (late September to late October) and is one of the three pilgrimage festivals. It commemorates the Israelites' living in temporary shelters in the wilderness following their exodus from Egypt (Lev. 23:43).

BOTTOMLESS PIT–*See* Abyss.

BOUNDARY STONE–A boundary stone (KJV: "landmark"; NRSV: "boundary marker") is an object used to mark the boundaries of property. Boundary stones were to remain in place over generations (Deut. 19:14). Moving a boundary stone was a serious offense; those who move boundary stones were cursed in the same breath as those who dishonor their parents and those who lead the blind astray (Deut. 27:16–18). Wisdom literature speaks strongly against those who move boundary stones. Job cites the moving of boundary stones as an indication of the depravity of humankind (Job 24:1–4). Proverbs assures that God will not allow such an act of theft to go unnoticed (Prov. 22:28; 23:10).

BOWELS–An approximate literal meaning of Hebrew and Greek terms used to refer to the seat of the emotions (sometimes translated as "intestines" or "stomach"). The literal meaning is apparent in a few passages (Ezek. 7:19; 2 Chron. 21:15–19; Jon. 1:17; Acts 1:18). More often the terms are used to refer to a variety of strong emotions (Jer. 31:20; Lam. 1:20; 2 Cor. 6:12; Phil. 1:8; Philem. 7). Elsewhere the words refer to the womb or are related to progeny (Gen. 25:23; 2 Sam. 16:11; Isa. 49:1).

Bozrah–**(1)** A city in northern Edom (Gen. 36:33; 1 Chron. 1:44), located thirty miles north of Petra at modern Buseirah. It controlled the traffic on the King's Highway. The city was protected by cliffs on three sides, making it almost unconquerable. It was periodically the capital of Edom. Isaiah, Jeremiah, and Amos prophesied that it would fall pending God's judgment on Edom (Isa. 34:6; 63:1; Jer. 49:13, 22; Amos 1:12). **(2)** A city in Moab mentioned in Jer. 48:24. Jeremiah prophesied that it would fall when Moab did. It is most likely the same place as Bezer, although its exact location is unknown.

Braiding–Both Paul and Peter exhort Christian women to adorn themselves not with "braided hair," expensive clothes, and fine jewels, but with an inner beauty expressed in good works and spiritual grace (1 Tim. 2:9–10; 1 Pet. 3:3–4 NASB, RSV). The terms used here refer not to simple hair weaves, but to the elaborate bejeweled coiffures of upper-class Greco-Roman women. The NIV uses the phrase "elaborate hairstyles," since the point is not the braids themselves but rather the ostentatious behavior and emphasis on outward beauty.

Bramble–One of several common thorny or prickly plants, also translated as "brier," "thorn," or "thistle." Brambles grew as weeds in grain fields (Job 31:40) and among ruins (Isa. 34:13). They were considered unattractive (Song 2:2), insignificant (Judg. 9:14–15; 2 Kings 14:9), and unproductive (Luke 6:44).

Branch–Besides its normal, literal usage, "branch" is often used figuratively in the Bible to refer to descendants. The image that is created is usually that of a tree or tree stump from which new growth ("the branch") emerges. The branch is thus both connected to the tree and yet still distinct and unique. In several OT passages the term "branch" is used to describe the coming Messiah, often stressing his descent from King David (Isa. 11:1; Jer. 23:5; 33:15; Zech. 3:8; 6:12–13; perhaps Isa. 4:2). Closely connected to the branch imagery of the Messiah is fruitfulness (Isa. 4:2; 11:1) and the dual concepts of justice and righteousness (Jer. 23:5; 33:15). Zechariah 6:12–13 states that "the Branch," clothed in majesty, will rebuild the temple and take his seat on the throne to rule. In Rom. 11:17–24 Paul uses the branch/tree imagery to explain how Israel (the natural branch) and the Gentiles (the ingrafted branch) both relate to the overall plan and people of God (the tree with its roots).

Bread–Generally made of grain, this staple of foods has been known to be in existence since prehistoric days, being mentioned in the oldest literatures of humanity. Though usually made of wheat, it can be made of any grain and also some kinds of beans or lentils.

To make bread, grain must be ground into flour, mixed with salt and water, kneaded into a dough, and baked. Most breads included a leaven to add substance. As a food staple, it became a symbol of hospitality (Neh. 13:1–2; Matt. 14:15–21) and community as people ate together (Acts 2:42). Bread was considered a gift from God, so it was treated with special deference. Unleavened bread was required during Passover feasts and in most occasions related to the worship of God. The "bread of the Presence" (KJV: "shewbread"), representing the twelve tribes of Israel in the temple, was made of unleavened bread (Exod. 25:30) with special flour and was carefully eaten by the priests.

Jesus used bread in the Lord's Prayer to represent asking God to meet our basic needs (Matt. 5:11), and he called himself the "bread of life" to show that he is the one who "gives life to the world," our ultimate sustenance (John 6:33–35). During this exchange with the Jews about the bread of life, Jesus foreshadows what takes place at the Last Supper with his disciples, suggesting that believers must "eat [his] flesh" (represented by bread) and "drink [his] blood" (represented by wine) (John 6:53–59; cf. Luke 22:19). Additionally, bread was used symbolically to represent those things that were present in daily life (Pss. 127:2; 80:5; Prov. 4:17; 20:17).

Bread of the Presence–*See* Bread.

Breastpiece of the High Priest–A pouch, nine inches square, woven of the same colorful material as the ephod. Gold rings were attached to each corner so that it could be firmly fastened to the ephod with gold cords at the top and blue cords at the bottom. Mounted on its front, in four rows, were twelve precious stones engraved with the names of the tribes of Israel and mounted in gold settings. Since it held the Urim and Thummim by which God revealed his judgments for Israel, it was sometimes called the "breastpiece of judgment." By wearing it, the high priest signified that he bore the names of all the tribes whenever he entered God's presence, and that he would bring God's judgments or announce his will to the people.

Breath–In the OT, the Hebrew words *ruakh* ("breath, spirit") and *neshamah* ("blast, spirit") are the standard terms, even collectively translated "wind." Constructively, these terms reflect the vibrant relationship between God and humankind. However, God's "breath" can also be an agent of judgment. So "breath/wind" is the invasive power of God—proof of his supremacy—capable of disruption or transformation of human life.

It is in human creation that God's breath is given one of its most dynamic illustrations. Formed of "dust," the human being must be enlivened by the Creator's breath. In the OT, human flesh remains dormant and helplessly passive until God breathes; then a living human being is animated (Gen. 2:7; 6:17; cf. Pss. 33:6; 104:29).

"Breath/wind" is also a powerful force in God's anger, when a "blast of breath from his nostrils" can undo and destroy (2 Sam. 22:16). Similarly, a "strong east wind" rolls back the Red Sea for the Israelites' crossing (Exod. 14:21), but the very same force is the undoing of Pharaoh's army, which was destroyed as God, Israel's warrior, "blew" with his "breath" (Exod. 15:10).

Not surprisingly, themes combining breath, wind, and spirit are also used to describe new creation (Ezek. 37:9). The life-generating force of the *ruakh*/spirit emerges in the NT as the Holy Spirit, manifested in wind, a breath, or Spirit (Gk. *pneuma*). At Pentecost "a violent wind came from heaven," enacting another creation (Acts 2:2). John clearly symbolizes Jesus' "breathing" on the disciples (John 20:22). Not only does this illustrate John's theology of being born "from above" (3:3 NRSV), but also "he breathed" reenacts the enlivening of Gen. 2:7. The two creations are connected: God's enlivening in Gen. 2:7 and Jesus' creation of eternal life following his own resurrection.

Breath of Life–*See* Breath.

Bribe–A gift given in order to influence a decision or judgment. The OT law prohibits giving a bribe with the result that a false judgment (the innocent proclaimed guilty or vice versa) is delivered (Exod. 23:8; Deut. 16:19; 27:25; see also Ps. 15:5). Some proverbs (Prov. 17:8; 18:16; 21:14), however, speak more positively about bribes (or gifts). Perhaps the circumstance of a gift is the issue. The giving of a gift in order to circumvent justice is wrong, but there are some situations where bribes can open doors to good ends.

Brick–Bricks are first mentioned in the Bible at Gen. 11:3 (the tower of Babel), which says that "they used brick instead of stone," a note that rings true to geographical differences in the use of bricks. In Mesopotamia, however, fire-hardened bricks could be used for monumental structures; thousands of these have survived. Bricks were made of mud or clay, often mixed with straw (Exod. 5:7), and could be dried in the sun for rudimentary purposes. Making bricks was hard labor, fitting for slaves (Exod. 1:14; 2 Sam. 12:31). Brick altars, like those of hewn stone, were not permitted in the worship of God (Exod. 20:24–25; Isa. 65:3).

Bride–In both Testaments of Scripture, marriage is used to illustrate the relationship between God and his chosen people. Isaiah and Jeremiah portray Israel as the bride of Yahweh, sometimes to emphasize his love for her, sometimes to lament her unfaithfulness to him. Isaiah says that Yahweh will one day rejoice over Israel "as a bridegroom rejoices over his bride" (Isa. 62:5; cf. 61:10). Jeremiah expresses God's disappointment that his bride (Israel) has lost her first love for him and even forgotten him (Jer. 2:2, 32). Hosea uses this metaphor repeatedly to proclaim Yahweh's undying love for his adulterous wife, the people of Israel (Hos. 1–3).

In the NT, the church becomes the bride of Christ, both in Paul's letters and in the book of Revelation (Rev. 21:2, 9; 22:17). Paul compares the church to a bride expressly in Eph. 5, where the love of Christ for his church sets an example for ordinary husbands: they must love their wives "as Christ loved the church"—that is, sacrificially (v. 25). In Revelation the church adorns herself with righteous acts for the sake of Christ, her groom (19:6). Further along in Revelation, the new Jerusalem itself becomes the "bride" of Christ, inhabited by his saved people, the church (21:9–10).

Brier–Being prickly and hardy, this plant carries negative connotations such as torment (Judg. 8:7; John 19:2), vexing enemies (Isa. 27:4; Ezek. 28:24), and judgment (Isa. 5:6; 7:23–25). It is also planted as a hedge for protection (Isa. 5:5).

Broad Wall–In Neh. 3:8; 12:38, a section of the rebuilt Jerusalem city wall is called the "Broad Wall." The name is now also used for the twenty-three-foot wide, eighth-century BC wall apparently constructed by Hezekiah (2 Chron. 32:2–5; Isa. 22:10), excavated in the 1970s.

Bronze—*See* Minerals and Metals.

Bronze Serpent–An early, tangible reminder of the goodness of God in rescuing his people from their sins (NIV: "bronze snake"). During the wilderness wanderings, the land of Edom lay in the path of the Israelites. The Israelites requested permission to pass through Edom, which the Edomites strongly denied (Num. 20:14–21). Forced to circle around Edom and head far out of their way, the Israelites began to complain yet again (Num. 21:4–5; see also Exod. 15:22–24; 16:1–3; 17:1–7). God responded by sending venomous snakes that killed many people (Num. 21:6). When the people admitted their sin and asked Moses to pray to God on their behalf, God commanded Moses to do a strange thing: he was to make a snake and put it on a pole. "Then when anyone was bitten by a snake and looked at the bronze snake, they lived" (21:9).

This seemingly insignificant and bizarre episode in Israelite history resurfaces twice in the Bible. The good king Hezekiah destroyed the bronze serpent during his purification of the land of Judah from idolatrous worship. The writer of Kings explains that the serpent, which had come to be called "Nehushtan," had itself become an idol, as the Israelites had been burning incense to it (2 Kings 18:4). Jesus also makes mention of the bronze serpent in his famous dialogue with Nicodemus. In speaking of his impending death, Jesus explains to Nicodemus that he, the Son of Man, must be lifted up from the earth, "just as Moses lifted up the snake in the desert" (John 3:14). Those who believe in Jesus will have eternal life because of his being lifted up—that is, crucified (see John 12:32–34). Jesus' reference to the bronze serpent emphasizes the simplicity of salvation through Christ. Just as the Israelites needed only to look to the bronze serpent, trusting in God's provision for their salvation from physical death, so also those who are dying in their sins need only look to the perfect sacrifice of Jesus Christ, trusting in God's provision for their salvation from spiritual death.

Brook of Egypt–*See* Rivers and Waterways.

Brotherly Love–The word brotherly love in Greek is *philadelphia*, which is composed of two parts: the first is one of the Greek words for "love" (*philia*), and the second part refers to the idea of a sibling (*adelphē, adelphos*).

Paul instructs the church at Rome to "love one another with brotherly affection" (Rom. 12:10 ESV) as a part of his description of the Christian life. He recognizes the supernatural origin of this new love among believers ("You yourselves have been taught by God to love each other"), compliments them on their success in this area, and yet appeals to them to continue to "do so more and more" (1 Thess. 4:9–10). The author of the book of Hebrews, writing to a church that was already counting the cost of persecution and was even then being tempted to give up the Christian faith, says simply, "Keep on loving one another as brothers and sisters" (13:1). Peter addresses this same topic (again to a persecuted church), admonishing them to "love one another deeply, from the heart," but also reminds them how this love needs to be built on a response of the will to the truth of the gospel and to flow from a right heart (or "purified") attitude (1 Pet. 1:22). Peter also offers still another appeal to press on in this area when he says, "Finally, all of you, have unity of mind, sympathy, brotherly love, a tender heart, and a humble mind" (3:8 ESV).

Bull–An uncastrated male bovine. The bull was an important symbol of the divine in Canaanite religion, and the infamous "golden calves" that were worshiped by the Israelites at Mount Sinai and then at Dan and Bethel were manifestations of this theology (see Ps. 106:20). In Ugaritic religion the god El was associated with the bull, and the god Baal with a bull calf. Although the Bible generally condemns the use of the bull as a depiction of the God of Israel, bull images were featured in the furnishings of Solomon's temple, including the twelve metal bulls that supported the Sea (1 Kings 7:25). Ahaz later sent these valuable objects as tribute to the king of Assyria (2 Kings 16:17).

Bulls were used in several important sacrifices, including in the consecration of priests (Exod. 29:1–37), the sin offering (Lev. 4:3), the Day of Atonement (Lev. 16:3), and the festivals of Weeks (Lev. 23:18), New Year (Lev. 28:11), Passover (Lev. 28:19), First Fruits (Lev. 28:27), and Booths (Lev. 29:13).

Bulls are powerful and dangerous animals (Ps. 22:12), and Israelite and Mesopotamian law codes mandated penalties for the owner of a bull that had harmed a person (Exod. 21:28–32) or another animal (Exod. 21:35–36).

Burial–Burial can refer to the ritual, body preparation, or interment.

Genesis in particular uses some formulaic phases: "died and was gathered to his people" and "rest with [one's] fathers/ancestors" (25:8; 35:29; 47:30; 49:33; cf. Job 14:10). In Abraham's death (Gen. 25:8), this "gathering" does not refer to his actual burial, since it occurs between his death and burial; nor was Abraham ever buried with his ancestors (cf. Num. 20:26 [Aaron]; Deut. 32:50 [Moses]). This idiom refers to joining one's ancestors in the realm of the dead. With communal notions, the phrase also refers to elements of family burial (similarly, "gathered to your people" [Num. 27:13]; "gathered to their ancestors" [Judg. 2:10]).

In Jacob's obituary he "gathered up" his feet and then was "gathered" to his people (Gen. 49:33 KJV), rich imagery because he had "gathered" his sons (cf. 49:1). This expression is also used of depositing the human remains in a collective family burial site (Judg. 2:10; 2 Kings 22:20; cf. Jer. 25:33).

In the genealogically sensitive books of Kings and Chronicles a formula is used for the kings: "X rested with his ancestors and was buried in Y." Here, "Y" can denote a place such as the City of David (1 Kings 2:10; 11:43; 14:31; 2 Chron. 16:13–14). Authors depart from this formula in order to describe a person's desecration, such as Jezebel; the dogs consumed her except for her skull, hands, and feet (2 Kings 9:37; cf. 1 Kings 21:23–24).

Jacob and Joseph receive specialized Egyptian embalming. Embalming preserved a more holistic persona through use of special fluids and wrappings for seventy days (Gen. 50:2–3, 26). Death usually required immediate burial, even for criminals (Deut. 21:1–9, 22–23; 1 Kings 13:24–30). Outside Israel, the inclusion of grave utensils (e.g., juglets, cooking pots, bowls, and jewelry) with the deceased was indicative of a person's status and needs in the afterlife. The OT prophets forbade certain practices of mourning such as self-mutilation (Lev. 21:1–6; cf. Amos 6:6–7).

In the NT, burial could include treatment with spices for odorific and purification reasons (Luke 23:56; John 19:40). Placed on a bench (*mishkab*, "resting place"), the body was covered in wrappings and a special facecloth (John 11:44). Familial respect required demonstration of grief with laments (Acts 8:2; cf. 1 Kings 13:29–30; Jer. 9:17–22).

Burning Bush–Moses' encounter with God at the burning bush was the first step in God's plan to bring his people, Israel, out of slavery. During Moses' time of alienation from Egypt (Exod. 2:11–15), the angel of the Lord manifested himself to Moses on Mount Horeb (Sinai) from a bush that was on fire but not being consumed. From within the bush, God spoke to Moses and ordered him to lead the Israelites out from Egypt. God further explained that his name is "I am who I am" (3:1–14). This incident forms the backdrop for the Jews' anger at Jesus in John 8:59: Jesus' reference to himself as "I am" (8:58) was an allusion to the encounter at the burning bush and thus a claim to be God.

Bushel–*See* Weights and Measures.

Byblos–An ancient Phoenician city, also known as Gebal, situated on a promontory of the foothills of Lebanon, about forty miles north of Sidon. Its historical significance as an international trade hub connecting Egypt, Greece, and Syria-Palestine has been demonstrated by ample evidence. Later, Byblos became a major distribution center for the Egyptian papyrus trade and supplied writing materials to the Greek world (thus the Greek name "Byblos," or "book," from which the English word "Bible" derives).

Byblos is mentioned in Josh. 13:5 as part of the land still unconquered. The men of Byblos aided the construction of the Solomonic temple (1 Kings 5:18). In an oracle against Tyre, Ezekiel mentions the men of Byblos as skillful shipbuilders (Ezek. 27:9). Byblos, or Gebal (ESV, NRSV, KJV), in Ps. 83:7 has been taken to denote a different place near Petra, southeast of the Dead Sea (based on statements from Eusebius and Josephus), but it is better understood as referring to the Phoenician city.

Byword–A traditional or popular saying used to show scorn. It can be used as a taunt or as a preeminent example of something bad, something that has come to ruin (1 Kings 9:7; Joel 2:17).

C

Cab–*See* Weights and Measures.

Caesar–The family name of the Roman emperors following Julius Caesar (100–44 BC). Emperors after Nero retained the title "Caesar," although they no longer belonged to the family line. The NT alludes to four Caesars: Augustus, also called "Octavian" (r. 31 BC–AD 14), called for the census (Luke 2:1) that brought Mary and Joseph to Bethlehem prior to Jesus' birth. Tiberius (r. AD 14–37) is named in Luke 3:1 and was the Caesar ruling when Jesus was questioned about paying taxes to Caesar (Matt. 22:17–21; Luke 20:22–25). The famine predicted by Agabus occurred during the tenure of Claudius (r. AD 41–54) (Acts 11:28), the emperor who prompted Aquila and Priscilla's relocation to Corinth (Acts 18:2) when he expelled the Jewish population from Rome (AD 49). Nero (r. AD 54–68) was the Caesar to whom Paul appealed (Acts 25:10) and from whose household Paul sent greetings to the Philippians (Phil. 4:22).

Caesarea–Built by Herod the Great between 22 and 10/9 BC and named in honor of Caesar Augustus, Caesarea was a major international seaport located on the Mediterranean coast about fifty-five miles northwest of Jerusalem. Also known as Caesarea Maritima or Caesarea Palestinae, it was built on the site of an earlier Phoenician trading station and town known as Strato's Tower.

After Herod's death in 4 BC, his eldest son, Archelaus, succeeded him as king. Augustus removed Archelaus from power in AD 6, and his kingdom, including Caesarea, was absorbed into the Roman Empire. The city was then made the seat of Roman government in the province of Judea. Pontius Pilate governed Judea from Caesarea when he presided over Jesus' trial.

Caesarea figures prominently in the establishment of Christianity, according to the book of Acts. Philip, a deacon in the Jerusalem church, appears to have brought Christianity to the city (8:4–40). At the beginning of Paul's ministry, threats from the Jews in Damascus forced Paul to flee to Caesarea and from there to Tarsus (9:30). Caesarea is where the centurion Cornelius and his household became the first Gentile converts, and where Peter received God's revelation regarding the acceptance of Gentiles into the kingdom of God (10:1–48).

Caesarea appears to have been an urban center for the early Christian movement. Paul came to the city at the end of his second and third missionary journeys (Acts 18:22; 21:8). On his way to Jerusalem, Paul stayed with Philip, who lived in Caesarea along with his four prophesying daughters (8:40; 21:8–9). It was in Caesarea that Paul made his decision to go to Jerusalem, despite Agabus's prophecy that the Jews would deliver him over to the Gentiles and the urging of Paul's companions and the local people for him not to go (21:10–13). Following Paul's arrest in Jerusalem, he was sent to Caesarea to appear before the governor Felix and remained imprisoned there for two years. When Felix was succeeded by Festus, Paul appealed to Caesar and was sent to Rome (25:11).

Caesarea Philippi–A city located about twenty-five miles north of the Sea of Galilee at the southwest base of Mount Hermon. In 20 BC the Roman emperor Octavian (r. 31 BC–AD 14) gave the area around Caesarea Philippi to Herod the Great, who made the town his capital. Herod's son Philip took control after his father's death, rebuilding the city as Caesarea in honor of Octavian's son Tiberius Caesar (in approximately 1 or 2 BC). During Philip's reign it was commonly called "Caesarea Philippi" (4 BC–AD 34) to avoid confusion, since other cities in the Roman Empire at that time were also called "Caesarea" (such as Caesarea Maritima).

Another of Herod the Great's sons, Agrippa I, ruled Caesarea Philippi for three years (AD 41–44), after which time it reverted to Roman rule until AD 53, when Agrippa II (the son of Agrippa I) was given control of the city (ruling for forty years, until AD 93). Agrippa II built a fortress there and renamed the city "Neronias" (after the emperor Nero), but this name did not become popular and quickly fell into disuse after Nero's reign ended.

The Roman emperor Titus stopped in Caesarea Philippi to rest his army after subduing the Jewish insurrection of AD 66–70. While there, Titus killed many captured Jews in public gladiatorial spectacles. The name of the town reverted back to the older name "Caesarea Paneas" in the second and third centuries AD and then simply to "Paneas" from the fourth century AD onward.

The towns Baal Gad (Josh. 11:17; 12:7; 13:5) and Baal Hermon (Judg. 3:3; 1 Chron. 5:23) were located in the region of what would become Caesarea Philippi. During Jesus' ministry, the town was populated mostly by Gentiles. The two explicit mentions of Caesarea Philippi in the Bible occur in parallel accounts in the Gospels: it was in the region of Caesarea Philippi that Peter made the memorable confession that Jesus is Israel's Messiah (Matt. 16:13–30; Mark 8:27–30; see also Luke 9:18–22).

Caesar's Household–Members of the Roman imperial palace staff who carried out the various logistical duties necessary to facilitate the emperor's rule over the empire. Such persons often were wealthy and influential beneficiaries of imperial favor, but large numbers of slaves were among their number as well. Inscriptions exist naming members of "Caesar's household," including many of the same names that appear in Rom. 16. Paul closes his letter to the Philippians with greetings from himself and "Caesar's household," thus indicating Rome as the probable origin of that letter (Phil. 4:22).

Caiaphas–High priest from AD 18 to 36/37. He is best known for presiding over the Jewish trial of Jesus. The Bible mentions him explicitly in Matt. 26:3, 57; Luke 3:2; John 11:49; 18:13, 24, 28; Acts 4:6. Gratus, a Roman prefect of Judea, appointed Caiaphas to the office, and Vitellius, a Roman legate of Syria, removed him from it. According to John 11:49–52, he prophesied about Jesus' death. He appears several times in the writings of Josephus, though conspicuously rarely considering the length of his tenure.

Cain–The first son of Adam and Eve, initially assigned Adam's task of working the land. His story is told in Gen. 4: After God favors his younger brother Abel's offering over his own, he becomes jealous, angry, and downcast (vv. 1–5). God offers him the hope of righteousness and caution against sin, but Cain murders his brother (vv. 7–8). Similar to his parents' reaction when confronted by God, Cain lies and pleads ignorance when God confronts him about Abel's death (v. 9), then receives a change in vocational assignment and is banished from God's presence (v. 14). He becomes a wanderer, and his lineage is prone to arrogance and deceit. The NT use of his name is related to selfishness and wickedness (Heb. 11:4; 1 John 3:12; Jude 11).

Calah–An Assyrian city built by Nimrod after establishing his kingdom (Gen. 10:11–12). The city is known as one of the four most important Assyrian cities, though it is specifically mentioned only in this one place in the Bible. The city, in modern times known as Nimrud, was situated on the Tigris River, about twenty miles south of Nineveh.

Caleb–One of the twelve spies sent into the promised land by Moses (Num. 13:1–14:45). He represented the tribe of Judah. When the spies returned, they reported that the land was beautiful and fertile, flowing with "milk and honey." However, they also described the inhabitants as fearsome and dangerous. The majority of the spies gave a counsel of despair, saying, "We can't attack those people; they are stronger than we are" (Num. 13:31). Caleb, supported by Joshua of Ephraim, gave a minority report, advising that they attack the land. The advice of the ten spies convinced the people who lacked faith in God's ability to give them victory. In response to their complaints, God determined that the generation of Israelites who came out of Egypt would die in the wilderness. The faithful spies, Caleb and Joshua, were exceptions, the only ones in their generation allowed to actually enter the promised land.

Caleb was forty when he served as a spy and eighty-five at the time the land began to be distributed to the tribes. Caleb came forward and asked that Joshua give him the land around Hebron. To actually possess the city, he successfully drove out the dreaded Anakites, who particularly put terror in the hearts of the Israelites (Josh. 14:6–15; 15:13–15).

Calf–Although the calf was not a principal animal used in the sacrificial system, there were significant occasions when a male calf or a heifer was slaughtered. These included the ordination offerings (Lev. 9:2–8) and the ritual for dealing with an unsolved murder (Deut. 21:3–8). A heifer was among the animals that Abram cut in pieces when God made the covenant (Gen. 15:9–18; cf. Jer. 34:18–19). As David brought the ark of the covenant to Jerusalem, a bull and a fattened calf were sacrificed (2 Sam. 6:13). Finally, when the prodigal son returned, the father slaughtered a fattened calf (Luke 15:23). Almost half of the thirty-six occurrences of "calf" refer to an idol.

Calvary–The name given to the site of Jesus' crucifixion. In the Greek NT the site is called "Golgotha," from the Aramaic term meaning "skull," which is translated in the Gospels as the "place of the skull." The Latin Vulgate then translates this phrase as *Calvariae locum* (Matt. 27:33; Mark 15:22; Luke 23:33; John 19:17–18), from which the English term "Calvary" derives. Golgotha could have been given its name because an outcropping of rock gave the place the appearance of a skull, but it seems more likely that Golgotha was a place habitually used for executions. The Bible specifies that Golgotha was outside Jerusalem, but not far from the city boundaries of Jesus' day (John 19:20; Heb. 13:12).

Camel–A large four-footed mammal that has been used by humans as a pack animal and for transportation since at least the second millennium BC. The camel found its greatest use in caravans, groups of traders that crossed deserts with goods in order to sell them in foreign markets.

Camels first appear in the Bible in Genesis in the patriarchal narratives, where they are a part of the pastoral assets (12:16). They are also featured prominently in the story of finding Rebekah to be Isaac's wife (24:10–36). Joseph was taken to Egypt by a caravan, which carried balm and myrrh in addition to human cargo (37:25). In the dietary regulations of Mosaic law, the camel is unclean and cannot be eaten (Lev. 11:4; Deut. 14:7). Camels continue to appear as beasts of burden and as livestock throughout the Bible in a number of contexts.

Camp, Encampment–Temporary homes for seminomadic peoples as well as military personnel.

After the exodus and during the wilderness journeys, the Israelites resided in this type of settlement (Exod. 14:2, 9; Num. 33; Deut. 2:14–15). Moses led the Israelites out of the camp to meet with God at Sinai (Exod. 19:16–17).

Each tribe had its own camp (Num. 2). Because of the presence of God in its midst, Israel's camp was to be holy. Leviticus and Deuteronomy contain laws regulating camp life (Lev. 14:3, 8; Deut. 23:10–11). Any unclean person or thing was to be put outside the encampment (Num. 5:1–4; Deut. 23:14). The angel of the Lord encamped around them (Ps. 34:7). The Israelite army encamped at numerous places during the conquest of Canaan (Josh. 4:19) and the monarchical period (1 Sam. 29:1).

The NT uses the Greek term *parembolē* to refer to the Israelite camp where animals sacrificed as sin offerings were "burned outside the camp" (Heb. 13:11–13). Since Jesus suffered outside the gate as a sacrifice for us, believers are called to join him outside the camp, "bearing the disgrace he bore." Revelation 20:9 speaks of "the camp of God's people."

Cana–A village of uncertain location near Nazareth, though Khirbet Qana is a possible candidate. Cana is mentioned only in John's Gospel. Though undistinguished (its name is always qualified as "Cana in Galilee"), it is given prominence as the place where Jesus performed his first and second signs (John 2:1, 11; 4:46). Nathanael, its only known citizen (John 21:2), raises its status further by becoming the first to confess Jesus as the Son of God and King of Israel (John 1:49).

Canaan–Son of Ham, grandson of Noah, and the father of the families that would become known as the Canaanites (Gen. 10:6, 15–19). Oddly, in the account of Ham's great sin against Noah (seeing his father's nakedness),

Noah cursed his grandson Canaan rather than his son Ham (Gen. 9:18–27). The explanations of such cursing vary, but the passage ultimately establishes the context by which the Bible explains the relationship of the Canaanites to the Israelites in the centuries that followed. The most plausible reasons for why Canaan rather than Ham was cursed center on the irrevocability of God's blessing of Ham in Gen. 9:1 or that Canaan played some undescribed role in the sinful act. The curse also included a promise of animosity between Canaan and the sons of Japheth (9:27). This element of the curse probably found fulfillment with the entrance of the Philistines (Sea Peoples) into the land at about the same time Israel was entering it under Joshua's leadership.

Canaan, Land of–A region generally identified with the landmass between ancient Syria and Egypt, including parts of the Sinai Peninsula, Palestine from the Jordan River to the Mediterranean, and southern Phoenicia (modern Lebanon).

In the Bible, the geographical reference "the land of Canaan" finds primary expression in Genesis through Judges. The promise to Abraham that his descendants would inherit the land of the Canaanites (Gen. 15:18–21) is the theological focal point of the uses of the term "Canaan" throughout these biblical books. Once that inheritance was achieved and Israel became a viable state, the term's use seems to serve the double purpose of being both a geographical marker and a reminder of the nature of its former predominant inhabitants. The prophets drew upon the term to remind Israel of the land's former status, both in its positive (Isa. 19:18) and negative (Isa. 23:11; Zeph. 2:5) connotations. The term is transliterated twice in the NT in the recounting of OT history (Acts 7:11; 13:19). One further connection between Canaan and the perspectives communicated concerning it in the OT is the apparent association of the land with corrupt trade practices. That is, while some believe that the word "Canaan" always meant "merchant" or some similar word, its use in Scripture suggests that the tradesmen of Canaan were of such disrepute in the recollection of ancient Israel that the term became a synonym for "unjust trader" (Job 41:6; Ezek. 16:29; 17:4; Zeph. 1:11; Zech. 14:21).

Capernaum–A fishing town located on the northwest shore of the Sea of Galilee (Matt. 4:13). The town was on an important trade route and was a center for commerce in Galilee. In Capernaum, Jesus called Levi (Matthew) from his "tax booth," probably a customs station for goods in transit (Mark 2:13–17; Matt. 9:9–13; Luke 5:27–32). There may also have been a military garrison in Capernaum, since the town's synagogue was built by a certain centurion whose servant Jesus healed (Matt. 8:8–13; Luke 7:1–10).

Capernaum served as Jesus' base of operations during his Galilean ministry. In Mark's Gospel, Jesus' teaching and healing ministry begins there (Mark 1:21–34), and this is where he returned "home" after itinerant ministry around Galilee (Matt. 9:1; Mark 2:1; 9:33). Although Peter and Andrew were originally from Bethsaida (John 1:44), they lived in Capernaum, and their fishing business was located there. It was here that Jesus healed Peter's mother-in-law (Mark 1:29–31) and a paralyzed man whose friends lowered him through a hole in the roof (2:1–12). Jesus later pronounced judgment against the town, together with Chorazin and Bethsaida, because of the people's unbelief despite the miracles they had seen (Matt. 11:23–24; Luke 10:15). Archaeologists have discovered a first-century home under a fifth-century church in Capernaum. Christian inscriptions in the home indicate that it was venerated by Christians, suggesting to many scholars that this was Peter's residence.

Caphtor–A place referred to in Deut. 2:23; Amos 9:7 as the original home of the Philistines. Jeremiah refers to the Philistines as "the remnant from the coasts of Caphtor" (Jer. 47:4). The location of Caphtor is uncertain but is widely accepted to be Crete. *See also* Caphtorites.

Caphtorites–According to Gen. 10:13–14; 1 Chron. 1:11–12 (NRSV: "Caphtorim"), a group of people descended from Noah's son Ham through Mizraim ("Egypt"). Elsewhere they are identified with the Philistines, who inhabited an area north of Egypt on the southern coast of Canaan (Jer. 47:4; Amos 9:7). According to Deut. 2:23, the Caphtorites migrated and dispossessed the land of the Avvites, which reached to the coast of Canaan as far west as Gaza. *See also* Caphtor.

Capital Punishment–*See* Crimes and Punishments.

Cappadocia–In ancient times, a sparsely populated region primarily composed of a large, high-altitude plateau in what is present-day central-eastern Turkey. The geographical region of Cappadocia was bordered in the north by the region of Pontus, in the east by the headwaters of the Euphrates River and portions of the Taurus Mountains, which also served as the region's southern boundary, and in the west by the regions of Pisidia and southwestern Galatia. Cappadocia marks the easternmost boundary of the broader region known today as Asia Minor, and thus it serves as a geographical point of transition between Europe and Asia. The Gospels are set in a time when Cappadocia was a Roman province, which it became in AD 17 under the emperor Tiberius (42 BC–AD 37). During this period, the region had few centers of urban life, and the majority of the population lived in small, widely scattered villages. Residents of Cappadocia are present in Jerusalem at Pentecost (Acts 2:9), and Christians in various regions of the Roman Empire, including Cappadocia, are greeted in the salutations at the beginning of 1 Peter (1:1).

Capstone–In the NIV "capstone" appears twice (Zech. 4:7, 10). Zechariah 4:7 uses the phrase *ha'eben haro'shah,* meaning "uppermost stone." In Zech. 4:10, the NIV interprets *ha'eben* as another reference to the capstone, although most other translations understand this as the weight suspended from a plumb line. *See also* Cornerstone.

Captivity–*See* Exile.

Carchemish–An ancient city predating biblical times. It was situated on the very northern portion of the Euphrates River, on its bend southward. The name means "fortress of Chemosh," the god of Moab.

There are three biblical references to Carchemish: 2 Chron. 35:20; Isa. 10:9; Jer. 46:2. In Isa. 10, in the midst of Isaiah's oracles of judgment against Israel, God declares that Assyria is "the club of my wrath" (v. 5), whom he will send to punish his faithless people. Assyria, however, has other plans, "to put an end to many nations" (v. 7). Assyria boasts of its might and compares its defeat of Kalno (in Syria) to the fall of Carchemish (v. 9), likely referring to its defeat at the hands of Sargon II.

The other two texts refer to a very important event in Israel's history. According to Jer. 46:2, it was in the fourth year of Jehoiakim (605 BC). Assyrian dominance of Mesopotamia was about to come to an end at the hands of the Babylonians under Nebuchadnezzar. The Egyptian pharaoh Necho II, wishing to maintain a buffer state between his land and this rising superpower, brought his armies to Carchemish in an effort to save the Assyrians.

According to 2 Chron. 35:20–36:1, King Josiah of Judah met Necho along the way and engaged him in battle. Necho was reluctant, as he had no quarrel with Judah, but Josiah was persistent, apparently thinking that an alliance between Judah and Babylon would be to his advantage. Josiah was shot by archers in battle and died in Jerusalem. Apparently, by the time Necho reached Carchemish, the remnant Assyrian army was defeated, and Nebuchadnezzar proceeded to defeat Necho. As a result, the city of Carchemish never fully recovered. But more important, this battle was decisive in swinging the balance of power away from Egypt and Assyria and toward Babylon, at whose hands Judah would, within a decade, start to be taken into exile. Jeremiah recounts Egypt's defeat in Jer. 49:2–12.

Carites–Mercenaries in the service of the house of David. The priest Jehoiada called on them to rid the land of Athaliah (2 Kings 11:4, 19). At one time they were thought to be foreign mercenaries (the Carians who served the Egyptians in the seventh and early sixth centuries BC), but this view is not widely held today. Although the name also occurs in the Hebrew text of 2 Sam. 20:23, most follow the Qere, which reads "Kerethites."

Carmel, Mount–The wooded mountain promontory on the Mediterranean, near modern Haifa. The name means "the garden." It forms a northern barrier to the coastal plain of Sharon. Mount Carmel provided the perfect stage for its most significant event, the confrontation between Elijah and the prophets of Baal (1 Kings 18), the god of storms and therefore agricultural produce. The mountain's high elevation meant that it was lush until a drought. When the prophets threatened that Carmel would wither, conditions were extreme (Isa. 33:9; Amos 1:2; Nah. 1:4).

Castor and Pollux–In Greek mythology, the twin sons of Zeus and Leda, and brothers of Helen of Troy. Elevated to the status of gods, they were thought to be responsible for the safety of those who traveled by sea (esp.

sailors) and thus were commonly represented on a ship's figurehead (or "ensign"). Acts 28:11 narrates that Paul finished his journey to Rome, via Puteoli, on an Alexandrian ship outfitted with such a figurehead (Gk. *Dioskouroi*, "Twin Gods").

Cauda–A small, sparsely populated island (KJV: "Clauda") twenty-three miles south of Crete. Modern Gavdos (or Gavdhos) is the southernmost Greek island. En route to Paul's Roman imprisonment, a hurricane wind blew his ship off course to the lee of Cauda, where the crew girded up for the storm (Acts 27:16).

Cenchreae–A seaport named for Cenchrias (a child of Poseidon) and located seven miles southeast of Corinth. Here Paul shaved his head as part of a vow he had made (Acts 18:18). Phoebe is called "a deacon of the church in Cenchreae" (Rom. 16:1).

Censer–A container for burning incense. In ancient Israel censers were bronze or gold vessels used to carry live coals to light fires for tabernacle and temple worship. Powdered incense was burned upon the live coals. Their use (or misuse) sometimes signified holy or unholy behavior. Thus, on the Day of Atonement the high priest preserved his life by obediently burning a censer of incense in the holy of holies (Lev. 16:12). Nadab and Abihu died after they offered incense in an unauthorized manner (10:1–7). Similarly, Korah and his followers died for usurping the priestly task of burning incense (Num. 16). Censers crafted for Solomon's temple were later carried off by the Babylonians who conquered Jerusalem.

Census–There are several censuses in Scripture, and their concern is not simply to account for the number of people or the number of men available for military service; they also have a literary and theological function.

In the book of Numbers there are two census accounts (actually, military registrations). These are important to the structure and theme of the book. The theme of Numbers has to do with the judgment on the first generation (the object of the census in Num. 1) and the hope for the second generation, which will enter the promised land (the object of the second census).

David conducted a census to measure his military power, but this is condemned by God and regarded as satanic (2 Sam. 24:1–17; 1 Chron. 21:1–30). For the Chronicler, any attempt to account for the total number of Israelite men twenty years and older, similar to the census in the book of Numbers, is regarded as challenging God's promise to make Israel as numerous as the stars (1 Chron. 29:23–26).

Ezra and Nehemiah contain census lists of the returnees from exile: under Zerubbabel, 42,360 men returned (Ezra 2:1–66; Neh. 7:4–73), and under Ezra, 1,496 men (Ezra 8:1–14).

In the NT, Jesus participates in the universal census that encompasses not only Israel but other nations as well—a census of the entire Roman world (Luke 2:1–7). The census motif reaches its fulfillment when a great multitude from every nation, tribe, people, and language will stand before the throne and in front of the Lamb, symbolized by the 144,000 from the twelve tribes of Israel, 12,000 from each tribe (Rev. 7:4–10).

Centurion–A commander of one hundred soldiers (a "century") in a Roman legion, with various tactical and logistical duties, including management of supplies and leadership in battle. Having the best training and most experience in battle, the sixty centurions of each legion served as the backbone of the Roman army. Centurions in the Bible include the centurion who, according to Jesus, had more faith than anyone in Israel (Matt. 8:5–13; Luke 7:2–9); Cornelius the generous God-fearer and supporter of the Jewish people of Caesarea Maritima (Acts 10); the centurion in charge of the soldiers at Jesus' crucifixion (Matt. 27:54; Mark 15:39, 44–45; Luke 23:47); and the various named and unnamed centurions throughout Acts (see Acts 22–27).

Cephas–*See* Peter.

Chaff–The tough outer covering of grain removed by threshing. It is inconsequential and of little substance. Biblical passages refer to the wicked as chaff blowing about in the wind (Job 21:18; Pss. 1:4; 35:5; Dan. 2:35; Hos. 13:3) or being burned in a fire (Isa. 5:24; Matt. 3:12; Luke 3:17).

Chaldea–Originally denoting the southern part of Babylonia, "Chaldea" is the name for the whole country of Babylonia. *See also* Babylon, Babylonia.

Chariot–A small, horse-drawn platform with various configurations throughout history with regard to size, construction, and purpose. The earliest known chariots are nearly three thousand years older than the racing chariots of the Roman Empire. They were bulky, four-wheeled carts pulled by mules instead of horses, making them very slow.

In the Bible, chariots often symbolize power and status (Gen. 41:43; Acts 8:26–40). For example, the "iron chariots" described in Josh. 17:16–18 evoked dread among the tribes of Israel preparing to enter the promised land. Psalm 20:7 sharply contrasts trust in God and trust in chariots, which are a symbol of human power. Perhaps the most vivid depiction of chariots in Scripture is that of Pharaoh's army descending upon the Israelites fleeing Egypt, and of his chariots' drivers sinking into the sea (Exod. 14–15).

Chemosh–The god of the Moabites (Num. 21:29; Jer. 48:46). The biblical evidence is one of the most important sources for information concerning Chemosh and the Moabite religion. Solomon built a high place for Chemosh (1 Kings 11:7), which was later desecrated by Josiah as part of his reforms (2 Kings 23:13). In Jeremiah's judgment of the nations, he condemns the people of Moab and Chemosh (Jer. 48). Important extrabiblical evidence concerning Chemosh is found primarily on the Moabite Stone, a ninth-century BC stela commemorating King Mesha's victory over Israel.

Cherub, Cherubim–"Cherubim" (Heb. *kerubim*) is the plural form of "cherub" (Heb. *kerub*), a winged heavenly creature, apparently different from (or a certain type of) an angel. Scholars are uncertain as to the original meaning of the word, but it is probably related to a word that means either "gatekeeper" or "intercessor." Cherubim appear as attendants around the throne of God or in some cases as gatekeepers, guarding the way to the presence of God.

God stationed cherubim to guard the entrance to the garden of Eden after he expelled Adam and Eve from the garden (Gen. 3:24). In this sense, the garden of Eden was a prototype of the temple, where the presence of God could be encountered. Later, in accordance with God's instructions, golden cherubim were constructed and placed on either side of the mercy seat on the ark of the covenant, the place where God declared, "I will meet with you [Moses]" (Exod. 25:18–22).

The decorations of the tabernacle and the later Solomonic temple incorporated artwork depicting representations of cherubim (Exod. 26:1, 31; 1 Kings 6:23–29; 7:29, 36; 8:6–7; 2 Chron. 3:14). Isaiah 37:16 describes God as sitting between the wings of the cherubim, and Ps. 18:10 describes him as flying on the wings of the cherubim.

The prophet Ezekiel gives an extensive description of "four living creatures" flying around the throne of God (1:4–21). Later, the prophet identifies these same creatures but refers to them as cherubim (10:1–22). *See also* Ark of the Covenant.

Children of God, Sons of God–*See* Son of God.

Chios–A large island with snow-covered mountains in the Aegean Sea, off the coast of Asia Minor to the west of Smyrna. At the end of his third missionary campaign, Paul's ship anchored off the coast of Chios en route from Mitylene to Samos (Acts 20:15). The chief city of the island was also called Chios.

Choinix–*See* Weights and Measures.

Chorazin–A city in Galilee that Jesus rebuked, along with Bethsaida and Capernaum, for its unbelief despite the miracles that he had performed there (Matt. 11:21; Luke 10:13).

Chosen People–*See* Election.

Christ and Christology–*See* Jesus Christ.

Christian–A word derived from the Greek term *Christos* ("anointed," "anointed one," "Messiah") with a Latin ending attached. It means "follower of Christ" and is used in the NT three times.

Acts 11:26 notes that the followers of Christ were first called "Christians" in Antioch, Syria, during Paul's initial ministry there. Acts does not elaborate, but the word "Christian" itself likely indicates that pagans coined the term to distinguish Christians from Jews as Christian practices brought increasing separation from the synagogues.

Acts 26:28 narrates the story of Paul's speech defending his ministry during a trial before Herod Agrippa in Caesarea Maritima. Agrippa somewhat sarcastically asks if Paul expects him to become a Christian, one who follows Christ.

Finally, 1 Pet. 4:16 praises suffering brought about through publicly identifying oneself as a

Christian, because such suffering is a participation in the suffering of Christ.

Chronicles, Books of–These books originally formed a single book. Chronicles tells the history of Israel from the creation of the world to the end of the Babylonian exile, focusing at length on the history of David and Solomon. Like Genesis, which opens the canon, Chronicles begins with creation (Gen. 1:1; 1 Chron. 1:1) and ends with a prophecy of a return to the land (Gen. 50:24; 2 Chron. 23) and the hope of redemption.

David and the Davidic kings. The main characters in Chronicles are the Davidic kings. Although the narrative begins with Saul as Israel's king (1 Chron. 10:1–3), he is quickly disposed of (10:4). David's kingship is immediately established (without the long struggle to become king as described in 1 Samuel) and is for Israel's benefit (1 Chron. 14:2). David is presented as the ideal monarch, who sought God with his whole heart and also instituted proper worship. Although Solomon builds the temple, in Chronicles David prepares for its construction (1 Chron. 22) and its administration (1 Chron. 23–25).

Presenting David as the founder of proper worship underscores the Chronicler's emphasis on the responsibility of Davidic kings to maintain proper worship in Israel. Some kings turned from proper worship (e.g., Manasseh), while others held true and restored it when it had been forsaken (e.g., Josiah). The Davidic king sat on God's throne (1 Chron. 17:14; 28:5; 29:23) and represented the people in prayer to God (2 Chron. 6:18–42). When northern Israel rejected the Davidic king, they rejected God (2 Chron. 13:4–12). This elevation of the importance of the Davidic monarchy held out hope of a coming Davidic king despite the current situation of Persian rule.

The temple and the Levites. Chronicles focuses on Israel's relationship to God, which is shown in the emphasis on the Davidic king as Israel's representative to God but is best expressed through the focus on the temple and its institutions. Chronicles shows how Israel's relationship to God was dependent on maintaining proper temple worship. The Levitical priesthood together with the Davidic king maintained the worship of God. The Levites even stepped in to preserve the Davidic line when it was threatened (2 Chron. 22:10–23:21), and only they could administer proper worship in the temple (26:16–18). Interestingly, this emphasis on Davidic kings and Levitical priests reflects the conditions of rule under which the original audience lived when they returned from exile (cf. Zech. 2:4).

All Israel. In Chronicles the term "all Israel" is used for northern Israel (2 Chron. 13:4), southern Judah (2 Chron. 11:3), or all the Israelites together (1 Chron. 11:1). For the Chronicler, "Israel" indicates a people who are in a special relationship with God and accountable to him. The Davidic king and the Levitical priests are important, but the people themselves are also accountable to God (e.g., 2 Chron. 11:3–4, 16–17; 13:14; 15:9–15). This allows the Chronicler to emphasize the responsibility of each generation to have a proper relationship with God.

The Chronicler encouraged his community by retelling the old story in new ways. The old story (Samuel-Kings) taught its audience why the exile happened (their sin), but the Chronicler's audience needed to be assured that God was still interested in them. Chronicles reminds the restoration community of the continuity between preexilic and postexilic times and their heritage as God's people and heirs of the promises to David. Whereas Samuel-Kings emphasized idolatry as the reason for the exile (2 Kings 17:7–18), Chronicles looks past this surface symptom to the root problem of "forsaking the Lord," characterized by neglecting their relationship with God through proper worship. "Seeking the Lord" calls for a complete response of his people to him.

Whereas Samuel-Kings explains the exile by the cumulative buildup of the sins of the monarchy (2 Kings 23:26; 24:3), in Chronicles the fate of Israel is never sealed. Any generation can seek God wholeheartedly and thereby receive blessing. The thematic verse for Chronicles is perhaps 2 Chron. 7:14: "If my people, who are called by my name, will humble themselves and pray and seek my face and turn from their wicked ways, then will I hear from heaven, and I will forgive their sin and will heal their land." The Chronicler's message demands a response in the present. In retelling the history of his people, his audience could see the cause-and-effect relationship between seeking and forsaking God and apply it to their current situation. They themselves were "all Israel" and needed to seek God wholeheartedly in proper worship. Only through faithfulness to God would Israel recapture the glory days of its past. In a message as applicable now as it was millennia ago, Chronicles calls for its readers to have a proper relationship with God and holds out expectation that blessing will follow.

Church–The nature of the church is too broad to be exhausted in the meaning of one word. To capture its significance, the NT authors utilize a rich array of metaphorical descriptions. Nevertheless, there are those metaphors that seem to dominate the biblical pictures of the church, five of which call for comment: the people of God, the kingdom of God, the eschatological temple of God, the bride of Christ, and the body of Christ.

The people of God. Essentially, the concept of the people of God can be summed up in the covenantal phrase: "I will be their God, and they will be my people" (see Exod. 6:6–7; 19:5; Lev. 26:9–14; Jer. 7:23; 30:22; 32:37–40; Ezek. 11:19–20; 36:22–28; Acts 15:14; 2 Cor. 6:16; Heb. 8:10–12; Rev. 21:3). Thus, the people of God are those in both the OT and the NT eras who responded to God by faith and whose spiritual origin rests exclusively in God's grace.

The kingdom of God. Many scholars have maintained that the life, death, and resurrection of Jesus inaugurated the kingdom of God, producing the overlapping of the two ages. The kingdom has already dawned but is not yet complete. The first aspect pertains to Jesus' first coming, and the second aspect relates to his second coming. In other words, the age to come has broken into this age, and now the two exist simultaneously. This background is crucial in ascertaining the relationship between the church and the kingdom of God, because the church also exists in the tension that results from the overlapping of the two ages. Accordingly, one may define the church as the foreshadowing of the kingdom. Two ideas flow from this definition: first, the church is related to the kingdom of God; second, the church is not equal to the kingdom of God.

The church and the kingdom of God are related. Not until after the resurrection of Jesus does the NT speak with regularity about the church. However, there are early signs of the church in the teaching and ministry of Jesus, in both general and specific ways. In general, Jesus anticipated the later official formation of the church in that he gathered to himself the twelve disciples, who constituted the beginnings of eschatological Israel—in effect, the remnant. More specifically, Jesus explicitly referred to the church in two passages: Matt. 16:18–19; 18:17. In the first passage Jesus promised that he would build his church despite satanic opposition, thus assuring the ultimate success of his mission. The notion of the church overcoming the forces of evil coincides with the idea that the kingdom of God will prevail over its enemies and bespeaks the intimate association between the church and the kingdom. The second passage relates to the future organization of the church, not unlike the Jewish synagogue practices of Jesus' day.

The church and the kingdom of God are not identical. As intimately related as the church and the kingdom of God are, the NT does not equate the two, as is evident in the fact that the early Christians preached the kingdom, not the church (Acts 8:12; 19:8; 20:25; 28:23, 31). The NT identifies the church as the people of the kingdom (e.g., Rev. 5:10), not the kingdom itself. Moreover, the church is the instrument of the kingdom. This is especially clear from Matt. 16:18–19, where the preaching of Peter and the church become the keys to opening up the kingdom of God to all who would enter.

The eschatological temple of God. Both the OT and Judaism anticipated the rebuilding of the temple in the future kingdom of God (e.g., Ezek. 40–48; Hag. 2:1–9). Jesus hinted that he was going to build such a structure (Matt. 16:18; Mark 14:58; John 2:19–22). Pentecost witnessed to the beginning of the fulfillment of that dream in that when the Spirit inhabited the church, the eschatological temple was formed (Acts 2:16–36). Other NT writers also perceived that the presence of the Spirit in the Christian community constituted the new temple of God (1 Cor. 3:16–17; 2 Cor. 6:14–7:1; Eph. 2:19–22; see also Gal. 4:21–31; 1 Pet. 2:4–10). However, that the eschatological temple is not yet complete is evident in the preceding passages, especially in their emphasis on the need for the church to grow toward maturity in Christ, which will be fully accomplished only at the parousia (second coming of Christ). In the meantime, Christians, as priests of God, are to perform their sacrificial service to the glory of God (Rom. 12:1–2; Heb. 13:15; 1 Pet. 2:4–10).

The bride of Christ. The image of marriage is applied to God and Israel in the OT (see Isa. 54:5–6; 62:5; Hos. 2:7). Similar imagery is applied to Christ and the church in the NT. Christ, the bridegroom, has sacrificially and lovingly chosen the church to be his bride (Eph. 5:25–27). Her responsibility during the betrothal period is to be faithful to him (2 Cor. 11:2; Eph. 5:24). At the parousia the official wedding ceremony will take place, and with it the eternal union of Christ and his wife will be actualized (Rev. 19:7–9; 21:1–2).

The body of Christ. The body of Christ as a metaphor for the church is unique to the Pauline literature and constitutes one of the most significant concepts therein (Rom. 12:4–5; 1 Cor. 12:12–27; Eph. 4:7–16; Col. 1:18). The primary purpose of the metaphor is to demonstrate the interrelatedness of diversity and unity within the church, especially with reference to spiritual gifts. The body of Christ is the last Adam (1 Cor. 15:45), the new humanity of the end time that has appeared in history. However, Paul's usage of the image, like the metaphor of the new temple, indicates that the church, as the body of Christ, still has a long way to go spiritually. It is not yet complete.

CILICIA–A Roman province located in the southeast of modern-day Turkey. Its capital was Tarsus, home of Paul (Acts 21:39; 22:3). Jews from Cilicia participated in the stoning of Stephen (Acts 6:9). The province of Cilicia is often mentioned in the NT as Paul traveled on his journeys (Acts 15:23, 41; 23:34; 27:5; Gal. 1:21). Due to his ministry there, Cilicia became a major center for Gentile Christians.

CIRCUMCISION–The custom of cutting the foreskin of the male genitalia as a religious rite. Egyptians practiced circumcision, as did the Ammonites, Edomites, Moabites, and nomadic Arabians (Jer. 9:25–26). Philistines, Assyrians, and Gentiles in general were uncircumcised (Judg. 14:3; Ezek. 32:17–32; Eph. 2:11).

Circumcision is first mentioned in the Bible as a sign of the covenant between God and Abraham (Gen. 17:10). God commanded that every male be circumcised at eight days old (Gen. 17:12; cf. 21:4; Lev. 12:3; Luke 1:59; 2:21). Circumcision was required for a male to participate in the Passover (Exod. 12:48) or worship in the temple (Ezek. 44:9; cf. Acts 21:28–29).

Metaphorically, circumcision goes beyond the physical sign (Rom. 2:28). Ultimately, the enemies of God, whether circumcised or not, will be slain and laid in the grave with the uncircumcised (Ezek. 32:32). Physical circumcision is of no avail if the heart remains "uncircumcised" (Jer. 9:25–26; cf. Rom. 2:25). Circumcision of the heart is accomplished when one loves God completely (Deut. 10:16; 30:6; Jer. 4:4; Rom. 2:29), but uncircumcised ears are disobedient (Acts 7:51). The circumcision accomplished by Christ occurs when the sinful nature is rejected (Col. 2:11). In him neither circumcision nor uncircumcision has any value; what counts "is faith expressing itself through love" (Gal. 5:6).

Controversy began in the NT church over whether Gentile believers should be circumcised (Acts 15:1–12). Evidently, a group existed that demanded circumcision (Acts 15:1; Titus 1:10). Paul argued that circumcision was not essential to Christian faith and fellowship (Gal. 6:15; Col. 3:11).

CISTERN–An artificial underground reservoir designed for collecting and storing water. Joseph was thrown into an empty cistern (Gen. 37:22–29), and Jeremiah was imprisoned in one (Jer. 38:6). Cisterns were good places to hide (1 Sam. 13:6), and one served as a place to dump corpses (Jer. 41:7–9). Like springs, cisterns were considered to be ritually clean (Lev. 11:36). Marriage fidelity is likened to drinking water from your own cistern (Prov. 5:15). On the other hand, Jeremiah describes covenant infidelity as rejecting "the spring of living water" for "broken cisterns that cannot hold water" (2:13).

CITIES OF REFUGE–Cities in the OT period that were divinely designated places of asylum to which a manslayer might flee for safety (Exod. 21:12–14). Refuge was provided in these cities for the manslayer from family members of the slain person who were seeking to avenge the death of their relative. According to the principle of *lex talionis* enshrined in OT revelation and subsequent Israelite law (Gen. 9:5–6; Exod. 21:12–14; Lev. 24:17), the death penalty applied to the willful murderer. In ancient Israel the sacred duty of punishing a murderer was placed in the hands of the closest relative of the murdered person ("the avenger of blood"). The manslayer was admitted to the city of refuge only after stating his case before the city's elders at the city gate (Josh. 20:4–5), for this provision applied only to those implicated in an accidental or unintentional death. This institution gave the accused person an opportunity to stand trial before a legal assembly and possibly be acquitted (Num. 35:12). After the death of the high priest (marking the end of an era), the acquitted manslayer was free to return home (Josh. 20). The manslayer who left the city before that time could be killed by the avenger of blood with impunity. More widely, the provision reflects the moral character of the God of Israel and the humane spirit of OT legislation that sought to limit vengeance and the blood feuds that easily resulted.

Cities of the Plain–Sodom, Gomorrah, Admah, Zeboyim, and Bela (also called "Zoar"), the cities of the plain (Gen. 14:2), were allied together against four kings invading from Mesopotamia. As the battle turned against them, they fled, and some fell into tar pits in the Valley of Siddim. Later, with the exception of Zoar, all these cities suffered cataclysmic destruction as God rained down burning sulfur on the entire plain in judgment against the sins of Sodom and Gomorrah (Gen. 19).

City Gates–In the ancient world, gates played a critical role in the defenses of a city. Gates usually were the weakest point in the walls of a city and therefore often the point of attack for siege armies. For a city to be strong, massive walls were not enough; it had to have strong gates.

City gates were also the location of judicial courts as well as the place where taxes were collected. Jeremiah 38:7 indicates that the king held court in one of Jerusalem's gates. When the OT prophets inveigh against injustice, they often refer to the city gates as the place for justice (Amos 5:15).

City of David–According to 2 Sam. 5:6–9 (see also 1 Chron. 11:5), David captured the "fortress of Zion" from the Jebusites and renamed it the City of David since his personal army captured it. The fact that it was the personal domain of the royal family rather than a tribal allotment made it an ideal capital of Israel, since it did not favor a particular tribe.

City of Palms–*See* Jericho.

Claudius–**(1)** A Roman emperor (born 10 BC), Claudius reigned from AD 41 until his death in AD 54. In AD 49 Claudius expelled all Jews from Rome because of Jewish riots instigated on account of "Chrestus" (probably Jesus Christ), which resulted in Aquila and Priscilla's move to Corinth (Acts 18:2). During Claudius's reign the prophet Agabus came to the church in Antioch predicting an empire-wide famine (11:28). **(2)** Claudius Lysias, the commander of the Roman military barracks in Jerusalem, who sent Paul under armed guard to stand trial before Felix in Caesarea Maritima (Acts 23:26).

Clay–Basic manufacturing material of fine-grained soil mixed with impurities. It is pliable when moist and hardens when baked. It was used for pottery (Lev. 6:28; 11:33; 15:12; Num. 5:17; Jer. 19:1; 32:14; 2 Cor. 4:7), building material (Lev. 14:42; Nah. 3:19), molds (1 Kings 7:46), sculpture (Dan. 2:33), and writing tablets (Ezek. 4:1). Clay is used metaphorically to illustrate weakness (Job 4:19; 13:12; 27:16) or lowliness of purpose (Lam. 4:2; 2 Cor. 4:7; 2 Tim. 2:20). The potter and his clay are likened to God and human creation (Job 10:9; 33:6; Isa. 29:16; 45:9; 64:8; Jer. 18:4; Rom. 9:21).

Clean, Cleanness–A holy God wants a holy people. He had described the nation of Israel as holy (cf. Exod. 19:5–6) but also wanted them to live holy lives and grow increasingly holy. Holiness came, in part, by keeping the law; an important part of the law was the concept of cleanness.

Cleanness does not refer to good hygiene, nor is it synonymous with morality, since a person could be unclean and still righteous. Cleanness allowed the OT believer to live a holy life and enabled that person to be made increasingly holy by "Yahweh, your sanctifier" (NIV: "the Lord, who makes you holy," Lev. 20:8; cf. 21:8, 15, 23; 22:9, 16, 32; 31:13). Impurity traveled along four channels: sexuality (various discharges; e.g., nocturnal emission, menstruation, childbirth), diet (e.g., eating certain types of animals), disease (e.g., skin diseases, mildew), and death (i.e., contact with animal or human corpses). Impurities occurring naturally and unavoidably in the course of life (e.g., menstruation) were tolerated, representing no danger to the person or community as long as they were promptly addressed. Other impurities had to be avoided at all costs or else grave consequences would result to the person and community.

One prohibited impurity arose from eating food declared off-limits by God. All meat had to be thoroughly bled before being eaten (Gen. 9:3–4; Lev. 17:10–14; Deut. 12:16, 23). Edible land animals must both have a completely divided hoof and chew the cud (Lev. 11:3; Deut. 14:6), while water creatures had to have both fins and scales (Lev. 11:9; Deut. 14:9). Most birds were acceptable for food (exceptions are given in Lev. 11:13–19; Deut. 14:11–18), as were most insects (Lev. 11:20–23; Deut. 14:19–20) and some crawling animals (Lev. 11:29–31, 41–42).

Why did God declare certain things clean and others unclean? Some suggest that the distinction is arbitrary; the rules are given as a test of obedience. Others argue that the original audience knew of reasons now lost to us. Still others believe that God was protecting his people from disease. It is true that certain kinds of meat improperly prepared can transmit disease, but not all laws can be explained this way. Some believe that God identified things as clean because they represented a state of normalcy (e.g., fish normally propel themselves with fins, so those lacking fins are abnormal and thus unclean). A related view considers things as clean or unclean based on what they symbolized. So, for example, God identified objects as unclean if they were associated with death (e.g., vultures, corpses) because he is for life. Here again, it is difficult to explain all the laws by appeal to normalcy or symbolism.

Ceremonial cleansing is not just a topic in the OT; it appears in the opening chapters of the Gospels. Mary underwent the required purification rituals after Jesus' birth (Luke 2:22–24), and Jesus "cleansed" people from leprosy, instructing them to carry out the Mosaic purification rituals (Matt. 8:2–4; Mark 1:40–42; Luke 5:12–14; 17:11–19; cf. Matt. 10:8; 11:5; Luke 4:27; 7:22).

In one of his confrontations with the Pharisees, Jesus signaled a departure from how these laws had been practiced. He announced, "Nothing outside a person can defile them by going into them. Rather, it is what comes out of a person that defiles them" (Mark 7:15), to which Mark adds an explanation: "In saying this, Jesus declared all foods 'clean'" (7:19). Peter's rooftop vision in Acts 10 reflects this same perspective, as do the church's decision regarding Gentile conversion (Acts 15) and Paul's comments to the church at Rome (Rom. 14:14, 20–21).

Clopas–*See* Mary.

Clouds–The OT depicts God as riding on a cloud (Judg. 5:4; Isa. 19:1; Pss. 18:11–12; 68:4; 104:3), and as the creator and sender of clouds: "Ask rain from the Lord in the season of the spring rain; from the Lord who makes the storm clouds, and he will give them showers of rain, to everyone the vegetation in the field" (Zech. 10:1 ESV [see also 1 Kings 18:44; Pss. 135:7; 147:8; Prov. 8:28; Isa. 5:6; Jer. 10:13]). Divine judgment is pictured as a dark storm (Isa. 30:30; Lam. 2:1; Nah. 1:3; Zech. 1:15).

At several crucial points God manifested his presence among the Israelites in the form of a cloud: in the wilderness (the "pillar of cloud" of Exod. 13:21 and elsewhere), on Mount Sinai (Exod. 19:9; 24:15), in the tabernacle (Exod. 40:34), in the temple at Jerusalem (1 Kings 8:10), and frequently in the visions of Ezekiel (e.g., Ezek. 1:4; 10:3).

The NT continues the imagery of the cloud as a manifestation of divine presence in the story of the transfiguration (Matt. 17:5; Mark 9:7; Luke 9:36), and also in depictions of Jesus as a cloud-rider in Matt. 26:64; Rev. 14:14 (see Dan. 7:13). Jesus was hidden by a cloud when he ascended (Acts 1:9), and believers will be caught up by clouds at his return (1 Thess. 4:17; Rev. 11:12).

Cnidus–*See* Asia Minor, Cities of.

Cohort–One-tenth of a Roman army legion, led by a captain, usually consisting of six hundred soldiers. Some auxiliary cohorts, with more infantry and cavalry than regular cohorts, were recruited from, and permanently stationed in, one specific imperial region (Matt. 27:27; John 18:1–13; Acts 10:1; 27:1).

Collection for the Poor–An action initiated by the apostle Paul to help poor Christians in Judea. For Paul, it expresses the core of the gospel: unity of Jew and Gentile in Christ and the nations coming to the God of Israel. He references it in Rom. 15:25–32; 1 Cor. 16:1–4; 2 Cor. 8–9; and possibly Gal. 2:10. Paul gives instructions to his predominantly Gentile churches to set aside funds for him to take to the Jewish Christians in Jerusalem. Doing so expresses the sacrificial other-oriented giving of Christ. Participating in this practice, especially in the midst of hardship, and giving of one's relative abundance to equalize the material situation with other Christians who have less manifests the saving grace of Christ at work among the givers (2 Cor. 8–9). Paul does not separate such material acts of grace from others associated with Christ's salvation.

Colossae, Colosse–*See* Asia Minor, Cities of; Colossians, Letter to the.

Colossians, Letter to the–Colossians is a letter sent by Paul to a church in Colossae when he was in prison. The letter was Paul's first direct contact with the church, which may have been started by one of his missionary associates, Epaphras (Col. 1:7). Epaphras was from Colossae (4:12), a city of Asia Minor located in the Lycus Valley, known for its fertile soil and green pastures. Colossae was a free city located on the main Roman road that ran from Ephesus and Sardis toward the east, and it was populated by native Phrygians, as well as Greeks, Romans, and Jews. More than likely, the church was founded during Paul's extended ministry in Ephesus, where persons from the region heard Paul's gospel and from where Paul sent missionary associates such as Epaphras into the surrounding cities (Acts 19). Tychicus, the letter carrier (Col. 4:7–8), was also one of Paul's associates from the same region; he decided to accompany Paul to Macedonia after the team left Ephesus (Acts 20:4).

The Colossians were doing several things that Paul found troublesome, as we learn from Col. 2. They were judging each other for not keeping certain dietary regulations and holy days (2:16). Some were claiming superiority through personal worship experiences that involved visions of angels (2:18). Some subscribed to strict discipline of the human body, punishing themselves through various acts of self-abasement in order to curb fleshly appetites (2:23) and enhance their worship experiences (2:18). It seems that many of them were trying to live by an expanded version of the divine command given in the story of Adam, Eve, and the forbidden fruit: "Do not handle! Do not taste! Do not touch!" (2:21). Paul recognized that all these claims and rules had the "appearance of wisdom" but in reality were nothing more than traditions based on "self-imposed" religion, and that such ascetic practices were useless in denying fleshly appetites (2:22–23). Where did the Colossians get all these strange ideas that led to such bizarre behavior?

Paul described the false teaching as an imprisoning "through hollow and deceptive philosophy, which depends on human tradition and the elemental spiritual forces" in opposition to the teachings of Christ (2:8). Because the Colossian church was made up primarily of Gentile converts (1:27), many interpreters argue that the problems resulted from the meshing of the gospel with local, pagan ways. The Phrygians were known for their fascination with magical rituals, the ability to manipulate the powers (earth, wind, fire, spirits, angels, often referred to as "elementary principles of the world") for human purposes.

Whatever the source of the false teaching referred to in Colossians, Paul attempts to correct the misbehavior of his Gentile converts by building an argument that the work of Christ is all-sufficient. Paul begins the letter by describing the person and work of Christ in cosmic terms (1:15–23). Next he recounts his role in the mission of Christ to bring the riches of the kingdom to Gentiles (1:24–2:5). After reminding the Colossians of their reception of the gospel, Paul juxtaposes the deceptive practices of the false teaching with the evidence of the work of Christ in them (2:6–23). Then he gives a number of instructions on what life in Christ is supposed to look like: in the church (3:1–17) and in the home (3:18–4:1). He concludes the letter with generic exhortations (4:2–6), specific instructions (4:7–9), and greetings (4:10–17). Finally, Paul signs the letter, obviously written by a secretary, with the simple request: "Remember my chains" (4:18)—a curious signature that makes the argument of his letter even more appealing.

It is ironic that Paul chose to describe the work of Christ in such grandiose terms, picturing him as a mighty ruler over all creation, even while the apostle was in prison—an undeniable sign of Roman sovereignty. In Col. 1, in some of the loftiest language Paul ever used to describe Christ's kingdom authority, the apostle reminds his converts that the Lord is "the image of the invisible God, the firstborn over all creation" (v. 15), an obvious reference to Christ's deity. Then Paul piles on the attributes, presenting Christ as the creator of all things, even angelic creatures (v. 16), the sustainer of all things (v. 17), the head of the church, the eternal one, the guarantor of the resurrection (v. 18), the fullness of God (v. 19), the reconciler of all things—the one who made peace with the enemies of God through his blood on the cross (vv. 20–22). Despite Paul's circumstances and what Rome may claim, the apostle holds fast to the irrepressible sovereignty of Christ's kingdom, displayed by Paul's perseverance in the midst of suffering and the full assurance that every Colossian believer is "fully mature in Christ" (vv. 22–29). Indeed, all the treasures of Christ's kingdom—love, knowledge, wisdom, discipline—are to be found in the life of his converts (2:1–5), unless someone "deludes" them into thinking otherwise.

In Col. 3, Paul tells how the Colossians draw upon the power of Christ when they "set [their] minds on things above, not on earthly things" (v. 2). The things on the earth are "sexual immorality, impurity, lust, evil desires and greed" (v. 5). Paul believes that his converts died with Christ ("hidden with Christ in God" [v. 3]) and therefore had set aside all these idolatrous practices when they put on the "new self," being conformed to the image of Christ (vv. 8–10). This renewal will be found in all believers, regardless of ethnicity (v. 11), and will result in peace for all. Indeed, Paul sees the "peace of Christ" as the undeniable evidence of his reign exhibited in the hearts of those who believe (vv. 12–15). And what would that peace look like? Believers will be patient, forgiving one another with hearts full of compassion, kindness, humility, gentleness, and love resulting in unity (vv. 12–14). Their worship of God will be characterized by songs of thankfulness and admonition, receiving the word with wisdom (v. 16). In their homes husbands, wives, and children will model deference and love, and masters and slaves will seek justice and fairness, as if they were serving Christ (3:18–4:1). The Colossians will be devoted to prayer, will treat outsiders fairly, and will be known for always speaking graceful words (4:2–6). In other words, where Caesar's empire has promoted Roman peace by enforcing Roman law in provinces, cities, and households, Paul believes that the peace of Christ will rule the hearts of his subjects, establishing a kingdom of love and unity, in word and deed, in the home as well as the church. So, in his final greetings, Paul talks about faithful slaves and beloved siblings as sources of encouragement in the ever-expanding work of the kingdom of God (4:7–17), making his simple request, "Remember my chains" (4:18), sound more like an act of defiance than a pitiful plea.

Compassion–Love for those who suffer. The OT often refers to God's compassion, especially toward those who, because of their sinfulness, deserve the opposite treatment. In Exod. 33:19 Yahweh takes pity on the Israelites after they have rebelled, making an idol for themselves and praising it for their deliverance. He renews his covenant with them, but he reminds them of his sovereignty in doing so: "I will have mercy on whom I will have mercy, and I will have compassion on whom I will have compassion" (cf. Rom. 9:15).

The NT points to God's compassion at significant junctures in the Gospels and the Epistles. Jesus himself has compassion for the crowds who "were harassed and helpless, like sheep without a shepherd" (Matt. 9:36). He takes pity on the crowds, healing their sick and feeding them miraculously (14:14–21; cf. 15:32). The same connection between compassion and healing occurs in Matt. 20:34; Mark 1:41, this time on an individual level. The apostle Paul underscores this attribute of God, raising it to a title of sorts. The Father of our Lord Jesus Christ is "the Father of compassion and the God of all comfort" (2 Cor. 1:3). James says that the Lord is "full of compassion and mercy" (5:11), and John depicts God as one who will wipe away every tear caused by persecution and trial (Rev. 7:17; 21:4). Because God is always dealing with broken sinners, his compassion for them coincides with his love (see Ps. 145:8); and this rescuing of the guilty sets an example for his people. They must go and do likewise, loving the unlovely, unwise, and even unrighteous.

Concubine–A concubine is a woman whose status in relation to her sole legitimate sexual partner is less than primary wife.

Reference to concubines is largely found in the Pentateuch (e.g., Gen. 22:24; 36:12) and monarchical texts (e.g., 2 Sam. 5:13; 1 Kings 11:3). The genealogies show that succession could move through concubines (Gen. 22:24; 1 Chron. 3:9). It is the kings who had concubines (1 Chron. 11:21), often guarded by eunuchs (2 Sam. 20:3; Esther 2:14). Therefore, access to the royal concubines functioned as a daring claim to the throne, exploited by interlopers (2 Sam. 12:11–12; 1 Kings 2:22–25). It took Nathan's allegorical story to show David his own greed of stealing another's "lamb" even though he already had many wives and concubines (2 Sam. 12:8; 16:21).

While concubines did care for the household (2 Sam. 20:2), their lower status is observed when David flees into exile, leaving the concubines "to take care of the palace" (2 Sam. 15:16), a role too dangerous for the royal wives.

Confession–In the OT, "to confess" is used in reference to verbal acknowledgment of one's sin or of God's name in faith. An object of confession is one's sins. Confession results in the cleansing of sin and the restoration of one's relationship with God (Lev. 5:5; Ps. 32:5). Solomon prays that God may forgive people's sin when they confess God's name (1 Kings 8:35). Moses, on the Day of Atonement, commands Aaron to lay "both hands on the head of the live goat and confess over it all the wickedness and rebellion of the Israelites" (Lev. 16:21).

Another object of confession is God's name. To confess the name of God means "to give thanks/praise" to God (Josh. 7:19). It involves not only negative matters such as sins and wrongdoings (Lev. 26:40; Prov. 28:13), but also positive ones such as God's name (1 King 8:33, 35; 2 Chron. 6:24, 26; Dan. 9:4). In this respect, confession conceptually involves a double function: to remove obstacles to fellowship with God, and to recover fellowship in covenantal faithfulness to God (1 Kings 8:33).

The double function of confession continues in the NT. John the Baptist exhorted people to confess their sins (Matt. 3:6). Epistles also emphasize the importance of confession of sins as a basis of atonement and purification (1 John 1:9; James 5:16). In the NT, the positive aspect of confession as confessing God's name is recast in terms of Jesus, who fulfilled the OT prophecies. Therefore, to "confess" Jesus as Lord is reckoned as confessing God's name so as to obtain salvation (Rom. 10:10 ESV, NRSV; NIV: "profess"). Verbal confession of Jesus in public is a means for spreading the gospel and witnessing to people about him. Thus, Paul regards his confession of God through Gentile evangelism as singing praises to God's name (Rom. 15:9).

Congregation–Primarily, the Israelite community united by a common bond to (or in covenant with) their God (Deut. 33:4; Josh. 8:35; 18:1; 1 Kings 8:5).

The terms also refer to Israelite gatherings for special purposes such as worship, war, lawcourt, and councils. They also refer to the assemblage of other peoples or beings such as divine beings, evildoers or enemies, beasts, and bees.

The NT uses both *ekklēsia* and *synagōgē* to refer to synagogue gatherings (Acts 7:38; 13:43). English versions translate both terms as either "congregation" or "assembly." These translations render the *ekklēsia* in Heb. 2:12 as either "assembly" or "congregation," whereas they translate *synagōgē* in James 2:2 as "assembly" or "meeting." *See also* Church.

Coniah–*See* Jehoiachin.

Conquest of Canaan–The Israelite conquest of the promised land is narrated in Numbers through 2 Samuel and includes key figures such as Moses, Joshua, Samuel, Saul, and David, although the main events of the conquest are described in Joshua and Judges.

The background for the Canaanite conquest is found in the Pentateuch narratives that describe the Israelites' exodus from Egypt and their trek toward Palestine. Indeed, the conquest is anticipated already in God's promise to Abraham that his descendants will become a mighty nation (Gen. 12:1–3; see also 15:16). The story describes God's initial command to quickly conquer the land after meeting them on Mount Sinai (Num. 13), and the people's rebellion caused by fear of the Canaanites, who are described as "giants in the land" (NLT). As a result, the Israelites are forced to wander in the Sinai wilderness until the entire generation dies (with the exception of Joshua and Caleb).

As narrated in the Bible, the conquest begins with defeat of the Midianites on the eastern side of the Jordan River under the leadership of Moses (Num. 31–32). Then, after Moses' death, the Israelites cross the Jordan River to attack Jericho (Josh. 1–7). After the miraculous destruction of Jericho, the Israelites move to Ai and encounter initial defeat due to one man's sin (Josh. 8). Later, after being tricked by the Gibeonites, the Israelites engage in battle with the five kings of the Amorites (Josh. 9–10). Finally, Josh. 11 describes the conquest of the northern part of the land and especially the military and strategically important city of Hazor.

The book of Judges relates fewer, more concentrated battles against different enemies, sometimes in offensive attacks and other times as defensive battles to preserve land control. The final stage of the conquest under David's kingship is described in 2 Sam. 1–8. After Saul's death, a short and violent confrontation takes place between Israelite forces still loyal to Saul's family and those loyal to David. Political power is consolidated with a few key assassinations, rather than through full-fledged war, orchestrated by David's men (there is some debate about how involved David was in these events). As a result, David, with the full support of the army (both the forces previously loyal to Saul and his own), takes the city of Jerusalem and then finally conquers the areas of the Philistines, the Ammonites, and the Moabites (areas that Saul had been unable to subdue). Thus, large-scale fighting for territory ends during David's reign.

Conscience–An innate awareness of wrong, with an inclination toward thinking and acting rightly. The OT describes moral awareness as a willingness to obey God's revealed will (Deut. 30:14; Ps. 1:1–2; Prov. 1:7). People are not presented as morally perfect, but, to the degree of their knowledge, they are expected to act rightly (Gen. 4:1–16; 1 Sam. 25:31). Abimelek, king of Gerar, appeals to ignorance because of Abraham's deception (Gen. 20:1–7). Job appeals to the purity of his conscience (Job 27:6).

Consecration–The process of effecting a transition to holiness, the state of being fit for the presence of God. Separation, or being set apart, while not the core meaning of consecration, is an associated notion (Num. 6:8; 1 Chron. 23:13). True consecration is not merely outward and symbolic but rather involves genuine covenantal obedience to God (Num. 15:40).

Consecration is closely related to purification—the removal of defilement (Exod. 29:36), dedication (particularly of buildings), and sanctification (particularly of people). God's glorious presence alone may render something holy (29:43–44). More commonly, a ritual act, such as washing (19:10) or anointing (29:36), serves to mark the transition to the new state.

Conversion–Conversion, signifying "to turn around" or a change of course in life, is closely related to repentance, although the two are by no means synonymous.

Both the OT and the NT present conversion as a crucial stage of God's saving work for people. The leading metaphor for conversion in the OT is turning back (from sin, to God; Isa. 55:7; Ezek. 14:6). The NT likewise uses the metaphor of turning. Another metaphor for conversion is that of birth, evidenced in concepts such as becoming God's children (Matt. 18:3), rebirth (1 Pet. 1:3), and being born again or born from above (John 3:3).

Conviction–In its more prominent use, "conviction" refers to the experience of becoming aware of one's guilt before God. Isaiah's vision of the throne of God provides a dramatic illustration of conviction. He describes the feeling of dread and self-revulsion that he experienced in the presence of God, who is holy: "'Woe to me!' I cried. 'I am ruined! For I am a man of unclean lips, . . . and my eyes have seen the King, the Lord Almighty'" (Isa. 6:5). After a miraculous catch of fish, when Peter recognized that Jesus was the Christ, his initial response was similar: "Go away from me, Lord; I am a sinful man!" (Luke 5:8).

Copper–*See* Minerals and Metals.

Cor–*See* Weights and Measures.

Corban–A transliteration of a technical term, *qorban*, used in reference to an offering to God throughout Leviticus and Numbers (e.g., Lev. 1:2; Num. 5:15). Mark 7:11 is set in the midst of an exchange where Jesus condemns the Pharisees for attempting to evade the true significance of the OT laws of Corban by greedily keeping money to themselves that should have been used to support elderly parents (cf. the parallel in Matt. 15:5–6, which uses the Greek word *dōron* ["gift"] rather than Corban).

Corinth–One of the largest, wealthiest, and most prestigious cities in ancient Greece. Corinth is located about fifty miles west of Athens on the narrow isthmus that connects mainland Greece with the Peloponnesus.

Corinth had two harbors and Paul sailed from one of them to Syria to end his second missionary journey (Acts 18:18). Corinth's location made it an international crossroads of commerce and travel. Because of the narrowness of the isthmus, it controlled the land routes between the Peloponnesus and mainland Greece.

Corinth boasted the most impressive acropolis in Greece, its Acrocorinth towering eighteen hundred feet above the city. The Acrocorinth served as a fortress and hosted temples, the most famous of which was the temple of Aphrodite, which in the old city (destroyed by the Romans in 146 BC) had boasted a thousand temple slaves and prostitutes. Its presence contributed to Corinth's reputation as an excessively immoral city. A Greek verb was coined, *korinthiazomai* (lit., "to Corinthianize"), which meant "to practice sexual immorality."

By the time of Paul's arrival, Corinth was one of the most important commercial centers in the entire Roman Empire and the largest city in Greece, with a free population of about 300,000 and an additional 460,000 slaves. Corinth had a significant Jewish population, especially after AD 49, when the Jews were expelled from Rome (Acts 18:2). During Paul's year and a half of ministry, he regularly argued in the synagogue (18:4). An inscription from the synagogue's lintel has been found. In AD 51 many of the Jews brought Paul before Gallio, the proconsul of Achaia, on charges of "persuading the people to worship God in ways contrary to the law" (18:13). As Paul stood at the *bēma* (judgment seat), Gallio dismissed the charges and expelled the Jews from the court (18:12–17). The *bēma*, a platform where speakers stood and citizens appeared before officials, has been located and identified by archaeologists. Archaeologists have also found near the theater an inscription that reads, "Erastus, in return for his aedileship, laid this pavement at his own expense." This is likely the same Erastus who was Corinth's city treasurer and who became a Christian (Rom. 16:23; 2 Tim. 4:20). Corinth played a significant role in Paul's ministry, as he visited it on multiple occasions (1 Cor. 12:14; 13:1), wrote 1–2 Corinthians to its church, and likely wrote Romans and 1–2 Thessalonians from there. Other early church leaders also ministered in Corinth, such as Apollos (Acts 19:1).

Corinthians, First Letter to the– First Corinthians is the first of two NT letters written by the apostle Paul to the Corinthian church. Paul visited Corinth on his second missionary journey (Acts 18:1–18) for a year and a half before leaving for Syria. This period can be dated quite precisely, since Acts mentions a court hearing before Gallio, proconsul of Achaia, who served in AD 51–52. Several years later, during Paul's third missionary journey, the Corinthian correspondence was written.

While in Ephesus, Paul heard of immorality in the church at Corinth and responded with a letter (1 Cor. 5:9). This letter is lost. About this time, three men from Corinth brought a financial gift to Paul (1 Cor. 16:17) along with a list of questions, which Paul answers in another letter (see 7:1). This letter, known to us as 1 Corinthians, is actually the second letter written by Paul to the church.

In chapters 1–6 Paul deals with a number of problems in the church at Corinth, including divisions, arrogance, immaturity, and immorality; then, in chapters 7–16 he answers the questions sent to him by the church. Not only are the members of this church not unified, but also they are at odds with Paul himself. Paul seeks to reestablish his authority over the church.

Problems in Corinth

Divisions. The church had divided sharply, aligning with different Christian leaders (1:12). There is no indication that this was encouraged by these leaders. Paul points out that it was not he who was crucified for them, and they were not baptized in his name. These groups had formed in the name of wisdom, each group boasting of the superiority of its leader's teaching.

Paul appeals to them to end their divisions and to be unified in mind and thought. Christ is the head of the church, and he cannot be divided. Human wisdom is not the cornerstone of the church. God's wisdom can only be known spiritually; the person with the Spirit of God understands the deep things of God (2:10–11). Those who think themselves wise by human standards should become "foolish" in the worldly sense in order to be wise spiritually (3:18).

Confronting immorality. Paul is appalled at the sexual immorality at the church: a man is sleeping with his own stepmother (5:1). This is forbidden in the Torah (Lev. 18:7–8) and even among pagan cultures. Worse than the sin, though, is the church community's response: they are proud, boasting even. It is not clear whether Paul refers to their generally inflated egos, a perverted sense of freedom in Christ, or the fact that they consider themselves so open-minded as to allow such a sin; what is clear is that Paul has attempted to deal with this before, in his first letter. Paul orders that the man be put out of fellowship (this he states four times) so that the man's spirit may be saved (5:5).

Lawsuits between believers. Conflicts in the church community had reached the point where church members were seeking resolution in secular courts. Paul shames the supposedly "wise" Corinthians for not solving their own problems. They are already defeated because they would rather be declared right by a nonbeliever than simply be wronged by a Christian brother or sister (6:7).

Immorality generally. The Corinthian church was begun when Paul abandoned his preaching to the Jews in Corinth and went instead to the Gentiles (Acts 18:6). Apparently, the new converts have continued with much of their pagan lifestyle, including visits to the temple prostitutes. To justify their behavior, the Corinthians had distorted Paul's theology of freedom: "I have the right to do anything," they say. Paul reminds them, "But not everything is beneficial" (6:12). Paul's corrective is for them to flee sexual immorality, because their bodies are not their own; they have been bought with a price (6:19–20).

Questions from Corinth

Paul then turns to questions brought him from the church, touching on many topics relevant for the church today.

Marriage. Some of the Corinthians were claiming that celibacy was a higher spiritual state than marriage. Paul agrees that there are benefits to celibacy and defends his own as a gift, but he also acknowledges the goodness of marriage (7:1–11). Marriage is the appropriate context for sexual energy to be expressed, and husbands and wives are responsible to each other sexually. For spiritual reasons they may abstain from sexual relations for a brief time and by mutual consent, but then they must come back together. Divorce is not condoned, except in the case of an unbelieving spouse leaving the marriage.

Each person's life should be lived in the situation in which he or she was called. A man should not seek to change from circumcision to uncircumcision or vice versa. Slaves should not seek freedom, and those who are free should remain so. Married couples should stay married; single believers should remain content in their singleness, though they do not sin by marrying.

Food sacrificed to idols. Most of the meat eaten in the ancient world came from pagan shrines and temples, where some of the animal was burned on the altar and the rest sold at a market. Some Christians believed that eating the pagan meat was like worshiping the god to which it was sacrificed. The question before Paul was, "Should Christians avoid meat from pagan sacrifices?"

Paul responds by saying that the idol is nothing, and the association of the food with an idol is irrelevant. Yet, because new believers may still associate the food with the idol and fall into sin, a Christian should avoid this meat in their presence. At a meal with an unbeliever, the food may be eaten freely unless its source in idol worship is made an issue. Then, for the sake of the unbeliever's conscience, the food must be refused.

Issues in worship. Paul's discussion on head coverings in chapter 11 is among the most difficult in the NT because the background and context are obscure to us. Clearly, the Corinthians were being inappropriate in dress or hairstyles in either a sexual or a religious context, or both. We can draw a principle from Paul's arguments: Christians should not blur the visual distinctions between the sexes, nor should they offend contemporary customs and fashion in a particular church. As with the food sacrificed to idols, one's effect on fellow Christians is paramount in one's actions.

Likewise in the Lord's Supper, the church must be unified in this central part of worship. The church was fracturing along class and economic lines when it came to the "love feast," a communal meal shared by the church in conjunction with the Lord's Supper. The rich were coming early to the meal and gorging themselves, while the poor had nothing to eat. Paul warns the church of God's severe judgment for such inequities and instructs them to all partake together (11:33).

Paul also applies the theme of unity to the gifts of the Spirit, but here it is diversity within unity. The many different gifts are given by the same Spirit and are intended for accomplishing God's work. Although some of the gifts are more spectacular, the greater gifts are faith, hope, and love.

The resurrection. To the question "Will there be a physical resurrection of the dead?" Paul gives an extensive explanation of the gospel message. The resurrection is central to the gospel; without it, Christian faith is in vain (15:14). But Christ was raised as the firstfruits of the dead, and in him all will be made alive (15:22). Christians will be raised with a glorified body, imperishable, powerful, and spiritual (15:42–44).

CORINTHIANS, SECOND LETTER TO THE–Part of the Corinthian correspondence, along with 1 Corinthians. These two letters are part of a larger body of correspondence written by the apostle Paul to the Corinthian church. Paul visited Corinth on his second missionary journey (Acts 18:1–18) for a year and a half before leaving for Syria. This period can be dated quite precisely, since Acts mentions a court hearing before Gallio, proconsul of Achaia, who served in AD 51–52. It was several years later, during Paul's third missionary journey, that the Corinthian correspondence was written.

While in Ephesus, Paul heard of immorality in the church at Corinth and responded with a letter (1 Cor. 5:9). This letter is lost. About this time, three men from Corinth brought a financial gift to Paul (1 Cor. 16:17) along with a list of questions, which Paul answers in another letter (see 1 Cor. 7:1). This letter is known to us as 1 Corinthians. Some time later, Paul heard that his letter had not solved many of the problems at Corinth, so he made a visit. This went very poorly (see 2 Cor. 2:1), and Paul sent a sorrowful letter (2 Cor. 2:3–4, 9; 7:8, 12). This letter is also lost, though some think that it may be preserved in 2 Cor. 10–13. When Paul heard later that the Corinthian church had repented and wished to reconcile with him, he was overjoyed and wrote yet again. This letter is known to us as 2 Corinthians. The sharp change in tone of chapters 10–13 perhaps represents a fifth letter reflecting ongoing friction with a strong minority faction within the church.

False teachers in the church at Corinth had attacked Paul's teaching and authority. Their charges can be seen in 2 Corinthians: Paul was fickle (1:17, 18, 23), proud and boastful (3:1; 5:12), worldly (10:2), unimpressive in appearance and speech (10:10; 11:6), confused and foolish (5:13; 11:16–19), dishonest (12:16–19), and "not a true apostle" (11:5; 12:11–12). Paul writes to defend his ministry and authority.

Paul gives a wonderful description of his apostolic ministry. He is a captive in Christ's triumphal procession, spreading the aroma of the gospel wherever he goes. This aroma is the smell of death to some, but life to others (2:16). He needs no letter of recommendation, as the church at Corinth is his letter, written on human hearts. The gospel is unlike the fading glory in Moses' face (see Exod. 34:33); in fact, relationship with God during the old covenant was accomplished only through a veil, which still covers hearts when Moses is read. Rather, Christians bask in the unveiled glory of the Lord and are transformed into the Lord's image with ever greater glory (3:18), carrying in their bodies the death of Jesus, so that the life of Jesus may be revealed in them (4:10).

The earthly consequence of this ministry is pain and suffering. Paul is constantly struggling, yet never defeated (4:8–9). But the spiritual reward is great: an eternal home with the Lord in heaven, with the Spirit given to him during this life as a deposit of what is to come (5:5).

Beginning with chapter 10, Paul's tone changes sharply, becoming much more aggressive as he defends his apostolic authority. His gentle nature in person, which may have been mistaken by some of the Corinthians for weakness, is really Christlikeness in Paul. He fights not as the world does, but rather on the spiritual level, with weapons that can demolish all arguments (10:4). He hopes that he will not have to unleash his power when he comes to see them, though he will if necessary (10:6).

Paul's opponents in Corinth have been exercising false authority beyond their rightful limits. They commend themselves and boast of their works. Paul promises to remain within the sphere assigned him by God, and he assures them that his sphere includes their church (10:13).

In chapter 11 Paul begins speaking "as a fool." His opponents apparently have referred to him as a fool, so he allows himself some latitude to do this. If he were a fool, he would boast of his accomplishments as an apostle. His opponents boast about themselves; Paul has more to boast about. He also is a Hebrew, a descendant of Abraham, and a servant of Christ; in fact, he is more. He has worked harder; he has been imprisoned more, beaten more, stoned, and shipwrecked; he has gone without food and water; he has been cold and naked. He has had visions and revelations, and he has been caught up in heaven and heard things that he may not repeat. Yet he would rather boast of his weakness, for his worldly weakness allows him to be strong in Christ. Paul should have been commended by the Corinthians, yet he has been reduced to having to defend himself boastfully.

During Paul's next visit, he will continue his habit of supporting himself, so as not to be a burden on the Corinthians (see Acts 18:3). He has not asked them to support him (though it was his right [see 1 Cor. 9]), yet they have accused him of trickery (12:16; see also 1:12). He hopes that he will not be forced to deal harshly with them, but they demand proof that Christ speaks through him (13:3). He would rather use the authority that God has given him to build them up, not tear them down (13:10).

Cornelius–A centurion in the Italian Regiment (cohort) of the Roman army who lived in Caesarea Maritima. Cornelius, whose generosity is notable and whose family are devout God-fearers, constantly engaged in prayer. In Acts 10:4–5 Cornelius receives a vision from

God to have Peter brought from Joppa to Caesarea to instruct him, his family, and close friends further in the truths of the gospel. Peter hesitates until he receives a vision from God that makes it clear the Gentiles are no longer unclean in light of Christ's reconciling work on the cross. Nonetheless, Peter and his Jewish Christian companions are astonished when the Holy Spirit falls upon all those who have just heard Peter's sermon. Those gathered are consequently baptized, since they have clearly received the Holy Spirit (see Acts 10–11). Cornelius thus appears in Acts as the confirming witness that God's salvation is for the Gentiles as well as the Jews.

Corner Gate–A gate of Jerusalem located on the western end of the city, guarding the east-west transverse valley. Joash king of Israel defeated Amaziah and destroyed the city wall between the Ephraim Gate and the Corner Gate (2 Kings 14:13; 2 Chron. 25:23). Uzziah rebuilt the gate with defensive towers (2 Chron. 26:9). The Corner Gate is the westernmost boundary of a future Jerusalem (Jer. 31:38; Zech. 14:10).

Cornerstone–An architecturally important stone, giving rise to its figurative uses. The architectural uses refer to either a capstone or a foundation stone. Long interlocking stones used to tie the corners of a building together for stability were topped off with a capstone, or "head of the corner" (1 Pet. 2:7 KJV, NRSV). The corner foundation stone was important for bearing weight and possibly for establishing the lines for the walls. Job 38:4–6 figuratively pictures God laying the earth's foundation and cornerstone. References to a cornerstone in Ps. 118:22; Isa. 28:16; Zech. 10:4 are taken as messianic. Zechariah looks forward to the ruler from Judah of the messianic age. In Isaiah's prophecy the corner foundation stone is of precious material and acts to ensure a true or square line. Like a good wall with aligned stones, the one who believes will not give way. Peter compares the church to believing, living stones built around Christ, the cornerstone (1 Pet. 2:4–6). Psalm 118 highlights an irony: a stone rejected early in the building process is chosen by God to be the corner capstone, a metaphor applied to Jesus six times in the NT (Matt. 21:42; Mark 12:10; Luke 20:17; Acts 4:11; Eph. 2:20; 1 Pet. 2:7). *See also* Capstone.

Council of Jerusalem–The teaching by some individuals in both Syrian Antioch (Acts 15:1) and in Jerusalem (15:5) that Gentile believers must be circumcised prompted the council of Jerusalem. The council, a meeting of the apostles and elders in Jerusalem in approximately AD 49, addressed matters regarding the relationship between Gentile Christians and the Mosaic law (15:6–29). Paul, Barnabas, Simon Peter, James the brother of Jesus, Silas, and Judas Barsabbas were among those present. The council acknowledged that salvation is by grace (15:11). In a letter dispatched to Gentile Christians, the council affirmed Gentiles' freedom from requirements of the law but required that they abstain from food sacrificed to idols, from blood, from the meat of strangled animals, and from sexual immorality (15:29). Some scholars believe that the council of Jerusalem is also described in Gal. 2:1–10.

Covenant–A pact/compact or an agreement (Heb. *berit*). The NT counterpart word is *diathēkē,* defined as a "legal disposition of personal goods."

The covenant is something that binds parties together or obligates one party to the other. Although there are legal implications associated with covenant, the relational aspect of covenant should not be overlooked. A covenant is best understood as a relationship with related legalities. Marriage, for example, is a covenant that establishes and defines a relationship. This perhaps explains why God chose from the realm of relationships among humans the covenant metaphor to establish and communicate his intent in divine-human relationships.

Some covenants are between persons of equal status (parity treaties); others are between a master and a servant (suzerainty treaties), between nations, between clans, and between a husband and a wife (Mal. 2:14). To "cut a covenant" at any level of society implies a solemn commitment to a relationship.

The most significant covenant relationship in the biblical material is the one between God and humankind. The uniqueness of Israel's covenant relationship with Yahweh in contrast to all surrounding nations is established on the basis of Deut. 32:8–9. Although Yahweh gave the nations their inheritance, he selected Israel for his own personal care; he established a relationship with the nation independent of and prior to the nation's association with his land.

Covenant is a dominant theme that gives cohesiveness to the structure of the OT and distinguishes the history of Israel. The phrase "covenant history" can be used to describe the biblical literature that recounts the events and episodes of Israelite life. It is a macrogenre that characterizes the historical narratives of the OT. Although this large literary corpus of historical narrative shares a covenant perspective, the individual books within the narrative corpus are noted for the attention they give to various aspects of the covenant relationship. For example, Gen. 12–50 develops the covenant promises of seed and blessing through a number of subgenres such as genealogies and family stories. Joshua, on the other hand, engages several military subgenres to recount the tension between the promise of land occupation and the responsibility of Israel to occupy the land. Covenant history is a realistic presentation of the tensions associated with the covenant relationship between Yahweh and the nation of Israel.

Finally, the psalms have a direct covenant connection emphasizing covenant worship. Psalm 119 (esp. vv. 57–64) is filled with covenant terms that relate to God's word (testimonies, laws, oath, judgments). Marching to the place of worship designated by the covenant is reflected in the Psalms of Ascent.

Although the covenant theme is less pervasive in the NT, its christological significance is profound. The NT highlights the significant messianic role of Christ in relation to the covenants. Paul references the new covenant in both books of Corinthians (1 Cor. 11:25; 2 Cor. 3:6). Each celebration of the Lord's Supper reminds us that the shed blood of Christ is the blood of the new covenant. The new covenant is cut in connection with or on the basis of his death, burial, and resurrection (1 Cor. 11:25). The writer of the book of Hebrews gives detailed attention to how the new covenant functions in contrast to the old Mosaic covenant. The writer explains that Jesus is the guarantor of a better covenant (7:22; 8:6–7). Finally, Paul indicates that we are now considered ministers of the new covenant ministry (2 Cor. 3:6).

Covenant of Salt–Grain offerings were seasoned with the "salt of the covenant" (Lev. 2:13). The sacred incense was to be salted (Exod. 30:35). Offering portions for the priests and Levites were given to them as "an everlasting covenant of salt" (Num. 18:19). The preservative quality of salt (or the fact that salt survives the sacrificial fire) symbolized the eternality of the covenant and undergirded Jesus' charge to believers to be "salt" (Matt. 5:13).

Covet, Covetous–To harbor an inordinate desire, especially for something belonging to someone else, often with intent to deprive that person of what is rightfully his or hers.

In the OT, the principal Hebrew term, *khamad*, indicates an unrestrained, selfish desire. A survey of its occurrences shows this desire directed most often toward things that belong to others or that are otherwise illicit (e.g., Josh. 7:21; Prov. 6:25; Mic. 2:2; but see Ps. 68:16: "God chooses").

Notably, the tenth commandment prohibits coveting another's possessions (Exod. 20:17; Deut. 5:21). It is unique among the Decalogue's latter commandments (Exod. 20:12–17) because it targets an inward attitude rather than outward acts.

In the NT, a principal Greek term, *epithymeō*, represents a strong desire generally. Paul uses it when referencing the tenth commandment (Rom. 7:7; 13:9), so that the Greek term is similar to the Hebrew one in meaning. In contrast, James 4:2 employs *epithymeō* broadly to refer to evil desires that promote strife. The exact meaning of this word is determined by context (cf. Matt. 13:17, where Jesus speaks of those who "longed" to experience what his disciples did).

Creation–The foundational story in all of the OT is the story of creation, found in Gen. 1–2. Throughout the history of interpretation there have been many approaches to understanding these chapters. In the modern world, discoveries from both science and archaeology have challenged some traditional convictions, and debates continue to rage. Still, what Gen. 1–2 communicates is generally clear: (1) it establishes Yahweh, the God of Israel, as the God by whose word all exists; (2) it presents for ancient readers a compelling argument for why they should worship Israel's God and not other gods of the ancient world.

Creature–Whether animal or human, "creature" assumes creator. God's unique creative activity is showcased in his majestic work: "creatures." While the infinite God is not confined in the lives of his creatures, both are linked in a relationship of fidelity (Ps. 104).

A creature is a gift and has an obligation of service (Ps. 150). Scripture celebrates divine rule and creaturely dependence (Ps. 96). Creatures have roles, and the liturgy of doxology revels in a cosmic and eschatological drama (Ps. 148; Isa. 40:12–31; 65:17–25). Humans are caretaking creatures (Ps. 8).

Creeping Thing–A translation of the Hebrew word *remes*, referring to a category of animals that includes reptiles, crawling insects, and other small animals that travel low to the ground. In the OT, such creatures are regularly distinguished from humans, large animals, livestock, flying animals, and fish, each of which constitutes its own class, and which, taken together with creeping things, represent all nonplant life. Creeping things are mentioned significantly in the creation account (Gen. 1:24–26) and in the Noah story (6:7, 20; 7:14, 23; 8:17, 19; 9:3). They are also found in 1 Kings 4:33; Pss. 104:25; 148:10; Ezek. 8:10; 38:20; Hos. 2:18; Hab. 1:14.

Cretans–Inhabitants of Crete. Apparently, many held Cretans in general to be of low morals. In order to bolster his argument against destructive teachers in Crete, Paul favorably quotes to Titus a saying from a Cretan "prophet": "Cretans are always liars, evil brutes, lazy gluttons" (Titus 1:12). The saying usually is attributed to the poet Epimenides of Crete (sixth century BC).

Crete–Crete is an island in the Mediterranean just off the coast of Greece, about 160 miles long and 35 miles wide in several places. It is a mountainous territory that has a known history dating back at least to 6000 BC.

The word for Crete in the OT is "Caphtor." As Moses recounts the division and settling of the land of Canaan, he makes note of a number of the inhabitants, one group being the Avvites, who lived near Gaza, near the Mediterranean Sea (Deut. 2:23). Their land was taken by the Caphtorites, from the island of Crete. Jeremiah prophesies that God will destroy the people of the coasts of Caphtor, or Crete (Jer. 47:4). The prophet Amos records God's message declaring his sovereignty over the nations, the Israelites, the Caphtorites (from Crete), and the Arameans (Amos 9:7).

Crete is referred to in the NT five times, four of these related to Paul's sailing to Rome for trial. Acts mentions that on the way to Rome the ship found shelter sailing under the lee of Crete. They sailed close to the coast of Crete, moving to the western part of the island in hopes of spending the winter there (27:7–13). Against Paul's warning, they chose to sail on, only to incur disaster. Afterward, Paul appeals to that event so that they might listen to him from then on (27:21–22).

Later, Paul returned to Crete for the purpose of evangelism and church planting. There he left his protégé Titus to carry on the work. The correction of the church at Crete and the instructions for ordaining elders occasion the book of Titus (1:5). Little is known of this church on Crete, only what can be inferred from the book of Titus. The church seems to have had problems similar to those faced by many of the other churches to which Paul ministered. Active there were rebellious and deceptive false teachers, whom Titus needed to silence. Paul reports that they were misleading whole families with their teaching. These teachers are said to have a Jewish connection. It is unclear what Paul means by this, but here he makes a surprising evaluation of these individuals by favorably citing a Cretan "prophet" who says that Cretans are "liars, evil brutes, lazy gluttons" (Titus 1:12–13). The connection between this evaluation and the problem of their false teaching is unclear, but Paul's characterization of the Cretans must have been in some way related to the type of false teaching that was occurring.

Crimes and Punishments–Unlike modern systems of jurisprudence, the Bible does not draw distinctions between criminal, civil, family, and religious law, either in its terminology or in its presentation of legal material. In the Bible, acts of deviance that are defined as criminal in virtually all societies are discussed alongside violations of a culturally specific, religious nature. For instance, the Ten Commandments prohibit murder and dishonoring parents (Exod. 20:12–13), as well as commanding Sabbath observance (Exod. 20:8–11). Any attempt to extract a system of criminal law from biblical materials must account for the fact that every culture defines deviance differently, with respect not only to specific acts but also to categories of deviance.

Capital Crimes

The Pentateuch mandates the death penalty for a wide variety of crimes. Often the mode of execution is unspecified. Where a particular mode is prescribed, the death penalty most often consisted of stoning (as in Num. 15:35) and less frequently of burning (Lev. 20:14) or shooting with arrows (Exod. 19:13).

Crimes incurring the death penalty include killing or murder (Exod. 21:12–14; Lev. 24:17; Num. 35:16), though the crime is aggravated or lessened depending on the intention behind it (Exod. 21:13–14) and whether a weapon is involved (Num. 35:16); attacking parents (Exod. 21:15); kidnapping and slave trading (Exod. 21:16; Deut. 24:7); cursing parents (Exod. 21:17; Lev. 20:9); negligence resulting in death (Exod. 21:29); bestiality (Exod. 22:19; Lev. 20:15–16); breach of the Sabbath (Exod. 31:14–15; Num. 15:35); child sacrifice (Lev. 20:2); adultery (Lev. 20:10; Deut. 22:22); incest (Lev. 20:11–12); homosexuality (Lev. 20:13); marrying a woman and her mother (Lev. 20:14); witchcraft (Exod. 22:18; Lev. 20:27); blasphemy (Exod. 24:16); unauthorized approach to the tabernacle (Num. 1:51); idolatry (Num. 25:5); false prophecy and divination (Deut. 13:5); presumptuous prophecy (Deut. 18:20); enticing others to idolatry (Deut. 13:6–10); false testimony in a capital case (Deut. 19:19); and contempt for authorities (Deut. 17:2; Josh. 1:18).

When the body of an executed criminal was displayed by hanging, it had to be removed by nightfall (Deut. 21:22). The death penalty was not to be applied vicariously to family members of criminals (Deut. 24:16). In OT texts, execution was to be carried out by the victims (Deut. 13:9), families of victims (the "avenger of blood" of Num. 35:19), or witnesses to the crime.

The NT mentions an official or professional executioner (Mark 6:27). Paul declares that the authorities rightly derive the power of the sword from God (Rom. 13:4).

Punishments for Noncapital Crimes

Corporal punishment. Beating as a criminal punishment is rare in the OT (Jer. 20:2; 37:15). Most OT references to beating occur in the context of the household, as a punishment for slaves or children. Deuteronomy 25:3 limits the number of strokes in a flogging to forty (see 2 Cor. 11:24). Flogging was commonly applied as a criminal punishment in Roman times, and it was a common mode of discipline within the Roman military (Acts 16:22; 2 Cor. 11:25; 1 Pet. 2:20).

Restitution. Crimes against property were punished by compelling the offender to make restitution by repaying, often in an amount that exceeded the actual damages, including in cases of theft or negligence (Exod. 21:33; 22:3–15); killing an animal (Lev. 24:18, 21); having sexual relations with a virgin not pledged to be married (Exod. 22:16); injuring a pregnant woman (Exod. 21:22); harming a slave (Exod. 21:26–27). Financial restitution could not be made for murder (Num. 35:31).

Retribution. The notion of the *lex talionis*, the law of retribution, is stated in Exod. 21:23–24: "life for life, eye for eye, tooth for tooth, hand for hand, foot for foot" (cf. Lev. 24:19–20; Deut. 19:21; Matt. 5:38). This formula appears in other ancient legal traditions. The idea of bodily mutilation may strike modern readers as barbaric, but such laws may actually have been relatively enlightened by ancient standards, as they imposed a proportional limit on retribution.

Incarceration. In modern societies, incarceration and probation account for the vast majority of the punishments resulting from criminal offenses. In the OT, incarceration is rarely mentioned apart from the imprisonment of war captives (e.g., Judg. 16:21) and political dissidents. Jeremiah was imprisoned several times for his criticism of the regime (Jer. 32:2; 37:15). Throughout the Bible, prisoners often are guarded by soldiers rather than by professional jailers.

Paul imprisoned Christians prior to his conversion (Acts 8:3), and he himself was imprisoned or placed under arrest several times (e.g., Acts 16:23; 20:23; 24:27; Rom. 16:7). John the Baptist was imprisoned after he criticized Herod (Mark 6:17). Again, in both cases, incarceration was used to silence and segregate someone whose free movement in society threatened political stability rather than to punish a common criminal. In Matt. 5:25–26 Jesus refers to imprisonment for an unspecified reason, though the threat that "you will not get out until you have paid the last penny" suggests that incarceration was a substitute for an unpaid fine or monetary penalty. This recalls Exod. 22:3, which mandates that a thief who could not make financial restitution for theft must be sold (as a slave).

Banishment and cities of refuge. A number of OT passages refer to the "cutting off" of a person from the community. It is not clear whether this language refers to exile or the death penalty; several of the crimes thus punished are known to be capital crimes in other texts.

The law of Num. 35:6–34 establishes six "cities of refuge" among the towns allotted to the Levites. To these cities an unintentional killer could flee from the "avenger of blood," a relative of the victim, until such time as the case could be adjudicated by the whole community. A killer who was found to have acted unintentionally and without malice could remain in the city of refuge, safe from retribution, until the death of the high priest, at which time the killer was free to return home with impunity.

Crispus–A synagogue ruler in Corinth (with or before Sosthenes; cf. Acts 18:17) who became a Christian, along with his entire household, after hearing Paul preach (18:8). He was one of the few Corinthian believers whom Paul himself baptized (1 Cor. 1:14–16).

Cross, Crucifixion–A cross is an upright wooden beam or post on which persons were either tied or nailed as a means of torture and execution. The Latin cross was shaped like a t and was the type most commonly used by the Romans. Jesus was crucified probably on a Latin cross, which allowed for a convenient place for a sign (called a *titlos* in John 19:19) to be placed above his head (Matt. 27:37 pars.).

Not long before the Romans took over Palestine, the Jewish ruler Alexander Jannaeus crucified about eight hundred Pharisees who opposed him in 86 BC. This gruesome event was out of character for the Jewish nation and was frowned upon by the Jews of the day as well as by the later Jewish historian Josephus. But it was the Romans who perfected crucifixion as a means of torture and execution. The Romans called crucifixion "slaves' punishment" because it was intended for the lowest members of society. It became the preferred method of execution for political crimes such as desertion, spying, rebellion, and insurrection. Roman crucifixion was common in NT times and extended well into the fourth century AD.

As for the significance of Jesus' crucifixion, the OT teaches that it is blood that makes atonement for sin (Lev. 17:11). Just as sacrificial lambs shed their blood on the altar for the sins of Israel, Jesus shed his blood on the cross for the sins of the world (John 1:29). The crucifixion of Jesus was the greatest atoning event in history. His blood, which provided the means for a new covenant, was poured out for many on the cross (Matt. 26:28). The cross, as gruesome as it was, was the means through which Christ died "for our sins" (Gal. 1:4). Jesus freely scorned the shame of the cross so that we might be reconciled to God by his shed blood (Col. 1:20; Heb. 12:2).

Jesus also bore the curse of God in our place when he died on the cross. The one who hangs on a tree is divinely cursed (Deut. 21:23). God's curse is a curse upon sin, death, and fallenness. Jesus took God's curse upon himself in order to redeem us from that curse (Gal. 3:13).

Jesus demonstrated the humble nature of his mission and ministry by his obedience to death, even death on the cross (Phil. 2:8). For Jesus the cross was not simply his martyrdom, as if he simply died for a worthy cause; it was the pinnacle example of obedience and love in the Bible. Jesus called his followers to take up a cross and follow his example of selfless sacrifice (Matt. 16:24). Jesus' cross is a symbol of his love, obedience, and selflessness.

Most of all, the cross reveals the unconditional love of God, who offered his Son as the atoning sacrifice for sin (John 3:16; 1 John 4:10). The brutal cross reveals the beautiful love of Jesus, who willingly laid down his life (1 John 3:16).

Crown–Headgear signifying honor, victory, power, or authority. A crown was worn by monarchs in the ancient world to designate their royal power, often including a golden headband with precious stones in it, as well as a turban.

There are two important types of crowns in the OT: the priestly and the royal. A royal crown first appears with Saul (2 Sam. 1:10) and is worn by monarchs after him, including David (2 Sam. 12:30; 1 Chron. 20:2; see also Pss. 21:3; 132:18) and Joash (2 Kings 11:12; 2 Chron. 23:11). The book of Exodus depicts a crownlike turban to which is affixed a golden "sacred emblem" bearing the inscription "Holy to the Lord," which is to be worn by the high priest (Exod. 28:36–37; 29:6; see also, e.g., 39:30; Lev. 8:9).

Zechariah 6:11–14 looks to a future messiah, "the Branch," who will be both priest and king, thus wearing a priestly and royal crown. Before his crucifixion, Jesus' tormentors place on his head a mock crown made of thorns (Matt. 27:29; Mark 15:17; John 19:2, 5). In the book of Revelation both godly and satanic figures wear crowns: the elders in heaven (4:4, 10), the rider of the white horse (6:2), the locusts from the Abyss (9:7), the woman clothed with the sun (12:1), the dragon and the beast (12:3; 13:1), the one "like a son of man" (14:14), and Christ himself (19:12).

Crown of Thorns–In each of the Gospels except Luke, Jesus' tormentors mock his kingly claims by placing on his head a crown made of thorns (Matt. 27:29; Mark 15:17; John 19:2, 5). The thorns probably were the rachis of a palm frond (*Phoenix dactylifera*), shaped into a radiating crown representing the light rays emanating from the heads of divinities. The "crown" was forced into the victim's skull, causing significant pain.

C

Cub–*See* Libya.

Cubit–*See* Weights and Measures.

Cumin–*See* Spices.

Cup–In the book of Psalms, "cup" signifies a person's divinely appointed lot in life (16:5–6; 23:5). The "cup of salvation" (Ps. 116:13) alludes to the wine poured out as part of the thank offering (Num. 28:7–8).

The most important theological use is the mainly prophetic (but also psalmic [e.g., Ps. 75:8]) image of the cup of God's wrath that wicked nations will drink (e.g., Isa. 51:17–23; Jer. 25:15–17, 28). The book of Revelation takes up this image (14:10; 16:19; 17:4; 18:6). This OT usage also stands behind the "cup" that Jesus must drink, to which he refers in the prediction of his death (Mark 10:38–39) and in his prayer in the garden of Gethsemane (Mark 14:36; cf. John 18:11: "Shall I not drink the cup the Father has given me?"). On the cross, Jesus as the substitute for sinners bore God's wrath.

Cupbearer–A high-ranking official in ancient Near Eastern courts. The cupbearer was responsible for serving wine at the king's table. Because of the possibility of plots and poisoning, a trustworthy individual was required for this position. His closeness to the king often gave him a position of great influence.

The "chief cupbearer" in the Joseph story (Gen. 40:1–2) likely supervised a staff. While in prison, the cupbearer, along with the baker, was attended by Joseph. Although Joseph asked the cupbearer to mention his plight to the pharaoh when the cupbearer was restored to his position, he forgot about Joseph for two years (Gen. 40:14, 23; 41:9–13). The cupbearer's closeness to the pharaoh, however, eventually allowed him to be influential in Joseph's rise to power.

Nehemiah was the cupbearer to Artaxerxes (Neh. 1:11) and highly esteemed. Nehemiah's financial resources (5:10, 17) may indicate that the position was well compensated.

Curse–*See* Blessing and Cursing.

Curtain–A cloth hanging used to construct temporary dwelling places, to function as an entrance, or to screen private places. The tabernacle was constructed from ten curtains woven from expensively dyed yarns, hung with blue cord, and fastened with gold clasps (Exod. 26:1–6). The surrounding tent was formed from eleven goatskin curtains (26:7–13). A curtain hung in front of the holy place, preventing entry except by the high priest on certain days, and then only after animal sacrifices were made and the sanctuary was sprinkled with blood (Lev. 16:2). At the time of Jesus' death, this curtain was torn in two, from top to bottom (Matt. 27:51), signifying a new freedom of access to God, which Jesus achieved by his blood (Heb. 10:19–20). When the earth is spoken of metaphorically as God's dwelling place, the heavens are described as the curtains that encompass it (Isa. 40:22).

Cush, Cushites–**(1)** An African kingdom located along the Nile River to the south of Egypt, in the region that is now part of the country of Sudan. Since the Greeks used the term "Ethiopia" in a generic sense to refer to everything south of Egypt, including Cush, and some historians occasionally refer to the Cushite kingdom as Nubia, English Bible versions occasionally translate the Hebrew term "Cush" as "Ethiopia" or "Nubia." Likewise, the NT character referred to as the "Ethiopian eunuch" (Acts 8:27) was not from modern Ethiopia but rather from this same kingdom on the Nile, south of Egypt, called "Cush" throughout the OT.

The OT prophets pronounce judgment on all the surrounding nations for their complicity in the attack on Israel and Judah by the Assyrians and Babylonians. Cush is included among the nations falling under this judgment. However, when the prophets look beyond the destruction to the time of messianic restoration, they paint a picture of people from all nations joining together to worship the true God. The prophets use the Cushites as one of their paradigm groups for this restoration.

That is, in the prophetic passages of future restoration, Cush often represents the future Gentile inclusion (Isa. 11:11; 45:14; Zeph. 3:9–10). In the NT, the Ethiopian eunuch (an official from Cush) is similar in several respects to Ebed-Melek in the book of Jeremiah (Acts 8:26–40). At a time when Jerusalem has rejected the message of God and is actively persecuting God's messengers (Acts 7:1–8:3), it is an Ethiopian (Cushite) official who believes. Thus, in a fashion similar to Ebed-Melek, this Ethiopian (Cushite) probably symbolizes the inclusion of Gentiles into the people of God.

(2) The superscription of Ps. 7 (7:1 MT) states that David sang this psalm to God concerning a Benjamite named "Cush," apparently one of David's enemies. It is not known why this individual and the Cushi of Zeph. 1:1, who apparently were Hebrews, were so named. Perhaps they were Cushites, or perhaps one of their parents was a Cushite. On the other hand, perhaps they were given the name in honor of a certain Cushite.

(3) Another reference to someone named "Cush" is in the puzzling passage Gen. 10:6–8 (restated in 1 Chron. 1:8–10). Genesis 10, however, is a notoriously difficult chapter to interpret. It consists largely of a genealogy, but the names used in the genealogy include those of individuals, peoples, countries, tribes, and cities. Some scholars think that the chapter is more about geopolitical alliances and geographical locations than about physical descent of individuals. In Gen. 10:6 Cush is said to be the father of Nimrod. Little is known for certain about Nimrod, but in Gen. 10:10–12 he is closely associated with various cities and kingdoms in Mesopotamia. Thus, some scholars associate this reference to Cush with some entity in Mesopotamia, perhaps a people known as the Cassites.

Cushan–Habakkuk 3 describes the itinerary of God from the mountain country of the southern Transjordan (v. 3). Along the way, he passes through Cushan and Midian (v. 7). Cushan is mentioned only here in the Bible. The context suggests that "Cushan" is a synonym for "Midian," in northern Arabia. The word sounds like *kush*, the biblical term for "Ethiopia."

Cushan-Rishathaim–King of Aram Naharaim, meaning "Aram of the Two Rivers," the Tigris and the Euphrates in northwest Mesopotamia. He is mentioned in Judg. 3:7–11. God allowed him to subjugate the Israelites because of their disobedience in turning from the worship of Yahweh to worship of Baals and Asherahs. Othniel, the first judge mentioned, went to war against Cushan-Rishathaim and delivered the Israelites. The name "Cushan-Rishathaim" means "doubly wicked Cushan" and is likely a pun on his real name.

Custodian–In Greco-Roman society, children were accompanied by a custodian (*paidagōgos*, lit., "pedagogue") who was entrusted with guardianship and instruction of the youth in goodness and morality. The judgment of the *paidagōgos* was considered to be the norm for the youth's actions. As such, the custodian was responsible for the social actions of the youth in public and could be punished for them when they were inappropriate. Libanius records one such incident: "Diogenes, on seeing a youth misbehaving, struck his paedagogus, adding: 'Why do you teach such things?'" (*Progymnasmata* 3).

The term *paidagōgos* is translated a variety of ways in the NT: "guardian" (NIV, ESV), "custodian" (RSV), "schoolmaster" or "instructor" (KJV), "tutor" (NASB), "disciplinarian" (NRSV), and so on. The apostle Paul refers to the law as a *paidagōgos* (Gal. 3:24–25) and to custodians or guardians (in contrast to fathers) in Christ (1 Cor. 4:15). The law's role in Israel's upbringing was to provide proper protection and guidance for growing up rightly. However, this custodial role was for Jews before the time of Christ, and now that Christ has come, no one needs or is required to submit to it in order to enter, remain, or go on in the Christian life.

Cyprus–The third-largest island in the Mediterranean Sea, located off the coasts of Syria and Asia Minor (modern-day Turkey). Cyprus is mentioned sporadically throughout the Bible, but in the OT it is referred to as "Kittim" (ESV, NRSV, NASB) or "Chittim" (KJV) (although sometimes the word "Kittim" is used to denote lands west of Palestine in general). In the NT, the island is called *Kypros* (Acts 11:19; 13:4; 15:39; 21:3; 27:4; cf. *Kyprios*, "Cypriot," in 4:36; 11:20; 21:16), whence the English name "Cyprus" (the word "copper" is derived from the Latin word for "Cyprus").

By the time the Romans took control of the island, Cyprus was host to a significant Jewish population, and Barnabas was originally from there (Acts 4:36). The persecution of believers in Jerusalem caused them to spread to Cyprus, and people from Cyprus traveled to Antioch spreading "the good news about the Lord Jesus" (11:19–20). On their first missionary journey, Paul and Barnabas traveled across the island, from the city of Salamis on the eastern side of the island to Paphos on the western side. In Paphos they met Bar-Jesus, a sorcerer and false prophet, "who was an attendant of the proconsul, Sergius Paulus" (13:7). When Bar-Jesus tried to dissuade the proconsul (who was the provincial ruler of Cyprus on behalf of the Romans) from accepting the gospel, Paul struck him blind (13:6–12). Following a disagreement during Paul's second missionary journey, Barnabas returned to Cyprus without Paul, accompanied by John Mark (15:36–41). Later, Paul passed by Cyprus twice while sailing elsewhere (21:3; 27:4).

CYRENE–A city on the coast of North Africa. During the NT period the city contained a large Jewish population. Simon the Cyrene was chosen to carry Jesus' cross (Matt. 27:32; Mark 15:21; Luke 23:26). Jews from Cyrene were present at Pentecost (Acts 2:10) and at the stoning of Stephen (6:9). Some Cyrenian Christians were prominent missionaries to Antioch (11:20; 13:1).

CYRENIAN–A person from the Roman province of Cyrenaica in Africa. Cyrenaica had a significant Jewish community, which maintained cultural ties with Jerusalem (Acts 6:9). Two Cyrenians are mentioned by name in the NT: Simon, the bearer of Jesus' crossbeam (according to tradition he may have become a Christian, along with his sons, Alexander and Rufus; Mark 15:21 pars.); and Lucius, a Christian teacher at Antioch (Acts 13:1). An ossuary was discovered in an Israelite burial cave for Cyrenian Jews that reads "Alexander son of Simon."

CYRUS–Cyrus II, better known as Cyrus the Great, was the founder and first ruler of the Persian Empire (559–529 BC).

After Cyrus assumed leadership of the Persians, he defeated the Medes (c. 550 BC) and combined the two states into one. He then defeated the Lydians (c. 546 BC), located in Asia Minor with a capital at Sardis, ruled at that time by the legendary King Croesus. Cyrus then turned his attention to the major prize, Babylon, whose kingdom extended from Palestine into Syria and across Mesopotamia. In 539 BC he defeated the army of Babylon under the leadership of its king, Nabonidus, then soon entered the city, which, according to Dan. 5, was ruled by Nabonidus's son and coregent, Belshazzar.

After inheriting the Babylonian empire and all its vassals, Cyrus issued a decree that allowed these subjugated people to return to their lands and rebuild their temples. This decree is described in what has come to be known as the Cyrus Cylinder, a record of major events in Cyrus's reign, but in the Bible the version is specifically directed toward the Jewish people (2 Chron. 36:23; Ezra 1:2–4). Soon thereafter, some, but not all, Jewish exiles began to return to Jerusalem under the leadership of Sheshbazzar and Zerubbabel.

Cyrus's impact on the people of God is described in Isa. 44:28–45:13 (esp. 45:1), where God refers to this foreign king as "his anointed" or "his messiah" (*mashiakh*). Such an honorific shows that it was really God himself who moved history to restore his people to their land.

Cyrus died in 530 BC while fighting the Massagetae in central Asia. His son Cambyses II inherited his vast empire from him at that time.

D

Dagon–Dagon is the chief god of the Philistines. The Philistines dedicated a "great sacrifice" to Dagon following their capture of Samson. This occurred in a temple at Gaza and was accompanied by testimony of Dagon's deeds (Judg. 16:23; cf. Exod. 15). First Samuel 5 recounts God's defeat of Dagon.

Damascus–A major city in ancient Syria (Aram) and the capital of modern Syria. Damascus is located fifty miles inland from the Mediterranean, east of the Anti-Lebanon mountains, northeast of Mount Hermon, and west of the Syrian Desert.

During the united monarchy, David incorporated Damascus into his kingdom after the Arameans from the city unsuccessfully came to the aid of Hadadezer of Zobah and were defeated by David in battle (2 Sam. 8:5–6; 1 Chron. 18:5–6). Later, Solomon's adversary Rezon son of Eliada, who had served under Hadadezer of Zobah, gathered a band of rebels, went to Damascus, and took control of the city (1 Kings 11:23–25).

After the division of the kingdom around 928 BC, little is known of Damascus until the biblical report that Asa of Judah appealed to Ben-Hadad I in Damascus for help in his war against Baasha of Israel. When Asa sent gifts of silver and gold and proposed a treaty, Ben-Hadad I (also known as Bir-Hadad I) complied with Asa's request and sent his army to attack Israel's northern cities (1 Kings 15:16–22; 2 Chron. 16:2).

Contacts between Ahab and Ben-Hadad II of Damascus are recounted in 1 Kings 20; 22. Chapter 20 notes that Ben-Hadad II gathered a coalition of thirty-two kings to besiege Samaria, but Ahab was able to defeat them. A second encounter left Ben-Hadad II requesting Ahab's mercy, offering to restore previously captured Israelite towns and to give Ahab access to Damascus. A third engagement pitted Ahab of Israel and Jehoshaphat of Judah against the Arameans at Ramoth Gilead and resulted in Ahab's death.

During and after Ahab's reign, both Elijah and Elisha became involved in the political affairs of Damascus: Elijah traveled to Damascus after his encounter with God at Horeb in order to anoint Hazael as future king of Aram (1 Kings 19:15). Later, Ben-Hadad II, informed of Elisha's presence in Damascus, sent his servant Hazael to inquire whether he would recover from an illness. However, Elisha used the opportunity to reluctantly predict Hazael's rise to kingship in Aram (2 Kings 8:7–15).

When he did rule as king (c. 842–806 BC), Hazael successfully expanded his empire into the territories of Israel and Judah during the reigns of Joram (2 Kings 8:28–29; 9:14–15), Jehu (10:32–33), and Jehoahaz of Israel (13:1–9), as well as Joash of Judah, who paid tribute to Damascus (12:17–18; cf. 2 Chron. 24:23).

After Hazael's death the kingdom of Aram, ruled by his son Ben-Hadad III (also known as Bir-Hadad), no longer remained the dominant power of the region. Jehoash of Israel was able to recapture Israelite territory (2 Kings 13:25), and the Assyrian king Adad-nirari III besieged Damascus and made the king pay tribute (c. 796 BC). Aram's weakened state was also apparent during the reign of Jeroboam II of Israel, who expanded Israel's border back to Damascus (2 Kings 14:28).

Rezin, Aram's last king (c. 740–732 BC), formed a coalition that included Pekah of Israel to fight Tiglath-pileser III of Assyria. When Rezin and Pekah attacked Ahaz of Judah and tried to replace him with a pro-coalition puppet named "Tabeel" (Isa. 7:6), Ahaz appealed to Assyria for help by sending gifts. Tiglath-pileser III complied with Ahaz's requests and attacked Damascus, deporting its inhabitants, putting Rezin to death, and annexing Aram into the Assyrian Empire (2 Kings 16:5–9). Although Damascus, with several surrounding cities, did attempt to rebel against Assyria in 720 BC, Sargon II was able to defeat them. From that point on, Damascus remained under control of the Assyrians, then the Babylonians, and then served as a provincial capital under the Persians.

Damascus is notable in the NT as the city to which Paul (then Saul) was traveling to persecute Christians when he encountered the risen Christ. After his conversion Paul stayed in Damascus until he had to escape the city by night because Jews were plotting to kill him (Acts 9:1–27; 22:3–16; 26:12–23; 2 Cor. 11:32–33). Paul also visited Damascus after his journey to Arabia (Gal. 1:17).

Dan–**(1)** The fifth of Jacob's twelve sons, and the namesake of one of Israel's twelve tribes, Dan was the first son of Bilhah, servant to Rachel.

(2) The city of Dan, originally known as Laish. After attacking the people of Laish (Leshem) and destroying the city, the Danites rebuilt it, settled there, and named it "Dan" after their forefather (Judg. 18:27–29; cf. Josh. 19:40–48).

Dan, Tribe of–One of the twelve tribes of Israel, the descendants of the fifth of Jacob's twelve sons, Dan, whose mother was Bilhah, Rachel's servant. Although Dan's early history included the notable Oholiab, a chief craftsman of the sanctuary built under the direction of Moses (Exod. 31:6; 35:34; 36:1, 2; 38:23), it was otherwise unremarkable.

Daniel–*See* Daniel, Book of.

Daniel, Book of–The book of Daniel contains gripping stories and complex visions of the end of history. While the former are easy to follow and provide clear moral lessons to readers, the latter are quite difficult to interpret. The book is set in a time when the people of God were living under the thumb of powerful pagan nations, and though varied in genre with six stories and four visions, the basic message of the book of Daniel is clear and repeated: in spite of present difficulties, God is in control and will have the victory. The book intends to instill in its readers a sense of calmness in the midst of crisis: although persecuted and/or living in a culture toxic to their faith, not only can they survive but they can also thrive.

Daric–Gold coin introduced by the Persian king Darius I (r. 521–486 BC), successor of Cyrus. Under Persia's influence, the daric is likely the first coin that Jews used. In 1 Chron. 29:7 darics are mentioned with respect to the funding of the first temple, thus indicating the Persian setting of Chronicles. According to Ezra 8:27, the twenty gold bowls of the second temple were valued at one thousand darics.

Darius–**(1)** Darius the Mede. He appears in the book of Daniel. Belshazzar, king of the Babylonians, was killed (we are not told how) after seeing the famous writing on the wall and exalting Daniel for interpreting the words (5:1–29). During his reign, Darius installed 120 satraps, who were accountable to three administrators, one of whom was Daniel. Daniel's success made the satraps and other administrators jealous, and they incited Darius to issue an edict that anyone praying to anyone other than Darius over a thirty-day period would be thrown into the lions' den. Upon hearing the decree, Daniel prayed openly and was arrested, which distressed Darius. After Daniel's miraculous deliverance, Daniel's accusers and their families were thrown into the lions' den, with deadly results, but Daniel prospered (6:1–28).

(2) Darius I (r. 521–486 BC), also known as Darius the Great. His rise to power is debated among historians, in part because the principal historical source is his own writing. He is the king under whom the temple was rebuilt (Ezra 4–6; Haggai; Zech. 1–8).

(3) Darius the Persian. He is mentioned in the OT only in Neh. 12:22. His identity is debated. He is considered to be either Darius III Codamannus (r. 336–331 BC) or Darius II Nothus (r. 423–404 BC).

Dathan–A descendant of Reuben through Eliab who, along with his brother Abiram, rebelled against Moses and Aaron with Korah son of Izhar. In one of the more memorable events of Israelite history, God executed judgment on Korah, Dathan, and Abiram by causing the earth to open up and swallow them and their families alive (Num. 16:1–35; 26:9–10; cf. Ps. 106:17).

David–The second king of Israel (r. 1010–970 BC), founder of a dynasty that continued with his son Solomon (r. 970–931 BC), who ruled all of Israel; subsequently the remaining "sons of David" ruled the southern kingdom, Judah, until 586 BC.

Human kingship is a late development in Israel, but a number of ancient texts anticipate the establishment of the institution (Gen. 17:6; Deut. 17:14–20) and specifically the rise of a king from Judah (Gen. 49:8–12; Num. 24:17). Thus, it is surprising that the first king of Israel is not from Judah, but from Benjamin. When the people ask Samuel for a king, he anoints Saul (1 Sam. 8–12), who proves to be a tremendous disappointment. He forfeits the establishment of his dynasty when he shows a lack of confidence in God by rashly offering prebattle sacrifices (13:13–14). God then rejects Saul as king because he does not execute God's full judgment against the Amalekites as he knows he should (15:23).

Eventually Saul's moment of judgment comes. Saul's final battle is against the Philistines, the major foreign force still inside the borders of the promised land. Both Saul and Jonathan meet their end on Mount Gilboa, and David sings songs that express his sadness over their deaths (1 Sam. 31–2 Sam. 1).

Even with Saul out of the way, David's rise to kingship is not easy. He is immediately crowned king of Judah (2 Sam. 2:1–7), but the northern tribes choose to follow Ish-Bosheth, the son of Saul. War erupts between the two kingdoms. Eventually, though, the powerful general Abner abandons his support of Saul's son, sealing the end of that dynasty. Ish-Bosheth is killed by his own men, and soon David becomes king over all Israel (5:1–5).

David's kingship leads to significant victories that, in essence, complete the conquest of Canaan by finally subduing all the internal enemies. His men take the city of Jerusalem from the Jebusites, and he makes it his capital (2 Sam. 5:6–16). He also defeats the Philistines, who have been a thorn in the side of Israel for years (2 Sam. 5:17–25; for other victories, see 8:1–14). In celebration, David brings the ark of the covenant to Jerusalem (2 Sam. 6).

The David narrative reaches its apex when God enters into a covenant with him that establishes his dynasty (2 Sam. 7; 1 Chron. 17). After David dies, his son will succeed him, and indeed his dynasty lasts for many hundreds of years (see below).

David is a good king, but not a perfect king. A turning point in his reign comes in 2 Sam. 11. Up to this point, David has been content with what God has given him. He does not grasp for anything that does not belong to him. However, when he sees the beautiful Bathsheba bathing, he sends messengers to bring her to his house, where the two have sexual intercourse and she becomes pregnant. In an attempt to conceal this sin of adultery, he orders the death of her husband, Uriah the Hittite. Thus, he adds the crime of murder to that of adultery.

David thinks that the sin is secret, but nothing is hidden from God, who sends his prophet Nathan to confront David (2 Sam. 12; cf. Ps. 51). The difference between Saul and David is not that the latter is perfect but rather that David, as opposed to Saul, repents when he sins. Thus, God allows his reign to continue. Even so, David feels the consequences of his sin. First, the son that Bathsheba bears from her illicit union with David is struck with illness and dies. And ever afterward, David's family life is troubled, with great impact on the political life of Israel. Son is pitted against son (Amnon and Absalom [2 Sam. 13]), as well as son against father (Absalom and David [2 Sam. 15–18]). Absalom temporarily deposes his father from the throne, but David eventually regains the kingship, though at the cost of the heartbreaking loss of his son.

Even at the very end, there is conflict within David's house. When David has grown old, another son, Adonijah, attempts to take the throne, with support from powerful people such as Joab and Abiathar. At the instigation of Bathsheba and Nathan, however, David places the son of his choosing, Solomon, on the throne (1 Kings 1). David then dies after a reign of forty-one years, seven in Hebron and the rest over all Israel (1 Kings 2:10–12).

David's greatest legacy is the dynasty that bears his name. Beginning with Solomon, however, his successors do not continue his spiritual legacy. Although a number of kings do some good, only Hezekiah (r. 727–698 BC) and Josiah (r. 639–609 BC) are given unqualified approval. Eventually, the Davidic rule comes to an end in Jerusalem at the hands of the Babylonians (586 BC). But God is not done with his redemptive purposes, and his promise to David is that he will have a ruler on the throne "forever" (2 Sam. 7:16). The NT recognizes that Jesus Christ is the fulfillment of this promise. He is the greater son of David, the one who is the Christ or Messiah, the anointed king. Jesus is the one who reigns forever in heaven. The life and the rule of David foreshadow the messianic rule of Jesus Christ.

Day of Atonement–*See* Festivals.

Day of the Lord–The "day of the Lord" is used to refer to the coming time when God will intervene powerfully and decisively in human history to bring about his promised plan.

Included in this "day" are several significant prophetic actions by God. First, the imminent judgments on Israel and Judah by the hand of the Assyrians and the Babylonians are included in the "day of the Lord" (Isa. 3:18–4:1; Amos 5:18–20). Likewise, merged into the "day of the Lord" is God's judgment on the foreign nations that conspired against Israel and Judah (Isa. 13:1–22; Obad. 15). Finally, the prophets will use the phrase "day of the Lord" to refer to that time of glorious future restoration and blessing that God will establish for both Israel/Judah and for the nations (Isa. 11:10–12; Joel 3:14–18). In this final context the "day of the Lord" is often tightly interconnected with the messianic promise.

In the NT, the phrase "day of the Lord" (Gk. *hēmera tou kyriou*) is used in much the same manner as in the OT. Some aspects of the day of the Lord were clearly fulfilled by the first coming of Christ. For example, the OT prophet Joel prophesies that on the day of the Lord, God will pour out his Spirit on all kinds of people (Joel 2:28–31), a prophecy that found fulfillment on the day of Pentecost (Acts 2:17–21). So the OT messianic prophecies connected to the day of the Lord sometimes find fulfillment in events surrounding Christ's first coming (as seen in the NT), while some await his future, second coming.

Deacon–*See* Offices in the New Testament.

Dead Sea–The large salt lake to the south of the Jordan River. The Bible refers to this lake as the Salt Sea (Num. 34:12 ESV), Sea of the Arabah (Josh. 3:16), and Eastern Sea (Ezek. 47:18), but not the Dead Sea. The Dead Sea is forty-two miles long and eleven miles wide. Located in the depths of the Jordan Rift Valley, the shore of the Dead Sea is the lowest point on earth, about 1,385 feet below sea level, and its waters are the second saltiest on earth. Because of the high salt content, nothing lives in the Dead Sea except microscopic organisms. Nevertheless, Ezekiel prophesied that its waters will be fresh and teeming with life (47:8–10). The Dead Sea is fed by the Jordan River, wadis such as the Arnon and the Zered, and springs such as En Gedi, but water escapes only through evaporation.

Dead Sea Scrolls–The Dead Sea Scrolls (DSS) were first discovered in 1947 by a Bedouin shepherd in a cave near Khirbet Qumran. Over the next several years, ten other caves were found by Bedouins (Caves 4, 11) and archaeologists (Caves 2, 3, 5, 6, 7, 8, 9, 10). The caves are numbered according to the order in which they were found: Cave 1 was found first, Cave 11 last. The scrolls are mostly written in Hebrew, but there are also a number in Aramaic and a few in Greek. There are thousands of fragments of over nine hundred scrolls. Some of the scrolls are virtually complete, while others are in tiny fragments smaller than a postage stamp.

The scrolls are our earliest manuscript witness to both the Hebrew OT and the Greek OT. They give us a glimpse into the beliefs of a Jewish sect thought to be composed of members of the Jewish party known as the Essenes and help us to understand the development of the Hebrew language.

Deborah–**(1)** The fourth judge of Israel, whose story is told in Judg. 4:1–5:31. While the period of judges was a time of ever-increasing moral darkness and spiritual confusion, Deborah was a paragon of virtue, wisdom, and piety. Her interaction with the military commander Barak, however, illustrates the problems of this time period.

(2) Rebekah's nurse, who died upon Jacob's return to Bethel. She was buried beneath an oak tree near Bethel (Gen. 35:8).

Decapolis–A federation of ten Greco-Roman city-states primarily situated east and south of the Sea of Galilee. The Decapolis was established by Pompey in 64 BC during the course of his invasion of Syria and Judea. It was to serve as a league for trade and defense.

Decapolites were among those who followed Jesus (Matt. 4:25). His healing of the deaf man by use of his own saliva also took place in this region (Mark 7:31–37). Although it is not explicitly mentioned, the Decapolis could be the "distant country" ("distant region" is a better translation) of the prodigal son (Luke 15:13–16). However, Jesus' most significant encounter in the Decapolis is his healing of the Gadarene demoniac (Matt. 8:28–34; Mark 5:1–20; Luke 8:26–39).

Dedication, Feast of–*See* Festivals.

Delilah–A non-Israelite woman, probably Philistine, who is best known for her role in the deception of her lover, Samson (Judg. 16:4). Enticed by the Philistine rulers' monetary bribe, Delilah is enlisted to find out the secret of Samson's strength. After lying three times, Samson succumbs to Delilah's constant nagging and reveals the truth: cutting off his hair would break his Nazirite vow, rendering him powerless. As a result, Samson is delivered, bald and bound, into the hands of the Philistines by Delilah, whose betrayal ultimately leads to Samson's final act, resulting in his own death along with many Philistines (Judg. 16:5–30).

Deliverance, Deliverer–Deliverance provides relief or escape from a detrimental situation or the prospect of adverse circumstances. Deliverance may come from God or humans and may be from physical temporal distress or spiritual in nature.

The principal example of deliverance in the OT is the exodus, God's deliverance of Israel from Egypt. The NT continues the exodus theme in that Jesus' death and resurrection, the foundation for salvation, coincide with the celebration of Passover. This constitutes deliverance in that all humanity is in slavery to the power of sin and subject to the penalty of death. Jesus' death and resurrection provide the possibility of deliverance, usually called "salvation," from the power of sin and death (1 Cor. 15:51–57; Gal. 1:4; Col. 1:13; 1 Thess. 1:10).

Throughout the Bible, God provides deliverers and is a deliverer (Judg. 3:15; 2 Sam. 22:2; 2 Kings 13:5; Ps. 40:17). The NT prefers the term "Savior," applying it to God the Father and to Jesus Christ.

Demas–A Gentile companion of Paul who sent greetings in Col. 4:14; Philem. 24. Paul refers to him as a "fellow worker" in Philem. 24; however, in 2 Tim. 4:10 Paul says that Demas deserted him because he "loved this world."

Demetrius–**(1)** A silversmith in Ephesus whose livelihood came from making "silver shrines" of the goddess Artemis (Acts 19:23–41). Worried that Paul's preaching would end his business and that of his fellow craftsmen, Demetrius stirred a local crowd into frenzied support of Artemis. As a result, Paul's missionary companions Gaius and Aristarchus were seized by the crowd and taken into the local theater. Calm came only with the intervention of the city clerk, who suggested that Paul had not actually spoken against Artemis, and that the proper place for Demetrius to air his grievances was a court. **(2)** In 3 John, a Christian of good repute in the church who was commended to the recipients of the letter with high praise (v. 12).

Demon–*See* Devil, Demons.

Demonic Possession–*See* Devil, Demons.

Denarius–A Roman silver coin that was the pay for a day's labor as well as the annual temple tax (see Matt. 22:15–22; Mark 12:13–17; Luke 20:20–26).

Derbe–*See* Asia Minor, Cities of.

Desert–*See* Wilderness.

Deuteronomy, Book of–Deuteronomy concludes the Torah. It is the fifth scroll or chapter of the work traditionally ascribed to Moses. Its title means "the second law." The name is appropriate in view of the fact that in it Moses takes a final opportunity, before the people go into the promised land and he ascends Mount Nebo to die, to speak to the people about their obligations before God. Many of the laws of the book, most notably the Ten Commandments (cf. Deut. 5 with Exod. 20), may be found in an earlier form elsewhere in the Torah, but there are many new laws as well. In essence, this final sermon by Moses takes the form of a covenant by which the people of God reaffirm their relationship to Yahweh.

The richness of Deuteronomy's message makes it hard to summarize the book. Yet behind the concept of a covenant/treaty stands the metaphor of God as a great king over his servant people. The various parts of the covenant feed into this idea. The preamble introduces the parties: God and Israel. Moses mediates the covenant between the two. The historical prologue then narrates the history of the relationship up to the present. The purpose is to make explicit how gracious the king has been toward his people in the past. This history provides the background for the next and longest section in Deuteronomy, the law. God has established this relationship with Israel by grace, and Israel should respond by obeying his commands. Law naturally leads to the curses and the blessings. If the Israelites obey, they will experience God's blessing, but if they disobey, they will feel his curse. Since the treaty/covenant is a legal document, there are witnesses, who will observe the relationship and, if Israel is disobedient, will confirm the justice of the judgment. This last section simply looks to the future maintenance of the covenant.

D

The Deuteronomic covenant is a reaffirmation of the covenant formulated at Sinai (Exod. 19–24), and as such it emphasizes the law. This law casts its long shadow over much of the biblical material that comes after Deuteronomy. For instance, the history that follows (Joshua, Judges, Samuel, and Kings, in contrast to Chronicles) seems to look at the history of Israel through the lens of the distinctively Deuteronomic law. Virtually every king is evaluated as to whether he keeps the law of centralization (a law, by the way, not found in earlier collections [Deut. 12]). Furthermore, some prophets (e.g., Jeremiah) bring their message of judgment specifically because the Israelites have broken the law of the covenant and therefore deserve the curses.

Thus, the significance of Deuteronomy is hard to overestimate. It is the capstone of the Pentateuch, and it informs the theology of much of the OT that follows.

Devil, Demons–In Gen. 3 the serpent entices humankind to sin. Not until Rev. 12:9 are we told explicitly that the serpent is Satan.

In the OT, "evil spirit" may be a heavenly being sent by God (1 Sam. 16:14–23; 18:10; 19:9; cf. 1 Kings 22:22–23). The OT engages in extensive rebuke of the superstitions of the surrounding nations that included belief in demons (Deut. 32:17; Ps. 106:37; perhaps Isa. 13:21; cf. Rev. 18:2).

Jesus' encounter with the devil in the wilderness recalls Adam and Eve's encounter with the serpent in Eden. The setting, significantly, is now a wasteland. The second man to walk the earth with no sin claims the right to take back the dominion that Adam passed to the serpent. Jesus can have the whole world (without the cross) if only he will submit to the devil's rule (Luke 4:5–7). Jesus rejects the offer. Later, he sees Satan's fall from heaven to earth (Luke 10:18; cf. Rev. 12:5–12). Whereas once the devil had access to God's courtroom, now his case is lost. His only recourse is murderous persecution. Between the ascension of the Son of Man (Acts 1:9) and the final judgment, this is understood to be the experience of Christ's people (Dan. 7:25; Rev. 12:17; cf. 1 Pet. 5:8).

Whereas the OT provides sparse information about Satan and his angels/demons, the NT opens with an intensity of activity. Demons are also called "evil spirits," and they are associated with physical illness, madness, and fortune-telling. In Acts 17:22 Paul describes his pagan Athenian listeners as "demon-fearers" (NIV: "religious"). Jesus' miracles demonstrate his lordship over Satan's regime as the demons flee in terror before him (Mark 1:23–26; 5:1–15). According to Paul, Christians are temples of the Holy Spirit (1 Cor. 6:19), and John urges believers to "test the spirits to see whether they are from God" (1 John 4:1), assuring them that they need not fear Satan or his forces, "because the one who is in you is greater than the one who is in the world." (1 John 4:4). On judgment day Satan will be cast into the lake of fire (Rev. 20:14–15) along with all of God's enemies.

Didrachma–The two-drachma (half-shekel) temple tax required annually of all Jewish males (Matt. 17:24–27).

Didymus–Surname of the apostle Thomas, meaning "twin." The term occurs only in the Gospel of John (11:16; 20:24; 21:2). "Didymus" is the Greek equivalent of the Aramaic "Thomas," which also means "twin."

Dinah–The daughter of Jacob and Leah (Gen. 30:21). Dinah was raped by Shechem in the Canaanite city of Shechem (Gen. 34). Dinah's action prior to the assault—leaving home to visit the Canaanite women—appears innocent but, in context, could be understood as improper. Her defilement led to the slaughter of the male residents of Shechem by Jacob's sons Simeon and Levi.

Diotrephes–An unruly church member rebuked by John for his malicious behavior and rejection of authority. He is assumed to be a powerful leader in the church, based on his authoritarian actions of excommunicating fellow Christians (3 John 9–10).

Disciple–The Greek term for "disciple," *mathētēs*, means "student." Like other rabbis and religious figures of the time, Jesus taught a group of such students (Matt. 9:14; 22:16; Mark 2:16; John 1:35; 4:1). The forms of address that Jesus' disciples used for him reflect the nature of the relationship: "rabbi" (Mark 9:5), "teacher" (Mark 9:38), and "master" (Luke 5:5). In addition to receiving instruction from Jesus, his disciples took care of his physical needs (Matt. 21:1; John 4:8), ate with him (Matt. 9:10; 26:18), performed exorcisms and healings (Matt. 10:1; Luke 10:17), baptized (John 4:2), controlled access to Jesus (Matt. 19:13; John 12:21), and traveled with him (Luke 8:1; John 2:12). On one occasion Jesus visited the house of Peter and healed Peter's mother-in-law (Matt. 8:14), which suggests that although the Gospels do not generally depict the private lives of Jesus or his disciples apart from their public ministry, the relationship among these men did not prevent the disciples from maintaining their own homes, families, and, probably, occupations.

Divided Kingdom–After the reigns of David and Solomon, who had held the Israelite tribes together in a fragile union, the kingdom split into north and south in 931 BC (1 Kings 11–12). The reasons for the division are given as Solomon's unfaithfulness (11:1–13) and his son Rehoboam's unreasonable expectations (12:1–15). Behind this lay a long history of rivalry among the tribes.

Retaining the name "Israel" (also known as "Ephraim"), the ten northern tribes had an unstable succession of kings for two hundred years until 722 BC, when the Assyrians brought the kingdom to an end with their deportation and resettlement program.

The southern kingdom of Judah (with the much weaker tribe of Benjamin) retained a Davidic line of kings until their removal and the destruction of the capital, Jerusalem, by the Babylonians in 586 BC.

Diviners' Tree–A notable tree used in pagan divination practices, visible from the entrance to the city of Shechem (Judg. 9:37). This may be the tree near which Abram built an altar after receiving God's promise regarding the surrounding land (Gen. 12:6–7). This may also be the tree under which Jacob buried his household's foreign gods and earrings (Gen. 35:4). These possible references cannot be verified.

Divorce–*See* Family.

Doeg–An Edomite, Saul's chief shepherd (though this may be a military title). Doeg was at the sanctuary at Nob when David arrived while fleeing Saul, and he saw Ahimelek provide David with bread and Goliath's sword (1 Sam. 21:6–9). Saul later complained of a conspiracy among his servants, so Doeg claimed that he also had seen Ahimelek inquire of Yahweh for David (1 Sam. 22:7–10). Ahimelek was condemned by Saul for this, and when no one else would act, Doeg executed him and the other priests from Nob (1 Sam. 22:16–19).

D

Dor–A port city on the Mediterranean coast located fourteen miles south of Haifa. Apparently settled around 2000 BC, it functioned as a major port for the Canaanites. The city, also called "Naphoth Dor," was located within the tribal allotment of Manasseh at the time of the Israelite conquest (Josh. 17:11). The Israelites defeated the king of Dor in battle during the conquest (Josh. 11:1–9; 12:23) but could not conquer and occupy the city at that time (Judg. 1:27). By the time of Solomon, Dor was identified as the home of the governor of Solomon's fourth administrative district (1 Kings 4:11), suggesting that David likely conquered the port during his earlier expansion. Dor probably was the primary port of the northern kingdom during the divided monarchy and served as the capital of the later Assyrian province of the same name. It continued as a significant port until the seventh century AD.

Dorcas–A benevolent seamstress in Joppa, characterized by her selfless deeds and described as a disciple (Acts 9:36). While Peter was in the nearby town of Lydda, Dorcas, or Tabitha (Aramaic), became ill and died. After burial preparations were performed on the body, two men went and asked Peter to heal Dorcas. He complied, traveled to Joppa, and raised her from the dead. Many people followed Jesus Christ because of this miracle (Acts 9:36–42).

Dothan–The Dothan Valley, at the southeastern end of the Carmel range, provided a vital connection between major coastal and Transjordanian routes. When Jacob sent Joseph to search for his brothers, in God's providence, he found them at Dothan. They sold him to the caravan of Midianite/Ishmaelite spice traders who "just happened" to be passing by en route to Egypt (Gen. 37:12–36). The international implications of Dothan's location are also evident in 2 Kings 6:8–23. Because Elisha was providing military information to the king of Israel, the king of Aram sent an army to surround Dothan, within the territory of Israel and not far from the capital of Samaria, in order to capture Elisha. They did not succeed, however, and Elisha's fearful servant was allowed to see the hills around the city full of horses and chariots of fire.

Dove–The rock dove was domesticated throughout the ancient Near East and used for carrying messages long before Roman times. It breeds prolifically, and its homing instinct brings it swiftly back to its dovecote (Isa. 60:8; Hos. 11:11) or the buildings or crevices where it nests (Jer. 48:28). Israel also has three species of turtledove (Heb. *tor*; Gk. *trygōn*), one being a summer migrant (Song 2:12; Jer. 8:7).

In Israel, the dove was considered clean for food and designated for sacrifice, often as a poor person's substitute for a lamb (Gen. 15:9; Lev. 1:14; 5:7, 11; 12:6, 8; 14:22, 30; 15:14, 29; Num. 6:10; Matt. 21:12; Mark 11:15; Luke 2:24; John 2:14, 16). The dove is first mentioned in Scripture when Noah sends out a dove from the ark (Gen. 8:8–12). In the NT, the dove is an image of purity (Matt. 10:16) and also symbolizes the Holy Spirit (Matt. 3:16; Mark 1:10; Luke 3:22; John 1:32), but in the Song of Songs, where the beloved, and in particular the beloved's eyes, are likened to doves (1:15; 2:14; 4:1; 5:2, 12; 6:9), it may also connote fertility.

The dove is also, however, mournful (Isa. 38:14; 59:11; Ezek. 7:16; Nah. 2:7), vulnerable (Ps. 74:19), and easily deceived (Hos. 7:11). When frightened, it takes flight to lonely places (Ps. 55:6; Isa. 60:8), which perhaps adds interest to the fact that Jonah's name literally means "dove."

Drachma–A drachma was originally a weight but later a coin. In Ezra 2 and Neh. 7 (between 450 BC and 350 BC), a drachma (NIV: "daric") is a standard weight of money, often identified with the ¼ troy ounce gold daric coin. In the NT, the drachma is a silver coin (Luke 15:8–9; cf. Josephus, *J.W.* 1.308) that was a typical day's wage for a laborer (Matt. 20:2; NIV: "denarius"). In the reigns of Augustus and Tiberius (27 BC–AD 37), drachma coins weighed 1/7 to 1/9 troy ounce, close to a silver denarius (Pliny the Elder, *Nat.* 21.109).

Dross–The scum that forms during the process of smelting metals, particularly silver (Prov. 25:4). It often is used figuratively for something that is impure or worthless. The psalmist compares "the wicked of the earth" to dross (Ps. 119:119).

Drusilla–Daughter of Agrippa I; great-granddaughter of Herod the Great; younger sister of Agrippa II and Bernice. According to Josephus (*Ant.* 20.137–47), Drusilla was stunningly beautiful, and she was envied by Bernice. Drusilla first wed Azizus, king of Emesa, for political reasons. Soon, however, Felix, the Roman governor of Judea, encountered Drusilla and fell in love with her. He approached her through his friend Simon, persuading her to transgress Jewish law, leave her husband, and marry him.

Acts 24:24 identifies Drusilla specifically as Felix's "Jewish" wife, which some interpret as communicating disapproval. She bore Felix one son, Agrippa, who was killed in AD 79 during the eruption of Vesuvius.

Dung Gate–*See* Gates of Jerusalem and the Temple.

Dura–Nebuchadnezzar commanded the worship of a golden statue on the "plain of Dura" in the province of Babylon (Dan. 3:1). Of numerous locations named similarly in the vicinity, none has been positively identified with this site. Further, *dura'*, an Aramaic term, probably means "fortification" and may refer to part of Babylon or its walls.

Dwarf–A person of unusually short stature. OT Levitical law considers dwarfs to be defective persons and thus prohibits them from drawing near the temple curtain or altar. Dwarfs are also prohibited from making food offerings to God. Dwarfs are, however, permitted to eat of the holy food (Lev. 21:20–22). Attention should be drawn to the fact, though, that some believe this Hebrew word refers to a "withered" part of the body, not a dwarf.

E

Eagle–The word "eagle" may represent more than one species of eagle and vulture, particularly the griffon vulture. A bird of prey, the eagle is classed among the unclean birds in the OT (Lev. 11:13). The eagle was considered one of the marvels of the world (Prov. 30:19), proverbial for its speed and power (Deut. 28:49; 2 Sam. 1:23; Ezek. 17:3), its inaccessibility among the high rocks (Job 39:27; Jer. 49:16), and its tutelage and protection of its young (Deut. 32:11). The eagle serves to illustrate the renewed strength of those whose hope is in God (Ps. 103:5; Isa. 40:31).

In Exod. 19:4 God brings his royal-priestly people to himself at Mount Sinai "on eagles' wings," while in Deut. 32:10–11 the eagle illustrates the divine protection of Israel. Because of its proverbial attributes and associations, the eagle is included in a number of visionary images (Ezek. 1:10; Dan. 7:4; Rev. 4:7; 8:13).

Earth, Land–Israel shared the cosmology of its ancient Near Eastern neighbors. This worldview understood the earth as a "disk" upon the primeval waters (Job 38:13; Isa. 40:22), with the earth having four rims or "corners" (Ps. 135:7; Isa. 11:12). These rims were sealed at the horizon to prevent the influx of cosmic waters. God speaks to Job about the dawn grasping the edges of the earth and shaking the evil people out of it (Job 38:12–13).

Israel's promised land was built on the sanctuary prototype of Eden (Gen. 13:10; Deut. 6:3; 31:20); both were defined by divine blessing, fertility, legal instruction, secure boundaries, and were orienting points for the world. Canaan was Israel's new paradise, "flowing with milk and honey" (Exod. 3:8; Num. 13:27). Conversely, the lack of fertile land was tantamount to insecurity and judgment. As Eden illustrated for Israel, any rupture of relationship with God brought alienation between humans, God, and the land; this could ultimately bring exile, as an ethically nauseated land "vomits" people out (Lev. 18:25, 28; 20:22; see also Deut. 4; 30).

For Israel, land involved both God's covenant promise (Gen. 15:18–21; 35:9–12) and the nation's faithful obedience (Gen. 17:1; Exod. 19:5; 1 Kings 2:1–4). Yahweh was the earth's Lord (Ps. 97:5), Judge (Gen. 18:25), and King (Ps. 47:2, 7). Both owner and giver, he was the supreme landlord, who gifted the land to Israel (Exod. 19:5; Lev. 25:23; Josh. 22:19; Ps. 24:1). The land was God's "inheritance" to give (1 Sam. 26:19; 2 Sam. 14:16; Ps. 79:1; Jer. 2:7). The Levites, however, did not receive an allotment of land as did the other tribes, since God was their "portion" (Num. 18:20; Ps. 73:26). Israel's obedience was necessary both to enter and to occupy the land (Deut. 8:1–3; 11:8–9; 21:1; 27:1–3). Ironically, the earth swallowed rebellious Israelites when they accused Moses of bringing them "up out of a land flowing with milk and honey" (Num. 16:13). As the conquest shows, however, no tribe was completely obedient, taking its full "inheritance" (Josh. 13:1).

Ebal–A mountain in north-central Israel overshadowing the city of Shechem on the north. Mount Ebal and its counterpart Mount Gerizim on the south form a natural amphitheater, eminently suitable for the covenantal ceremony commanded by Moses (Deut. 11:29; 27:1–13) and carried out by Joshua and the Israelites (Josh. 8:30–35). *See also* Gerizim.

Ebed-Melek–A Cushite official, probably a military officer, in Jerusalem during the Babylonian siege (587–586 BC). The prophet Jeremiah is arrested and placed into

E

a dungeon/pit with King Zedekiah's permission (Jer. 38:1–13). Ebed-Melek confronts the king and obtains permission to remove Jeremiah from this pit, probably saving his life. God commends Ebed-Melek, declaring that Ebed-Melek will be delivered because he trusted in God (Jer. 39:15–18).

Ebenezer–Ebenezer usually is associated with a symbol of God's help in the past and an encouragement for continued trust. This is based on 1 Sam. 7:12: "Samuel took a stone and set it up between Mizpah and Shen. He named it Ebenezer [lit., 'stone of help'], saying, 'Thus far the Lord has helped us.'" Ebenezer is also an unknown location in western Palestine where Israel had been defeated and subsequently lost the ark of the covenant to the Philistines (1 Sam. 4–5).

Eber–A descendant of Shem, son of Shelah, father of Peleg, and ancestor to Jesus (Gen. 10:21–31; 11:14–17; 1 Chron. 1:18–25; Luke 3:35). As hinted in Gen. 10:21, Eber seems to be the source for the name "Hebrew" for that particular line of Semitic people (a name similarly derived from "Shem").

Ecbatana–Also known as Achmetha (modern Hamadan), located about 160 miles southwest of modern Tehran, Iran. The single reference to Ecbatana in the OT comes in Ezra 6:2, where a document thought to be in Babylon is later found to have been deposited in Ecbatana.

Ecclesiastes, Book of–The book of Ecclesiastes is about the meaning of life. There are two speakers in the book. The main speaker goes by the name Qohelet, which is variously translated as "the Teacher" (NIV, NLT) or "the Preacher" (KJV, ESV). He speaks in the first person ("I Qohelet") from 1:12–12:7, and he describes his search for meaning in pleasure (2:1–11), wisdom (2:12–17), work (2:18–23; 4:4–6), wealth (5:10–6:9), and political power (4:9–12). He concludes that there is no meaning. He believes that death (see reasoning in 2:12–17 for instance), injustice (7:15–22), and the inability to discern the proper time (3:1–15; 9:11–12) renders everything meaningless. Accordingly, he urges everyone to enjoy whatever joy they can find in life (carpe diem!, 2:24–26; 3:12–14; 3:22; 5:18–20; 8:15; 9:7–10).

The other voice is that of an unnamed wise man who is speaking about Qohelet ("He Qohelet"). His comments introduce Qohelet in 1:1–11 and then summarize and evaluate his thought in 12:8–14. He is speaking to his son (12:12) and using Qohelet's ideas as a basis to teach his son an important lesson about life. In brief he tells his son that Qohelet is right to conclude that life is meaningless as long as you stay "under the sun"—that is, approach life apart from a vital relationship with God. In conclusion, though, he urges his son to adopt a perspective different from Qohelet's—namely, to "fear God and keep his commandments" as well as to remember that "God will bring every deed into judgment" (12:13–14).

The book of Ecclesiastes challenges the attempt to find the meaning in life in anything except God himself. Anything else (work, pleasure, money, etc.) is an idol that will only lead to an empty and meaningless life.

Eden–The region within which was situated the primeval garden, the setting of the story of the creation in Gen. 2 and of the fall in Gen. 3. Although numerous attempts have been made to identify its intended location (Turkey, North Africa, the Persian Gulf), the information we can glean from the references to Eden, the rivers that flow from it, and the regions they encompass is insufficient for locating Eden in relation to known geography. It is simply "in the east" (Gen. 2:8).

Eden is portrayed as a mountainous region (Ezek. 28:13–14). Four rivers flow from it: the Pishon and the Gihon, which are unknown, and the Tigris and the Euphrates in Mesopotamia (Gen. 2:10–14). This may be compared with other ancient Near Eastern portrayals of rivers flowing from the mountain dwelling of the gods.

The name "Eden" may be connected with a Hebrew word for "luxury, delight," though another suggestion is that it derives from a Sumerian word meaning "steppe, plain." The garden in Eden is also referred to as the "garden of the Lord" (Gen. 13:10; Isa. 51:3) or the "garden of God" (Ezek. 28:13; 31:8–9), or (in a visionary reappearance) as "paradise," from a Persian word for "garden" (Rev. 2:7).

The garden is depicted as a sanctuary or holy space (Ezek. 28:14) into which humanity is invited on God's terms to act as God's agents. It contains the tree of the knowledge of good and evil and the tree of life (Gen. 2:9).

As a picture of fertility, Eden holds out the prospect of a reversal from a desolate state (Isa. 51:3).

E

Edom–"Edom" denotes Esau (Gen. 25:30; 36:1, 8, 19), or the Edomites collectively (Num. 20:18, 20–21; Amos 1:6, 11; 9:12; Mal. 1:4), or the land occupied by Esau's descendants, formerly the land of Seir (Gen. 32:3; 36:20–21, 30; Num. 24:18). Edom was renowned in Israel for its wisdom (Jer. 49:7; Obad. 8), and the book of Job seems to reflect an Edomite setting.

The region stretched from the Zered Valley to the Gulf of Aqabah (about one hundred miles) and extended to both sides of the Arabah, the great depression connecting the Dead Sea to the Red Sea (Gen. 14:6; Deut. 2:1, 12; Josh. 15:1; Judg. 11:17–18; 1 Kings 9:26). It is a dry, mountainous area with peaks rising to 3,500 feet. Though not a fertile land, it has cultivable areas (Num. 20:14–18). The name is derived from the Semitic root meaning "red, ruddy," perhaps because of the reddish color of the sandstone in that region.

Following the OT, it seems that Esau's descendants migrated to the land of Seir and in time became the dominant group, incorporating the original Horites (Gen. 14:6) and others into their number. Esau had already occupied Edom when Jacob returned from Harran (Gen. 32:3; 36:6–8; Deut. 2:4–5; Josh. 24:4). Tribal chiefs emerged here quite early (Gen. 36:15–19, 40, 43; 1 Chron. 1:51, 54), and the Edomites had kings "before any Israelite king reigned" (Gen. 36:31; 1 Chron. 1:43–51).

We know from the OT that after the exodus Israel was denied permission to travel by the King's Highway (Num. 20:14–21; 21:4; Judg. 11:17–18). Still, Israelites were forbidden to abhor their Edomite brothers (Deut. 23:7–8). Joshua allotted the territory of Judah up to the borders of Edom (Josh. 15:1, 21), but the Israelites were not allowed to encroach on their lands.

Despite the brotherly relationship between Edom and Israel, the biblical evidence shows that the relationship between Edom and Israel was one of continuous hostility from the time of the Israelite kings. King Saul fought the Edomites (1 Sam. 14:47), and David conquered Edom and put garrisons throughout the land (2 Sam. 8:13–14). Edom was subjugated by Israel during the time of David but seems to have regained independence in the eighth century BC.

The prophets of Judah were very bitter against later Edom because of its stance in the destruction of Jerusalem by Babylon (587/586 BC), and they predicted Edom's destruction (e.g., Obadiah). The oracle of Mal. 1:2–4 indicates that by the time of its writing, Edom was in ruin. The archaeological evidence supports the fall of Edom by the end of the sixth century BC, and there is evidence that the Nabateans (an Arabian tribe) forced their way into Edom and replaced the Edomites, many of whom went westward to southern Judea (later Idumea [cf. 1 Macc. 5:3, 65]), while others may have been absorbed by the newcomers. By 312 BC the area around Petra was inhabited by Nabateans.

Edrei–A principal stronghold of Og of Bashan, one of two Transjordanian rulers the Israelites defeated under Moses (Josh. 13:12). Edrei was the site of this battle (Num. 21:33–35; see also Deut. 3:1). Joshua 13:31 describes Edrei and Ashtaroth as "royal cities" of Og and places both in the tribal territory of Manasseh (specifically, of the subtribe of Makir [see Judg. 5:14]). Joshua 19:37 mentions a distinct "fortified city" of Edrei in the territory of Naphtali.

Eglon–The obese Moabite king who, after enlisting the aid of the Ammonites and the Amalekites, defeated Israel and ruled over them for eighteen years. He was assassinated by the Israelite judge Ehud, who deceived Eglon and plunged a small sword into his stomach. Following Eglon's death, Israel defeated the Moabites and ended their oppressive rule (Judg. 3:12–30).

Egypt–Egypt is one of the earliest ancient civilizations. The first development of writing took place simultaneously in both Egypt and ancient Sumer around 3000 BC.

Ancient Sumer and Egypt were river valley cultures. Sumer was located in Mesopotamia (southeast Iraq), Egypt in the Nile Valley (northeast Africa). The Nile Valley was well suited for long-term growth and cultural success for three reasons. First, the annual flooding of the Nile (July to October) brought sediment and nutrients from up river to the fields of the Nile Valley. The water also washed the salts out of the soil. These brought great fertility to the valley and allowed the same fields to be farmed year after year for millennia without exhausting the land. Second, the Nile provided a central highway for transporting people and goods across Egypt, thus facilitating internal trade and communication. Third, Egypt was surrounded by a buffer zone of desert regions to the east, west, and south, which hindered foreign invasion. Ancient Egyptians called the fertile land of the Nile Valley the "black land" and the desert regions the "red land." They also divided the land into "upper" and "lower" Egypt. Upper Egypt (from the first cataract northward to Memphis) was in the higher southern elevations of the Nile River (the Nile flows from south to north). Lower Egypt was made up of the Nile Delta region. Only a pharaoh who controlled and unified both could take the epithet "king of upper and lower Egypt."

Egypt had an ancient and long history, but the following summary will only address Egypt as it comes into contact with biblical history.

First Intermediate period (2134–2040 BC) and Middle Kingdom (2040–1640 BC). After the death of Pepy II came economic collapse due to drought and falling tax revenues. These led to political collapse, and power was split among many competing factions. This time of instability is known as the First Intermediate period; it ended when the Eleventh Dynasty pharaoh Mentuhotep II reunified Egypt and reestablished a strong central government. It is likely around the time of the end of the First Intermediate period (2134–2040 BC) and the beginning of the Middle Kingdom (2040–1640 BC) that Abraham visited Egypt and later Joseph, Jacob, and his family entered Egypt. The famous Beni Hasan tomb painting of this period shows a caravan of Semitic peoples moving into Egypt, wearing multicolored clothing. In this period the position of vizier (prime minister) grew to prominence. One vizier, Amenemhet, succeeded to the throne of Egypt. Joseph filled the role of vizier in the biblical account (Gen. 41:39–40). Also dating from this period are turquoise mines in the Sinai region that have the earliest known Semitic inscription. Written on the mine walls in Proto-Sinaitic, this inscription may be the earliest alphabetic script in existence.

Second Intermediate period (1640–1550 BC). At the end of the Middle Kingdom, Egypt again fell into a fractured political situation with the decline of the pharaoh's power. A Semitic people, the Hyksos (Egyptian for "foreign rulers" or "shepherd kings"), invaded the Nile Delta region and established their capital at Avaris. The Seventeenth Dynasty continued to rule Upper Egypt in the south while the Hyksos were in power. Although the Israelites were servants of Pharaoh from the beginning (keeping his flocks), they were not enslaved until later. It may have been a Hyksos pharaoh or a New Kingdom pharaoh who enslaved them to hard labor.

New Kingdom (1550–1069 BC). The last king of the Seventeenth (Theban) Dynasty, Kamose, attacked the Hyksos, but it was his successor, Ahmose, who drove them out and reunified Egypt. Ahmose is considered the first pharaoh of the Eighteenth Dynasty. It may have been Ahmose or one of his successors who enslaved the Hebrews. During the first half of the New Kingdom, Egypt was at the height of its power and wealth. During this period Egyptians began to call their king "Pharaoh," meaning "great house." The Eighteenth Dynasty pharaoh Thutmose III and his son Amenhotep II are good candidates for an early-date exodus (c. 1446 BC). A later king of the Eighteenth Dynasty, Akhenaten, moved the capital to Amarna and shifted his allegiance from Amun-Re, the sun god, to sole worship of the god Aton (sun-disk). For this reason, many identify him as the first monotheist. Akhenaten may have made this move in order to defund the temples and priestly orders that had grown very wealthy and powerful over time. His reforms did not last, and the worship of Amun-Re was restored by his successor, Tutankhamen. The Nineteenth Dynasty warrior Ramesses II is the likely pharaoh of a late-date Exodus (c. 1250 BC).

Third Intermediate period (1069–664 BC). This period was a time of weak and divided government, with capitals in the north and the south. Pharaoh Siamun has been conjectured to be King Solomon's father-in-law, who conquered Gezer and gave it to Solomon as a dowry (c. 960 BC; 1 Kings 9:16). Later, Sheshonq (biblical Shishak), a Libyan pharaoh of the Twenty-second Dynasty, came to the throne and campaigned against Solomon's son Rehoboam, plundering Jerusalem in the process (1 Kings 14:25; 2 Chron. 12:2; cf. 1 Kings 11:40). The African Cushite pharaohs of the Twenty-fifth Dynasty (760–664 BC) ruled the north for a little more than a century but failed to defend against the waves of Assyrian conquest in the seventh century BC.

Late Kingdom period (664–525 BC). The Twenty-sixth (Saite) Dynasty (ruling from the Delta city of Sais) reunified Egypt under native Egyptian control. Pharaoh Necho II tried to support a declining Assyria as a buffer against the Babylonian onslaught but was unsuccessful (c. 609 BC). However, in the process Necho killed King Josiah of Judah in battle at Megiddo and placed one of Josiah's sons, Jehoiakim, as a vassal upon the throne of Judah (2 Kings 23:29–35; cf. 2 Chron. 35:20–36:8; Jer. 46:2). After the Babylonian destruction of Judah/Jerusalem (587/586 BC) and the murder of their Jewish governor, Gedaliah, a group of Jewish exiles fled to Egypt. This group forced the prophet Jeremiah to go with them to Egypt (Jer. 40:1–43:7). A small group of Jewish exiles eventually found their way to a tiny island in the upper Nile, Elephantine, where they established a temple and community; there they worked as mercenaries.

Persian period (525–332 BC). Cambyses II, king of Persia and son of Cyrus the Great, conquered Egypt in 525 BC. His successor, Darius I, ruled Egypt benevolently and resumed the construction of temples and canals. However, Egypt revolted against Persian rule several times, ultimately winning independence in 404 BC with the help of Greek allies. The last native Egyptian pharaoh was Nectanebo II, who ruled in 359–343 BC. However, this period of Egyptian independence was short-lived, with Persia reestablishing control in 343 BC.

Hellenistic-Roman period (332–30 BC; 30 BC and beyond). Alexander the Great conquered Egypt in 332 BC. After Alexander's death, his general Ptolemy took control of Egypt and ruled as pharaoh. From Alexander's conquest to the death of Cleopatra, Egyptian rulers were of Greek descent. After Cleopatra's death (30 BC), Rome annexed Egypt into its empire and governed the country until the fall of the Roman Empire. A large contingent of Jews lived and prospered in the Delta city of Alexandria in this period.

EGYPTIAN, THE–Hearing Paul speak Greek, a Roman tribune mistook him for "the Egyptian," who had recently led four thousand terrorists into the wilderness (Acts 21:37–38). The first-century Jewish historian Josephus corroborates the event and adds supplemental detail (*J.W.* 2.261–63; *Ant.* 20.169–72). He claims that the Egyptian was a "false prophet," a messianic "imposter," who deceived an even larger body of people ("thirty thousand" [*J.W.* 2.261] or a "multitude of the common people" [*Ant.* 20.169]). Like the exodus generation, these people wandered in the wilderness, before eventually gathering on the Mount of Olives to besiege Jerusalem. The Egyptian claimed that the city's walls would fall at his command. However, the Roman procurator Felix attacked preemptively. Although the Egyptian escaped, most of his followers were killed or imprisoned.

EHUD–The second judge, or deliverer, of Israel appointed by God to relieve his people from foreign oppression—in this case, the Moabites. In Judg. 3:15 Ehud, a Benjamite, is said to be left-handed. Ehud is sent by the Israelites to present a tribute to Eglon, the obese king of Moab. Following the presentation, however, Ehud deceives Eglon by claiming that he has a secret message for him, and when alone, Ehud assassinates the king with a small sword. Ehud escapes unnoticed and rallies Israel to defeat the Moabites (Judg. 3:5–4:1).

EKRON–One of the five chief cities of the Philistines, listed as part of the territory of Judah but not taken by Israel at the time of the distribution of the land to tribes (Josh. 13:3; 15:11, 45–46; Judg. 1:18), though it bordered Dan (Josh. 19:43).

Upon the defeat of Hophni and Phinehas, the ark of the covenant was taken to the temple of Dagon in Ashdod. After God demonstrated his displeasure, the Philistines sent the ark to Ekron, where God greatly afflicted the people until they sent it back to Israel (1 Sam. 5).

Ekron served as the entry point from Israel to Philistia, as witnesses the account of the pursuit of the Philistine army to the "gates of Ekron" (1 Sam. 17:52) after David defeated Goliath.

In 2 Kings 1, King Ahaziah is accused of worshiping Baal-Zebub, the god of Ekron. The prophets pronounced oracles announcing the destruction of this city (Jer. 25:20; Amos 1:8; Zeph. 2:4; Zech. 9:5, 7).

ELAH–**(1)** The wicked son and successor of Baasha. Elah ruled Israel for two years (1 Kings 16:6–14). **(2)** A valley in the Judean foothills where David killed Goliath (1 Sam. 17), some twelve miles west-southwest of Bethlehem. As one of several fertile valleys in this region between the Philistines on the coastal plain and the Israelites in the hill country, the Elah Valley was a natural battleground between the two peoples.

ELAM–Elam is one of the oldest of the ancient civilizations, lasting from 2700 BC to

E

539 BC. Ancient Elam originally consisted of kingdoms on the Iranian Plateau, centered in Anshan. Later, Susa in the Khuzistan lowlands became prominent in documentation of the Elamite civilization.

Elam appears in various books of the Bible (e.g., Ezra 4:9; Isa. 11:11; 21:2; 22:6; Jer. 25:25; 49:34–39; Ezek. 32:24; Dan. 8:2; Acts 2:9), including Gen. 14, where Kedorlaomer, king of Elam, is mentioned as one of the kings of the east who defeated the five kings of Sodom and Gomorrah. During the Achaemenid period, in which the traits of Elamite civilization were still strong, "Elam" was used as a general reference to the Persian province on the Iranian plateau (e.g., Dan. 8:2: "I saw myself in the citadel of Susa in the province of Elam"). In the NT era, Elam, albeit long gone from history, occupied an established place in the view of world history seen as a sequence of world empires (cf. Acts 2:9).

Elath–This fortified harbor town, near Ezion Geber at the northern extremity of the Gulf of Aqabah (modern Aqabah), was a way station on the important trade routes to southern Arabia, Africa, and India. It is often identified with El Paran in Gen. 14:6.

Due to its importance for the profitable trade with southern Arabia and beyond, control over Elath was a prized object for Israel, Edom, and other rival powers. King Solomon, for instance, built Ezion Geber close to Elath and dispatched the lucrative "ships of Tarshish" from there with the help of Phoenician sailors (1 Kings 9:26–28; cf. Ps. 48:7). It is possible that the intention of Shishak's campaign in the Negev was to cut off these trade activities, since the Egyptians were the only competitors to Israel's shipping on the Gulf of Aqabah. Later Judean kings, such as Jehoshaphat and Uzziah, rebuilt the Red Sea port to resume trade with southern Arabia, although with much less success (2 Chron. 20:36; 26:2). Elath was handed over to the Edomites during the Syro-Ephramite war.

Eldad–One of the seventy elders of Israel appointed to share the burden of leadership with Moses (Num. 11:26–27). He and Medad began to prophesy within the Israelite camp when the Spirit rested upon them, hence validating their appointment as elders of Israel.

Elder–The term "elder" is used variously in Scripture to describe an older man, a person of authority, or an appointed leader in a church office.

Old Testament. The first instance of "elder" in the OT is in Exod. 3:16, where Moses calls the elders of Israel to gather together. These men, seventy in number, most likely were the heads of different families in Israel (Num. 11:16, 24; Deut. 19:12; 21:19). The term "elder" likely indicates both their function as leaders and their age. They were gifted leaders, but they were also wiser because of their experiences in life.

Elders exercised civic and judicial authority in Israel's cities and towns. They made judgments of various kinds, such as disciplining a rebellious son (Deut. 21:18–21), clearing the reputation of a young virgin girl who may have been slandered (22:13–19), and urging obedience to the law and commands of God (27:1).

New Testament. *See* Offices in the New Testament.

Eleazar–The third son of Aaron, who succeeded his father as the second high priest after his older brothers Nadab and Abihu disqualified themselves by offering incense different from that which God commanded (Lev. 10:1–7). Eleazar had assisted his father and Moses against a rebellion of other Levites who wanted equal status with the priestly family of Aaron (Num. 16:36–40). Aaron failed to enter the promised land because he and Moses rebelled against God at the rock of Meribah (Num. 20:1–13). On Mount Hor, and in the presence of Moses, Aaron took off his high priestly garments and put them on his son Eleazar. Eleazar was the high priest during the conquest and, along with Joshua, cast the sacred lots to determine where each tribe should settle (Josh. 14:1–5). Upon Eleazar's death, his son Phinehas succeeded him as high priest.

Election–The choice or selection of a person or group, especially God's determination of who will be saved.

On occasion, the language of being "elect" is used as a description of Christ, or perhaps even a title. Isaiah, in one of his Servant Songs, gives a description that is probably best taken as a veiled reference to Christ in his unique relationship with the Father: "Here is my servant, whom I uphold, my chosen [or 'elect'] one in whom I delight; I will put my Spirit on him, and he will bring justice to the nations" (Isa. 42:1). There is similar usage in the NT, where Jesus is described in 1 Pet. 2:6 (using a quotation from Isa. 28:16): "For in Scripture it says: 'See, I lay a stone in Zion, a chosen [or "elect"] and precious cornerstone, and the one who trusts in him will never be put to shame.'"

Many times the word "elect" is used in Scripture as a synonym for believers. For example, Jesus speaks of the future time when "he will send his angels with a loud trumpet call, and they will gather his elect from the four winds, from one end of the heavens to the other" (Matt. 24:31).

Eli–The chief priest of Israel at the tabernacle at Shiloh toward the end of the period of judges (1 Sam. 1:1–4:22). He is described as both physically and spiritually flabby. He is not evil, just spiritually undiscerning. Also, he fails to discipline his two sons, Hophni and Phinehas, who are wicked. He ends badly when his sons, who are leading the army against the Philistines, are defeated and killed. When he gets the news, Eli falls off a log and breaks his neck. Even so, his descendants continue as priests until the time of David. At that time, though, the prophetic announcement comes to fulfillment, and the priesthood passes from his descendant Abiathar and goes to Zadok (1 Kings 2:27, 35).

Eliakim–Another name for Jehoiakim. *See also* Jehoiakim.

Eliezer–A servant of Abram from Damascus (Gen. 15:2). He probably was Abram's adopted son and potential heir of his household (15:4–5).

Elihu–The son of Barakel who mysteriously appeared and restarted the discussion after Job and his three friends had finished. After listening to his elders, he became angry with Job for justifying himself and with the friends because they had no answer (Job 32:2–5). His lengthy speeches (Job 32:6–37:24), emphasizing God's sovereignty, set up God's final response from the whirlwind.

Elijah–A prophet raised up by God during the reign of Ahab of Israel (ninth century BC) in order to counter fast-rising idolatry fueled by the king and his foreign-born wife, Jezebel.

False worship at this time focused on Baal, a major Canaanite deity who was the god of fertility, having power over dew, rain, lightning, and thunder. Thus, as people turned to Baal for these life-giving forces, God shut up the heavens so there would be no rain in Israel (1 Kings 17:1). God also at this time sent Elijah the Tishbite to confront the king.

Through the performance of miraculous acts, Elijah demonstrated that God was with him. The first such act was multiplying the food supplies of a widow who provided him with food. Even more dramatically, he prayed for the woman's son when the child died, and the dead boy began to breathe again (1 Kings 17:17–24).

Elijah's most dramatic moment came when he confronted Ahab and his many Baal prophets on Mount Carmel (1 Kings 18). Yahweh fought Baal on the latter's terms. The object was whether Yahweh or Baal could throw fire from heaven to light the altar fire. Baal was purportedly a specialist at throwing fire (lightning), and his prophets went first. However, because Baal did not really exist, they failed. When Yahweh's turn came, Elijah increased the stakes by pouring water on the wood. Yahweh, the one true God, threw fire from heaven, which burned the sacrifice, wood, stones, and dirt, and even dried up the water. Soon thereafter, God opened up the skies so that it rained again. Even so, Ahab and then his son Ahaziah (2 Kings 1) continued to worship Baal.

Elijah was a devoted servant of Yahweh. Before Elijah passed from this life, God introduced him to his successor, Elisha. When the end came, he did not die but rather was caught up to heaven (2 Kings 2:1–18)—only the second person reported to leave this life without dying (cf. Enoch in Gen. 5:21–24).

Toward the end of the OT period, the prophet Malachi announced the coming day of the Lord (Mal. 4:5–6). As a precursor to that day, God would send the prophet Elijah as a forerunner. Some people thought that Jesus was Elijah (Matt. 16:14; Mark 6:15; 8:28; Luke 9:8, 19), but Jesus is the one who ushers in the kingdom of God. John the Baptist was his forerunner, and so it was he who is rightly associated with Elijah (Matt. 11:13–14). Indeed, his wilderness lifestyle and ministry echoed those of Elijah. At the Mount of Transfiguration, Elijah appeared to Jesus along with Moses; these two wilderness figures represented the prophets and the law (Matt. 17:1–13; Mark 9:2–13; Luke 9:28–36).

Elimelek–A man from Bethlehem of the tribe of Judah and the husband of Naomi. The story of Ruth begins as if it is about Elimelek, who takes his family to Moab during a famine. When he dies, the focus of the story shifts to Naomi (Ruth 1:1–5).

Eliphaz–One of Job's three friends and interlocutors, identified as a Temanite (Job 2:11). Teman is one of the sons of Esau's son Eliphaz (Gen. 36:11). The participation of Eliphaz in the wisdom discussion of Job is appropriate, as the line of Teman was known elsewhere in the Bible for its sages (Jer. 49:7). Eliphaz is prominent among Job's three friends, and he speaks three times (Job 4–5; 15; 22). God spoke to Eliphaz as a representative of the three friends (42:7).

Elisha–Prophet, coworker of and then successor to Elijah. Both men resisted the Baal worship that infected the northern kingdom during the reign of Ahab and his successors (Ahaziah, Jehoram, Jehu, Jehoahaz, and Jehoash) in the latter half of the ninth and first half of the eighth centuries BC.

Elisha began as a disciple of Elijah, whom God had used to confront Ahab and Jezebel's prophets of Baal on Mount Carmel (1 Kings 18). When Elijah was taken to heaven, Elisha succeeded him (2 Kings 2:19–23). God accredited Elisha as prophet and demonstrated his authority through miracles. Many of the miracles involve water, such as making the bitter water of Jericho drinkable (2 Kings 2:19–23) and raising an ax head from the bottom of the Jordan River (6:1–7). These miracles were implicitly directed at Baal and his supporters, since Baal was thought to be a god who specialized in providing and controlling the waters.

Elisha also demonstrated God's power and compassion with acts such as providing a poor woman with olive oil (2 Kings 4:1–7), curing a Syrian general of leprosy (2 Kings 5), and even raising a child from the dead (4:8–37).

God also told the prophet to anoint Hazael, king of Syria, and Jehu, a military man who usurped the throne of Israel (2 Kings 8:7–15; 9:1–13). God used these men to bring a violent conclusion to those leaders who promoted the worship of Baal.

Elisha's miracles continued even after his death. Some Israelites threw a dead man's body in Elisha's grave, and when it touched Elisha's bones, the man sprang back to life (2 Kings 13:20–21).

Elizabeth–The mother of John the Baptist. She was a descendant of Aaron and the wife of Zechariah (Luke 1:5). She and her husband are described in Luke 1 as righteous but barren in their old age. When Zechariah had the opportunity to serve in the temple and burn incense, an angel prophesied that he and Elizabeth would have a son, and they would name him "John." Elizabeth was the relative of Mary the mother of Jesus (Luke 1:36), but the Bible does not specify how they were related. Mary visited Elizabeth when both were pregnant, and Elizabeth was filled with the Spirit when she heard Mary's voice. She called Mary "the mother of my Lord" (Luke 1:43).

Eloi, Eloi, Lama Sabachthani–The Aramaic translation of Ps. 22:1, which Jesus cried out on the cross (Matt. 27:46; Mark 15:34), meaning, "My God, my God, why have you forsaken me?" Jesus may have continued on and quoted the rest of the psalm. The Gospel writers, in any case, pattern part of their account of the crucifixion on elements of Ps. 22.

El Shaddai–*See* God; Shaddai.

Elymas–A Jewish sorcerer and false prophet serving Sergius Paulus, the proconsul of Cyprus (Acts 13:4–12). Attempting to prevent the proconsul from believing the message of Paul and Barnabas, he was stricken with temporary blindness. He was also known as Bar-Jesus ("son of salvation" [Acts 13:6]). The name "Elymas" may be a transliteration of a Semitic word equivalent to the Greek *magos*, "magician" or "sorcerer" (Acts 13:8).

Elyon–*See* God.

Emmaus–A village approximately seven miles (sixty stadia in the Greek text) from Jerusalem. The village is of particular note because of Luke's account of two disciples walking to Emmaus from Jerusalem and their encounter with the risen Christ (Luke 24:13–32). It is located at the eastern end of the Ayalon Valley.

Emperor Worship–Originally, Roman emperors did not allow themselves to be worshiped directly. Instead of accepting direct worship, most emperors only accepted veneration of their *genius* ("spirit"), on the pattern of household religion. Divinization was initiated by the succeeding emperor and approved by the Roman senate. Divine honors were not automatically conferred, as the example of the unpopular Domitian (AD 51–96) illustrates.

Caligula (AD 12–41) was the first Roman emperor to demand personal veneration as a god. However, he and Domitian were the only emperors who required full-fledged worship while still alive.

The cult of the emperor was as much political as religious. The empire-wide cult united diverse cultures and people, provided a test of loyalty to the emperor, and enabled those who desired influence to display their commitment to imperial power. Many Jews and Christians were viewed suspiciously as unpatriotic because they refused to venerate the emperor.

The language of emperor worship has many striking parallels with NT language applied to Jesus Christ. Emperors received such titles as "savior," "lord" (see Acts 25:26 KJV), "god," and "son of god" in return for their acts of deliverance for peoples throughout the empire. The word *parousia* ("coming") was used in ancient writings and inscriptions to describe the triumphant arrival of an emperor to a welcoming city in language very similar to that used to describe the second coming of Christ. Even more remarkable is the ascription of the word *euangelion* ("gospel, good news") to major events in the life of the emperor, especially important military victories that led to relative peace throughout the empire.

The book of Revelation narrates a time when emperor worship was a pressing temptation for the Christian churches spread throughout the Roman Empire. If, as is likely, Rev. 17:7–14 is a cryptic reference to Rome, then the prohibitions against worshiping the beast in 13:4, 8; 14:9–10 are calls for Christians to remain steadfast in their refusal to worship the Roman emperor, a refusal that could easily result in a death sentence.

ENDOR–A town located in the territory assigned to western Manasseh (Josh. 17:11) and associated with modern Endor or Khirbet Salsafe. Mentioned three times in the OT (Josh. 17:11; 1 Sam. 28:7; Ps. 83:10), Endor was the residence of the woman—a spiritist, medium, or witch—whom Saul consulted to contact the spirit of Samuel on the night before his last battle against the Philistines at Gilboa (1 Sam. 28:7–25).

EN GEDI–A luxuriant oasis located west of the Dead Sea midway between Qumran and Masada. Four springs (David, Arugot, Shulamit, and Ein Gedi) cause the ravine to flow with water year-round, offering a stark contrast to the barren land surrounding it.

En Gedi is mentioned six times in the OT (Josh. 15:62; 1 Sam. 23:29; 24:1; 2 Chron. 20:2; Song 1:14; Ezek. 47:10), but is most famous as the site where David hid from Saul. King Saul entered one of En Gedi's caves to relieve himself, and David and his men were hiding farther back in the same cave.

ENOCH–**(1)** The son of Cain after whom Cain named a city (Gen. 4:17). **(2)** The son of Jared and the father of Methuselah in Seth's line. According to Gen. 5:23, he lived 365 years, conspicuously shorter than others in the genealogy. Most interpret Gen. 5:24 as saying that God took Enoch to the heavenly realm, without death, due to Enoch's piety. In the NT, Jude 14 assumes that he wrote or prophesied part of *1 Enoch*, a collection of Second Temple Jewish apocalyptic writings.

ENOSH–A grandson of Adam, a son of Seth, and the father of Kenan (Gen. 5:6–11; 1 Chron. 1:1–2), also listed in Luke's genealogy of Jesus (Luke 3:38). The ungodliness of Lamech in Cain's lineage (Gen. 4:23–24) is contrasted by a comment on a return to godliness at the time when Enosh was born (Gen. 4:25–26).

EPAPHRAS–Epaphras evangelized his hometown of Colossae and ministered in nearby Laodicea and Hierapolis (Col. 4:13). Paul highlighted Epaphras's devotion to prayer, and he called him a "servant of Christ Jesus" (4:12), "fellow servant" and "faithful minister" (1:7), and "fellow prisoner" (Philem. 23). Epaphras shared information about the Colossian church with Paul prior to Paul's letter to them. Although "Epaphras" is a shortened form of "Epaphroditus," he is not the man of that name referenced in Phil. 2:24; 4:18.

EPAPHRODITUS–Mentioned only in Philippians, Epaphroditus was a messenger of that church who brought a gift to Paul and served his needs on their behalf (4:18). Paul's words about Epaphroditus reflect a deep personal relationship and close association in the work of the gospel (cf. 2:30). For Paul, Epaphroditus was a brother, a fellow worker, and a fellow soldier (2:25). While serving Paul, he became ill and was close to death; this troubling news reached the church in Philippi, which was distressing to Epaphroditus and made Paul eager to send him there (2:26–30).

Ephah–*See* Weights and Measures.

Ephesians, Letter to the–Rising above the ordinary routine of church life, Paul pens a majestic letter calling Christians to remember what God has done for them in Christ and to walk worthy of their calling. Ephesians stands as an extremely significant and intensely practical book for today's church.

Letter opening (1:1–2). The letter opens in typical fashion by naming the author and the audience before adding a greeting. Paul, an "apostle of Christ Jesus by the will of God," writes to God's people in Ephesus (and surrounding cities). He greets his readers with "grace and peace," themes that appear throughout the letter.

Praise for spiritual blessings in Christ (1:3–14). Ephesians explodes in adoration and praise: "Praise be to [or 'blessed be'] the God . . . who has blessed us . . . with every spiritual blessing in Christ." God's people praise him for their election (1:4–6), for their redemption and wisdom to understand God's master plan (1:7–12), and for sealing them with the Holy Spirit (1:13–14). Each section ends with a similar phrase, "to the praise of his glory" (1:6, 12, 14), showing that the triune God in his essential character (his glory) is worthy of highest praise.

Prayer for spiritual understanding (1:15–23). After praising God for his blessings, Paul now asks for spiritual wisdom that his audience might comprehend those blessings (as described in both the previous section and the rest of the letter). As the Spirit enlightens their hearts, they come to know the hope of God's calling, the glory of God's inheritance, and the greatness of God's power (1:18–19), which was supremely displayed in Jesus Christ's resurrection and exaltation (1:20–23).

New life in Christ (2:1–10). Paul now turns his attention to the new life available in Christ (2:1–10). First, he offers a lengthy description of a person's spiritual state without Christ (2:1–3). Second, he explains how God came to the rescue of such helpless and hopeless people. Moved by his love and mercy, God has mysteriously allowed believers to participate in Christ's death, resurrection, and exaltation (2:4–6). God's purpose in saving people was to demonstrate the "riches of his grace" expressed to us in Jesus (2:7). There is perhaps no better summary of this salvation message than 2:8–10: the basis of salvation is God's grace, the means of receiving salvation is faith, and the result of salvation is good works.

New community in Christ (2:11–22). God not only has given new life to individuals in Christ but also has created a new community, composed of both Jews and Gentiles. As Gentiles, the Ephesians' condition outside of Christ was desperate: no Messiah, no connection to God's people, no promise of salvation, no hope, and no relationship with God (2:11–12). But now they have been brought near through Christ's sacrifice on the cross (2:13). In Christ, Jews and Gentiles have now been reconciled to each other in a new spiritual community (2:14–18). They are full-fledged members of God's kingdom and God's family. What is more, they are even part of God's holy temple (2:19–22).

Paul's unique role in God's plan (3:1–13). After describing God's strategy to unite Jewish and Gentile believers in Christ, Paul begins to pray for these believers (3:1). Almost immediately, however, he breaks off his prayer to explain more about God's "secret plan" or "mystery" and his own role in that plan. Only the grace and power of God could transform a persecutor of the church into one of the church's great leaders (3:2–9). Now God is using his multicultural church to announce his manifold wisdom to the heavenly powers (3:10–11). Since God is using Paul to fulfill his purpose, no one should be discouraged by Paul's sufferings (3:12–13).

Paul's prayer for the new community (3:14–21). Paul now resumes his prayer (3:1) and asks that God may strengthen believers by the Holy Spirit in their inner being according to his glorious riches (3:16). They will know the prayer has been answered when Christ feels at home in their hearts and they experience his indescribable love more and more. The final purpose of the prayer is that they be filled with the "fullness of God" or become like Christ (3:17–19; cf. 4:13). Although it may appear that Paul has asked for too much, the doxology in 3:20–21 affirms that God is able to do more than can be imagined.

New walk in Christ (4:1–6:20). God's gift of new life and his creation of a new community in Christ (chaps. 1–3) call for a new walk (chaps. 4–6), a walk in unity (4:1–6), a walk in holiness (4:17–32), a walk in love (5:1–6), a walk in light (5:7–14), an exhortation to walk carefully (5:15–6:9), and a walk in the Lord's strength (6:10–20). The important Greek word *oun* ("then, therefore") in 4:1 marks a transition from the blessings and privileges of the church (chaps. 1–3) to the conduct and responsibilities of the church (chaps. 4–6). Obedience comes as a response to God's grace.

Letter closing (6:21–24). Paul concludes with a commendation of Tychicus, the letter carrier, and a benediction of peace, love, and grace.

Ephesus, City of–*See* Asia Minor, Cities of.

Ephod–The ephod (only in the OT) was a garment, perhaps a vest or tunic, worn over the shoulders and extending at least to the waist, covering front and back. It is most closely associated with the Israelite priesthood. The eighty-five priests at Nob wore linen ephods (1 Sam. 22:18), and the expression "to wear an ephod" is used as a virtual synonym for "to serve as a priest" (2:28; 14:3).

Ephphatha–A Hellenized form of the Aramaic for "Be opened!" Jesus said this in healing a man who was unable to hear or speak (Mark 7:34). It is one of several Aramaic words or phrases recorded in the Gospels.

Ephraim–Joseph's second son, who received a greater blessing than did his older brother, Manasseh, when they were adopted by Jacob (Gen. 41:52; 46:20; 48:5, 20). Ephraim's descendants formed one of the tribes of Israel. *See also* Ephraim, Tribe of.

Ephraim, Hill Country of–The part of the hill country in north-central Israel allotted to the large, powerful tribe of Ephraim (Josh. 16). In Jeremiah, it is referred to as the "hills of Ephraim" (4:15; 31:6; 50:19); the KJV uses the term "Mount Ephraim." This part of the hill country included cities such as Shechem (Josh. 20:7), Shiloh, and Joshua's home of Timnath Serah (Josh. 24:30). The region was largely composed of high, rugged hills that made for difficult travel. Since the area had only been sparsely settled before the Israelite conquest, the Ephraimites had to clear the natural forestation (Josh. 17:15–18) in order to take advantage of the naturally fertile soil.

Ephraim, Tribe of–One of the tribes of Israel, descended from Joseph's second son, Ephraim (Gen. 46:20). Occasionally, the tribes of Ephraim and Manasseh were described together as the tribe of Joseph (Deut. 33:13), but usually they were listed separately in censuses, tribal movements, and territorial descriptions (Num. 2:24). The territory of Ephraim included the central hill country, with Manasseh to the north and Benjamin to the south (Josh. 16). The territory of Ephraim played a prominent role during the period of the judges. Deborah held court in the hill country of Ephraim (Judg. 4:5). The Ephraimites contended with Gideon (Judg. 8:1) and later went to war with Jephthah (12:4). Ephraim played a role in the revolts against David, with Absalom being killed in Ephraim (2 Sam. 18:6) and Sheba being from Ephraim (20:21). Ephraim grew in prominence to represent the entire northern kingdom (Isa. 7:2; Ezek. 37:16).

Ephraim Gate–*See* Gates of Jerusalem and the Temple.

Ephrath, Ephrathah–**(1)** Ephrath is the location where Rachel, Jacob's beloved wife, died giving birth to Benjamin while they were in the process of moving from Bethel to Bethlehem (Gen. 35:16, 19). Genesis 35:19 adds the editorial comment that Ephrath is the same location as Bethlehem, although it is possible that the two were separate towns at first and that only later Ephrath was absorbed into Bethlehem. This story and its identification of Ephrath with Bethlehem is repeated in Gen. 48:7 when Jacob blesses his children before his death. By the time of the prophet Micah, the two place names had become synonymous. Micah's famous messianic promise that the ruler would come from a small town, and not Jerusalem, praised "Bethlehem Ephrathah" (Mic. 5:2).

(2) David, when preparing to fight Goliath, is recorded as "the son of an Ephrathite named Jesse" (1 Sam. 17:12). Later in the same chapter David says that he is a son of "Jesse of Bethlehem" (1 Sam. 17:58). Thus, the designation between location and being a descendant of Ephrath is blurred (of course, most members of a clan would have lived closely together). This is also the case in Ruth 1:2 when Naomi's husband and sons are recorded as being Ephrathites from Bethlehem, thus tying the name "Ephrathah" to the geographic location of Bethlehem (see also Ruth 4:11). Similarly, Caleb's name is associated with Ephrathah in 1 Chron. 2:24, where it is recorded that

E

Hezron, Caleb's father, dies at Caleb Ephrathah. Because "Caleb Ephrathah" is an unusual place name (cf. KJV: "Calebephratah"; NRSV: "Caleb-ephrathah") and the Hebrew syntax of this verse is awkward, some prefer to emend the text, giving, for example, "After the death of Hezron, Caleb had relations with Ephrathah, the widow of his father Hezron, and she bore him Ashhur, the father of Tekoa" (NAB).

Ephron–A Hittite, the son of Zohar, who owned the cave of Machpelah near Mamre, which later was named "Hebron." Abraham negotiated with Ephron to buy Machpelah in order to have a place to bury his wife, Sarah. Following custom, Ephron offered to give the cave to Abraham, who, also following custom, offered full price (four hundred shekels) for the cave (Gen. 23:7–20). It is recorded that Abraham also was buried in the cave (25:9–10). According to Jacob, in his farewell message before dying, Isaac, Rebekah, and Leah were also buried there, and he desired to be buried there as well (49:29–32). Today Machpelah, or the Cave of the Patriarchs, is a heavily visited shrine, located in the modern city of Hebron.

Esarhaddon–Esarhaddon replaced Sennacherib as king of Assyria after some brief internal strife (2 Kings 19:37 // Isa. 37:38). During his reign (680–669 BC), western areas such as Phoenicia and Palestine were fairly stable. He resettled foreigners in Palestine (Ezra 4:2).

Esau–The firstborn son of Isaac and Rebekah, the twin brother of Jacob, and the father of the Edomites (Gen. 25:25–26; 36). Unlike Jacob, Esau was red and hairy in appearance (hence his name [25:25]), a skillful hunter by trade, and loved by his father, Isaac.

Before the birth of the twins, Rebekah received a prophecy that the two sons would represent nations, and that the older, Esau, would serve the younger, Jacob (Gen. 25:23). This reversal of events was brought about through the trickery of Jacob and Rebekah. Jacob bargained for Esau's birthright, which the famished Esau traded for food. Rebekah cleverly disguised her beloved son, Jacob, to feel and smell like Esau in order to fool her blind husband, which allowed Jacob to steal Esau's blessing. Esau plotted to kill Jacob, who possessed his birthright and blessing.

Rebekah intervened to save Jacob by urging Isaac to send Jacob away to Paddan Aram to take a wife from her father's home (Gen. 27:42–28:5). As a result, Jacob's wife-to-be would not be a grief to his parents like Esau's foreign wives, Judith and Basemath (26:34). Upon hearing of his parents' disapproval, Esau added another foreign wife, Mahalath, apparently out of spite (28:8–9). Esau never exacted revenge on his brother, even though Jacob greatly feared this fate (32:3–21). Instead, the two brothers met peacefully following Jacob's departure from Paddan Aram (33:4), and again in order to bury their father (35:29).

Genesis 36 describes Esau as the father of the Edomites, who inhabited the hill country of Seir in Edom (also Deut. 2:4–6). Even though Jacob and Esau resolved their differences, there was continued strife between the two nations that they represent, fulfilling the earlier prophecy. Edom also figures prominently within the prophetic corpus (see Obadiah; Mal. 1:2–4). Further, the relationship between Jacob and Esau and their father is used as a type in the NT (Rom. 9–11), and Esau is used to represent the godless (Heb. 12:16).

Eschatology–Eschatology is the study of last things. The word "eschatology" comes from the Greek word *eschatos*, meaning "last." From this same Greek word is derived the term "eschaton," which is sometimes used to refer to the end times.

Eschatology deals with such future events as the end of the world, Jesus' return, the resurrection, the final judgment, and the afterlife in heaven or hell. The tribulation and the millennium also belong to eschatology, but their timing and nature vary with different views. Although from one perspective human history entered its final phase in NT times so that people today are already living in the "last days," eschatology normally focuses on the unfulfilled prophecies that remain still in the future for present-day believers.

Essenes–*See* Jewish Parties.

Esther–*See* Esther, Book of.

Esther, Book of–The purpose of the book of Esther is to explain how the Feast of Purim originated. At this time, Purim becomes one of the annual festivals of the Jewish people. It is the celebration of a time when God delivered his people from an almost certain end.

The story begins with a great banquet (chap. 1). King Ahasuerus throws a feast for all the important people of his kingdom. At the climactic point of the celebration, he calls for his queen, Vashti, so that all his subjects can see her great beauty. She refuses, creating a crisis. After all, this banquet likely had as its purpose the assertion of the king's authority over his leaders, and this disobedience could not be tolerated. Vashti is deposed, and the search begins for a new queen. The king takes full advantage of this opportunity and tries out many beautiful young women in his kingdom, but none is as outstanding as Esther. Her selection as queen provides background for the action that follows.

In the meantime, Esther's relative Mordecai also has an experience that carries importance later in the story. Mordecai foils an assassination plot against the king. At this point in the narrative, his action is simply given as information (2:21–23).

The reader is also introduced to one more major character in the book, Haman the Agagite. He is a powerful, evil figure. He hates Mordecai for refusing to show him the respect that he feels is his due (3:1–6). So he determines to kill not just Mordecai but all the Jewish people in the empire. Accordingly, Haman convinces the king to allow him to set a date when all the Jews might be killed. Lots (Heb. *purim*, from an Akkadian loanword) are cast to choose the date, about a year later (3:7–15).

Mordecai catches wind of the plot and explains the dire situation to Esther. He pleads with her to approach the king to inform him of the plot. Esther hesitates, until Mordecai reminds her that she will not escape the consequences just because she is queen (chap. 4). In the context of this discussion, Mordecai speaks the most famous words of the book when he asks, "Who knows but that you have come to your royal position for such a time as this?" (4:14).

This scene raises the question of who is the hero of the story. Although Mordecai and Esther perform admirable acts, there is a force behind the scenes that the narrative does not name but subtly and certainly makes clear is the hero. It is none other than God himself. The coincidences that follow are just too great to be attributed to chance.

First, Esther is given permission to approach the king, and she successfully invites him to a feast along with Haman (5:1–8). This invitation fuels Haman's pride. Soon thereafter, the king has difficulty sleeping and asks that the royal annals be read to him. Coincidentally, or so it seems, the part of the annals chosen informs the king of Mordecai's earlier service in foiling the assassination plot. The king is told that nothing has yet been done to honor Mordecai for his act (6:1–3).

The next morning, Haman comes to court having just constructed a huge gallows on which to execute his enemy Mordecai. When asked by the king what he should do to honor a person whom the king has desired to honor, Haman thinks that it is he who will receive the honor, so he piles up honor after honor. When informed that Mordecai is the one, and that he, Haman, would take a role in honoring him, Haman realizes that his own doom is assured (6:4–14).

Sure enough, at the banquet Esther informs the king of the underside of Haman's plot. The result is that Haman is killed on the gallows built for Mordecai, yet another ironic reversal in the book (chap. 7).

A problem persists, however. The king has determined a date for the destruction of the Jews, and a decree of a Persian king is irreversible. Although the king cannot reverse his decision to allow the killing of the Jewish people, he can, and does, issue a second decree, permitting the Jewish people to defend themselves (chap. 8). On the fateful day, the Jews are victorious over their enemies, the final and climactic ironic reversal (9:1–19). Purim is established as an annual festival to celebrate this fact (9:20–32).

A deeper significance to this conflict is recovered once it is realized that this is a story of unfinished business. The attentive reader recognizes that Mordecai's membership in the clan of Kish (2:5) connects him with Saul, since Kish was Saul's father. On the other hand, Haman is an Agagite (3:1) and therefore related to the Amalekite king Agag, whom Saul, against God's instructions, did not immediately kill (1 Sam. 15). The story actually begins during the wilderness wandering, when the Amalekites tried to kill off the Israelites before they entered the promised land. At that time, God determined that the Amalekites should be judged and eradicated (Exod. 17:16; Deut. 25:17–19). That a Saulide (Mordecai) defeats an Amalekite (Haman) has deep significance in the past.

Ethan–Ethan the Ezrahite, son of Kishi (or Kushaiah) through the Levitical line Merari. He was a singer appointed by the Levites to the bronze cymbals (1 Chron. 15:19) and subsequently appointed to leadership by David after the ark of the covenant was returned to Jerusalem (1 Chron. 6:44). According to its inscription, Ps. 89 was composed by Ethan. Ethan had a reputation for being wise, though not as wise as Solomon (1 Kings 4:31).

Ethbaal–Ethbaal, a priest of Astoreth, reigned for thirty-two years as king of Tyre and Sidon, where he expanded Phoenician commercial activities. His daughter Jezebel married Ahab, king of Israel (1 Kings 16:31), an alliance that served to introduce Ahab and Israel to Baal worship. The name "Ethbaal" means "Baal is with him."

Ethiopia–The ancient Greeks used the term "Ethiopia" (lit., "the burnt faces") to refer to all regions south of Egypt. Thus they lumped all of black Africa into this term. The leading black African kingdom that interacted regularly throughout the biblical period with the nations in Mesopotamia, Palestine, and the entire Mediterranean region was the kingdom of Cush, located just to the south of Egypt, above the fourth cataract on the Nile River (*see* Cush, Cushites).

Ethiopian Eunuch–The Ethiopian eunuch, who appears in Acts 8:26–40, is from an African kingdom centered at the city of Meroe, located on the Nile just to the south of Egypt. Acts 8:27 states that he is in charge of the treasury of the Kandake, queen of the Ethiopians. "Candace" was the name used by all the queens of the Cushite kingdom at Meroe. Roman records from 23 BC document negotiations between the Roman general Gaius Petronius and a queen named "Candace" ruling over a kingdom at Meroe, on the Nile River.

Eucharist–*See* Lord's Supper.

Eunice–The Jewish mother of Timothy, Eunice was a Christian believer from Lystra in Asia Minor whose unnamed husband was Greek (Acts 16:1). Paul credits both Eunice and Timothy's grandmother Lois for instilling faith in his young disciple (2 Tim. 1:5).

Eunuch–Generally, a castrated official in a royal court serving a queen (2 Kings 9:30–32) or a king's harem (Esther 2:14–15). Ebed-Melek, an Ethiopian eunuch, along with Baruch, is the only person recorded as responding positively to Jeremiah (Jer. 38:7–13; 39:15–18). The Mosaic law did not permit eunuchs to enter sacred spaces (Deut. 23:1). But the prophet Isaiah (Isa. 56:3–5) promises salvation to eunuchs, the fulfillment of which began when Philip the evangelist shared the gospel with a eunuch from Ethiopia, who was immediately baptized into the church (Acts 8:26–40). Jesus uses the term metaphorically to describe those who make themselves eunuchs for the kingdom, probably a reference to celibacy (Matt. 19:12).

Euodia–A woman in the church at Philippi who was encouraged by Paul to settle her disagreement with Syntyche (Phil. 4:2). Paul commended Euodia and Syntyche, who "contended at my side in the cause of the gospel" (4:3). These women likely held leadership roles in the church of Philippi, and thus their disagreement merited mention in the Letter to the Philippians. They may have been hosts of house churches or perhaps deacons. The nature of their disagreement remains unclear in the text.

Euphrates and Tigris Rivers–*See* Rivers and Waterways.

Euroclydon–In Acts 27:14 the KJV rendering of the Greek word *Euroklydōn* (the earliest manuscripts have *Eurakylōn*, and there are other variations), referring to the "northeaster" storm that resulted in the wreck of the ship transporting Paul to imprisonment in Rome. "Euroklydon" means "storm from the east," while the preferred transliteration of the hybrid Greek-Latin word, "Euraquilo," means "northeast wind."

Eutychus–While Paul was preaching in Troas, this young man fell asleep and fell from his upstairs window seat (Acts 20:7–12). He was "picked up dead," but Paul revived him. Thus Luke portrays Paul as able to raise a boy from the dead in the tradition of Elijah and Elisha (1 Kings 17:21–22; 2 Kings 4:34–35).

Evangelism–Evangelism is the proclamation of the "evangel" (Gk. *euangelion*), the good news, of Jesus Christ. The content of the evangel includes Jesus' birth, which was announced as good news to Zechariah by the angel Gabriel (Luke 1:19) and by the angels to the shepherds (Luke 2:10). The good news speaks of the reality of Jesus' resurrection (Acts

17:18), is described as a message of grace (Acts 20:24) and reconciliation to God through the sacrificed body of Christ (Col. 1:22–23), and includes the expectation of a day of divine judgment (Rom. 2:16). Paul preached the gospel (from Old English *gōdspel*, "good news") message, which he claimed had its origin with God, not humans (Gal. 1:11–12). He summarizes this message in 1 Cor. 15:3b–5: "that Christ died for our sins according to the Scriptures, that he was buried, that he was raised on the third day according to the Scriptures, and that he appeared to Cephas, and then to the Twelve." The introduction to the Gospel of Mark (1:1) may indicate that this written gospel could serve evangelistic purposes.

Eve–*See* Adam and Eve.

Evil-Merodach–*See* Awel-Marduk.

Excommunication–A form of communal discipline characterized by expulsion from the community of the faithful. Jewish communities practiced excommunication, defined as being cut off from the people of Israel, and it is mentioned in connection with a number of transgressions: eating yeast during Passover (Exod. 12:15), failing to heed the call to return following the exile (Ezra 10:8), performing an improper sacrifice (Lev. 17:8–9), and others. David calls for his enemies to be cut off from the people of Israel (Ps. 109:13). In Jesus' day, excommunication could take the form of anything from a light censure to death. The Sanhedrin held the power of excommunication in serious cases, but to kill an offender required the authority of the Gentile rulers. Thus, the punishment of death for blasphemy put upon Jesus could not be exercised by the Sanhedrin alone.

Exile–The dislocation of a people group from its homeland. In the Bible, exile usually refers to two events in Israel's history: the Assyrian exile of the northern kingdom in 722 BC and the Babylonian exile of the southern kingdom around 586 BC.

Exodus–*See* Exodus, Book of.

Exodus, Book of–In the first chapter we see connections to Genesis, which tell us that we cannot read Exodus in isolation. For example, Exod. 1:1 closely parallels Gen. 46:8. The latter speaks of the Israelites going down into Egypt, and the former picks up on this theme, thus reminding us that Israel's presence in Egypt was not an accident and that Exodus is a continuation of the story begun in Genesis. Likewise, the use of creation language in Exod. 1:7 (the Israelites were fruitful, multiplying, becoming numerous, filling the earth; compare to Gen. 1:21, 28; 8:17; 9:1) signals that Israel's impending drama is somehow connected to creation. That point is made clearer in the chapters that follow. Perhaps most central is the crossing of the Red Sea. As in Gen. 1:9, where the dry land appears where once there was water, here the dry land (Exod. 14:21) appears to make a path through the sea.

There is, in fact, a fair amount of Exodus that plays on this theological theme of creation and the reversal of creation. In ancient Near Eastern conceptions of creation, water represented chaos. The gods' role was to tame the chaos so that the earth could be inhabited. Separating the land from the primordial sea was an important part of that, and this is reflected in the biblical account in Gen. 1. The flood in Gen. 6–9 is a reversal of that creative act, where God allows the waters of chaos to come crashing down on his creation, thus making it uninhabitable again. Exodus continues this theme, but here creation is called upon to aid the Israelites in their escape, whereas it is used against the Egyptians. The ten plagues, for example, are declarations that Israel's God controls the cosmos, whereas Egypt's gods stand by helplessly. The plague of darkness in particular is a graphic reversal of what God had done in Genesis, the creation of light and the separation of light from darkness. Israel's deliverance from Egypt is, in other words, another act of creation: the same God who brought order to cosmic chaos in Gen. 1 is now unleashing the forces of creation to save his people and punish their enemies. And whereas Pharaoh's Egyptians are able to reproduce the first sign and the first two plagues, it is only Israel's God who can end the plagues and restore order to chaos.

Israel has been delivered from Egypt for a purpose, and that purpose begins to become clear in the chapters that follow their departure. The newly created people of Israel are not delivered from Egypt so that they can be "free" from bondage. The key struggle in the opening chapters of Exodus, indeed, the whole reason for the ten plagues, is to determine to whom Israel belongs, whether to Pharaoh or to Yahweh, Israel's God. The Hebrew word

E

'abad can mean both "serve" (in the sense of servitude) and "worship." In a wonderful play on words, the question being asked in the opening chapters is "Whom will Israel *'abad*, Pharaoh or Yahweh?" But Yahweh claims his people, not so that they can be liberated to go where they please, but rather so that they are free to move from serving/worshiping Pharaoh to serving/worshiping Yahweh on Mount Sinai.

Law. It is important to understand that the law was given to the Israelites after they had been redeemed from Egypt, not before. The law is a gift to those who have been saved. It is not something to be followed in order to become saved. Israel is, as we read in Exod. 4:22–23, God's son. This is why Israel was delivered from Egypt, and this is why Israel was given the gift of the law.

The purpose of the law, therefore, was not to prove to God that his people were somehow worthy of his covenant with them. The law was given so that Israel would be molded into a new people, one whose hearts were wholly devoted to God and so could be the instrument through which not only Israel but also the nations themselves would be blessed (see Gen. 12:1–3). As Exod. 19:6 puts it, Israel is to become a "kingdom of priests"—that is, the "holy nation" that would perform the mediatorial role of blessing the nations. The law, therefore, was not a burden but a delight, a gift from God to a redeemed people.

Tabernacle. The section on the tabernacle begins in chapter 25 and extends to the end of the book, chapter 40. In between is an important episode, the rebellion involving the making of the golden calf. Just as the law represents much more than "rules to live by," the tabernacle is more than just a building for sacrificing animals. The importance of the tabernacle can be seen by focusing on some key elements.

Chapters 25–31 provide the list of instructions for the tabernacle. For centuries, rabbis and biblical scholars have noticed a pattern in these chapters. Seven times the phrase is repeated "The Lord said to Moses," and the seventh time is in 31:12 to introduce the topic of Sabbath observance. Just like the creation of the cosmos in Gen. 1, the tabernacle is a product of a six-stage creative act ("And the Lord said") followed by rest. Some have suggested that the tabernacle is a microcosm of creation: for example, cherubim are worked into the curtains, so to look up is to look at the heavens; the lampstand is a sort of tree of life, as in the garden of Eden. To be in the tabernacle is to be in touch with creation as it was meant to be, in the garden apart from the chaos of life outside.

Chapters 35–40 relay how the instructions are carried out. This section begins with reference to the Sabbath (35:1–3), which is how the first section ends. In between, we find the episode of the golden calf (chaps. 32–34), which is about false worship. The Israelites nearly succeed in undoing all that God had planned in bringing his people out of Egypt. Still, through Moses' intervention, God's plan is not thwarted, and so chapter 35 does not miss a beat, picking up where chapter 31 leaves off, with the Sabbath. Some scholars see here a pattern of creation (chaps. 25–31), fall (chaps. 32–34), and redemption (chaps. 35–40).

The tabernacle is an important theological entity in Exodus: it is heaven on earth. It is a truly holy space where God communes with his holy (law-keeping) people. This is the ultimate purpose of the exodus: to create a people who embody God's character and who worship him in purity. Then God would be with his people wherever they go (40:36–38).

Exorcism–The act of expelling demons from afflicted persons, places, and objects.

There is no record of exorcism in the OT. In the NT, Jesus considered delivering people from demons to be central to his proclamation of the kingdom of God: "But if it is by the Spirit of God that I drive out demons, then the kingdom of God has come upon you" (Matt. 12:28). He used no formula or ritual; on his own authority he simply commanded the demons to leave, and he attributed his success to God. He also extended to his disciples the authority to expel demons in his name (Luke 10:17), dependent upon their faith (Matt. 17:17–20). Even a nondisciple was found performing exorcisms in Jesus' name (Mark 9:38), and when Jesus was told about it, he refused to forbid it.

Jesus is not shown struggling against the demons; he simply spoke, and they obeyed, even at a distance (Mark 7:30). Often the demons recognized Jesus (e.g., Mark 5:7); sometimes they left the person with Jesus' permission. Although Jesus' exorcisms are listed along with healing miracles, the NT differentiates between exorcism and healing (e.g., Matt. 10:8); not every disease is considered to have been caused by demons, nor is every possessed person described in terms of illness.

Philip's ministry in Samaria was enhanced by his casting out demons and healing the sick (Acts 8:6–7). In Acts 16:18 Paul performs an exorcism "in the name of Jesus Christ." But while the ministry of Paul was so profound that articles associated with him were effective in exorcisms (Acts 19:11–12), the Jewish sons of Sceva were themselves overcome when they invoked the names of Jesus and Paul in an attempted deliverance (19:13–16). In the longer (and inauthentic) ending of Mark, the ability to cast out demons is promised to all believers (Mark 16:17).

Expiation–"Expiation" refers to the atonement of sin and the removal of guilt, while "propitiation" refers to the appeasement or satisfaction of wrath. Both ideas are present in the one Greek word *hilasmos* (and its cognates) used in the LXX and the NT. It is difficult to translate *hilasmos* into English using one corresponding word, so two words, "expiation" and "propitiation," are often used. This is problematic because neither term precisely captures the nuances of the Greek word. The problem persists because, as noted above, "expiation" and "propitiation" have different meanings in English. Because no single English word conveys the full sense of *hilasmos*, "expiation" and "propitiation" are conveniently combined in the NIV's "sacrifice of atonement" or "atoning sacrifice" (Rom. 3:25; 1 John 2:2; 4:10).

Ezekiel–*See* Ezekiel, Book of.

Ezekiel, Book of–The book of Ezekiel is widely recognized as one of the most idiosyncratic of the OT prophetic books. Some rabbis prohibited anyone under the age of thirty from reading portions of the book (i.e., the visions of God's glory in chapters 1 and 10 might lead to dangerous speculations about the mystery of God). Ezekiel includes a number of main themes.

The sovereignty of God. The book emphasizes God's sovereignty over all as Ezekiel challenged the false theology of his fellow Jewish exiles, which held that Yahweh, bound by covenantal oath, could not destroy Jerusalem. The formulaic expression (with variations) "After X occurs, then you/they will know that I am the Lord/I have spoken" occurs over sixty-five times in the book to emphasize God's intervention in human events, including the exile and restoration (e.g., 7:27; 13:23; 29:16), to uphold the covenant and establish his kingdom.

The holiness of God. Israel's sins had obscured God's holiness in the sight of their neighbors (20:9). God's holiness required both punishment of Israel's sins and the continuation of his covenantal relationship with his people. God's purging judgment and restoration would be a fulfillment of his covenantal obligations and would display his holiness (20:40–44; 28:25; 36:16–32).

Hope in the midst of judgment. God's covenantal faithfulness would include restoration after judgment (chaps. 33–39). The final temple vision (chaps. 40–48) gives a picture of the restoration using typological images and cultural idioms with which the people were familiar.

Ezion Geber–A town located at the northern end of the Gulf of Aqabah. The Bible locates it "near Elath in Edom, on the shore of the Red Sea" (1 Kings 9:26). However, the precise location is debated.

From David to the end of the monarchy, control over Ezion Geber oscillated between Judah and Edom. David may have first captured it when he subdued Edom (2 Sam. 8:13–14). With the help of the Phoenicians, Solomon built a fleet of ships at Ezion Geber that brought immense wealth into Israel (1 Kings 9:26–28). After Solomon's death, it may have been destroyed during Pharaoh Shishak's invasion (1 Kings 14:25–26). Edom reasserted control over it until Jehoshaphat, in alliance with Ahaziah, built at Ezion Geber a fleet of merchant vessels, which God destroyed because of Ahaziah's wickedness (2 Chron. 20:36–37). This is the last time Ezion Geber is mentioned by name.

From this point onward, nearby Elath is the focus of events in the area. Uzziah's father defeated the Edomites, allowing Uzziah to build up Elath (2 Kings 14:22; 2 Chron. 26:1–2). The Syrians briefly controlled the area, but the Edomites reclaimed control until the Babylonian period (2 Kings 16:6). Elath was abandoned in the fourth century BC, and a Nabatean site developed farther east near Aqabah.

Ezra–*See* Ezra, Book of.

Ezra, Book of–The evidence is clear that the books of Ezra and Nehemiah originally formed a single book. It is not until the Middle

Ages that manuscripts show a division between the two.

The book of Ezra is named after Ezra, a self-described priest and teacher (7:11) of the Lord. This man was commissioned by the Persian king Artaxerxes I (r. 464–424 BC) to reestablish the law of the Lord in the land of Judah.

The book of Ezra begins where Chronicles ends, with the decree by King Cyrus of Persia that the Jews be allowed to return to the land. The first six chapters narrate the events of the first phase of that return, from 539 until 515 BC. Zerubbabel and Sheshbazzar are the leaders of the people at this time, and their initial goal is to rebuild the temple. Once they start, however, opposition sets in, and the work stops. However, motivated in large part, as we know, by the prophets Haggai and Zechariah, the people finish the work, and the second temple becomes functional.

Nonetheless, over fifty years later, when the story of Ezra begins (Ezra 7–10), the condition of the people of God is not promising. King Artaxerxes of Persia allows Ezra, a priest and teacher, to lead a return back to Judah with the express purpose of reestablishing the law in the land. When he arrives, he finds that there are sinful practices such as illegitimate intermarriage between Jews and Gentiles, and he works to reestablish the purity of the people. The story of Ezra continues in the book of Nehemiah, where he is seen leading the people in a great renewal of the covenant as they reaffirm their commitment to obey God's law (Neh. 8–10).

EZRAHITE–This name occurs in 1 Kings 4:31 and in the superscriptions to Pss. 88–89. "Ezrahite" possibly signifies a clan name. Ethan and Heman, wise men worthy of mention as a standard for measuring the wisdom of King Solomon, were Ezrahites.

F

Fair Havens–Fair Havens is a harbor on the south-central coast of Crete. The ship carrying the apostle Paul to Rome stopped there after encountering difficult sailing from Cnidus (Acts 27:7–13). Paul pressed to spend the winter there, but he was overruled by the captain because of the port's perceived deficiencies.

Faith, Faithfulness–Faith in the context of the OT rests on a foundation that the person or object of trust, belief, or confidence is reliable. Trust in Yahweh is expressed through loyalty and obedience. The theme of responsive obedience is emphasized in the Torah (Exod. 19:5). In the later history of Israel, faithfulness to the law became the predominant expression of faith (Dan. 1:8; 6:10). OT faith, then, is a moral response rather than abstract intellect or emotion.

Faith is a central theological concept in the NT. In relational terms, faith is foremost personalized as the locus of trust and belief in the person of Jesus Christ.

In the Gospels, Jesus is spoken of not as the subject of faith (as believing in God), but as the object of faith. In the Synoptic Gospels, faith is seen most often in connection with the ministry of Jesus. Miracles, in particular healings, are presented as taking place in response to the faith of the one in need of healing or the requester. In the Gospel of John, faith (belief) is presented as something that God requires of his people (6:28–29).

In the book of Acts, "faith/belief" is used to refer to Jews and Gentiles converting to following the life and teachings of Jesus Christ and becoming part of the Christian community. The book correlates faith in Christ closely with repentance (Acts 11:21; 19:18; 20:21; 26:18).

Paul relates faith to righteousness and justification (Rom. 3:22; 5:11; Gal. 3:6). In Ephesians faith is shown as instrumental in salvation: "For it is by grace you have been saved, through faith—and this not from yourselves, it is the gift of God" (2:8).

In Hebrews, faith is described as "being sure of what we hope for and certain of what we do not see" (11:1). Faith thus is viewed as something that can be accomplished in the life of the believer—a calling of God not yet tangible or seen. To possess faith is to be loyal to God and to the gospel of Jesus Christ despite all obstacles. In the Letter of James, genuine works naturally accompany genuine faith. Works, however, are expressed in doing the will of God. The will of God means, for example, caring for the poor (James 2:15–16).

In 1 Peter, Christ is depicted as the broker of faith in God (1:21), whereas in 2 Peter and Jude faith is presented as received from God (2 Pet. 1:1). In the Letters of John "to believe" is used as a litmus test for those who possess eternal life: "You who believe in the name of the Son of God, . . . you have eternal life" (1 John 5:13).

Fall–"The fall" refers to the events of the first human couple's sin in the garden of Eden (Gen. 2–3). Although the word "fall" does not occur in the account, Christians have used the term to describe it, taking their cues from Paul's writings (esp. Rom. 5:12–21). The term is important because it reflects an interpretation that the events in the garden are the entrance of human sin and that the sin has universal effects on humankind.

Family–People in the Bible were family-centered and staunchly loyal to their kin. Families formed the foundation of society. The extended family was the source of people's status in the community and provided the primary economic, educational, religious, and social interactions.

Marriage and divorce. Marriage in the ancient Near East was a contractual arrangement between two families, arranged by the bride's father or a male representative. The bride's family was paid a dowry, a "bride's price." Paying a dowry was not only an economic transaction but also an expression of family honor. Only the rich could afford multiple dowries. Thus, polygamy was minimal. The wedding itself was celebrated with a feast provided by the father of the groom.

The primary purpose for marriage in the ancient Near East was to produce a male heir to ensure care for the couple in their old age. The concept of inheritance was a key part of the marriage customs, especially with regard to passing along possessions and property.

Marriage among Jews in the NT era still tended to be endogamous; that is, Jews sought to marry close kin without committing incest violations (Lev. 18:6–17). A Jewish male certainly was expected to marry a Jew. Exogamy, marrying outside the remote kinship group, and certainly outside the *ethnos,* was understood as shaming God's holiness. Thus, a Jew marrying a Gentile woman was not an option. The Romans did practice exogamy. For them, marrying outside one's kinship group (not *ethnos*) was based predominantly on creating strategic alliances between families.

Greek and Roman law allowed both men and women to initiate divorce. In Jewish marriages, only the husband could initiate divorce proceedings. If a husband divorced his wife, he had to release her and repay the dowry. Divorce was common in cases of infertility (in particular if the woman had not provided male offspring). Ben Sira comments that barrenness in a woman is a cause of anxiety to the father (Sir. 42:9–10). Another reason for divorce was adultery (Exod. 20:14; Deut. 5:18). Jesus, though, taught a more restrictive use of divorce than the OT (Mark 10:1–12).

Children and parenting. Childbearing was considered representative of God's blessing on a woman and her entire family, in particular her husband. In contrast to this blessing, barrenness brought shame on women, their families, and specifically their husbands.

Children were of low social status in society. Infant mortality was high. An estimated 60 percent of the children in the first-century Mediterranean society were dead by the age of sixteen.

Ancient Near Eastern and Mediterranean societies exhibited a parenting style based on their view of human nature as a mixture of good and evil tendencies. Parents relied on physical punishment to prevent evil tendencies from developing into evil deeds (Prov. 29:15). The main concern of parents was to socialize the children into family loyalty. Lack of such loyalty was punished (Lev. 20:9). At a very early stage children were taught to accept the total authority of the father. The rearing of girls was entirely the responsibility of the women. Girls were taught domestic roles and duties as soon as possible so that they could help with household tasks.

Family identity was used as a metaphor in ancient Israel to speak of fidelity, responsibility, judgment, and reconciliation. In the OT, the people of Israel often are described as children of God. In their overall relationship to God, the people of Israel are referred to in familial terms—sons and daughters, spouse, and firstborn (Exod. 4:22). God is addressed as the father of the people (Isa. 63:16; 64:8) and referred to as their mother (Isa. 49:14–17).

The church as the family of God. Throughout his ministry, Jesus called his disciples to follow him. This was a call to loyalty (Matt. 10:32–40; 16:24–26; Mark 8:34–38; Luke 9:23–26), a call to fictive kinship, the family of God (Matt. 12:48–50; Mark 3:33–35). Jesus' declaration "On this rock I will build my church" (Matt. 16:18) was preceded by the call to community. Entrance into the community was granted through adopting the values of the kingdom, belief, and the initiation rite of baptism (Matt. 10:37–39; 16:24–26; Mark 8:34–38; Luke 9:23–26, 57–63; John 1:12; 3:16; 10:27–29; Acts 2:38; 16:31–33; 17:30; Rom. 10:9). Jesus' presence as the head of the community was eventually replaced by the promised Spirit (John 14:16–18). Through the Spirit, Jesus' ministry continues in the community of his followers, God's family—the church. *See also* Adoption.

FARM, FARMING–*See* Agriculture.

FARMER–*See* Agriculture.

FASTING–Fasting, often linked with prayer, was one avenue of appeal to God in the face of crises, both national and personal. Moses ascended to Mount Sinai and was with God forty days and nights without eating bread or drinking water, both before and after the Israelites' sin with the golden calf (Exod. 34:28; Deut. 9:8–18). David fasted when his son was dying (2 Sam. 12:15–23). Esther called all the Jews of Susa to fast for three days before she ventured before the king (Esther 4:15–17). Joel called the people to repentance and fasting as the land was devastated by a locust plague (Joel 1:13–14; 2:12). Forty days of fasting, an echo of Moses' experience, prepared Jesus to face the devil's temptations (Matt. 4:1–11 pars.).

The OT prophets criticized Israelites who presumed that their religious obligations were met simply by fasting (Isa. 58:1–10; Zech. 7:1–5). When asked why his disciples did not fast and pray, Jesus indicated that sometimes fasting is inappropriate (Matt. 9:14–17 pars.). Luke recorded an addition to Jesus' statement about new wine in old wineskins: "No one after drinking old wine wants the new, for they say, 'The old is better'" (Luke 5:39), perhaps suggesting that the accumulation of fasting practices was "new wine" and they ought simply to observe the Day of Atonement.

Father–*See* Family; God.

Fatherless–*See* Poor, Orphan, Widow.

Fear of Isaac–A term that Jacob applied to God in Gen. 31:42. "Fear of Isaac" is found in parallel with "the God of my father" and "the God of Abraham" (cf. Gen. 32:9). The word "fear" in these cases carries the sense "dread" or "terror." See also Exod. 15:16; Deut. 2:25; 1 Chron. 14:17. With reference to God, see 1 Sam. 11:7.

Feasts–*See* Festivals.

Felix–The Roman governor of Judea when Paul was arrested in Jerusalem (Acts 21:27–36). He presided over Paul's subsequent trial at Caesarea (23:3–24:27). Felix treated his prisoner with leniency and deferred judgment on the case. Several days later, Felix, along with his wife, Drusilla, listened to Paul discourse on the Christian faith, and his conscience became alarmed by what Paul taught (24:24–25). Felix dismissed Paul, but later he sent for Paul often to talk with him, hoping thereby to secure a bribe (24:26). Caught between his greed and his desire to keep favor with the Jews, Felix kept Paul in custody for a further two years until Porcius Festus became governor (24:27).

Fellowship–The common experience/sharing of something with someone else.

The close and intimate fellowship that the members of the Trinity experience with one another (John 10:30; 14:10; 16:14–15; 17:5) is something that Jesus prays for his people to experience themselves (17:20–26). He asks that believers "may be one, Father, just as you are in me and I am in you. May they also be in us so that the world may believe that you have sent me" (17:21). Just as the Father is in Jesus and Jesus is in the Father, believers are described as being in both the Father and the Son. The stated purpose for such fellowship is twofold: that the world may know and believe that the Father has sent the Son, and that the Father loves believers even as he has loved the Son (17:21, 23). Central to this fellowship between God and believers is the sharing of the glory that the Father and the Son experience (17:22). Jesus expresses similar truths in John 15:1–11 when he speaks of himself as the true vine and his followers as the branches who must remain in him because "apart from me you can do nothing" (v. 5).

Paul frequently speaks of the believer's fellowship with Christ, even though he rarely uses the word "fellowship" to speak of this reality. It is God who calls the believer into fellowship with Christ (1 Cor. 1:9), but such fellowship involves both the "power of his resurrection and participation in his sufferings, becoming like him in his death" (Phil. 3:10). When believers celebrate the Lord's Supper, they are participating in the body and blood of Christ (1 Cor. 10:16–17). Far more frequently, Paul expresses the concept of fellowship with Christ by his use of the phrase "with Christ." Believers have been crucified, buried, raised, clothed, and seated in the heavenly realms with Christ (Rom. 6:4–9; 2 Cor. 13:4; Gal. 2:20–21; Eph. 2:5–6; Col. 2:12–13; 3:1–4). They also share in the inheritance that Christ has received from the Father (Rom. 8:16–17) and one day will reign with him (2 Tim. 2:12).

The fellowship that believers have with one another is an extension of their fellowship with God. John wrote, "We proclaim to you what we have seen and heard, so that you also may have fellowship with us. And our fellowship is with the Father and with his Son, Jesus Christ" (1 John 1:3). Just as walking in darkness falsifies a believer's claim to fellowship with God, so also walking in the light is necessary for fellowship with other believers (1:6–7). Paul

F

strikes a similar note when he says, "Do not be yoked together with unbelievers. For what do righteousness and wickedness have in common? Or what fellowship can light have with darkness? What harmony is there between Christ and Belial? Or what does a believer have in common with an unbeliever?" (2 Cor. 6:14–15). The point is not to avoid all contact with unbelievers (cf. 1 Cor. 5:9–10), but rather that the believer is so fundamentally identified with Christ that to identify with unbelievers should be avoided.

From the earliest days of the church, believers found very tangible ways to demonstrate that their fellowship was rooted in their common faith in Jesus. Immediately after Pentecost, "they devoted themselves to the apostles' teaching and to fellowship, to the breaking of bread and to prayer. . . . All the believers were together and had everything in common" (Acts 2:42–44). This common experience led believers to voluntarily sell their possessions and share with any who had a need (2:45; 4:32). This meeting of very practical needs was motivated by a common experience of God's abundant generosity in freely giving his Son (Rom. 8:32). The self-sacrificial sharing of resources became a staple of the early church (Rom. 12:13; Gal. 6:6; 1 Tim. 6:18) and provided an opportunity for Paul to demonstrate the unity of the church when he collected money from Gentile churches to alleviate the suffering of Jewish Christians in Judea (Rom. 15:26–27; 2 Cor. 8–9).

FESTIVALS–The Israelites gathered regularly to celebrate their relationship with God. Such festivals were marked by communal meals, music, singing, dancing, and sacrifices. They celebrated, conscious that God had graciously brought them into a relationship with him. Within this covenant he had committed himself to act on their behalf both in regular ways, such as the harvest, and in exceptional ways, such as deliverance from Egypt. At the festivals, Israel celebrated God's work in its past, present, and future and reaffirmed its relationship with this covenant God.

We know of Israel's festivals from several calendars in the Mosaic legislation (Exod. 23:14–17; 34:18–23; Lev. 23; Num. 28–29; Deut. 16:1–17), calendars further clarified by the prophets (e.g., Ezek. 45:18–25; Zech. 14), and narrative material (e.g., 2 Kings 23:21–23).

Passover and the Festival of Unleavened Bread. Israel's religious calendar began with Passover, the day set aside to commemorate deliverance from Egypt. Occurring in spring, this single day was joined with a weeklong celebration known as the Festival of Unleavened Bread, during which all males were required to make a pilgrimage to the sanctuary and offer the firstfruits of the barley harvest (Lev. 23:9–14). Israel observed Passover with rituals that reactualized the night God's destroyer spared the Israelites in Egypt. A lamb was killed, and its blood was put on the doorposts of the homes and on the bronze altar in the sanctuary. The lamb was roasted and served with unleavened bread and bitter herbs while those partaking—dressed in their traveling clothes—listened to the retelling of the exodus story. No yeast was to be found anywhere among them, no work was to be done on the first and last days of the festival, and offerings were to be brought to the sanctuary (Num. 9:1–5; Josh. 5:10–11; 2 Kings 23:21–23; 2 Chron. 30; 35:1–19).

Early Christians associated Jesus' death with that of the Passover (Paschal) lamb (1 Cor. 5:7–8), encouraged by Jesus' comments at the Last Supper (described by the Synoptic Gospels as a Passover meal [e.g., Matt. 26:17–30]). Perhaps Jesus meant to emphasize that just as Passover and the Festival of Unleavened Bread reminded God's people of his deliverance and provision, his followers would find true freedom and full provision in him.

The Festival of Weeks. Also known as the Festival of Harvest, the Day of Firstfruits, or Pentecost (because it occurred fifty days after Passover), the Festival of Weeks took place on the sixth day of the third month (corresponding to our May or June). This marked another occasion when all Jewish men were required to come to the sanctuary. They were to bring an offering of the firstfruits of the wheat harvest, abstain from work, and devote themselves to rejoicing in God's goodness.

Early in the NT period, if not before, this festival also became associated with the giving of the law on Mount Sinai. The Jews who assembled in Jerusalem on the day of Pentecost as described in Acts 2 came to celebrate not only God's provision but also the revelation of his nature and will. Significantly, God chose this day to send the Holy Spirit, the One who would produce a harvest of believers and reveal God more fully to the world.

The Festival of Tabernacles. So important was the Festival of Tabernacles (also known as the Festival of Ingathering or the Festival of Booths) that Israel sometimes referred to it as "the festival of the LORD" (Judg. 21:19) or simply "the festival" (cf. 1 Kings 8:65). Held from the fifteenth to the twenty-first of the seventh month (September–October), this was the third of the three pilgrimage festivals. For that week, Israel lived in booths to remind them of their ancestors' time in the wilderness. They also celebrated the fruit harvest. They were to "take the fruit of majestic trees, branches of palm trees, boughs of leafy trees, and willows of the brook; and you shall rejoice" before God for seven days (Lev. 23:40 NRSV). Avoiding all work on the first and last days of the festival, they were to mark the week with sacrifices, celebration, and joy. Also, every seventh year the law was to be read at this festival (Deut. 31:10–11).

John 7 records Jesus' secretive departure to Jerusalem for the Festival of Tabernacles, where he spent several days teaching in the temple courts. It was on the last and greatest day of the festival when Jesus invited those thirsty to come to him and drink.

The Festival of Trumpets. Occurring on the first day of the seventh month (September–October), this feast marked the beginning of the civil and agricultural year for the Jews; it was also referred to as Rosh Hashanah (lit., "head/beginning of the year"). Observed as a Sabbath with sacrifices and trumpet blasts, this day was intended for rest and to begin preparations for the coming Day of Atonement. The Mishnah makes this connection more explicit by identifying the Festival of Trumpets as the day when "all that come into the world pass before [God] like legions of soldiers" or flocks of sheep to be judged (*m. Ros. HaSh.* 1:2).

The Day of Atonement. Some festivals, like Passover, looked back to what God had done or was doing for his people; other festivals, like Trumpets and the Day of Atonement (Yom Kippur), focused on the relationship itself. The latter was marked by repentance and rituals designed to remove the nation's sins and restore fellowship with God. Coming ten days after the Festival of Trumpets, this was a solemn occasion during which the Israelites abstained from eating, drinking, and other activities. This was the only prescribed annual fast in the Jewish calendar, though other fasts were added in the fourth, fifth, seventh, and tenth months to mourn the Babylonian exile (Zech. 7:3, 5; 8:19).

In Leviticus, God clarified the purpose of this day: "On this day atonement will be made for you, to cleanse you. Then, before the LORD, you will be clean from all your sins" (16:30). Not only would the people be purified but so also would the sanctuary, so that God could continue to meet his people there. Sacrifices were offered for both priest and people, and the blood was taken into the most holy place. Only on Yom Kippur could this room be entered, and only by the high priest, who sprinkled blood on the cover of the ark of the covenant. Leaving that room, he also sprinkled blood in the holy place (16:14–17) and then on the bronze altar in the courtyard.

Yom Kippur was marked by another ritual that symbolized the removal of Israel's sins, this one involving two goats. One goat, chosen by lot, was offered as a sacrifice to God. The high priest placed his hands on the other goat and transferred to it the sins of the nation. He then released the goat into the wilderness, for "the goat will carry on itself all their sins to a remote place" (Lev. 16:22).

The book of Hebrews uses the symbols of Yom Kippur to describe Jesus' death. As the high priest entered the most holy place, so Jesus entered God's presence, carrying not the blood of bull and goat but his own. His once-for-all death at the "culmination of the ages" (Heb. 9:26) not only allows him to remain in God's presence (10:12) but also gives us access to God's presence as well (10:19–22).

Sabbath Year. Every seven years, the Israelites were to observe a "Sabbath of the land" (Lev. 25:6 ESV), a time for the land to rest. They could not sow fields or prune vineyards, but they could eat what grew of itself (25:1–7). Deuteronomy 15:1–11 speaks of all debts being canceled (some would say deferred) every seventh year, presumably the same year the land was to lie fallow. When Israel was gathered at the Festival of Tabernacles during this Sabbath Year, the law of Moses was to be read aloud. The Chronicler described the seventy years of Babylonian exile as "sabbaths" for the land, perhaps alluding to the neglect of the Sabbath Year (2 Chron. 36:21; cf. Lev. 26:43). Those returning from exile expressed their intent to keep this provision (Neh. 10:31), and it appears to have been observed in the intertestamental period (see 1 Macc. 6:48–53; Josephus, *Ant.* 14.202–10).

This year seems intended to maintain the fertility of the land and to allow Israel's economy to "reset," equalizing wealth and limiting poverty. Observing such a provision took great faith and firm allegiance, for they had to trust God for daily bread and put obedience above profit. Rereading the law at the Festival of Tabernacles reminded the Israelites of God's gracious covenant and their required response.

Jubilee. God instructed Israel to count off seven "sevens" of years and in the fiftieth year, beginning on the Day of Atonement, to sound a trumpet marking the Jubilee Year. As in the Sabbath Year, there was to be no sowing and reaping. Further, the land was released from its current owners and returned to those families to whom it originally belonged. Individual Israelites who had become indentured through economic distress were to be freed. The assumption underlying the Jubilee Year was that everything belonged to God. He owned the land and its occupants; the Israelites were only tenants and stewards (Lev. 25:23, 55). As their covenant Lord, he would provide for their needs even during back-to-back Sabbath Years (Lev. 25:21). The year began on the Day of Atonement, perhaps to emphasize that the best response to God's redemptive mercy is faith in his provision and mercy to others. Although the Jubilee Year is commanded in the Mosaic law and spoken about by the prophets (Isa. 61:1–2; Ezek. 46:17), rabbis, and Jesus (Luke 4:18–19), Scripture is silent on how or if Israel observed this year.

New Moon. The beginning of each month was marked with the sounding of trumpets, rejoicing, and sacrifices (Num. 10:10; 28:11–15). There is some indication that work was to be suspended on this day, as on the Sabbath (Amos 8:5), and that people gathered for a meal (1 Sam. 20:5, 18, 24, 27). By faithfully observing this day, Israel was in a position to properly observe the remaining days, set up, as they were, on the lunar calendar. Paul learned of some in Colossae who were giving undue attention to New Moon celebrations (Col. 2:16).

Purim. Beyond the festivals commanded in the law of Moses, the Jews added two more to their sacred calendar, one during the postexilic period and one between the Testaments. Both commemorated God's deliverance of his people from their enemies. A wave of anti-Semitic persecution swept over the Jews living in Persia during the reign of Xerxes (486–465 BC). God delivered his people through Esther, and the Jews celebrated this deliverance with the festival of Purim. Their enemies determined when to attack by casting lots, so the Jews called this festival "Purim," meaning "lots." It was celebrated on the fourteenth and fifteenth days of the twelfth month (February–March) with "feasting and joy and giving presents of food to one another and gifts to the poor" (Esther 9:22).

Festival of Dedication. During the intertestamental period, the Jews came under great persecution from the Seleucids, who outlawed the practice of Judaism and desecrated the Jerusalem temple. After recapturing the temple, the Jews began the process of purification. On the twenty-fifth day of their ninth month, in the year 164 BC, the Jews

> rose at dawn and offered a lawful sacrifice on the new altar of burnt offering which they had made. The altar was dedicated, to the sound of hymns, zithers, lyres and cymbals, at the same time of year and on the same day on which the gentiles had originally profaned it. The whole people fell prostrate in adoration and then praised Heaven who had granted them success. For eight days they celebrated the dedication of the altar, joyfully offering burnt offerings, communion and thanksgiving sacrifices. . . . Judas [Maccabees], with his brothers and the whole assembly of Israel, made it a law that the days of the dedication of the altar should be celebrated yearly at the proper season, for eight days beginning on the twenty-fifth of the month of Chislev [December], with rejoicing and gladness. (1 Macc. 4:52–56, 59 NJB)

This festival is also called "Hanukkah" (from the Hebrew word for "dedicate") or the Festival of Lights, to recall the lighting of the lamps in the temple. The rabbis told how these lamps were lit from a small quantity of oil that miraculously lasted eight days until more could be consecrated. John 10:22–39 describes events from Jesus' life that took place at the Festival of Dedication.

FESTUS–Porcius Festus served as procurator (governor) of Judea from about AD 59 to 62, succeeding Marcus Antonius Felix (governed AD 52–59). Felix had imprisoned Paul in Caesarea Maritima as a political favor to a group of Jews who desired Paul's death, and Festus did not release him (Acts 24:27). Paul stood trial before Festus, but he appealed to be tried in Rome before Caesar's court, contrary to his opponents' desire that he be tried in Jerusalem (see Acts 25–26). Festus granted Paul's request, but first he remanded him to King Agrippa, before whom Paul presented his defense before being sent to Rome for trial (Acts 27–28).

Field of Blood–*See* Akeldama.

Fiery Serpent–*See* Venomous Serpent.

Firmament–In the understanding of the ancient Hebrew people, the firmament was a great vaulted ceiling that covered the earth. It was thought that the universe consisted of a great expanse of water beneath the earth, which sat like a disk on top of it. Above, there was another great expanse of heavenly waters, which was held back from the earth by a large dome, the substance of which was like stretched and beaten metal (Job 37:18). The prohibition of idols in Exod. 20:4 reflects this worldview. Holes in this dome allowed water to fall on the earth (Gen. 7:11; Ps. 78:23–24), and celestial bodies such as the sun and the stars were set within the dome and moved along it (Gen. 1:14–18). In Ezekiel's vision of the four creatures, the firmament was "sparkling like ice" (Ezek. 1:22).

First and Last–*See* Alpha and Omega.

Firstborn–The first child born to a married couple. In the OT it most commonly refers to the first male child, upon whom special privileges were bestowed. The OT describes some of the privileges associated with being the firstborn son: he would receive a double portion of the inheritance (a privilege codified in the law in Deut. 21:17), the paternal blessing (Gen. 27; 48:17–19), and other examples of favoritism (e.g., Gen. 43:33). The importance ascribed to the firstborn is also attested in the legislative requirement that the firstborn—people, animals, and produce—belong to Yahweh (Lev. 27:26; Deut. 15:19; and of people, note Num. 3:12–13), so stressing his primacy over Israel.

"Firstborn" language is also used figuratively in the OT. It is used of Israel as Yahweh's firstborn in Exod. 4:22–23, wherein Pharaoh's failure to release Yahweh's firstborn results in the destruction of Egypt's firstborn. God also declares the Davidic king to be his firstborn son in Ps. 89:27, highlighting the special favor that he would enjoy. "Firstborn" language can also be used figuratively to describe anything that receives a greater share, such as "the firstborn of Death" in Job 18:13 (NRSV) and "the firstborn of the poor" in Isa. 14:30 (NRSV).

Somewhat surprisingly, God does not adhere to the significance of primogeniture, frequently bestowing his favor on those who were not firstborn: Abel over Cain, Isaac over Ishmael, Jacob over Esau, Joseph and Judah over Reuben, Ephraim over Manasseh, Moses over Aaron, David over his brothers, and Solomon over Adonijah.

The NT presupposes an understanding of the significance of the firstborn. Jesus is specifically identified as Mary's firstborn (Luke 2:7, 23). However, the description extends beyond mere notions of human primogeniture when Jesus is described as "firstborn over all creation" (Col. 1:15) and "firstborn from among the dead" (Col. 1:18; cf. Rev. 1:5). These expressions, in line with figurative use of "firstborn" language in the OT, express Jesus' privileged place in both creation and the new creation.

Firstfruits–The earliest ripening produce of the harvest (Exod. 23:16; Neh. 10:35) or, more generally, the highest-quality portion of any produce or manufactured commodity (Num. 15:20).

The firstfruit of the harvest is a symbol and harbinger of God's blessing. Thus, God commands that sacrifices take place in which the "best of the firstfruits" are offered to him in thanksgiving and praise (Exod. 34:26; cf. Lev. 23:17; Deut. 26:2). The same principle applies to manufactured goods (Deut. 18:4), and all these events are accompanied by feasts and festivals (Exod. 23:16). Such ceremonial worship takes on renewed importance in the return from the exile, where they are connected to God's worldwide rule and his claim upon the firstborn (Neh. 10:35–37; cf. Exod. 13:2–16).

Paul uses this OT background to metaphorically describe the resurrection, God's final "harvest" of the earth. Jesus Christ, by virtue of his resurrection from the dead, is "the firstfruits of those who have fallen asleep" (1 Cor. 15:20; cf. Rom. 8:29). The resurrection of Christ is the guarantee of an abundant harvest to come, in which those united to Jesus will be similarly raised into abundant life. There is therefore a two-part order to a single resurrection harvest: "Christ, the firstfruits; then, when he comes, those who belong to him" (1 Cor. 15:23).

Furthermore, since Jesus' own resurrection has already taken place, believers, who are sealed with Christ through "the firstfruits of the Spirit," enjoy now a foretaste of the abundant life to come (Rom. 8:23; cf. 2 Cor. 1:22; 5:5). Believers are therefore encouraged to live as those who have been born again by faith, "that we might be a kind of firstfruits of all he created" (James 1:18). Similarly, Paul sometimes uses the term "firstfruits" to describe the first converts in a region (Rom. 16:5; 1 Cor. 16:15 KJV), symbolizing the expectation of fruitful ministry and the intimation of worldwide salvation.

Flesh and Spirit–Throughout both Testaments the word "flesh" usually refers to the physical body of both humans and animals, while the word "spirit," although less specific, generally refers to the persona of an individual, that part of a human that relates most closely to God. Contrasting these, the prophet Isaiah says that the enemy Egyptian horses are "flesh and not spirit," and so he implies that the spirit is stronger than the flesh. Isaiah says that those living in Jerusalem should put their trust in God and not the flesh (Isa. 31:3).

Probably the most specific instance of flesh and spirit being discussed together is in John 3:6, where the author quotes Jesus saying, "Flesh gives birth to flesh, but the Spirit gives birth to spirit." English translations capitalize the first of the two occurrences of the Greek word *pneuma* ("spirit") in this verse, inferring that it is the Spirit of God who gives birth to the human spirit. Jesus tries to explain to Nicodemus that a person must be born again by the Spirit of God, much as a human birth produces human flesh.

Flood–Recounted in Gen. 6:5–9:19, the flood is the event whereby God destroys all creatures except for Noah, his family, and a gathering of animals. The account is highly literary and God-centered. It opens and closes with Noah's three sons (6:10; 9:18–19). Noah's obedience is highlighted (7:5, 9, 16). God is the protagonist, and Noah remains silent.

In Gen. 6:5–22, God observes the grand scale of human wickedness, determines to destroy all life, and selects righteous Noah to build an ark. God's "seeing" is judicial investigation (6:5, 13) that counters the sons of God who "saw" (6:2), just as his pained heart counters humankind's wicked heart (6:5–6). God's second statement, "I will wipe from the face of the earth the human race" (6:7), is his judicial sentence (cf. 3:15–19), affecting all life in the domain of human care (1:28; cf. Job 38:41; Ps. 36:6; Hos. 4:3; Joel 1:20).

The earth's corruption and violence (Gen. 6:12–13) reflect a spectrum of evil that has despoiled a creation that was once "very good" (1:31; cf. 6:17; 7:21; 8:17; 9:11). God's destruction responds to the moral corruption of the earth. The ark is a rectangular vessel designed for floating rather than sailing (6:14–15). Noah builds a microcosm of the earth to save its life. The boat's windowlike openings and three decks reflect the cosmology of Gen. 1 (heavens, water, earth [cf. 6:16]). God makes a promise that Noah will survive and receive a covenant from God (6:18), fulfilled in the Noahic covenant following the flood (9:9, 11, 14–17).

Genesis 7:1–24 recounts the boarding of the ark and then the rising waters. Two numbering systems are used by the narrator in the flood narrative: one for dates of Noah's age (day, month, year) and one for periods between flood stages. Both systems number between 365 and 370 days. The flood is portrayed as a reversal of the second and third days of creation. Watery boundaries that God once separated collapse (cf. 1:6–10). The rising flood is described in three phases: rising and lifting the ark (7:17), increasing greatly and floating the ark on the surface (7:18), and covering all the high mountains (7:19). Total destruction is amplified by reversing the order of creation—people, animals, birds (7:23)—with "all/every" occurring repeatedly in 7:21–23.

Genesis 8:1–22 recounts the disembarking and Noah's sacrifice. Genesis 8:1 is the structural and theological center, with God fulfilling (= "remember") his covenant promise for Noah's safety. The ark rests on one mountain within the range in eastern Turkey (Kurdistan). The earth's drying occurs as a process (8:3, 5, 9, 11, 13, 14), and echoes of creation reappear (e.g., "wind" [8:1; cf. 1:2]). Although the old curse is not lifted (cf. 5:29), God promises not to add to it (8:21). The flood has not reformed the human heart; it has only stopped the violence. God's oath of restoration reaffirms the seamless rhythm of seasons that compose a full year (8:22).

Genesis 9:1–19 recounts the restoration of world order. Since murder was part of the antediluvian violence (6:11, 13), God's law recalibrates earthly morality (9:5). God's second postdiluvian speech encodes his plan for the broader preservation of creation (9:8–17).

"My rainbow" is God's confirming sign (9:13). The meteorological phenomenon of the storm is now harnessed as an image of peace. The cosmic warrior "hangs up" his bow in divine disarmament. Humankind now shares the responsibility of justice with God, illustrated in Noah's first speech of cursing and blessing (9:20–27).

Folly–*See* Fool, Foolishness.

Food Sacrificed to Idols–"Food sacrificed to idols" refers both to the part of pagan sacrifices that was burned for a god and what was left over, whether eaten at a temple meal or sold in a market. Since most meat in the first century was butchered at temples, Christians faced the dilemma of whether to eat it. At times, NT writers viewed it as spiritual adultery and forbade it, along with sexual immorality (Rev. 2:14, 20). At other times, believers were encouraged not to partake of it in order to preserve Christian harmony. Thus, when the members of the Jerusalem council determined that Gentile believers need not convert to Judaism, they included eating food sacrificed to idols among the four things to be avoided because they were particularly repulsive to Jews (Acts 15:20). In a setting where Jewish scruples were less influential, some Corinthian believers concluded that eating sacrificed meat would compromise their faith, since demons behind the idols received the offerings. Others felt free to eat such meat, trusting their knowledge that since idols were not really gods, meat sacrificed to them remained unaffected. Although Paul permits the purchase of meat in a market, since all things belong to the Lord (1 Cor. 10:25–26; cf. Ps. 24:1), and allows eating whatever unbelievers serve without asking questions, he rejects open participation in pagan sacrifices as incompatible with participation in the Lord's Supper (1 Cor. 10:21). He further exhorts his readers to set aside their freedom to eat meat if it would harm the conscience of either weaker believers or unbelievers (1 Cor. 8; 10:27–32).

Fool, Foolishness–Generally speaking, in Scripture the word "fool" is used to describe someone in a morally deprived state. It does not, as in contemporary American usage, refer to a person's lack of intellectual ability or to one whose actions convey those of a buffoon. Terms for "fool" appear all through Scripture, but wisdom literature contains the highest concentration. Proverbs uses over half a dozen words to describe the fool. All of them indicate some kind of moral breach and fall on a scale from the most morally hardened to the naive.

Obstinacy, recalcitrance, and closed-mindedness characterize the morally dense fool. Such individuals have no use for advice from others because they are "wise in their own eyes" (Prov. 3:7; cf. 12:15; 16:2). Fools frequently scoff at correction and rebuke (9:7–8, 12; 13:1; 14:6; 15:12; 19:25; 20:1; 21:11, 24; 22:10; 24:9). They manifest arrogance (21:24). Fools do not learn from their own mistakes or those of others but instead often repeat them (26:11). One of the main problems is that fools "lack sense," which ultimately implies that they lack character (see 6:32; 7:7; 9:4, 16; 10:13, 21; 11:12; 12:11; 15:21; 17:18; 24:30). Such a person consistently makes poor decisions and loses the appetite and passion necessary for acquiring wisdom.

According to the book of Proverbs, three qualities make up the essential nature of the fool. First, the fool is unwilling to learn by means of discipline (3:11–12; 17:10), or formal instruction (17:16), or a word of advice (12:15), or personal experience (26:11). Second, the fool lacks self-control. Both the speech (15:2) and the behavior (14:16) of fools demonstrate a lack of restraint. They take the path of least resistance to easy money (1:8–19) and easy sex (7:6–27). Third, the fool is the one who rejects the fear of the Lord (1:7).

In the NT, the fool is the one who does not trust in God or in the power that God displays through the resurrection of Christ (Luke 24:25; Rom. 1:22; 1 Cor. 15:36). Jesus makes references to the fool when he tells the stories of the wise and foolish builders (Matt. 7:24–27) and the wise and foolish maidens (Matt. 25:1–13). Paul uses the term "foolish" to rebuke the Galatians for their refusal to accept the gospel (Gal. 3:1). However, in his correspondence with the church in Corinth, Paul reverses the conventional understanding of folly and uses it as a rhetorical strategy to communicate his message. He speaks of the message of the cross as foolishness to the world (1 Cor. 1:18). On another occasion, in order to argue against the arrogance of his opponents, Paul engages in "a little foolishness" (2 Cor. 11:1) as he boasts about his ministry, which is riddled with failure (2 Cor. 11–12).

Footstool–There are seven references in the OT to "footstool," only one of which is literal (2 Chron. 9:18); the other six are variously figurative. In 1 Chron. 28:2 the ark of the covenant is apparently referred to as God's footstool (though this imagery clashes somewhat with other texts that seem to regard the ark as the seat of his throne). Psalm 99:5 commands worship at God's footstool, perhaps referring to the temple (so also Ps. 132:7; Lam. 2:1). In Isa. 66:1 God declares that the earth is his footstool (seeing the universe as his temple). In Ps. 110:1 God tells the anointed king that he will make his enemies "a footstool for your feet." Paintings from ancient Egypt depict Pharaoh's footstool adorned with carvings of conquered enemies, and correspondence from both Egypt and Mesopotamia indicates that vassals referred to themselves as the king's footstool.

In the NT, all the references to "footstool" are quotations of, or allusions to, the aforementioned OT passages (Matt. 5:35; Luke 20:43; Acts 2:35; 7:49; Heb. 1:13; 10:13).

Footwashing–A common form of hospitality offered to travelers in biblical times. A host offered a basin full of water so that a guest's feet could be cleaned upon entrance into the home. The dusty and dry climate of Palestine made footwashing important, as people often walked along dirt roads with nothing more than sandals on their feet. Footwashing was so common that hosts who failed to offer this basic expression of hospitality and comfort were severely criticized (Luke 7:44).

Although a staple of hospitality, footwashing was considered the lowliest of activities performed by a servant. It was so demeaning that Jews did not wash the feet of other Jews but rather left the task to Gentile slaves. More often, travelers simply washed their own feet rather than having the chore performed for them (Gen. 18:4; 19:2; 43:24; Judg. 19:21; Luke 7:44).

Because footwashing was performed by a person of inferior social status for a superior (1 Sam. 25:41), it would be unthinkable to reverse this socially accepted norm in a culture saturated with relative social status. So for Jesus, a superior, to perform this demeaning chore for his disciples, his inferiors, makes his object lesson all the more dramatic (John 13:5–17). Jesus washed his disciples' feet to show them that no role is too lowly for him to show the extent of his love (13:1). Peter learned the necessity of spiritual cleansing when Jesus washed his feet (13:8). Jesus also taught his disciples the importance of following his example in their own lives by washing one another's feet (13:14). No act of service is too lowly for Christ's followers, and no one is too great to perform such a humble act.

Foreigner–A person or group of people whose birthplace is other than the location in which they are currently residing. Genesis records God's covenant relationship with Abraham and his promise to create a vast nation from Abraham's offspring (Gen. 17:8–20). In the OT context, a foreigner is a person not born into the nation of Israel, determined by lineage traceable to Jacob, son of Isaac, son of Abraham. Foreigners in the land of Israel were allowed to partake of the Passover only if it was done in accordance with Israelite law (Exod. 12:48; Num. 9:14). The relationship between foreigners and the nation of Israel was not hostile. In fact, God reminds Israel of their own sojourn in Egypt and gives specific laws for the fair treatment of foreigners in their midst (Exod. 23:9; Lev. 19:10, 33–34; 23:22; 25:35; Deut. 10:19).

In the NT, the apostle Paul uses the concept with respect to a person's relationship to the kingdom of God. In Ephesians he refers to those without Christ as being "excluded from citizenship in Israel and foreigners to the covenants of the promise" (Eph. 2:12), meaning that they exist outside of God's kingdom. Conversely, those believing in Christ have received "adoption as children" (Gal. 4:5 NRSV), meaning that they are no longer foreigners and are now counted as citizens of God's kingdom, as the offspring of the king clearly are.

Foreknow, Foreknowledge–In systematic theology, "foreknowledge" usually refers to the doctrine that God knows all things, events, and persons before they exist or occur and that this knowledge has been his from all eternity. No single Hebrew term in the OT corresponds to the English term; the concept is expressed rather on the phrase or sentence level. In the NT, the Greek verb *proginōskō* and noun *prognōsis* are translated "foreknow" and "foreknowledge," respectively. Recently in evangelical circles there has been intense debate as to whether foreknowledge and omniscience are in fact taught in the biblical texts.

Forgiveness–Biblically speaking, to forgive is less about changing feelings (emotions) and more about an actual restoration of a relationship. It is about making a wrong right, a process that usually is both costly and painful.

To capture the biblical sense, the English word "pardon" may prove more helpful.

Forgiveness expresses the character of the merciful God, who eagerly pardons sinners who confess their sins, repent of their transgressions, and express this through proper actions. Forgiveness is never a matter of a human right; it is exclusively a gracious expression of God's loving care. Human need for forgiveness stems from actions arising from their fallen nature. These actions (or nonactions), whether done deliberately or coincidentally, destroy people's relationship with God and can be restored only by God's forgiving mercy (Eph. 2:1).

Under the Mosaic covenant, sin placed offenders under God's wrath among the ungodly. Rescue from this fate could be obtained by God's forgiveness alone, which was attained through repentance and sacrifice. Although sacrifice was necessary to express true repentance, it is a mistake to consider it a payment that could purchase God's forgiveness (1 Sam. 15:22; Prov. 21:3; Eccles. 5:1; Hos. 6:6). The forgiveness of God remains his free, undeserved gift.

Although the sacrificial system is done away with, or rather completed, through Christ (Heb. 10:12), NT teaching continues to recognize conditions for forgiveness. Since forgiveness restores relationship, the offender remains involved and must desire the restoration (Luke 13:3; 24:47; Acts 2:38). God does not grant his forgiveness without consideration of the offending party.

Jesus expresses this most clearly in the parable of the prodigal son (Luke 15:11–24). The son rebels against his father, squanders his wealth, and violates their relationship. The gracious and loving father remains willing to restore the relationship, but the reunion does not occur until the prodigal replaces rebellion with repentance; then, before he can even utter his sorrow, the eager father welcomes him back to a restored relationship. God remains free to forgive or not forgive, but, because of God's nature and mercy, sinners can rest assured of God's relationship-restoring forgiveness when they seek it in repentance. The forgiveness that God grants is full and restores things to an "as before" situation (cf. Ps. 103:12; Jer. 31:34), a point that the older son in the parable (Luke 15:25–32), who exemplifies religious self-righteousness, did not comprehend.

Fortunatus–A Corinthian Christian mentioned along with Stephanus and Achaicus in 1 Cor. 16:17–18 as having "supplied what was lacking" from the Corinthians and having "refreshed" Paul's spirit. Fortunatus, Stephanus, and Achaicus visited Paul in Ephesus and probably delivered a letter from Corinth. Paul encouraged the Corinthians to honor them. It is likely that these three men delivered the letter that we know as 1 Corinthians to the church at Corinth.

Fortune and Destiny–In Isa. 65:11 the prophet castigates those who forsake God and "spread a table for Fortune [Heb. *gad*] and fill bowls of mixed wine for Destiny [*meni*]," thus worshiping Gad and Meni, pagan gods of fate. The prophecy asserts that the fate of such persons is actually in the hands of Israel's God: "I will destine you for the sword, and all of you will fall in the slaughter" (Isa. 65:12).

Forum of Appius–The Forum of Appius (KJV: "Appii Forum") was a market station forty-three miles south of Rome on the Appian Way. Some Roman believers traveled to this town to meet Paul on his way to imprisonment in Rome (Acts 28:15).

Fountain–In Proverbs, the phrase "fountain [*maqor*] of life" refers to the mouth of a righteous man (10:11), the law of the wise (13:14; cf. 18:4), the fear of the Lord (14:27; cf. Ps. 36:9), and understanding (Prov. 16:22). Similarly, Jer. 2:13 describes God as a fountain of living water, an idea echoed in Rev. 21:6. In Prov. 5:18 the fountain (along with wells, cisterns, streams, and springs) symbolizes the fecundity of marriage.

The "fountains of the deep" mentioned in Gen. 7:11; 8:2 (NIV: "springs of the deep"); Prov. 8:28 refer to a particular aspect of ancient cosmology: the notion that the terrestrial earth is supported by pillars (see Job 9:6; Ps. 75:3) above a subterranean sea. In the story of the great flood, the "fountains" of this sea, the "great deep," were a source of the waters of the flood.

Fountain Gate–*See* Gates of Jerusalem and the Temple.

Frankincense–*See* Spices.

Freedmen, Synagogue of the–A synagogue in Jerusalem whose members argued with Stephen. After they were unable to prevail over Stephen, they instigated the accusations that led to his stoning. The Synagogue of the Freedmen was named for those who had been liberated from slavery, and some have identified the freedmen as descendants of Pompey's prisoners. Pompey was the Roman general who seized control of Judea for Rome in 63 BC.

Freewill Offering–Occurring approximately twenty-two times in the OT, this term refers to sacrifices presented to God not by prescription or external compulsion, but from a motivation within the heart of the offerer. Some examples are the contributions that the Israelites made for building the tabernacle (Exod. 35:29; 36:3), gifts for the first temple (2 Chron. 31:14), and gifts for the construction of the second temple (Ezra 2:68). These gifts could either be monetary or animal offerings. The concept of the freewill offering may stand behind some of Paul's teaching about giving in the Corinthian letters.

Frontlets–In Exod. 13:16; Deut. 6:8; 11:18 the KJV renders the Hebrew word *totapot* as "frontlets" (NIV: "symbol"; NRSV: "emblem"), referring to the binding of God's commandments on one's forehead. The literal reading of this led to the custom of *tefillin* (a word found in *Targum Onqelos*, the Peshitta, and rabbinic literature), a pair of small leather boxes worn by Jews during prayer. Specific Scripture verses (Exod. 13:1–16; Deut. 6:4–9; 11:13–21) were written on small scrolls and placed in each box. The NT refers to tefillin as "phylacteries" (from the Gk. verb for "guard, keep"). In Matt. 23:5 Jesus condemned individuals who called attention to themselves by making their phylacteries "wide."

Fruit–Literally, fruit is the seed-bearing part of a plant. It constitutes an important part of the diet in the ancient Near East. Common fruits are olives, grapes, and figs, though many other varieties of fruit are also available, including apples, apricots, peaches, pomegranates, dates, and melons. Fruit trees play a prominent role as a food source in God's creation and preparation of the garden of Eden (Gen. 1–3). The law prohibits the Israelites from cutting down their enemy's fruit trees (Deut. 20:19). The abundance of fruit trees characterizes the land that God has prepared for Israel (Deut. 8:8; Neh. 9:25) as well as the final restoration (Ezek. 47:12; Joel 2:22; Rev. 22:2).

One aspect of fruit is that it grows from a plant. This use of the term is often extended to represent what emerges from something else. Thus, fruit may represent offspring, whether human or animal (Deut. 7:13; 28:4), one's actions (Matt. 7:16–20), the result of one's actions or choices (Prov. 1:31; 10:16; Jer. 17:10), or words coming from one's mouth (Prov. 12:14; Heb. 13:15). In the NT especially, producing much fruit symbolizes performing deeds that are pleasing to God (Matt. 3:8; 13:23; Mark 4:20; John 15:16; Rom. 7:4; Col. 1:10). Those who live by the Spirit produce the fruit of the Spirit (Gal. 5:22–23). The apostle Paul speaks of the first converts in a particular region as being firstfruits, probably referring to their conversion as the result of the gospel being preached in the area (Rom. 16:5; 2 Thess. 2:13).

Fulfill, Fulfillment–The various Hebrew and Greek words that express the idea of fulfillment occur hundreds of times in the Bible, and the concept often is present even when the specific word is not. At the basic level, fulfillment indicates a relationship between two (or more) things in which the second is said to "fill up" the significance of the first. Frequently this takes the form of a specific promise that is said to be fulfilled when the person, object, or event referred to comes to pass. There are countless examples of this type of fulfillment, some of which even quote the specific promise that is being fulfilled. The seventy years of Babylonian captivity prophesied by Jeremiah (Jer. 29:10) are said to be fulfilled when Cyrus permits the Jews to return to the land (Ezra 1:1–4). Jesus' birth in Bethlehem (Matt. 2:1–6) fulfills the promise of a ruler who will shepherd Israel (Mic. 5:2).

But the concept of fulfillment goes beyond specific promises that are then said to be fulfilled in a particular person, object, or event. In the broadest sense of the term, one can say that the NT fulfills what the OT promises. After his resurrection, Jesus reminds his disciples, "Everything must be fulfilled that is written about me in the Law of Moses, the Prophets and the Psalms" (Luke 24:44). He then provides a summary of the entire OT message: "The Messiah will suffer and rise from the dead on the third day, and repentance for the forgiveness of sins will be preached in his name to all nations, beginning at Jerusalem" (Luke 24:46–47).

Fuller's Field–*See* Washerman's Field.

Fullness of Time–This expression appears in Gal. 4:4; Eph. 1:10 NRSV (although with variation in the Greek: *chronos* in the former, *kairos* in the latter). In Gal. 4 the context suggests that God sent Christ at the most opportune time. In Eph. 1 the expression is more apocalyptic and looks forward to the occasion when this fullness takes place. There it designates the entirety of the era from the coming of Christ to the final culmination of all things. In Ephesians the fullness is both already present and awaiting its ultimate arrival when Christ returns and finalizes his rule.

G

Gaal–The son of Ebed who came to Shechem along with his brothers to incite the citizens against Abimelek (Judg. 9:26–29). When the governor Zebul reported this rebellion to Abimelek, Abimelek attacked Shechem at dawn and drove Gaal and his brothers out of the city (9:30–41).

Gabbatha–An English rendering of the Greek transliteration of an Aramaic place name from the root *gbb*, probably meaning "high" or "elevated." John gives this and the Greek name, *Lithostrōton* ("stone pavement"), together in describing Jesus' trial before Pilate (John 19:13). Such a structure was commonly found in the marketplace of Roman cities. The exact location of the one in Jerusalem is unknown, but it is likely to have been on the east side of Herod's palace.

Gabriel–An angel who first appears in the book of Daniel (8:16; 9:21). Gabriel functions as the spokesperson for God to the prophet, and in particular he explains the meaning of the visions that Daniel experienced. Although not mentioned by name in Dan. 10, he is likely the angel who comes to Daniel with the aid of Michael, another angel, to inform Daniel of the meaning of the vision recounted in Dan. 11. Gabriel is also sent to Zechariah and to Mary to inform them of the significance of the births of, respectively, John (the Baptist) and Jesus (Luke 1:19, 26).

Gad–**(1)** A son of Jacob, born to Zilpah, Leah's maidservant. He was one of Jacob's twelve sons, destined to become a tribe of Israel. His name can mean "luck," and this is the etiology given in Gen. 30:11. **(2)** Another Gad, found in 2 Sam. 24, is called "David's seer" (v. 11). He was the prophet who confronted David about the census he had taken and offered him three choices: famine, foes, or plague. Gad instructed him to buy Araunah's threshing floor and build an altar there. When this was done and sacrifice made, the blight ended. Much earlier, he had advised David to return to the land of Judah during his tenure as persona non grata in Saul's court (1 Sam. 22:5). **(3)** There is another Gad mentioned in Isa. 65:11, sometimes translated "Fortune," as in the NRSV: "But you who forsake the Lord, who forget my holy mountain, who set a table for Fortune and fill cups of mixed wine for Destiny"—here perhaps the name of a god worshiped by some Israelites.

Gad, Tribe of–One of the twelve tribes of Israel, descended from Gad, a son of Jacob born to Leah's maidservant Zilpah. After the conquest of Canaan, the tribe of Gad (sometimes referred to as the "Gadites") settled with the Transjordanian tribes, between Manasseh to the north and Reuben to the south. Sometimes the Bible equates the land with part of Gilead (Num. 32:25–26). One of its important cities was Ramoth Gilead (Josh. 21:38), where king Ahab was mortally wounded. Gad remained part of Israel until the kingdom came to an end, and its inhabitants eventually were taken into exile by the Assyrians.

Gadarenes–One of three principal variant names in all three Synoptic Gospels for the region where Jesus healed demoniacs after sailing with his disciples across the Sea of Galilee (Matt. 8:28–34; Mark 5:1–20; Luke 8:26–39). *See* Gerasenes.

Gaius–**(1)** Paul's missionary companion (along with Aristarchus) who was apprehended by an angry Ephesian crowd until being released at the urging of the city clerk

(Acts 19:29). This is likely the same Gaius who traveled with Paul into Macedonia (20:4). **(2)** A member of the church in Corinth who was baptized by Paul (1 Cor. 1:14) and who showed great hospitality to the entire Corinthian church during Paul's time in that city (Rom. 16:23). **(3)** An elder in the church addressed by the author of 3 John who is praised for his faithfulness to the gospel (v. 1).

Galatia–An ethnic-geographic area in northern Asia Minor inhabited primarily by peoples of Gaulic and Celtic extraction since the mid-fourth century BC. In 25 BC the Romans conferred provincial status not only on the northern ethnic-geographic Galatian area, but also on parts of Pontus, Phrygia, Pisidia, and Lycaonia, farther to the south. Some of the towns that Paul visited on his first missionary journey (Acts 13–14) were in the southern part of this area: Antioch, Iconium, Lystra, and Derbe. Very little evidence remains attesting to the presence of either Jews or Christians in the Roman provincial area of Galatia in the first or second century AD, beyond reference in the NT and Christian writings drawing from the NT.

The location of the Galatian churches to which Paul writes in his letter to the Galatians remains a thorny problem. On the one hand, the address (Gal. 1:2) naturally seems to indicate the ethnic-geographic area of the north. On the other hand, if one takes Acts seriously, Paul never traveled in that area and thus had no chance to proclaim the gospel to the ethnic Galatians. Even Acts 16:6 places Paul over 125 miles southwest of this area. Thus, some scholars adopt the South Galatian hypothesis: Paul addresses his letter to people living in the southern part of the Roman province of Galatia and its environs.

Galatians, Letter to the–Galatians is often understood as the letter teaching justification by faith in Christ alone. Paul inveighs against false teachers who teach Christians to supplement the work of Christ with their own keeping of the law as part of earning salvation.

Greeting (1:1–5). When Paul hears of this situation among the Galatian churches, he writes them a frustrated letter. He commences by stressing how Jesus, through giving himself for our sins, is God's means for delivering us from the present evil age (1:3–4).

The law-defined gospel is a different gospel (1:6–10). Paul continues by making clear his point of view: despite what the other teachers say, their law-defined gospel is in fact a damnable "different gospel" (1:6–10; all translations are the author's).

Paul's gospel is straight from God (1:11–24). While the other teachers may claim that their gospel comes from the authoritative Jerusalem church, Paul explains that his gospel comes straight from God and not from other men (1:11–24).

The Jerusalem apostles recognize Paul's law-free gospel (2:1–10). However, when he had met with the Jerusalem apostles, they had recognized his law-free gospel (1:18–2:10). Indeed, they had not forced Titus to be circumcised (2:3).

Paul and Peter on whether Gentiles should live like Jews (2:11–21). Paul then narrates an account of an incident that speaks directly to the Galatian situation (2:11–21). Previously in Antioch Peter had acted so as to imply that Gentiles would have to live like Jews (e.g., keep the law) in order to truly be unified with God's people (2:11–14). Paul, however, has rebuked Peter (2:14). Paul continues with a speech about how Gentiles are made righteous ("justified") not within the space demarcated by the "works of the law," but rather within the faithfulness of Jesus the Messiah (2:15–16). The works of the law, or the duties commanded by the law, do not define those who are "righteous"—that is, God's true people who will be saved. Rather, the faithfulness of Christ defines God's true people, the ones who believe in Jesus.

Works of the law or Christ's faithfulness? (3:1–5). So far, Paul has not addressed the powerful scriptural arguments and appeals to the law as a means to self-mastery through which the opposing teachers have gained influence. As becomes clear from the rest of the letter, Paul does not anchor his counterarguments ultimately in interpretations of the Jewish Scriptures, possibly because the scriptural arguments of the opposing teachers would have more cogency. Again, they draw on understandings about Gentiles that they can easily ground in the God of Israel's sacred writings. Paul instead appeals directly to how the Galatians have experienced salvation initially. Have they received and experienced the workings of the Spirit "out of/from the works of the law, or from the message of (Christ's) faithfulness" (3:1–5)? Paul, of course, knows that the answer is "from the message of Christ's faithfulness" (often translated as "hearing with faith") apart from the works of the law.

Paul addresses the situation in Galatia (3:6–4:31). For the rest of 3:6–4:31, Paul continues to address the situation in Galatia within the cultural codes and kinds of concerns sketched above. In 3:6–13 Paul launches into a densely packed excursus of scriptural arguments to set up an answer to his rhetorical question "Does he who supplies the Spirit to you and works miracles among you do so out of/from the works of the law, or from the message of (Christ's) faithfulness?" (3:5). He sets up the answer to his question, which comes in 3:14, by focusing on the nature of the Galatians' Abrahamic sonship—that is, the nature of their identity as the God of Israel's special people. Paul argues that Christ's faithfulness, and not the law, defines their Abrahamic sonship.

In 4:1–7 Paul restates parts of his preceding discussion in a different way, introducing the language of slavery. In 4:12–20 Paul returns to reminding the Galatians of their past experience with himself and the gospel. Paul has embodied Christ to them, and they to him. He has brought them Christ in his weakness, and they have accepted him as such. Their turn to the opposing teachers marks a departure from how they first received Paul.

Summary and restatement of Paul's argument (5:1–12). In 5:2–6 Paul quickly summarizes the substance of his arguments thus far, while in 5:7–12 he resummarizes the situation.

The faithfulness of Christ and communal living (5:13–6:10). In 5:13–6:10 Paul finally depicts the positive content of the faithfulness of Christ for the Galatians. This section, in which Paul focuses on how the Galatians live communally, has been his driving focus all along. Not only must he offer something in place of the law for self-mastery in order to wrench the Galatians from the influence of the opposing teachers, but also Paul considers it absolutely necessary for the Galatians to live together in ways embodying Christ's other-oriented, cross-shaped faithfulness (2:19–20; 4:19; 5:13–6:10). Paul does not view the law simply as a neutral, ineffectual means to self-mastery; rather, he thinks that the law will positively work death, slavery, and irrational passions, the things that would bar the Galatians from inheriting the kingdom of God (5:22). Thus, 5:13–6:10 is the most important part of the letter for Paul. All his earlier arguments serve his purposes here.

Conclusion and summary (6:11–18). Paul concludes in 6:11–18, summarizing most of his main points. The law and circumcision now count for nothing; only faithfulness working through love and new creation in Christ count for anything (5:6; 6:15).

For Paul in Galatians, the other-oriented, cross-shaped faithfulness of Christ offers a more concrete communal identity and practical way to life than the law ever could. The faithfulness of Christ and Spirit define the Galatians as a people of the new creation. Justification in Galatians involves more than the traditional doctrine. It involves the unification associated with the fruit of the Spirit, not the division and strife of the works of the flesh/law. It relates to and establishes the conditions for the radical and tangible other-oriented and cross-shaped communal faithfulness (of Christ) that must define God's people.

GALEED–An English rendering of the Hebrew word *gal'ed*, meaning "witness pile" (Gen. 31:47–48). The patriarch Jacob chose "Galeed" as the name for the pile of stones that he and his clan erected as a memorial of the covenant between Jacob and his father-in-law, Laban. The pile also marked the boundary that neither was to cross in order to harm the other. The Aramaic-speaking Laban instead used the equivalent Aramaic term "Jegar Sahadutha."

GALILEE–The northern region of Israel. Determining the region's precise boundaries is difficult, but in Jesus' time it appears to have encompassed an area of about forty-five miles north to south and twenty-five miles east to west, with the Jordan River and the Sea of Galilee forming the eastern border. Josephus divides the region into Upper and Lower Galilee. Upper Galilee contains elevations of up to about four thousand feet and is composed mostly of rugged mountains, while Lower Galilee reaches a maximum height of about two thousand feet and is characterized by numerous fertile valleys. Lower Galilee was the site of most of Jesus' ministry.

Galilee appears several times in the OT (e.g., Josh. 20:7; 1 Kings 9:11; 1 Chron. 6:76). It was part of the land given to the twelve tribes (Josh. 19). Since Galilee was distant from Jerusalem, which played the most prominent part in Jewish history, much of its history is not mentioned in the OT. Many of the references that do occur are military references, such as Joshua's defeat of the kings at the waters of Merom (Josh. 11:1–9) and the Assyrian removal of the northern kingdom of Israel (Isa. 9:1). However, its great beauty, particularly of mountains such as Carmel, Hermon, and Lebanon, was the source of numerous images and metaphors in the poetic and prophetic literature (e.g., Ps. 133:3; Isa. 33:9; 35:2; Jer. 46:18).

Galilee figures more prominently in the NT. Jesus came from Nazareth in Galilee and conducted much of his early ministry there. Luke specifically identifies Galilee as the place where Jesus' ministry began before spreading to Judea (Luke 23:5; Acts 10:37). Galilee is also portrayed as the place where Jesus will reunite with his disciples following the resurrection (Mark 16:7) and where he gives them the Great Commission (Matt. 28:16–20).

Galilee, Sea of–*See* Sea of Galilee.

Gallio–The proconsul of Achaia in the years AD 51–52. He was the brother of the Stoic philosopher Seneca, with whom he shared a reputation for anti-Semitism. In Acts 18:12–17, the Jews of Corinth bring Paul before Gallio's tribunal with the charge of persuading people to worship against the law. Since the charge is brought before the Roman proconsul, this probably refers to Roman law, not Jewish. Under Roman law, Judaism enjoyed the status of being a *collegium licita* (recognized religion), and so its members were exempt from the obligations of emperor worship. Christianity did not enjoy this status, and the Jewish prosecutors wanted Paul's preaching to be seen as part of a *religio illicita* (illegal religion).

Gamaliel–Gamaliel, who is mentioned in Acts 5:34; 22:3, was a member of the Sanhedrin, a Pharisee, and a teacher of the law. He is reputed to have been the grandson of the famous sage and scholar Hillel (according to later tradition). He was a member of the Hillel party of the Pharisees, who were renowned for their more liberal interpretation of Scripture when compared with the more conservative Shammai party. In Acts 5:34–40 Gamaliel intervenes at the trial of the apostles before the Sanhedrin with a reasoned speech. Paul acknowledges him as his teacher in Acts 22:3.

Gate–A controlled point of entry into an otherwise enclosed area such as a city (Gen. 34:24; Ps. 122:2; Acts 9:24), camp (Exod. 32:26–27), tabernacle court (Exod. 35:17), palace (2 Kings 11:19), temple area (Jer. 36:10; Ezek. 40), prison (Acts 12:10), or house (Acts 10:17).

In the OT, the city gate has a central role in that city's military, economic, judicial, political, and religious aspects of life. A key component of the defense system of a city, the gate consists of doors fortified with bars (Judg. 16:3; Ps. 107:16; Nah. 3:13) and keeps invading armies out while also serving as the point of departure and return for the city's army (2 Sam. 18:4; cf. God the warrior entering in Ps. 24:7–8). The gate also may serve as the location where news of the battle is delivered (1 Sam. 4:18; 2 Sam. 18:24). The destruction of the city gate usually means the destruction of the city (Isa. 24:12).

In the economic life of the city, the gate functions as a place of commerce (Gen. 23; 2 Kings 7:1) and music (Lam. 5:14). At the entrance to the city gate, the city elders assembled daily to hear cases and render judgment (Job 29:7; Prov. 24:7). Along with the elders, there might be additional witnesses (Ruth 4:1–11; Ps. 69:12). For criminal cases, the gate may also be the location where punishment is enacted (Deut. 17:5; 22:24). Thus, the gate is to be a place where all people can come to obtain justice (2 Sam. 15:2–4; Isa. 29:21; Amos 5:15). The gate may hold a seat reserved for the king (2 Sam. 19:8) as well as the king's officials (Esther 2:19–21; 3:2–3). The city gate might also contain shrines to various gods (2 Kings 23:8; cf. Acts 14:13).

Some references to gates refer to those of the temple area (Ezek. 44; 46; Pss. 100:4; 118:19–20). In Ezek. 48 the temple area is to have twelve gates, each named after a tribe of Israel (Ezek. 48:30–35; cf. Rev. 21:12–25). The prophet Jeremiah proclaims the word of the Lord from both the city gate(s) (Jer. 17:19–27) and the temple gate(s) (7:1–4).

In the NT, Jesus raises the dead son of a widow at the town gate (Luke 7:11–17) and heals a lame man near the Sheep Gate (John 5:1–15). Peter heals a crippled man near the temple gate (Acts 3:1–10). Jesus mentions gates in his teaching, including a call to enter through the narrow gate of life (Matt. 7:13–14), and his parable of the sheep and the gate, in which Jesus refers to himself as the gate (John 10:1–18). *See also* City Gates.

Gates of Jerusalem and the Temple–The gates of Jerusalem and the temple have varied throughout history. Gates usually were given names that represented their function, activity, or the direction of travel. Most of what we know of gates during OT times is derived from Nehemiah's inspection and description of the destroyed city.

Jerusalem contained several gates during the OT period. On the eastern wall was the Fountain Gate. Just south of this gate was the Potsherd Gate, later becoming the Dung Gate. On the southwest corner was the Valley Gate. On the northern wall were the Ephraim Gate (later called "Middle Gate") and possibly the Fish Gate.

Gates that were either associated with or near the temple were the Muster Gate, Horse Gate, Gate of the Guard, and the Water Gate (possibly also called "East Gate"), the temple gate facing the north, New Gate, Horse Gate, and the upper Benjamin Gate (also Sheep Gate?).

Josephus recounts ten gates associated with the temple: four each on the north and south and two on the east. The gate that led to the court of the women may have been the Beautiful Gate (Acts 3:2), and the gate between the court of the women and the court of Israel probably was the Nicanor Gate. The Todi Gate was on the north; the Coponius Gate (Barclay's Gate), Wilson's Arch, and Warren's Gate were on the west. The south side of the Temple Mount had two large gates: the Double Gate and the Triple Gate. Josephus mentions only two city gates: the Gate of the Essenes and the Gennath Gate.

Gath–One of the five major cities of the Philistines, each of which was ruled by its own lord (Josh. 13:3). Gath was situated close to the border of Judah. Since the Hebrew word *gat* means "winepress" and occurs in the names of several places (e.g., Gath Rimmon, Gath Hepher, Moresheth Gath), there may have been other towns of this name. Some of the biblical references (e.g., 1 Chron. 7:21; 8:13) may not be to Philistine Gath.

At the time of the conquest, Gath (mentioned in the Amarna letters of the fourteenth century BC) was inhabited by the formidable Anakites, whom Joshua failed to dislodge (Josh. 11:21–22; see also Deut. 1:28; 9:2), and in David's day it still boasted warriors of great height and strength (2 Sam. 21:19–22; 1 Chron. 20:5–8). However, it was also one of the cities that God afflicted with tumors when the captured ark of the covenant was stored there (1 Sam. 5:8–9; 6:17), and the mighty Goliath of Gath was no match for God's anointed (1 Sam. 17:8–58).

On two occasions David fled from Saul to Achish, king of Gath. The first time, he was so scared of Achish that he feigned insanity and escaped as soon as he could (1 Sam. 21:10–22:1; cf. the superscription to Ps. 56). The second time, he settled down with six hundred men and their families to deceive Achish in a different way: he used Gath as a base to attack Israel's other enemies (1 Sam. 27:1–30:31), all the while claiming that he was wreaking revenge on Saul. When Achish himself defeated Saul and Jonathan, David was horrified by the thought that the town of Gath would hear of their deaths and gloat (2 Sam. 1:20). His horror is poetically echoed in Micah's eighth-century BC lament over a doomed Judah (Mic. 1:10).

David seems nevertheless to have made friends as well as enemies in Gath. Obed-Edom the Gittite was blessed rather than cursed when the ark was kept at his house before its final journey to Jerusalem (2 Sam. 6:10–11; 1 Chron. 13:3). After David had conquered Gath (1 Chron. 18:1), the six hundred Gittite mercenaries in his army were among his most loyal followers (2 Sam. 15:18–22).

Gath seems to have changed hands fairly frequently thereafter. We know that Achish ruled it in Solomon's day, when Shimei retrieved his runaway slaves from there (1 Kings 2:39–46), and that it was again in Philistine hands when Uzziah broke down its walls (2 Chron. 26:6). In between, however, we are told that Rehoboam of Judah fortified it (2 Chron. 11:8), and that in Joash's reign Hazael of Aram conquered it (2 Kings 12:17). The fact that Amos mentions Gath as "in Philistia" (Amos 6:2) but does not group it with the other four cities of the Philistines (1:6–8) may mean that it was under Israelite control at the time. Assyrian records from the eighth century BC describe several campaigns against rebellious Philistine cities, including the city of Gath (Annals of Sargon II).

Gaza–Gath is strategically situated in southern Palestine near the Egyptian border and is approximately three miles from the Mediterranean Sea.

In the Late Bronze Age (1550–1200 BC), Gaza was under the control of Egypt. It is first mentioned in the annals of Thutmose III as the provincial capital of Canaan, and it functioned as an Egyptian administrative center in the Amarna and Taanach letters. At the beginning of the Iron Age (1200 BC), the Sea Peoples (esp. the Philistines) took control of this coastal region. This scenario is reflected in Deut. 2:23, which states that the Caphtorites (i.e., the Philistines) displaced the Avvites. Joshua 11:22 also states that after the Israelite conquest, the giant Anakim only remained in Gaza, Gath, and Ashdod (they were most likely assimilated into Philistine culture, perhaps as mercenaries). These three cities, along with Ekron and Ashkelon, compose the Philistine Pentapolis (Josh. 13:3; 1 Sam. 6:17–18). The Pentapolis remained unconquered at the end of Joshua's life (Josh. 13:3), even though Ekron, Ashdod, and Gaza were included in Judah's allotment (15:45–47). The Judahites took brief control of Gaza, Ashkelon, and Ekron, which they were unable to maintain due to the Philistines' employment of "iron chariots" on the plains (Judg. 1:18–19). During the period of the judges, Gaza is prominently featured in the exploits of Samson. The city is described as having a gate and a multistoried temple (Judg. 16:1–3, 26). After David's conquests of the Philistines, King Solomon is said to have dominion over a vast region including Gaza (1 Kings 4:24). In the second half of the eighth century BC, Gaza became an Assyrian vassal (under Tiglath-pileser III). King Hezekiah also briefly subdued the region (2 Kings 18:8), but Gaza remained an Assyrian vassal until the end of the seventh century, when the city was briefly occupied by Pharaoh Necho II and then fell to Nebuchadnezzar (see Jer. 47:1–2, 5). Gaza is mentioned in a number of prophetic oracles against Philistia (Jer. 25:20; 47:1; Amos 1:6–7; Zeph. 2:4; Zech. 9:5). It appears only one time in the NT, when Philip is traveling toward Gaza and encounters the Ethiopian eunuch (Acts 8:26).

Geba–Situated on the eastern edge of the central Benjamin Plateau, Geba (modern Jeba) and its sister city, Mikmash (Mukhmas), were about six miles north of Jerusalem on a significant route from the Jordan Valley up into the hill country.

The name "Geba" comes from the Hebrew three-letter root meaning "hill" and is sufficiently similar to "Gibeah" that some have suggested that Geba, Geba of Benjamin (1 Sam. 13:16), Gibeah (Judg. 19–20), Gibeah of Benjamin (1 Sam. 13:2, 15; 14:16), and Gibeah of Saul (e.g., 1 Sam. 10:26; 11:4) are the same location. The best reading of the texts, however, indicates that Geba and Gibeah are at least two separate locations (1 Sam. 13:2–3; Isa. 10:29). Gibeah of Saul is Tell el-Ful, approximately two miles south of Jeba.

During the early years of Saul's monarchy, the Philistines had an outpost at Geba, between the forces of Saul at Mikmash and those of Jonathan at Gibeah of Benjamin (1 Sam. 13:2–3). When they lost Geba to Jonathan, they regrouped at Mikmash, across the pass. Jonathan and his armor-bearer set out from Geba, descended into the wadi, climbed up the other side, and attacked and conquered the Philistine outpost (1 Sam. 14).

King Baasha of the north created a stranglehold on the southern kingdom by seizing Ramah, a critical crossroad point north of Jerusalem between Geba and Mizpah. Asa, king of the south, appealed to Ben-Hadad of Aram, who attacked the northern border of Baasha's territory. Asa wrested control of Ramah back from Baasha and fortified both Geba to the east and Mizpah to the west, making certain to hold the access routes to the central Benjamin Plateau from both east and west (1 Kings 15:16–22).

Gedaliah–The son of Ahikam and grandson of Josiah's scribe, Shaphan. After the exile of Zedekiah, he was appointed as governor over Judah by Nebuchadnezzar of Babylon in 587 BC (2 Kings 25:22–26; Jer. 39:14; 40:5–41:18). He not only protected the prophet Jeremiah but also gave the people similar advice, telling those who remained in Judah to serve the Babylonians. He ignored the warning of Johanan about an assassination plot and, after ruling for only two months, was killed by Ishmael, a representative of Baalis king of the Ammonites. A seal from Lachish appears to refer to him: "belonging to Gedaliah, who is over the house."

Gehazi–The servant of Elisha the prophet. Gehazi figures prominently in the stories of Naaman and the Shunammite woman. He was likely also the servant with Elisha whose eyes were opened to see the protecting heavenly horses and chariots of fire (2 Kings 6:17).

The Shunammite woman provided hospitality for Elisha, who sought to provide a favor in return. When Gehazi pointed out that she had no son, Elisha prophesied that she would have one the following year, which she did. Years later the boy died, and Gehazi took Elisha's staff to place upon the boy until Elisha came and brought him back to life (2 Kings 4). After Naaman was healed of leprosy, Gehazi pursued Naaman with a contrived story designed to get clothing and silver from him. As punishment for his presumption, he became a leper (2 Kings 5:20–27).

Gehenna–*See* Hell.

G

Gemariah–**(1)** The son of Hilkiah, he was one of two envoys to Nebuchadnezzar of Babylon and the Judean exiles there (Jer. 29:3). **(2)** The son of Shaphan, a high official, he had a chamber at the temple (Jer. 36:10–12). Gemariah allowed the scribe Baruch to read Jeremiah's prophecies (36:10) and later tried to stop King Jehoiakim from burning Jeremiah's scroll (36:25).

Genesis, Book of–The book of Genesis ("Origins") is well named because it provides the foundation for the rest of the Bible and speaks of the beginnings of the world, humanity, sin, redemption, the people of God, covenant, marriage, Sabbath, work, and much more. Genesis is the first chapter of the Pentateuch, a five-part story of the origins of the nation of Israel. Genesis is the preamble to that account, leading up to the pivotal moment of the exodus and the move toward the promised land.

The primeval history (Gen. 1:1–11:26). The book opens with an account of creation given in two parts. Genesis 1:1–2:4a provides a creation account that describes the six days in which God created the heavens and the earth, followed by a seventh day of rest. Genesis 2:4b–25 then provides a second account of creation, this time with a focus on the creation of Adam and Eve. Genesis 3 then narrates the first sin of humanity, which introduces sin and death into the world. Genesis 4–11 provides four additional stories (the murder of Abel by Cain, the intermarrying of the "sons of God" with the "daughters of men," the flood, and the tower of Babel). These stories show a creation gone wrong, God's move to start over again with Noah and his family, and the persistence of sin thereafter. All of this leads to the story of the patriarchs, where God's plan to set things right takes a decisive turn. These stories are connected by genealogies that mark the march of time as well as provide significant theological commentary.

The patriarchal narrative (Gen. 11:27–36:43). The middle section of the book of Genesis turns its attention to the patriarchs, so called because they are the fathers of the nation of Israel. The style of the book changes at this point, so that rather than following the story of all the world and moving at a fast pace, the narrative slows down and focuses on God creating a people to obey him and to bring blessing to the whole world (12:1–3). God now determines to restore the blessing lost at Eden by reaching the world through the descendants of one individual, Abraham.

Abraham's father, Terah, took Abram (as Abraham was then known), Abram's wife Sarai (Sarah), and Terah's grandson Lot and left Ur and settled in Harran in northern Mesopotamia. No explanation is given why. While they are settled in Harran, God commands Abraham to leave there and travel to Canaan. God promises that he will make him a great nation (implying land and many descendants), and that he will be blessed and will be a blessing to the nations (12:1–3). That blessing requires Abraham and Sarah to have children, and this sets up much of the drama of his story. Often Abraham reacts in fear and not faith, but at the end of his story he has a solid confidence in God's ability to take care of him and bring all the promises to fulfillment (Gen. 22).

Isaac, not Ishmael (Abraham's son through Sarah's maidservant Hagar; see Gen. 16), is the conduit of the promises to future generations. Even so, Isaac is not a highly developed character in the book of Genesis, although his near sacrifice in Gen. 22 is certainly a matter of great interest. The episode in his life that receives the lengthiest attention is the courtship with Rebekah (Gen. 24), and there the focus is primarily on her.

The account of Isaac's life gives way to an account of his son Jacob. Jacob is a complex character. The first episodes of his story are about how he, the younger, inherits the blessing and becomes the conduit for the promise rather than his older brother, Esau. Jacob becomes an example of how God uses the foolish things of the world to accomplish his purposes. That the story of the patriarchs is a preamble to the story of the founding of Israel becomes obvious when Jacob's name is changed to "Israel" after he fights with God (32:22–32) and his wives give birth to twelve sons, who give their names to the twelve tribes of Israel.

The Joseph story (Gen. 37–50). The third section of Genesis focuses on the twelve sons of Jacob, in particular Joseph. A main theme seems to be God's providential preservation of the family of the promise, in the context of a devastating famine. Joseph himself expresses the theme of this section at the end of the narrative, after his father dies and his brothers now wonder whether he will seek revenge against them. He reassures them by his statement that although they had meant their actions to harm him, he knows that God has used these very actions for good, for the salvation of the family of God (50:19–20). Yes, they had just wanted to get rid of him, but God has used their jealousy to bring Joseph to Egypt. The wife of his owner had wanted to frame him for rape, but God has used this false accusation in order to have him thrown into jail, where he meets two of Pharaoh's chief advisers. He had demonstrated to them his ability to interpret dreams, so when the chief cupbearer is restored to a position of influence, he can advise Pharaoh himself to turn to Joseph to interpret his disturbing dreams. These dreams have allowed Pharaoh, with Joseph's help, to prepare for the famine. Joseph has risen to great prominence in Egypt, so when the famine comes, he is in a position to help his family, and the promise can continue to the next generations.

Among other secondary, yet important, themes of the Joseph narrative are the rising prominence of Judah and the lessening significance of Reuben. Judah at first is pictured as self-serving (Gen. 38), but by the end of the story he is willing to sacrifice himself for the good of his father and family (44:18–34). This story thus demonstrates why the descendants of Judah have dominance over the descendants of the firstborn, Reuben, in later Israelite history. Also, the Joseph story recounts how Israel came to Egypt. This sets up the events of the book of Exodus.

Gennesaret–On the northwestern shore of the Sea of Galilee, Gennesaret (Matt. 14:34) gives its name to the surrounding fertile plain and to the lake (Luke 5:1).

Gentiles–The word "Gentiles" is often used to translate words meaning "nations" or "peoples."

In general, within the OT, Gentiles are not God's people. God chose Israel to be his people, not other nations (Deut. 7:6–8; 10:15; 26:18–19). Israelite ancestry determines membership in the covenant people. Some writings thus forbid Gentiles from becoming part of God's people (Ezra 9–10; Neh. 13).

The OT more commonly envisions Gentiles experiencing covenant blessing through Israel if they functionally become Israelites by keeping the law, including the parts we understand as ceremonial-ritual law. The law is that special life-giving and regulating aspect of the covenant that God revealed to Israel, which defines Israel (Lev. 18:1–5; 20:22–26; Deut. 4:1–8, 32–40; 6:24–25; 8:1–6; 10:12–11:32; 30:11–20; Josh. 1:7–9; Neh. 9:29; Pss. 119; 147:19–20; Ezek. 20:9–13, 21).

Such law/Israel-centered conditions for Gentiles relate to a broader OT understanding: God will reach and restore the world through Israel, the locus of his saving activity. God will bless the nations in and through Abraham's descendants, Israel (Gen. 12:1–3; 17:4–6; 22:18; 26:4; 28:14). This covenant specifically involves keeping the law (e.g., circumcision [Gen. 17:9–14]). Some passages depict this happening through the nations being subject to Israel (Gen. 49:8–12; Num. 24:9, 17–19; Isa. 11:10–16; 14:2; 54:3). In other passages the nations will be blessed by Israel's God as they come to Israel, bring back exiled Israel, serve Israel, present Israel with their own wealth, and/or fear Israel's God (Isa. 45:23; 49:22–23; 51:4–5; 55:5; 60:3–16; 61:5–6; 66:12–13, 18–21; Mic. 7:12–17; Zech. 2:11; 8:22–23). Other passages further elucidate the law-defined nature of such Gentile participation in the God of Israel's salvation (Exod. 12:48; Isa. 56:1–8; Jer. 12:14–17; Zech. 14:16–21). The portrait of the nations "flowing" up the mountain of God associates Gentile participation in God's salvation explicitly with the law (Isa. 2:2–5; Mic. 4:1–5).

Situating Jesus and early Christianity within this matrix of Gentile sensitivities is illuminating. As the Jesus movement spread across the Mediterranean, proclaiming the ultimate salvation of the God of Israel in and through Jesus the Messiah, questions about how Gentiles experience this salvation of the Jewish God had paramount importance.

Some Christians, in line with traditional readings of the OT, thought that Gentiles must keep the law, becoming Jews to experience the God of Israel's salvation in Jesus (Acts 11:1–3; 15:1, 5; Paul's opponents in Galatia). Gentiles, after all, were separated from God and his salvation promises to Israel (Rom. 9:4–5; Eph.

G

2:11–13; 1 Pet. 2:10). They stood under God's condemnation, especially because they were controlled by their passions and sin, lacking self-mastery and the ability to live rightly (Rom. 1:18–32; Eph. 4:17–19; 1 Thess. 4:5; 1 Pet. 1:14, 18).

However, various NT authors, such as Paul, contend that Gentiles need not keep the law, functionally becoming Jews, in order to participate in God's ultimate salvation in Jesus. Christ, the climax of Israel itself, has replaced the law's centrality and ultimacy with himself and his death and resurrection (Rom. 10:4). Through being united to Christ by the Spirit, Gentiles are, apart from the law, grafted into true, redefined Israel and become Abraham's descendants, inheriting God's promised salvation for Israel (Rom. 3:21–4:25; 8:1–17; 9:30–10:17; 11:13–32; Gal. 2:11–4:7; Eph. 2:11–22; 3:4–6). In Christ, by the Spirit, Gentiles attain self-mastery over their passions and sin and thus live rightly before God, inheriting the kingdom of God in Christ (Rom. 6:1–8:30; 1 Cor. 6:9–11; Gal. 5:16–26; 1 Thess. 4:3–8). Various NT writings thus reconfigure the situation of Gentiles with respect to Israel's God because of what God did in Christ.

Debates about Gentiles, the law, salvation, and what Christ means for these issues persisted after Paul. Early Christians lacked an unequivocal saying from Jesus on the matter, and not all accepted Paul and some other NT writings.

GERAH–*See* Weights and Measures.

GERAR–The site where Abraham deceived Abimelek king of Gerar by claiming that his wife, Sarah, was his sister (Gen. 20:1–2). Isaac would also make the same claim with respect to his wife, Rebekah (26:7). In the Table of Nations, Gerar is used as a geographical border for the southern extremity of Canaan (10:19). In the time of King Asa, when Zerah the Cushite came out to attack him, Asa and his army pursued them as far as Gerar and destroyed all the villages around it (2 Chron. 14:13–14). The ancient site is located between Beersheba and Gaza.

GERASA–An ancient city located on the east side of the Jordan River, known today as Jerash. This largely Hellenistic city was located on the strategically vital north-south King's Highway. Gerasa was annexed by Roman Syria and later joined to the Decapolis. Josephus locates the city on the eastern border of Perea (*J.W.* 3.47). Jesus healed a demoniac in this region (Matt. 8:28–34; Mark 5:1–20; Luke 8:26–39). The problem with the miracle story is that Gerasa is some forty miles southeast of the Sea of Galilee, which is too distant from the shoreline where the events transpired. Mark and Luke probably mean the "region of Gerasa," and the event could have transpired in Gadara (Matt. 8:28) or Gergesa (according to some manuscripts), which are closer to the Sea of Galilee. *See also* Gadarenes.

GERASENES–One of three principal variant names in all three Synoptic Gospels for the people of the region where Jesus healed demoniacs after sailing with his disciples across the Sea of Galilee (Matt. 8:28–34; Mark 5:1–20; Luke 8:26–39). *See also* Gadarenes; Gerasa; Gergesenes.

GERGESENES–One of three principal variant names (also Gadarenes, Gerasenes) in all three Synoptic Gospels for the people of the region where Jesus healed demoniacs after sailing with his disciples across the Sea of Galilee (Matt. 8:28–34; Mark 5:1–20; Luke 8:26–39).

GERIZIM–The twin peaks of Mount Gerizim and Mount Ebal stand about forty miles north of Jerusalem in Samaria and flank the entrance to the Nablus Valley, the location of biblical Shechem. Gerizim, the southern mountain, rises 2,889 feet above sea level, and Ebal, the northern mountain, 3,083 feet. Together, they form a natural amphitheater.

Shechem was of strategic importance in antiquity because it sat on one of three major north-south trade routes through Canaan—the Ridge Route—and provided the only east-west passage in that area to the mountains of Ephraim. Abram took this route into the promised land, where the great trees of Moreh at Shechem became his first recorded stop. It was there, between Gerizim and Ebal, that he heard the voice of God and built an altar (Gen. 12:6–7). Although Shechem is rich in biblical history (e.g., Gen. 33:18–19; 34:2–26; Josh. 24:32; Judg. 8:31–9:57), each of the two mountains has specific individual significance.

Upon their entry into the promised land, Moses had commanded the Israelites to proclaim the blessings of obedience to the law on Mount Gerizim, and the curses of disobedience to the law on Mount Ebal (Deut. 11:29). Moses had further commanded that they build an altar of uncut stones on Ebal to bear the words of the law written in plaster (27:1–8). Moses had also specified that those six tribes descended from Jacob's wives stand on Gerizim, and the five tribes descended from the maidservants plus Reuben (Gen. 49:4) stand on Ebal (Deut. 27:11–14). After the conquest of Jericho and Ai, Joshua led a covenant renewal at the twin peaks, thereby fulfilling the Mosaic requirements (Josh. 8:30–35).

The final explicit mention in the OT of Mount Gerizim occurs in Judges. There, Jotham son of Gideon challenged the Shechemites for their loyalty to his half brother, the treacherous Abimelek (Judg. 9:7–21). A ledge about halfway up the mountain is popularly called "Jotham's Pulpit."

The character of Mount Gerizim changed after the exile, when the Samaritans emerged as a separate people group at enmity with the Jews. The Samaritan Pentateuch substitutes Gerizim for Ebal in Deut. 27:4, so the Samaritans constructed their own temple there in the fourth century BC, during the reign of Alexander the Great (it later was destroyed by John Hyrcanus in 128 BC). During her conversation with Jesus, the woman at Jacob's Well in Sychar, near Shechem, brought up the topic of ancestral worship on Mount Gerizim (John 4:4–38, esp. v. 20). *See also* Ebal.

GERSHOM–The elder son of Moses and Zipporah, born in Midian (Exod. 2:22; 18:3; 1 Chron. 23:15). His name, given by Moses, means "sojourner there," reflecting Moses' status as an alien in Midian. This Gershom is named as an ancestor of Jonathan, the priest of Micah and subsequently of the Danites (Judg. 17:7–18:30), as well as an ancestor to Shubael, called both chief and officer over the treasuries (1 Chron. 23:16; 26:24). *See also* Gershon.

GERSHON–Along with Kohath and Merari, Gershon was one of the three sons of Levi, and thus the ancestor of a group of Levites (Gen. 46:11). His name is spelled "Gershon" in Genesis, elsewhere in the Pentateuch (Exod. 6:16–17; Num. 3:17, 21), and in the initial listing of the genealogy in 1 Chron. 6 (v. 1). However, in the Hebrew the spelling reverts to "Gershom" in the remainder of the genealogy (1 Chron. 6:16, 17, 20, 43, 62, 71; see NIV mg.). *See also* Gershom; Gershonites.

GERSHONITES–The descendants of Gershon (also spelled "Gershom") son of Levi (Gen. 46:11) were Libni (also known as Ladan) and Shimei and their descendants (Num. 3:18, 21; 1 Chron. 6:17, 43; 23:7–11). During the wilderness period they were responsible for all activities concerning the tabernacle coverings, screens, and hangings (Num. 3:25–26; 4:21–28; 7:6–7). They also carried the ark of the covenant (Num. 10:17; 1 Chron. 15:7, 11–15). *See also* Gershon.

GESHEM–An Arab, king of Qedar, who resisted Nehemiah's efforts to rebuild Jerusalem's wall. He and his associates (Sanballat and Tobiah) appealed to the Persian king but ultimately were unsuccessful (Neh. 2:19; 6:1–2, 6). During the Persian period the Qedarites were located to the south of Palestine and in the Nile Delta region of Egypt. A reference to Geshem has been found on a silver container discovered at Tel el-Maskhuta in Egypt. "Gashmu" is an alternate spelling in Neh. 6:6 (see KJV).

GESHUR–An agricultural region east of the Sea of Galilee, settled about 2000 BC, whose population was not expelled during the Israelite conquest (Josh. 13:11, 13) and increased in the eleventh century BC. As an independent Aramean kingdom, Geshur allied with David when he married the Geshurite princess Maakah (2 Sam. 3:3). Their son Absalom lived in Geshur for three years after killing his half brother Amnon (2 Sam. 13:37–38). Geshur later allied with Aram-Damascus to capture Israelite territory in Gilead (1 Chron. 2:22–23), but it was decimated by the Assyrian king Tiglath-pileser III in 734 BC.

GETHSEMANE–The place where Jesus, after agonized prayer, was betrayed by Judas and arrested by Jewish authorities. The name comes from the Aramaic word for "oil press," and Gethsemane probably had an olive orchard and an oil press. It likely was located near the Mount of Olives (Matt. 26:30; Mark 14:26; Luke 22:39), although its precise location is unknown.

Only Matthew and Mark specifically call the place "Gethsemane" (Matt. 26:36; Mark 14:32); Luke does not mention Gethsemane, but he does, with them, indicate that the events took place on the Mount of Olives (Luke 22:39). John describes the site as a garden, although he also does not mention it by name (John 18:1).

In Gethsemane, the disciples fell asleep after Jesus warned them against temptation. Jesus prayed three times for deliverance, but he resisted temptation and remained obedient to the will of God.

Gezer–Located in the Aijalon Valley, Gezer guarded the route from the seacoast up to Jerusalem. Gezer (Tell Jezer, Tell Jazari) is a mound, thirty-three acres in size, situated in the foothills of Judah. It is known from biblical, Egyptian, and Assyrian sources. Gezer was a major Canaanite city-state throughout the second millennium BC. The city was destroyed around 1500 BC and rebuilt during the Late Bronze Age, when it came under Egyptian hegemony. Joshua defeated the king of Gezer, who was part of a Canaanite coalition (Josh. 10:33). Gezer remained in Canaanite hands throughout the period of the judges (Josh. 16:10; Judg. 1:29), even though it formed the boundary for Ephraim's tribal allotment (Josh. 16:3) and was assigned as a Levitical city (Josh. 21:21). David fought against the Philistines near Gezer (2 Sam. 5:25; 1 Chron. 20:4).

Gezer was conquered by Egypt and given as a dowry to Solomon. Solomon fortified Gezer along with Jerusalem, Hazor, and Megiddo (1 Kings 9:15–17). Gezer was destroyed by Shishak (c. 950–925 BC). It was rebuilt and destroyed by the Assyrians under Tiglath-pileser III (733 BC). Gezer became known as Gazara in the Hellenistic period and became an important city for the Hasmonean rulers.

Ghost, Holy–*See* Spirit, Holy.

Gibeah–A town located within the borders of the tribe of Benjamin. Gibeah is infamous as the setting where the men of the city raped and murdered the concubine of a Levite who had lodged in the city for the night. In response to this brutal act, an army of Israelites from all the other tribes engaged in battle against Gibeah and the Benjamites, killing all but six hundred men and burning the city (Judg. 19–20). Hosea refers to these events when he compares the sins of Israel in his time to the depravity of Gibeah (Hos. 9:9; 10:9).

Gibeah was the hometown of Saul (1 Sam. 10:26; 15:34; Isa. 10:29), and as such it played a central role during his reign. It was to Gibeah that the elders of Jabesh sent messengers to Saul requesting help (1 Sam. 11:1–5), and from Gibeah that Saul directed his campaign against the Philistines (1 Sam. 13–14). Later, David handed over two of Saul's sons and five of his grandsons to the Gibeonites to be hanged in Gibeah in retaliation for Saul's misdeeds (2 Sam. 21:5–6). The final biblical references to Gibeah appear in Isaiah and Hosea in connection with the impending invasion of Assyria (Isa. 10:29; Hos. 5:8).

Gibeah of God–The site identified by the prophet Samuel as the location of Saul's encounter with a group of prophets and his subsequent filling by the Spirit of the Lord (1 Sam. 10:5–6). Other versions render the Hebrew phrase *gibe'at ha'elohim* as "hill of God" (KJV, NASB) or "Gibeath-elohim" (NRSV). *See also* Gibeah.

Gibeon–The town of Gibeon has been located at the site of el-Jib, an Arab village, about five and a half miles north of Jerusalem.

Gibeon first appears in the Bible when the Gibeonites, using old clothes, old shoes, and moldy bread, pretended to be foreigners from far away and tricked Joshua into a peace treaty. Joshua honored the treaty, although he relegated the Gibeonites to do menial labor (Josh. 9:3–10:15). When their neighbors attacked the Gibeonites, the Israelites fulfilled their obligations and went to the Gibeonites' defense (Josh. 10:1–15).

Gibeon factors in several events during the lives of Saul, David, and Solomon. Men loyal to Saul's household and David's men faced off in a strange contest around the "pool of Gibeon." Twelve pairs of men fought, with each contest resulting in both men dying (2 Sam. 2:12–17). In James Pritchard's excavations of Gibeon, he found what is undoubtedly the pool referred to in this story. The pool was thirty-seven feet in diameter and eighty-two feet deep, with a spiral staircase on the side. The pool gave the city access to freshwater within its walls. It was part of the water defenses of the city, which also included a tunnel leading to a spring that provided additional water to the city. Gibeon was also the site of several of the events in Absalom's revolt against David.

Gibeon also was an important cultic center and high place in the early monarchy. The tabernacle was situated in Gibeon for some time (1 Chron. 16:39). God twice appeared to Solomon at Gibeon. Once, God appeared in order to ask Solomon what he wanted, to which Solomon responded that he wanted wisdom (2 Chron. 1:2–13). On another occasion, God assured Solomon that he had heard his prayer (1 Kings 9:2–9). This second encounter with God took place after the construction of the temple, which suggests that Gibeon was religiously important even after the temple was built. Gibeon is recorded as one of the cities captured by Shishak during his campaign against Israel shortly after the death of Solomon.

Although Gibeon is rarely mentioned after the partition of the kingdom, the archaeological data suggest that the city was a vital economic asset during the entire monarchy. Gibeon was also the site of Gedaliah's assassination. Gedaliah was the Babylonian-appointed Jewish governor after the destruction of Jerusalem. Some Gibeonites were taken to Babylon during the exile and then returned with Nehemiah to help him build Jerusalem's wall (Neh. 3:7–8).

Gideon–The fifth judge described in the book of Judges (6:1–8:35). After Deborah's victory over the Canaanites, Israel again falls into sin, so God turns Israel over to a new oppressor, the Midianites and their allies.

In the past, when Israel has repented as they do in Judg. 6:7, God has immediately brought them a judge to rescue them. This time, however, God first sends a prophet, who berates them for their continual apostasy (6:8–10). Still, the narrative next focuses on Gideon, whom God commissions to rescue Israel from Midian (7:14). Like Barak before him (4:8), however, Gideon does not immediately agree, but rather sets conditions for his participation, asking for a sign. Even after receiving the sign, he first of all acts only locally, tearing down his father's idolatrous shrine and building a proper altar to Yahweh (6:26–27). Although the people want to punish Gideon out of fear of the Midianites, his father defends him and renames his son "Jerub-Baal," which means "Let Baal contend with him" (6:32).

At this point, the conflict grows more serious as the Midianites and their allies amass against Israel. Even after the Spirit of the Lord comes upon Gideon, he still sets conditions on God asking for yet another sign, this time putting a fleece in front of God and asking that it be wet while the ground is dry. Even though God meets this condition, Gideon demands a second trial, and only after that is successful does he proceed.

The successful battle against the Midianites is best known for the prebattle dismissal of many of the Israelite troops. Many respond to Gideon's call to arms. As God demands, Gideon insists that fearful troops leave, but even after ten thousand men leave, twenty-two thousand remain. Ultimately, God instructs Gideon to have the troops drink from the waters of the Wadi Harod. The three hundred who drink water by lapping it with their hands to their mouths are chosen, and with these Gideon wins a great victory. There is nothing special about these three hundred troops. God knows that Gideon has a propensity to self-glorification ("by my hand" [Judg. 6:36]), and God wants to ensure that Israel will not boast in its own strength and will know that it is God who has brought deliverance.

Although Gideon is hesitant and apparently distrustful in answering God's call, events during and after the battle show his true nature. His humility is in evidence (cf. Judg. 6:15) when he refuses the Israelites' request to be their king (though later he names one of his sons "Abimelek," meaning "My father is king"), insisting that God alone will rule them (8:22–23). However, a request of his own becomes an occasion for Israel to plunge back into idolatry when he fashions an ephod from plundered enemy gold, which the Israelites then worship (8:24–27). Even so, the book of Hebrews (11:32) considers him an example of faith.

Gift of Tongues–Both speaking in tongues and interpreting tongues are listed among the various gifts of the Spirit that God may choose to give to believers according to his will (1 Cor. 12:10, 28).

The first-century Corinthian church exercised a variety of spiritual gifts, including the gift of tongues. When Paul writes to that church, he includes teaching designed to correct various abuses of these spiritual gifts. A lengthy discussion about spiritual gifts in 1 Cor. 12–14 affirms the practice of speaking in tongues in the Corinthian assembly under certain conditions (14:39–40) while also relegating it to a status lower than the gift of prophecy (14:5). By its very nature, Paul asserts, those who speak in tongues are not understood by their human audience; utterances in tongues speak to God, not to human beings (14:2). Therefore, on its own, glossolalia cannot edify those who hear it unless an interpretation is also provided for them. For this reason, Paul directs the Corinthians to other spiritual gifts (14:6) that can function to build up the church (14:12). Nonetheless, Paul affirms the practice of glossolalia in the Corinthians' public worship when it is limited to two or three speakers, when it is done in an orderly manner with the speakers taking turns, and when it is coupled with interpretation so that the church can be edified by its message (14:26–27).

Gihon–**(1)** The second of the four rivers that stemmed from the garden of Eden (Gen. 2:13). The identity of the Gihon River is unknown, though much debated. Scholars taking its reference to be more literal in its geography have argued for locations in Mesopotamia, assuming the ancient river to be long since dried up. Still others, believing this portion of Genesis to be more symbolic in intent, have argued for different locations from Egypt to India and even in Jerusalem itself.

(2) A spring located southeast of Jerusalem's Old City. It lies on the eastern perimeter of the City of David in the modern village of Silwan. The Gihon spring was the primary source of water for Jerusalem in ancient times. Because of the Gihon's importance, a series of underground water systems was constructed to make use of its waters. One of these is King Hezekiah's (727–698 BC) tunnel, which brought Gihon's waters to the Pool of Siloam (2 Kings 20:20; 2 Chron. 32:30). It was at the Gihon that David had Solomon anointed to be king over Israel (1 Kings 1:28–48). The spring is also mentioned in connection to the wall that King Manasseh (698–642 BC) rebuilt (2 Chron. 33:14).

Gilboa–A crescent-shaped hill at the northern end of the Israelite hill country where it borders the strategic and open Jezreel Valley. Gilboa's location made it a natural staging ground for military action. Gideon brought his troops to the spring of Harod (Judg. 7:1) at the base of Gilboa before defeating the Midianites camped across the valley. Later, King Saul brought his troops to Gilboa to battle the Philistines camped across the valley, only to die with his sons on Gilboa (1 Sam. 28:4; 31:1, 8; 2 Sam. 1:6, 21).

Gilead–The southern section of the Transjordan, with the Jordan River to the west, Bashan to the north, Ammon to the east, and Moab to the south. The Jabbok River ran across it from east to west, and "Gilead" could be used either more widely to describe the whole area or more narrowly to describe the land either south or north of the Jabbok. It was a high, fertile region, famed for its healing balm and spices (Gen. 37:25; Jer. 8:22; 46:11) as well as its pastures and livestock (Num. 32:1; 1 Chron. 5:9; Song 4:1; 6:5).

Gilgal–The most famous place of this name was not far from Jericho. However, archaeologists have not been able to identify the site definitively in modern times.

Gilgal was Israel's first camp after crossing the Jordan, marked by a cairn of twelve stones from the riverbed (Josh. 4:19–20). It was called "Gilgal" because this sounds like the Hebrew word *galal*, meaning "to roll away." When the people had been circumcised and had celebrated their first Passover in the promised land, God told them that he had "rolled away the reproach of Egypt" (5:9). It was at this base camp that Israel settled the question of Caleb's inheritance (14:6–14) and fell for the Gibeonites' deception (Josh. 9), and from which they set out on their southern campaign (Josh. 10). In the next generation, the angel of the Lord went up from there to Bokim to confront them with their sinfulness (Judg. 2:1).

The prophet Samuel visited Gilgal regularly to judge the people (1 Sam. 7:16), as well as to offer sacrifice (10:8) and to proclaim Saul as king (11:14–15). David returned to his kingdom through Gilgal after Absalom's death, effectively retracing Joshua's steps (2 Sam. 19:15, 40). Later, Elijah and Elisha passed through Gilgal just before Elijah miraculously crossed the Jordan eastward and Elisha then miraculously crossed back (2 Kings 2:1–14). On his return to Gilgal, Elisha removed poison from stew and multiplied bread for the famine-stricken people (2 Kings 4:38–44).

The stones at Gilgal were meant to be a perpetual reminder of God's faithfulness in the conquest (Josh. 4:21–24; Mic. 6:5). However, when Ehud turned back at Gilgal to assassinate Ekron, they were already described as "the stone images [i.e., idols] near Gilgal" (Judg. 3:19). It was there that Saul forfeited his kingship first by offering sacrifice himself instead of waiting for Samuel to do so (1 Sam. 13) and then by setting aside captured livestock for sacrifice rather than destroying them according to God's instructions (1 Sam. 15). By the eighth century BC, Gilgal was one of the cult sites of the northern kingdom and was notorious for false worship (Hos. 4:15; 9:15; 12:11; Amos 4:4; 5:5).

Girgashites–Descended from Ham the son of Noah (Gen. 10:16), the Girgashites comprised one of the original tribes of Canaan whose land was promised to Abraham (15:21). They were defeated by Joshua in the conquest (Josh. 24:11).

Gittith–A transliteration of a Hebrew word used in the superscriptions of Pss. 8; 81; 84. Its significance is uncertain. The word might designate a musical instrument or a musical sign denoting how the psalms were to be sung.

Gleaning–Mosaic law prohibited farmers from harvesting the crops—usually grain, grapes, or olives—on the edges and corners of their land, going through the crops a second time, or picking up that which fell on the ground (Lev. 19:9–10). This prohibition was a means of providing for the poor and strangers among the people and for those who could not own land, who were then allowed to glean, or gather, what was left behind by the harvesters (Ruth 2:6–9). The prophets used gleaning figuratively to represent destruction (Isa. 17:5; Jer. 6:9; Mic. 7:1).

Glory–The tangible presence of God, experienced as overwhelming power and splendor. The main Hebrew word referring to glory, *kabod,* has the root meaning "heavy" (1 Sam. 4:18), which in other contexts can mean "intense" (Exod. 9:3; NIV: "terrible"), "wealthy" (i.e., "heavy in possessions" [Gen. 13:2]), and "high reputation" (Gen. 34:19; NIV: "most honored"). When used of God, it refers to his person and his works. God reveals his glory to Israel and to Egypt at the crossing of the sea (Exod. 14:4, 17–19). He carefully reveals his glory to Moses after Israel's sin with the golden calf in order to assure him that he will not abandon them (33:12–23).

In the NT the glory of God is made real in the person of Jesus Christ (John 1:14; Heb. 1:3). He is, after all, the very presence of God. When he returns on the clouds, he will fully reveal God's glory (Matt. 24:30; Mark 13:26; Luke 21:27).

Gnashing of Teeth–The act of grating or grinding one's teeth together. The phrase is frequently found in the OT as an expression of anger. Most often the wicked gnash their teeth toward the righteous (Pss. 35:16; 37:12; 112:10; Lam. 2:16). In the teaching of Jesus, the gnashing of teeth is associated with a place of future punishment, especially in the Gospel of Matthew (8:12; 13:42, 50; 22:13; 24:51; 25:30). In the NT, gnashing of teeth is often associated with the place of outer darkness, where there is weeping. In this case, the gnashing of teeth may be an expression of anger and hence the continual refusal to repent. In the context of punishment, the picture may also express futility in the face of judgment.

God–For Christians, God is the creator of the cosmos and the redeemer of humanity. He has revealed himself in historical acts—namely, in creation, in the history of Israel, and especially in the person and work of Jesus Christ. There is only one God (Deut. 6:4); "there is no other" (Isa. 45:5). Because "God is spirit" (John 4:24), he must reveal himself through various images and metaphors.

The OT refers to God by many names. One of the general terms used for God, *'el* (which probably means "ultimate supremacy"), often appears in a compound form with a qualifying word, as in *'el 'elyon* ("God Most High"), *'el shadday* ("God Almighty"), and *'el ro'i* ("the God who sees me" or "God of my seeing"). These descriptive names reveal important attributes of God and usually were derived from the personal experiences of the people of God in real-life settings; thus, they do not describe an abstract concept of God.

The most prominent personal name of God is *yahweh* (YHWH), which is translated as "the Lord" in most English Bibles. At the burning bush in the wilderness of Horeb, God first revealed to Moses his personal name in sentence form: "I am who I am" (Exod. 3:13–15). Though debated, the divine name "YHWH" seems to originate from an abbreviated form of this sentence. Yahweh, who was with Moses and his people at the time of exodus, is the God who was with Abraham, Isaac, and Jacob. According to Jesus' testimony, "the God of Abraham, the God of Isaac, and the God of Jacob" is identified as the God "of the living" (Matt. 22:32). Hence, the name "Yahweh" is closely tied to God's self-revelation as the God of presence and life.

Many of God's attributes are summarized in Exod. 34:6–7: "The Lord, the Lord, the compassionate and gracious God, slow to anger, abounding in love and faithfulness, maintaining love to thousands, and forgiving wickedness, rebellion and sin. Yet he does not leave the guilty unpunished; he punishes the children and their children for the sin of the parents to the third and fourth generation."

The Christian God of the Bible is the triune God. God is one but exists in three persons:

the Father, the Son, and the Holy Spirit (Matt. 28:19). The Son is one with the Father (John 10:30); the Holy Spirit is one with God (2 Sam. 23:2–3). All three share the same divine nature; they are all-knowing, holy, glorious, and called "Lord" and "God" (Matt. 11:25; John 1:1; 20:28; Acts 3:22; 5:3–4; 10:36; 1 Cor. 8:6; 2 Cor. 3:17–18; 2 Pet. 1:1). All three share in the same work of creation (Gen. 1:1–3), salvation (1 Pet. 1:2), indwelling (John 14:23), and directing the church's mission (Matt. 28:18–20; Acts 16:6–10; 14:27; 13:2–4).

G

God-Fearer–A technical term in NT times for a non-Jew who feared and recognized Israel's God, the true God, but stopped short of becoming a full-fledged Jewish proselyte (Acts 10:2, 22; 13:16, 26).

Gog and Magog–This infamous pair is known to most readers of the Bible from Rev. 20:8. They stand for all the nations of the world, which are enticed by Satan to attack the saints in the end times. This text universalizes Ezek. 38–39, where "Gog, of the land of Magog, the chief prince of Meshek and Tubal" (38:2–3), is the commander of a coalition (38:2–7) to be gathered in an unprovoked attack on a restored, defenseless Israel. He acts not on his own initiative but rather is impelled and ultimately destroyed by God (38:21–23; 39:2–6). Some have suggested that the mysterious Gog derives from the historical figure Gyges, a seventh-century BC king of Lydia located in western Asia Minor, or Gaga, a god mentioned in the Ras Shamra texts of ancient Ugarit. Others believe that the name "Gog" is derived from "Magog," since Magog, the land "in the far north" from which Gog came (Ezek. 38:2, 15; 39:6), can be translated as "place of Gog." Magog is associated in the Table of Nations (Gen. 10:2) with Meshek and Tubal, eponymous sons of Japheth whose territories are presumed to lie somewhere in the vicinity of modern Turkey.

Gold–*See* Minerals and Metals.

Golden Calf–Made by Aaron while Moses was on Mount Sinai, the golden calf was an image fashioned from gold jewelry donated by the Israelites, who grew impatient waiting for Moses as he spent forty days and nights receiving instructions from God (Exod. 32). It became an object of idolatrous worship and a cause of corrupt behavior.

Moses' response on seeing the image is to smash the two tablets containing the Ten Commandments, signifying the end of the covenant between God and Israel. He burned the image, pulverized it, scattered it on the water, and made the Israelites drink it. While initially it seemed uncertain whether there could be any future for the covenant, Exod. 33–34 serves to resolve this.

The episode of the golden calf lived long in Israel's memory as the paradigm instance of apostasy (Ps. 106:19–20; Acts 7:41). King Jeroboam I repeated the offense, setting up golden calves at Dan and Bethel (1 Kings 12:28) to discourage citizens of the northern kingdom from traveling to the southern capital Jerusalem, where their allegiance might switch to the Davidic king.

Golgotha–*See* Calvary.

Goliath–Goliath was the Philistine champion whom David killed in one-on-one combat with a stone hurled by a sling (1 Sam. 17). David's victory led to a rout of the Philistines and personal rewards and prominence in Israel. Goliath was considered a giant. While the MT measures him at 9′ 6″ (NRSV: "six cubits and a span"), another textual tradition (preserved in the DSS, the LXX, and Josephus [*Ant.* 6.171]) gives his height as 6′ 9″ ("four cubits and a span"). From a copying perspective, the 6′ 9″ height is easier to explain as original. The average Israelite was about 5′ 3″, but Saul was head and shoulders taller, perhaps 6′.

Gomer–The wife of Hosea the prophet. God commanded Hosea to marry Gomer, though he also describes her as "an adulterous wife" (Hos. 1:2). The purpose behind God's command was to provide an illustration of his own relationship with his people, which, like a marriage, was to be intimate and exclusive. Israel, however, was worshiping other gods, just as Gomer was sleeping with other men.

Gomorrah–*See* Sodom and Gomorrah.

Good News–*See* Gospel.

Goshen–A region in northeast Egypt along the eastern Nile Delta. The extent of the region is uncertain, but it is identified with the area around Wadi Tumilat up to Lake Timsah. Ramesses II built his capital on the ruins of the Hyksos capital Avaris and called it Pi-Ramesses, which is probably the same Rameses that the Israelite slaves built (Exod. 1:11). Goshen was either roughly equated with the "land of Rameses" or a part of it (Gen. 47:6). Joseph settled his family there because it was "the best of the land," good for tending herds, and was near him (Gen. 45:10, 18; 46:34). Goshen later became the place of Israel's enslavement. While Egypt faced the plagues, Goshen was spared (Exod. 8:22).

Gospel–The English word "gospel" translates the Greek word *euangelion*, which is very important in the NT, being used seventy-six times. The word *euangelion* (*eu* = "good," *angelion* = "announcement"), in its contemporary use in the Hellenistic world, was not the title of a book but rather a declaration of good news. *Euangelion* was used in the Roman Empire with reference to significant events in the life of the emperor, who was thought of as a savior with divine status. These events included declarations at the time of his birth, his coming of age, and his accession to the throne. The NT usage of the term can also be traced to the OT (e.g., Isa. 40:9; 52:7; 61:1), which looked forward to the coming of the Messiah, who would bring a time of salvation. This good news, which is declared in the NT, is that Jesus has fulfilled God's promises to Israel, and now the way of salvation is open to all.

Governor–The English word "governor" is used to translate a number of Hebrew words. The term indicates one who has been designated with authority over a certain region, especially under the rule of a king or emperor.

There are several notable governors in the OT. After being sold into slavery in Egypt, Joseph was exalted to governor of Egypt, second only to the king. Thus, his brothers bowed before him (Gen. 42:6). Solomon, during his reign, established twelve governors, each one responsible for supplying provisions to the king one month out of the year (1 Kings 4:7), and Solomon received tribute from them (1 Kings 10:15; 2 Chron. 9:14).

One notable governor was Gedaliah, ruler of the Jewish remnant left in Judah during the deportation, who reported to the king of Babylon (Jer. 40:11). Later, he was assassinated by Ishmael (41:2). This provoked great fear, causing some to flee to Egypt (41:17–18).

Another notable individual who governed the Jewish people upon their return to Jerusalem after the captivity was Sheshbazzar, governor under Cyrus (Ezra 5:14). He had been entrusted with the vessels for the house of God in Jerusalem that had been taken by Nebuchadnezzar (1:7–8). This same Sheshbazzar had begun building the foundation of the temple by the legal decree of Cyrus the king (5:14–6:6). Subsequently, Zerubbabel (under Darius I) became governor and completed the foundation and the rest of the temple (Ezra 3–6; see also Hag. 1:1–15). He and the other workers are said to have had their spirits stirred to do the work (Hag. 1:14).

Nehemiah, who led the people in restoring the wall of Jerusalem for the safety and restoration of the city, was governor over his people (under Artaxerxes I) and had a true heart of compassion toward the poor. His sympathy for them was so deep that he did not take the regular allotment of food and other goods that the other governors took by right (Neh. 5:14–15). The governors who had gone before ruled and taxed heavily. Nehemiah deemed this an illegitimate way to live among God's people. At the reading of the law along with Ezra the priest and the other Levites, Nehemiah directed the attention of the people to the proper response to the word of God (8:9–10).

In the NT, the most common word for governor is *hēgemōn*. As in the OT, governors were appointed by higher authorities who delegated to them the authority to rule.

The office of governor was very important in Israel during the NT period. Herod the Great had ruled Israel during the years 37–4 BC. At his death in 4 BC, three of his sons took over the kingdom with the approval of Caesar Augustus. Archelaus ruled Judea and Samaria, Herod Antipas (Herod the Tetrarch) was tetrarch of Galilee and Perea, and Philip was tetrarch of Iturea and Traconitus (see Luke 3:1; Josephus, *J.W.* 2.93–97). The Jewish people revolted against Archelaus in the ninth year, and he was stripped of his rulership and banished in AD 6 (Josephus, *J.W.* 2.111). His kingdom was turned into a Roman province, with Coponius ruling as governor. From this time until the reign of Herod Agrippa I, Judea was ruled by a line of governors (called "prefects" or "procurators"). In AD 41 Herod Agrippa I began to rule and eventually governed roughly the same territory as did Herod the Great, his grandfather. His rule, however, lasted only three years. In the period AD 44–66 governors again ruled in Judea, among them Felix and Festus, with whom the apostle Paul had audience.

Of note among these governors was Pontius Pilate, appointed in AD 26 by Tiberius. Pilate's fortunes seemed to wax and wane with those of General Sejanus, with whom he shared many political and social views. When he first arrived in Palestine, Pilate provoked protests by secretly bringing army standards bearing the images of Roman emperors—idols in Jewish eyes—into Jerusalem (Josephus, *Ant.* 18.55–59). On another occasion demonstrations broke out when Pilate used money from the temple treasury to build an aqueduct for Jerusalem (18.60–62). Pilate sent soldiers to surround and attack the protestors, many of whom were killed. Luke 13:1 refers to a similar episode near the Temple Mount in which Pilate massacred some Galileans, "whose blood Pilate had mixed with their sacrifices." Typical of the Romans, Pilate met protest with ruthless and overwhelming force. At Jesus' trial, though Pilate knew that Jesus was innocent (John 18:38), he condemned Jesus to crucifixion to avoid antagonizing the religious leaders. This kind of action was characteristic of Pilate. He was an unscrupulous and self-seeking leader who loathed the Jewish leadership but feared antagonizing them. Josephus notes that during the tumult of the Samaritans (to assemble at Mount Gerizim), Pilate put them to flight, killing some of them. The Samaritans complained about Pilate's murderous ways to Vitellius, who was friendly to them, and he recalled Pilate to Rome to answer before Tiberius, but Pilate took so long getting there that Tiberius was dead when he finally arrived (Josephus, *Ant.* 18.85–89). Pilate was eventually removed from office, and we hear nothing else from him.

Two other Judean governors who appear in the NT are Felix and Festus, who played a role in the apostle Paul's trial (Acts 24–26). Felix's wife, Drusilla, was a Jewess, and she was with him at Paul's second hearing. On this second occasion Paul reasoned powerfully with Felix, so much so that Felix became frightened about the future and sent Paul away. His fear notwithstanding, Felix sought to exploit the situation for monetary gain (no doubt bribes were common), but Paul made no response. Two years later Felix was replaced by the next governor, Porcius Festus. Festus heard the defense of Paul (Acts 26) and sent him to Rome after his appeal, though both Festus and Herod agreed that Paul could have been set free had he not appealed to Caesar (Acts 26:30–32).

Goyim–*See* Gentiles.

Gozan–A city-state to which many Israelites were deported by the Assyrians following the defeat of the northern kingdom of Israel and Samaria in 722 BC (2 Kings 17:6; 18:11; 19:12; 1 Chron. 5:26). Gozan probably was located in northwestern Mesopotamia on the Habor River, one of the tributaries of the Euphrates (identified as the "river of Gozan" in 1 Chron. 5:26; today, the Khabur River).

Grace–Grace is the nucleus, the critical core element, of the redemptive and sanctifying work of the triune God detailed throughout the entire canon of Scripture. The variegated expressions of grace are rooted in the person and work of God, so that his graciousness and favor effectively demonstrated in every aspect of the created realm glorify him as they are shared and enjoyed with one another.

The biblical terminology informing an understanding of grace defines it as a gift or a favorable reaction or disposition toward someone. Grace is generosity, thanks, and good will between humans and from God to humans. Divine expressions of grace are loving, merciful, and effective. The biblical texts provide a context for a more robust understanding of divine gift. The overall redemptive-historical context of grace is the desire of the eternal God to bring glory to himself through a grace-based relationship with his creation. The Creator-Redeemer gives grace, and the recipients of grace give him glory.

Great Sea–*See* Mediterranean Sea.

Greece–Ancient Greece was a federation of several loosely affiliated city-states located on the islands of the Aegean Sea, the land south of the Balkan Peninsula, west Asia Minor, and Crete.

The Minoan civilization (c. 2000–1400 BC). Archaeological evidence shows that as early as the fourth millennium BC there were already human inhabitants in the Aegean basin. Early migrants from Asia Minor came to settle in Crete (c. 2600 BC) and started its civilization at Knossos and Phaistos. It was called "Minoan," after the mythical king Minos. The Minoan civilization reached its peak around 1600 BC, when sophisticated palaces, highly developed metal work, and fine pottery were produced. The popular religion was the worship of the Mother Goddess. Not only did the Minoans excel in arts and crafts, but also they were literate and developed a syllable-based (non-Greek) writing system known as Linear A. Minoan culture came to a sudden end around 1400 BC, probably due to internal turmoil, natural disasters, and foreign invasion.

The Mycenaean civilization (c. 1450–1200 BC). The Mycenaeans may have arrived in the Early or Middle Bronze Age, and eventually they took over the Cretan palace settlement in 1450 BC and thus dominated the Aegean region for a time. The discovery of the city of Mycenae gave rise to the name "Mycenaean." During this period, the Greek mainland enjoyed prosperity. While retaining their own culture, the Mycenaeans were greatly influenced by the Minoans, as indicated by their pottery, luxury items, and religious symbolism. They were great engineers who built remarkable bridges and citadels. One of the finest examples of their handiwork was the gold masks that were buried together with their warriors. They employed a form of Greek language, known as Linear B, evidence of which has been discovered at Knossos, Pylos, Tiryns, Mycenae, Thebes, and elsewhere. Between 1250 and 1150 BC, for unknown reasons, all the Mycenaean palace citadels were destroyed.

The Age of Expansion (c. 1200–800 BC). Already in the thirteenth century, the Greeks were scattered all over the eastern Mediterranean, as far as the coast of southern Palestine. Migration increased around 1200 BC, driven by population growth and the accompanying demand for food and space, which led to colonization in other regions. By the eighth century BC, great cities (e.g., Troy) along the northwest coast of Asia Minor had been taken by the Aelions. The Dorians dominated the south of the Balkan Peninsula and eventually founded Sparta, while the Ionians settled in the east-central area of the Balkan Peninsula and founded Athens. This period was known as the Dark Age because of a lack of cultural advancements, and the art of writing was largely lost after the Mycenaean civilization was destroyed.

The Archaic period (c. 800–500 BC). Great changes took place in this period. The rise of the city-state (*polis*) not only provided stability, where leagues were formed among individual city-states, but also brought forth the establishment of institutions such as gymnasiums, symposiums, and temples. Trading with the Phoenicians allowed the Greeks to adopt and perfect their alphabet. Military defense was enhanced with huge city walls, and architecturally sophisticated buildings of various kinds were constructed. The first Olympian games were held during this period, in 776 BC. Science and philosophy began to be taught; lyric poetry expressing human emotions was created; and various gods (e.g., Zeus) were honored in their sanctuaries, which were overshadowed by mystery religions in the sixth century BC (e.g., Demeter, Dionysus, and Orpheus).

Greek settlements were established in southern Italy, the northern Aegean, and along the northern coast of Africa. At this time, two important city-states representing two very different cultures came into the picture. Sparta was made up of unwalled villages and ruled by kings, while Athens was a walled city governed first by the aristocrats, later by tyrants. Sparta was famous for its disciplined army, while Athens boasted of its superior naval force. The social structure of Sparta produced a political system that upheld the interest of the states, while Athens developed a legal system that laid the foundation for democracy.

Perhaps most important in this age were the Persian Wars. As the Greeks continued to expand into the southern Balkan Peninsula and to the north of the Black Sea, and to establish colonies in the Mediterranean, they encountered the superpower of that time. By 500 BC, Darius I of Persia controlled the Greek world, except the mainland of the Balkan Peninsula. Although on several occasions the Persians tried to invade mainland Greece, Athens (in alliance with Sparta) was able to successfully defeat them, rendering them powerless for a long period.

The Classical period (c. 500–338 BC). After the Persian Wars, Greek civilization advanced significantly into what is now known as Classical Greece. Political leadership shifted from Sparta to Athens, which held naval hegemony, dominating the Aegean islands and the coast of Asia Minor. According to the Athenian historian Thucydides, the growth of Athenian power, which posed a threat to neighboring city-states, caused the Peloponnesian War (c. 431–404 BC). With the aid of the Persians, Sparta defeated Athens, tearing down its Long Walls, which guarded the city, and its port of Piraeus, and making it an ally.

This period was a golden age for the Greeks, with the flowering of democratic institutions, architecture, literature, and art. Massive buildings were constructed, such as the Parthenon (447–438 BC), the Athena Nike (427–424 BC), the Erectheion (421–407 BC) on the

Acropolis, and the Theseion (449 BC) on the Agora. Greek writings of history, poetry, philosophy, comedy, and tragedy flourished. Thanks to the works of great historians such as Herodotus and Thucydides, events that transpired in ancient Greece have been made known to us. The four greatest Greek playwrights, Aeschylus, Aristophanes, Euripides, and Sophocles, were products of this period. Some of the greatest plastic arts were produced during this time, such as the statue of Athena Promachos (458 BC). Great thinkers, such as Socrates and Plato, were born during this period. The end of the Classical period of Greece, however, was marked with endless civil wars and wars with outside forces.

The Hellenistic period (338–146 BC). Philip II of Macedon defeated the Greeks at the battle of Chaeronea in 338 BC and took control of the entire Balkan Peninsula. His son Alexander the Great further expanded his territory all the way to India. Although his empire crumbled after his death (at the age of thirty-three), Alexander contributed so much to the furtherance of Greek culture and language that this age is known as the Hellenistic period, a time when Greek culture and language became widespread and dominant. Greece became a region of Macedon until 196 BC, when Rome declared it independent.

The Roman period (146 BC–AD 330). In 148 BC Rome defeated Macedon, making it a Roman province. Two years later, Rome further took control of Greece, and in 46 BC the province of Achaia was created. These two provinces were not only strategic for Rome; they also became the centers of the NT church. The Greek language became the lingua franca and the language of the NT. Paul's second and third missionary journeys brought him to Macedonia and Achaia (Acts 16:11–20:6). During the Roman period, Greece continued to be a cultural and intellectual center, and Greek influence even went beyond that of early Christianity.

Grief and Mourning–Grief is great sadness or sorrow or the circumstances that produce such; mourning refers to expressions of grief. Grief and mourning are often thought of in conjunction with death, but they may occur with regard to any personal or national tragedy (2 Sam. 13:19), the impending prospect of tragedy (Esther 4:3; Isa. 37:1), or repentance prompted by prophetic word of tragedy, sorrow over sin, or both.

The expressions of mourning in the Bible include weeping (Gen. 23:2), wailing (Esther 4:3; Isa. 15:3; Mark 5:38), tearing clothes and wearing sackcloth (Gen. 37:34; 2 Sam. 3:31), lying on the ground (2 Sam. 13:31), putting dust and ashes on the head or sitting on dust and ashes (Ezek. 27:30), fasting (2 Sam. 3:35; 12:16), singing songs of lament (2 Sam. 1:17–27; 3:32–35), pulling hair out of one's beard (Ezra 9:3), cutting the hair (Jer. 7:29), uncovering the head (Lev. 10:6), removing sandals (Ezek. 24:17, 23), covering the lips or mouth (Ezek. 24:17, 22; Mic. 3:7), and employing professional mourners (Jer. 9:17; Matt. 9:23; Mark 5:38). Some pagan mourning practices were prohibited, such as slashing the body, cutting patterns into the body (tattooing?), and the somewhat obscure act of making the forehead bald (Lev. 19:28; Deut. 14:1; cf. 1 Kings 18:28).

Guest–One who receives hospitality at another's home or table. Hospitality was a matter of honor in ancient times. It was shameful to mistreat a guest (Judg. 19:23). A guest received special portions at the table (1 Sam. 9:22–24; Esther 1:3), although the guest of a Levitical priest was not allowed to eat the sacred offering (Lev. 22:10). Job's misfortunes alienated him from his guests (Job 19:15), but the guests of the metaphorical Woman Folly fared worse (Prov. 9:18).

Guests abound in Jesus' parables about banquets and weddings (Matt. 22:10–11; Mark 2:19; Luke 14:16; 19:7). Jesus himself was often a guest (Luke 7:49; 14:7; 22:11; John 2:10). King Herod's misguided concern for his dinner guests caused the death of John the Baptist (Matt. 14:9; Mark 6:22, 26).

Guile–Deceitful cunning, usually employed in taking advantage of others through scheming and underhanded methods (e.g., Exod. 21:14; Pss. 32:2; 34:13; 55:21; 2 Cor. 12:16 KJV; 2 Macc. 12:24; 1 Pet. 2:1 NRSV). Although Nathaniel is not initially impressed with Jesus' messianic credentials, Jesus nevertheless praises him for his straightforwardness: "Behold an Israelite indeed, in whom is no guile" (John 1:47 KJV [NIV, NRSV: "no deceit"]). The reference to an Israelite may be a pun on the meaning of Jacob's name, which means "deceiver" (see Gen. 25:26; 27:35–36; cf. Gen. 28:12 with John 1:51). Judas Iscariot is an unfortunate contrast (John 12:6). God cannot lie (Titus 1:2), and therefore his word is without guile or "pure" (cf. 1 Pet. 2:1–2; 3:10).

Guilt–Although the concepts of sin and guilt often overlap, a basic distinction between the two can be established. In the biblical sense, sin is basically violation of divine stipulations (what a person does or does not do), whereas guilt is the resulting state, or one's "legal" status (what that person has become as a result). In essence, one commits sin and becomes guilty (Hab. 1:11).

The state of being guilty is further distinguished from the punishment that it draws, because one can be pronounced guilty and still be exempted from punishment. Nor should guilt be mistaken for the emotional response of the culprits toward themselves and their victims. No matter how sincere it may be, remorse does not eliminate the guilt.

In the biblical sense, guilt is something objective and separate from the will or intention of the culprit. One can pay back debt and render the obligation fulfilled. One cannot, however, cancel one's own guilt. In the sacrificial system of the OT, the offender must perform restitution to the victim and also give a guilt offering to God. This reflects the notion that in committing sinful acts in violation of God's laws, the culprit has offended not only the victim but also God. This is what David means in Ps. 51:3–4 (with his sin in full display before God, David realizes that he has sinned against God and God alone).

This is why those who scoff at the guilt offering are fools (Prov. 14:9). By doing this, they insult God's being and character. Such a biblical view of guilt implies that forgiveness and restoration should come from without, from source(s) other than the culprit and victim. The Bible affirms that the only one capable of offsetting the cost of human sin is the sinless Christ, "the Lamb of God who takes away the sin of the world" (John 1:29). His life was laid on the cross and offered as the acceptable sacrifice for the totality of guilt, and as a result it freed those who believe in him from the obligation of the guilt.

Guilt Offering–*See* Sacrifice and Offering.

Gymnasium–In the ancient world, a place for physical training and Greek education. Paul used the activities of the gymnasium as metaphors for Christian living: running (1 Cor. 9:24–27), boxing (1 Cor. 9:26), and wrestling (Eph. 6:12). In 1 Tim. 4:8 Paul uses the Greek term *gymnasia* to mean "physical training" and acknowledges its value.

H

Habakkuk–*See* Habakkuk, Book of.

Habakkuk, Book of–Habakkuk prophesied, as did Jeremiah, Ezekiel, and Zephaniah, during the turbulent period that saw the rise of the Babylonians and the ultimate destruction of Jerusalem. Like them, he was a warning sign that judgment was coming. On the other hand, he is unlike these other prophets in that his initial burning concern is how God is executing judgment: by means of a people seemingly more wicked than those being punished.

The book begins with the prophet's laments and God's responses. The laments of the prophet express questions about the justice of God. How can God allow internal (1:2–4) and external (the Babylonians; 1:12–17) wickedness to succeed? God responds that the wicked eventually will receive what is due them, but he is going to use the Babylonians to bring judgment on his people. In the light of these truths, God tells Habakkuk (and through him all readers) that "the righteous will live by his faith" (2:4 NASB [cf. Gen. 15:6]), just as Abraham did. God eventually will judge those whom he uses to bring punishment on his people (2:6–20). The final section (chap. 3) is a magnificent, and perhaps ancient, poetic portrait of God the warrior that Habakkuk includes in his work. In this way, the prophet records his own acceptance of God's ways in the world.

Hadad–*See* Baal.

Hadadezer–The king of Zobah defeated by David. In David's time, Hadadezer's sphere of influence extended southward to the northern Transjordan and eastward to the Upper Euphrates. Hadadezer encountered David's army in battle on three occasions. First, when David sent an army under the command of Joab against the Ammonites, who had insulted David's ambassadors, the Aramaean coalition army led by Hadadezer marched to the relief of the besieged city of Rabbath at the request of the Ammonites (2 Sam. 10:1–14). Second, when Hadadezer, unwilling to lose face after being routed by Joab, raised a new army "from beyond the River" under the command of Shobach, David himself moved to Helam and defeated the Aramean army (10:15–19). Third, David later took vengeance on Hadadezer for his interference in the Ammonite war (8:3–8) by invading the heartland of Hadadezer's realm. These campaigns by David against the Arameans and the Ammonites resulted in his securing control of the King's Highway.

Hades–A transliteration of the Greek word referring to the place of the dead. In addition to referring to the place of the dead, the term sometimes is used to signify death itself.

The Greek word *hadēs* is used ten times in the NT, and English translations vary in their rendering of the term. For example, the NIV translates it as "Hades" (Matt. 11:23; 16:18; Luke 10:15; 16:23; Rev. 1:18; 6:8; 20:13–14) or "the realm of the dead" (Acts 2:27, 31). It is occasionally used in conjunction with the idea of a place of punishment or torment (Luke 16:23), though the NT more frequently uses the Greek word *geenna* (a transliteration of Aramaic) when indicating future punishment in the afterlife. It is much more common to find *hadēs* associated with death, such as the four occasions in Revelation where the two concepts are linked together (1:18; 6:8; 20:13–14).

Hagar–The Egyptian maidservant whom Sarah offered to her husband, Abraham, as a solution to her own infertility (Gen. 16). When Hagar became pregnant, she treated Sarah disrespectfully, resulting in Hagar's dismissal. On instruction from the angel of the Lord, Hagar returned and bore Ishmael when Abraham was eighty-six years old. While Hagar received God's promise that her son would have many descendants, he was not the one through whom God's promises to Abraham would be fulfilled (Gen. 12:1–3; 15:4; 17:19). Following the birth of Isaac to Abraham and Sarah, the tension between the two women resulted in Sarah sending Hagar and Ishmael off into the desert, where God reaffirmed his commitment to Ishmael (Gen. 21:9–19).

Paul uses Hagar and Sarah to represent two covenants. Hagar represents the covenant given on Mount Sinai, the law that brings slavery and characterizes the earthly Jerusalem. The child born to Sarah as a result of God's promise represents the citizens of the heavenly Jerusalem, who are free (Gal. 4:22–27).

Haggai–*See* Haggai, Book of.

Haggai, Book of–The book of Haggai is the tenth book in the collection known as the Minor Prophets or the Book of the Twelve. Haggai was a contemporary of Zechariah, and the two prophets had an overlapping purpose: to encourage their generation to rebuild the temple. Though short and similar in theme to Zechariah, Haggai has its own interests, and it repays close reading.

The oracles of Haggai are clearly and specifically dated, so modern readers know that they reflect his prophetic ministry during a four-month period in 520 BC. The historical background to his message begins with the early return from exile under Sheshbazzar and Zerubbabel, the latter being frequently mentioned in Haggai. Soon after the return, the altar was rebuilt, and sacrifices began to be offered in the temple area, but the temple itself was still in disarray. The focus of Haggai's concern is that God wants his people to get busy reconstructing the temple. They have been hesitant, according to Haggai, because of their own economic struggles. God, through Haggai, tells his people that they must first take care of their religious obligations, and then God will bless them with personal well-being.

In addition, Zerubbabel plays an important role in the prophecy of Haggai. He is a descendant of David and a leader in postexilic Judah. His presence may have given rise to the expectation of the reestablishment of the Davidic monarchy, or at least that seems to be the implication of the last verses of the book, based on 2 Sam. 7:1–11.

Half-Shekel Tax–Paid in March for the upkeep of the temple, particularly the sacrifices (Matt. 17:24–27 [NIV: "two-drachma temple tax"]; cf. Josephus, *Ant.* 18.312). The law required every male who was twenty-years-old and older who came out of Egypt to give a half shekel (Exod. 30:13–16). Nehemiah made the tax annual, but at one-third shekel (Neh. 10:32). The amounts stated in the law and in the cycle of Nehemiah were eventually conflated. Even Jews living in the Diaspora paid the tax (Philo, *Embassy* 156; *Let. Aris.* 40).

Hallelujah–Hebrew "hallelujah" means "praise the Lord." This phrase has become idiomatic for Christian communities, so that the Hebrew pronunciation of "hallelujah" and its use as an exclamation of praise have been preserved. The phrase occurs twenty-four times in the Psalms, beginning at Ps. 104:35, and appears the most frequently in the last five psalms (Pss. 146–150).

Ham–The second of Noah's three sons, his descendants included Cush, Mizraim (Egypt), Put, and Canaan. After Ham informed his brothers that he saw their naked father, Noah cursed Ham's son Canaan, who was possibly involved. The name can designate one branch of Ham's descendants, the Egyptians, or their land (Pss. 78:51; 105:23, 27; 106:22).

Haman–*See* Esther, Book of.

Hamath–A Hittite city strategically positioned on the Orontes River and the main trade route running south from Asia Minor. Located about halfway between Damascus and Aleppo, it is frequently mentioned with reference to Israel's northern border—"the entrance to Hamath" or Lebo Hamath (Num. 13:21; 1 Kings 8:65). David received tribute from its king (2 Sam. 8:9–10), and Solomon built storage cities in the area (2 Chron. 8:4). During the exile, some Israelites settled there (Isa. 11:11), and some of its inhabitants were similarly transported to Samaria (2 Kings 17:24).

Hamstring–The act of cutting the large tendon in the back of a horse's hind leg (also oxen in Gen. 49:6) in order to make the animal unusable for combat. Joshua obeyed God's command to hamstring captured horses (Josh. 11:6, 9 [so as not to rely on military ability?]), but David was less thorough (2 Sam. 8:4; 1 Chron. 18:4).

Hanamel–The son of Shallum, Jeremiah's uncle. Jeremiah purchased a field in Anathoth from his cousin Hanamel to redeem it during the Babylonian invasion of Jerusalem (Jer. 32:7–9, 12). This action expressed faith in God's promise to restore the people to the land.

H

Hananel–A tower along the northern wall of Jerusalem. It appears that the tower was between the Sheep Gate and the Fish Gate (Neh. 3:1). The exact location is uncertain. Jeremiah predicted that the tower would be rebuilt (Jer. 31:38), and Nehemiah records that the tower was indeed rebuilt and consecrated with the newly reconstructed wall of Jerusalem (Neh. 3:1; 12:39). The Nehemiah passage may have been intended to demonstrate the fulfillment of this promise; however, Jeremiah's promise says that the city will never again be destroyed (Jer. 31:40). After Jerusalem's destruction in AD 70, the rebuilding led by Nehemiah cannot be seen as the final fulfillment of Jer. 31:38. Zechariah speaks of the tower as part of the elevated Jerusalem in God's eschatological kingdom (Zech. 14:10). This tower may have literary significance, alluding to the certainty of God's eschatological promises.

Hanani–**(1)** A prophet who prophesied against King Asa of Judah because Asa trusted the military might of the Arameans rather than trusting in God. Because of this prophecy, Asa had Hanani put into prison (2 Chron. 16:7–10). **(2)** The brother of Nehemiah who reported to Nehemiah the sad state of the wall in Jerusalem (Neh. 1:2). Later, Nehemiah placed him in charge of the gate of Jerusalem (Neh. 7:2).

Hananiah–**(1)** The son of Azzur from Gibeon, he was a false prophet in the time of the prophet Jeremiah. He took the yoke off the neck of Jeremiah and broke it, saying that the "yoke of Babylon" would be broken, which is contrary to Jeremiah's prophecy. Because Hananiah led people to believe lies, he died in the seventh month of that year in accordance with the prediction of Jeremiah (Jer. 28). **(2)** One of three godly companions of Daniel. His name was changed to "Shadrach" by the Babylonians (Dan. 1:6–7, 11, 19; 2:17).

Handbreadth–*See* Weights and Measures.

Hannah–The mother of Samuel and one of two wives of Elkanah from Ramathaim. She was regularly provoked by his other wife, Peninnah, who had children, because God had closed her womb (1 Sam. 1:6). But one year, while worshiping at Shiloh, she prayed for a son, whom she promised to dedicate to God (1:9–11). Although the priest Eli mistook her distress for drunkenness, he subsequently blessed her. She later gave birth to Samuel and dedicated him (1:26–28), and annually she provided him with a robe (2:19). Hannah's prayer (2:1–10) is often noted for its resemblance to the later prayer of Mary the mother of Jesus (Luke 1:46–55), both of which celebrate God's humiliation of the rich and powerful and exaltation of the poor and lowly.

Hanukkah–*See* Festivals (Festival of Dedication).

Hanun–King of the Ammonites. After Hanun's father, Nahash, died, David sent messengers to comfort him because of Nahash's relationship with David (2 Sam. 10:1–2; 1 Chron. 19:1–2), but Hanun did not trust David's intentions, humiliated the messengers, and incited a war against Israel. Israel won and conquered the Ammonites (2 Sam. 12:30–31; 1 Chron. 20:1–3).

Haran–A son of Terah and brother of Abraham. He was the father of Lot as well as of Milkah and Iskah. Haran died in Ur of the Chaldeans, where he was born, before Terah took his family and set out for Canaan (Gen. 11:26–32).

Hardness of Heart–Hardness of heart describes a spiritual condition of active resistance against God and his ways. In a certain sense this kind of resistance is found in every human being ever since the fall in Gen. 3. Every human being inherits a sin nature from Adam (Rom. 5:12–14) that naturally and inevitably imparts a predisposition to sin.

One of the puzzles and mysteries of Scripture is that God himself is often described as being the one who hardens the hearts of various individuals. Pharaoh in the exodus story is a classic illustration. In Exod. 4:21 God says to Moses, "I will harden his [Pharaoh's] heart so that he will not let the people go." Other times, more ambiguous language is used, such as in 7:13, where "Pharaoh's heart became hard." Still other times, Pharaoh himself is described as being actively involved in this process, such as "when Pharaoh saw that there was relief, he hardened his heart and would not listen to Moses and Aaron" (8:15). The best way to understand this situation is to see hardness of heart as a combination of the active will of fallen human beings and the mysterious workings of a sovereign God. (Salvation and spiritual growth are similar spiritual realities in that both of these also involve a mysterious combination of God's direct involvement in people's lives and the necessity of their own human response.) Since the Bible so frequently warns against the danger of a hardened heart, there are clearly genuine opportunities for people to cry out to God for mercy and deliverance from this awful situation.

Harem–A harem typically was a large group of women (wives, concubines, virgins, plus any small children) associated with a king; they lived together in a secluded, restricted area of his palace and often were attended by eunuchs. Harems were common in the royal courts of the ancient Near East, including in Israelite royal life (2 Sam. 3:7; 5:13; 12:11; 19:5; 21:11; 1 Kings 11:3–4; 1 Chron. 3:9; 2 Chron. 11:21; Ps. 45:14; Eccles. 2:8).

Harlot–*See* Sex, Sexuality.

Harod–A valley and spring in northern Israel where Gideon assembled his troops before the battle recorded in Judg. 7. The narrow Harod Valley connects the Jezreel Valley and the Jordan Rift Valley between the cities of Jezreel and Beth Shan. This fertile valley boasts several springs, including the spring of Harod (7:1). Here, before Gideon's army went into battle and defeated the Midianites, God reduced their numbers based on how the soldiers drank from the spring. After the battle, the Midianites fled southeast down the Harod Valley on their way back across the Jordan River. Years later, King Saul assembled his army in the same vicinity before his final, deadly battle with the Philistines (1 Sam. 28; 31).

Harran–A city or region approximately sixty miles north of the confluence of the Euphrates and the Balikh rivers. Abraham moved from Ur to Harran en route to Canaan (Gen. 11:26–12:5). There, Eliezer acquired Rebekah as a wife for Isaac (24:1–67), and Jacob later resided, marrying Leah and Rachel (29:1–30).

Harvest–The harvest was a major event on the yearly calendar of Israel's agrarian society (Lev. 25:11; Judg. 15:1; Ruth 1:22; 2 Sam. 21:9–10). Life was dependent on the harvest. As a result, God set certain rules with respect to the harvest to help the Israelites keep proper priorities. Every seven years and every fiftieth year, the people were to give the land a rest (Exod. 23:10; Lev. 25:20–22). The people were to rest on the Sabbath, even during the harvesttime (Exod. 34:21). Some portions of crops were to be left in the field so that the poor might have food (Lev. 19:9; 23:22; Deut. 24:21). The people were to acknowledge God as the source of the harvest by offering the first of the produce (Lev. 23:10). Celebrating the harvest was commanded (Exod. 23:16; Deut. 16:15; Isa. 9:3). Planning for the harvest was a mark of wisdom (Prov. 6:8; 10:5; 20:4). Even as a good harvest was the blessing of God (Ps. 67:6; Isa. 62:9), so a bad harvest was a curse from God and the plight of a fool (1 Sam. 12:17; Job 5:5; Prov. 26:1; Isa. 18:4–5; Jer. 8:13, 20; Joel 3:12; Mic. 6:15). Failure to acknowledge God for the harvest was a sin (Jer. 5:24).

The harvest is often used in Scripture as an analogy. The prophets talk about the negative harvest of idolatry (Isa. 17:11). Israel is called the firstfruits of God's harvest (Jer. 2:3). Hosea uses the idea of harvest to indicate that God's people have a future (Hos. 6:11). In the Gospels, the harvest is used as an analogy for those needing to hear the good news (Matt. 9:37–38), for the end times (Matt. 13:24–30; Rev. 14:15), and for a lesson about unfaithful leadership (Matt. 21:33–46; 25:24). In the remainder of the NT, the harvest analogy usually refers to Christian growth and salvation (Rom. 1:13; 1 Cor. 9:10–11; 2 Cor. 9:10; Gal. 6:9; Heb. 12:11; James 3:18).

Harvest, Feast of–Another name for the Feast of Weeks (cf. Exod. 23:16; 34:22; NIV: "Festival of Harvest/Weeks"). *See also* Festivals: The Festival of Weeks.

Havilah–A land surrounded by the Pishon River and used to describe the location of the garden of Eden. It is characterized by its abundance of fine gold, bdellium, and onyx stones (Gen. 2:11–12). Although the passage is somewhat enigmatic, it appears that Havilah lies outside the garden. Havilah is used elsewhere in connection with Shur to describe the boundaries of the land of the Ishmaelites (Gen. 25:18) and the geographical extent of Saul's victory over the Amalekites (1 Sam. 15:7). Havilah lies outside the land of Israel. It likely refers to some part of Arabia or to Arabia in general, since this region is characterized by gold, bdellium, and onyx stones and is associated with the Ishmaelites; its name may be associated with the name of a region in southwest Arabia.

H

Hazael–The king of Damascus around 842–800 BC, Hazael was a high officer of Ben-Hadad before he seized the throne by assassinating him (2 Kings 8:7–15). Although Hazael was a usurper, whom Assyrians called "the son of a nobody," his reign brought the kingdom of Damascus to the zenith of its power. The Israelites, however, remembered him as the perpetrator of horrible cruelties against them (2 Kings 8:12). Thus, later, when Amos predicted vengeance upon Damascus, he foretold that fire would consume "the house of Hazael" (Amos 1:4).

In 2 Kings 9:15–17 Hazael appears as the ally of Yahwism against Baalism. He indirectly aided Jehu's coup against Joram (9:14–15). After successfully withstanding an attack by Shalmaneser III (841 BC), he turned to menace the kingdoms of both Israel and Judah throughout the reigns of Jehu and Jehoahaz. He took the whole of the Transjordan south up to the Moabite frontier (10:32–33) and reduced the Israelite army to a minimum (13:7). Joash king of Judah had to bribe Hazael with the treasures stripped from the temple and the palace to save Jerusalem (12:17–18). After Hazael's death, he was succeeded by his son Ben-Hadad III, which prompted Jehoash son of Jehoahaz to take back the land Hazael had taken from his father (13:24–25). Hazael's empire came to an end when the Assyrian king Adad-nirari III conquered Damascus in 796 BC.

Hazor–**(1)** From both a biblical and an archaeological point of view, the most important place named "Hazor" was at modern Tell el-Qedah, a site in the Huleh Valley some eight miles north of the Sea of Galilee. The site was occupied beginning in the third millennium BC (Early Bronze Age). The Middle Bronze Age city was destroyed by burning, but the site was rebuilt in the Late Bronze Age (sixteenth to thirteenth centuries BC) and flourished as a Canaanite city-state. This city was destroyed in the thirteenth century BC in an event that some have correlated to the conquest of the land under Joshua (Josh. 11:13 [see below]). The city was built up and fortified again during the period of the Israelite monarchy, under Solomon (1 Kings 9:15) and again under the northern Omride dynasty. Following the destruction by the Assyrian king Tiglath-pileser III (2 Kings 15:29), the site served as an Assyrian garrison before finally being abandoned in the fourth century BC.

Hazor figures prominently in several biblical accounts. As noted above, Hazor is among several cities that Joshua was supposed to have conquered (Josh. 11:13). In the case of Hazor, the destruction of the city by burning is noted as an exceptional circumstance. The king of Hazor was named "Jabin" (Josh. 11:1), a name that appears later in the time of Deborah and Barak, when Hazor was once again a center of Canaanite power (Judg. 4:2, 17) and hostile toward the Israelites. Although archaeological discoveries do not uniformly corroborate the biblical descriptions of the overall program of Joshua's conquest (Ai and Jericho are notable problems), the evidence at Hazor of a massive destruction by fire in the late thirteenth century BC suggests a historical underpinning for Josh. 11:13. In terms of broader biblical chronology, this correlation presupposes a late date for the exodus.

Hazor once again rises to prominence in biblical history in the war waged by Deborah and Barak, when it is again ruled by a powerful Canaanite king named "Jabin" (Judg. 4:2 [ostensibly in the Iron Age I period, 1200–1000 BC]).

The tenth century BC saw the construction of massive fortifications at Hazor, including a large gate. Following the biblical account, this evidence belongs to Solomon's program of building throughout the country and corresponds to the identification of Hazor as one of several regional administrative capitals (1 Kings 9:15). The "Solomonic" city was destroyed in the late ninth century, possibly as a part of the invasion of the Aramean king Ben-Hadad (1 Kings 15:20 [Hazor is not mentioned, though it is encompassed in the region more generally described; see also Josh. 19:36–37]).

The Bible does not describe a subsequent rebuilding of the city, but it was again destroyed by the Assyrian king Tiglath-pileser III in 732 BC (2 Kings 15:29), an event evidenced in the archaeology of the site. The repeated destructions of Hazor testify to the importance of its site along the "Way of the Sea" from Egypt to the northern Levant.

(2) Jeremiah 49:28–33 describes Nebuchadnezzar's campaign against "Kedar and the kingdoms of Hazor." Based on the association with Kedar and the description of Hazor as "a nation that has neither gates nor bars" (49:31), and a people with camels and herds (49:32), the Hazor of this passage appears to be a nomadic tribal entity rather than the heavily fortified city of Solomonic times.

HEADSTONE–*See* Capstone.

HEART–Physiologically, the heart is an organ in the body, and in the Bible it is also used in a number of metaphors.

Metaphorically, the heart refers to the mind, the will, the seat of emotions, or even the whole person. It also refers to the center of something or its inner part. These metaphors come from the heart's importance and location.

Mind. The heart refers to the mind, but not the brain, and in these cases does not involve human physiology. It is a metaphor, and while the neurophysiology of the heart may be interesting in its own right, it has no bearing on this use of language. Deuteronomy 6:5 issues the command to love God with all one's heart, soul, and strength. When the command is repeated in the Gospels, it occurs in three variations (Matt. 22:37; Mark 12:30; Luke 10:27). Common to all three is the addition of the word "mind." The Gospel writers want to be sure that the audience hears Jesus adding "mind," but this addition is based on the fact that the meaning of the Hebrew word for "heart" includes the mind.

The mental activities of the metaphorical heart are abundant. The heart is where a person thinks (Gen. 6:5; Deut. 7:17; 1 Chron. 29:18; Rev. 18:7), where a person comprehends and has understanding (1 Kings 3:9; Job 17:4; Ps. 49:3; Prov. 14:13; Matt. 13:15). The heart makes plans and has intentions (Gen. 6:5; 8:21; Prov. 20:5; 1 Chron. 29:18; Jer. 23:20). One believes with the heart (Luke 24:25; Acts 8:37; Rom. 10:9). The heart is the site of wisdom, discernment, and skill (Exod. 35:34; 36:2; 1 Kings 3:9; 10:24). The heart is the place of memory (Deut. 4:9; Ps. 119:11). The heart plays the role of conscience (2 Sam. 24:10; 1 John 3:20–21).

It is often worth the effort to substitute "mind" for "heart" when reading the Bible in order to grasp the mental dimension. For example, after telling the Israelites to love God with all their heart, Moses says, "These commandments that I give you today are to be upon your hearts" (Deut. 6:6). Reading it instead as "be on your mind" changes our perspective, and in this case the idiom "on your mind" is clearer and more accurate. The following verses instruct parents to talk to their children throughout the day about God's words. In order for parents to do this, God's requirements and deeds need to be constantly on their minds, out of their love for him. Similarly, love for God and loyalty are expressed by meditation on and determination to obey his law (Ps. 119:11, 112). The law is not merely a list of rules; it is also a repository of a worldview in which the Lord is the only God. To live consistently with this truth requires careful, reflective thought.

Emotions and attitude. The heart, as the seat of emotion, is associated with a number of feelings and sentiments, such as gladness (Exod. 4:14; Acts 2:26), hatred (Lev. 19:17), pride (Deut. 8:14), resentment (Deut. 15:10), dread (Deut. 28:67), sympathy (Judg. 5:9), love (Judg. 16:15), sadness (1 Sam. 1:8; John 16:6), and jealousy and ambition (James 3:14). The heart is also the frame of reference for attitudes such as willingness, courage, and desire.

HEAVEN–The present abode of God and the final dwelling place of the righteous. The ancient Jews distinguished three different heavens. The first heaven was the atmospheric heavens of the clouds and where the birds fly (Gen. 1:20). The second heaven was the celestial heavens of the sun, the moon, and the stars. The third heaven was the present home of God and the angels. Paul builds on this understanding of a third heaven in 2 Cor. 12:2–4, where he describes himself as a man who "was caught up to the third heaven" or "paradise," where he "heard inexpressible things." This idea of multiple heavens also shows itself in how the Jews normally spoke of "heavens" in the plural (Gen. 1:1), while most other ancient cultures spoke of "heaven" in the singular.

Although God is present everywhere, God is also present in a special way in "heaven."

During Jesus' earthly ministry, the Father is sometimes described as speaking in "a voice from heaven" (Matt. 3:17). Similarly, Jesus instructs us to address our prayers to "Our Father in heaven" (6:9). Even the specific request in the Lord's Prayer that "your kingdom come, your will be done, on earth as it is in heaven" (6:10) reminds us that heaven is a place already under God's full jurisdiction, where his will is presently being done completely and perfectly. Jesus also warns of the dangers of despising "one of these little ones," because "their angels in heaven always see the face of my Father in heaven" (18:10). Jesus "came down from heaven" (John 6:51) for his earthly ministry, and after his death and resurrection, he ascended back "into heaven," from where he "will come back in the same way you have seen him go into heaven" (Acts 1:11).

Given this strong connection between heaven and God's presence, there is a natural connection in Scripture between heaven and the ultimate hope of believers. Believers are promised a reward in heaven ("Rejoice and be glad, because great is your reward in heaven" [Matt. 5:12]), and even now believers can "store up for [themselves] treasures in heaven" (6:20). Even in this present life, "our citizenship is in heaven" (Phil. 3:20), and our hope at death is to "depart and be with Christ, which is better by far" (1:23). Since Christ is currently in heaven, deceased believers are already present with Christ in heaven awaiting his return, when "God will bring with Jesus those who have fallen asleep in him" (1 Thess. 4:14).

Heavenly City–*See* Heaven.

Heavenly Council–The idea of the divine council appears throughout the literature of the ancient Near East, including the OT. Taking various forms, it generally involves numerous deities subservient to an overall patriarchal divine figure (or couple)—for example, El in Ugaritic materials, and Yahweh in the OT.

The heavenly council appears in the OT, though the lower tiers have been collapsed into one other tier of divinities subservient to Yahweh. Psalm 82 constitutes a classic example. God upbraids the lower gods for not executing their ruling tasks properly. It also reflects the common notion of lower gods ruling over peoples or other aspects of creation (see also Deut. 32:8–9). Another example of the divine council, in 1 Kings 22:5–28, highlights the role of the prophet as one granted access, through vision, who proclaims its decisions. Job 1–2 and Zech. 3 also provide glimpses of the divine council interacting. Note here the "sons of God" in Job 1:6 (KJV; NIV: "angels"), perhaps reflecting the divine family aspect of the council. See also the "Let us" or "us" passages from the divine voice in Genesis, wherein Yahweh communicates with the rest of the deities about actions to undertake (1:26; 3:22; 11:6–7). Numerous other passages in the OT manifest the notion of the divine council, either referring directly to it or indicating the existence of other deities alongside Yahweh and envisioning their council together. In the Second Temple period and within apocalyptic thought, the lower deities begin more consistently to be conceived of as angels. The Bible generally assumes the existence of other deities but views them as creatures rather than the Creator and restricts worship to the one true God.

Heber–A Kenite who separated himself from his people and lived at the great tree in Zaanannim near Kedesh (Judg. 4:11). He was married to Jael, who rescued Israel from their Canaanite oppressors. Taking advantage of the fact that Jabin, the Canaanite king, was on friendly terms with the Kenites, Jael lured the fleeing Sisera, commander of Jabin's army, into her tent. After hiding him and giving him a drink, she pounded a tent peg through his temple while he slept (4:17–21).

Hebrews, Letter to the–The Letter to the Hebrews and the Letter to the Romans constitute the two great pillars of theology in the NT. Hebrews brings a high Christology and increases Christian understanding of Christ's role as priest and pioneer of faith. From this book, deductions can be made regarding the early church's understanding of OT interpretation and its view of typology.

Hebrews ends like a letter, but it does not begin like one. In particular, it lacks the names of the writer and the recipients. From the content, though, it is evident that this work is meant for a certain audience, familiar with the author. The author shows a loving pastoral concern for his readers, teaching them, exhorting them, and rebuking them when necessary. He gives them models of faith to encourage them and instructs them to encourage one another. The author describes the work as "my word of exhortation" (13:22). The book is often identified as a sermon.

The letter is, strictly speaking, anonymous. No author is mentioned, and few clues as to his identity exist. He is known by his readers (13:19) and has a pastor's heart for them (6:9). He and his audience are second-generation Christians; that is, they did not hear Jesus during his ministry but rather are dependent upon those who did (2:3). He is a companion of Timothy (13:23) and thus possibly in the circle of Paul. The original readers almost certainly were a house church, part of a network of churches in an urban setting, likely either Jerusalem or Rome, with Rome being slightly preferred.

The author brings his unique perspective to the work of Christ—his special roles as both high priest and sacrifice. Because Jesus lives forever, he has a permanent priesthood (7:24), which is not a function of his ancestry but rather is "on the basis of the power of an indestructible life" (7:16). He meets the requirements of a priest, being "holy, blameless, pure, set apart from sinners, exalted above the heavens" (7:26). He is a "priest forever, in the order of Melchizedek" (7:17, quoting Ps. 110:4). Melchizedek is a once-mentioned figure from Gen. 14:18. He was the king of Salem, a "priest of God Most High." Abraham, and by extension Levi, paid him a tithe and received a blessing from him. Therefore, Melchizedek is superior to Levi, and his priestly order is superior to Levi's. This priesthood, in fact, replaces the Levitical priesthood because the earlier priesthood could not produce perfection (Heb. 7:11), being "weak and useless" (7:18).

The Levitical priests had offered their sacrifices repeatedly, year after year, first for their own sins, then for those of the people. They had used the blood of bulls and goats to cleanse the tabernacle and accessories, because without the shedding of blood there can be no forgiveness of sin (9:22). There had been many priests, as death claimed each one. The priests, in all their weaknesses, had been appointed by the law. The sanctuary in which they serve is a "copy and shadow" of what is in heaven (8:5).

In contrast to the Levitical high priest, Jesus sits at "the right hand of the throne of the Majesty in heaven" (8:1) and serves in the true tabernacle not made by human hands. He has been appointed not by the law but by the oath of God, which came after the law. He has no need to offer sacrifices day after day; his sacrifice was "once for all" (7:27), coming at the culmination of the ages to do away with sin (9:26). In fact, the repeated nature of the Levitical sacrifices serves as proof of their ineffectiveness. Had they been effective, they would have ceased. But "it is impossible for the blood of bulls and goats to take away sins" (10:4), even when offered in accordance with the law (10:8). The worshipers had been left with the same guilty consciences. Christ had "entered the Most Holy Place once for all by his own blood" and obtained eternal redemption for all believers (9:12), sprinkling their hearts to cleanse them from guilty consciences (10:22).

Because of this, Christ is the mediator of the new covenant, prophesied in Jer. 31:31, which is superior to the Mosaic covenant. The first covenant has been made obsolete and will soon disappear (Heb. 8:13), as the new covenant is "established on better promises" (8:6). The tabernacle had been designed to demonstrate that there was no way into the most holy place for anyone but the high priest. Now, the blood of Jesus has opened a way through the curtain, allowing believers to "draw near to God with a sincere heart and with the full assurance of faith" (10:22).

Hebron–A city located in the Judean hills eighteen miles south-southeast of Jerusalem, identified with modern El-Khalil in the West Bank, in an area well supplied with water from nearby wells and springs. Hebron (also known as Kiriath Arba) played a significant role in OT narratives. After Lot chose to dwell in Sodom, Abram settled near the oaks of Mamre in Hebron (Gen. 13:18). When Sarah died, Abraham purchased land in Hebron for her burial (Gen. 23). Both Isaac and Jacob lived in Hebron, and from there Jacob sent Joseph to inquire about his brothers' welfare (35:27; 37:14). When Moses sent twelve spies into the promised land, their glimpse of the large inhabitants of Hebron significantly influenced their negative report about the prospects for invasion (Num. 13:22, 33).

During the period of the conquest, Hebron's king was among five kings whom Joshua killed after they attacked Gibeon (Josh. 10). Joshua went on to fight at Hebron, destroying the city and its Anakite inhabitants (11:21). The city was then deeded to Caleb (15:13), but later it was given to the Levites and became a city of refuge (20:7; 21:13).

Hebron played a prominent role during the united monarchy. After Saul died, God instructed David to go to Hebron. There the men of Judah anointed him as king, and he reigned from there for seven and a half years (2 Sam. 2:1–11). During this time, several sons were born to David in Hebron, and it was there that Joab, David's commander, murdered Abner in revenge for his brother's death (2 Sam. 3; 1 Chron. 3:1–4). When David's authority became widely recognized, the elders of all the Israelite tribes came to Hebron and anointed him king over all Israel. He then moved his capital to Jerusalem after capturing it from the Jebusites (2 Sam. 5:1–10; 1 Chron. 11:1–9). When Absalom later conspired to become king, he chose Hebron as his headquarters (2 Sam. 15:1–10).

Hebron is next mentioned as one of the cities that Rehoboam fortified for the defense of Judah (2 Chron. 11:10) and as one of the locations where returning exiles settled (Neh. 11:25).

HEIFER–A young cow, typically one that has not produced offspring. Heifers assisted people by plowing (Deut. 21:3) and producing milk, which could be curdled into cheese (Isa. 7:21). Samson compares the animal allegorically to his wife (Judg. 14:18). Jeremiah does the same with Egypt, which will be tormented by a Babylonian gadfly (Jer. 46:20). Hosea compares Israel to a stubborn heifer (Hos. 4:16). The lives of heifers were required for special sacrifices (Gen. 15:9; 1 Sam. 16:1–2). Their sacrifice also purged bloodguilt from the land as a consequence of murder when the culprit was unknown (Deut. 21:1–8). Through an elaborate ritual, the ashes of a red heifer were mixed with water for purification from uncleanness caused by coming into contact with a corpse (Num. 19:1–22; cf. Heb. 9:13).

HELIOPOLIS–The name "Heliopolis" is Greek for "city of the sun." The Greek name for the city referred to in Hebrew as "On" or "Aven" (Gen. 41:45, 50; 46:20; cf. Ezek. 30:17) (the Hebrew spellings are similar). It is one of the oldest cities in Lower Egypt, dating from the predynastic period.

Heliopolis was the center of worship for Re, the sun god, and Atum, the creator god. The priests of Heliopolis were among the most powerful in Egypt. They officiated at all the major festivals and produced one of the major versions of Egyptian religion and mythology. The prominence of the priesthood is reflected in the description of Joseph marrying Asenath, the daughter of Potiphera, the priest of On (Gen. 41:45, 50; 46:20). The Egyptians called the city by a name that means "city of pillars." Its temples were embellished with many obelisks, to catch the first rays of the morning sun. Jeremiah prophesied the destruction of the obelisks and temples in Heliopolis (Jer. 43:13; cf. Ezek. 30:17). The city flourished as a seat of learning until it was eclipsed by Alexandria.

HELL–The place where the lost are assigned by God to eternal punishment of both body and soul (Matt. 10:28). This agony of eternal torment in hell is the greatest of all possible tragedies.

This topic of the afterlife unfolded only gradually in Scripture. "Gehenna" originally referred to the Valley of Hinnom near Jerusalem, the location of the notorious sacrificial offerings of children by fire to the god Molek by Ahaz (2 Chron. 28:3) and Manasseh (2 Chron. 33:6). Later, the meaning of this term was extended to the place of fiery punishment in general. Still later, the geographic location of this place of punishment was shifted to under the earth, but the idea of fiery torment continued. By NT times, the Pharisees clearly believed in the punishment of the wicked in the afterlife.

It is primarily in the teachings of Jesus that the reality of a place of eternal punishment comes into clear focus. Jesus describes hell as involving unquenchable fire (Matt. 18:8–9; Mark 9:42–43, 48), a place where the worm does not die (Mark 9:48). Jesus also pictures the extreme anguish of those who suffer the ultimate punishment of being "thrown outside, into the darkness, where there will be weeping and gnashing of teeth" (Matt. 8:12).

The idea of a severe eternal punishment for the lost is also taught by the apostles. At the return of Christ, those living outside a proper relationship with God will experience sudden destruction (1 Thess. 5:3) when the angels will come "in blazing fire" and "punish those who do not know God and do not obey the gospel of our Lord Jesus" (2 Thess. 1:6–9). The author of Hebrews speaks of the "fearful expectation of judgment and of raging fire that will consume the enemies of God" (Heb. 10:27). Revelation describes how "the smoke of their torment will rise for ever and ever" (Rev. 14:11), and how the ungodly will be cast into "the fiery lake of burning sulfur" (21:8).

HELLENISM–Traditionally, the noun "Hellenism" refers to the phenomenon of so-called Greek cultural influence, especially in the eastern Mediterranean, in the aftermath of Alexander the Great. As Alexander conquered the Near East, he worked to establish Greek culture and institutions within the conquered cities and areas. Over time, native populations adopted Greek culture in varying degrees. The adjective "Hellenistic" thus represents something as a part of this phenomenon, usually indicating some form of a "native" culture having a veneer of "Greek" culture. Although differences exist, scholars of antiquity understand the Hellenistic period to commence shortly after Alexander the Great, toward the end of the fourth century BC, and to conclude sometime in the several centuries after Christ.

All forms of ancient Judaism of which we are aware were Hellenized to some degree. To some extent they manifested a mixture of cultural practices, even at the level of patterns of thought. Thus, all forms of Judaism, including that practiced by Jesus, the authors of the NT, and other early Christians, were to some extent Hellenistic. Setting Jesus and the writings of the NT within the broad matrix of Jewish-Hellenistic practices and ways of understanding the world aids in understanding them.

For example, Jewish apocalyptic thought and literature developed and continued taking shape among Jewish specialists within Hellenistic cultural mixing. Its semidualistic views of the world along with its various conceptions of the afterlife make sense as part of broader Hellenistic views. Jesus and other early Christians explicitly taught and wrote about God's salvation in Christ within such Hellenistic-Jewish apocalyptic matrices. Thus, Paul's apocalyptic conceptions of the afterlife, redefined around Christ, in 1 Cor. 15 involve understandings of the resurrection body in categories common to Hellenistic philosophy. It will be a body composed of the lighter heavenly substances associated with the upper divine realm and not the heavier flesh-and-blood substances of the lower world, just as most Hellenistic philosophical sensitivities conceived afterlife possibilities for existence. In this way, Paul's Jewish apocalyptic belief of the God of Israel's end-time blessing of resurrection, which happened first and foremost in Christ, also completely involved broader Hellenistic views. Jesus and early Christians lived in the Hellenistic world of long-standing and continuous cultural mixing.

HELLENISTS, HELLENISTIC JEWS–The Hellenists, or "Hellenistic Jews," mentioned in Acts 6:1 are Greek-speaking Jewish Christians who immigrated back to Israel and are distinguished from the native-born, Aramaic-speaking "Hebraic Jews." The two groups are involved in a dispute over the distribution of food among widows. The principal spokesperson of the Hellenists is Stephen, who is later martyred for his faith (Acts 7; his opponents are also Hellenistic Jews [6:9]). The same Greek word is used to refer to Greek-speaking Jews in Antioch (9:29) and to non-Christian, Greek-speaking Gentiles (11:20; NIV: "Greeks"). Paul himself was a Hellenistic Jew, born in Tarsus in Cilicia (21:37; 22:3). It is evident from Paul's life that being a Hellenist did not necessarily mean he was less committed to Jewish laws and customs (see Phil. 3:5–6).

HEMAN–**(1)** A worship leader during the time of King David (1 Chron. 16:42), a descendant of Levi through Kohath and Joel (1 Chron. 6:33). Heman was one of King David's seers, which involved prophesying as well as musical worship (1 Chron. 25:1, 4–5). Two of Heman's famous colleagues were Asaph and Jeduthun. **(2)** A descendant of Judah through Zerah (1 Chron. 2:6) whose name appears in the inscription of Ps. 88 as "Heman the Ezrahite." He was known for his wisdom (1 Kings 4:31). Some have suggested that he is the same person as in 1 Chron. 6:33; 16:42; 25:1, 4–5.

HEMORRHAGE–The word "hemorrhage" is sometimes used to refer to a "flow of blood" or "discharge of blood" related to a woman's reproductive organs (Lev. 12:7; cf. Matt. 9:20), which rendered her ritually unclean. The impurity of menstruation made a woman unclean for seven days and was transmitted to anyone or anything she touched (Lev. 15:19–24). Thus, sexual intercourse with a woman during this period was prohibited (Lev. 18:19; 20:18; cf. Ezek. 22:10). A woman suffering from irregular or prolonged bleeding was considered clean only after the bleeding had ceased for seven days (Lev. 15:25–28). Jesus healed a woman who had been suffering from bleeding for twelve years (Matt. 9:20–22; Mark 5:25–34; Luke 8:43–48). Instead of Jesus becoming unclean by her touching his garment, the power of his holiness cleansed her. The woman, who had been excluded from worshiping in the temple due to her physical "uncleanness" (Lev. 15:31), was transformed by grace and now a member of Jesus' new family.

Hephzibah–**(1)** The mother of King Manasseh of Judah and presumably the wife of Hezekiah (2 Kings 21:1). **(2)** A symbolic name, meaning "my delight is in her," that God gives to Jerusalem after the return from exile (Isa. 62:4). The name provides a contrast with Jerusalem's earlier names, "Deserted" and "Desolate." It is God's declaration that he will once again take delight in Jerusalem.

Herald–A messenger commissioned to deliver a proclamation on behalf of a royal personage or God. King Nebuchadnezzar's herald announces that all subjects must worship a golden statue or else be thrown into a blazing furnace (Dan. 3:4). God instructs Habakkuk to record his oracle regarding the future destruction of Babylon on a tablet so that it might be delivered by a herald (Hab. 2:2). Paul was appointed as an apostle and a herald of the gospel to the Gentiles (1 Tim. 2:7; 2 Tim. 1:11).

Herbs, Bitter–*See* Bitter Herbs.

Hermes–**(1)** A Greek deity (equivalent to the Roman god Mercury) associated with science and eloquence, he was said to have appeared with the god Zeus around Lystra (Ovid, *Metam.* 8.611–724). A crowd in Lystra identified Paul as Hermes and Barnabas as Zeus after Paul healed a man who could not walk (Acts 14:8–12). **(2)** A Christian greeted by Paul (Rom. 16:14). He is not specified as Jewish (cf. Rom. 16:7, 11, 21), and in Rome the name "Hermes" was typical of (former) slaves.

Hermogenes–An apostacized believer whom Paul names while writing from prison (2 Tim. 1:15). Paul claims that Hermogenes, Phygelus, and everyone else in the province of Asia have deserted him. Paul's disappointment with Hermogenes is mentioned in the context of his exhortation not to be ashamed of suffering for the sake of the gospel.

Hermon, Mount–The highest mountain in ancient Israel, with its highest peak reaching over 9,200 feet. Due to its height, its peak is snow-covered year-round, causing abundant dew in comparison to the arid land in that region, with its melting ice serving as a major source of the Jordan River.

The Canaanites referred to Hermon as Sirion or Senir (Deut. 3:9), as do some biblical texts (e.g., 1 Chron. 5:23). It is located above the Lebanon Valley (Josh. 11:17) and above Mizpah (11:3), where Joshua pursued the Canaanite kings and defeated them at the Waters of Merom (11:1–7). Hermon is identified with the modern Jebel es-Sheik (Arabic for "mountain of the sheik"), about thirty miles southwest of Damascus.

Hermon is mentioned fifteen times in the Bible (Deut. 3:8, 9; 4:48; Josh. 11:3, 17; 12:1, 5; 13:5, 11; Judg. 3:3; Pss. 42:6; 89:12; 133:3; Song 4:8; 1 Chron. 5:23). It is known for its lions and leopards (Song 4:8) and pine trees (Ezek. 27:5). It is praised for its dew (Ps. 133:3) and mentioned in reference to other mountains (89:12), the Jordan River (42:6), and the power of God (29:6). Hermon is not mentioned in the NT, but due to its geographical proximity to Caesarea Philippi, some have suggested it was the location for Jesus' transfiguration, which Mark 9:2 locates on a "high mountain."

Herod–Several kings of the Jews, related by birth, had the name "Herod." The Herods formed a royal dynasty that flourished during the time of Christ and the early church. The founder of the dynasty was Antipater, who was appointed by Caesar in 47 BC as procurator of Judea. The Herods, being partly Edomite (descended from Esau) as well as loyal servants of Rome, were never fully accepted by their Jewish subjects. The family history was characterized by lust, intrigue, and bloodshed. They opposed the Christian faith, sometimes violently, being responsible for the attempted murder of Jesus (Matt. 2:16), the beheading of John the Baptist (Matt. 14:1–12), and the execution of the apostle James (Acts 12:2).

(1) Herod I (Herod the Great), son of Antipater, known as King Herod (Matt. 2:1; Luke 1:5). He ruled Palestine in the years 37–4 BC with Roman consent. A skillful politician, he managed to retain the favor of Rome by deftly switching allegiances when necessary. A capable ruler in some respects, he engaged in extensive building works. His finest project was the beautification of the temple, which he hoped would win Jewish favor. The rabbis would later say, "Whoever has not seen Herod's building has not seen anything beautiful."

His rule, however, was marred by paranoia, suspicion, and cruel jealousy. He had some of his wives and sons killed for suspected plotting. In Matthew's Gospel he is visited by wise men looking for "one who has been born king of the

Jews." Subsequently, he massacred the male infants of Bethlehem, trying to rid himself of this new, royal challenger (Matt. 2:1–11). Upon his death, his kingdom was divided among three of his sons, Herod Antipas, Herod Archelaus, and Herod Philip.

(2) Herod Antipas, son of Herod the Great, also known simply as Herod or as Herod the tetrarch (Matt. 14:1; Luke 3:19). He was given jurisdiction over Galilee and Perea, which he ruled from 4 BC to AD 39 (Luke 3:1). For this reason, when Pilate heard that Jesus came from Galilee, he sent him to Antipas for questioning (Luke 23:6–12).

He is infamous for his role in the death of John the Baptist, which later haunted him (Matt. 14:1–12; Mark 6:14–29). Jesus referred to him as "that fox," alluding to his predatory destructiveness for having killed John the Baptist, who criticized him for taking his half brother's wife, Herodias, in marriage. He also sought to kill Jesus (Luke 13:31–32). Jesus warned the disciples of the yeast of Herod (Mark 8:15). Yeast was a metaphor sometimes used to describe how evil spreads and corrupts the whole person, perhaps a reference to Herod's lust for Herodias and his murderous opposition to God's word and Son. (*See also* Antipas.)

(3) Herod Archelaus, ethnarch of Judea, Samaria, and Idumea (4 BC–AD 6) and son of Herod the Great (Matt. 2:22). (*See also* Archelaus.)

(4) Herod Philip, son of Herod the Great and Cleopatra of Jerusalem; he was tetrarch of Iturea and Traconitis in the years 4 BC–AD 34 (Luke 3:1). He rebuilt Paneas and named it "Caesarea Philippi" after the emperor and himself (Matt. 16:13; Mark 8:27). Apparently, he married his niece Salome III, the daughter of Herodias and his half brother Herod son of Mariamne II.

(5) Herod (Philip), son of Herod the Great and Mariamne II; he was married to Herodias, who left him for his half brother Antipas (Matt. 14:3; Mark 6:17; Luke 3:19). Though sharing a common name, this is a different son of Herod the Great than the Herod Philip of Luke 3:1.

(6) Herod Agrippa I, grandson of Herod the Great, also called "King Herod" in Scripture (Acts 12:1). At the height of his power (r. AD 37–44), he ruled an area coextensive with that of his grandfather. He persecuted the early church, killing James the brother of John. Encouraged by the Jews, he imprisoned Peter, intending to put him on trial, until an angel of God miraculously intervened to free him. He died prematurely in Caesarea when struck down for not giving glory to God (Acts 12:20–25).

(7) Herod Agrippa II (reigned in Chalcis AD 48–52, in Iturea AD 52–c. 93), the son of Herod Agrippa I. Prompted by the governor Festus, he gave audience to the apostle Paul to make his defense. He rejected Paul's attempt to persuade him of the truth of the Christian faith (Acts 25:13–27; 26).

Herodians–*See* Jewish Parties.

Herodias–The unscrupulous wife of Herod Antipas who instigated the beheading of John the Baptist (Matt. 14:1–12; Mark 6:14–29). Herodias deserted her first husband, Herod Philip, son of Herod the Great and Mariamne II, to marry his half brother Herod Antipas (Matt. 14:3; Mark 6:17; Luke 3:19). When John the Baptist publicly denounced the legality of the marriage (cf. Lev. 18:16; 20:21), Antipas imprisoned him and Herodias sought revenge. Opportunity came through her daughter, Salome, whose dancing so pleased Antipas that he foolishly swore an oath promising anything she wanted.

Herodion–A Christian living in Rome to whom Paul sends greetings and calls "my relative" (Rom. 16:11; NIV: "fellow Jew"). This description could denote a blood relation, but since Paul uses the same Greek term (*syngenēs*) to describe at least five other individuals (Rom. 16:7, 21) and elsewhere in the letter to refer to fellow Jews (Rom. 9:3), it more likely indicates a kinsman of the same race. The name implies a connection with Herod's household.

Herod's Palace–Herod the Great (73–4 BC) built a number of palaces throughout his kingdom, including those in Jerusalem, Caesarea, Jericho, the Herodium, and Masada, but two play an important role in the NT. The only explicit NT mention of "Herod's palace" (Acts 23:35) refers to the palace (or praetorium) built by Herod in Caesarea Maritima, which was used during the period of Acts as the headquarters of Roman governors in Judea. When Paul was rescued from a group of his Jewish opponents plotting to kill him (Acts 23:12–22), the governor Felix held Paul in Herod's Palace until his Jewish accusers arrived from Jerusalem to charge him face-to-face (Acts 23:35).

Another of Herod's palaces was the magnificent residence built to provide protection for the Upper City of Jerusalem. This palace consisted of two main buildings, each with banquet halls, baths, and accommodation for hundreds of guests. It was surrounded by groves, canals, ponds, and fountains. This palace became the official residence of the Roman governors who came to Jerusalem during the major Jewish festivals, and it is likely that Jesus' Roman trial before Pilate took place here in the palace's courtyard, or praetorium (Mark 15:16; cf. John 18:28, 33; 19:9). This is more likely than the traditional location at the Antonia Fortress overlooking the temple, since Pilate is unlikely to have been staying in the somewhat spartan barracks of Antonia.

HESHBON–A Moabite city that Sihon the Amorite king captured and made his royal capital (Num. 21:26–30). When Israel requested permission to pass through his territory, Sihon refused and instead attacked the Israelites. However, under the leadership of Moses, Israel defeated Sihon and captured Heshbon (Num. 21:21–31; Deut. 2:24; Josh. 12:2; Judg. 11:19–26).

The city appears to have changed hands many times throughout biblical history. Initially, the city was distributed to the tribe of Reuben, which "rebuilt" the city (Num. 32:37). Subsequently, Heshbon was passed over to the tribe of Gad (Josh. 13:27), which then assigned it to the Levites (Josh. 21:39). Judges 11:26 notes that Israel occupied Heshbon and surrounding settlements for several centuries. However, Judg. 3:14–30; 11:13–28 assert that the kingdoms of Ammon and Moab controlled the region (though not mentioning Heshbon particularly) at different times. By the time of Isaiah (and later in the time of Jeremiah), Moab had recaptured Heshbon (e.g., Isa. 15:4; Jer. 48:2), possibly under King Mesha during the height of Moabite prosperity. Josephus notes that by the time of Alexander Jannaeus, Israel had again conquered Heshbon (*Ant.* 13.397). The region of Heshbon is noted for its vineyards, wells, grasslands, and pools (Num. 21:22; Isa. 16:8–9; Song 7:4).

HEZEKIAH–The fourteenth ruler of the kingdom of Judah (727–698 BC). He was the son of Ahaz, an impious king, but Hezekiah reversed his father's religious policies and worked hard at promoting true worship of Yahweh. Though not perfect, he, along with Josiah, is remembered as one of the two best kings to rule Judah.

He was not sole ruler of Judah until 715 BC, and he was serving as coregent with Ahaz when the northern kingdom fell to the Assyrians in 722 BC (2 Kings 18:9–12). Perhaps the fate of the northern kingdom led Hezekiah to initiate religious reform in Judah.

Although Judah was not incorporated into the Assyrian Empire when the northern kingdom fell, it was always under that great kingdom's shadow and threat, likely paying annual tribute. It appears that Hezekiah participated in an area-wide revolt against Assyria after the death of Sargon II in 705 BC. In response, the new Assyrian king, Sennacherib, threatened Jerusalem in 701 BC. The Assyrian army successfully took many Judean cities, and its envoys appeared at the walls of Jerusalem. The prophet Isaiah assured Hezekiah that the capital would not fall, and it did not (2 Kings 18:17–19:37; 2 Chron. 32:1–23; Isa. 36–37).

According to 2 Kings 20:20, Hezekiah constructed a tunnel that brought water inside the walls of the city. The tunnel still exists today and takes the water from the Gihon spring to the Pool of Siloam. It is a remarkable engineering achievement, and an inscription found on the wall inside the tunnel indicates that it was built during Hezekiah's reign.

After the Assyrian siege, Hezekiah fell sick, and Isaiah announced that he would die (2 Kings 20:1–11; Isa. 38). Hezekiah turned to God in prayer, and God granted him fifteen additional years of life, giving the king the remarkable sign of the sundial whose shadow moved backward.

Even Hezekiah, though, had his bad moments. After showing a Babylonian leader, Marduk-Baladan, the temple treasures, thus revealing an inclination to trust foreign powers rather than God, Hezekiah heard from Isaiah that his descendants would suffer the consequences of his action (2 Kings 20:13–21; Isa. 39).

HIDDEKEL–The third of four rivers mentioned stemming from the river originating from the garden of Eden (Gen. 2:14), flowing east from Eden to Assyria. Whereas the KJV transliterates the Hebrew *khiddeqel*, more-recent versions use the better-known name of this river, "Tigris." The other three rivers are Pishon, Gihon, and Euphrates. Hiddekel/Tigris is also the site of Daniel's vision in the third year of Cyrus (Dan. 10:4).

Hiel–The man from Bethel who rebuilt Jericho (1 Kings 16:34). He sacrificed his two sons, Abiram and Segub (or lost them to natural causes), and buried them under the foundation and city gates of Jericho respectively in fulfillment of the prophetic word pronounced by Joshua (Josh. 6:26).

Hierapolis–*See* Asia Minor, Cities of.

Higgaion–In Ps. 9:16 (9:17 MT) the Hebrew word *higgayon* appears to be a technical musical term and thus is transliterated as "Higgaion." The same Hebrew word elsewhere is translated as "meditation" (Ps. 19:14 [19:15 MT]), "melody" (Ps. 92:3 [92:4 MT]), and "mutter" (Lam. 3:62). The word appears to be derived from the verb *hagah*, which means "to meditate, speak" (e.g., Ps. 1:2). It may refer to a reflection set to meditative music.

High Places–In the OT, "high places" were places of worship, probably so named because hilltops were the preferred sites for such shrines (though alternative explanations are offered). They do not imply the presence of a temple building, but rather might consist simply of outdoor altars and could be associated with other religious objects such as sacred stones and fertility symbols (1 Kings 14:23). In the only description we have of the appearance of high places, they are disparaged as being "gaudy" (Ezek. 16:16).

Before Israel entered the land of Canaan, such shrines were centers of pagan fertility religion, the worship of the Baals. The Israelites were instructed that, on entering the land, they were to destroy all such shrines (Num. 33:52; Deut. 33:29). This they failed to do, and although not every Israelite high place had Canaanite origins, it appears that many did. Perhaps because of their Canaanite background and the continued presence of some Canaanite worshipers in Israel's midst, the high places, while notionally becoming places of Yahweh worship for Israel (2 Kings 17:32; 18:22; 2 Chron. 33:17), were places where this worship was debased by pagan associations and practices, even to the extent of child sacrifice (Jer. 7:31) and prostitution (if this is to be taken literally in Ezek. 16:16; 43:7). The worship of Yahweh at these shrines became indistinguishable from Baal worship (2 Kings 17:11; 23:5), and some were specifically erected to foreign gods (1 Kings 11:7; Jer. 32:35). While perhaps deliberately not called a "high place," the altar that Elijah repaired on Mount Carmel became a focal point for calling for an end to such syncretism (1 Kings 18).

High Priest–*See* Priests.

Hin–*See* Weights and Measures.

Hinnom, Valley of–*See* Hell.

Hippopotamus–*See* Behemoth.

Hirah–The Adullamite friend of Judah whom the latter was visiting when he met his Canaanite wife (Gen. 38:1–2, 12, 20–23).

Hiram, Huram–The king of Tyre, contemporary with David and Solomon (tenth century BC). The Bible states that Hiram was on friendly terms with David (1 Kings 5:1), probably indicating a treaty relationship between their two kingdoms. Hiram provided both materials and laborers to aid in the building of David's Jerusalem palace (2 Sam. 5:11). Similarly, Hiram aided Solomon in the construction of the Jerusalem temple, providing "cedar and juniper logs" (1 Kings 5:8) and craftsmen. In return, Solomon paid Hiram wheat and oil on a yearly basis (5:11). Israelite buildings from this period show signs of Phoenician influence in their style and design. Most scholars believe that Solomon's temple was designed by Phoenician craftsmen, guided by Israelite models and concerns.

After the temple was completed, Solomon gave Hiram twenty Galilean villages in exchange for 120 talents of gold (1 Kings 9:10–14). However, Hiram was displeased by the transaction. Some speculate that Solomon was forced by debt to give these cities to Hiram in order to raise capital, though 2 Chron. 8:2 claims that Hiram gave these cities to Solomon, perhaps understanding Hiram's displeasure as implying their return.

Hiram and Solomon also pursued joint commercial maritime ventures. Hiram supplied veteran sailors for Solomon's newly constructed fleet (1 Kings 9:28), and their two fleets sailed together (1 Kings 10:22; 2 Chron. 8:18). These seafaring expeditions dealt in luxury items such as precious metals, ivory, and exotic animals (1 Kings 10:22).

Hireling–A laborer who contracted himself out for temporary jobs ("hireling" is used in the KJV, whereas more-recent versions use "hired man/worker, laborer"). It could be as short-term as one day. In the OT, there are warnings against oppressing hirelings, since they were among the socially disadvantaged (Deut. 24:14–15; Mal. 3:5). Jesus told a parable about workers hired throughout the day, all of whom received the full day's wage, to teach God's grace-oriented approach to rewarding his servants (Matt. 20:1–16). Elsewhere, the hireling became a metaphor for uncaring "shepherds" motivated by self-interest (John 10:11–15).

Hittites–The name "Hittite" derives from the name of the Hittite homeland: Hatti. The Bible refers to "children (daughters) of Heth" and "Hittite" or "Hittites."

According to the Bible, the Hittites descended from Canaan (Gen. 10:15; 1 Chron. 1:13 [the NIV reads "Hittites" for the proper name "Heth"]) and were destined to be subjugated—for example, by the Israelites (see Gen. 9:25–27). Genesis portrays the patriarchs in regular contact with Hittites, through which we learn of several Hittite individuals. Abraham purchased a cave and surrounding field from "Ephron the Hittite" (Gen. 23). Esau took Hittite wives (27:46); however, discrepancies exist concerning their names and ethnicities (cf. 26:34; 28:9; 36:2–3).

The OT consistently mentions the Hittites among those peoples whom the Israelites would dispossess upon entering the promised land (Gen. 15:18–21; Exod. 3:8). Yahweh vowed to drive them out before the Israelites (Exod. 23:28 [cf. v. 23]), while the Israelites were instructed to eradicate their presence from the land (Deut. 7:1–2; 20:17). The Israelites only partly succeeded, eventually settling among the other peoples (Judg. 3:5–6).

During this time, the Hittites are depicted as occupying the central hill country between the coastal plain to the west and the Dead Sea to the east (Num. 13:29; Josh. 9:1), though Josh. 1:4 refers to the entire region of Canaan and Transjordan as "the Hittite country." This perhaps recalls Hittite influence upon the region, revealing a generic or political (versus ethnic) use of the term.

Further references pertain to the monarchic period. David had several close Hittite associates: Ahimelek, of whom nothing else is known (1 Sam. 26:6), and Uriah, Bathsheba's husband and a member of David's bodyguard (2 Sam. 11:3; 23:39). Under Solomon's reign Hittites were conscripted for forced labor (1 Kings 9:20). Solomon also conducted trade between Egypt and Hittite states to the north (10:29), taking for himself Hittite wives (11:1). The final reference to extant Hittites comes from Joram's reign, in the mid-ninth century BC (2 Kings 7:6).

During the exile and afterward, the Hittites became a byword (Ezek. 16:3, 45), exemplifying practices from which pious Jews sought to distance themselves (Ezra 9:1).

Hivites–A people descended from Ham, one of Noah's sons, through the Canaanites (Gen. 10:17). They were indigenous inhabitants of the promised land, usually referred to along with others (e.g., Amorites, Hittites, Perizzites, Jebusites) who were to be dispossessed by Israel (e.g., Exod. 3:8; 23:23; Deut. 7:1). They lived primarily near the Lebanese mountains (Judg. 3:3) and Mount Hermon (Josh. 11:3). Despite God's command to drive the Hivites out, they continued to inhabit these regions in the time of David (2 Sam. 24:7).

Hobab–*See* Jethro.

Holy–Holiness is an attribute of God and of all that is fit for association with him. God alone is intrinsically holy (Rev. 15:4). God the Father is holy (John 17:11), as is the Son (Acts 3:14), while "Holy" is the characteristic designation of God's Spirit (Ps. 51:11; Matt. 1:18). God's name is holy (Luke 1:49), as are his arm (Ps. 98:1), ways (Ps. 77:13), and words (Ps. 105:42).

With reference to God himself, holiness may indicate something like his uniqueness, and it is associated with attributes such as his glory (Isa. 6:3), righteousness (Isa. 5:16), and jealousy—that is, his proper concern for his reputation (Josh. 24:19).

God's dwelling place is in heaven (Ps. 20:6), and "holy" functions in some contexts as a virtual equivalent for heavenly (11:4). God's throne is holy (47:8), and the angels who surround it are "holy ones" (89:5; cf. Mark 8:38).

A corollary of God's holiness is that he must be treated as holy (Lev. 22:32)—that is, honored (Lev. 10:3), worshiped (Ps. 96:9), and feared (Isa. 8:13).

While "holy" is sometimes said to mean "set apart," this does not appear to be its core meaning, though it is an associated notion (Lev. 20:26; Heb. 7:26). Holiness, as applied to people and things, is a relational concept. They are (explicitly or implicitly) holy "to the Lord" (Exod. 28:36), never "from" something.

The symbolic representation of God's heavenly palace, the tabernacle (Exod. 40:9), and later the temple (1 Chron. 29:3), and everything associated with them, are holy and the means whereby God's people in the OT may symbolically be brought near to God. For God to share his presence with anything or anyone else, these too must be holy (Lev. 11:44–45; Heb. 12:14).

The OT system of worship involved the distinction between unclean and clean, and between common and holy, and the means of effecting a transition to a state of cleanness or holiness (Lev. 10:10). People, places, and items may be made holy by a process of consecration or sanctification, whether simply by God's purifying presence (Exod. 3:5) or by ritual acts (Exod. 19:10; 29:36).

God's faithful people are described as holy (Exod. 19:6; 1 Pet. 2:9). In the OT, this is true of the whole people of God at one level, and of particular individuals at another. Thus, kings (Ps. 16:10), prophets (2 Kings 4:9), and in particular priests (Lev. 21:7) are declared to be holy. While the OT witnesses to some tension between the collective holiness of Israel and the particular holiness of its designated leaders (Num. 16:3), the latter were intended to act as models and facilitators of Israel's holiness.

Holy Ghost–*See* Spirit, Holy.

Holy of Holies–The main structure of the tabernacle and later the temple consisted of two rooms, the holy place and the holy of holies, the latter otherwise known as the "Most Holy Place" (Exod. 26:33–35; 1 Kings 6:19–21). The ark of the covenant was placed in this room, which was entered by the high priest once a year on the Day of Atonement (Lev. 16).

Holy One of Israel–A descriptive title emphasizing God's holy nature and his special relationship to his people, Israel. The title occurs thirty-two times in the OT in 2 Kings, Psalms, Isaiah, and Jeremiah. As a favorite designation in the book of Isaiah, the title occurs twelve times in chapters 1–39 and fourteen times in 40–66.

Holy Place–One of two major sections in Israel's tabernacle, the holy place housed several sacred objects, including the lampstand, the table of consecrated bread, and the altar of incense (Exod. 25:23–39; 30:1–10; Heb. 9:2–3). A special curtain in the holy place separated this chamber from the most holy place, which contained the ark of the covenant, thereby protecting the latter from defilement (Exod. 26:33).

Holy Spirit–*See* God; Spirit, Holy.

Holy Spirit, Sin against the–A sin described by Jesus as unforgivable (Matt. 12:31–32; Mark 3:28–30; Luke 12:10). While in many ways mysterious, it is identified as blasphemy and involves the conscious and deliberate attribution of the work of God's Spirit to the power of the devil.

Holy War–Also known as *kherem* warfare or Yahweh war. The term "holy war," though never used in the Bible, characterizes well the wars that Israel fought at God's command, particularly those within the promised land. God is present with Israel in war, and thus the battlefield becomes holy ground. God gives Israel instructions concerning the waging of war in Deut. 7, 20.

Homer–*See* Weights and Measures.

Hope–At times simply indicating a wish (2 Cor. 11:1), in the Bible the word "hope" most often designates a disposition of soul, the grounds for one's hope, or the outcome for which one hopes. At its core, biblical hope is hope in God, rooted in God's covenant faithfulness (Ps. 62:5–8; Jer. 14:8; 17:13; Rom. 4:18; 5:1–5). Hope trusts God in the present and lives even now on the strength of God's future accomplishments (Gal. 5:5; Heb. 11:1).

In the NT, hope is closely associated with Christ and his saving work. Christians now live by hope in Christ (Eph. 1:12; 1 Pet. 1:3; 3:15); indeed, he is "Christ Jesus our hope" (1 Tim. 1:1), and his future appearing is "the blessed hope" (Titus 2:13). Thus, hope refers to eschatological glory (2 Cor. 3:11–12; Eph. 1:18). It is "the hope of the resurrection" (Acts 23:6; cf. 24:15; 26:6–9), our transformation into Christ's likeness (1 John 3:1–3). That expectation stimulates various hopes for God's plans to be realized in one's own or others' lives (1 Cor. 9:10, 13; Phil. 2:19, 23; 2 Tim. 2:25; 2 John 12). So hope is named repeatedly as an essential Christian attribute (Rom. 12:12; 15:4, 13; 1 Cor. 13:13).

Hophni–One of the two sons of the priest Eli at Shiloh (1 Sam. 1:3). Hophni and Phinehas were corrupt priests: they abused worshipers by demanding more than their priestly share (2:12–17) and had sexual relationships with women serving at the sanctuary (2:22). After they rejected their father's rebuke (2:23–25), their judgment was announced in 1 Sam. 2:27–36. This was fulfilled when both died in battle (4:11).

Hophra–Known as Apries in Greek historical texts, he was an Egyptian pharaoh of the Twenty-Sixth Dynasty (r. 589–570 BC). In 587 BC, during a period of Egyptian-Babylonian competition in Syria-Palestine, Hophra sent his army north and temporarily drove away the Babylonian army that was besieging Jerusalem (Jer. 37:5 [Hophra is the unnamed pharaoh]). He is named once in the Bible (Jer. 44:30), where Jeremiah predicts that Hophra would be vanquished by the Babylonian king Nebuchadnezzar, just like the rebellious Judahite king Zedekiah. Those Judeans who had fled from Nebuchadnezzar to Hophra's Egypt had misplaced their trust. Hophra later was assassinated.

Hor, Mount–The mountain where Aaron died and was buried (Num. 20:22–29; 33:37–39; Deut. 32:50). In Deut. 10:6 it is called "Moserah" (meaning "chastisement"), probably because it was due to Aaron's earlier sin that he died there (cf. Num. 20:24; Deut. 32:51).

Horeb–*See* Sinai, Mount.

Horites–The inhabitants of the Mount Seir region. "Horites" may be the biblical name for the Hurrians. The Hurrians were Semites. They were one of the people groups defeated by Kedorlaomer in the time of Abraham (Gen. 14:6).

Esau and his descendants, the Edomites, conquered the Mount Seir region and forcibly removed the majority of the Horite people in a manner that paralleled the conquest of the Canaanites by the Israelites (Deut. 2:12, 22). However, some early intermarriage apparently took place between Esau and the Horites (Gen. 36:2). Apparently, some of the Horites (Hivites) were living in the area of Canaan (Exod. 3:8, 17; 13:5; 33:2; 34:11; Deut. 20:17; Josh. 3:10; 9:1; 11:3; 12:8; 24:11). Genesis 10:17 lists the Horites (Hivites) as descendants of Canaan. Shechem, who raped Jacob and Leah's daughter Dinah, is said to be a Horite (Hivite; Gen. 34:2).

Hormah–A location first mentioned in the book of Numbers, when the Israelites disobeyed God's word and were defeated and beaten all the way to Hormah by the Canaanites and the Amalekites, as predicted (Num. 14:45; Deut. 1:44). In addition to being a specific location, "Hormah" (Heb. *kharemah*) can also have a generic meaning as "place of destruction [*kharemah*]." In Num. 21:1–3 the Israelites completely destroyed Canaanite cities, and the place or cluster of cities is called "Hormah" (21:3). It was evidently rebuilt and later conquered by Joshua, as the list indicates (Josh. 12:14). Hormah was allotted to Judah (Josh. 15:30) and then reassigned to Simeon (Josh. 19:4; 1 Chron. 4:30) as its tribal inheritance. Later, Judah and Simeon collaborated to defeat and destroy the Canaanite city Zephath, and so they renamed it "Hormah." It is one of the cities to which David sent his share of booty taken from the Amalekites (1 Sam. 30:30). Its location has been variously conjectured as Tell esh-Sheriah, about twelve miles northwest of Beersheba; Tell el-Milh, about seven miles northeast of Beersheba; Tell Masos; Tell Ira.

Horn–The Hebrew term for "horn" refers to a bony protrusion on an animal's head, like those belonging to the ram (Gen. 22:13), ox (Deut. 33:17), and goat (Dan. 8:5). More broadly the term indicates any hornlike projection, as in "ivory tusks" (*qarnot shen*, lit., "horns of tooth" [Ezek. 27:15]).

In the OT, horns are emblematic of vitality and strength. David praises Yahweh as "the horn of my salvation"—that is, a mighty deliverer (2 Sam. 22:3 = Ps. 18:2). The appellation evokes Yahweh's special commitment to uphold the king's horn (see 1 Sam. 2:10; Pss. 89:24; 132:17). The king is similarly identified as the horn of his people (Pss. 89:17–18; 148:14), denoting both his role as protector and his duty to uphold justice. As instruments of defense and dominance among animals, horns especially symbolize martial prowess (Deut. 33:17; 1 Kings 22:11). This sense figures in pronouncements of judgment upon Israel (Lam. 2:3, 17) and hope for Israel's restoration (Mic. 4:13).

In Daniel's visions, "horn" designates rulers (7:24), and kingdoms (8:22), which figure in the schematized portrayal of history.

Among them, the "large horn" (8:8, 21) signifies Alexander the Great, while the four horns (8:22) represent the dissolution of his empire following his death. The "little/small horn" (7:8; 8:9–12) signifies Antiochus IV Epiphanes (see 8:23–25). In Zechariah's vision (1:18–21), "horn" generally indicates nations that oppress Judah.

In the NT, the Greek word *keras* exhibits a semantic range similar to Hebrew *qeren*. Jesus is "a horn of salvation" for all Israel (Luke 1:69). Revelation 9:13 mentions "the four horns of the golden altar" that stands before God; elsewhere, "horn" symbolizes the power of the Lamb or of the red dragon (5:6; 12:3) or designates eschatological rulers (17:12).

Horse–Horses first appear in the Bible in Gen. 47:17 as a part of the livestock traded for grain under Joseph's supervision during a time of famine. Due to the military role of horses and the need to depend on God alone, the king of Israel was forbidden to hold great numbers of horses (Deut. 17:16), and the people were commanded not to obtain horses from the principal supplier of the time, Egypt, which happened despite the prohibition (2 Chron. 1:16). King David first introduced chariots to the armies of Israel when he kept one hundred chariot horses out of a large number he had captured from the kingdom of Zobah (2 Sam. 8:3–4). The use of chariots expanded under Solomon, and he is said to have owned as many as twelve thousand chariot horses (1 Kings 4:26). He also built specific chariot cities in order to solidify Israel's defenses (1 Kings 10:26). This move was deeply unfaithful, however, and was denounced by the prophets as an indulgence in pagan luxury and sinful self-reliance. Isaiah proclaimed, "Woe to those who go down to Egypt for help, who rely on horses, who trust in the multitude of their chariots and in the great strength of their horsemen, but do not . . . seek help from the Lord" (Isa. 31:1). The very real military advantages that came from chariot warfare gave God's people a reason, however false, to trust their own power rather than the provision of God.

Horses are often mentioned as a literary image meant to evoke speed, energy, and strength (Ps. 20:7). Jesus' own entry into Jerusalem was on a donkey rather than a horse, emphasizing the nonmilitary nature of his messiahship (Matt. 21:5). In Rev. 6:1–8 horses of different colors represent four judgments of God upon the earth.

Horse Gate–*See* Gates of Jerusalem and the Temple.

Hosanna–The cry of the crowds at Jesus' triumphal entry into Jerusalem (Matt. 21:9, 15; Mark 11:9–10; John 12:13), meaning literally "Save, now" (Heb. *hoshi'ah na'*). The term comes from Ps. 118:25–26, which reads, "Lord, save us. . . . Blessed is he who comes in the name of the Lord." In using "hosanna," the people are identifying Jesus as the Messiah. The unusual use of the word as an exclamation of praise in the Gospels indicates that "hosanna" may have been used as a word of praise by early Christians, who then carried that new meaning back into the Gospel accounts.

Hosea–*See* Hosea, Book of.

Hosea, Book of–The book of Hosea is one of the twelve Minor Prophets, but among these books Hosea is preeminent. It is the longest and appears first canonically, and it was one of the first of all the prophetic books to be written down. The emotive poetry depicting God's heartbreak over the trauma of his broken relationship with his people is hardly matched anywhere else in Scripture.

The first verse sets the book into the reigns of Jeroboam II of Israel (784–748 BC) and Uzziah (769–733 BC), Jotham (758–743 BC), Ahaz (733–727 BC), and Hezekiah (727–698 BC) of Judah. It is difficult to pinpoint when it was during the reign of Jeroboam II that Hosea began his ministry or how far into the reign of Hezekiah he served. Scholars generally date Hosea's ministry between 760 and 720 BC.

God's initial commission to Hosea to marry the prostitute Gomer serves as the frame on which to hang the content of the book. God's primary message is that the people of Israel have been unfaithful to the covenant that they had initially established at Sinai after he had delivered them from enslavement in Egypt. God had said that he would be their God, and Israel would be his people (Exod. 6:7), so they had made a covenant that the people promised to obey (24:1–8). Just as Hosea's heart has been broken by the unfaithfulness of his wife, God has been devastated by Israel's adulterous behavior. Gomer gives birth to three children: Jezreel ("God Sows"), Lo-Ruhamah ("Not Pitied"), and Lo-Ammi ("Not My People"). The name of each child has significance in the book: "Jezreel" because God is going to judge Jeroboam's house for the blood shed by his great-grandfather Jehu in the valley of Jezreel (see 2 Kings 9:36–37; 10:6–7, 11); "Not Pitied" because God will no longer show mercy to the nation; "Not My People" because he is no longer their God and they are no longer his people. The themes of sowing (Hos. 2:23; 8:7; 10:12), God showing pity (2:1, 4, 23; 14:3), and Israel as the people of God (2:1, 23; 4:6, 8, 12; 6:11; 11:7) reappear throughout the book.

The book cycles through patterns of accusation, punishment, and hope. God accuses his people of being unfaithful to their covenant. This unfaithfulness takes two primary forms: worship of foreign idols and reliance on foreign nations. Despite their commitment to follow God's laws, they have blatantly broken the first two commandments: have no other gods, and make no idols (Exod. 20:3–4). The first ruler of the northern kingdom of Israel, Jeroboam I, had constructed two calves of gold, one in Dan and one in Bethel (1 Kings 12:25–33), similar to the one made by Aaron in the wilderness (Exod. 32:4). Jeroboam I's golden calves have survived beyond the reign of Jeroboam II and contributed to Israelite apostasy during the period of the entire northern monarchy. The book of Hosea specifically condemns calf worship (8:5–6; 10:5), which even took the form of kissing the calves (13:2). Israel's idolatry also involved consulting blocks of wood instead of God (4:12), joining themselves to idols (4:17), constructing idols of silver and gold (8:4), and sacrificing to idols (10:5).

Israel's sins provoke God's anger (5:10; 8:5; 13:11) and prompt him to declare that he will punish his people (1:4; 2:13; 4:9; 5:2, 9; 8:13; 9:7, 9; 10:10). The punishment sent by God specifically targets Israel's king, though it is difficult to be certain which one. Jehu's house is the subject of the first royal condemnation (1:4–5), which may refer to the assassination of Zechariah, Jeroboam II's son (2 Kings 15:8–10). The king is called to listen to the judgment because it pertains to him (Hos. 5:1). Some of Israel's kings have already fallen (7:7), which may refer to the period of monarchical instability after Jeroboam II. Eventually, Israel's king will be completely cut off (3:4; 10:3, 7, 15; 13:10), which happened in 722 BC, when Assyria destroyed the capital Samaria.

In the midst of accusation and punishment, the book also includes words of hope, specifically that Israel will return to its God, and their relationship will be restored. Three times the people are called to return to God: in the beginning (2:14–23), in the middle (6:1–3), and at the end of the book (14:1–3). God views his people not only as his wife but also as his children (11:1–4), and he promises that because of his compassion his anger will cease (11:8–9) and he will lead his children as they return to their homes (11:11). In a surprising twist, immediately after telling Hosea to give the three children names signifying judgment (1:4–9), God declares that Israel will be called the "children of the living God," and the children's names change to "Ammi" ("My People") and "Ruhamah" ("Pity") (1:10–2:1 NET). God also promises that the people of Israel will be as numerous as the sand of the seashore (1:10), recalling his promise to Abraham (Gen. 22:17).

Hoshea–The son of Elah, he was the last king of the northern kingdom, Israel (733–724 BC). He attained the throne through assassinating Pekah (2 Kings 15:30). When Shalmaneser, the king of Assyria, discovered that Hoshea had stopped paying him tribute, he imprisoned Hoshea and laid siege to Samaria. The Assyrians eventually captured the city and sent the Israelites into exile (2 Kings 17:1–6).

Hospitality–The practice of receiving strangers in order to offer provision and protection was an important concept in many of the cultures throughout the time period of both Testaments.

Hospitality first appears in Abraham's care of the strangers who visit him in Gen. 18. The strangers in turn reveal God's imminent fulfillment of his promise to provide a child to Abraham and Sarah. Thus, they return the good favor and kindness that they have received, which is the expected pattern of mutual goodwill that characterizes hospitality.

The unusual hospitality of Rebekah in offering water for Abraham's servant's camels distinguishes her as the wife whom God had appointed for Isaac (Gen. 24:1–49).

Part of the sin of Sodom and Gomorrah is that the men violate hospitality norms by demanding that the visiting angels have sex with them, which is in deep contrast to Lot's attempt to welcome and protect the visitors (Gen. 19:1–9; see also Ezek. 16:49–50).

A conviction of the people of Israel is that God is their host in the promised land (Lev. 25:23). Jesus frequently is the beneficiary of the hospitality of others in the Gospels, and he sends out his disciples relying on it (Luke

9:1–4; 10:1–9). The messianic banquet is a theme of Jesus' teaching on the kingdom of God (Matt. 8:11; 22:1–14; Luke 14:16–24). Hospitality is also commanded to be an aspect of early Christian communities, and it is a spiritual gift (Rom. 12:8, 13; Heb. 13:2; 1 Pet. 4:9).

Host of Heaven–A KJV phrase used to describe the heavenly bodies or heavenly beings. The NIV prefers "starry host(s)," "multitudes of heaven," or "stars in the heavens/sky," but "host of the heavens" does occur in Dan. 8:10. The Hebrew phrase, *tseba' hashamayim*, means literally "army of the heavens." The connection between the celestial elements and an army comes in conjunction with God's role as the commander of the Israelite forces (Josh. 5:13–15; Judg. 5:23). There are times when the Bible portrays the celestial elements as part of God's military retinue, fighting on his behalf. The stars fight from heaven against Sisera (Judg. 5:20), and in the Israelites' battle against the Amorites, the sun and the moon are commanded to stand still (Josh. 10:12–13; cf. Hab. 3:11). Based on these passages, the phrase may have had some military background.

The most frequent use of the phrase "host of heaven" is to describe a condemned object of Israelite worship. It is likely that from their association with God's council, these celestial elements gained an independent status and were worshiped apart from God. At times the "host of heaven" appears to refer to the stars alone; the NIV therefore translates it as "stars in the sky" (Deut. 17:3; Jer. 33:22; cf. Jer. 8:2) or "starry hosts" (2 Kings 23:5). At other times the phrase refers to the totality of the heavenly bodies (Deut. 4:19 [NIV: "heavenly array"]; cf. 2 Kings 21:3, 5). Based on the distribution of the phrase, and its occurrence primarily in documents narrating the Assyrian period (2 Kings 17:16; 21:3, 5; 23:4–5; Jer. 19:13; Zeph. 1:5), there is likely a direct correlation between the worship of the host of heaven and Israel's Assyrian vassalage in the seventh century BC. The extent of Assyrian impact on Israelite religion is debated, but it is likely that astral worship—that is, worship of the starry hosts—flourished in this period due to the influence of the Assyrians, a culture entrenched in worship of the astral powers.

Huldah–A faithful prophetess of God serving during the time of King Josiah. When Josiah discovers the book of Deuteronomy while cleaning out the temple, he sends his advisers to inquire of God about the judgments in the book. They go to Huldah, who is identified as a prophet. In typical prophetic fashion, she delivers the word of the Lord (2 Kings 22:14–20), underscoring judgment on the disobedient and unrepentant but blessing on those, like Josiah, who have a repentant heart.

Humility–In the OT, humility often refers to people of low social status, the disenfranchised, and those who suffer oppression and poverty (e.g., Prov. 22:22–23; Amos 2:7; Zech. 7:10). Scripture sometimes associates those socially marginalized with the ethical dimension of humility, thus making the social status equivalent to a subjective spiritual quality (Pss. 22:26; 37:11–17; 146:7–9; Zeph. 3:11–13). Social humiliation, however, does not necessarily lead to humility as a virtue. In a number of instances in the OT, the two remain distinct. In its subjective quality, humility involves submission to one in authority, usually to God (Exod. 10:3; Deut. 8:2–3, 16; Ps. 119:67, 71, 75). On some occasions humility is related to the act of repentance before God (e.g., Zeph. 2:1–3). When paired with "fear of the Lord," humility implies a person who lives in a posture of pious submission before God (Prov. 15:31–33; 22:4).

Such is the case with Moses, whom the writer of Numbers describes in the following way: "Now Moses was a very humble man, more humble than anyone else on the face of the earth" (Num. 12:3). Moses' humility in this situation is displayed in his intimate relationship with, and by his submissive attitude toward, the sovereign God (12:4–9).

In the NT, Christians take Christ as their model of humility (Matt. 11:29; Phil. 2:6–11). The NT writers also call on Christians to humble themselves before God (James 4:10; 1 Pet. 5:5–6) as well as others, including their enemies (Rom. 12:14–21; Phil. 2:3).

Hur–**(1)** An important leader in the time of the exodus. While Joshua was fighting against the Amalekites in Rephidim, Aaron and Hur helped Moses keep his hands raised for the Israelites' victory (Exod. 17:10–13). While Moses was away at Mount Sinai, he put Aaron and Hur in charge (24:14). **(2)** A Judahite and the grandfather of Bezalel, who worked on the tabernacle with his divinely gifted craftsmanship (Exod. 31:2; 35:30; 38:22; 2 Chron. 1:5). He was a descendant of Caleb, whose wife was Ephrath, and he was the grandfather of

Bethlehem (1 Chron. 2:19–20; 2:50; 4:1, 4). Josephus and Jewish tradition made him the husband of Miriam and identified him with the Hur of Exod. 17:10–13; 24:14. **(3)** One of the five kings of Midian killed along with Balaam as the Israelites applied "the LORD's vengeance" on the Midianites for having seduced them in the "Peor incident" (Num. 31:3, 16; cf. 25:16–18). These kings are recorded as the princes who allied with Sihon, an Amorite king (Josh. 13:21).

HURRIANS–*See* Horites.

H

HUSBAND–*See* Family.

HUSHAI–A friend of David from the Arkite clan, located near the northern border of Benjamin near Ataroth (see Josh. 16:2). Hushai met David to join him as he fled from Jerusalem because of Absalom's rebellion. Having just prayed that the advice of Absalom's highly regarded counselor Ahithophel be thwarted, David persuaded Hushai to stay behind as a spy. He assigned Hushai to pretend loyalty to Absalom but to report to him through the priests Zadok and Abiathar (2 Sam. 15:30–37). Hushai successfully feigned loyalty to Absalom (16:16–18) and gained his trust. Ahithophel advised hot pursuit of David, anticipating that he and the people with him would be weary. But Absalom also consulted Hushai. Painting a picture of David as a trapped, fierce warrior, he persuaded Absalom to take the time to gather an overwhelming force, and then he reported this to the priests, who passed the word to David (17:7–16). Hushai's action saved David's life.

HYMENAEUS–A leader in the church of Ephesus who opposed Paul and his teaching. He was among those who rejected sound doctrine with "seared" consciences (1 Tim. 4:2) and in doing so "suffered shipwreck with regard to the faith" (1:19). Paul responded by excommunicating ("handed over to Satan") Hymenaeus and Alexander so that they "be taught not to blaspheme" (1:20). But Hymenaeus continued to destroy others' faith by teaching falsely that the resurrection had already occurred (2 Tim. 2:17–18). Paul charged Timothy to avoid such godless teaching and to gently instruct his opponents (2 Tim. 2:16, 25).

HYMN–A song of worship and praise to God. The NIV only uses the word once in the OT, in Ps. 40:3, referring to a "hymn of praise" to God. The Hebrew word behind this phrase is *tehillah*, which is common in the OT and is elsewhere translated simply as "praise," especially in the psalms. Psalms were part of Israel's worship, and so such "hymns of praise" to God are more common than the English suggests.

The content of these hymns is not laid out for modern readers, but it involves things such as thanksgiving, gratitude, or generally giving God due recognition for who he is (e.g., Ps. 66:2) and what he has done (e.g., 106:2, 12).

In the NT, the word occurs only a handful of times in the NIV, and there is very little indication what these hymns were about. Here too, generally we can say that a hymn is a particular type of song of praise to God.

In Matt. 26:30; Mark 14:26, Jesus and the disciples sang a hymn at the conclusion of the Lord's Supper. Since this meal was patterned after the Passover, it is likely that one or more of the Hallel psalms (Pss. 111–118) were sung. ("Hallel" means "praise" in Hebrew and is related to *tehillah*.) The Greek word behind this use in the Gospels, *hymneō*, is the origin of the English word "hymn." In Acts 16:25 Paul and Silas sang hymns at midnight while in prison, although we are told nothing about their content.

In 1 Cor. 14:26 Paul is instructing his readers about orderly worship. According to the NIV, one of the elements of worship includes hymns, although the Greek word here is *psalmos* (the word used to refer to the book of Psalms in Luke 20:42; 24:44; Acts 1:20; 13:30), which the KJV renders there as "psalm." There is certainly significant overlap between hymns and psalms, since both involve praising God, but evidently there is some distinction too, as can be seen in Eph. 5:19 and Col. 3:16, where Paul makes a distinction between "psalms, hymns, and songs from the Spirit." Perhaps these terms do not reflect clearly marked categories in Paul's mind. In Eph. 5:19 all three are directed to God "from [the] heart," and in Col. 3:16 they are sung with "gratitude," both of which reflect the use of psalms in the OT.

HYSSOP–The Hebrew word translated "hyssop" occurs ten times in the OT, five of them in Lev. 14. Although there is some question regarding the identity of the plant, it clearly is small, in contrast to the cedar of Lebanon (1 Kings 4:33). When branches of hyssop are bundled together, the leaf structure holds liquids. Hyssop was used to sprinkle the blood of the Passover lamb on the lintels and doorposts of the Israelite houses (Exod. 12:22). Its use in conjunction both with sprinkling blood on persons and houses affected by infectious skin diseases and mildew (Lev. 14) and with burning the red heifer (Num. 19:1–6) suggests that its aromatic properties were also significant in countering the stench of blood and burning flesh. Hyssop was used to sprinkle the purification water from the heifer on objects and individuals that had come in contact with a corpse (Num. 19:18). The impact of these ceremonial purification rites gave hyssop symbolic significance; it represented cleansing from sin (Ps. 51:7) and humility.

The English word "hyssop" comes from the Greek word *hyssōpos,* itself of Semitic origin. At the crucifixion, in response to Jesus' cry "I thirst," a sponge soaked in vinegar was lifted on a branch of hyssop to Jesus (John 19:29). If the plant is of the small herb variety, lifting the sponge on a branch of hyssop seems unlikely. Some suggest that the Greek really is a similar word that means "javelin" (*hyssos*). Others maintain that John, who is the only evangelist to mention the hyssop, is more interested in the symbolic aspects of hyssop and the connection to Passover with the death of Jesus, the Passover Lamb. The combination of purity and humility may be why John included it in the crucifixion scene. The author of Hebrews enhanced the description of the covenant ratification ceremony (Exod. 24:1–8) by including the ritual elements of scarlet wool and hyssop from Num. 19 and Lev. 14 along with water and the blood of sacrificial animals (Heb. 9:19).

I

I Am–The divine name, YHWH, revealed to Moses (Exod. 3:14) is related to *hayah*, the Hebrew verb for "to be." The LXX renders this name with the phrase "I am" (*egō eimi*), which later OT writings employ as a title for God (Isa. 43:25; 51:12; 52:6).

A significant feature in the Fourth Gospel is John's record of seven predicated "I am" statements within Jesus' teaching: "I am the bread of life" (6:35); "I am the light of the world" (8:12); "I am the gate for the sheep" (10:7); "I am the good shepherd" (10:11); "I am the resurrection and the life" (11:25); "I am the way and the truth and the life" (14:6); and "I am the true vine" (15:1). With each metaphor Jesus expresses a contrast between himself and another. For instance, Jesus' claim to be the bread of life differentiates him from the manna that appeared in the wilderness (6:49), while his identification as the good shepherd stands in contrast to the hired hand who abandons the sheep in a time of trouble (10:12–13). In these instances "I am" is likely an intentional choice meant to echo the divine name and reveal Jesus' relationship of unity with God the Father.

The meaning of additional unpredicated but emphatic "I am" declarations in Greek by Jesus is debated (Mark 6:50; 14:62; Luke 24:39; John 6:20; 8:24, 28, 58; 13:19; 18:5). In response to Jesus' declaration of "I am," the high priest accuses him of blasphemy (Mark 14:64), the Jews desire to stone him (John 8:59), and the officials who come to arrest him "[draw] back and [fall] to the ground" (John 18:6). These reactions suggest that at least some who heard Jesus utter these words interpreted them as his claim to equality with God (cf. John 5:18).

Ibzan–A "minor judge" from Bethlehem (Josh. 19:15) who had thirty sons and thirty daughters (Judg. 12:8–10; cf. 10:3–4; 12:13–14). His children married people from outside his clan. He led Israel for seven years and was buried in Bethlehem.

Ichabod–The son of Phinehas and the grandson of Eli the high priest. Phinehas died battling the Philistines, who also captured the ark of the covenant, the news of which caused the death of Eli. Upon hearing of the deaths of her father-in-law and husband and that the ark had been captured, Phinehas's wife went into labor and gave birth to a boy. Saying, "The glory has departed from Israel, for the ark of God has been captured," she named the boy "Ichabod," which means "where is the glory?" or "no glory" (1 Sam. 4:19–22).

Iconium–*See* Asia Minor, Cities of.

Iddo–The author of a chronicle or book of prophecies known to the author of Chronicles (2 Chron. 9:29 [as read in the Masoretic tradition]; 12:15; 13:22). This Iddo is described as a "seer" or a "prophet" and is cited in connection with the late tenth-century kings Solomon, Jeroboam, Rehoboam, and Abijah (Abijam). His literary work is described as "visions," "words," and as a "midrash" (a study or commentary). He may have collaborated with Shemaiah (2 Chron. 12:15).

Idol, Idolatry–An image or likeness of a deity, whether carved from wood, molded from metal, or even formed in one's mind.

In contrast to other ancient religions, the Bible rejects worship of all images as incompatible with worship of God. This includes images of Yahweh, since he is transcendent and cannot be represented by anything in creation. As Moses reminded Israel, they saw no form at Sinai but only heard God's voice (Deut. 4:12).

No form can adequately represent Yahweh, as he is incomparable. The Bible similarly forbids worshiping images of other deities because it elevates them to the status reserved for God alone. Thus, the second commandment prohibits making and worshiping idols in the image of anything found in heaven, on earth, or in the water (Exod. 20:4–5).

By NT times, idol worship was no longer a problem for Jews, but it remained an important issue for the growing church because many believers came from idolatrous backgrounds. Thus, the apostles included idolatry in lists of sins to be judged, warned their readers to flee from it, and addressed eating food sacrificed to idols. Indicating that idolatry went beyond worship of images, they linked it with the love of money (Matt. 6:24) and greed (Col. 3:5). The NT authors believed that their readers could turn from idols to worship the true and living God, praised them for doing so, and looked to the time when all idol worship would cease.

Idumea–A transliteration of *Idoumaia*, the Greek name for Edom (e.g., Gen. 36:16 LXX; Mark 3:8), the land given by God to Esau (Gen. 32:3), whose descendants were called "Edomites." In NT times this was the homeland and critical power base of Herod the Great. After his death, Idumea was ruled by Archelaus and then Agrippa I. After Rome's destruction of Jerusalem in AD 70, Idumea was absorbed into the province of Judea and ceased to exist as such.

Illyricum–A Roman province northwest of Macedonia along the eastern coast of the Adriatic Sea. It was the westernmost of the Roman provinces established across the northern part of the Balkan Peninsula, encompassing present-day Albania and the former Yugoslavia. Paul mentions Illyricum as the outermost boundary of his missionary journeys and proclamation of the gospel at the time of his writing of the Epistle to the Romans (Rom. 15:19). It is unclear whether Paul had traveled northward into the Illyricum province or only up to its southern border with Macedonia. His visit to its borders or interior may be implied in Acts 20:2. Paul's associate Titus traveled to Dalmatia, the region of southern Illyricum (2 Tim. 4:10).

Image, Nebuchadnezzar's–A vision of a multimetaled statue seen by Nebuchadnezzar in a dream, the significance of which is interpreted by Daniel after the failure of the Babylonian wise men to do so (Dan. 2). The statue's head was made of gold, the chest and arms of silver, the belly and thighs of bronze, the legs of iron, and the feet a mixture of iron and baked clay (see 2:31–45). As the vision continues, a rock is cut out of the earth and then crushes the weak feet, causing the entire statue to crumble. Daniel interprets this dream as anticipating the succession of human kingdoms and the rock that destroys them as representing the kingdom of God, but he does not identify any of the kingdoms beyond the first, which he identifies as Nebuchadnezzar's (Babylon).

Image of God–That humankind has been created in the image of God indicates its unique status above the animals because of a special similarity with God. This status authorizes humankind to rule the earth and requires respect toward people. The particulars of what the phrase "image of God" means have been understood in many ways.

The phrase is rather rare. It first appears in Gen. 1:26–27, and the same or similar phrases occur in five more verses (Gen. 5:1, 3; 9:6; 1 Cor. 11:7; James 3:9) that refer back to it. The NT also refers to Christ as the image of God and to believers becoming like the image of Christ.

The passages that refer back to Gen. 1:26–27 emphasize honor and respect for human individuals. Humans are to dominate the earth, not one another. They should not kill one another; otherwise they become subject to the death penalty (Gen. 9:6), and they should not curse others but instead treat them with honor (James 3:9). But the motif has no real prominence other than being in the beginning of the Bible. After Gen. 9:6, the OT does not use the phrase "image of God." The concept of human rule appears (e.g., Ps. 8), but the expression "image of God" is more a subpoint under a larger topic than it is a heading for biblical teaching.

In the NT, Jesus is twice identified by the Greek equivalent to the Hebrew phrase "image of God" (2 Cor. 4:4; Col. 1:15). Especially in the context of Col. 1:15, the emphasis is on Christ's deity and so part of a different topic, despite the similar wording. The two verses about believers that refer to the likeness of God and the image of the Creator (Col. 3:10; Eph. 4:24) deal with moral behavior and the sanctification of the believer (cf. Rom. 8:29;

2 Cor. 3:18). Although they do not directly refer to Gen. 1, they do address the common metaphor that humankind, by sinning, marred its imaging of God. To be conformed to the image of Christ restores how humanity images God in the world.

Immanuel–A transliteration of the Hebrew phrase *'immanu 'el*, which means "God is with us." This name is a reminder of God's presence, and although the name "Immanuel" appears in the Bible only a few times (Isa. 7:14; 8:8; Matt. 1:23; cf. Isa. 8:10), the theme of God's presence is one of the most prevalent in Scripture.

Immortality–The OT cryptically mentions Enoch (Gen. 5:24) and Elijah (2 Kings 2:1–12) ascending into heaven without passing through death or Sheol. Otherwise, mortality is presented as part of the universal human condition, a result of Adam and Eve's disobedience (Gen. 2:17; 5:1–32).

In the creation story, God warns Adam that if he eats from the tree of the knowledge of good and evil, he will die that very day (Gen. 2:17). But despite eating from the tree, Adam lives on physically for almost a millennium (Gen. 5:5), and so this sin-begotten death describes separation from God. Jesus will overcome this separation at the cross (Luke 23:43; cf. Matt. 10:28 par.). For those who trust this work—believe in his name—death is already overcome because they are reconciled with God. Life is no longer bound, as it were, to brain activity, but rather is unbound in the immortal being of God. By reconciling others to God, Jesus is able to promise eternal life (John 3:15, 36; 5:24). Indeed, John writes his Gospel to advance this promise (20:31).

Three NT assertions need to be taken into account in ascertaining biblical perspectives on immortality: (1) God is immortal (Rom. 1:23; 1 Tim. 1:17); (2) God alone is immortal (1 Tim. 6:16); (3) God grants immortality to those who seek him (Rom. 2:7; 1 Cor. 15:53–54; 2 Tim. 1:10). These assertions are important in distinguishing immortality from the idea of the continued existence of some part of the human makeup after the death of the body. The word "immortality" should be reserved to refer to the existence of body and soul together for eternity. Human beings, therefore, do not intrinsically possess immortality; it must be granted by God.

Imperishable, Imperishability–The property or state of not being subject to decay or deterioration, and thus heavenly. "Imperishability" (Gk. *aphtharsia*) and immortality are closely linked; note that the Greek adjective for "imperishable," *aphthartos*, can be translated "immortal" (e.g., Rom. 1:23). Often the Bible contrasts the imperishable with the perishable. Thus, Paul contrasts the perishable earthly body with the imperishable resurrection body (1 Cor. 15:42, 50–55) and an imperishable reward with a perishable reward (1 Cor. 9:25 NRSV, NET). Peter explains that the believer's new birth is "not of perishable seed, but of imperishable, through the living and enduring word of God" (1 Pet. 1:23).

Impurity–*See* Clean, Cleanness.

Impute, Imputation–The word "impute" means "to think of, regard, reckon, or credit something to someone that comes from another." The language comes from the business world, where records are kept indicating credits and debits to a person's account.

In the NT, the clearest passages teaching imputation are found in Paul's writings. Drawing upon Gen. 15:6 and Ps. 32:1–2, he asserts that God imputes righteousness to the believer apart from works (Rom. 4:1–8). Because of Adam's rebellion, sin and guilt were imputed to all humankind, while at the same time Christ's obedience is imputed to all his people (5:12–21). Imputation makes it clear that salvation is entirely the work of God. It is only on the basis of Christ's righteousness that the believer can be justified in God's court of law. Far from being an abstract theological concept, it is the very basis upon which the believer relates to God.

Incarnation–The term "incarnation" refers to something being "enfleshed" (Lat. *in carne*). In the context of Christian teaching, "incarnation" expresses what happened when Jesus, who had been with God for all eternity, stepped onto the historical scene as a human being (John 1:14; Col. 1:19; Heb. 2:14; 1 John 1:1–2). The Greek NT uses *en sarki* ("in flesh") repeatedly as a reference to Jesus' human nature. Hymns such as 1 Tim. 3:16 show the confessional character of Christ's incarnation, giving it strong theological significance (cf. the similar confessional emphasis of Phil. 2:5–11). The defining power of such confessions comes to the fore strongly in 1 John 4:3 (cf. 2 John 7), where John deems those who reject genuine incarnation to be filled with the spirit of the antichrist. Paul understands Jesus' work on the cross in light of the incarnation (Col. 1:22; cf. 1 Pet. 4:1) and considers incarnation the reason Christ could accomplish what the law of Moses could not (Rom. 8:3; Eph. 2:15).

Incense–A compound of aromatic spices closely related to the daily life of Israel. It became synonymous with "frankincense" at a later time. Aromatic spices were used in Israel for cosmetics (Prov. 7:17; Song 5:5) and for medical (Jer. 8:22; 46:11; 51:8) purposes but occupied a special place in Israelite worship when used as incense. Incense was professionally compounded (Exod. 30:34–35) and was offered on the golden altar by the high priest twice a day (Exod. 30:7–8; cf. Luke 1:8–11) and on the Day of Atonement (Lev. 16:12–13; cf. 10:1–2). Prayers offered with the smoke of the incense guaranteed acceptance by God (Deut. 33:10; cf. Gen. 8:21; Exod. 29:18; Ezek. 20:41). In Ps. 141:2, prayers are said to ascend to God like incense, providing a background to the book of Revelation, where incense represents the prayers of the saints (Rev. 5:8; 8:3–4).

Incense Altar–*See* Altar; Tabernacle, Tent of Meeting.

Incest–Incest can be defined as sexual intercourse or sexual contact between close relatives that is considered by society to be illegal, immoral, or socially taboo. The Bible has no term analogous to the English word "incest."

The strongest prohibitions against incest are in Lev. 18; 20; Deut. 27. What Israelite society could not control, God oversaw. In Lev. 18:16–23 the entire unit moves gradually from incestuous unions to other illicit expressions. The consequences of incest are, according to OT legislation in Leviticus, the defilement of the land itself (18:24–30), death (20:11–12), childlessness (20:21), and banishment from the covenant community (20:17; cf. Matt. 18:15–18; 1 Cor. 5:2, 5, 13).

Incorruptible, Incorruption–*See* Imperishable, Imperishability.

India–The northwestern region of the subcontinent of southern Asia. India marked the eastern boundary of Ahasuerus's territory (Esther 1:1; 8:9), but it was connected to the biblical world primarily through trade. The Seleucids employed "Indian drivers" on elephants (1 Macc. 6:37). Nard, the fragrant oil that Mary pours over Jesus' feet, is derived from a root that grows in the mountains of northern India (John 12:3; cf. Song 1:12; 4:13; Mark 14:3).

Ingathering, Feast of–*See* Festivals.

Inheritance–***Family.*** In the ancient world every culture had customs for the passing of wealth and possessions from one generation to the next. In ancient Israel special provisions were made for inheriting land upon the death of the father. The firstborn son received a double portion; the rest was divided equally among the remaining sons. If a man lacked sons, priority went to the following in order: daughters, brothers, father's brothers, next of kin (Num. 27:1–11). The OT provides guidance for additional circumstances (Gen. 38:8–9; Num. 36:6; Lev. 25:23–24; Deut. 21:15–17; 25:5–10; Ruth 2:20; 3:9–13; 4:1–12), with an overriding concern for the stability of the family and the retention of the land within a tribe. Under Roman law during the NT period, an heir had legal standing even while the father was still alive; his status was based on birth or adoption rather than the father's death.

Old Testament. Even more prominent than family inheritance is the assertion that God gave the land of Canaan to Abraham and his descendants as an inheritance (Gen. 12:7; 15:18–21; 17:8; Num. 34:1–29; Deut. 12:10). This inheritance is God's gracious gift, not something that Israel earned by its righteousness (Deut. 9:4–7). Descriptions of the land ("flowing with milk and honey") and its fertility portray this gift as a new Eden, where God will dwell with his people (Exod. 3:8, 17; Lev. 20:24; Num. 16:13–14; Deut. 11:9–12). In some texts the language of inheritance moves beyond the land of Canaan to an international scope. In Ps. 2:8 the anointed king recounts God saying to him, "Ask me, and I will make the nations your inheritance, the ends of the earth your possession." This expansion of inheritance from the land of Canaan to the ends of the earth prepares the way for a similar expansion in the NT (see Rom. 4:13).

God's relationship with Israel is also described in terms of inheritance. On the one hand, Israel is described as God's inheritance (Deut. 32:9; 1 Sam. 10:1; 1 Kings 8:51–53); on the other hand, God is Israel's inheritance (Pss. 16:5; 73:26; Jer. 10:16; 51:19). This mutuality expresses the intimacy of God's relationship with Israel.

New Testament. Inheritance language is taken up in the NT and expanded in a variety of ways. First and foremost, Jesus Christ is the "heir of all things," the Son to whom the Father has given all authority in heaven and on earth (Matt. 28:18–20; Heb. 1:2–5). Through their union with Christ, believers share in Christ's inheritance (Rom. 8:17), having been qualified by the Father to share in that inheritance (Col. 1:12). What believers inherit is described in various ways: the earth (Matt. 5:5), eternal life (Luke 10:25), the kingdom (1 Cor. 6:9–10; James 2:5), salvation (Heb. 1:14), blessing (Heb. 12:17; 1 Pet. 3:9). This inheritance was enacted by the death of Christ and sealed by his blood (Heb. 9:15–28). Believers experience the benefits of this inheritance through the Spirit now (Eph. 1:14, 18), but its fullness is reserved in heaven and awaits the consummation (1 Pet. 1:4–6).

Iniquity–*See* Sin.

Innocents, Slaughter of the–Matthew reports that in an attempt to kill the infant Jesus, Herod the Great ordered the slaughter of the boys in Bethlehem and its vicinity who were two years old or younger, adding that the extent of the slaughter was calculated to correspond with the information Herod learned from the magi regarding the time of Jesus' birth (Matt. 2:16). Jesus escaped only because his parents fled to Egypt for the duration of Herod's life (he died in 4 BC). Matthew regards this event as the fulfillment of Jer. 31:15.

Insects–The Bible is full of teeming creatures and swarming things. These creatures, insects, often play significant roles in the stories and the events described in them. From the first chapter of the Bible to the very last book, these flying, creeping, hopping, and crawling things are prominent.

Terms for Insects

Insects are described in the Bible with both general and specific terms. In the OT, there are three general terms for insects and twenty terms used to refer to specific types of insects. In the NT, two different types of insects are referenced: gnats and locusts.

The two most common general terms for insects are variously translated. Terms and phrases used to describe them include "living creatures" (Gen. 1:20), "creatures that move along the ground" (Gen. 1:24–26; 6:7, 20; 7:8, 14, 23; 8:17, 19; Lev. 5:2; Ezek. 38:20; Hos. 2:18), that which "moves" (Gen. 9:3), "swarming things" (Lev. 11:10), "flying insects" (Lev. 11:20–21, 23; Deut. 14:19), "creatures" (Lev. 11:43), "crawling things" (Lev. 22:5; Ezek. 8:10), "reptiles" (1 Kings 4:33), "teeming creatures" (Ps. 104:25), "small creatures" (Ps. 148:10), and "sea creatures" (Hab. 1:14). The other general term for insects is used with reference to swarms of insects, typically flies (Exod. 8:21–22, 24, 29; Pss. 78:45; 105:31). Specific insects named in Scripture are listed below.

Ants. Ants are used in Proverbs as an example of and encouragement toward wisdom. In 6:6 ants serve as an example for sluggards to reform their slothful ways. Also, in 30:25 ants serve as an example of creatures that, despite their diminutive size, are wise enough to make advance preparations for the long winter.

Bees. Bees are used both literally and figuratively in Scripture. Judges 14:8 refers to honeybees, the product of which becomes the object of Samson's riddle. The other three uses of bees in the OT are figurative of swarms of enemies against God's people (Deut. 1:44; Ps. 118:12; Isa. 7:18).

Fleas. Fleas are referenced in the OT only by David to indicate his insignificance in comparison with King Saul (1 Sam. 24:14; 26:20). The irony of the comparison becomes clear with David's later ascendancy.

Flies. The plague of flies follows that of gnats on Egypt (Exod. 8:20–31). Although the gnats are never said to have left Egypt, the flies are removed upon Moses' prayer. In Eccles. 10:1 the stench of dead flies is compared to the impact that folly can have on the wise. In Isa. 7:18 flies represent Egypt being summoned by God as his avenging agents on Judah's sin. In addition, one of the gods in Ekron was named "Baal-Zebub," which means "lord of the flies" (2 Kings 1:2–3, 6, 16). The reference to Satan in the NT using a similar name is likely an adaptation of the OT god of Ekron (Matt. 10:25; 12:24, 27; Mark 3:22; Luke 11:15, 18–19).

Gnats. Gnats are distinguished from flies in the OT, though the distinction is not always apparent. Gnats are employed by God in the third plague on Egypt (Exod. 8:16–19), while flies form the means of punishment in the fourth plague. The two are listed together in Ps. 105:31 and appear parallel, though the former may be a reference to a swarm. Gnats were also used by Jesus to illustrate the hypocrisy of the Pharisees and the scribes (Matt. 23:24).

Hornets. The Bible uses hornets in Scripture as an agent of God's destruction. The term occurs three times in the OT. In each occurrence these stinging insects refer to God's expulsion of the Canaanites from the land that God promised to his people. The first two times, Exod. 23:28 and Deut. 7:20, hornets are used in reference to a promise of what God will do; the third time, Josh. 24:12, they illustrate what God did.

Locusts. Of particular interest is the use of locusts in the Bible. The term or a similar nomenclature occurs close to fifty times in the NIV. Locusts demonstrate a number of characteristics in Scripture. First, they are under God's control (Exod. 10:13–19). As such, they have no king (Prov. 30:27). They serve God's purposes. Second, locusts often occur in very large numbers or swarms (Judg. 6:5; Jer. 46:23; Nah. 3:15). At times, their numbers can be so large as to cause darkness in the land (Exod. 10:15). Third, in large numbers these insects have been known to ravage homes, devour the land, devastate fields, and debark trees (Exod. 10:12–15; Deut. 28:38; 1 Kings 8:37; 2 Chron. 7:13; Pss. 78:46; 105:34; Isa. 33:4; Joel 1:4–7). Due to their fierceness, they were compared to horses (Rev. 9:7). Fourth, locusts hide at night (Nah. 3:17). Finally, certain types of locusts were used as food.

Moths. Moths are referred to seven times in the OT and four times in the NT. Job uses moths to illustrate the fragility of the unrighteous before God (4:19) and the impermanence of their labors (27:18). The other references to moths in Scripture present them as the consumers of the wealth (garments) and pride of humankind as a means of God's judgment (Job 13:28; Ps. 39:11; Isa. 50:9; 51:8; Hos. 5:12; Matt. 6:19–20; Luke 12:33; James 5:2).

Functions of Insects in Scripture

As food. Insects also are mentioned in Scripture as food. Certain types of locusts are listed as clean and eligible for consumption. The NT describes the diet of John the Baptist, which consisted of locusts and wild honey—a diet entirely dependent on insects (Matt. 3:4; Mark 1:6). The OT also notes Samson enjoying the labor of bees as food (Judg. 14:8–9).

Used figuratively. Most often, insects are used figuratively in Scripture. They are used in the proverbs of Scripture to illustrate wisdom. The sages wrote about ants (Prov. 6:6; 30:25), locusts (Prov. 30:27), and even dead flies (Eccles. 10:1) both to extol wisdom and to encourage its development in humankind.

Another figurative use of insects is in the riddle about bees and honey posed by Samson to the Philistines (Judg. 14:12–18). As noted above, Samson ate honey (Judg. 14:8–9; cf. 1 Sam. 14:25–29, 43). Also, Scripture describes the promised land as a place of "milk and honey."

Insects also are used to symbolize pursuing enemies (Deut. 1:44; Ps. 118:12; Isa. 7:18), innumerable forces (Judg. 6:5; 7:12; Ps. 105:34; Jer. 46:23; Joel 2:25), insignificance (Num. 13:33; 1 Sam. 24:14; 26:20; Job 4:19; 27:18; Ps. 109:23; Eccles. 12:5; Isa. 40:22), vulnerability (Job 4:19), God's incomparable nature (Job 39:20), the brevity of life (Ps. 109:23), wisdom and organization (Prov. 30:27), and an invading army (Isa. 7:18; Jer. 51:14, 27), and they are employed in a taunt against Israel's enemies (Nah. 3:15–17), a lesson on hypocrisy (Matt. 23:24), and an image of eschatological judgment (Rev. 9:4–11).

INSPIRATION OF SCRIPTURE–In biblical and systematic theology, "inspiration" is one of several descriptions of God's involvement in the production of Scripture. It is not an exhaustive description of the many ways in which divine revelation is mediated.

Taken as a description of "all Scripture" (as in 2 Tim. 3:16), inspiration must necessarily encompass such diverse modes of revelation as words audibly spoken or dictated by God and written down by humans (i.e., dictation: "the LORD said to Moses," "thus says the LORD"), words spoken by angels, texts in which a divine or angelic voice is entirely obscured by the voice and identity of the human author (e.g., the letters of Paul), and, in the vast majority of cases, texts that are essentially anonymous, invoking no human author or divine author in particular. Moreover, any catalog of divinely inspired texts must include not only direct quotations of God's speech but also occasional letters (the NT Epistles), prayers directed to God by humans (the Psalter), divine oracles given through prophets, the results of historical research (e.g., Luke 1:1–4; 1 Kings 14:19), and anthological texts that were collected and edited over a long period of time, often by unnamed individuals or groups of individuals.

Thus, the inspiration of Scripture must be regarded as a concept that is applied in the broadest possible way to the materials of Scripture. While the doctrine of inspiration constitutes a strong statement concerning the authority and divine authorship of Scripture, it must remain highly flexible with regard to the particular modes and literary products of divine revelation in Scripture.

Insurrection–A revolt against governmental authority. David leads an insurrection against Saul (1 Sam. 19–31; see 2 Sam. 18). Barabbas, the prisoner whom Pilate releases in response to the crowd seeking Jesus' crucifixion, probably is a terrorist captured during another insurrection (Mark 15:7; Luke 23:19, 25). In Acts, the Pharisee Gamaliel mentions an insurrection led by Judas the Galilean against Rome (Acts 5:37), and a Roman army officer asks Paul, "Aren't you the Egyptian who started a revolt and led four thousand terrorists out into the desert some time ago?" (21:38).

Intercession–The act of advocating before the powerful on someone's behalf (Gen. 23:8–9), especially turning to God in prayer to seek God's favor for others in crisis (2 Sam. 12:16). While it is a prerogative of prophets (Gen. 20:7; Num. 12; Amos 7:1–6), priests (Ezra 6:9–10), and kings (1 Chron. 21:17; 2 Chron. 30:18; Jer. 26:19), intercession is a ministry that belongs to all the people of God (Acts 12:5; Eph. 6:18; 1 Tim. 2:1; James 5:16).

Interest–The practice of loaning money with interest was common in the ancient Near East, but Israelites under the Mosaic covenant were prohibited from charging interest to their kinfolk. Lending with interest was permissible in commercial transactions with foreigners but was forbidden in all cases among Israelites (Deut. 23:19–20). This ban on interest protected the poor from being exploited by creditors. Leviticus 25:36–37 stresses the moral responsibility of Israelites to fear God and help their poor kinfolk rather than take advantage of them by exacting interest or profit (cf. Exod. 22:25; Neh. 5:7).

Intertestamental Period–The name given to the historical period between the Old and New Testaments (fifth century BC–first century AD). It is also known as the Second Temple period. The first Jewish temple, completed by Solomon around 960 BC, was destroyed by the Babylonians in 587/586 BC. The second temple, completed by Zerubbabel in 516 BC (and expanded later by Herod the Great), was eventually destroyed by the Romans in AD 70. The intertestamental period is roughly, then, the period from the return of the Babylonian exile to the dawn of the Christian era.

Ira–A Jairite and a priest during David's time (2 Sam. 20:26). Some consider this position to be civil rather than religious, a chief adviser or minister. Others view the role as one of personal priest to David, a kind of palace chaplain.

Irijah–The son of Shelemiah, he served as the captain of the guard under Zedekiah king of Judah (Jer. 37:13). After Jeremiah prophesied the Babylonian destruction of Jerusalem, he started to leave the city in order to receive his share of the property in Benjamin. However, Irijah saw Jeremiah at the Benjamin Gate and accused him of deserting the people and joining the Babylonians. Based on this faulty assumption, Irijah arrested Jeremiah and brought him before the officials, who subsequently beat the prophet and placed him in prison (37:13–15).

Iron–*See* Minerals and Metals.

Isaac–Along with Abraham and Jacob, Isaac is a central character in the narratives of Gen. 12–35. Isaac is the offspring of Abraham and Sarah, the fulfillment of a promise from God of an heir for Abraham (15:4). The promise of offspring is one component in a set (protection and land being some of the others), the provisions of a covenant between God and the patriarchs (12:1–3; 17:1–8; 26:2–5). The name "Isaac" is associated with the verb for "laugh" (21:3–7), referring to Sarah's reaction upon hearing the promise of a child coming well beyond her childbearing years (18:9–15). Sarah's incredulity, and Abraham's sympathy to it, may be witnessed by their attempt to enact fulfillment to the promise through the insemination of Hagar, Sarah's slave (16:1–4, 16).

In the narratives of Gen. 12–35 Isaac is the least prominent of the patriarchs. The main event of his life is encapsulated in the incident known as the Akedah, the "binding" (22:1–19). Abraham demonstrates his loyalty to God by complying with a command to offer Isaac as a sacrifice on Mount Moriah. After an initial inquiry about the absence of a sacrificial beast, Isaac (apparently) passively follows Abraham's directions in compliance with God's will. A divine emissary, however, halts Abraham's actions just prior to the slaying of Isaac.

The procurement of Isaac's wife, Rebekah, by Abraham's servant is found in Gen. 24:1–67. Like Abraham, Isaac describes his wife as a sister in order to deflect danger to his person (26:6–11; cf. 12:10–16; 20:1–18). Rebekah bears two sons to Isaac, Esau and Jacob (25:21–26). Through the instigation and cooperation of Rebekah, Jacob tricks Isaac into conferring a blessing upon him, one originally intended for Esau (27:1–30).

Isaiah–*See* Isaiah, Book of.

Isaiah, Book of–The first of the Major Prophets in the canon, the book of Isaiah is one of the longest books in the Bible. This, coupled with the NT's frequent use of Isaiah, has contributed to the book's great importance in Christian tradition. Isaiah contains some of the most memorable passages in Scripture, with its majestic poetry and evocative sermons making it a literary masterpiece.

The authorship of Isaiah has been one of the most debated issues in biblical interpretation. Ancient tradition credited the eighth-century BC prophet Isaiah with the entire sixty-six chapters. However, an early Jewish tradition in the Talmud claims that "the men of Hezekiah" compiled Isaiah, showing their awareness that the book did not come entirely from Isaiah. Most scholars today, including many evangelical scholars, conclude that the book of Isaiah is the end result of a history of composition that began in the eighth century BC (so-called First Isaiah [1–39]), continued in the sixth century BC during the exile (Second Isaiah, chaps. 40–55), and then was completed after the exile (Third Isaiah, chaps. 56–66).

Isaiah has a literary structure similar to that of Ezekiel, Zephaniah, Joel, and the Greek translation of Jeremiah. The first section is concerned with judgment on Israel (chaps. 1–12), the second with judgment on foreign nations (chaps. 13–23), and the third records prophecies of hope and salvation (chaps. 24–27). This structure purposefully places hopeful oracles of comfort after the judgment oracles. Some view the entire book of Isaiah as following this pattern (chaps. 1–12, judgment on Israel; chaps. 13–35, judgment on other nations; chaps. 40–66, oracles of comfort). However, both of these schemes are somewhat forced, since each section is slightly mixed (there are oracles of salvation in chaps. 1–12, prophecies against Judah in chaps. 13–23, and judgment oracles in chaps. 56–66). However, in broad outline it is helpful to recognize this structure.

Isaiah 1–39

Structure and themes. The structure of chapters 1–39 is quite complex. However, the prophecies and historical narratives concerned with Isaiah's day are roughly in chronological order (e.g., prophecies and events occurring during the reign of King Ahaz [6:1–8:22] precede those during Hezekiah's reign [36:1–39:8]). The structure of these chapters alternates between threat and promise (e.g., chap. 1 = threat; 2:1–4 = promise of hope; 2:5–4:1 = threat; 4:2–6 = promise of hope). Analogously, the main themes of these chapters alternate between threat and promise.

Holiness. A major theme of Isaiah is God's holiness, as evidenced in its favorite title for the Lord, "Holy One of Israel." While the original idea underlying holiness was physical separation and did not have an ethical dimension (e.g., temple prostitutes in the ancient Near East were called "holy women"), a different concept of holiness emerges in chapter 6, the account of Isaiah's call. Since 6:1–9:7 is the only part in the book with autobiographical narration, these chapters probably come from an original memoir of Isaiah himself. The memoir is surrounded by judgment oracles with a repeated element, "Yet for all this, his anger is not turned away, his hand is still upraised" (5:25; 9:12, 17, 21; 10:4), suggesting that the memoir as a whole was inserted between these oracles to explain God's anger recorded in 1–12. God's mandate to Israel was to "be holy, because I am holy" (Lev. 11:44–45), but Israel failed to follow this command. In the presence of the holy God, Isaiah realized his own sinfulness and the sinfulness of his people (6:5), connecting the concepts of holiness and righteousness.

The remnant. Already in the first chapter we see the emergence of two groups within Israel: the wicked, who will be punished, and a remnant, who will be redeemed (1:27–31). This focus on the remnant was one way in which Isaiah saw hope for Israel despite the coming judgment that he predicted. The remnant theme highlights the apparent tension between God as holy and God as redeemer: God's holiness is upheld through the judgment on Israel, but God's character as savior is witnessed through the remnant that is redeemed.

A coming messianic king. The section 6:1–9:7 dates from the time of the Syro-Ephraimite war, and it appears that Isaiah wrote it down (8:16) when Ahaz refused his counsel. The memoir emphasizes the rejection of the Davidic king Ahaz and predicts the birth of a royal son who would replace Ahaz and bring freedom from oppression (9:1–7). This dissatisfaction with the reigning Davidic king was the seedbed for messianic expectations and is the background for the messianic trilogy of 7:14–16; 9:2–7; 11:1–9. While some of these passages may have originally referred to Hezekiah, he falls short of these messianic expectations, leaving the community of faith awaiting another anointed one (messiah). Ominously, chapter 39 describes Hezekiah's entertaining guests from Babylon, perhaps implying an alliance between the two nations. Hezekiah's actions prompt Isaiah to predict the Babylonian exile (39:6–7), providing a fitting segue to chapters 40–66.

Isaiah 40–55

A message to the exiles. Second Isaiah was written near the end of the exilic period for those who were deported by Nebuchadnezzar to Babylon. Although the exiles in Babylon were settled in communities (Ezek. 3:15) and allowed to build houses and farm the land (Jer. 29:5–7), they had no temple for worship, and many of the exiles probably saw the destruction of Jerusalem and their temple as the end of God's action on their behalf. The gods of Babylon appeared to have won the victory. The exiles' faith was flagging, and even those who did not abandon worship of Israel's God simply clung to the past and expected nothing new from him.

Contrary to these expectations, Second Isaiah proclaims that God is doing something new for his people and bringing an end to the exile (40:1; 55:12). The role of Cyrus in this deliverance is highlighted, with explicit and implicit reference made to the Persian king (41:2–3, 25; 44:28; 45:1–4, 13–14). However, amid the oracles of comfort there is also a challenge to Israel, which is somehow resistant to the message. To break down this resistance, the prophecy has a sustained rhetoric against idol worship, with some quite hilarious sections ridiculing idol makers (44:9–20). Israel needed to realize that only Yahweh is God and to trust that he will redeem Israel for his purposes. Chapters 1–39 allude to the redemption of Israel (1:27; 35:9), and chapters 40–66 reveal more of how this redemption will take place: the work of "the servant."

The servant. Several poems featuring an anonymous "servant" (42:1–9; 49:1–12; 50:4–11; 52:13–53:12) are often referred to as the Servant Songs. As far back as the Ethiopian eunuch (Acts 8:34), interpreters have struggled with how to identify "the servant." At times, Israel is explicitly identified as the servant (Isa. 41:8–9; 42:19 [2×]; 43:10), yet the servant clearly also has individual features, suggesting that a person was to fill the role. Some have suggested Cyrus because 42:1 says that the servant "will bring justice to the nations," and Cyrus is described as conquering nations (41:2, 25; 45:1). However, despite all the talk of Cyrus, the text never explicitly applies the term "servant" to him, which can hardly be by chance. Alternatively, the servant could be the prophet who speaks in these chapters (as the Ethiopian eunuch speculated), since he was destined for his mission before his birth (49:1) and equipped for a mission involving prophetic speech (49:2) and had received divinely revealed knowledge (50:4).

Yet the Servant Songs are also messianic and look forward to a future anointed one who will fulfill the role of the servant fully. In the NT, Jesus is presented as the new Israel (cf. Matt. 2:15 with Hos. 11:1) who truly fulfills the role of the servant (John 12:38, quoting Isa. 53:1; Matt. 8:17, quoting Isa. 53:4). However, Paul appears to hold to a collective interpretation of the songs, as he sees himself as the servant in some instances (Acts 13:47; Rom. 15:21; Gal. 1:15). Both the individual and the collective interpretations are legitimated in the NT, as both Jesus (individual) and the church (collective), which is Christ's body, fulfill the role of the servant.

Isaiah 56–66

In 539 BC Cyrus allowed the exiles to return home to rebuild Jerusalem and its temple (Ezra 1:1–4). Despite many obstacles, the temple was finished in 515 BC. Even with this success, living in the land was challenging (see Malachi), with factions among the people, economic troubles, hypocritical worship (Isa. 58:1–14), and problems with corrupt leaders (56:9–57:13). It was for this postexilic community that Third Isaiah was written (probably before the reforms of Ezra and Nehemiah in 445 BC brought lasting change to the desperate situation).

Unlike in chapters 40–55, where Israel needs to be roused from its despair by the imminent actions of God, in chapters 56–66 the people are pleading with God to help them (59:11; 62:7). In chapter 59 the prophet declares that God's delay in helping his people is due not to his inability but rather to the sins of the people, which are described, confessed, and lamented.

In many ways, Third Isaiah unites the themes of First Isaiah and Second Isaiah. Second Isaiah emphasizes the inbreaking of a new age that contrasts with the old. The former things are remembered, but the new thing that God was doing—the return from exile—is stressed. However, in Third Isaiah the deliverance from Babylon is seen as merely a foretaste of God's promise, which is now identified as a new heaven and earth (chaps. 65–66). Third Isaiah looks forward to the new things that are still ahead.

First Isaiah predicts a Davidic messiah who would rule in righteousness (9:1–7; 11:1–9) and a faithful remnant that would respond in trust (10:20; 28:16). Second Isaiah does not continue with these themes, instead turning attention to the "servant" whose suffering and death would atone for Israel (53:4–5). However, Third Isaiah links First Isaiah's faithful remnant with obedient "servants" who take on the mission of the Suffering Servant in Second Isaiah. This interpretation sets the direction for the NT's identification of the royal messiah of chapters 1–39 as the servant of chapters 40–55 (Luke 24:26; Acts 8:32). Third Isaiah thus unites and reinterprets the book as a whole.

It is fitting that Jesus read the opening verses of Isa. 61 in the synagogue at the beginning of his ministry. Like Third Isaiah, he united prophecies of both the messianic Davidic ruler of First Isaiah and the Suffering Servant of Second Isaiah, taking on both roles himself. Third Isaiah ends with a glorious future pictured for the Jewish community as they function as priests in the world (61:6). Similarly, Christ's body, the church, now functions in these same roles in the world (cf. Acts 13:47; Rev. 5:10).

Iscariot–An epithet or appellation for the disciple named "Judas" who betrayed Jesus (Matt. 10:4; Mark 3:19; Luke 6:16). A word of uncertain derivation, it may signify "man of Kerioth," a city in southern Judea (so the alternate textual readings at John 6:71; 12:4; 13:2, 26; 14:22: "from Kerioth"), the plural of "city," or an Aramaic adaptation of the Latin *sicarius*, "assassin" or "terrorist." The latter would place him with the Sicarii, a group of terrorists who murdered Roman sympathizers with curved swords (Acts 21:37–38; Josephus, *J.W.* 2.254; *Ant.* 20.186).

Ish-Bosheth–A son of Saul who became king at Mahanaim following his father's death, although Judah was loyal to David (2 Sam. 2:8–11). His original name was "Esh-Baal" (1 Chron. 8:33; 9:39), probably changed to avoid having "Baal" appear in his name (cf. Hos. 2:16–17 NRSV); "Ish-Bosheth" means "man of shame." Ish-Bosheth is perhaps to be identified with Saul's second son, Ishvi (1 Sam. 14:49), and he was absent from Mount Gilboa when Saul died (31:2). His power depended upon Saul's general Abner, who had placed him on the throne. He weakened his position when he accused Abner of having a sexual relationship with Saul's concubine Rizpah, leading Abner to defect to David (2 Sam. 3:7–11). Ish-Bosheth was murdered by two of his captains, Rechab and Baanah (2 Sam. 4:5–7), but the chronology of 2 Sam. 2:10–11 suggests that the kingdoms did not immediately unite under David.

Ishmael–**(1)** The son of Abraham and Hagar (Gen. 16:11–16; 17:18–26; 21:8–21; 25:12–17; 28:9; 36:3; 1 Chron. 1:28–31), and the progenitor of the Ishmaelites. **(2)** Son of Nethaniah and chief officer of the royal house who assassinated Gedaliah, the Babylonian-appointed governor of Judah, and then fled to Egypt (2 Kings 25:23–26).

Ishmaelites–The ethnic group said to be the descendants of Ishmael's sons from Gen. 25:12–16. They are mentioned a few times in the OT, including an appearance as the traders who take Joseph down to Egypt (Gen. 37:25–36; see also Gen. 39:1; Judg. 8:24; Ps. 83:6). In Gen. 37, these traders are also called Midianites, often understood as a subgroup of Ishmaelites. The Ishmaelites maintained a Bedouin lifestyle and were a considerable power in the northern Arabian Desert, with their rise to prominence beginning in the eighth century BC and finally fading in the third century. Both Jewish and Islamic traditions consider the Ishmaelites (and Ishmael) to be the origins of the Arab people.

Israelites–The designation "Israelites" signifies the nation of Israel, which can be traced back to the children of Jacob (Gen.

46:8; cf. Exod. 1:9; Num. 1:45). To distinguish themselves from foreigners, Israelites called themselves *'ibrim*, "Hebrews" (Gen. 43:32; Exod. 10:3). During the period of the divided kingdom, the name "Israelites" was used to refer to the Ephraimites (2 Kings 17:6; 18:11); during the Second Temple period, it took on a religious orientation (Sir. 46:10; 47:2; Jdt. 4:11; 2 Macc. 1:25–26). In the NT, true Israelites are not necessarily those descended from Israel or Abraham but rather those who trust in Jesus Christ, who is the fulfillment of God's promise to Abraham (Rom. 9:4–8; Gal. 4:21–31; cf. Rev. 21:12).

Issachar–**(1)** The ninth son of Jacob, his fifth by Leah (Gen. 30:17–18). Issachar, whose name sounds like the Hebrew phrase "hired man," was so named because Leah "hired" her husband to impregnate her by giving to Rachel some mandrakes that Reuben (Leah's son) had gathered. The patriarch Issachar does not figure prominently in the patriarchal stories of Genesis. The blessing of Issachar in Gen. 49:14–15 reflects the history and folklore of the tribe that bore his name rather than any biblical story. **(2)** The seventh of Obed-Edom's eight sons, temple gatekeepers (1 Chron. 26:5).

Issachar, Tribe of–One of the twelve tribes of Israel, descended from the ninth son of Jacob, by Leah. The censuses in Num. 1:29; 26:23 indicate Issachar was the third or fourth largest tribe. The territory of Issachar lay southwest of the Sea of Galilee, including the Jezreel Valley (Josh. 19:17–23). In the period of the judges, soldiers of Issachar came to the aid of Deborah and Barak (Judg. 5:15), and the judge Abimelek was an Issacharite (Judg. 10:1). Baasha was also an Issacharite (1 Kings 15:27).

Italian Cohort–A Roman military unit of six hundred soldiers, one-tenth of a legion. The Gentile centurion Cornelius was an officer of the Italian Cohort in Caesarea Maritima (Acts 10:1), the capital of Palestine under Roman rule. Cornelius commanded a smaller military unit called a "century," an eighty-man subset of the Italian Cohort. "Italy" (Gk. *Italia*) was then, as now, the name of the country of which Rome is the capital.

Italy–The peninsular region roughly corresponding to the modern southern European nation of the same name. Acts 18:2 recounts Paul's meeting of Aquila and Priscilla, who were forced to move from Italy to Corinth because of the emperor Claudius's edict expelling all Jews from Rome. Italy was Paul's destination as he sailed as a prisoner to the imperial courts of Rome after appealing to Caesar in his trial before Porcius Festus (Acts 25:11; 27:1, 6). On this journey, Paul landed in Puteoli and traveled by land through Italy, heading to Rome (Acts 28:12–16). Cornelius the centurion was an officer of the Italian Cohort of the Roman army (Acts 10:1). Hebrews 13:24 includes a greeting from Italian Christians.

Ithamar–The fourth son of Aaron and Elisheba (Exod. 6:23), he, along with his three brothers, was ordained to serve as a priest (Num. 3:2–4; 1 Chron. 24:1–2). Due to the death of Nadab and Abihu, which resulted from their offering an unauthorized sacrifice (Lev. 10:1–2; Num. 26:60–61), Eleazar and Ithamar were the only sons of Aaron left to serve as priests. According to Exod. 38:21, Ithamar directed the recording of the materials used for the tabernacle. He was also specifically placed over the work of the Gershonite and Merarite clans, both of which were appointed to serve in and carry the tent of meeting (Num. 4:28, 33; 7:8).

Ithiel–Along with Ucal, he is mentioned as a recipient of the words of Agur (Prov. 30:1). Both his and his counterpart's names may have symbolic meaning in the proverb. The Hebrew is obscure, and the names are absent in the LXX and have been variously translated (e.g., NRSV: "I am weary, O God, I am weary, O God. How can I prevail?"). Some scholars translate them not as names but as part of a confession of weakness by Agur.

Ittai–A Gittite soldier and commander of six hundred men who joined with King David and his men as they were fleeing Jerusalem, which had been overtaken by Absalom. Despite his recent arrival and against David's noble objections, Ittai remained faithful to David, earning him David's confidence (2 Sam. 15:19–22). As David prepared for the battle that would claim Absalom's life, he named Ittai as commander of a third of his forces, making him equal to Joab and Abishai (2 Sam. 23:29 [NIV: "Ithai"]). He is not subsequently mentioned.

Iturea–A predominantly Gentile territory north of Galilee at the base of Mount Hermon (present-day Syria). It is mentioned by name only once, as one of two territories ruled by Herod Philip, half brother of Herod Antipas (Luke 3:1).

Ivory–Ivory artifacts from the Chalcolithic, Late Bronze, and Iron Ages, as well as the Greco-Roman and Byzantine periods, have been found in the Levant. This material was African and Asian elephant tusk, and hippopotamus tusk or teeth from Egypt. Herds of elephants are thought to have roamed Syria into the Iron Age. Ivory was also brought from other locales (2 Chron. 9:17, 21). Ivory objects were luxury items and symbols of wealth (1 Kings 22:39; Amos 3:15; 6:4) and were considered to be of great beauty (cf. Song 5:14; 7:4). Bone was also a medium for some fine objects, but more often for utilitarian items such as awls, pins, spindle whorls, and handles.

J

Jabal–The son of Lamech and Adah, and the brother of Jubal (also born to Adah) and Tubal-Cain (born to Lamech and Zillah). Jabal is identified as "the father of those who live in tents and raise livestock" (Gen. 4:20).

Jabbok–A key tributary of the Jordan River, flowing about thirty-seven miles. The Jabbok is the modern Wadi Zarqa in the Transjordan. Famously, Jacob wrestled with "a man" at the Jabbok (Gen. 32:22–27), memorialized by the narrator's wordplays: "Jabbok" (*yabboq*), "Jacob" (*ya'aqob*), and "he wrestled" (*ye'abeq*).

Jabesh Gilead–The exact location of the town Jabesh Gilead is unknown, but biblical descriptions place it in the northwest Gilead region. It may have been located near the Wadi Yabis. Both Tell el-Maqlub and Tell Abu Kharaz have been suggested as possible sites. Jabesh Gilead played prominent, if tragic, roles in three biblical events. Judges 19–20 records how the gross immorality of some men from Benjamin resulted in the other Israelite tribes attacking and nearly destroying the tribe of Benjamin. Because the people of Jabesh Gilead failed to assemble with the Israelite tribes at Mizpah (Judg. 21:8), all of its people were killed except for four hundred virgins, who were given as wives to the surviving Benjamites. Years later, 1 Sam. 11 records Saul, a Benjamite, saving Jabesh Gilead from the Ammonites. When the people of Jabesh Gilead heard that the Philistines had hung the corpses of Saul and his sons on the wall of Beth Shan, their warriors traveled all night to retrieve them and give them an honorable burial at Jabesh (1 Sam. 31:11–12). David blessed them for their bravery and kindness to Saul (2 Sam. 2:4–6).

Jabin–In the Bible, Jabin appears to be the name of two different rulers. **(1)** The king of Hazor during Joshua's "northern campaign." He formed a coalition of Canaanite kings who battled the Israelites at the Waters of Merom (Josh. 11:1–5). God gave victory to the Israelites, Jabin was killed, and Hazor was burned (Josh. 11:6–14). **(2)** The "king of Canaan, who reigned in Hazor" during the war of Deborah (Judg. 4:2). He was defeated, and his commander, Sisera, was killed by Jael (Judg. 4:14–23).

Jacob–Renamed "Israel" by God (Gen. 32:28), he was the son of Isaac and Rebekah and was the father of twelve sons, whose descendants became the twelve tribes. Half the book of Genesis (25:19–49:33) narrates his story and that of his sons. The middle chapters of Genesis focus on his struggles with his brother, Esau, and with his uncle Laban, and the later chapters focus on his children Dinah, Judah, and particularly Joseph during his time in Egypt.

Jael–A Kenite woman, the wife of Heber. The Kenites were allied with the Canaanites, whose king was Jabin and whose chief commander was Sisera. God raised up Deborah as a judge to initiate the overthrow of the Canaanites, who were oppressing his people. Barak, Israel's chief military officer, should have received the glory, but because of his reluctance to take on the job alone, God promised the glory to a woman (Judg. 4:9). That woman turned out to be Jael, a non-Israelite woman, whose people had friendly relationships with the Canaanites. As Sisera fled after being defeated on the battlefield, he sought refuge in the tent of Jael, who lured him to sleep and then killed him with a tent peg (Judg. 4:17–22). In the victory song sung by Deborah and Barak, she is praised for this act (Judg. 5:24–27).

Jairus–The father of a twelve-year-old girl whom Jesus raised from the dead (Matt. 9:18–26; Mark 5:21–43; Luke 8:40–56). All three Synoptic accounts of this story record that Jesus, on his way to Jairus's house, healed a woman who had suffered with a hemorrhage for twelve years. Only Mark and Luke name Jairus and identify him as a synagogue leader; Matthew, who shortens the story in several respects to include only the basic elements, merely calls him "a synagogue leader."

Jakin–One of two pillars erected by Solomon and Hiram in the temple (1 Kings 7:21; 2 Chron. 3:17). Together with the other pillar, Boaz, the names form a prayer: "May he [the Lord] establish strength in him [Solomon]" ("Jakin" means "he establishes," and "Boaz" means "may strength be in him"). The pillars did not support anything; thus, they appear to be symbolic and to demonstrate that the temple belonged to Yahweh. *See also* Boaz.

Jambres–*See* Jannes and Jambres.

James–The name "James" is a form of the name "Jacob" (Heb. *Ya'aqob*; Gk. *Iakōbos*), which was very popular in the first century. In the NT there are five individuals named "James."

(1) James the son of Zebedee and the older brother of John. He was martyred by Herod Agrippa I in AD 40 (Mark 1:19; 3:17; Acts 12:2).

(2) James the son of Alphaeus we know very little about other than that he is consistently listed among the disciples (Mark 3:18; Matt. 10:3; Luke 6:15; Acts 1:13).

(3) James "the younger" (Mark 15:40), whose mother, named "Mary," appears in Mark 16:1 just as the "mother of James." In church tradition, he is sometimes identified with James the son of Alphaeus.

(4) James the father of Judas (Luke 6:16; Acts 1:13) is mentioned only to distinguish this Judas from Judas Iscariot.

(5) James the brother of Jesus was an early leader of the Jerusalem church (Matt. 13:55; Mark 6:3; Acts 12:17; 15:13–31; 21:18; 1 Cor. 15:7; Gal. 1:19; 2:9, 12; Jude 1). A number of Jesus' family members became prominent leaders in the early Christian movement in Palestine, James being the most prominent.

James, Letter of–The Letter of James has been hailed as possibly the earliest, most Jewish, and most practical of all NT letters. James 3:13 aptly communicates the book's theme: "Who is wise and understanding among you? Let them show it by their good life, by deeds done in humility that comes from wisdom."

Some readers of this letter have observed a seeming contradiction between James's call for good works and Paul's insistence on salvation by grace through faith apart from works (cf. James 2:14–26 with Eph. 2:8–10). The discussion is complicated by James's argument that a faith without works cannot "save" and by his observation that Abraham was justified by what he did, not by faith alone (James 2:14, 20–24). Paul, by contrast, maintains that Abraham was justified exclusively by faith (Rom. 4:1–3).

Referring rhetorically to people who claim to have faith but have no deeds, James asks, "Can such faith save them?" (2:14). That is, can the kind of faith that results in no works be genuine? The expected answer is no. The kind of faith that produces no works cannot be genuine faith; rather, it is "dead" (2:17, 26) and "useless" (2:20). This kind of faith is "by itself," meaning that it produces no lasting fruit (2:17). James's point is that genuine faith will produce good works in the believer's life. By way of contrast, a mere profession is not necessarily an indication of genuine faith. Even demons believe in God, but they are not saved; the kind of belief that they exhibit is merely an acknowledgment of God's existence (2:19).

According to James, Abraham was justified not in the sense of first being declared righteous, but rather in the sense that his faith was demonstrated as genuine when he offered up Isaac (2:21). Paul, on the other hand, argues that salvation is obtained not through works but rather by faith alone. He quotes Gen. 15:6 to show that Abraham trusted God and was declared righteous several years before he offered up Isaac (Rom. 4:3).

According to Paul, Abraham was justified (declared righteous) before God when he believed God's promise (Gen. 15:6), but for James, he was justified in the sense of giving observable proof of salvation through his obedience to God. Whereas Paul refers to the point and means of positional salvation, James refers to a subsequent event that confirmed that Abraham was justified.

J

It is important to keep in mind that each author wrote with a different purpose. Paul wrote against Judaizers, who taught that a man had to be circumcised and keep the OT law to be saved. James was warning against a mere profession of faith that leads to self-deception (1:22). John Calvin correctly expressed the biblical teaching that faith alone saves, but that kind of faith does not remain alone; it produces good works (cf. Rom. 3:21–6:14; Eph. 2:8–10; Titus 2:11–14; 3:4–7).

Jannes and Jambres–Jewish tradition identifies Jannes and Jambres as the magicians who opposed Moses in his early encounters with Pharaoh (Exod. 7:11–12, 22). The author of 2 Timothy mentions their names in connection with Moses as examples of false teachers who oppose the truth (3:8).

Japheth–One of the sons of Noah, listed last in most lists (Gen. 9:18; 10:1) but also listed as the older brother of Shem (Gen. 10:21; or younger [see NIV mg.]). The third son, Ham, is said to be the youngest (Gen. 9:24). Along with his wife, Japheth was one of eight persons saved on Noah's ark (1 Pet. 3:20). After Japheth acted nobly with his brother Shem by covering up his sleeping and naked father, Noah gave a blessing to Japheth, asking God to extend his territory and bless his offspring. His name means "widespread" or "God will enlarge." Japheth had seven sons, and it is suggested that his descendants settled in eastern Europe and northern Asia (Gen. 10:2–5).

Jashar, Book of–A written document, twice mentioned in the OT, recounting Joshua's appeal for the sun and the moon to stand still (Josh. 10:12–13) and David's lament over the deaths of Saul and Jonathan (2 Sam. 1:17–27). The book is mentioned as though well known.

Jason–**(1)** A Thessalonian who was likely a Hellenistic Jew converted under Paul's preaching. He hosted Paul and was consequently taken into custody and posted bond (Acts 17:1–9). **(2)** A Jewish Christian present with Paul in Corinth when he wrote Romans (Rom. 16:21). The association of Jason with Sosipater (Rom. 16:21) and of Sopater (= Sosipater) with Thessalonica (Acts 20:4) makes it likely that he is the same Jason as in Acts 17:1–9.

Jebus–*See* Jebusites.

Jebusites–A people group who dwelled in the land of Canaan. They were descended from Canaan (Gen. 10:15–16). God wished to destroy them when Israel invaded (Exod. 23:23). They occupied the hills and Jerusalem, also called "Jebus," in the central region of Canaan (Josh. 15:63; Judg. 1:21). Their king, Adoni-Zedek, organized a coalition of kings to attack Gibeon and Israel (Josh. 10). Though victorious, the Israelites were never able to drive out the Jebusites. They remained in control of Jerusalem until it was conquered by David's men (2 Sam. 5:6–9). Araunah, a Jebusite, sold David his threshing floor so that David could build an altar there (2 Sam. 24:18). The Jebusites were made slave laborers by Solomon (1 Kings 9:20–21).

Jedidiah–Through the prophet Nathan, God gave the name "Jedidiah" to Solomon (2 Sam. 12:25). This additional name, meaning "loved by the Lord," unquestionably established Solomon's favored status as one to succeed David as king and become an ancestor of Jesus.

Jeduthun–A Levite musician stationed at the tent where the ark of the covenant was placed during David's reign (1 Chron. 16:38–41; 25:1–6). He also played instruments at the temple dedication (2 Chron. 5:12). His son Obed-Edom was one of the gatekeepers for the tent. He was an ancestor of Levites who helped Hezekiah purify the temple (2 Chron. 29:14), of Levites present during Josiah's rededication of the temple (where he is listed as David's seer [2 Chron. 35:15]), as well as of some of those who resettled in Judah after the exile (1 Chron. 9:16; Neh. 11:16). The superscriptions of Pss. 39; 62; 77 mention a Jeduthun who is the director of music, likely this same person.

Jehoahaz–**(1)** King of Israel (r. 814–800 BC), the son of King Jehu (2 Kings 10:35). He apparently did not worship Baal, but he did not completely eradicate idolatry from Israel during his reign (2 Kings 13:2). For much of his reign he was subject to the Aramean kings and had a pitifully small army (2 Kings 13:7). His deliverance from Aram did not substantially change his attitude toward God. **(2)** A son of King Josiah and Hamutal, he became king of Judah in 609 BC after Pharaoh Necho of Egypt killed Josiah at Meggido. Jehoahaz, who "did evil in the eyes of the Lord" (2 Kings

23:32), reigned for three months before Necho took him as prisoner to Egypt, where he died (2 Kings 23:29–35; 2 Chron. 36:1–4). He is also known as Shallum (1 Chron. 3:15).

Jehoash–Jehoahaz's son and a king of Israel (2 Kings 13:10–25; 14:8–16; 2 Chron. 25:17–24 [KJV: "Joash"]). The Bible records him as a king unfaithful to God who followed the sins of Jeroboam. He had an encounter with the dying Elisha in which he failed to follow the prophet's directions carefully and was granted only a partial victory over Hazael of Aram. He also went to war with King Amaziah of Judah and attacked Jerusalem, sacking the temple and destroying a large part of Jerusalem's wall. The Chronicler attributes Amaziah's defeat to his disobedience of God.

Jehoiachin–The nineteenth of the twenty monarchs of Judah (r. 597 BC), he was a grandson of Josiah and an ancestor of Jesus (Matt. 1:11–12: "Jeconiah"). His brief reign is recorded in 2 Kings 24:8–17; 2 Chron. 36:8–10. He became ruler at age eighteen, and, like many other ruling members of his family (uncles Jehoahaz and Zedekiah, and father Jehoiakim), he "did evil in the eyes of the Lord" (2 Kings 24:9). He reigned only three months before being exiled to Babylon by Nebuchadnezzar in 597 BC. During this deportation Nebuchadnezzar exiled many Judeans and looted the temple, fulfilling the prophecy of Isaiah to Hezekiah over a hundred years earlier (2 Kings 20:17–18). Jeremiah prophesied the end of Jehoiachin's reign and dynasty (Jer. 22:24–30 [MT: "Coniah"]). He was finally released from imprisonment in 562 BC by Awel-Marduk of Babylon (2 Kings 25:27–30; Jer. 52:31–34). Babylonian tablets record prison rations for him and his sons during his exile.

Jehoiada–The high priest who organized the revolt that placed Joash, the last living male heir of the time in the line of David and the rightful king, on the throne (r. 836–798 BC). According to 2 Chron. 22:11, Jehoiada was married to Joash's aunt Jehosheba; thus Jehoiada was Joash's uncle. Jehosheba saved Joash during an attempt by Queen Athaliah, Joash's grandmother, to kill all other members of the royal family and secure her own claim to the throne. Jehoiada organized the coup d'état by using the temple guard, who killed Athaliah when she came to investigate the noise made by the guards and the people as Jehoiada crowned Joash king and charged him to follow the covenant (2 Kings 11; 2 Chron. 22–23).

Jehoiakim–The second of King Josiah's sons to rule over Judah (r. 609–598 BC), his mother was Zebidah. He "did evil in the eyes of the Lord" (2 Kings 23:37), and his eleven-year reign is recorded in 2 Kings 23:34–24:6; 2 Chron. 36:4–8. He was twenty-five when Pharaoh Necho of Egypt deposed his brother Jehoahaz and made him king, changing his birth name, "Eliakim," to "Jehoiakim." He initially gave tribute to Egypt, but he became a Babylonian vassal when Nebuchadnezzar defeated Necho in 605 BC. Jeremiah prophesied exile and death because of his greed and oppression of the poor (Jer. 22:13–19). Jehoiakim burned Jeremiah's scroll and attempted to arrest the prophet, but God thwarted him (Jer. 36:20–26). He did, however, kill the prophet Uriah (Jer. 26:20–23). Jehoiakim ignored Jeremiah's advice and rebelled against Babylon, so Nebuchadnezzar retaliated first by sending small military bands, then besieging Jerusalem and capturing Jehoiakim. He probably died in exile.

Jehonadab–The son of Rekab, he joined with Jehu in the purge of Ahab's family during Jehu's coup d'état. He also helped Jehu kill all the priests of Baal in the temple of Baal in Samaria (2 Kings 10:15, 23). Although it is historically unverifiable, he apparently is the founder of the Rekabite community. They refused to drink wine with Jeremiah because they had vowed to follow the instructions of their ancestor Jehonadab to refrain from drinking wine, building houses, sowing seed, and planting vineyards (Jer. 35 [NRSV: "Jonadab"]). Jeremiah's oracle uses them as an example of faithfulness, while he condemns Judah for its unfaithfulness. *See also* Jonadab.

Jehoram–**(1)** An alternate name for Joram, king of Israel, Ahab's son (r. 851–842 BC). **(2)** King of Judah (r. 846–843 BC), Jehoshaphat's son. It is likely that he served as coregent with his father early in his reign. He was married to Athaliah, daughter of Ahab and Jezebel. This marriage likely sealed a treaty with Israel established by his father. He was also noted for his apostasy and his inability to subjugate Edom. He was not given the traditional honorable burial reserved for kings (2 Kings 8:16–24; 2 Chron. 21:4–20). **(3)** One of two priests commissioned by King Jehoshaphat to teach "the Book of the Law of the Lord" throughout Judah (2 Chron. 17:8–9). *See also* Joram.

Jehoshaphat–The fourth king of Judah (r. 867–846 BC), coming to the throne on the death of his father, Asa (1 Kings 22:1–50; 2 Kings 3:1–27; 2 Chron. 17:1–21:1). He was a good king who loved God, but not a perfect king. He removed most, but not all, forms of false worship from the land of Judah. He entered into a formal treaty with King Ahab of Israel and sealed it with a marriage between his son Jehoram and Athaliah daughter of Ahab. From a religious point of view, this alliance was not healthy, because although Jehoshaphat remained faithful, his son came under the influence of the Baal worship favored by Ahab and his family. From a political point of view, Jehoshaphat was the junior partner of this relationship (vassal) and often had to lend his support to Ahab against his enemies, particularly the Arameans.

Jehoshaphat, Valley of–A wide valley in which an assembly of all nations will take place (Joel 3:2, 12). It is to be equated with the Valley of Decision (Joel 3:14), the place where God decides the fate of the peoples of the world. The proper name "Jehoshaphat" means "Yahweh judges." A geographical identification is impossible and beside the point, for the name of the valley is simply symbolic for the place of final divine judgment. King Jehoshaphat's victory in 2 Chron. 20 may in part explain the expression. Also, in 2 Chron. 19 Jehoshaphat established a Judean judicial system.

Jehosheba–Daughter of Jehoram, king of Judah (r. 846–843 BC); sister of Ahaziah, king of Judah; and wife of Jehoiada the priest. Jehosheba saved the infant Joash from the massacre of Ahaziah's sons by his mother, Athaliah. Jehosheba hid Joash for six years, until he was revealed by Jehoiada and crowned the rightful king of Judah (2 Kings 11:1–12).

Jehovah Jireh–In Gen. 22:1–19 Abraham obeys God and prepares to sacrifice his son Isaac, but an angel of the Lord intervenes and provides a ram as a substitute for Isaac. As a result, Abraham names the place "Jehovah Jireh" (Heb. *yhwh yir'eh*), meaning "Yahweh provides" (v. 14 [NIV: "The Lord Will Provide"]).

Jehovah Nissi–After Joshua and the Israelites defeated the Amalekites in Rephidim, Moses erected an altar and called it "Jehovah Nissi" (Heb. *yhwh nissi*), meaning "Yahweh is my banner" (Exod. 17:15 [NIV: "The Lord is my Banner"]). The suggestion is that the people should rally around God as an army gathers around its banner.

Jehovah Shalom–After Gideon was terrified at seeing an angel of the Lord, God said to him, "Peace! Do not be afraid" (Judg. 6:23). In response, Gideon built an altar in Ophrah and named it "Jehovah Shalom" (Heb. *yhwh shalom*), meaning "Yahweh is peace" (Judg. 6:24 [NIV: "The Lord Is Peace"]). It is equivalent to "Yahweh is well disposed."

Jehovah Shammah–In Ezekiel's vision of the new Jerusalem, restored and glorified, the city is called "Jehovah Shammah" (Heb. *yhwh shammah*) (Ezek. 48:35; cf. Rev. 21:3). It means "Yahweh is there" (NIV: "The Lord Is There") and emphasizes the importance of God's presence in the midst of his people when he returns to the forsaken temple.

Jehovah Tsidqenu–According to Jeremiah, the "righteous Branch" of David will be known by the name "Jehovah Tsidqenu" (Heb. *yhwh tsidqenu*), meaning "Yahweh (is) our righteousness" (Jer. 23:6; 33:16 [NIV: "The Lord Our Righteous Savior"]). In his days "Judah will be saved and Israel/Jerusalem will live in safety." This symbolic name of the messianic king contrasts with that of the last king of Judah, Zedekiah ("Yahweh is righteousness"), who was an unworthy bearer of that name.

Jehu–**(1)** King of Israel, son of Jehoshaphat (r. 842–814 BC). He carried out a bloody purge of the Omride dynasty, killing Joram, Ahaziah, Jezebel, and around seventy other individuals associated with Omri's family and administration (2 Kings 9:1–10:27). Although he had great influence in ending Baal worship in Israel (2 Kings 10:28), his methods are identified in Scripture as being overzealous and therefore against the will of Yahweh (Hos. 1:4). He also failed to distance himself from the sins of his predecessors and retained the golden calves of Dan and Bethel (2 Kings 10:28–31). He is known from archaeology by the inclusion of his likeness on the Black

Obelisk of Shalmaneser III, which ironically identifies him as "Jehu, son of Omri."

(2) A prophet in the time of King Baasha of Israel, he foretold and then witnessed the demise of Baasha (1 Kings 16:1–12). He also apparently interacted with King Jehoshaphat of Judah and charged him with sin for his alliance with Ahab (2 Chron. 19:2–3). It is also reported that the prophet functioned as a sort of court recorder for the kingdom of Jehoshaphat, and that his work served as a source for the Chronicler (2 Chron. 20:34).

Jemimah–The first of three daughters born to Job after his ordeal had ended and God restored him (Job 42:14). The daughters were famed for their beauty, and Job granted them, as well as their brothers, an inheritance. The name "Jemimah" probably is related to an Arabic word meaning "dove" or "turtledove."

Jephthah–The son of Gilead, he judged Israel for six years (Judg. 11:1–12:7). Like David, he was a military hero, surrounded by outlaws, and descended from a prostitute. After the people of Gilead convinced Jephthah to lead them in battle, he first attempted to establish a truce by reminding the king of Ammon that Israel took the Ammonites' land only after they had attacked Israel first. His message was ignored, so Jephthah vowed that if God gave him victory over Ammon, he would sacrifice whatever he first saw coming out from his house on his return home. After his victory, out to greet him first was his daughter, his only child. Since she allowed herself to be sacrificed as the only child of her father, parallels can be drawn between her, Isaac, and Jesus. Jephthah is mentioned alongside other heroic judges in Samuel's farewell address (1 Sam. 12:11) and in the book of Hebrews' hall of faith (Heb. 11:32).

Jeremiah–*See* Jeremiah, Book of.

Jeremiah, Book of–Jeremiah is a complex book with many themes. One of the central ideas, however, is covenant. The Bible often uses the idea of a covenant to describe the relationship between God and his people. A covenant is a divinely initiated and defined agreement. God makes promises and calls on his people to observe certain requirements. Research has found that the biblical covenants are close in form and concept to ancient Near Eastern treaties between the kings of superpowers and those of much less powerful nations (vassal treaties). The powerful, sovereign king announces the law to the vassal, and it is accompanied by curses and blessings. If the vassal obeys, then the king gives a reward, but if the vassal disobeys, then the king issues punishment.

There is a series of covenantal relationships between God and his people (Noah [Gen. 9]; Abraham [Gen. 12:1–3; 15; 17]; Moses [Exod. 19–24]; David [2 Sam. 7]), but most relevant for our understanding of Jeremiah is the covenant with Moses as reaffirmed in Deuteronomy. The Mosaic covenant emphasizes law (see Deut. 5–26) and has an extensive section of curses and blessings (Deut. 27–28).

Jeremiah and many of the other prophets may be styled "lawyers of the covenant." God sends them to his people when they disobey the law. Their job is to warn the people to change their lives and live in conformity with God's will or else the curses of the covenant will come into effect.

Jeremiah's oracles focus on warning the people that they are covenant breakers, particularly in the matter of worshiping false gods (Jer. 10–11). The hope is that the people will repent and thus avoid the most extreme punishment. But it is not only the judgment oracles that are related to the covenant; so too are the salvation oracles. In Jer. 31:31–34 the prophet announces that God will replace the old covenant with a new one, which will be more internal, more intense, and more intimate.

Jericho–Jericho, "the city of palm trees" (Deut. 34:3; Judg. 3:13; 2 Chron. 28:15), is located about four miles west of the Jordan River and about ten miles north of the Dead Sea. It is located about 850 feet below sea level on a narrow plain across from one of the major Jordan River crossings. Its location was crucial to protect this important east-west route. Immediately behind the city the land rises quickly into a mountainous region known as the Judean Wilderness.

Jericho is possibly the earliest continuously inhabited city in the world, with archaeological finds going back perhaps as early as 9000 BC. Jericho is most famous for being the first city defeated by the Israelites during the conquest under Joshua (Josh. 5:13–6:27).

Jeroboam–**(1)** The first ruler of the northern kingdom (r. 928–907 BC) (1 Kings 11:26–14:20). The son of Nebat, he was a

J

hardworking royal servant, so Solomon gave him responsibility over the northern labor force. The prophet Ahijah declared to Jeroboam that to punish Solomon for apostasy, God would give him the ten northern tribes, leaving Solomon's son Rehoboam with only Judah and Benjamin. When Solomon sought to kill him, Jeroboam fled to Egypt. After Solomon's death, he returned and requested that Rehoboam reduce the workload for the Israelite laborers. Rehoboam, ignoring the advice of the elders and following the counsel of his peers, rudely refused the request of Jeroboam and the people. The ten northern tribes rebelled and made Jeroboam king, and he reigned for twenty-two years.

Jeroboam set up two golden calves, one in Bethel and one in Dan (for the wilderness parallel, see Exod. 32:4), to prevent the northerners from traveling to the temple in Jerusalem to worship. A man of God condemned the sanctuary at Bethel, prophesying that a future king named "Josiah" would destroy it. When he attempted to seize the prophet, Jeroboam's hand was stricken, but after the king's entreaty the prophet restored it. When Jeroboam's son Abijah became ill, the prophet Ahijah delivered a judgment against his son, who soon died, and against his dynasty. After Jeroboam's death, his son Nadab ruled for only two years before being killed by the usurper Baasha. Jeroboam's sanctuaries are mentioned in the condemnation of fifteen other evil northern rulers; they survived the fall of Samaria in 722 BC, but eventually Josiah destroyed the Bethel sanctuary as prophesied (2 Kings 23:15).

(2) The thirteenth ruler of the northern kingdom (r. 784–748 BC; 2 Kings 14:23–29). He was the son of Jehoash and a great-grandson of Jehu. Despite doing "evil in the eyes of the Lord" (v. 24), he received a favorable prophecy from the prophet Jonah, restored the borders of the northern kingdom, and was one of the longest-reigning rulers of Israel or Judah (forty-one years). During his reign, Aramean and Assyrian domination over Israel subsided, which resulted in wealth and prosperity for the upper classes, but oppression and injustice of the marginalized. Amos condemned these practices and prophesied the end of Jeroboam's house (Amos 7:8–11), which was fulfilled when his son Zechariah was killed by the usurper Shallum after reigning only six months.

Jerub-Baal–*See* Gideon.

Jerusalem–The central city and capital of ancient Israel. Throughout its history, the city has also been referred to variously as Zion, Jebus, Mount Moriah, and the City of David.

The name "Jerusalem" occurs more than 650 times in the OT, particularly in the history of Israel, and in the NT more than 140 times. The OT prophets used the city as a symbol of God's dealing with his people and his plan. Jerusalem is viewed collectively as God's abode, his chosen place, and his sovereignty, while its destruction is also representative of God's judgment on apostasy among his people (e.g., Jer. 7:1–15; 26:18–19; Mic. 3:12). The rebuilding of the city represents the hope and grace of God (e.g., Isa. 40:1–2; 52:1, 7–8; 60–62; Jer. 30:18–19; 31:38–39; Ezek. 5:5; Hag. 2:6–8; Zech. 8:3–8). Like the writers of the OT, the NT authors spoke of Jerusalem in metaphorical and eschatological terms. Paul used Jerusalem to contrast the old and the new covenants (Gal. 4:24–26), and the writer of Hebrews used it as the place of the new covenant, sealed through the blood of Jesus (Heb. 12:22–24). In Revelation the concept of a new Jerusalem is related to the future kingdom of God (Rev. 3:12; 21:1–22:5).

Jerusalem is located in the Judean hill country, about 2,700 feet above sea level. It borders the Judean desert to the east. The city expanded and contracted in size over various hills and valleys. There are two major ridges (Eastern and Western Hills) separated by the Tyropoeon Valley. The Eastern Hill contains a saddle, the Ophel Hill, and north of this is the traditional site of Mount Moriah, where later the temple was constructed. The Eastern Hill was always occupied, since the only water source is the Gihon spring, located in the Kidron Valley. Two other ridges were important for the city, as they were used for extramural suburbs, cemeteries, and quarries. To the east is the Mount of Olives, which is separated from the Eastern Hill by the Kidron Valley. To the west of the Western Hill is the Central Ridge Route, separated by the Hinnom Valley.

Jerusalem Council–*See* Acts of the Apostles.

Jerusalem Temple–Temples have always been the domain and house of the gods throughout the ancient Near East. The temple played an important role in the social, religious, and political life of ancient Israel. The Jerusalem temple was originally built by

Solomon in 953 BC and was destroyed by the Babylonian king Nebuchadnezzar in 586 BC. After the exile, the temple was rebuilt and then rededicated by Zerubbabel in 515 BC (Ezra). Herod the Great significantly expanded and changed the temple, but it was eventually destroyed by the Romans under the direction of Titus in AD 70.

The temple was the dwelling place of Yahweh. It was the domain of the religious leaders, priests, and Levites. It also represented the relationship/covenant between God and the nation of Israel. Various kings used the temple for their political maneuvering and attempts to shift the religious worship of the nation. The temple was the visible presence of God and embodied the political and religious aspirations of the people. The temple sat on top of a sacred mountain.

JESHURUN–A poetic term meaning "the upright one" that appears in the Song of Moses (Deut. 32:15), the Blessing of Moses (Deut. 33:5, 26), and a prophecy of Isaiah of Babylon (Isa. 44:2). Used in parallel with "Jacob" and "Israel," it refers poetically to the people of Israel.

JESSE–From Bethlehem, he was the father of David and a descendant of Ruth the Moabite (Ruth 4:17); 1 Sam. 22:3 implies that Jesse fled to Moab on one occasion. The Gospels recognize him as an ancestor of Jesus (Matt. 1:5–6; Luke 3:32). Prior to the anointing of David, Samuel was sent to Jesse (1 Sam. 16:1) to choose from among his eight sons (1 Sam. 17:12). Like the father of Samuel (1 Sam. 1:1), Jesse is called an "Ephrathite," a name associated with Bethlehem (1 Sam. 17:12; cf. Ruth 1:2; Mic. 5:2). Isaiah alludes to the Davidic dynasty as a "Root of Jesse" (Isa. 11:1, 10).

JESUS CHRIST–The founder of what became known as the movement of Jesus followers or Christianity. For Christian believers, Jesus Christ embodies the personal and supernatural intervention of God in human history.

Birth and childhood. The Gospels of Matthew and Luke record Jesus' birth in Bethlehem during the reign of Herod the Great (Matt. 2:1; Luke 2:4, 11). Jesus was probably born between 6 and 4 BC, shortly before Herod's death (Matt. 2:19). Both Matthew and Luke record the miracle of a virginal conception made possible by the Holy Spirit (Matt. 1:18; Luke 1:35). Luke mentions a census under the Syrian governor Quirinius that was responsible for Jesus' birth taking place in Bethlehem (2:1–5). Both the census and the governorship at the time of the birth of Jesus have been questioned by scholars. Unfortunately, there is not enough extrabiblical evidence to either confirm or disprove these events, so their veracity must be determined on the basis of one's view regarding the general reliability of the Gospel tradition.

On the eighth day after his birth, Jesus was circumcised, in keeping with the Jewish law, at which time he officially was named "Jesus" (Luke 2:21). He spent his growing years in Nazareth, in the home of his parents, Joseph and Mary (2:40). Of the NT Gospels, the Gospel of Luke contains the only brief portrayal of Jesus' growth in strength, wisdom, and favor with God and people (2:40, 52). Luke also contains the only account of Jesus as a young boy (2:41–49).

Baptism, temptation, and start of ministry. After Jesus was baptized by the prophet John the Baptist (Luke 3:21–22), God affirmed his pleasure with him by referring to him as his Son, whom he loved (Matt. 3:17; Mark 1:11; Luke 3:22). Jesus' baptism did not launch him into fame and instant ministry success; instead, Jesus was led by the Spirit into the wilderness, where he was tempted for forty days (Matt. 4:1–11; Mark 1:12–13; Luke 4:1–13). Mark stresses that the temptations immediately followed the baptism. Matthew and Luke identify three specific temptations by the devil, though their order for the last two is reversed. Both Matthew and Luke agree that Jesus was tempted to turn stones into bread, expect divine intervention after jumping off the temple portico, and receive all the world's kingdoms for worshiping the devil. Jesus resisted all temptation, quoting Scripture in response.

Matthew and Mark record that Jesus began his ministry in Capernaum in Galilee, after the arrest of John the Baptist (Matt. 4:12–13; Mark 1:14). Luke says that Jesus started his ministry at about thirty years of age (3:23). This may be meant to indicate full maturity or perhaps correlate this age with the onset of the service of the Levites in the temple (cf. Num. 4:3). John narrates the beginning of Jesus' ministry by focusing on the calling of the disciples and the sign performed at a wedding at Cana (1:35–2:11).

Galilean ministry. The early stages of Jesus' ministry centered in and around Galilee. Jesus presented the good news and proclaimed that the kingdom of God was near. Matthew focuses on the fulfillment of prophecy (Matt. 4:13–17). Luke records Jesus' first teaching in his hometown, Nazareth, as paradigmatic (Luke 4:16–30); the text that Jesus quoted, Isa. 61:1–2, set the stage for his calling to serve and revealed a trajectory of rejection and suffering.

All the Gospels record Jesus' gathering of disciples early in his Galilean ministry (Matt. 4:18–22; Mark 1:16–20; Luke 5:1–11; John 1:35–51). The formal call and commissioning of the Twelve who would become Jesus' closest followers is recorded in different parts of the Gospels (Matt. 10:1–4; Mark 3:13–19; Luke 6:12–16). A key event in the early ministry is the Sermon on the Mount/Plain (Matt. 5:1–7:29; Luke 6:20–49). John focuses on Jesus' signs and miracles, in particular in the early parts of his ministry, whereas the Synoptics focus on healings and exorcisms.

During Jesus' Galilean ministry, onlookers struggled with his identity. However, evil spirits knew him to be of supreme authority (Mark 3:11). Jesus was criticized by outsiders and by his own family (3:21). The scribes from Jerusalem identified him as a partner of Beelzebul (3:22). Amid these situations of social conflict, Jesus told parables that couched his ministry in the context of a growing kingdom of God. This kingdom would miraculously spring from humble beginnings (4:1–32).

The Synoptics present Jesus' early Galilean ministry as successful. No challenge or ministry need superseded Jesus' authority or ability: he calmed a storm (Mark 4:35–39), exorcized many demons (5:1–13), raised the dead (5:35–42), fed five thousand (6:30–44), and walked on water (6:48–49).

In the later part of his ministry in Galilee, Jesus often withdrew and traveled to the north and the east. The Gospel narratives are not written with a focus on chronology. However, only brief returns to Galilee appear to have taken place prior to Jesus' journey to Jerusalem. As people followed Jesus, faith was praised and fear resolved. Jerusalem's religious leaders traveled to Galilee, where they leveled accusations and charged Jesus' disciples with lacking ritual purity (Mark 7:1–5). Jesus shamed the Pharisees by pointing out their dishonorable treatment of parents (7:11–13). The Pharisees challenged his legitimacy by demanding a sign (8:11). Jesus refused them signs but agreed with Peter, who confessed, "You are the Messiah" (8:29). Jesus did provide the disciples a sign: his transfiguration (9:2–8).

Jesus withdrew from Galilee to Tyre and Sidon, where a Syrophoenician woman requested healing for her daughter. Jesus replied, "I was sent only to the lost sheep of Israel" (Matt. 15:24). Galileans had long resented the Syrian provincial leadership partiality that allotted governmental funds in ways that made the Jews receive mere "crumbs." Consequently, when the woman replied, "Even the dogs eat the crumbs that fall from their master's table," Jesus applauded her faith (Matt. 15:27–28). Healing a deaf-mute man in the Decapolis provided another example of Jesus' ministry in Gentile territory (Mark 7:31–37). Peter's confession of Jesus as the Christ took place during Jesus' travel to Caesarea Philippi, a well-known Gentile territory. The city was the ancient center of worship of the Hellenistic god Pan.

Judean ministry. Luke records a geographic turning point in Jesus' ministry as he resolutely set out for Jerusalem, a direction that eventually led to his death (Luke 9:51). Luke divides the journey to Jerusalem into three phases (9:51–13:21; 13:22–17:10; 17:11–19:27). The opening verses of phase one emphasize a prophetic element of the journey. Jesus viewed his ministry in Jerusalem as his mission, and the demands on discipleship intensified as Jesus approached Jerusalem (Matt. 20:17–19, 26–28; Mark 10:38–39, 43–45; Luke 14:25–35). Luke presents the second phase of the journey toward Jerusalem with a focus on conversations regarding salvation and judgment (Luke 13:22–30). In the third and final phase of the journey, the advent of the kingdom and the final judgment are the main themes (17:20–37; 19:11–27).

Social conflicts with religious leaders increased throughout Jesus' ministry. These conflicts led to lively challenge-riposte interactions concerning the Pharisaic schools of Shammai and Hillel (Matt. 19:1–12; Mark 10:1–12). Likewise, socioeconomic feathers were ruffled as Jesus welcomed young children, who had little value in society (Matt. 19:13–15; Mark 10:13–16; Luke 18:15–17).

Passion week, death, and resurrection. Each of the Gospels records Jesus' entry into Jerusalem with the crowds extending him a royal welcome (Matt. 21:4–9; Mark 11:7–10; Luke 19:35–38; John 12:12–15). Luke describes Jesus' ministry in Jerusalem as a time during which Jesus taught in the temple as Israel's Messiah (19:45–21:38).

In Jerusalem, Jesus cleansed the temple of profiteering (Mark 11:15–17). Mark describes the religious leaders as fearing Jesus because the whole crowd was amazed at his teaching, and so they "began looking for a way to kill him" (11:18). Dismayed, each segment of Jerusalem's temple leadership inquired about Jesus' authority (11:27–33). Jesus replied with cunning questions (12:16, 35–36), stories (12:1–12), denunciation (12:38–44), and a prediction of Jerusalem's own destruction (13:1–31). One of Jesus' own disciples, Judas Iscariot, provided the temple leaders the opportunity for Jesus' arrest (14:10–11).

At the Last Supper, Jesus instituted a new Passover, defining a new covenant grounded in his sufferings (Matt. 26:17–18, 26–29; Mark 14:16–25; Luke 22:14–20). He again warned the disciples of his betrayal and arrest (Matt. 26:21–25, 31; Mark 14:27–31; Luke 22:21–23; John 13:21–30), and later he prayed for the disciples (John 17:1–26) and prayed in agony and submissiveness in the garden of Gethsemane (Matt. 26:36–42; Mark 14:32–42; Luke 22:39–42). His arrest, trial, crucifixion, death, and resurrection followed (Matt. 26:46–28:15; Mark 14:43–16:8; Luke 22:47–24:9; John 18:1–20:18). Jesus finally commissioned his disciples to continue his mission by making disciples of all the nations (Matt. 28:18–20; Acts 1:8) and ascended to heaven with the promise that he will one day return (Luke 24:50–53; Acts 1:9–11).

Jethro–The father of Zipporah, the wife of Moses. He is thus best known as the father-in-law of Moses. Moses came into contact with Zipporah and her father as he fled from Egypt (Exod. 2:11–25). Jethro is identified from the start as a "priest of Midian" (Exod. 2:16). Midian was not a nation-state but rather an area occupied by nomadic shepherds. The area is in northern Arabia on the east side of Aqaba.

Jewish Parties–Five of the important parties in ancient Judaism were the Pharisees, the Sadducees, the Essenes, the Zealots, and the Herodians. The first three seem to have first emerged in reaction to the rise of the Hasmonean priest-kings in the mid-second and first centuries BC, and the other two in response to the occupation of Palestine by the Romans and their establishment of the Herods as the rulers of Israel.

Pharisees. In the Synoptic Gospels, the Pharisees were one of the groups that opposed Jesus. It seems that the Pharisees most strongly opposed Jesus on issues related to their received tradition, which they considered to be as binding as the OT law. Two such legal issues were ceremonial washings before meals and working on the Sabbath. All three Synoptic Gospels narrate the Pharisees questioning Jesus concerning his and his disciples' failure to follow the tradition of the elders by eating with "unclean"—that is, "unwashed"—hands (Matt. 15:1–2; Mark 7:1–5; Luke 11:39–41). Concerning breaking the Sabbath, the Pharisees confronted Jesus on various occasions, such as when Jesus healed on the Sabbath (Matt. 12:9–14; Mark 3:1–5; Luke 6:6–11) and when his disciples picked grain while walking through a field (Matt. 12:1–8; Mark 2:23–28; Luke 6:1–5).

In response to accusations concerning breaking the traditions of the elders, Jesus affirmed the priority of mercy in the face of human need that supersedes laws concerning the Sabbath by saying that the Sabbath was made for humans, not humans for the Sabbath (Mark 2:27), or that the Son of Man (Jesus) was Lord of the Sabbath (Matt. 12:8; Mark 2:28; Luke 6:5). He also said that God desires mercy, not sacrifice (Matt. 12:7).

Jesus' critique of the Pharisees concentrated on their neglecting mercy toward fellow humans for the sake of their tradition. This is especially clear in Matthew, where Jesus' critique of the Pharisees includes indictments against them for concentrating on the fine points of the law but neglecting justice and mercy (12:7; 23:23).

In the Gospel of John, the Pharisees are again usually depicted as adversaries of Jesus and also in league with other Jewish authorities in plotting to arrest and kill Jesus (7:32; 11:47–57). One passage suggests that they were divided concerning Jesus (9:16). One Pharisee, Nicodemus, came to Jesus by night (John 3), defended Jesus before his peers (7:50), and brought spices to prepare Jesus' body for burial after his death (19:39).

The Pharisees were not always antagonistic toward Jesus. From time to time, they were on the same side of an issue, such as Jesus' confrontation with the Sadducees over the resurrection (Luke 20:27–40). Nicodemus, mentioned above, was quite sympathetic toward Jesus. The apostle Paul identifies himself as a Pharisee in regard to keeping the law in Phil. 3:5; Acts 26:5, and in a confrontation with Jerusalem authorities in Acts 23:6. Also, some early Christians were said to be Pharisees (Acts 15:5).

Sadducees. The Sadducees were an elite group of Jews connected with the priesthood. "Sadducee" probably means "Son of Zadok," a descendant of the high priest Zadok from the time of David. Some members of the Qumran community used the term "Son of Zadok" as a self-designation as well, suggesting some common ancestry, if not direct identification, of the Sadducees and some members of the Qumran community.

The Sadducees are mentioned in the Synoptic Gospels, but not in John, although the "chief priests" who plotted against Jesus with the Pharisees (e.g., John 11:46) probably were Sadducees. All three Synoptic Gospels relate the narrative in which the Sadducees posed the hypothetical question concerning whose wife a woman would be in the resurrection if she outlived seven husbands. Jesus answered that they understood neither the Scriptures nor the power of God, and that God was the God of the living and not the dead (Matt. 22:23–33; Mark 12:18–27; Luke 20:27–40).

The book of Acts confirms that the Sadducees were closely connected to the priesthood 4:1; 5:17), and that they disputed with the Pharisees over the resurrection (23:6–8).

Essenes. Josephus delineates the beliefs of the Essenes as follows: (1) They ascribed every happening to God. (2) They believed in the immortality of the soul.

Zealots. Scholars tend to use "Zealots" as a general term to refer to three different groups mentioned by Josephus: brigands, Sicarii (Assassins), and Zealots. The three groups have different political ideologies and emerged at different times in the first century. They can all be described as revolutionaries.

Herodians. The Herodians are mentioned three times in the Gospels. They are reported to have plotted, along with the Pharisees, to kill Jesus after he healed a man with a withered hand (Mark 3:6). They are also described, along with the Pharisees, as trying to trap Jesus concerning the lawfulness of paying taxes to Caesar (Matt. 22:16; Mark 12:13).

The Herodians were aristocrats who supported the Herodian dynasty and the Romans, whose support made that dynasty possible. There seems to be some overlap between the Herodians and the Sadducees; Mark 8:15 has Jesus warning his disciples concerning the leaven of the Pharisees and the leaven of Herod (some ancient witnesses read "Herodians"), whereas the parallel in Matt. 16:6, 11 has Jesus warning his disciples concerning the Pharisees and the Sadducees. Their religious beliefs may have been similar to those of the Sadducees. Too little information about them exists to permit drawing strong conclusions. One can safely say, however, that the Herodians were pro-Roman aristocrats who joined forces with the anti-Roman Pharisees in opposing Jesus.

Jezebel–The foreign-born wife of Ahab, a ninth-century BC king of Israel. Jezebel was the daughter of King Ethbaal of Sidon. She was a devout worshiper of the god Baal, whose religion she promoted in Israel after marrying Ahab. Many people were persuaded to add the worship of Baal to the worship of Yahweh, the true God of Israel. God raised up two prophets during this time, Elijah and Elisha, who resisted the encroachment of her false religion.

Jezebel was evil and a worshiper of false gods. In the NT she became an exemplar of wickedness. Revelation 2:20 associates a woman prophet in Thyatira with Jezebel because she was leading the people astray by her teaching.

Jezreel–**(1)** A fertile valley extending west from the northern city of Jezreel (Greek form, Esdraelon) and possibly also east to the Jordan. This is the location of Gideon's attack on the Midianites (Judg. 6:33). **(2)** A city in Issachar's territory about eighteen miles southwest of the Sea of Galilee (Josh. 19:18). **(3)** One of Hosea's sons. The name initially points symbolically to the judgment on Jehu's dynasty for his massacre in Jezreel (Hos. 1:4–5). In Hos. 2:22–23 this name is reinterpreted as a picture of restoration, playing both on the natural fertility of the Jezreel Valley and the meaning of "Jezreel," "God sows."

Joab–A nephew of King David through his sister Zeruiah (1 Chron. 2:16–17). His brothers were Abishai and Asahel, and his cousin was Amasa, all of whom were important military commanders. Joab himself was the most famous military leader of them all. He became the leader of David's army after he was the first to take up David's challenge to defeat the Jebusite city of Jerusalem (1 Chron. 11:4–9).

Joab won many impressive battles for David (2 Sam. 2:12–32; 10:1–19). He often served the interests of David, even trying to persuade David not to take a census that he knew would provoke God's anger (2 Sam. 24:1–9; 1 Chron. 21:1–6). On some occasions he gave David bad advice—for instance, counseling him to take Absalom back into the court (2 Sam. 14:1–33). However, he sometimes acted in his own interests, and not those of his king, country, or God. He killed Abner, the commander of the northern army, in revenge (2 Sam. 3:22–39) and even murdered his own cousin Amasa (2 Sam. 20:7–13).

Joab met his end when he supported Adonijah's attempt to succeed David. When David's choice, Solomon, became king, he sent Benaiah to kill Adonijah. When news of Adonijah's death reached Joab, he fled to the tabernacle and took hold of the horns of the altar (1 Kings 1:50). Solomon ordered Benaiah to kill Joab, and he did so in the tabernacle because Joab refused to come out (1 Kings 2:29–31, 34).

Joanna–The wife of Chuza, the manager of Herod Antipas's household. Joanna was cured by Jesus of either illness or demon possession, and she was among the women who traveled with Jesus during his ministry and provided support for him (Luke 8:1–3).

Joash–**(1)** Ahaziah's son and a king of Judah (2 Kings 11–12; 2 Chron. 22:10–24:27). He is described as the only surviving descendant of Ahaziah (and the line of David) after Athaliah's (Jehoram's wife and Joash's grandmother) purge of the royal line. The priest Jehoiada protected Joash in the temple until he was seven years old, at which time Jehoiada was able to organize a rebellion against Athaliah and place Joash on the throne. Joash is given a favorable description largely due to his allegiance to the temple (as evidenced by his renovation of the temple) and the priesthood. According to the Chronicler, Joash strayed away from God after Jehoiada's death. By the time of the end of his reign, Joash was so politically weak that he was assassinated by some of his own servants.

(2) A variation of "Jehoash" (Jehoahaz's son and a king of Israel) in 2 Chron. 25:17–24 (KJV, ESV, NRSV). *See* Jehoash.

Job–*See* Job, Book of.

Job, Book of–The question of undeserved suffering has plagued humanity for as long as we have written records, as is demonstrated by several ancient Mesopotamian literary compositions going back to Sumerian times. Today too we wonder why bad things happen to good people. The book of Job raises this issue in the person of Job, a pious and blameless man who suffers unspeakable tragedies. However, the question of why Job suffers leads to an even more important question: Where can wisdom be found?

The genre of the book is a debate, the topic being the nature and source of wisdom. The various parts of the book contribute to this debate, beginning with the prose prologue (1:1–2:13) that introduces Job as a perfect wise man (1:1, 8–10). God presents Job as an example of a godly and wise man to "the Satan" (or "the accuser," best understood as one of God's angels, not the devil). No matter his exact identify, the accuser does not question Job's character, but he does challenge his motivation. He believes that Job is righteous because God rewards him. God accepts the challenge and allows the accuser to harm his possessions and family, followed by a second round of suffering where the accuser afflicts by taking away his health. Job, however, persists in his proper attitude toward God. At the end of the prologue, we also hear of Job's three friends, who move in to offer sympathy and support. They sit with him for seven days in silence.

Job is the first to break the silence, and what he says unsettles his friends. He complains about his present condition, cursing the day of his birth (Job 3). Job's complaint triggers a debate about the cause of Job's suffering as well as the best prescription to solve his problem (Job 4–31).

The three friends keep repeating the same argument. Job suffers because he is a sinner. They represent a traditional retribution theology, which states that if you sin, you suffer; therefore, if you suffer, then you must have sinned. The solution is obvious. Job needs to repent (4:7–11; 11:13–20). For his part, Job knows that he has not sinned in such a way to deserve to suffer as he is. But this creates a theological problem for him, since he too believes in the same theology of retribution held by the three friends. Thus, in his mind, God is unjust (9:21–24). Accordingly, his solution is to find God and present his case before him (23:2–7).

Although the subject of their debate is Job's suffering, the heart of it concerns wisdom. Who is wise? Who has the correct insight into

Job's suffering? Both Job and the friends set themselves up as sources of wisdom and ridicule the wisdom of the other (11:12; 12:1–3, 12; 13:12; 15:1–13). The question "Who is wise?" dominates the book.

After their debate, a new character surprisingly emerges from the background. Elihu has observed the debate silently, but now he feels compelled to speak (Job 32–37). He is young and thus has deferred to the wisdom of the elderly, but he has been sorely disappointed. Now he realizes that wisdom is not always a matter of age, but comes from "the spirit in a person" (32:8). The reader expects a new argument from this brash young man, but instead Job is treated to another blast of the retribution theology of the three friends: Job suffers because he is a sinner (34:11, 25–27, 37).

Elihu represents another type of person who claims wisdom. Rather than age, he believes the spirit in a person gives wisdom. However, he comes up with the same old descriptions and solutions. This viewpoint is critiqued by silence; he is ignored. No one responds to his unpersuasive opinion.

At the end of chapter 31, Job had expressed his wish for an audience with God. Now he gets his wish. God appears in a whirlwind, an indication of his displeasure, and challenges Job's purported wisdom: "Who is this that obscures my plans with words without knowledge?" (38:2). God then bombards Job with a series of questions that he cannot possibly answer, since he is not God. God also describes how he is the one who distributes and withholds power and wisdom to his creatures.

He never addresses the reasons for Job's suffering or the question of suffering in general. That is not the main purpose of the book. He asserts his wisdom, thus answering the question of the book: "Who is wise?" Only God is wise. What is the proper response to God's wisdom and power? Repentance and submission, and thus Job responds two times (40:3–5; 42:1–6).

The epilogue raises a number of interesting questions for the interpreter. After Job repents, God restores his health and prosperity beyond what he had enjoyed at the beginning of the book. Does this not concede to the argument of the three friends and Elihu? All along they have been urging him to repent and be restored. However, such an interpretation misses a key point. Job has not repented of any sin that had led to his suffering in the first place. No, he has passed that test. However, as time wore on, he had grown impatient with God. He never takes the counsel of his wife to "curse God and die" (2:9), but he does question God's justice without ever breaking relationship.

A second issue concerns God's statement that Job has "spoken the truth about me" (42:8). Did God not just spend two chapters criticizing him? The best way to understand this comment is to understand it as God's affirmation not of every word that Job has spoken about him, but rather of how Job has responded to God in the end. After all, he had never abandoned God, even in his darkest hour.

Jochebed–The wife of Amram and the mother of Moses, Aaron, and Miriam (Exod. 6:20; Num. 26:59). She is not mentioned by name in the narrative in Exod. 2, where she puts the infant Moses in a basket and floats him down the Nile. By God's providence and the actions of Miriam, Moses' sister, Jochebed becomes the paid nursemaid for her son after he is rescued by Pharaoh's daughter. Jochebed and her husband are listed as examples of faith in Heb. 11:23.

Joel–*See* Joel, Book of.

Joel, Book of–Joel is the second of the twelve Minor Prophets. The book is best known for its frightening depiction of God's judgment in the form of a locust plague and the stirring description of that future day when God will pour his Spirit out on all people (2:28–32).

Joel is a collection of prophetic oracles. Like most prophetic books, the book has both judgment and salvation oracles, although there are more salvation oracles than usual. The first chapter describes an actual locust plague that Joel understands to be a judgment on the people of God. The second chapter also speaks of a locust plague, but this time the locusts are a metaphor for future devastation by a human army. On this basis, Joel calls for the people's repentance and also places before the people a picture of God's future salvation, which includes judgment on the other nations.

Joel uses a recent locust plague to paint a picture of the devastation of a coming day of judgment, referred to here and elsewhere in the prophets as the "day of the Lord" (2:1; see also Amos 5:18–20). This vivid and horrifying teaching on judgment is intended not simply to frighten readers but also to encourage their repentance. As frightening as Joel's language about judgment seems, his language of future salvation is encouraging to an even greater degree.

Johanan–An army officer who survived the conquest of Judah by King Nebuchadnezzar (2 Kings 25:23). In Jeremiah he plays a significant role among the remnant of Jews who were not carried off into exile. Loyal to Gedaliah, who was appointed by the Babylonians as administrator of Judah in 587 BC (Jer. 40:8), Johanan unsuccessfully warned him of an assassination plot by Ishmael (Jer. 40:13–16; 41:1–3). Having saved a group of Jews from further treachery by Ishmael, Johanan subsequently became their leader (Jer. 41:11–18). He and the rescued Jews, however, refused to obey the word of God that came through Jeremiah to remain in the land and instead went down into Egypt, forcibly taking Jeremiah with them (Jer. 42:1–43:7).

John–A common name in first-century Judaism. The Greek name *Iōannēs* comes from the Hebrew name "Yohanan." **(1)** The Baptist or Baptizer, he was the son of the priest Zechariah and Elizabeth. (*See* John the Baptist.) **(2)** The son of Zebedee, he was an apostle originally belonging to the inner circle of the twelve main disciples of Jesus. (*See* John the Apostle.) **(3)** John Mark, a cousin of Barnabas (Col. 4:10) and the son of Mary (Acts 12:12). (*See* Mark, John.) **(4)** The elder. Both 2 John and 3 John claim authorship by "the elder" (2 John 1; 3 John 1). Traditionally, all three Johannine Letters, the Gospel of John, and sometimes the Revelation of John have been attributed to John the apostle. However, modern scholarship often attributes 2 John and 3 John, and sometimes 1 John, to "the elder"—John the elder. **(5)** The seer, the author of the book of Revelation (see 1:1, 4, 9; 22:8). Some scholars ascribe the authorship of Revelation to John the apostle, in line with the view of the church father Irenaeus. Other scholars ascribe the writing of Revelation to a certain John the elder. The book of Revelation does not further identify the author. However, the author is among the prophets, a seer, and his name is "John"—hence, John the seer.

John, First Letter of–First John is a letter written to reassure Christians of the security of their salvation in Christ. The letter contrasts the truth of the original gospel taught by the author with the heretical doctrines of traveling teachers who sought to instill doubt and fear in the churches. The incarnation takes center stage as the climactic confession of Christianity (1 John 4:2–3). Christian love flows out of God's ultimate example of love in the atoning death of Christ.

First John repeats many of the same themes as the Gospel of John. The historical reality of the incarnation of Christ is a central theme in 1 John (1:1–3). The incarnation is rooted in history and cannot be divorced from that foundational fact. Christ's "atoning sacrifice" is another foundational fact of Christian belief; however, it is not simply that Christ died a sacrificial death, but that he did so "for our sins" (2:2; 4:10). The author explains the meaning of the atonement to help build the salvation confidence of the struggling Christians. In a number of places the author places special stress on the forgiveness of sins that comes through Jesus' blood. His death "purifies us from all sin" (1:7). He came to take away sin and to destroy the work of the devil (3:5, 8).

Love is another resounding theme. Christians are to love one another in concrete ways, reflecting the sacrificial love of Christ (2:16–18). Love is rooted in God and ultimately demonstrated at the cross (4:9). We will never find what love means if we start from the human end. We must start from the cross, where we see the love of God (4:10). The author reminds his readers that they have the Holy Spirit and have no need for further instruction by the false teachers (2:20–21, 26–27). The Spirit of God is the Spirit of truth, who bears witness that Jesus is Christ in the flesh (4:2, 6). Competing spirits should be tested and rejected as "antichrist" if they fail to confess Christ (4:3).

John, Gospel of–Traditionally appearing after Matthew, Mark, and Luke in the NT canon, the Gospel of John is also referred to as the Fourth Gospel. Because of its many unique features, John is often discussed in distinction from the other three Gospels, which are grouped together as the Synoptic Gospels.

The Gospel of John states its purpose in 20:31: "But these [signs] are written that you may believe that Jesus is the Messiah, the Son of God, and that by believing you may have life in his name."

For this reason, the Gospel of John clearly focuses on the person, work, and identity of Jesus Christ. John intends to clarify and affirm exactly who the Messiah/Christ/Son of God really was and why he came. For John, the answer is evident: Jesus Christ is the physical manifestation of God, and he came to be crucified.

The thesis statement of the Fourth Gospel appears at the close of the opening prologue: "the one and only Son, who is himself God" has "made him [the Father] known" (1:18). John demonstrates this by affirming that what God is, the Word is (1:1); what the Father does, the Son does (5:19); the Son and the Father are one (10:30); the Son speaks what the Father has told him (8:28; 12:49; 14:10); and the Son is in the Father, and the Father is in the Son (14:10–11). The climactic statement, then, is Jesus' proclamation: "Anyone who has seen me has seen the Father" (14:9).

Several proposals have set forth various secondary intentions for the Gospel of John. Many of these have some measure of legitimacy, though it is difficult to establish any of them as forthright in the mind of John. For example, it has been suggested that the Fourth Gospel was written to combat a growing form of gnosticism. Although this Gospel has traces of evidence that support this contention, and there is even some external evidence in its favor, it is difficult to establish that this was an explicit intention of John. Gnosticism as a developed system did not arise until the second century. Others have argued that this Gospel was written as an anti-Jewish polemic. A close reading, however, suggests that this was not one of John's purposes. Perhaps the most plausible secondary proposition is that John's Gospel was written to complement the Synoptic Gospels.

John, Revelation of–*See* Revelation, Book of.

John, Second Letter of–Second John is a follow-up letter to 1 John, sent to one of the churches involved to warn it about the heretics who were trying to deceive people. The elder exhorts the church to have nothing to do with the false teachers and to continue to walk in the truth and to follow God's command to love one another (vv. 4–6).

Second John continues the main themes of 1 John: love, obeying God's commands, walking in the truth, and Christians as "children." One additional theme is hospitality. The readers are warned not to let these deceivers teach in their house church (vv. 10–11). Fellowship and hospitality are extended only to those who acknowledge that Jesus Christ has come in the flesh.

John, Third Letter of–Third John is a second follow-up letter to 1 John, sent to Gaius to commend him for extending hospitality to traveling preachers of good standing. Third John also commends the actions of Demetrius while condemning those of Diotrephes.

Like 2 John, 3 John centers on the themes of love, obeying God's commands, walking in the truth, and Christians as "children," but it deals in more detail with the matter of hospitality (vv. 6–10).

John Mark–*See* Mark, John.

John the Apostle–John, along with his brother James, was a son of Zebedee and a fisherman, and a disciple of Jesus (known as the Beloved Disciple). He was first called to be a disciple when Jesus passed along the shore of Galilee (Matt. 4:21; Mark 1:19–20; Luke 5:10). The fishing boat belonging to John's family contained hired men, indicating that he left behind a profitable fishing trade (Mark 1:20). Jesus surnamed John and his brother James "Boanerges," meaning "sons of thunder" (Mark 3:17), likely a reflection of their boisterous temperament.

John's passionate temperament may be reflected in the Gospels in his attempt to confront potential opposition (Mark 9:38–41; Luke 9:49–50) and his desire to bring heavenly fire down upon those who rejected Jesus (Luke 9:54). James and John requested seats of honor in Jesus' kingdom (Mark 10:37–40). Matthew clarified this event by naming James and John's mother as the one voicing the request, something befitting the cultural setting (Matt. 20:20–22). As part of Jesus' inner group of disciples, along with James and Peter, John was allowed to witness Jesus' actions on certain critical occasions: raising a child from the dead (Mark 5:37–43), his transfiguration (Matt. 17:1–2; Mark 9:2; Luke 9:28–30), and his agony in the garden of Gethsemane (Matt. 26:36–38; Mark 14:32–34; Luke 22:39–40).

John was among the disciples who stayed in Jerusalem in the upper room prior to Pentecost (Acts 1:13–14). John next was seen after Pentecost with Peter in accounts of the healing of a crippled beggar (3:1–11) and the two of them being arrested for proclaiming the gospel (4:1–23).

John is said to have authored the Fourth Gospel (John 21:20–24). In addition to the Gospel of John, tradition attributes the Johannine Letters and, in some cases, the Revelation of John to the apostle John.

John the apostle is understood in his older days to have been a member of a community with disciples of his own, commonly known as the Johannine Community. Within this community the teachings of John about Jesus were preserved and written down. In addition, his correspondence was preserved—1 John, 2 John, and 3 John.

John the Baptist–A Jewish prophet at the time of Jesus, he was the son of priestly parents (Zechariah and Elizabeth), executed by Herod Antipas, and identified as "John" (a common Jewish name), often with the title "the Baptist" or "the Baptizer," the latter possibly being the older title.

John the Baptist unwaveringly maintained that he was sent to introduce the Son (or Chosen One) of God, who would baptize with the Holy Spirit (John 1:33–34; cf. Matt. 3:11–12 pars.). This one was not named, but the Baptist was told how he would know him: "The man on whom you see the Spirit come down and remain is the one" (John 1:33). Thus, the Baptist could claim, "I myself did not know him" (John 1:31), more likely meaning that the Baptist did not know Jesus was the one until the Spirit descended on him (1:32). It is less likely that John meant that he had not met his cousin previously (Luke 1:39–45). Jesus accepts (and validates) the Baptist's proclamation both at the beginning of his ministry (Mark 1:9) and again later (Luke 16:16; John 5:35; 10:41).

After his imprisonment, the Baptist seems less certain of his earlier identification of Jesus as the coming one (Matt. 11:2–3). It should also be noted that John had not disbanded his disciples. After his death, some continued to preach his baptism of repentance as far away as in Ephesus (Acts 18:24–26; 19:1–7). Similarly, Jesus' last description of the Baptist is ambiguous. It is guarded but still complimentary (John 5:32–36; 10:41) and even lofty: "Among those born of women there has not arisen anyone greater than John the Baptist"; however, Jesus' next statement could be interpreted to mean that the Baptist was not yet part of the coming kingdom: "Yet whoever is least in the kingdom of heaven is greater than he" (Matt. 11:11). Like everyone else, John was confused by Jesus' preaching ministry. Jesus was not acting like the Messiah they were expecting (Luke 7:18–20). The Gospels offer no final verdict on the Baptist.

Jonadab–**(1)** The son of Shimeah, David's brother. He devised the scheme that helped his cousin Amnon seduce and rape Tamar, Amnon's half sister (2 Sam. 13:3–5). Later he advised David of Amnon's death (2 Sam. 13:32–35). **(2)** The son of Rekab, he instructed his descendants to become nomadic and not to engage in agriculture or drink wine (Jer. 35 [here spelled as both *yonadab* and *yehonadab* in Hebrew; NIV: "Jehonadab"]). Apparently, he is Jehonadab in 2 Kings 10, where he aids Jehu in the bloody purge of Ahab's family and the extermination of Baal worshipers in Samaria.

Jonah–*See* Jonah, Book of.

Jonah, Book of–The book of Jonah is best known for its "large fish," commonly and mistakenly called a "whale." Jonah is the fifth book among the twelve Minor Prophets. The other eleven books are collections of prophetic oracles, but Jonah is a story about a prophet. In this, it is more like the accounts of Elijah and Elisha in the book of Kings than it is like a regular prophetic book. Jonah tells the story of a gracious God, a reluctant and resentful prophet (who represents God's hard-hearted people Israel), and repentant sinners.

One of the interesting features of Jonah is the way it contrasts Gentiles and Jonah, who apparently functions as a representation of Israel. While Jonah resists the will of God, the Gentiles appear spiritually sensitive. While Jonah sleeps during the divinely sent storm, the pagan sailors anxiously determine the divine purpose behind their trouble. While Jonah refuses and then reluctantly announces the destruction of Nineveh, the king of Nineveh leads his people (and even the animals!) in a ritual of repentance.

In this way, the book rebukes Jonah (and Israel) for its lack of spiritual sensitivity and concern. The book also illustrates God's grace toward the nations. After all, Israel's election was to be a conduit of blessing to the nations (Gen. 12:1–3; cf. Isa. 42:6; 49:6). Although Assyria was a horrible oppressor, God's grace is shown to such people.

In a word, the book of Jonah teaches that God is not just the God of Israel. He is the God of Israel, the God of Nineveh, and the God of the whole universe.

J

Jonathan–**(1)** A priest who served the idolatrous shrine at Dan. According to the best textual traditions, he was a descendant of Moses, though the MT changes "Moses" to "Manasseh" out of embarrassment at the association (Judg. 18:30).

(2) The oldest son of Saul, the first king of Israel. As such, he would have been heir to the throne, but his father's actions compromised the dynasty (1 Sam. 13:13–14). Jonathan's great integrity throws into contrast his father's meanness, particularly in regard to David. Jonathan's military skill and bravery were notable. He led his father's army in victory against the Philistine garrison at Geba (1 Sam. 13:1–7). Even though he was a loyal son, his paranoid father treated him poorly and even suspected him of collaborating with his enemy David (1 Sam. 20:30–33).

Although David and Jonathan were fast friends, they did not conspire against Saul, so Jonathan helped David escape his father's murderous plans. Indeed, Jonathan expressed his deep love for David by handing over to him his robe, tunic, sword, bow, and belt, a gift that may even have indicated his belief that David, not he, should be the next king (1 Sam. 18:4). Even so, Jonathan stayed with his father until the end. Jonathan died at his father's side as they fought the Philistines at Mount Gilboa (1 Sam. 31:1–3). David deeply mourned the loss of his dear friend, whose love was "more wonderful than that of women" (2 Sam. 1:26).

(3) The son of Abiathar, who was high priest at the time of David. Jonathan functioned as a spy for David during the rebellion of Absalom (2 Sam. 15:27, 36; 17:17, 20). He and his father sided with the Adonijah faction, so when Solomon became king, they were disenfranchised from the high priesthood in favor of Zadok (1 Kings 1:42–45).

Joppa–A seaport along the Mediterranean coast just south of the modern city of Tel Aviv that served the Israelites and others during the periods covered by both Testaments.

Joppa's importance is reflected in ancient historical sources, including the Bible. Egyptian and Assyrian texts describe the city's conquest in the fifteenth and eighth centuries BC respectively. Joppa was located within the tribal allotment of Dan (Josh. 19:46) but probably did not come under Israelite control at least until the conquests of David. David's son Solomon used Joppa to import materials from Phoenicia for the temple (2 Chron. 2:16); Jonah (1:3) boarded a ship at Joppa apparently heading to the western Mediterranean; the returnees from exile imported building materials through Joppa to rebuild the temple (Ezra 3:7).

The NT contains several references to Joppa (all in Acts), even after Caesarea had been completed and began to serve as the region's primary port. The early Christian community was present in Joppa, as indicated by the stories of Peter raising Tabitha from the dead (Acts 9:36–43) and of Peter's vision at the home of Simon the tanner in Joppa that led him to preach to Cornelius the centurion at Caesarea (Acts 10:1–11:18).

Joram–King of Israel (r. 851–842 BC), Ahab and Jezebel's son (2 Kings 3:1–3). His reign was troubled by the rebellion of Moab and Syria, two of his father's vassal states. He was killed, along with Ahaziah king of Judah (r. 843–842 BC), in Jehu's purge of the Omride dynasty (2 Kings 9:14–29).

Jordan River–*See* Rivers and Waterways.

Joseph–**(1)** The eleventh son of Judah and the first by Jacob's beloved wife, Rachel (Gen. 30:24; 35:24).

Joseph was Jacob's favorite, and so Jacob "made an ornate robe for him" (37:3). While shepherding with his brothers, Joseph had a dream indicating that he would one day rise to prominence over them. This was too much for his brothers to bear, and so they decided, after some deliberation, to throw him into a cistern and, rather than kill him, sell him to passing Ishmaelite/Midianite merchants (37:25–28).

Upon arriving in Egypt, Joseph was sold to Potiphar, an official of Pharaoh, and then thrown in jail after Potiphar's wife falsely accused him of making sexual advances (chap. 39). While in jail, he accurately interpreted the dreams of Pharaoh's cupbearer and baker (chap. 40). Two years later, he was called upon to interpret Pharaoh's dreams (chap. 41). Joseph's ability to interpret dreams plus his administrative skills saved Egypt from famine, which resulted in his elevation to being "in charge of the whole land of Egypt" (41:41).

It was the famine that brought Joseph's family to Egypt to find food, which eventually led to their warm reunion, though not without some testing on Joseph's part (chaps. 42–45). After Joseph made himself known to his brothers, they reconciled and sent for the elderly

Jacob, who was awaiting news in Canaan. Thus, Jacob and his twelve sons lived in Egypt, and their descendants were eventually enslaved by a king "to whom Joseph meant nothing" (Exod. 1:8).

Joseph died in Egypt and was embalmed (Gen. 50:20–26). The exodus generation took his bones out of Egypt (Exod. 13:19), and he was later buried in Shechem (Josh. 24:32).

(2) The husband of Mary, mentioned only by name in Jesus' birth stories in Matthew and Luke. According to Matt. 1:16, Joseph is a descendant of David, which establishes Jesus' royal bloodline. Luke's genealogy (3:23–38) downplays Jesus' relationship to Joseph. In Matthew, Joseph is a recipient of several divine communications by means of dreams, announcing Mary's conception (1:18–25) and commanding the flight to Egypt (2:13) and the return to Nazareth (2:19–23). In Luke, Joseph takes Mary to Bethlehem to give birth (2:4–7), presents Jesus in the temple for consecration (2:21–24), and brings Mary and Jesus to Jerusalem for the Passover feast when Jesus is twelve (2:41–52).

(3) A Jew from Arimathea, a secret follower of Jesus and member of the Sanhedrin who did not agree to put Jesus to death (Luke 23:50–51; John 19:38). He asked Pilate for Jesus' body, wrapped it in linen, and placed it in his own tomb (Matt. 27:57–60). **(4)** Also known as Barsabbas or Justus, he was one of the two men proposed to take Judas Iscariot's place among the disciples (Acts 1:23).

Joshua–**(1)** The son of Nun and the servant of Moses. As a military commander, Joshua fought against the Amalekites (Exod. 17:8–13). He became an assistant to Moses and accompanied him up and then down the mountain of God (24:13; 32:17). Joshua also kept watch over the tent of meeting (33:11).

Moses sent Joshua, Caleb, and ten others as spies to explore the land of Canaan (Num. 13). At this point, Moses also changed his name from "Hoshea" to "Joshua" (13:8, 16). Because Joshua and Caleb trusted that God would help Israel conquer Canaan, God vowed that only these two of that rebellious generation would enter the promised land (14:30). God also commanded Moses to commission Joshua as his successor. So in the presence of all Israel Moses laid his hands upon Joshua and set him apart for the task (27:15–23).

Joshua's character as a leader is demonstrated throughout the book that bears his name. Among other things, Joshua served as a brilliant military leader (Josh. 1–12), an administrator (Josh. 13–21), and a religious leader (Josh. 24). He led the Israelites across the Jordan and presided at the allotment of land. In all of this, Joshua was "strong and courageous" (1:6), just as God and the people encouraged him to be (1:6–7, 9, 18). At the end of his life he was called, like Moses, "the servant of the Lord" (24:29). The people served God throughout the lifetime of Joshua (Judg. 2:7).

(2) A high priest and one of the leaders of Israel who survived the Babylonian captivity and was permitted by an edict of Cyrus to return to Jerusalem (Ezra 2:2; Neh. 7:7). He was a contemporary of Haggai and Zechariah.

Together with Zerubbabel, Joshua helped to restore worship for the returned exiles (Ezra 3:2) and with the sometimes hazardous work of rebuilding the temple (Ezra 3:8–9; 4:3; 5:2). The high priests descended from him are listed in Neh. 12:10, but other descendants are named as guilty of intermarriage with foreign wives (Ezra 10:18). In the book of Zechariah he is the subject of two visions where he serves as a representative of Israel (Zech. 3:1–10) and as a type of Christ (6:9–15).

Joshua, Book of–The book of Joshua narrates that at God's command, the Israelites, under Joshua's leadership, entered the promised land at its midpoint from the east, just north of the Dead Sea. After undergoing a period of spiritual preparation (1:1–5:12), they defeated the powerful city of Jericho and, after a devastating setback, the small town of Ai. After falling for a ruse, they entered into a treaty relationship with the Gibeonites. This completed their conquest of the middle territory, thus cutting the Canaanite city-states in half.

Then the kings of the independent city-states of the southern portion of the land gathered together and attacked the Gibeonites, now in treaty relationship with Israel. Joshua responded by attacking the armies of the south now outside their walled cities. God the warrior gave them the victory, making his presence known through lethal hailstones and by stopping the sun and the moon in their tracks. Consequently, the kings of the north assembled together, and again God fought for Israel to complete the conquest of the land. Throughout the narrative of the conquest, the emphasis continues to be on God the warrior, the one true power behind Israel's military victories.

Few modern readers venture into the second part of the book (chaps. 13–24), filled as it is with lists of cities and descriptions of tribal boundaries. Nonetheless, this material has great theological significance. As Israel took possession of the land, the ancient promises to Abraham were beginning to come to realization. God's promises were being fulfilled. Through the casting of lots, the individual tribes received their specific inheritance. As their boundaries were rehearsed and the cities in the territories lovingly named, the Abrahamic promises were becoming concrete. We are to imagine great joy and celebration among those who saw the fulfillment of the promises.

The book of Joshua ends with yet another great covenant reaffirmation (chap. 24). With the impending death of their great leader Joshua in sight, the tribes renewed their commitment to follow Yahweh into the new era.

Josiah–The king of Judah (r. 640–609 BC). Although his father (Amon) and grandfather (Manasseh) were evil and worshiped false gods, Josiah "did what was right in the eyes of the Lord and followed completely the ways of his father David, not turning aside to the right or to the left" (2 Kings 22:2). Indeed, according to 2 Kings 21:24–23:30; 2 Chron. 33:25–35:27, no one among the kings of Judah, not even Hezekiah, surpassed Josiah in terms of his piety.

Josiah's name first appears centuries before he was born. First Kings 13:2 records the words of an unnamed prophet who announced that Josiah would destroy the golden calf shrine that Jeroboam I dedicated. This altar was built in the second half of the tenth century BC. The fulfillment of this prophecy is recorded in 2 Kings 23:15–18.

The high point of his religious reform took place in his eighteenth year, when he ordered the purification of the temple. Up to that time, the temple had housed idolatrous objects. During the repair, the priest Hilkiah discovered the Book of the Law. The reaction to this book suggests that it was Deuteronomy or a part thereof, which presumably had been suppressed by the previous wicked administrations.

Although he was a good king, Josiah had a sad conclusion to his life. He was killed in 609 BC when he attempted to block the march of Pharaoh Necho up the coast as the latter tried to bolster the Assyrian forces at Carchemish.

Jotham–**(1)** The youngest son of Gideon (Jerub-Baal). After Gideon's death, Abimelek, who was his son through his concubine from Shechem, sought to gain control of Israel by executing Gideon's seventy other sons and Abimelek's rival heirs. Jotham alone escaped, by hiding. Even as the Shechemites were pronouncing Abimelek king, Jotham emerged atop Mount Gerizim and delivered a message of warning and judgment to the people of Shechem in the form of a parable of trees and a thornbush. His message, though unheeded, was vindicated three years later as God brought judgment on the people of Shechem (Judg. 9:5–57). **(2)** Son of King Azariah (Uzziah) and his successor to the throne of Judah. He reigned sixteen years and did "right in the eyes of the Lord" (2 Kings 15:34). It was during Jotham's reign that Tiglath-pileser III (r. 744–727 BC), king of Babylon, rose to prominence.

Jubal–One of two sons born to Lamech by his wife Adah (Gen. 4:21). He is referred to as "father of all who play stringed instruments and pipes," which probably designates him both as the instruments' inventor and as the founder of the musical arts.

Jubilee–*See* Festivals.

Judah–The fourth son of Jacob (Gen. 35:23). The meaning of his name is debated, but his mother, Leah, links it to "praise" (29:35). He persuaded his brothers to sell Joseph instead of killing him (37:26–27). He also guaranteed the safety of Benjamin when the brothers returned to Egypt to purchase food (43:1–10). In spite of his despicable behavior with his daughter-in-law Tamar (Gen. 38), his father's blessing included the promise of kingship (49:10).

Judah, Kingdom of–Also known as the southern kingdom, the kingdom of Judah began when the northern tribes of Israel seceded from David's kingdom due to the continuation of Solomon's economic policies by his son Rehoboam.

In the tenth and ninth centuries BC, Judah was marked by its ongoing conflicts with Israel to its north. In the eighth century BC, Israel's Omride dynasty exerted considerable influence on Judah, to the extent that around 845 BC Athaliah, daughter of Israel's King Ahab, became the disputed queen of Judah. With the rise of the Assyrian Empire in the late eighth century BC, Israel was destroyed (resulting in a large influx of refugees from the north), and Judah became little more than a vassal state of Assyria, with large tributes due the Assyrians. Soon afterward, King Hezekiah revolted against the Assyrians. This brought major repercussions against Judah, including the destruction of the Lachish fortress and the decimation of most of the population outside Jerusalem, but the kingdom was still left intact (by keeping a king on the throne).

As the Assyrian Empire succumbed to the rising power of the Babylonians, Josiah was able, for a short time, to initiate a reformation in Judah, extending his political power and the boundaries of Judah over much of the land of the former kingdom of Israel. For reasons that are not clear, Josiah attempted to stop an advancing Egyptian army from joining the Assyrians in a bid to defeat the Babylonians, and as a result the Egyptians gained control of the kingdom of Judah. The Egyptians appointed Jehoiakim king, and he remained faithful to Egypt despite Egypt's defeat by the Babylonians. Jehoiakim revolted against the Babylonians, believing that the Egyptians would come to his rescue. The Babylonians came, but the Egyptians did not, and as a result the Babylonians destroyed the city of Jerusalem in 586 BC.

The destruction of Jerusalem effectively ended the kingdom of Judah, which became a province of Babylon. After the Persians defeated the Babylonians, Judah became the Persian province of Yehud and remained so for another two hundred years.

Judah, Tribe of–Descendants of Judah, the fourth son of Jacob. The tribe of Judah had special prominence throughout the OT and was often a political and military leader among the tribes. Joshua 15 describes the geographic territory of the tribe as the land between the Dead Sea and the Mediterranean Sea, with a northern border roughly a straight line from the northernmost point of the Dead Sea directly west to the Mediterranean Sea. The southern border similarly was roughly a straight line from the southernmost point of the Dead Sea west to the Mediterranean Sea. In 2 Kings 23:8, Judah is described as encompassing the area from Geba (about eight miles north of Jerusalem) to Beersheba (about forty miles south of Jerusalem). As a premonarchical tribe, Judah never realized its borders but rather occupied the hill country in the eastern part of the described area. The Philistines controlled the coastal plains areas and hampered Judah's expansion. They were not subdued until the time of David.

Contributing to this independent nature was the hilly geography of the area, which naturally isolated it from the rest of Israel. The tribe of Judah has a relatively short history because even before the time of David's consolidation of the tribes, the distinction between the tribe of Judah and the area that would later become the kingdom of Judah was beginning to be blurred. This was further exacerbated with the revolt of Absalom, which further divided the kingdom ideologically between the northern tribes and Judah. Finally, with the death of Solomon, the tribe's distinction was essentially lost, as the new kingdom of Judah—which encompassed the tribal areas of Judah along with much of Benjamin, Simeon, parts of the old Jebusite kingdom (including Jerusalem), and some of the Philistine kingdom—was formed.

Judaizers–Judaizers continued to observe the Jewish practices of circumcision, the food laws, the Sabbath, and the other feasts and festivals alongside their new faith in Jesus as the Messiah. In particular, they believed that salvation was for the Jews, and that anyone who wanted to experience salvation needed to become aligned with all the OT Jewish practices. Paul, more than anyone else, saw the dangers in this movement and rightly condemned even Peter himself when he saw that Peter and others "were not acting in line with the truth of the gospel"; Paul "said to Peter in front of them all, 'You are a Jew, yet you live like a Gentile and not like a Jew. How is it, then, that you force Gentiles to follow Jewish customs?'" (Gal. 2:14). Judaizers suffered a significant defeat at the council of Jerusalem, when James and the Jerusalem church ruled that Gentiles did not have to be circumcised in order to be saved (Acts 15).

Judas–**(1)** One of the apostles identified as "Judas son of James" (Luke 6:16; Acts 1:13) and "Judas (not Judas Iscariot)" (John 14:22), probably the same person as Thaddaeus (Matt. 10:3; Mark 3:18). **(2)** A leading Jerusalem believer and prophet, "Judas called Barsabbas" (i.e., "son of the Sabbath" or "son of Sabbas"; possibly a relative of "Joseph called Barsabbas" in Acts 1:23). Along with Silas, he was sent with Paul and Barnabas to add verbal testimony to the letter to the Gentile Christians from the apostles and elders after the Jerusalem council (Acts 15:22, 27, 32). **(3)** One of the twelve disciples chosen by Jesus, he betrayed Jesus. *See* Judas Iscariot.

Judas Iscariot–One of the twelve disciples chosen by Jesus (Matt. 10:4). He is identified beforehand as the one who would betray Jesus (Mark 3:19) and is noted as having a devil (John 6:66–71). John further attributes his betrayal of Jesus to Satan (John 13:2, 27), and Luke asserts that before the betrayal Satan entered into Judas (Luke 22:3).

Peter notes that Judas's punishment, death, and abandonment of office were predicted by David in the psalms (Acts 1:15–20). Speaking euphemistically, Peter remarks that Judas went to his own place, no doubt a reference to hell (1:25).

Jude–*See* Jude, Letter of.

Jude, Letter of–Jude clearly asserts the sovereignty of God as a basis for Christian assurance, since it is God who keeps the believer (vv. 1, 24). He speaks in absolute terms of the believer's blamelessness in Christ on judgment day (v. 24). By contrast, those who adhere to another gospel are deviants who violate God's created order. The Christian response is to hold firm to the gospel and reject false teaching vigorously. Jude's defense of the faith is exemplary. He has extensive knowledge of his opponents' literature, myths, and teachings and is able to use this against them. Like Peter, he points his readers back to the eyewitness testimony of the apostles (vv. 3, 17), who predicted such challenges as an ongoing issue for Christians until Jesus returns. He urges believers to work together to maintain right doctrine, behavior, and an attitude of love (vv. 20–21) and to apply the grace of the gospel even to their opponents in hope of their salvation (vv. 22–23). Jude's final words (vv. 24–25) constitute one of the most beautiful and reassuring doxologies of the Bible.

Judges, Book of–Judges covers the period between the death of Joshua and the rise of the monarchy in Israel. It was a turbulent period, as the people did not seem to have any center in God. The bulk of the book narrates the stories of judges, mostly military leaders, whom God sent to Israel on those occasions when they turned to him for help (Othniel, Ehud, Shamgar, Deborah, Gideon, Jephthah, and Samson). The book also includes brief mentions of judges who are not associated with violent actions against the enemy (Tola, Jair, Ibzan, Elon, and Abdon [10:1–5; 12:8–15]), as well as the story of an abortive attempt to establish kingship during this time (Abimelek [chap. 9]).

Indeed, the stories of the judges who were deliverers tend to follow a relatively set pattern. They begin with the sin of the people, which leads to their oppression by a foreign power. The suffering of the people shocks them into realizing that they need God, and they turn to him for help. In such instances, God responds by giving the people a judge, really a military leader, who then delivers them from the power of their oppressors. However, after a period of peace, the people sin again, and another oppressor takes control.

The two stories in the appendix of the book of Judges simply add emphasis to the dark picture painted in the body of the book. These are two accounts of family sins that expand into national tragedies. Individuals from the tribe of Levi, the priestly tribe dedicated to special service to God, play a particularly negative role in the appendix.

This phrase "in those days Israel had no king" (17:6; 18:1; 19:1; 21:25) is repeated throughout the appendix of the book and alerts the reader to one of the major themes of the book. Who will be the human leader of the people of God? The imperfect judges and the fragmentary condition of the tribes as well as their sad spiritual state cause the reader to yearn for something better: the rise of divinely appointed kingship in Israel. The books of Samuel and Kings, which follow, narrate the promise and ultimate failure of kingship, which itself will lead to the expectation of something even more, the Messiah.

Judgment–Of several Hebrew words for "judgment," two are important here.

The word *shepet* is used of God, who brings the judgments upon the Egyptians in the plagues (Exod. 6:6; 7:4; 12:12). Ezekiel prophesies God's judgment on Israel and other nations (e.g., Ezek. 5:10; 16:41; 25:11). The word is also applied to human beings, as the Syrians execute judgment on Israel (2 Chron. 24:24).

The most frequent noun is *mishpat*. Abraham is noted for *mishpat*, "judgment/justice" (Gen. 18:19). God by attribute is just (Gen. 18:25); he shows justice toward the orphan and the widow (Deut. 10:18) and brings judgment on behalf of the oppressed (Ps. 25:9). At the waters of Marah, God makes a judgment, an ordinance for the people (Exod. 15:25). Similarly, the *mishpatim*, "judgments/ordinances," become law for life in Israel (Exod. 21:1). In making judicial judgments, the Israelites are to be impartial (Lev. 19:15), and they are to use good judgment and justice in trade (Lev. 19:35; Prov. 16:11). Israel will be judged for rejecting God's judgments (Ezek. 5:7–8) and worshiping false gods (Jer. 1:16). Those accused of crime will come to judgment/trial (Num. 35:12). The children of Israel come to their judges for judgment (Judg. 4:5). God will bring each person to a time of judgment regarding how his or her life is spent (Eccles. 11:9).

One key word in the NT is *krisis*. It has a range of meaning similar to *mishpat*. In the NT, judgment is rendered for thoughts and words as well as deeds (Matt. 5:21–22; 12:36). Future, eschatological judgment is a key theme for Jesus (Matt. 10:15; 11:22, 24; 12:42), Paul (2 Thess. 1:5), and other NT writers (Heb. 9:27; 10:27; 2 Pet. 2:9; 3:7; 1 John 4:17; Jude 15; Rev. 14:7). Jesus himself will be the judge (John 5:22). The only way to avoid condemnation is by having eternal life in the Messiah (John 5:24).

Another key word in the NT is *krima*. It may refer to condemnation (Matt. 7:2; Rom. 3:8) or to judgment, again including the eschatological judgment (Acts 24:25). *Krima* is the word most frequently used by Paul. He also often presents judgment as already realized (e.g., Rom. 2:2–3; 5:16). In the later epistles judgment may be realized as well (2 Pet. 2:3; Jude 4). James points out that not many should presume to be teachers, because they will be judged more strictly (James 3:1).

JUDGMENT DAY–The book of Revelation concludes with a harrowing vision of final judgment. On that day, when the God of all creation sits on his great white throne and holds court, the dead will rise and answer for their deeds, whether good or bad (20:11–13). The record of each person's conduct appears in books, one of which is the Book of Life (20:12–13). Anyone whose name does not appear in the Book of Life is thrown into the lake of fire (20:15).

The apostle Paul refers to this same event in Acts 17:30–31. All human beings will face their scheduled day in court, as God certified by raising Christ from the dead. It will be a day of wrath, among other things, when God's righteous anger against sin is fully displayed (Rom. 2:5). In the presence of this God, Isaiah proclaimed himself to be ruined because of his sinfulness before the one who is called "Holy, holy, holy" (Isa. 6:1–5). We therefore confess with the author of Hebrews, who says, "It is [and will be] a dreadful thing to fall into the hands of the living God" (Heb. 10:31).

JULIUS–A Roman centurion of the Imperial Regiment who was responsible for conveying Paul and other prisoners from Caesarea to Rome (Acts 27:1). Julius played a small but providential role in showing kindness to Paul, arranging for a ship, ignoring Paul's advice not to sail in dangerous conditions, and saving Paul's life by preventing the other soldiers from killing the prisoners when they shipwrecked (Acts 27:3, 6, 11, 42–44).

JUNIA, JUNIAS–Paul mentions Junia (along with Andronicus) as "prominent among the apostles" (Rom. 16:7 NRSV). Among contemporary evangelicals, debate surrounds both her name and Paul's description of her. Some argue that the name is properly "Junias" and thus masculine, or that Paul terms this person as "well known among the apostles." However, it is likely that the name is "Junia," a feminine name.

JUSTICE–The concept of justice pervades the Bible, especially, though not exclusively, the OT. The biblical concept of justice is an embodiment of two contemporary concepts: righteousness and justice. The former designates compliance with the divine norm, while the latter emphasizes conformity to a societal standard of what is right and equitable. Focusing exclusively on the latter hinders the correct understanding of justice in the biblical sense.

The source of justice is God himself. It flows from his essential character as one who is both just and righteous, whose actions are flawless, perfect, upright, and just (Deut. 32:4; 1 Sam. 12:7; 2 Sam. 22:31; Job 37:23; Ps. 89:14). God is the righteous lawgiver, hence the one who establishes the norm for right conduct (Deut. 4:4–8; Ps. 19:7–9). He requires justice of all his creatures (cf. Gen. 9:5–6; Exod. 21:12, 28–29). God also judges righteously (Gen. 18:25; 1 Kings 8:32; Ps. 9:4, 9; Jer. 9:24) and defends and vindicates the weak and oppressed (Deut. 10:18; Ps. 103:6). The responsibility of maintaining justice in the human community, however, he delegates to its leaders, such as civil magistrates or political officials, and requires them to execute this responsibility with integrity, equity, and impartiality (Deut. 1:16–17; 16:18–20; Ps. 82:2–4; Prov. 31:8–9; John 7:24; 1 Pet. 2:13–14). God's requirement of justice in the human community is not limited to its leaders only; it is incumbent upon everyone therein (Ps. 15:1–5; Mic. 6:8; Zech. 7:9; 8:17; Matt. 23:23).

J

Justification–The word "justification" occurs only five times in the Bible (NIV), but related words comprise significant themes in both Testaments. Justification is often related to a legal setting in both Jewish and Greco-Roman contexts, with its judge, defendant, evidence, criteria for evaluating the evidence, verdicts, and the implications of verdicts. This is a good word picture for justification and is used in the Bible itself. As long as the legal picture is extended to everyday affairs, moral and ethical concerns, and different criteria for evidence evaluation, it is a fine starting point for understanding the doctrine of justification.

Extraordinary justification in the NT is characteristic of the apostle Paul. Luke's report of Paul's synagogue sermon in Pisidian Antioch concludes with a brief overview of extraordinary justification (Acts 13:38–39). Paul proclaims that forgiveness of sins is available through Jesus. Every person trusting in Jesus is being justified "from all things from which you could not be justified by the law of Moses" (NKJV). The forgiveness of sins leads to the verdict "innocent" even though sinners apart from Christ are guilty before God of their unrighteous deeds.

Justification and righteousness are important themes in Paul's letter to the Romans. At the beginning of the letter, Paul declares that he is not ashamed of the gospel because it is the power of God that brings salvation to all who believe. In the gospel the righteousness of God is revealed, a righteousness that is by faith (Rom. 1:16–17). Paul argues in Rom. 1:18–3:20, a section abounding with righteousness language, that all humanity, Gentile and Jew, is under the power of sin (3:10), that no one is righteous (e.g., 3:10–18). All are subject to condemnation (i.e., the declaration of "guilty" and "unrighteous" [cf. 5:16]) rather than justification (i.e., the declaration of "innocent" and "righteous"). No human will be justified before God by works of the law; the law provides knowledge of sin (3:20).

The state resulting from this unrighteousness and sin is God's wrath (e.g., Rom. 1:18). It is into this situation, this sad state of affairs where all have sinned and fallen short of the glory of God, that the righteousness of God, God's saving activity long anticipated in the OT, is revealed in the person and work of Jesus Christ (3:21; 10:3). This righteousness is from God (3:22), a righteousness not related to human fulfillment of Mosaic law or righteousness of one's own (Rom. 3:21; 9:31–32; 10:4; Phil. 3:6, 9; cf. Eph. 2:8–9). This righteousness comes from God by trust in Christ (Rom. 3:22; 5:1; 9:30; 10:10; Phil. 3:9). By trust in Christ, God justifies each human in his freely given grace, whereby the human is redeemed from unrighteousness and sin (Rom. 3:24).

K

Kadesh, Kadesh Barnea–"Kadesh" means "holy" or "sacred." This city was located between the Wilderness of Paran and the Wilderness of Zin in the northeast of Sinai (Num. 20:1; 33:36). It is first mentioned by the name "En Mishpat" ("spring of judgment")—within the context of the war of four kings (Amraphel of Shinar, Arioch of Ellasar, Kedorlaomer of Elam, and Tidal of Goyim) against five kings (Bera of Sodom, Birsha of Gomorrah, Shinab of Admah, Shemeber of Zeboyim, and the king of Zoar)—as the area where Kedorlaomer and his allies defeated the Amalekites. Abraham joined in this conflict to rescue Lot from being taken captive (Gen. 14:1–16).

Hagar, the Egyptian servant of Sarai, fled to a spring in the wilderness between Kadesh and Bered after she was found to have conceived a child by Abram. It was here that she received the promise of Ishmael's birth (Gen. 16:11–14).

Moses sent the twelve spies out from Kadesh to survey the promised land of Canaan. The negative report of ten of those spies caused the people to hesitate to take the land (Num. 13:26). For this lack of faith, the Israelites were required to wander in the wilderness for forty years, spending thirty-eight of those years at Kadesh (Deut. 2:14). It was here that Moses' sister Miriam died and was buried (Num. 20:1).

At Kadesh the Israelites complained about their lack of water (Num. 20:2–5). Moses was instructed by God to take his staff and to tell the rock to yield water (20:6–8). But instead, Moses struck the rock with his staff twice. The water flowed out abundantly, but Moses was punished for his disobedience by not being allowed to bring the Israelites into the land (20:11–12).

The Israelites were encamped at Kadesh when the king of Edom denied them passage through his land (Num. 20:14–21). The site eventually became the southern border of the territory allotted to the tribe of Judah (Josh. 15:1–3).

Kandake–This term, rendered "Candace" in most English versions, is not a proper name but rather a title (similar to "Pharaoh" or "Caesar") borne by a series of Ethiopian queens. The Kandake under whom the Ethiopian eunuch was treasurer (Acts 8:27) was probably Amantitare, who ruled in AD 25–41 in Meroe, located on the Nile in Upper Nubia.

Kedorlaomer–A king of Elam during the time of Abram. He and three other kings subdued five kings rebelling against Kedorlaomer's rule, routing them in the Valley of Siddim, a tar-filled lowland at the south end of the Dead Sea. When Abram heard that his nephew Lot had been captured in battle, he set out with his men and pursued Kedorlaomer, ultimately recovering Lot and the spoils that Kedorlaomer's forces had taken (Gen. 14:1–16).

Kenites–A clan whose name likely is related to an Aramaic word meaning "smith," they were a nomadic group probably skilled as blacksmiths. The land of the Kenites was included in the covenantal promise of God to Abraham (Gen. 15:19). Moses' father-in-law was a Kenite and a priest of Midian (Judg. 1:16; Exod. 3:1), suggesting some kind of relationship between the two. The Kenites played a role as allies of Israel from the Mosaic period through the time of the judges and into the monarchy. The non-Israelite Balaam prophesied the downfall and captivity of the Kenites (Num. 24:21–22). Jael, the woman who killed Sisera by driving a tent peg into his temple, was the wife of a Kenite who had separated from the Kenites (Judg. 4:11, 17). The widespread geographical area of the Kenites' habitations and the individual Kenites who separated and were associated with various peoples support the suggestion that these people were itinerant smiths who maintained their separate identity and were not completely absorbed by other peoples.

K

Kenizzites–A clan whose name probably deriving from Kenaz, a descendant of Esau who was an Edomite chieftain (Gen. 36:11, 15, 42), they were one of the ten peoples whose territory God promised to deliver to the descendants of Abraham (Gen. 15:19). The Kenizzites lived in the Negev, the southern desert area that was part of the territory of Judah after the conquest. They may have been related to the Kenites, who were skilled in metalworking (1 Chron. 4:13–14). Caleb was the son of Jephunneh, a Kenizzite, which apparently indicates marriage with a woman from the tribe of Judah (Num. 32:12; Josh. 14:6, 14; 15:3).

Kerethites–Although their name indicates they may have originated from Crete, they were a Philistine group (Ezek. 25:16; Zeph. 2:5) whose territory apparently was south of the main Philistine region, with an identifiable area within the Negev (1 Sam. 30:14). A group of them served as troops under David (2 Sam. 8:18; 20:7, 23) and were notable for their loyalty to him during Absalom's rebellion (2 Sam. 15:18–23).

Kesitah–A unit of value or measurement ("to divide up, measure"), equivalent unknown, which the NIV renders as "piece of silver." Jacob bought land from the Shechemites for one hundred kesitahs (Gen. 33:19; Josh. 24:32; see NIV mg.). Job received a kesitah from each of his friends and family after his restoration (Job 42:11; see NIV mg.).

Keturah–Abraham's second wife, apparently taken after Sarah's death (Gen. 25:1; called "Abraham's concubine" in 1 Chron. 1:32). She was the mother of six sons of Abraham (including Midian), but they were not regarded with the same favor as Isaac. Abraham gave them gifts and sent them away to the east country (Gen. 25:6).

Kidron Valley–This deep ravine (and the brook running through it during heavy rains) is located between Jerusalem to the west and the Mount of Olives to the east. David crossed the brook as he fled Jerusalem to escape the rebellion of his son Absalom (2 Sam. 15:23). Solomon warned Shimei not to cross the brook or he would die (1 Kings 2:37). Reformer kings destroyed idols here (Asa [1 Kings 15:13]; Hezekiah [2 Chron. 29:16; 30:14]; Josiah [2 Kings 23:4–6]). Jesus crossed the Kidron Valley after the Last Supper on his way to the garden of Gethsemane (Matt. 26:36; John 18:1).

King, Christ as–The NT begins with the claim that Jesus is the "son" or descendant of King David, presupposing the significance of the biblical narrative about the kings of Israel for understanding the gospel (Matt. 1:1, 6; see also Rom. 1:3; 2 Tim. 2:8). The epithet also creates an almost immediate conflict with Herod the Great (Matt. 2:1–2), who was given the title "King of the Jews" by the Roman senate in 40 BC, although he was not a Jew. Herod unsuccessfully attempts to kill the infant king, but Jesus finally is executed by the Roman prefect Pontius Pilate as "King of the Jews" (Matt. 27:37 pars.).

The popular Jewish emphasis on a violent overthrow of Rome probably explains why in the Gospels Jesus himself does not emphasize his kingship in his ministry, except for the explicit fulfillment of Zechariah's prophecy of a humble king riding into Jerusalem on a donkey (Matt. 21:1–9 pars.; cf. Zech. 9:9; see also Isa. 62:11). However, following his resurrection and final instructions to his disciples, Jesus ascends to the right hand of the Father (Luke 24:50–51; Acts 1:6–11; 2:33–36), a coronation ceremony foretold in the psalms (Pss. 2; 110). He presently reigns from heaven (Rev. 1:5; cf. Matt. 28:18), but he will return to make his authority explicit on earth, which includes the dispensing of justice (2 Thess. 1:5–12). His rule is present, however, in the lives of those who obey him and wherever the Holy Spirit is manifested.

King, Kingdom–A kingdom signifies the reality and extent of a king's dominion or rule (Gen. 10:10; 20:9; Num. 32:33; 2 Kings 20:13; Esther 1:22). Some kingdoms were relatively small; others were concerted attempts to gain the whole world.

A kingdom presupposes monarchy, rule by an individual, human authority. Although kings only have as much authority as their armies and the general populace allow, they nevertheless exercise an almost absolute power, which invites either profound humility or hubris. Royal arrogance, unfortunately, is the primary motif characterizing kings in the Bible (e.g., Dan. 3).

God originally intended Israel to be governed as a theocracy, ruled by the one, true, living God (but see Gen. 17:6; Deut. 17:14–20). Israel was to be a "kingdom of priests" (Exod. 19:6), but the people demanded a king (1 Sam. 8:1–22). However, even when God granted their request, God remained King over the king and even retained ownership of the land (Lev. 25:23, 42, 55). The Israelite king was nothing more than God's viceroy, with delegated authority. With few exceptions, most of the kings of Israel and Judah were corrupted by authority and wealth and forgot God (1 Sam. 13:13–14; 15:28; Matt. 14:6–11). But God made a covenant with David, so that one of his descendants would become a coregent in a restored theocracy, the kingdom of God (2 Sam. 7:1–29; Pss. 89:3; 132:11). In contrast to David's more immediate descendants, this coming king would return to Jerusalem humble and mounted on a donkey (Zech. 9:9; cf. Isa. 62:11). The Gospels present Jesus Christ as this king (Matt. 21:1–9 pars.). Those who are likewise humble will inherit the land with him (Matt. 5:5).

Kingdom of God–The kingdom of God is a major theme in the Bible. While the theme is most fully developed in the NT, its origin is the OT, where the emphasis falls on God's kingship. God is king of Israel (Exod. 15:18; Num. 23:21; Deut. 33:5; Isa. 43:15) and of all the earth (2 Kings 19:15; Pss. 29:10; 99:1–4; Isa. 6:5; Jer. 46:18). Juxtaposed to the concept of God's present reign as king are references to a day when God will become king over his people (Isa. 24:23; 33:22; 52:7; Zeph. 3:15; Zech. 14:9). This emphasis on God's kingship continues throughout Judaism and takes on special significance in Jewish apocalypticism and its anticipation of the kingdom of God in the age to come, which abandoned any hope for present history. Only at the end of the age will the kingdom of God come. This idea of God's kingdom is further developed throughout the NT.

Kings, Books of–The books of Kings recount the history of Israel from the time of Solomon (c. 970 BC) to the destruction of Jerusalem in 586 BC. Kings continues the narrative of 2 Samuel, with 1 Kings 1:1–2:11 concluding the story of David. The book has many references back to David (see the promises to David in 2 Sam. 7:1–17; 1 Kings 8:14–26), and prophecy spoken in earlier books reaches its fulfillment only in Kings (e.g., prophecy against Jericho [Josh. 6:26; 1 Kings 16:34] and against the house of Eli [1 Sam. 2:27–36; 3:11–14; 1 Kings 2:27]), showing that it is actually part of a larger historical work beginning in Joshua and ending in 2 Kings.

Kings is primarily concerned with proper worship and faithfulness to God. David set the standard of having a heart "fully devoted to the Lord" (1 Kings 15:3) and is the measuring stick by which all the southern kings are judged. Thus, Solomon is contrasted with David when Solomon falls away from God (1 Kings 11:4), and when Hezekiah trusts in God, he is compared with David (2 Kings 18:3). In northern Israel Jeroboam and Ahab are the models of the degenerate king. Jeroboam is known for setting up golden calves (1 Kings 12:28) in northern Israel to be used in the worship of Yahweh, and Ahab is infamous for his promotion of Baal worship in Israel (1 Kings 16:30–33). In Kings, when kings of Israel are assessed, they are often said to partake in Jeroboam's sins (2 Kings 10:31) or judged for doing "as Ahab king of Israel had done" (2 Kings 21:3; see also 8:18, 27; 21:3). This apostasy culminates in the destruction of the northern kingdom by Assyria in 722 BC (2 Kings 17).

Prophets are prominent in the story of Kings, with both famous (Isaiah, Elijah, Elisha) and anonymous prophets (e.g., 1 Kings 13) playing important roles as bearers of the prophetic word of God. Many short-term prophecies are fulfilled in the story of Kings (e.g., 1 Kings 13:11–32), where the reader can perceive a pattern of prophecy and fulfillment that helps to structure the story of Kings. The way a prophecy is fulfilled is often surprising (see the prophecy of 1 Kings 20:42 and its fulfillment in 1 Kings 22:34–35). The prediction of Josiah's birth and reform centuries in advance ties together the beginning of Kings with one of the most significant events near the end of the book. This shows how historical events are at the mercy of the Lord of history and his prophetic word.

King's Highway–This major ancient Near Eastern trade route began in Heliopolis, Egypt, and cut across the Sinai Peninsula to Aqaba (on the shores of the Red Sea). It then headed straight north to Damascus (on the Transjordan side), ending at Resafa on the upper Euphrates River. It was crucial to the trade of Edom, Moab, Ammon, and Syria. Some of the more important cities along this trade route were Heliopolis (Egypt), Clysma (modern Suez), Eilat, Aqaba, Medeba (modern Madaba), Rabbah/Philadelphia (modern Amman), Gerasa, Bozrah, Damascus, and Tadmor. It is mentioned three times in the Bible (Num. 20:17, 19; 21:22), generally referring to the major route through Moab and Ammon.

Kinnereth–A large lake in northern Israel. It was the eastern border of Canaan and part of the western boundary of the tribal territory of Gad. Kinnereth (Deut. 3:17; Josh. 11:2; cf. NIV mg. for Num. 34:11; Josh. 12:3; 13:27) was also known as the Sea of Gennesaret (Mark 6:53; Luke 5:1), the Sea of Tiberius (John 6:1; 21:1), and the Sea of Galilee (Matt. 15:29; Mark 1:16).

Kinsman–In the OT, a relative within an association of families that together compose a clan (e.g., Lev. 25:48–49). Sometimes translated as "fellow Israelite" or "relative" (Lev. 25:25, 35, 47–48, but not 25:14–15), a kinsman is more literally a "brother" who has certain responsibilities for aiding another of his kin in times of hardship, especially when a portion of the clan's land is involved (see Josh. 13:24–31). The greatest responsibility falls to the closest of kin, the *go'el*, the "kinsman-redeemer" (Ruth 4:1–8 [NIV 1984]; cf. Job 19:25; NIV: "guardian-redeemer").

When hard economic times force a kinsman to sell some property (or rather lease it [cf. Lev. 25:15–16]), the kinsman-redeemer is to redeem what has been sold, thus keeping the land with the clan (25:25). The poorer kinsman may then work for the kinsman-redeemer in order to pay off the debt, though the relationship of both individuals is to remain that of brothers and not become that of a master and a slave (25:39–46). If a poor man sells himself to an alien's clan, a kinsman should purchase him so that he can work within his own clan (25:47–49). The kinsman-redeemer also has the duty of avenging the blood of a murdered kinsman (Num. 35:21).

The role of a kinsman-redeemer in Israelite society is displayed in the book of Ruth. Boaz, a kinsman of Naomi and her widowed daughter-in-law Ruth, meets with the kinsman-redeemer to discuss the acquisition of the land of Ruth's deceased husband, Naomi's son Mahlon. Although the kinsman-redeemer at first agrees to redeem the land (Ruth 4:1–4), he changes his mind when Boaz points out that along with the land would come Ruth and the responsibility to maintain the name of Mahlon (Ruth 4:5–6; cf. Deut. 25:5–10). As next in line, Boaz acquires the land, Ruth, and the responsibility to maintain Mahlon's name on the property (Ruth 4:7–10).

God, who owns all the land (Lev. 25:23–24) and who views all of Israel as his clan (Ps. 74:2), accepts the role of redeemer (*go'el*) (e.g., Ps. 19:14; Isa. 41:14; 43:14).

Kir–The Hebrew name for a Mesopotamian city, Der (the Akkadian word meaning "wall"), which is situated east of the Tigris River, on the border between Sumer and Elam (Persia). This is the location of modern al-Badrah in Iraq. Kir and Elam are portrayed together in military array against Judah in Isaiah's oracle concerning Jerusalem (Isa. 22:6). It is the place from which the Arameans migrated to Syria. This migration, along with emigration of the Philistines from Caphtor, is likened to the Israelites' exodus from Egypt—all declared as being accomplished by Yahweh (Amos 9:7). The descendants of those first immigrants were exiled back to Kir when King Tiglath-pileser III of Assyria conquered Damascus during the reign of King Ahaz of Judah (2 Kings 16:9; Amos 1:5). *See also* Kir Hareseth.

Kir Hareseth–Appears in various forms in the Hebrew text: Kir Heres (Jer. 48:31, 36), Kir Hares (Isa. 16:11), Kir Hareseth (Isa. 16:7), and Kir Haraseth (2 Kings 3:25). All of these forms refer to the same city, Kir Hareseth. Some scholars also identify Kir in Moab (Isa. 15:1) with this city. This was a major fortified stronghold of Moab, possibly the capital. It was mentioned by the prophets Isaiah (Isa. 16:7, 11) and Jeremiah (Jer. 48:31) in their words of judgment for Moab. The city is associated with modern Kerak, located about fifty miles southeast of Jerusalem and eleven miles east of the Dead Sea. It is situated on a strategic hill surrounded by steep valleys. King Jehoram of Israel, King Jehoshaphat of Judah, and the king of Edom joined forces to combat King Mesha of Moab, who had rebelled against the king of Israel (2 Kings 3:5). They were successful in overthrowing the Moabite cities and finally had cornered Mesha in Kir Hareseth. Mesha tried to break through the besiegers with seven hundred swordsmen, but he failed. Finally, he offered up his oldest son, his heir, as a burnt offering on the wall of the city. Because of this, a great wrath came against Israel, and they withdrew from pursuing Mesha and returned to their own land (2 Kings 3:4–27). Later, the Babylonian destruction of Kir Hareseth was prophesied as punishment from the hand of God (Isa. 15:1; 16:7, 11; Jer. 48:31, 36).

Kiriath Arba–*See* Hebron.

Kiriath Jearim–This city, whose name means "city of forests," is also known as Kiriatharim (Ezra 2:25 [NIV: "Kiriath Jearim"]), Baalah (Josh. 15:9), Baalah in Judah (2 Sam. 6:2), Jaar (Ps. 132:6), and Kiriath Baal (Josh. 15:60; 18:14). It is one of the cities of the Gibeonites, who tricked Joshua into a treaty for peace (Josh. 9:17). This city was part of the inheritance allotted to the tribe of Judah (15:9).

The tribe of Dan encamped at Kiriath Jearim when it went out to seek its inheritance (Judg. 18:12). After being returned by the Philistines, the ark of the covenant remained here for twenty years until David moved it to Jerusalem (1 Sam. 6:21–7:2). When David first attempted to relocate the ark from Kiriath Jearim to Jerusalem, Uzzah was struck dead because he touched the ark as it was moved improperly (2 Sam. 6:1–8). The faithful prophet Uriah, a contemporary of Jeremiah, was from Kiraith Jearim (Jer. 26:20). Exiles from Kiriath Jearim returned from the Babylonian captivity with Zerubbabel (Neh. 7:29). The Romans built an outpost over the ruins and garrisoned the Tenth Legion here.

Kish–**(1)** A Benjamite from Gibeah, the son of Abiel and the father of Saul (1 Sam. 9:1–2). According to 1 Chron. 8:33; 9:39, however, Ner was the father of Kish. Some suggest that Kish was the son of Ner and a grandson of Abiel. **(2)** A Benjamite ancestor of Mordecai (Esther 2:5), likely the same person as the Kish of 1 Sam. 9:1–2.

Kishon–A river, whose name means "bending" or "curving," that is fed by several wadis that meet four miles northeast of Megiddo and extends for twenty-three miles. Kishon was the scene of the defeat of Sisera by the armies of Deborah and Barak (Judg. 4:7, 13; 5:19, 21). Later it was the site of Elijah's execution of the prophets of Baal after the contest on Mount Carmel (1 Kings 18:40).

Kittites–According to Gen. 10:4; 1 Chron. 1:7, the Kittites were the descendants of Javan, along with Elishah, Tarshish, and the Rodanites. Most translations read "Kittim," and some treat it as the name of an individual (e.g., ESV, NASB, NKJV). Elishah is identified with the island of Cyprus, Tarshish with the coast of Spain, and the Rodanites may refer to the island of Rhodes. The Kittites are associated with the port of Kition (modern Larnaca) in Cyprus. Kition was a Phoenician port during the reign of Solomon. Biblical references speak of the coastlands (Jer. 2:10; Ezek. 27:6) as well as the land of Kittim (Isa. 23:1, 12 [NIV: "land of Cyprus"]). They were sea peoples vying for trade in the Mediterranean during the second millennium BC. Balaam (Num. 24:24) saw them as a military threat. During the first millennium BC the designation came to refer generally to the Greeks.

Kohathites–Descendants of the Levite Kohath (Num. 26:58–59). During the wilderness journey, they were responsible for transporting the tabernacle and its contents and also for its maintenance (Num. 3–4). Chronicles reports that some of the Kohathites participated in the purification of the temple under Hezekiah (2 Chron. 20:19) and led musical services at the sanctuary during the monarchic period (1 Chron. 6:33; 2 Chron. 20:19; 34:12). But there are no biblical psalms ascribed to this group as there are for their relatives the Korahites. Like the Korahites, they were bakers of the sacred bread during the postexilic period (1 Chron. 9:32).

Korah–A Levite, the son of Izhar, of the family of Kohath (Exod. 6:21; Num. 16:1). Numbers 16 tells how Korah, along with the Reubenites Dathan, Abiram, and On, led a rebellion of 250 Israelite chiefs against Moses and Aaron. They challenged the validity of the Aaronic priesthood and claimed that the entire congregation was holy and fit to perform the priestly functions. They also questioned the authority of Moses over all the tribes because he was not from the tribe of Reuben, the firstborn of Israel.

Moses was then directed by Yahweh to have the congregation move away from the dwellings of Korah, Dathan, and Abiram. Moses went to Dathan and Abiram, and they came

K

out and stood at the entrance of their tents along with their households. Then the ground opened up and swallowed Korah, Dathan, Abiram, and all that belonged to them (their households and their goods). The sons of Korah, however, did not die (see Num. 26:11). Fire came down from Yahweh and consumed the 250 men with the censers. The censers were taken by Eleazar, the son of Aaron, and hammered into plates to cover the altar as a sign to the Israelites that only the descendants of Aaron should draw near to burn incense before Yahweh. *See also* Korahites.

Korahites–The descendants of the Levite Korah, grandson of Kohath (Exod. 6:24; Num. 16:1; 26:11, 58), not the Edomite Korah (Gen. 36:5, 16). They were a guild of temple singers during the monarchic period, residing certainly in the southern kingdom but also possibly in the northern kingdom. They appear in the superscriptions of Pss. 42–49; 84–85; 87–88, which focus on the themes of Zion, rescue from trials and estrangement from God, and God's faithfulness as a refuge for his people. In postexilic times they were gatekeepers at the temple and bakers of the sacred bread (1 Chron. 9:19, 31).

Kozbi–Daughter of a Midianite tribal chief, Zur (Num. 25:15). Kozbi was executed by Phinehas after an Israelite man, Zimri, brought her into his tent in front of Moses and the whole assembly of Israel. After following them into the tent, Phinehas stabbed Zimri and Kozbi with a spear. Their deaths brought an end to a plague in Israel (Num. 25:8–9).

L

Laban–Rebekah's brother (Gen. 24:29) and Rachel and Leah's father (29:16). Laban is involved in the betrothal of Rebekah to Isaac (24:29–51), but he is best known for his deceitfulness and trickery, especially in his dealings with his nephew Jacob (29:1–31:55).

Laban is characterized by this type of self-centeredness throughout the narrative. He continued to cheat Jacob, knowing that Jacob was the key to his own prosperity. Jacob remained in Laban's home for twenty years (Gen. 31:41) but afterward fled with his family and possessions. Laban stopped Jacob on the way, and the two made a covenant (31:43–54).

Lachish–Lachish was in the foothills of the Shephelah, thirty miles to the southwest of Jerusalem, and it controlled the road that ran from the north to the south hill country.

We first hear of Lachish in the OT at the time of the conquest when, under its king Japhia, it formed part of a coalition of five Amorite city-states. Joshua defeated the coalition, killed the kings, and totally destroyed the cities (Josh. 10:1–35; 12:11). After the conquest, Lachish was allotted to the tribe of Judah (15:39), but there is no archaeological evidence of Israelite occupation until the time of the monarchy.

During the monarchy, Lachish was the most important of a double line of fortified cities guarding the western approaches to Jerusalem. It probably was one of Solomon's chariot cities (1 Kings 9:19; 10:26) and certainly was fortified by Rehoboam (2 Chron. 11:9). Amaziah fled to Lachish from a conspiracy against him in Jerusalem, but he was followed and killed there (2 Kings 14:19; 2 Chron. 25:27). When Sennacherib of Assyria invaded Judah in Hezekiah's reign, he besieged and captured Lachish, making it his headquarters for further threats against Jerusalem, which were miraculously averted in answer to prayer (2 Kings 18:13–19:37; 2 Chron. 32:1–22; Isa. 36–37).

After the Babylonians destroyed and burned the city, archaeological evidence suggests it lay abandoned for some time. Nehemiah reports that it was resettled after the return from exile (Neh. 11:30). Archaeological remains from the Persian and Hellenistic periods indicate that this rebuilding (Level I) was in use until the second century BC.

Laish–A city in the upper Jordan Valley in far northern Israel, conquered by the tribe of Dan during the time of the judges and renamed "Dan" (Judg. 18:2, 7–10, 27–29). In Josh. 19:47 the original name is given as "Leshem" instead of "Laish." The location is identified with Tel Dan, the site of several copious springs that form the headwaters of the Jordan River. Excavations show that settlement began about 3000 BC, and a sudden change in the material culture at the time of the judges probably reflects the Danite conquest.

Lamb–*See* Lamb of God.

Lamb of God–A title of Jesus used in the Gospel of John, the Letters of John, and the book of Revelation.

The phrase first appears in John 1:29, where John recognizes Jesus as the one "who takes away the sin of the world," and then again in John 1:36, when John's outcry causes two of his disciples to become the first followers of Jesus.

The main reference is to the Passover feast, during which John places the passion narrative, at which a lamb is slaughtered and eaten. This is a celebration and an echo of the original Passover, in which the Hebrew people smeared lamb's blood on the frames of their doors so that the judgment upon Egypt's firstborn would not strike the Hebrews (Exod. 12:1–15). The salvation that John envisions, however, is different from the exodus narrative in many respects. The enemy from which God's people are saved is no longer a geopolitical oppressor but rather sin itself. Israel has now been expanded to contain the entire human race. The "lamb" has undergone quite a transformation and is now to be identified with the Messiah and even God himself. For NT believers, Jesus' death and resurrection are a completion of the Passover. Rather than saving one people from one specific danger, God's salvation reaches universal efficacy in Jesus Christ, taking away the sin of the world.

The other figure that feeds meaning into "Lamb of God" is the Suffering Servant of Isa. 53. Isaiah says, "He was oppressed and afflicted, yet he did not open his mouth; he was led like a lamb to the slaughter, and as a sheep before her shearers is silent, so he did not open his mouth" (53:7). John perhaps means to fulfill this verse specifically in John 19:9. Lambs were also a part of the cultic worship of Israel and were acceptable for more than one offering (e.g., Lev. 3:7; 4:32; 5:6).

Lamech–**(1)** A descendant of Cain and the husband of both Adah and Zillah, and thus the first polygamist (Gen. 4:18–24). After killing a man who had wounded him, he sings to his wives, boasting of his violent deed. He has three sons: Jabal, the first herdsman; Jubal, the first to play the harp and the flute; and Tubal-Cain, the first metalworker. **(2)** A descendant of Seth, a son of Methuselah, and the father of Noah (Gen. 5:25–31). He prophesied that Noah would bring relief from the curse on the ground. Genesis records his life span as 777 years. He is listed as an ancestor of Jesus (Luke 3:36).

Lamentations, Book of–Though brief, Lamentations is memorable for its powerful poetic expression of deep mourning over tremendous loss.

As Lamentations passionately considers the destruction of Jerusalem, it sees God as an enemy (2:5). Israel has experienced God as a warrior, winning the victory for it against incredible odds. One only has to think of the crossing of the Red Sea or the conquest of Canaan to remember this. However, here God is seen as a warrior against his people.

Lamentations does acknowledge that God has turned his anger against his people in this way because of their sin (1:8, 14, 18; 3:40–42). Even so, this theme, though present, is not the major response to God's punishment. The primary response is to describe the horrible suffering experienced by God's people with the hope of garnering God's pity. Interestingly, the book ends not on a strong note of resolution but with a rather pitiful plea: "Restore us to yourself, Lord, that we may return; renew our days as of old unless you have utterly rejected us and are angry with us beyond measure" (5:21–22).

Even so, the theological message of Lamentations is not purely negative. There is also hope, but it is expressed only briefly. In the heart of the book (3:22–33), the poet expresses his assurance that God does not abandon those who turn to him for help. This section indicates that they do expect that God will forgive them and restore them.

Lamp, Lampstand–Lamps were commonly found in family dwellings (2 Kings 4:10; Matt. 5:15). They also played an important role in the tabernacle and temple (Exod. 25:31–39; 1 Kings 7:49), where they not only illuminated their interiors but also, having the shape of a tree, symbolically evoked memories of Eden. Lamps could be carried or placed on a shelf or stand. Since they could hold only enough olive oil to burn for several hours, a woman who ensured that "her lamp does not go out at night" would have been particularly diligent (Prov. 31:18).

The Bible frequently uses lamp or light metaphorically. It can symbolize life (Job 18:6; 21:17; Prov. 13:9; 20:20; 24:20) or the continuation of the Davidic line (2 Sam. 21:17; 1 Kings 11:36; 15:4; 2 Kings 8:19). Jesus is the light of the world, who gives spiritual life (John 8:12; 9:5; 12:46; cf. 1:9; 3:19). John the Baptist was a lamp illuminating the way to the Messiah (John 5:35). Jesus' followers should shine as lights so that the world can see their good works and praise God (Matt. 5:14–16). God's word is a lamp to guide one's way (Ps. 119:105; Prov. 6:23). God himself is a light who enables people to live in difficult times (2 Sam. 22:29; Job 29:3). In one of Jesus' parables, the foolish virgins who did not prepare enough oil to keep their lamps burning serve as a warning for people to be ready for Christ's return (Matt. 25:1–13).

Land–*See* Earth, Land.

Laodicea–*See* Asia Minor, Cities of.

Last Supper–According to the Gospels and Paul, Jesus had a final meal with his closest followers the night before his crucifixion, which is remembered as the "Last Supper" (Matt. 26:26–29; Mark 14:22–25; Luke 22:15–20; 1 Cor. 11:23–26; cf. John 13:1–30, which mentions the meal but describes and focuses on Jesus washing his disciples' feet and elaborates on the betrayal by Judas Iscariot).

Law–In general, Torah (Law) may be subdivided into three categories: judicial, ceremonial, and moral, though each of these may influence or overlap with the others. The OT associates the "giving of the Torah" with Moses' first divine encounter at Mount Sinai (Exod. 19–23) following the Israelites' deliverance from the land of Egypt, though some body of customary legislation existed before this time (Exod. 18). These instructions find expansion and elucidation in other pentateuchal texts, such as Leviticus and Deut. 12–24, indicating that God's teachings were intended as the code of conduct and worship for Israel not only during its wilderness wanderings but also when it settled in the land of Canaan following the conquest.

More specifically, the word "law" often denotes the Ten Commandments (or "the Decalogue," lit., the "ten words") (Exod. 34:28; Deut. 4:13; 10:4) that were delivered to Moses (Exod. 20:1–17; Deut. 5:6–21). These commandments reflect a summary statement of the covenant and may be divided into two parts, consistent with the two tablets of stone on which they were first recorded: the first four address the individual's relationship to God, and the last six focus on instructions concerning human relationships. Despite the apparent simplistic expression of the Decalogue, the complexity of these guidelines extends beyond individual acts and attitudes, encompassing any and all incentives, enticements, and pressures leading up to a thing forbidden. Not only should the individual refrain from doing the prohibited thing, but also he or she is obligated to practice its opposite good in order to be in compliance.

Laying On of Hands–Laying hands on someone/something has two literal uses and two with symbolic significance. (1) Literally, to take something (e.g., Exod. 22:8–11; Esther 9:10–16; Matt. 26:51; Luke 9:62) or someone—that is, to make an arrest (e.g., Neh. 13:21; Matt. 26:50; Mark 14:46; Luke 20:19; 21:12; 22:53; John 7:30, 44; Acts 4:3; 5:18; 12:1; 21:27). (2) Literally, to lay hands on persons (or things) so as to hurt or destroy them (e.g., Gen. 22:12; 37:22; 1 Sam. 22:17; 24:5–13; 26:9–23; Job 1:12; 9:33; Isa. 11:14; Jer. 15:6; Ezek. 39:21). (3) Laying a hand over one's mouth as a symbolic gesture of amazement (Mic. 7:16) or humility (Job 40:4). (4) A gesture to symbolize the transfer of something from one person to another. Transfer symbolism applications include the transfer of representative identity in sacrificing (e.g., Exod. 29:10–19; Lev. 1:4; 16:21; Num. 8:10–12; 2 Chron. 29:23–24), of authority in commissioning (ordination) (e.g., Num. 27:18–23; Deut. 34:9; Acts 6:6; 13:3), of blessing (e.g., Gen. 48:13–20; Matt. 19:13–15), of life and health (e.g., Matt. 8:3, 15; 9:18, 25, 29; 20:34; Mark 6:5; 7:32–33; 8:22–26; 16:18; Luke 4:40; 7:14; 13:13; 22:51; Acts 8:17; 9:12, 17; 28:8), and of the Holy Spirit and spiritual gifting (Acts 8:17–19; 9:17; 19:6; 1 Tim. 4:14; 2 Tim. 1:6).

Lazarus–**(1)** The brother of Mary and Martha and a resident of Bethany, his story is told in John 11:1–44, and he appears again in John 12:1–11 at a supper given in Jesus' honor. Lazarus is described as one whom "Jesus loved," prompting speculation that he is to be identified as "the disciple whom Jesus loved" (cf. John 13:23; 19:26; 20:2–3, 8; 21:7, 20–24). When an illness led to Lazarus's physical death, Jesus traveled to Bethany and grieved. Four days after Lazarus's death, Jesus asked mourners to remove the tombstone, prayed, and called for Lazarus to come out. Miraculously restored to life, Lazarus emerged from the tomb still wrapped in his grave clothes.

(2) A beggar in one of Jesus' parables (Luke 16:19–31). Generally, characters in parables are literary creations and remain unnamed. The naming of Lazarus may suggest that he was a historical figure, but it may also serve to emphasize the role reversal between the named Lazarus and the unnamed rich man, who overlooked him in life but sought his aid after death.

Leah–The older of Laban's two daughters (Gen. 29:16) and a wife of Jacob (29:23). The biblical description of Leah, whose name means "cow," is not altogether flattering. Her marriage to Jacob resulted from Laban's deception of Jacob, who expected to marry Laban's younger, more attractive daughter, Rachel, which he did soon thereafter (29:26–28). Genesis explicitly says that Jacob loved Rachel more than Leah (29:30). However, God, because Leah was less loved, opened her womb (29:31). As a result, she bore six of Jacob's sons, Reuben, Simeon, Levi, Judah, Issachar, and Zebulun (35:23), and also a daughter, Dinah, who is the subject of Gen. 34. Leah's fertility was the cause of the barren Rachel's strife (Gen. 29–30). Needless to say, a palpable tension is depicted between the two sisters, who also relinquished their maidservants to Jacob as secondary wives for the purpose of having more children. Leah was buried in the cave at Machpelah with Abraham, Sarah, Isaac, and Rebekah (49:30–31).

Leaven–In biblical Israel, leaven used for making bread was a fermented lump of dough saved from an earlier batch. Like sourdough starter, it was added to a new batch of bread, which rose due to the fermentation process. Although the word "yeast" is found in some translations of the Bible, there is no clear evidence that ancient Israel was familiar with it.

Biblical teaching often views leaven as something to avoid. This may be because fermentation was linked with corruption, which to Israel implied uncleanness. Leaven was prohibited during Passover and the Feast of Unleavened Bread to remind the people of Israel that they left Egypt in haste, with no time for bread to rise (Exod. 12:15–20, 39). Leavened bread was forbidden in burnt offerings (Lev. 2:11). It was allowed, however, when brought as firstfruits, a thank offering, a peace offering, or as a wave offering during the Feast of Weeks (Lev. 2:12; 7:13; 23:17). This was possibly because it would be eaten by the worshipers and priests and not burned on the altar.

In the NT, leaven usually retains its negative connotations. Jesus instructed his disciples to beware the leaven—the teaching—of the Pharisees and the Sadducees (Matt. 16:6–12). Paul taught that the sin of one, like leaven, could corrupt the many (1 Cor. 5:6–8). He also wrote that legalism perverts the gospel just as leaven works through a batch of dough (Gal. 5:9). Positively, Jesus compared the growth of God's kingdom to leaven, which invisibly spreads through a large quantity of dough (Matt. 13:33).

Lebanon–Biblical Lebanon is the region that consists of two parallel mountain ranges north of Israel, whose boundaries are very similar to modern-day Lebanon. The south-southwest range is called "Lebanon," and the north-northeast range "Anti-Lebanon" (i.e., "all Lebanon to the east" [cf. Josh. 13:5]). Between the two ranges is the Valley of Lebanon, where the city of Baal Gad was located (Josh. 11:17; 12:7). At the southern end is Mount Hermon, where the snowcapped peaks probably gave rise to its name, which in Hebrew means "to be white" (Jer. 18:14).

Important to the present discussion is the metaphorical use of the term "Lebanon," particularly in the OT, where the term occurs over seventy times (the name does not appear in the NT). First, associated with the mountainous range in the region, Lebanon evokes images of glory, fertility, and abundance. For example, the high elevation gives Lebanon the sense of majesty and glory (Isa. 35:2; 60:13; cf. 2 Kings 19:23), which is further equated with the glory of Jerusalem (Isa. 60:13; Ezek. 17:3, 22; cf. Isa. 10:34; Zech. 11:1) and the restored Israel (Zech. 10:10–11; cf. Jer. 22:6). The melting snows, plus the annual rainfall, ensure abundance and fertility (Ps. 104:16; Song 4:15; Jer. 18:14; cf. Ps. 72:16). The glory of Lebanon is linked with Sharon, Bashan, and Carmel in the territory of Israel (Isa. 2:13; 35:2; cf. Isa. 33:9; Nah. 1:4).

Second, of all the coniferous trees in the forest of Lebanon, cedars receive the greatest attention and have been regularly used to indicate stature and beauty. For example, their sweet smell describes the desirability of renewed Israel (Song 4:11; Hos. 14:7), and their magnificence reminds one of the beautiful trees in Eden (Ps. 104:16; Ezek. 31:9, 16). These towering evergreens are a fitting image of humankind. The righteous people are compared to a cedar of Lebanon (Ps. 92:12–15); the legs of the bridegroom are as noble as the cedars (Song 5:15); and even kings, both Davidic (Isa. 14:8; Ezek. 17:3) and foreign (Isa. 10:34; Ezek. 31:3–18), as well as their subjects (Judg. 9:15), are likened to the cedars of Lebanon. Quite often, they are symbols of political entities (Isa. 2:13; 40:16), such as Judah (Ezek. 17:3), Assyria (Ezek. 31:3), and Tyre (Ezek. 27:5).

Third, Lebanon, together with its forest, is used to depict negative images. For example, all its glories and riches combined are not enough for a sacrificial offering to God (Isa. 40:16). The barrenness of Lebanon is the result of

God's judgment (Isa. 33:9). Prophetic oracles are often associated with Lebanon. The cutting down or withering of the choicest trees is spoken of as judgment against the proud (Isa. 2:13; 33:9; Ezek. 31:15; Nah. 1:4), against the wicked nation of Tyre (Ezek. 27:1–9), and against Judah (Jer. 22:6–7).

Lebbaeus–*See* Thaddaeus.

Legion–A Roman army division consisting of approximately six thousand soldiers. Jesus once encountered a demon-possessed man who, when asked his name, replied, "My name is Legion, . . . for we are many" (Mark 5:9). Jesus cast the evil spirits out of the man and into a herd of pigs, and the entire herd, about two thousand animals, drowned (Mark 5:1–20; Luke 8:26–39). When Peter attempted to fight those who arrested Jesus in the garden of Gethsemane, Jesus ordered him to put away his sword, saying that he could immediately have twelve legions of angels at his disposal (Matt. 26:53).

Lemuel–A foreign king who is the source of a collection of wise sayings that he learned from his mother. The sayings are recorded in the book of Proverbs (31:1–9). The main topics addressed in this teaching focus on drinking and women, two areas that are likely to tempt leaders. Commentators generally agree that the geographical designation of Lemuel's kingdom is Massa, a region of Arabia. Beyond this, little is known concerning the king's identity.

Leprosy–It is important to distinguish biblical leprosy, which was primarily a discoloration of the skin, from Hansen's disease, what we today call "leprosy." Lepers were ritually impure, which caused them to be ostracized by other Israelites and banished from God's presence (Lev. 13:45–46). Jesus cleansed several people from leprosy (Matt. 8:1–4 pars.; Luke 17:11–19). Of special significance is his willingness to touch the leper, which, were it not for the emanating purity of the Holy Spirit, would have rendered him impure. But instead the leper was purified.

Levi–A great-grandson of Abraham, grandson of Isaac, and the third son of Jacob by Leah (Gen. 29:34). Levi's sons were Gershon, Kohath, and Merari (46:11). The Israelite Levites were descended from Levi. Levi's only notable act was a brutal slaughter to avenge his sister Dinah's honor. When Shechem violated Dinah (34:2), Levi and his brother Simeon duped all the males of the city in which Shechem lived by suggesting that they will be able to marry Israelite women, such as Dinah, if they will first be circumcised. As the men of the city lay in pain from the procedure, the two brothers killed the unsuspecting men (Gen. 34). From his deathbed, Jacob cursed Levi and his brother Simeon for their actions (49:5–7).

Leviathan–A transliteration of a Hebrew word (*liwyatan*) that refers to some kind of sea creature, variously mentioned in OT passages extolling God for his mighty work and power (Job 3:8; 41:1–34; Pss. 74:14; 104:26; Isa. 26:20–27:1). Leviathan is usually depicted as a multiheaded and chaotic dragon that wreaks havoc upon the cosmos and can be slain only by the gods. Drawing on this mythological background, Ps. 74:14 praises God because during his work of creation he "crushed the heads of Leviathan and gave it as food to the creatures of the desert." None of these passages implies the actual existence of the creature described; on the contrary, they draw on this material to metaphorically accent God's unique and preeminent authority over the forces of chaos. Revelation may draw on this imagery as well, for God alone is able to destroy the beast and the seven-headed dragon (12:3; 13:1; 19:20) and thereby bring peace to the earth.

Levites–One of the twelve tribes of Israel, descended from Jacob's third son, Levi. The smallest of the tribes during the wilderness wanderings, the Levites provided Israel with the priests who offered sacrifices to God and other ministers who cared for the tabernacle and its sacred furnishings. The term "Levite" is somewhat fluid in meaning, sometimes referring solely to the nonpriestly descendants of Levi and other times including the Aaronic priests. When used in the first manner, the Levites are almost always portrayed as assisting the priests in the service of the tabernacle or temple.

Levitical Cities–Forty-eight cities allocated to the Levites in lieu of a larger inheritance of land like those afforded the other tribes of Israel (Josh. 13:1–14:5). The cities are listed in Josh. 21:1–42; 1 Chron. 6:54–81. Included with the cities on the lists are six cities of refuge designated for fugitives from violent reprisal—the designated duty of the nearest male relative to the deceased—in cases of homicide without intent (Num. 35:6, 13–15). However, in cases of murder the boundaries of these cities offered no protection from the penalty of death. The cities of refuge were located on either side of the Jordan Valley (three on each side), facilitating access from the various parts of the nation.

Leviticus, Book of–The title "Leviticus" means "matters pertaining to the Levites," the priestly tribe of Israel. Thus, topics such as sacrifice and ritual laws that deal with food, skin disease, mildew, and incest are prominent. Although the story line is hard to keep in mind in the midst of all the laws, the Israelites are still wandering in the wilderness, and one of the most notable events of this period is the ordination of the priests and Levites. Most of these topics are foreign and seemingly irrelevant to contemporary audiences. However, as an example, sacrifice and priesthood not only are fundamental theological concepts in the OT but also are important for understanding the NT, where Jesus is proclaimed as the ultimate sacrifice and the ultimate priest. It is impossible to grasp fully this NT teaching without understanding the theology of Leviticus.

Most of the laws of Leviticus concern worship of the holy God of Israel, who is present in the camp. The book of Leviticus thus teaches that God is separate from the present world, and that only those who are also freed from the taint of sin are permitted to enter into his presence. This works out in three areas: the sacrificial system, the priesthood, and purity.

Leviticus describes five sacrifices (chaps. 1–7): the burnt offering, the grain offering, the fellowship offering, the sin offering, and the guilt offering. The description of these sacrifices focuses on performance rather than significance, so modern readers must engage in some measure of guesswork as to what these sacrifices meant to those who performed them. Nonetheless, it is fairly clear that there are three main functions to these sacrifices: atonement, gift, and fellowship. The burnt offering, for instance, emphasizes atonement. When sin has broken the covenant relationship with God, a person may offer a burnt offering in order to atone, or restore relationship. The grain offering is a gift to God the king. Indeed, the Hebrew word for "grain offering" is more literally translated as "tribute." Finally, with the fellowship offering (or peace offering), we see the third important function of sacrifice: fellowship. After all, the priest and the worshipers actually eat most of this sacrifice. Elsewhere in the Pentateuch, we see that more than one type of sacrifice is offered at the same time. The sin and the guilt sacrifices, like the burnt sacrifice, emphasize atonement and the restoration of the covenant relationship.

God is holy, separate from the present sinful world, and the priests live and minister in their realm. They too are holy or set apart. We see this in the very clothes that they are given when they are ordained. The fabric is similar to the fabric of the tabernacle itself. Many of the laws are directed toward the priests themselves. They must be holy because their job is to preserve the holiness of the camp. The story of the sin of Nadab and Abihu (chap. 10) illustrates God's intolerance of priestly irregularities.

A major concern of the laws of Leviticus involves cultic purity, or cleanness. Food (chap. 11), childbirth (chap. 12), skin diseases and mildew (chaps. 13–14), and bodily discharges (chap. 15) are a few of the many topics treated in the book in connection with cleanness. God was present in the camp; the priests had to maintain the camp's purity.

The reason why something or someone was considered clean or pure is not always clear to the modern reader.

Libnah–A town in the Shephelah conquered by Joshua (Josh. 10:29) and then allotted to the tribe of Judah (Josh. 15:42). However, later it is mentioned as one of the Levitical cities allotted to the sons of Aaron (Josh. 21:13; 1 Chron. 6:57). The city revolted from Judean rule under King Jehoram (2 Kings 8:22), but it was again under Judean control during King Hezekiah's reign when it was attacked by the Assyrian king Sennacherib (2 Kings 19:8; Isa. 37:8). Libnah is last mentioned as the hometown of King Josiah's wife, Hamutal, the mother of both Jehoahaz (2 Kings 23:31) and Zedekiah (2 Kings 24:18; Jer. 52:1).

Libya–There are different Hebrew words rendered as "Libya." In the Bible, Libya is sometimes referred to as "Put" (KJV: "Phut") (Gen. 10:6; Ezek. 27:10). Libyans served in the army of Egypt and Ethiopia (2 Chron. 12:3; 16:8; Nah. 3:9). Ezekiel prophesied that Libya (KJV: "Chub") and other nations would be ruined (Ezek. 30:3–5). One of its cities was Cyrene, home of Simon who was forced to carry the cross of Christ (Matt. 27:32; Mark 15:21; Luke

23:26). Libyans were present at Peter's sermon on the day of Pentecost (Acts 2:10).

Life, Book of–An image of heavenly record keeping (Luke 10:20), a book with the names of all who have lived. If one fails to be included among the "righteous," one's name is then erased, "blotted out" (Ps. 69:28; see also Exod. 32:32; Rev. 3:5; 20:15).

Light–God begins his creation with light, which precedes the creation of sun, moon, and stars and throughout Scripture is an unqualified good (Gen. 1:3–5, 15–18; Exod. 10:23; 13:21). In the ancient world, people rarely traveled at night and usually went to bed soon after sunset. The only light in the home was a small oil lamp set on a stand, which burned expensive olive oil. Light is a biblical synonym for life (Job 3:20; John 8:12). Seeing the light means living (Ps. 49:19; see also Job 33:30). Conversely, darkness is often a symbol of adversity, disaster, and death (Job 30:26; Isa. 8:22; Jer. 23:12; Lam. 3:2).

John, who offers perhaps the most profound meditations on light, claims that God is light (1 John 1:5). The predicate appropriates the intrinsic beauty of light, a quality that draws people's hearts back to the author of beauty. For the apostle, light represents truth and signifies God's will in opposition to the deception of the world (John 1:9; 12:46). Light stands for purity and signifies God's holiness as opposed to the unrighteousness of the world (John 3:19–21). Light is where God is, and it radiates from the place of fellowship between God and his creation (John 1:7).

Likeness–The word "likeness" is used in various contexts. The foundational concept of likeness, however, is found in Gen. 1:26: "Let us make mankind in our image, in our likeness." This announces the high status of humans as the pinnacle of God's creation (also Gen. 5:1–2). Genesis 5:3 says that Adam fathered Seth "in his own likeness, in his own image," employing both words found in 1:26. The precise meaning of this has been much debated. Three things are to be noted. First, the expression "let us," versus "let there be," implies a personal aspect. It refers to the human capacity to relate to God in worship and obedience of his word (2 Cor. 4:4; Eph. 4:24). Second, the word "likeness" describes human beings as not simply representative of God but representational. Humankind is the visible, corporeal representative of the invisible, bodiless God. Third, being in God's likeness/image sets human beings apart from everything else that God has made. Humankind's supremacy and uniqueness are emphasized.

Linen–A type of cloth woven with fibers from the flax plant. Common in Palestine and known for its strength, coolness, and remarkable whiteness, linen served many uses, especially in the tabernacle (Exod. 25–28; 35–36; 38–39). Both wealthy and common people wore linen garments, but luxurious fine linens were worn by the rich (Isa. 3:23; Ezek. 16:10; Luke 16:19; Rev. 18:12, 16). In NT times, the Jews extensively used linen burial shrouds, as at Jesus' burial (Matt. 27:59; Mark 15:46; Luke 23:53; John 19:40; 20:5–7).

Lintel–The horizontal beam on top of a doorway. God commanded the Israelites to sprinkle lamb's blood on their doorposts and lintels in preparation for the first Passover, the sight of which would identify the Israelite houses and spare them the destruction that God would bring upon the Egyptians (Exod. 12:7, 22–23 NRSV [NIV: "top of the doorframe"]). The lintel was part of a five-sided doorjamb for the olive-wood entrance door of Solomon's temple (1 Kings 6:31 NRSV). Birds would roost on the lintels of Nineveh's deserted doorways after its destruction (Zeph. 2:14 KJV).

Lo-Ammi–A transliteration of the Hebrew phrase "not my people" (*lo' 'ammi*), the name of Gomer and Hosea's third child (Hos. 1:9). While this name symbolizes a stunning reversal of Israel's relationship with God, a message of hope follows this declaration, promising that the child's name will be changed to "Ammi," "my people" (Hos. 2:23). *See also* Lo-Ruhamah.

Locust–*See* Insects.

Lo Debar–A city that lay just east of the Jordan River. Scholars have suggested that Debir, mentioned in the tribal allotment to Gad (Josh. 13:26), may be the same city (the Hebrew here for "of Debir" is spelled with the same consonants as the Hebrew for "Lo Debar"). Mephibosheth was staying in Lo Debar at the house of Makir son of Ammiel when David was seeking to show kindness to a member of Saul's family after Saul's death. Summoned by David, Mephibosheth traveled southwest to Jerusalem and settled there, "because he always ate at the king's table" (2 Sam. 9:1–13).

As David and his men fled from Absalom during Absalom's rebellion, they came to Mahanaim, in the vicinity of Lo Debar, where Makir son of Ammiel came with Shobi son of Nahash from Rabbah of the Ammonites (present-day Amman, Jordan) and Barzillai the Gileadite from Rogelim to offer the weary fugitives a wide variety of provisions (2 Sam. 17:27–29). The northern kingdom later conquered Lo Debar in an unrecorded battle, which led to an ungodly joy and pride that Amos criticized (Amos 6:13).

L

Log–*See* Weights and Measures.

Logos–A Greek term meaning "word," a title given to Jesus Christ that indicates his preexistent divine nature and his identity as the climactic revelation of God (John 1:1, 14; 1 John 1:1; Rev. 19:13).

Lois–The devout Jewish Christian maternal grandmother of Timothy. Paul praises her faith as a legacy to both her daughter Eunice and her grandson (2 Tim. 1:5).

Lord–The Hebrew word for "Lord," *yhwh* (usually pronounced "Yahweh"), occurs more than 6,800 times in the OT and is in every book except Ecclesiastes and Esther. "Yahweh" is God's personal name and is revealed as such in Exod. 3:13–14. God tells Moses to declare to the Israelites in Egypt, "I am has sent me to you" (3:14). The Hebrew behind "I am" connotes active being; the Lord is the one who is there for his people and, in the book of Exodus, does so through miraculous events (14:13–14). This demonstrates the close association between one's name and one's character in the ancient world.

In the NT, the majority of occurrences of "Lord" (*kyrios*) appear in Luke-Acts and the writings of Paul, perhaps due to the predominantly Hellenistic audiences of these texts, who would know well its Greco-Roman connotations. As for Paul, the use of "Lord" by Luke may point to the deity of Jesus. In the Lukan birth narrative, Elizabeth wonders why "the mother of my Lord should come to me?" (Luke 1:43; cf. 7:19; 10:1). In Acts 1:21 the name "Jesus" is preceded by the definite form of "Lord," reflecting an oft-repeated confessional title in Acts and Paul (Acts 15:11; 20:35; 2 Cor. 1:2). According to some, if Matthew intends a divine connotation by his use of the term "Lord," it is more oblique. For instance, in Matt. 4:7 Jesus quotes Deut. 6:16, where "the Lord" is Yahweh and not Jesus (cf. Matt. 9:38).

For Paul, a particularly important component of the lordship of Jesus is his resurrection, through which he becomes "the Lord of both the dead and the living" (Rom. 14:9; cf. 1:4), and his return marks the "day of the Lord," which in the OT was the day of Yahweh (1 Thess. 5:2; cf. 5:23). Exactly how Jewish Christians could attribute such a status to Jesus and yet maintain a strict monotheism remains a matter of considerable debate. Is Christ included in the identity of the Godhead, or is he an intermediary figure (of which Second Temple Judaism had many), possessing a quasi-divine status? If Jesus is an intermediary figure, then his authority to do that which only Yahweh can (such as forgiving sins and fulfilling roles originally referring to God) suggests a very close identification between Yahweh and Jesus himself.

Lord's Day–*See* Sabbath.

Lord's Prayer–This prayer, found but not named as such in Matt. 6:9–13; Luke 11:2–5, is a version of the Jewish Qaddish prayer revised around the theme of the kingdom of God and is a paradigmatic model of prayer given by Jesus to his followers.

The prayer can be broken up into a number of petitions. First is the petition addressed to God as Father and self-sanctifier. God is invoked as Father, and his name represents both his character as a loving father and his authority as the master over all creation. The prayer is theocentric, and it reads literally "let your name be sanctified," which is a plea that God's holiness will become more and more evident.

The second petition is for God to finally establish his kingdom. The "kingdom of God" is more akin to God's reign, rule, or government. It is referred to rarely in the OT (e.g., Dan. 2:44; Obad. 21); much more prominent is the theme of God as "king."

Third is the petition for daily provision of physical needs. The "daily bread" petition looks to God as the provider and caregiver of his people. Elsewhere in the Sermon on the Mount/Plain, Jesus preaches dependence on God as a means of escaping the worry and lure of wealth and money (Matt. 6:25–33 // Luke 12:22–34). Bread was a powerful symbol for sustenance and life (e.g., Prov. 22:9; Lam. 2:12; John 6:35, 48; Sir. 29:21; 34:25).

Fourth is the petition for divine forgiveness in coordination with mutual forgiveness among the community of Jesus' followers. The prayer does not ask God to forgive persons who then in turn forgive others; rather, in reverse, the prayer implies that God forgives in the same way that humans forgive each other (Matthew) or on the basis of humans forgiving each other (Luke).

Fifth is the petition to be spared eschatological tribulation and the malevolence of Satan. The prayer could constitute a plea for help in the face of personal trials and struggles in the believer's life and in the journey of discipleship (e.g., 1 Cor. 10:13; James 1:2), or it could denote a request to be kept from the eschatological ordeal that will precede the final and full establishment of the kingdom of God (e.g., Mark 14:36, 38; Rev. 3:10).

Lord's Supper–The meal of remembrance instituted by Jesus Christ during the Passover celebration (Matt. 26:26 pars.) prior to his crucifixion. While with his disciples, Jesus took bread and broke it and said, "Take and eat; this is my body" (Matt. 26:26). After this, he took wine, gave thanks, and then gave it to them and said, "This is my blood of the covenant, which is poured out for many for the forgiveness of sins" (Matt. 26:28). After Jesus' death and resurrection, this breaking of bread and drinking of wine in his memory became a primary symbol of Christianity (1 Cor. 11:26). The apostle Paul had harsh things to say to the Corinthian church for inappropriately celebrating the Lord's Supper, for some went hungry while others became drunk (1 Cor. 11:17–26), and thus the whole point of Jesus' sacrificial death was lost.

Lo-Ruhamah–A transliteration of the Hebrew phrase "not pitied," or "not loved" (*lo' rukhamah*), it occurs in Hos. 1:6 as the God-given name of Gomer and Hosea's second child, a daughter. Lo-Ruhamah's name indicates the perilous status of the northern kingdom before God in the time leading up to the exile. This pity carries the connotation of God's motherly compassion for Israel, as other instances of the root word for this name are translated "compassion" and "womb." Significantly, in Hos. 2:23 God changes her name from "Not Loved" to "Loved," showing his endangered but enduring compassion on Israel.

Lot–A nephew of Abraham (Gen. 11:27–14:16) and a resident of Sodom (18:16–19:38). When God called Abraham to go to Canaan and leave his family behind, he still took Lot with him. Lot, however, proved to be a burden to his uncle in several aspects. Tensions arose between their herders, so Abraham graciously allowed Lot to choose his land first. Lot selected the fertile area near Sodom, just south of the Dead Sea, where he settled. When Lot and his family and property were captured in battle by King Kedorlaomer of Elam and his three allies, Abraham rescued his nephew, defeated the coalition, and restored Lot's entire household.

When forewarned of God's intentions to destroy Sodom, Abraham attempted to convince God not to destroy the city if ten righteous people could be found there. Presumably, Abraham's efforts were based on his desire to protect Lot, who resided there. Apparently, not even ten righteous people were found in the city, but before the city was to be destroyed, two angels were sent to warn Lot and his family. When the messengers arrived, Lot would not allow them to spend the night in the town square, to protect them from the men of Sodom. All the men of the city surrounded Lot's house and demanded that the guests be brought out so that they could have sex with them. Instead, Lot offered his two daughters. However, the angels struck the Sodomites outside with blindness, which frustrated their efforts, so they left Lot, his guests, and his daughters alone.

The next morning, the angels forced Lot and his wife and daughters out of the city, and then God rained sulfur and fire from heaven on Sodom and Gomorrah. Lot's wife refused to heed the angel's warning, and when she turned back to look, she became a pillar of salt. Lot's two daughters, fearing that they would be unable to marry, got their father drunk, committed incest, and became pregnant, thus Lot became the father (and grandfather) of Moab and Ben-Ammi, ancestor of the Ammonites (Gen. 19:37–38). Jesus used the example of Lot, his wife, and the city of Sodom to illustrate how the kingdom of God will come (Luke 17:28–32). Lot's sins relative to his daughters apparently are ignored in 2 Pet. 2:7, where he is called "righteous Lot."

Lots–Possibly made of stone or wood, lots apparently were shaken or tossed from a container to help make decisions, on the assumption that God(s) directed the outcome (Prov. 16:33). Many peoples throughout the ancient Near East cast lots. Surprisingly, available sources do not make clear what exactly the lots were and how people cast them.

One finds the casting of lots in both Testaments in a number of different situations. Sometimes the lot was used to uncover truth about who had committed some wrong in the past (Achan [Josh. 7:14, 18]; Jonathan [1 Sam. 14:41–42]). Other times Israelites used lots to determine God's choice (Saul as king [1 Sam. 10:20–21]; Matthias as a disciple [Acts 1:26]) or to divide things, such as tribal allotments of land (Num. 26:55–56). Tasks and services could be determined by casting lots (Levitical service at the temple [1 Chron. 26:13–16]; who would live in rebuilt Jerusalem [Neh. 11:1]). Non-Israelites also cast lots to determine guilt (Jon. 1:7), divide property captured in war (Nah. 3:10), and determine the best date for an event (when to massacre Jews [Esther 3:7; 9:24]). The concept that God directed the course of events also led to figurative use of the term "lot" as one's fate in life (Ps. 16:5; Jer. 13:25). *See also* Urim and Thummim.

Love Feast–The "love feast" (*agapē*) was a common meal shared by early Christians in conjunction with their celebration of the Eucharist, the Lord's Supper. The term occurs in Jude 12 and, in some manuscripts, 2 Pet. 2:13. This type of gathering for fellowship evidently was a common feature of early Christianity. Jude exhorts the community to which he writes to rid itself of the immoral, godless people who "are blemishes at your love feasts." A similar group appears to be infiltrating the "love feast" referred to in 2 Pet. 2:13. In 1 Cor. 11:17–34 is described some form of a common meal that included the Eucharist (cf. Acts 20:7), and it is likely that the Eucharist was very much a part of the love feasts mentioned in Jude and 2 Peter.

Love of God–The Bible uses the metaphor of marriage to describe God's covenant relationship with his people (Isa. 54:5–8). This metaphor captures the intimate character of the relationship that God desires to have with his people. Marriage is the most intimate human relationship in two ways. First, marriage is a relationship in which knowledge is the most intimate. A spouse can see many of the flaws that are hidden from others. Thus, each spouse must accept and love the other for who that person is, in spite of his or her imperfections. Second, the depth and passion of the expressions of love are most intimate in marriage. Consequently, there is no greater pain than that caused by unfaithfulness to this covenant.

Sadly, as the story of the OT unfolds, God's "wife" betrays him. How so? His people worship idols in their hearts (Ezek. 14:1–5). Because God is jealous for the exclusive love of his people, idolatry is spiritual unfaithfulness. God wants both the allegiance and the affection of their hearts to be reserved exclusively for him. The people continue the formalities of worship, but their hearts have turned away from God. The book of Hosea illustrates the sense of betrayal that God feels when his people are spiritually unfaithful. God tells Hosea to marry a woman who will be unfaithful to him. Subsequently, she leaves Hosea for one lover after another. This story is intended to give God's people a vivid picture of how painful their spiritual betrayal of him is. His heart is crushed by the rebellious and idolatrous condition of his people. Hosea's wife ends up on the market as a prostitute, and God tells him to buy her back and love her again.

The story of God's love for his people is expanded by what the Father did centuries later when he sent Jesus to pay the ransom for the sins of his people so that they might be healed of their rebellion and receive eternal life (John 3:16; 17:24). The death and resurrection of Christ were necessary because sin had to be atoned for. This love is a free gift that comes to the one who trusts in Christ for forgiveness of sin and a new heart. The new heart inclines one to please God. The gift of the Spirit enables one to bear the "fruit" of love (Gal. 5:22–23). As Abraham's engrafted children (Gal. 3:7), believers are called by God to live as pilgrims on their way to a heavenly promised land (Heb. 11:9–10; 1 Pet. 2:11).

Christ modeled genuine love by serving us (Mark 10:42–45). His love should motivate us and enable us to practice sacrificial service toward others (Matt. 22:39; 1 John 3:16). It should also cause us to practice forbearance, long-suffering, and forgiveness toward those who wrong us (Matt. 18:21–35). It should cause us to repay evil with good (Rom. 12:14). Our love for truth should motivate us to act in the best interests of others (1 Cor. 13:4–8) in the hope that they may become reconciled to God (2 Tim. 2:24–26).

Lucifer–Some translations (e.g., KJV), following the Vulgate, translate as "Lucifer"

(Lat. "light-bearer") the epithet of the king of Babylon in Isa. 14:12 (NIV: "morning star"). Originally, the term referred to Venus (the "shining one"), which appears as one of the brightest objects in the night sky. In medieval Christian theology Isa. 14:3–23 was interpreted (in light of Luke 10:18) as a history of the figure called "Satan" or "the devil" in the NT and in a handful of OT texts. As a result, the name "Lucifer" was applied to this figure.

Luke–*See* Luke, Gospel of.

Luke, Gospel of–The Gospel of Luke has been traditionally known as the Gospel that portrays Jesus as the perfect man who came to bring salvation to all humanity (2:32; 3:6; 4:25–27; 9:54; 24:47). This thematic focus is captured in the frequent use of the words "gospel" or "good news" (1:19; 2:10; 3:18; 4:18, 43; 7:22; 8:1; 9:6; 16:16; 20:1) and "salvation" (1:69, 71, 77; 3:6; 19:9). By way of contrast, the word "salvation" does not appear in either the Gospel of Matthew or the Gospel of Mark. The author aptly summarizes the focus of the third Gospel in Luke 19:10: "For the Son of Man came to seek and to save the lost."

Luke is unique among the Gospel writers in declaring his purpose at the outset of his writing. He informs his readers that he has used several sources available to him when composing his Gospel. These sources were written by "eyewitnesses and servants of the word" and were already being handed down to others (1:2). Luke maintains that he investigated these sources thoroughly and gleaned from them the information that he then put into an "orderly account" (1:3). Luke's purpose was to instruct Theophilus about the "certainty" of the events that surrounded the life and ministry of Jesus the Messiah (1:4). The chronological data provided in 1:1–4; 2:1; 3:1–2 reinforce this purpose.

Luke records more information about the birth and early years of Jesus than any of the other canonical Gospels. The account begins some four hundred years after the last events of the OT with the angel of the Lord announcing to Zechariah the birth of John the Baptist, the forerunner of the Messiah (1:11). Six months later the angel Gabriel announces to Mary the birth of Jesus, the heir to the throne of David who "will reign over Jacob's descendants forever" and whose "kingdom will never end" (1:26, 31–33). Historically, Luke ties Jesus' birth to the reign of Caesar Augustus and his ministry to the rule of Tiberius Caesar (2:1; 3:1). His interpretation of these events is that God has prepared salvation "in the sight of all nations" (2:30–31) and "all people will see God's salvation" (3:6). In these early chapters the narrator links Christ's humanity and his salvation purpose all the way back to Adam (3:23–38). Yet the humanity of Jesus is carefully balanced with his deity. The term "Lord" is used nineteen times in reference to God at the beginning of the Gospel, but it is also applied to Christ in 2:11. In Gabriel's announcement to Mary, the child is called "the Son of the Most High" (1:32). He was recognized as such also by demons (4:34, 41; 8:28), by Jesus himself (10:22; 22:70), and by God the Father (3:22; 9:35).

The writer also accentuates the ministry of the Holy Spirit by revealing that key characters such as John the Baptist, Mary, Elizabeth, Zechariah, Simeon, and Jesus were filled with the power of the Spirit (1:15, 35, 41, 67; 2:25–27; 3:16, 22; 4:1, 14, 18; 24:49).

In chapters 4–9, Luke chronicles Jesus' ministry in Galilee. His early miracles and ministry serve as messianic credentials that substantiate his authority and message, demonstrating that he is the Messiah and that in him the kingdom of God has drawn near (1:33; 4:40–43; 6:20; 7:28; 8:1, 10; 9:2, 11, 27, 60, 62). Prayer is a discipline that Jesus practices from the beginning of his ministry to the end (3:21; 5:16; 6:12; 9:18, 29; 22:32, 40–42). The Messiah's initial popularity is countered by jealousy and growing opposition, especially from the religious establishment (4:28–30, 36–37; 5:15, 20–22, 26; 6:11; 7:16, 30, 39). In these early chapters, Jesus calls his disciples and begins to prepare them for the full implication of what it will mean to follow him (5:1–11, 27; 6:12–16).

In 9:51–19:27, Luke records an extended account of Jesus' journey toward Jerusalem from Galilee. This section contains several parables and narratives not found in any of the other Gospels. Throughout this section the narratives, miracles, and parables point to a Messiah who came expressly to seek out and save the lost, especially the disadvantaged, the underprivileged, and those outside the Jewish establishment, such as the Samaritans, women, children, notorious sinners, and the poor. Luke records more about Jesus' view of money and material things than any other book of the NT. Joy and salvation characterize the ministry of the Messiah (1:14; 8:13; 10:17, 21; 13:17;

15:5, 9, 32; 17:15–16; 19:37). But the establishment in Israel, particularly the Pharisees, rejects his claims (4:28–29; 5:21–24, 30; 6:7–11; 7:30, 39; 8:36–37; 9:7–9, 53; 10:25, 29; 11:15–16, 37–53; 13:31; 14:1; 15:1; 16:14). As this rejection and opposition increase, he begins to reveal to his followers his coming death and calls them to an ever-increasing commitment to his purpose and person (9:22–26, 57–62; 10:1–3; 14:25–35).

Once Jesus reaches Jerusalem, the stage is set for the official presentation of the king to the nation (19:28–44). But rather than joyfully accepting the Messiah, the nation's leaders hotly contest his claims (19:39; 20:1–2, 19, 20, 27). Jesus weeps over the city (19:41) and announces its future judgment and his future coming in glory (21:6–36). Luke brings his narrative of Jesus' ministry to a close by recording the events that lead up to the death of the Messiah: the betrayal by Judas (2:1–6), the Last Supper (22:7–23), Jesus' arrest (22:47–53), the denial by Peter (22:54–62), Jesus' crucifixion, and finally his death and burial (23:26–56). However, this unjust and tragic end is trumped by Jesus' glorious resurrection (24:1–12). Luke alone records the postresurrection conversation on the Emmaus road, where Jesus reveals himself to the two disciples and subsequently explains his victory over death (24:25–26, 45–49). The account closes with the Messiah's ascension into heaven (24:50–53), preparing the reader for the sequel that continues in the book of Acts (Acts 1:1–5).

Lydia–A "dealer in purple cloth" "from the city of Thyatira" who believed and was baptized when Paul came to Philippi on his second missionary journey (Acts 16:14). Luke records that Lydia was "a worshiper of God," a designation that he uses elsewhere only in Acts 18:7. The description is similar to "God-fearing," which applied usually to devout Gentile followers of the Jewish God (Acts 10:2; 17:17).

Paul shared the gospel with Lydia and her female companions at a place of prayer near a river. God "opened her heart to respond to Paul's message" (Acts 16:14), and Lydia became the first named Christian convert in Europe. Lydia then invited Paul and his companions to stay at her house (16:15), indicating that she was a woman of some means. Paul, Luke, and the rest of the missionary band seem to have stayed at Lydia's house until they left Philippi (16:40).

Lydia's hometown, Thyatira, over two hundred miles from Philippi, is home to one of the seven churches of Revelation (Rev. 2:18–29).

Lysias–A Roman tribune who provided a military escort for Paul's transportation to Caesarea to appear before the governor Felix (Acts 23:23–25). Lysias sent a letter to Felix explaining the reasons for the arrest. Subsequently, Felix suspended judgment on Paul's case until Lysias arrived in Caesarea (Acts 24:22).

Lystra–*See* Asia Minor, Cities of.

M

Maakah–The mother of Abijah, second king of Judah, also identified as the daughter of Absalom (1 Kings 15:2 [NIV: "Abishalom," a variant of "Absalom"; see NIV mg.]) and the wife of Rehoboam (2 Chron. 11:20–21). In 2 Chron. 13:2 too she is identified as the mother of Abijah, but here as a descendant of Uriel of Gibeah, likely avoiding a negative reference to Absalom. She is also mentioned as the grandmother of the third king of Judah, Asa. Asa deposed his grandmother because she worshiped false gods (1 Kings 15:10; 2 Chron. 15:16).

Macedonia–The territory linking the Balkans with the Greek Peninsula. Though its borders shifted through its history, Macedonia stood north of Thessaly and mainland Greece, east of Epirus, and west of Thrace. Its topography is dominated by mountains and coastal plains along the Thermaic Gulf and northern shore of the Aegean Sea.

From the time that Paul received his vision of a Macedonian man calling him to proclaim the gospel (Acts 16:9), Macedonia played a significant role in Paul's journeys and the early church. He established three churches there and wrote three letters to them (Philippians and 1–2 Thessalonians). Several of Paul's companions were Macedonians, including Sopater, Aristarchus, Secundus, and Jason (Acts 17:4–7; 20:4). In Paul's correspondence he spoke of Macedonia at least sixteen times in six different letters. Answering the Macedonian call during his second missionary journey, Paul arrived in Philippi, which was "a Roman colony and a leading city of that district of Macedonia" (Acts 16:12). There he led Lydia, the first known European convert, to the gospel. After casting an evil spirit out from a slave girl, Paul and Silas were imprisoned, and they led the Philippian jailer and his family to the gospel (Acts 16:16–40). Lydia and the Philippian church generously supported Paul's ministry and the church in Jerusalem (Rom. 15:26–27; 2 Cor. 8:1–5; Phil. 4:15–17).

Paul then traveled along the paved Via Egnatia to Thessalonica, where he established a church composed of "some" Jews and a "great many" Greeks and leading women (Acts 17:4). He stayed there at least three Sabbaths before opposition drove him to Berea (17:1–9), where many examined the Scriptures and more eagerly accepted the gospel (17:11). From Berea, he left Macedonia for Athens and Corinth in Achaia. Paul later returned to Macedonia during his third missionary journey (20:1–6).

Machpelah–A cave at Hebron purchased by Abraham as a burial place for his wife Sarah (Gen. 23). Machpelah became the burial site for most of the patriarchs and their wives. Abraham and Sarah, Isaac and Rebekah, and Jacob and Leah were buried in the same cave (Gen. 49:31). By starting this family burial site in Canaan, Abraham marked Canaan as the ancestral homeland for future Israelites, as opposed to Ur or Harran, where his family had lived earlier.

Magdalene–*See* Mary.

Magog–*See* Gog and Magog.

Magor-Missabib–After being punished as a false prophet by the priest Pashhur, Jeremiah renames him "Magor-Missabib," which means "terror on every side" (Jer. 20:1–6). Since the priest epitomizes the sins of Judah as well as the Judeans' resistance to God's message through Jeremiah, he also represents the punishments that will come not just to him but to all Judeans.

Mahanaim–This city, whose name means "two camps," was named by Jacob when he met the angels of God right before his encounter with God at Peniel (Gen. 32:2). After the conquest and settlement, Mahanaim was located on the border of Gad and Manasseh and set aside as a Levitical city (Josh. 13:26, 30; 21:38). It served as the capital for Saul's son Ish-Bosheth until his murder led to the unification of David's kingdom (2 Sam. 2:8, 12, 29). David sought refuge here when pursued by Absalom and used it as his headquarters when fighting against his son (2 Sam. 17:24, 27; 19:32). Solomon made it the seat of one of his administrative districts (1 Kings 4:14). Situated east of the Jordan and north of the Jabbok Rivers, its precise location remains uncertain. According to Song of Songs 6:13 the woman asks the man why he looks at her as on the "dance of Mahanaim," which is better translated the "dance of two war camps." Whatever the translation, the context makes it clear she is referring to the fact that he cannot take his eyes off of her.

Maher-Shalal-Hash-Baz–A name whose precise translation is disputed but means something close to "the spoil speeds, the prey hastens." God commanded Isaiah to give one of his sons this name as part of a prophecy that Judah would soon be delivered from the Syro-Ephraimite threat (Isa. 8:1–4). The prophecy found fulfillment when Assyria plundered Ephraim in 733 BC and conquered Damascus in 732 BC. The birth of Maher-Shalal-Hash-Baz can therefore be dated with some confidence to 734 BC.

Mahlon–The first husband of Ruth the Moabite (Ruth 4:9). When famine struck Judah, Mahlon traveled with his family to Moab in search of food (1:1–2). There, Mahlon took Ruth as his wife, but he died after living about ten years in Moab (1:4–5). Ruth's second husband, Boaz, maintained Mahlon's name and property by taking Ruth as his wife and fathering a son on Mahlon's behalf (Ruth 4:10, 17; cf. Deut. 25:5–6).

Malachi, Book of–Malachi is one of the last prophetic voices in the OT. It is likely for this reason that it is the last of the twelve Minor Prophets, the last book in the entire OT, at least in the English (based on the Septuagint) order of books. In the Hebrew canon it concludes the second of three parts of the Hebrew Bible, the Nebiim, or Prophets.

Since the prophet comes from the period after the judgment of the exile, it is sad to see that he addresses the sin of the people and thus threatens further judgment. Intriguingly for the Christian, the book ends with the promise that Elijah will come before that great day of judgment, a promise that the NT authors see fulfilled in the person of John the Baptist, whose ministry comes as a prelude to the appearance of Jesus Christ (Matt. 3; Mark 1:1–8; Luke 3; John 1:19–34).

As is typical of the biblical prophets, the covenant is at the center of Malachi's prophetic proclamation. Three covenants in particular are cited: the covenant with Levi (2:8), the covenant of the fathers (2:10), and the covenant of marriage (2:14). God's people have violated these covenants. God loves them in a special way, but they do not return that love. Their sin breaks their covenant relationship; thus the prophet warns them of the possibility of future judgment. Even so, God is also a redeemer, and so Malachi also presents a vision of future restoration. He foresees a day when God will intervene in the world, bringing victory to those who obey God's laws and punishment to those who do not (3:1–5; 4:1–6).

Malta–An island of strategic importance about sixty miles south of Sicily in the Mediterranean Sea, Malta was famous in ancient times for shipwrecks. It is the location of Paul's shipwreck on his way to Rome for trial (Acts 28:1). After the shipwreck, Paul was stuck on the island for three months and was taken care of by the island's residents. Here Paul was bitten by a viper but suffered no ill effects. Today St. Paul's Bay is the accepted location of the shipwreck.

Mammon–A transliteration of the Greek rendering of the Aramaic noun *mamōnas*, which signifies "wealth" and is translated by the NIV as either "money" or "worldly wealth" (Matt. 6:24; Luke 16:9, 11, 13). Only Jesus uses the term in the Bible. Since the early church retained the Aramaic, it is likely that the word itself retains significance. Jesus warns, "You cannot serve both God and mammon [NIV: 'money']" (Matt. 6:24 KJV). In this case, mammon is placed in parallel with God, which suggests that it has taken on the significance of an idol. Like all false gods, mammon promises pleasure to worshipers but ultimately enslaves them. However, Jesus also uses the term in a broader sense, "worldly wealth," where it is not necessarily possessive and can be mastered and shrewdly redirected to advance the kingdom of God (Luke 16:9, 11).

Mamre–A site near Hebron where Abraham settled (Gen. 13:18; 14:13; 18:1). Its location was identified in association with "great trees." Abraham acquired a burial area in Machpelah, described as being in the vicinity of Mamre (23:17, 19; 25:9; 49:30; 50:13), where a number of the patriarchs and matriarchs were buried. Later, Isaac lived in the area (35:27). A man named "Mamre" helped Abraham defeat a coalition of eastern kings (14:24); perhaps the site was named after him.

Manasseh–**(1)** A son of Joseph and grandson of Jacob. He was Joseph's firstborn, but Jacob blessed Ephraim his brother over Manasseh (Gen. 48:13–20). Joseph received a double portion over his brothers because the two tribes of Israel traced their ancestry back to him through his two sons. In keeping with Jacob's blessing, the tribe of Ephraim overshadowed the tribe of Manasseh (*see* Manasseh, Tribe of).

(2) The fourteenth king of Judah (698–642 BC), his rule was so wicked that it secured the doom of his kingdom (2 Kings 20:21–21:18; 2 Chron. 32:33–33:20).

The account of his rule in 2 Kings focuses exclusively on the perversity of his leadership and the negative consequences that flowed from his reign. Many kings promoted or tolerated the worship of pagan deities, but only Manasseh is associated with the practice of child sacrifice, offering up his own son (2 Kings 21:6). He "also shed so much innocent blood that he filled Jerusalem from end to end" (2 Kings 21:16). Such sin elicited a strong reaction from God, who announced that he would "wipe out Jerusalem as one wipes a dish, wiping it and turning it upside down" (2 Kings 21:13).

Interestingly, 2 Chronicles, a postexilic historical work, expands our knowledge about this king to include the account of his end-of-life conversion. This story is absent from 2 Kings because that book tells the history of God's people in order to explain why they were in exile. Manasseh's change of life happened when his Assyrian overlords, angry over an unspecified offense, dragged him to their capital with a hook in his nose. Because of Manasseh's change of heart, God blessed the remainder of his reign, although God did not reverse the judgment of destruction that his sins evoked against Judah (Jer. 15:4).

Manasseh, Tribe of–One of the twelve tribes of Israel. Along with Ephraim, it is traced to Joseph rather than Jacob. Manasseh and Ephraim were the two sons of Joseph, each of whom received a tribal portion (resulting in Joseph getting a double portion) along with the sons of Jacob (Gen. 48). At the same time, Manasseh, the older brother, lost his birthright to Ephraim when Jacob crossed his hands and put his right hand on Ephraim when giving the inheritance. This follows the tradition in Genesis of the younger son supplanting the older. The exact status of the tribe of Manasseh is a complex issue, but it is clear that Manasseh and Ephraim were rivals for status and power during the early northern kingdom monarchy. Based on the land descriptions in the book of Joshua, Manasseh would have had the largest tribal territory. It also uniquely had land on both sides of the Jordan River, which may have contributed to Manasseh being one of the least unified tribes in Israel. Many of the most important cities of the northern kingdom were located in Manasseh, including the capital cities of Shechem and Samaria and the major military cities of Megiddo and Jezreel.

Manger–A container or basin that holds the feed for domesticated farm animals such as cattle, sheep, or horses (Prov. 14:4; KJV: "crib"). For want of a room at the inn, Mary wrapped Jesus in cloths and placed him in a manger shortly after his birth (Luke 2:7). Nearby, shepherds were told by angels that Christ the Lord had been born in Bethlehem, and that the sign to them would be a baby wrapped in cloths lying in a manger (2:12). They journeyed to Bethlehem and found Jesus just as the angels had said (2:16).

Manna–Miraculous, heavenly bread that God rained down for the Israelites to eat during their wilderness wanderings (Exod. 16:1–35). The word *manna* likely comes from the Hebrew phrase *man hu'* ("What is it?"), reflecting the Israelites' puzzled response to God's gracious provision (Exod. 16:15). It resulted from a layer of dew that fell on the camp at night and evaporated in the morning, leaving fine flakes resembling frost on the ground (Exod. 16:14;

M

Num. 11:9). Manna was white like coriander seed and tasted like wafers made with honey and olive oil (Exod. 16:31; Num. 11:8). It could be crushed into a paste and then either boiled or baked (Num. 11:8).

Manoah–The father of Samson (Judg. 13:24; 16:31). The Samson story in Judges begins with an introduction of his father, Manoah, a Danite from Zorah whose wife was barren (13:2). An angel of the Lord appears to Manoah's wife, who is nameless throughout the narrative, and declares that she will have a son and that he must be raised as a Nazirite. Manoah requests that the Lord send this "man" again, which he does. Manoah and his wife finally realize the identity of the angel of the Lord after he has disappeared in the flames of their sacrifice (13:9–21).

Mara–Meaning "bitter," this name is chosen by Naomi following the death of her husband and sons. Upon her return to Bethlehem, she requests that the people call her "Mara" because God has made her life bitter (Ruth 1:20–21).

Marah–An Israelite encampment in the Desert of Shur (Exod. 15:23) that was reached following a three-day journey after the Israelites crossed the Red Sea (Num. 33:8). The name means "bitter" and describes the bitter, brackish water found there. The Israelites complained against Moses because of the water, and God instructed him to cast a tree into the water, which made it sweet and drinkable. The exact location of Marah is debated and cannot be established with certainty.

Maranatha–Paul uses this term in 1 Cor. 16:22 (KJV; see NIV mg.) when closing that letter. "Maranatha" is actually two Aramaic words, *marana tha*, meaning "Our Lord, come." Two similar passages suggest that eschatological hope may be a key factor. Near the end of Revelation, the author writes, "Come, Lord Jesus" (Rev. 22:20). Also, Paul, discussing the Lord's Supper, refers to proclaiming the Lord's death "until he comes" (in 1 Cor. 11:26). Both of these references are in Greek, but they suggest the future aspect to the early Christian's hope for Christ's return, which fits with translating "Maranatha" as "Come, O Lord." The use of an Aramaic formula indicates an early reference to Jesus in a way normally reserved for God.

Mark, Gospel of–Mark's Gospel is a fast-paced, action-packed narrative that portrays Jesus as the mighty Messiah and Son of God, who suffers and dies as the servant of the Lord—a ransom price for sins. Mark's purpose is to provide an authoritative account of the "good news" about Jesus Christ and to encourage believers to follow Jesus' example by remaining faithful to their calling through persecution and even martyrdom. A theme verse is Mark 10:45: "For even the Son of Man did not come to be served, but to serve, and to give his life as a ransom for many."

Mark's narrative may be divided into two main parts. The first half of the story demonstrates that Jesus is the mighty Messiah and Son of God (1:1–8:26); the second half reveals that the Messiah's role is to suffer and die as a sacrifice for sins (8:27–16:8).

Unlike Matthew and Luke, Mark does not begin with stories of Jesus' birth but instead moves directly to his public ministry. As in the other Gospels, John the Baptist is the "messenger" who prepares the way for the Messiah (cf. Isa. 40:3; Mal. 3:1). John preaches a baptism of repentance for the forgiveness of sins and announces the "more powerful" one, the Messiah, who will come after him (1:7). When Jesus is baptized by John, the Spirit descends on him, empowering him for ministry. After his temptation (or testing) by Satan in the desert, Jesus returns to Galilee and launches his ministry, proclaiming the "good news" (gospel) that "the time has come. . . . The kingdom of God has come near" (1:15).

During his Galilean ministry, Jesus demonstrates extraordinary authority in teaching, healing, and exorcism. He calls fishermen from their occupation, and they drop everything and follow him (1:16–20). He claims authority to forgive sins (2:10) and authority over the Sabbath command (2:28). He reveals power over natural forces, calming the sea (4:35–41), walking on water (6:45–52), and feeding huge crowds with a few loaves and fishes (6:30–44; 8:1–13). The people stand "amazed" and "astonished" (a major theme in Mark) at Jesus' teaching and miracles, and his popularity soars.

Jesus' authority and acclaim provoke opposition from the religious leaders of Israel, who are jealous of his influence. The scribes and Pharisees accuse him of claiming the prerogative of God (2:7), associating with undesirable sinners (2:16), breaking the Sabbath (2:24), and casting out demons by Satan's powers (3:22). They conspire to kill him (3:6).

A sense of mystery and awe surrounds Jesus' identity. When he calms the sea, the disciples wonder, "Who is this?" (4:41), and King Herod wonders if this might be John the Baptist risen from the dead (6:16). Adding to this sense of mystery is what has come to be called the "messianic secret." Jesus silences demons who identify him as the Messiah and orders those he heals not to tell anyone what has happened. This secrecy is not, as some have claimed, a literary device invented by Mark to explain Jesus' unmessianic life; rather, it is Jesus' attempt to calm inappropriate messianic expectations and to define his messianic mission on his own terms.

The critical turning point in the narrative comes in 8:27–33, when Peter, as representative of the disciples, declares that Jesus is the Messiah. The authority that Jesus has demonstrated up to this point confirms that he is God's agent of salvation. Yet Jesus startles the disciples by announcing that his messianic task is to go to Jerusalem to suffer and die. Peter rebukes him, but Jesus responds, "Get behind me, Satan! . . . You do not have in mind the concerns of God, but merely human concerns" (8:33). Jesus will accomplish salvation not by crushing the Roman occupiers, but by offering his life as a sacrifice for sins.

In the second half of the Gospel, Jesus journeys to Jerusalem, three times predicting that he will be arrested and killed (8:31–32; 9:31; 10:33–34). The disciples repeatedly demonstrate pride, ignorance, and spiritual dullness (8:33; 9:32–34; 10:35–41), and Jesus teaches them that whoever wants to be first must become last (9:35); that to lead, one must serve (10:45); and that to be Jesus' disciple requires taking up one's cross and following him (8:34).

When he comes to Jerusalem, Jesus symbolically judges the nation by clearing the temple of merchants (11:15–17) and by cursing a fig tree (representing Israel), which subsequently withers (11:12–14, 20–21). He engages in controversies with the religious leaders (chaps. 11–12) and teaches the disciples that Jerusalem and the temple will be destroyed (chap. 13). Judas Iscariot, one of Jesus' own disciples, betrays him. Jesus is arrested and brought to trial before the Jewish Sanhedrin, which finds him guilty of blasphemy. That council turns Jesus over to the Roman governor Pilate, who accedes to his crucifixion (chaps. 14–15).

The crucifixion scene in Mark is a dark and lonely one. Jesus is deserted by his followers, unjustly condemned, beaten by the soldiers, and mocked by all. Apparently deserted even by God, Jesus cries out from the cross, "My God, my God, why have you forsaken me?" (15:34). Yet the reader knows by this point in the story that Jesus' death is not the tragedy that it seems. This is God's means of accomplishing salvation. Upon Jesus' death, the curtain of the temple is torn, opening a new way into God's presence. The Roman centurion at the cross cries out, "Surely this man was the Son of God!" (15:39). The death of the Messiah is not a defeat; it is an atoning sacrifice for sins. Three days later Jesus rises from the dead, just as he has predicted. When Jesus' women followers come to the tomb, the angel announces, "He has risen! He is not here" (16:6). Jesus the Messiah has turned tragedy into victory and has defeated sin, Satan, and death.

Mark, John–Patristic evidence identifies John Mark (Mark) as the author of the second Gospel. The house of Mark's mother, Mary, served as a place for early Christians in Jerusalem to meet and pray (Acts 12:12). Mark followed his cousin Barnabas from Jerusalem to Antioch and joined Barnabas and Paul on their first missionary journey (Acts 13:5), working with them in Cyprus. When they left for the mainland of Asia Minor, Mark returned to Jerusalem (13:13). Later, when Paul and Barnabas wished to return to the churches that they had established, Barnabas wanted to take Mark again, but Paul objected because of Mark's prior desertion (Acts 15:38). Paul and Barnabas differed so markedly on this point that they parted ways, with Barnabas and Mark going to work in Cyprus, while Paul and Silas traveled elsewhere. The NT tells nothing more of Mark for ten years. The former disagreement apparently was resolved, for Mark was later present with Paul in Rome and received Paul's recommendation to the Colossian church (Col. 4:10). Paul also speaks positively of Mark's use in ministry (2 Tim. 4:11). It is quite likely that Mark was associated with Peter during this same period in Rome (1 Pet. 5:13).

Marriage–*See* Family.

Mars Hill–A rocky hill in Athens near the Acropolis, also known as the Areopagus. Mars was the Roman god of war; Ares was his Greek equivalent. "Areopagus" means "Hill of

Ares." The hill is mentioned as the place where Paul answered questions posed by Athenian philosophers (Acts 17:19), though most contemporary translations use "Areopagus," which also referred to the supreme moral tribunal in Athens. It is unclear whether Paul actually spoke from the hill itself, but it is certain that he was addressing the council.

Martha–The sister of Mary and Lazarus, who lived in Bethany (John 11:1–2). In Luke 10:38–42 and John 12:1–8, Martha is depicted as interested only in preparing and serving food to her houseguest, Jesus. As such, she is contrasted with Mary, who spends her time with Jesus. In Luke 10 Martha even enlists Jesus' help in requesting that Mary join her in completing the necessary work. Jesus, however, declares that Martha is "worried and upset about many things" (v. 41) and Mary's actions are more desirable. In a separate account (John 11:1–44), Mary and Martha send word to Jesus that their brother, Lazarus, is sick. Jesus delays the journey to Bethany in order to demonstrate the glory of God, which results in his raising Lazarus from the dead. Upon hearing of Jesus' eventual arrival, Martha goes out to meet him and questions the timing of his journey. In their dialogue, Jesus confirms Martha's faith in him (John 11:27), but before Jesus performs the miracle, she experiences doubt.

Mary–**(1)** The most important Mary of the NT is the mother of Jesus, who becomes pregnant through the Holy Spirit while still a virgin. In contrast with Matthew's birth narrative, where the emphasis falls on Joseph, Luke's focuses on Mary. Luke's Gospel introduces Mary as the one to whom God sends the angel Gabriel (1:26–27). Gabriel announces that Mary will be the mother of the Messiah from David's line, who will reign over the house of Jacob and have a unique father-son relationship with God. Mary responds in humble obedience as "the Lord's servant" (1:29–38). When she visits her relative Elizabeth, Mary breaks forth in the Magnificat, a song praising God for caring for the humble, humbling the mighty, and remembering his covenant with Abraham (1:46–55).

After the birth of Jesus and the visit from the shepherds, Mary "treasured up all these things and pondered them in her heart" (2:19). An old man, Simeon, announces that although Jesus will be a light of revelation for the Gentiles and Israel's glory, Mary will be deeply grieved, and her soul will be pierced by a sword (2:35). This is the first hint in Luke's Gospel that Mary's child, the Messiah, will suffer. In the only episode from Jesus' childhood in the Gospel, Mary scolds her son for remaining in the temple while his family traveled back to Galilee (2:48). In Luke's Gospel, Mary is a humble and obedient woman who reflects deeply about her experiences surrounding the birth of Jesus and cares greatly for him as well. Beyond the birth narratives, Mary does not figure as a prominent character in the Gospels. In John's Gospel, Jesus speaks sternly to his mother when she wants him to perform a miracle before his "hour has . . . come" (2:4); however, at the crucifixion, Mary is present, and Jesus places her into the care of the Beloved Disciple (19:25–27). Later traditions about Mary's immaculate conception, perpetual virginity, sinlessness, and roles as co-mediator of salvation and answerer of prayer are not taught in the Bible.

(2) Another Mary mentioned in the Gospels is the sister of Martha, who is praised by Jesus for not busying herself with domestic duties as Martha does, but rather sits at the feet of Jesus, "listening to what he said" (Luke 10:39–40). This same Mary is mentioned on another occasion as the one "who poured perfume on the Lord and wiped his feet with her hair" (John 11:1–2; cf. 12:1–8). The Synoptic Gospels record a similar event in which a woman, left unnamed, anoints either the feet of Jesus (Luke 7:36–50) or his head (Matt. 26:6–13; Mark 14:3–9). With the exception of Luke, it seems as though John, Matthew, and Mark are recording the same event. In each of these three, Jesus associates the anointing with the preparation of his body for burial.

(3) Mary Magdalene makes a brief appearance during the ministry of Jesus, and Luke describes her as one who had been cured of seven demons (Luke 8:2). It is quite unlikely that she is the "sinful" woman of the preceding narrative (7:37–50), an association that has given rise to the erroneous belief that Mary Magdalene was a prostitute. She is the first to witness the empty tomb (John 20:1). Likewise, she is the first to see the resurrected Lord and is commanded to go and tell the disciples about his resurrection (John 20:11–18; cf. Matt. 28:1; Mark 16:1–6; Luke 24:1–10). She is even present for the crucifixion (Matt. 27:56) and the burial of Jesus' body (Matt. 27:61).

(4) Mary the mother of James and Joses (Matt. 27:56; Mark 15:40) is one of two other

Marys who, like Mary Magdalene and Mary the mother of Jesus, appear at the crucifixion. She may be the same person as #5.

(5) Mary the wife of Clopas (John 19:25) is the second of the two other Marys who, like Mary Magdalene and Mary the mother of Jesus, appear at the crucifixion. She may be the same person as #4.

Massah–A location on the journey toward Mount Horeb (Sinai) where the Israelites grumbled against God because they had no water. Moses called the place Massah ("testing") and Meribah ("quarreling") because of their complaining (Exod. 17:7). Still, at God's direction, Moses struck the rock at Horeb, and water flowed out. All subsequent references to Massah in the biblical text are about this incident (Deut. 6:16; 9:22; 33:8; Ps. 95:8). Subsequent references to Meribah, however, concern another incident (e.g., Num. 20:13, 24; Deut. 32:51; 33:8). *See also* Meribah.

Matthew–*See* Matthew, Gospel of.

Matthew, Gospel of–Matthew's Gospel appears first in almost every extant witness to the NT, and it was considered the preeminent Gospel by the early church. It is the Gospel most quoted by the early church fathers. Of the four Gospels, Matthew's is most oriented toward a Jewish audience.

The miraculous beginnings of Jesus (1:1–4:11). Jesus' genealogy and childhood show him to be the fulfillment of OT prophecy. His baptism demonstrates this fulfillment; his forty days of testing in the desert identify him with Israel.

Ethical teachings and miracles (4:12–10:42). This section begins with a geographical change, as Jesus returns to Galilee. Having instructed his disciples, he sends them out as an extension of his own mission.

Confrontation and reactions (11:1–16:20). This section also involves a change of geography. Jesus first is questioned by John's disciples, then by the Pharisees, and finally by the people in his own town. The questions are resolved by Peter's confession.

The messiah must suffer (16:21–20:28). This is the third section that begins "from that time on Jesus began to. . . ." Jesus explains to his disciples that he will die at the hands of the Jews but be raised on the third day. This section includes the transfiguration and many parables concerning judgment and reward. The climax is at the end, when Jesus declares that he has come "to give his life as a ransom for many."

Jesus claims authority and receives praise (20:29–25:46). Another geographical shift occurs, as Jesus and his disciples leave Jericho. Jesus acknowledges the title "Lord, Son of David," cleanses the temple, and argues with the Pharisees about the source of his authority. The parables concern sonship and responses to authority. The Pharisees try to entrap Jesus. Jesus teaches about authority, then rebukes the Pharisees. Chapter 24 describes the consequences of the ultimate rejection of authority. The climax is the parable of the sheep and the goats.

The death of Jesus (26:1–27:66). Matthew's Gospel has built-in intensity up to the passion narrative. This section builds again within itself, from the anointing of Jesus in Bethany to the hush as the tomb is closed and sealed.

The resurrection of Jesus (28:1–28:20). The accounts of the resurrection and postresurrection appearances are brief but significant and contain several details not found in the other Synoptics.

Matthias–The apostle chosen to replace Judas Iscariot (Acts 1:15–26). After Judas's death, Peter called upon the approximately 120 believers in Christ to designate another apostle, one who had been with the apostles from the time of Jesus' baptism by John to Jesus' ascension. The choice of a new apostle would fulfill David's words concerning Judas (see Pss. 69:25; 109:8b). After praying for God's guidance, the believers cast lots, and Matthias was chosen over the other nominee, "Joseph called Barsabbas (also known as Justus)" (v. 23).

Meat Sacrificed to Idols–Meat, or food, sacrificed to idols refers to animal offerings to pagan deities. Consumption of this meat was prohibited for Gentile converts by the Jerusalem council (Acts 15:29; 21:25) because it was linked to pagan worship, especially when combined with sexual immorality (cf. Ezek. 18:5–6, 15; 22:9; Rev. 2:14, 20). However, the ban eventually created problems for Christians (e.g., dining out), as most meat markets in the Greco-Roman world obtained their inventory from local temples (Rom. 14:21; 1 Cor. 8; 10:18–33). Paul therefore modified the teaching by upholding the prohibition in cases where eating the meat violated

M

one's conscience, harmed Christian witness, or caused a weaker Christian to stumble, but relaxing it in cases where partaking was a social courtesy or otherwise separated from pagan practice.

Medes, Media–Media was a country located to the south of the Caspian Sea, to the east of the Tigris River and Zagros Mountains, to the west of Parthia, and to the north of Elam. The northern portion of the modern country of Iran occupies the same area, although at the height of Media's power, the kingdom included parts of modern-day Iraq and Turkey. The best-known city was Ecbatana. The people of Media, the Medes, lived on the steppes and were known among the neighboring countries for their excellent horses.

The Medes and Media figure most prominently in the biblical books of Daniel and Esther. Daniel began his exile and rise to fame under the Babylonians but finished his prophetic career under the rule of the Medo-Persian Empire. Both Daniel and other prophets foresaw this change of governance and the Medes' part in the conquest of Babylon (Isa. 13:17; 21:2; Jer. 51:11, 28; Dan. 5:28). The importance of the Median contribution to the culture and governance of the new empire is manifest in the fact that the Medo-Persian ruler Darius is called "the Mede" in Dan. 11:1 due to his mixed ancestry (cf. Dan. 9:1). Indeed, the idea that an established law could not be changed even by the king himself (cf. Esther 1:19) seems to be a Median contribution to the empire and was the political tool used by Daniel's enemies to have him thrown into the lions' den (Dan. 6:8, 12).

Many of the exiled Jews from Judah chose to settle in Media instead of return to Judah, and a portion of their story is recounted in the book of Esther. Esther 1:3 notes that "the military leaders of Persia and Media" were among those present at a great feast of Ahasuerus (Xerxes I). Similarly, in Esther 1:14 the king's closest advisers are labeled "nobles of Persia and Media," indicating the unity of the two countries and the cultural mix among the high officials. The same was true of the high-ranking women in the land (Esther 1:18).

Jews from Media who recognized the Median language being spoken by the Spirit-filled disciples are mentioned in Acts 2:9. Thus, although the country had ceased to be a dominant power in the world, its language and culture were still present during the NT period.

Mediator–One who serves as a facilitator of reconciliation between two parties. The role of a mediator was taken by different individuals and offices in the OT, as seen in Abraham interceding for Sodom and Gomorrah (Gen. 18:22–32), Moses asking God to forgive Israel (Exod. 32:31–32), and the Israelites begging Moses to speak to God on their behalf (Exod. 20:19). In addition, judges, prophets, kings, and priests assumed intermediary functions at times. Mediation functions bidirectionally: from God to humans, and from humans to God. The prophets are quintessentially the first kind of mediators (God to humans), while the priests took, mostly, the second function (humans to God).

In the NT, the role of mediator is given to Christ, since he alone, as God incarnate, is qualified for it (the "one mediator between God and mankind" [1 Tim. 2:5]). This implies that insomuch as reconciliation between sinful humankind and a holy God is conceivable, Christ alone can facilitate that mediation.

Mediterranean Sea–The major body of water dividing Europe and Africa, extending eastward from the Atlantic Ocean well over two thousand miles to the western shore of Israel. The Mediterranean is almost completely surrounded by land. Though in some places this sea has a width of six or seven hundred miles, it is only nine miles wide at the Strait of Gibraltar, which gives access from the Mediterranean to the Atlantic Ocean. Situated between the Middle East, Europe, and Africa, the Mediterranean Sea made possible a quicker means of trade between these three great landmasses.

The Mediterranean Sea (known as the Great Sea, the Western Sea, and the Sea of the Philistines) plays a major role for Israel in both Testaments. It is noted as the Western boundary for the inheritance of Israel (Deut. 11:24; Josh. 1:4) and thus forms the border of Judah (Josh. 15:12, 47). In the NT, the Mediterranean Sea is mentioned in Acts, where Luke relates the story of Simon Peter staying with Simon the tanner in Joppa, which is "by the sea" (10:6, 32). And later in Acts, Luke chronicles the path of the ship taking Paul to Rome, a trip on the Mediterranean starting from Caesarea and passing through Myra, Cnidus, Crete, Malta (after shipwreck in a storm), Syracuse, Rhegium, Puteoli, and Three Taverns (the latter two are in Italy) before concluding in Rome (27:1–28:14).

Medium–A person who serves as a conduit for communicating with the dead (more commonly today called a "psychic"). In the OT, this term is almost always paired with "spiritist." The law delivered to the Israelites by Moses compares a patron of these practitioners to a prostitute (Lev. 20:6). The practice defiles patrons (Lev. 19:31), making them detestable to God (Deut. 18:11–12), and the law prescribes excommunication from the community (Lev. 20:6) and death by stoning (Lev. 20:27) as punishment for such acts. Such activity is considered characteristic of the other nations (Deut. 18:11–12; Isa. 19:3) and therefore inappropriate for the Israelites.

In accordance with this overriding negative attitude toward them, Saul expels the mediums and spiritists from Israel (1 Sam. 28:3). Nevertheless, when Saul seeks a prophetic word regarding his imminent encounter with the Philistines and is unable to receive one from God by the usual means, he asks for a medium (28:5–7).

Megiddo–A major city in the north of Israel that guards a strategic pass of the international highway known as the Via Maris, which connected Egypt and Mesopotamia. Its location explains why it was so large and the site of many ancient battles.

Megiddo appears for the first time in the Bible when Josh. 12:21 mentions its king as one of the many defeated by the Israelites (presumably as part of the northern coalition). Joshua 17:11 says that it was part of Manasseh, though it was not conquered until later (Judg. 1:27). The Song of Deborah describes it as being near the location of a battle between Israel and the Canaanites (Judg. 5:19). We do not get the account of the Israelite takeover of Megiddo, but we know that Solomon (tenth century BC) controlled it and fortified it along with Hazor and Gezer. It is listed in the fifth administrative district of Solomon (1 Kings 4:12).

Jehu's agents wounded King Ahaziah of Judah, who fled to Megiddo, where he died (2 Kings 9:27). The Assyrian king Tiglath-pileser III conquered parts of northern Israel in the middle of the eighth century BC and created a new province of his empire, Magiddu. In 609 BC, King Josiah of Judah died there trying to stop the Egyptians under Necho from reinforcing the Assyrians against Babylon (2 Kings 23:29; 2 Chron. 35:22).

The area around Megiddo began to be called "Har Megiddo" ("mountain of Megiddo"). In Greek this became "Armageddon," and in Rev. 16:12–16 it is associated with the final future battle between the forces of God and the forces of evil.

Melchizedek–A mysterious individual who is referenced twice in the OT and once in the NT. In Gen. 14:18–20 Melchizedek is a priest of El Elyon (God Most High), possibly a reference to the Canaanite god El but here used as a title for Yahweh. He is said to be from "Salem," which could be a shortened form of "Jerusalem." Melchizedek brings out bread and wine to Abram, blesses him, and receives one-tenth of Abram's spoils that Abram had acquired from his successful military campaign against the eastern kings. The royal oracle of Ps. 110 holds a declaration of the Davidic king as an eternal priest "in the order of Melchizedek" (v. 4). This phrase is later applied to Jesus by the writer of the book of Hebrews to emphasize the superiority of Jesus' priesthood over the Levitical priesthood. In Heb. 7:1–17 Melchizedek is described as the "king of righteousness" and the "king of peace" (v. 2); he is said to have been birthed "without father or mother" and is described as one who has existed eternally, thus resembling the Son of God (v. 3). This description draws not only on Gen. 14 and Ps. 110 but also on the description of Melchizedek as a heavenly figure that appears also in the DSS (11Q13). While Melchizedek's identity and function remain a mystery, all three biblical passages refer to him in order to proclaim the work of God.

Memorial–In the Bible the word "memorial" is used in two primary senses. First, it can refer to something meant to provoke a worshiper's remembrance. The Israelites erected a monument of stones as a memorial to remind their descendants that God had stopped the flow of the Jordan River (Josh. 4:7). Similarly, the Passover feast was a memorial to the Israelites of God's deliverance (Exod. 12:14 KJV, NET). God could even speak of his name as a memorial (Exod. 3:15 KJV, NET).

Second, a memorial can be an act of worship whereby God favorably remembered a worshiper and his or her offering (Lev. 5:12; Acts 10:31). Memorial portions were burned before God in grain offerings (Lev. 2:1–2) and certain sin offerings (5:11–13); the remainder of these offerings was consumed by the priests. In the NT, God considered Cornelius's prayers and gifts to the poor to be a memorial offering (Acts 10:4).

M

Memphis–An Egyptian city, no longer in existence, located about fifteen miles southwest of Cairo. It was the site of the palaces of most of the pharaohs mentioned in the Bible. "Memphis" is the Greek name of the city, and, with the exception of Hos. 9:6 (*mōp*), the town goes by the name "Noph" (*nōp*) in the OT, although many modern translations use the Greek name throughout. Notably, both Jer. 46:14–19 and Ezek. 30:13–19 prophesy against the city and predict its destruction. Historically, Egypt and Israel had a rather tumultuous relationship, but Jeremiah's and Ezekiel's particular invective may have concerned Memphis's refusal to join with the southern kingdom in its rebellion against the Babylonians. At least one of Jeremiah's prophecies after the destruction of Jerusalem is directed toward some Jews who have settled in Memphis (Jer. 44:1). Memphis was also the center of the Apis cult, which worshiped the image of a bull. Some scholars have tried to link the story of the golden calf in Exod. 32 to this particular cult, but the connections seem dubious.

Menahem–The son of Gadi, he was the sixteenth king (r. 747–737 BC) of the northern kingdom, Israel. Menahem's rise to power was marked by violence and cruelty. His predecessor, Shallum son of Jabesh (also a usurper of the throne), had reigned only one month in Samaria when Menahem went up from Tirzah and killed him. Menahem then brutally attacked the city of Tiphsah, where "he ripped open all the pregnant women" (2 Kings 15:16).

Menahem's ten-year reign was "evil in the eyes of the Lord" (2 Kings 15:18). Having obtained the throne in the thirty-ninth year of Azariah of Judah (c. 747 BC), he followed in the sins of his predecessors. Tiglath-pileser III (Pul) of Assyria invaded Israel during Menahem's reign, but Menahem was able to avoid takeover and even "strengthen his own hold on the kingdom" by paying one thousand talents of silver to the Assyrian king (2 Kings 15:19), which he raised by taxing the wealthy men of Israel. Menahem died a natural death, and his son Pekahiah succeeded him as king. See 2 Kings 15:13–22.

Mene, Mene, Tekel, Parsin–At King Belshazzar's feast in the book of Daniel an apparitional hand appeared and wrote a mysterious inscription on the wall. According to the Aramaic text, it read *mene' mene' teqel uparsin* (Dan. 5:25). Daniel alone was able to identify God as the source of the message, read the writing, and decipher its significance (Dan. 5:24–28).

Menorah–A lampstand, principally the seven-branched lampstand built initially for use in the tabernacle (Exod. 25:31–39) and placed in front of the inner curtain that shielded the ark of the covenant (27:21). The menorah has the decorations of an almond tree and, as a tree in the midst of the place where God makes his presence known to humans, is to remind Israel of the garden of Eden. The menorah was to stay lit twenty-four hours a day (Lev. 24:1–4). It is the central symbol of the Jewish festival of lights, Hanukkah.

Mephibosheth–**(1)** A son of Jonathan and a grandson of Saul, he became lame at the age of five when his nurse dropped him as she fled after hearing of the deaths of Saul and Jonathan (2 Sam. 4:4). His name is more correctly "Merib-Baal" (1 Chron. 8:34), but the books of Samuel usually change names compounded with *ba'al* ("master" [perhaps originally referring to Yahweh]) to *bosheth* ("shame"). Because of his covenant with Jonathan (1 Sam. 20:15), David arranged for Mephibosheth to live at the palace with him and restored his estates (2 Sam. 9). Later, he spared him from the execution of Saul's descendants (2 Sam. 21:7) when addressing the famine caused by Saul's killing of some Gibeonites.

During Absalom's rebellion, Mephibosheth's steward Ziba met David and gave him provisions, claiming that Mephibosheth believed that the rebellion would see the throne returned to him (16:1–4), resulting in David handing the estates across to Ziba. But Mephibosheth was among the first to meet David on his return, and he claimed that Ziba had deceived him (19:24–30). Samuel does not resolve their conflicting testimonies, perhaps to reflect the information available to David, who then divided the estates between them.

(2) A son of Saul, born to his concubine Rizpah, and one of seven descendants of Saul executed by David to avert famine because of Saul's actions against the Gibeonites (2 Sam. 21:8–9).

Merab–The older of Saul's two daughters (1 Sam. 14:49). When Saul offered her to David as his wife, David hesitated because his family and clan were undistinguished (1 Sam. 18:17). Merab married Adriel of Meholah.

Saul's younger daughter, Michal, fell in love with David, and Saul offered her as wife to David in a bizarre plot to kill him off. Merab's sons with Adriel were given by David to be executed by the Gibeonites because Saul transgressed an agreement made between them and Joshua (2 Sam. 21:8; see Josh. 9).

Mercy–Mercy is a distinguishing characteristic of the nature of God. God is called "the Father of mercies" (2 Cor. 1:3 NRSV [NIV: "Father of compassion"]). God is "rich in mercy" (Eph. 2:4; cf. 2 Sam. 24:14; Dan. 9:9). God's mercy was demonstrated in his covenantal faithfulness to his people (1 Kings 8:23–24; Mic. 7:18–20). God redeemed the oppressed Israelites from slavery under Pharaoh because of his mercy, which was stirred when he heard their groaning and cry for help.

Jesus Christ lived a life full of mercy. He is, in a sense, the bodily manifestation of God's mercy. Jesus expressed deep mercy whenever he saw the sick and the lost. The writers of the Gospels describe Jesus' demonstrations of mercy when he healed the blind, the lame, the deaf, the leprous, the demon-possessed, and the dead (Matt. 9:36; 14:14; 20:34; Mark 1:41; 5:19; 6:34; 8:2; Luke 7:13; John 11:33). Jesus especially had compassion on the crowds, who did not have a spiritual leader, and he compared them to "sheep without a shepherd" (Matt. 9:36).

What is the proper response to God's mercy and compassion? God expects believers to show the same kind of mercy toward other people. One of the best examples is the parable of the unmerciful servant (Matt. 18:23–35).

Mercy Seat–The mercy seat, or "atonement cover" (NIV, NLT), was the cover on the ark of the covenant in the tabernacle and the place of atonement for Israel (Exod. 25:21). It was made of pure gold, forty-five inches long, and twenty-seven inches wide (25:17). Above the mercy seat were two cherubim made of gold, one at each end (25:18–20). There, God spoke with Moses (Num. 7:89). Upon entering the holiest place, the priest was required to burn incense over the mercy seat; otherwise, he would face judgment and die (Lev. 16:13). On the Day of Atonement the blood of the bull and the goat was sprinkled on the mercy seat.

In the NT, the Greek term *hilastērion* is used for the mercy seat itself (Heb. 9:5) and for the "sacrifice of atonement" or "propitiation" (Rom. 3:25), the blood of which was dripped onto the mercy seat. In Rom. 3:25 Christ himself is identified as the *hilastērion*, the sacrifice of atonement for our sins.

Meribah–Meribah ("quarreling") is another name for Massah ("testing"), a location on the journey toward Mount Horeb (Sinai) where the Israelites grumbled against God because they had no water; Moses struck the rock at Horeb, and water flowed out (Exod. 17:7). Subsequent references to Meribah concern a similar incident in Kadesh after the Israelites had journeyed on from Horeb (Num. 20:13, 24; 27:14; Deut. 32:51; 33:8; Pss. 81:7; 95:8; 106:32). On this occasion Moses and Aaron, in getting water out of the rock, failed to honor God as holy, and for this they were denied entrance into Canaan. *See also* Massah.

Mesha–The king of Moab who, along with his father, Chemosh-yatti, was a vassal of the northern kingdom of Israel during the reigns of the northern Israelite kings Omri, Ahab, Ahaziah, and Joram (c. 885–840 BC). When Ahab died, Mesha rebelled against Ahab's son Ahaziah, withholding the annual tribute of one hundred thousand lambs and the wool of one hundred thousand rams (2 Kings 3:4–5). Ahaziah died after a brief reign and was replaced by his brother Joram, who enlisted King Jehoshaphat of Judah to help him attack Moab and restore it to servitude (2 Kings 3:7). In the 2 Kings 3 account, Joram and Jehoshaphat attacked and utterly defeated Moab, but Mesha they besieged in the city of Kir Hareseth. Mesha could not escape, so he sacrificed his own son in plain view on the wall of the city to appease his god, Chemosh. This sacrifice disgusted the armies of Israel and Judah, and they left for home. Mesha considered this as Chemosh's divine deliverance due to his sacrifice, and he erected a stela, known as the Moabite Stone.

Meshach–The Babylonian name given to Mishael by Nebuchadnezzar's chief official, Ashpenaz, as part of an attempt to turn him into a Babylonian official (Dan. 1:7). Along with Abednego and Shadrach, he is a Judahite companion of Daniel.

Meshek–**(1)** The sixth of Japheth's seven sons (Gen. 10:2; 1 Chron. 1:5). Listed in the Table of Nations, the descendants of Japheth inhabited Asia Minor, and Meshek's name is given to a region there. In Ps. 120:5 Meshek is placed in parallel with Kedar, perhaps bringing

M

to mind a distant, warring people. Meshek and Tubal are linked together as trading partners (of slaves and copper vessels) with Tyre (Ezek. 27:13), and both are mentioned as part of the kingdom of Magog, ruled by Gog (38:2; 39:1). **(2)** A grandson of Shem, the eponymous ancestor of an Aramean tribe (1 Chron. 1:17). In Gen. 10:23, most Bible versions follow the Hebrew text in rendering his name as "Mash" (see NIV mg.). He is listed in the Table of Nations as the eponymous ancestor of a Syrian tribal group, possibly associated with Mount Masius (Tur Abdin), near the source of the Euphrates River in northern Mesopotamia, or with Akkadian Mashu, the Lebanon and Anti-Lebanon ranges of the Epic of Gilgamesh.

Mesopotamia–The fertile region of the Tigris and Euphrates valleys, bordered on the north by the Taurus Mountains and on the east by the Zagros Mountains (modern Iraq). The region extends from Turkey to the Persian Gulf.

Messiah–The English word "messiah" derives from the Hebrew verb *mashakh,* which means "to anoint." The Greek counterpart of the Hebrew word for "messiah" (*mashiakh*) is *christos,* which in English is "Christ."

In English translations of the Bible, the word "messiah" ("anointed one") occurs rarely in the OT. In the OT, kings, prophets, and priests were "anointed" with oil as a means of consecrating or setting them apart for their respective offices. Prophets and priests anointed Israel's kings (1 Sam. 16:1–13; 2 Sam. 2:4, 7).

The expectation for a "messiah," or "anointed one," arose from the promise given to David in the Davidic covenant (2 Sam. 7). David was promised that from his seed God would raise up a king who would reign forever on his throne. Hopes for such an ideal king began with Solomon and developed further during the decline (cf. Isa. 9:1–7) and especially after the collapse of the Davidic kingdom.

The harsh reality of exile prompted Israel to hope that God would rule in such a manner. A number of psalms reflect the desire that an ideal son of David would come and rule, delivering Israel from its current plight of oppression. Hence, in Ps. 2 God declares that his son (v. 7), who is the Lord's anointed one (v. 2), will receive "the nations [as] your inheritance, the ends of the earth your possession" (v. 8). God promises that "you will rule them with an iron scepter; you will dash them to pieces like pottery" (v. 9; see NIV footnote). Jesus demonstrates great reticence in using the title "Messiah." In the Synoptic Gospels he almost never explicitly claims it. The two key Synoptic passages where Jesus accepts the title are themselves enigmatic. In Mark's version of Peter's confession (8:29), Jesus does not explicitly affirm Peter's claim, "You are the Messiah," but instead goes on to speak of the suffering of the Son of Man. Later, Jesus is asked by the high priest Caiaphas at his trial, "Are you the Christ, the Son of the Blessed One?" (Mark 14:60). In Mark 14:62, Jesus answers explicitly with "I am," while in Matt. 26:64, he uses the more enigmatic "You have said so." Jesus then goes on to describe himself as the exalted Son of Man who will sit at Yahweh's right hand.

Jesus no doubt avoided the title because it risked communicating an inadequate understanding of the kingdom and his messianic role. Although the Messiah was never a purely political figure in Judaism, he was widely expected to destroy Israel's enemies and secure its physical borders. *Psalms of Solomon* portrays the coming "son of David" as one who will "destroy the unrighteous rulers" and "purge Jerusalem from Gentiles who trample her to destruction" (*Pss. Sol.* 17.21–23). To distance himself from such thinking, Jesus never refers to himself as "son of David" and "king of Israel/the Jews" as other characters do in the Gospels (Matt. 12:23; 21:9, 15; Mark 10:47; 15:2; John 1:49; 12:13; 18:33). When Jesus was confronted by a group of Jews who wanted to make him into such a king, he resisted them (John 6:15).

In Mark 12:35–37, Jesus also redefines traditional understandings of the son of David in his short discussion on Ps. 110:1: he is something more than a mere human son of David. Combining Jesus' implicit affirmation that he is the Messiah in Mark 8:30 with his teaching about the Son of Man in 8:31, we see that Jesus is a Messiah who will "suffer many things and be rejected by the elders, the chief priests, and the teachers of the law" (8:31) and through whom redemption will come (10:45). Jesus came not to defeat the Roman legions, but to bring victory over Satan, sin, and death.

Methuselah–Dying at 969 years of age, he is the oldest human reported in the Bible. He lived before the flood and was the son of Enoch and the father of Lamech (Gen. 5:25–27). He is remembered later in Scripture in the opening genealogy of Chronicles (1 Chron. 1:3) and in Luke's genealogy of Jesus (Luke 3:37).

Methushael–A descendant of Cain, he was the great-grandson of Enoch and the father of Lamech (Gen. 4:18 [KJV: "Methusael"). Some scholars consider "Methushael" to be a variant of "Methuselah," the son of Enoch and the father of Lamech in the lineage of Seth (Gen. 5:21, 25).

Micah–**(1)** A man from the hill country of Ephraim during the period of the judges (Judg. 17–18). It is ironic in this story that a man whose name points to the incomparability of Yahweh is portrayed as a thief and as one who established an idolatrous cult shrine (Judg. 17:1–5). This story graphically illustrates how in the time of the judges "everyone did as they saw fit" (Judg. 17:6). **(2)** A prophet from Moresheth in the Judean Shephelah (Jer. 26:18; Mic. 1:1). A contemporary of Isaiah, he prophesied in the late eighth century BC during the reigns of Jotham, Ahaz, and Hezekiah.

Micah, Book of–Micah, the sixth of the Minor Prophets, presents a powerful message of judgment and salvation. The book contains several memorable passages, including a dramatic call for justice, mercy, and humility (6:6–8).

Micah was commissioned to bring a message of judgment against his generation. They had sinned and deserved punishment. Legal language is found in Micah's oracles, as he was sent by God to press a case against those who had broken the law of the covenant (see 1:2; 6:1–5). He speaks against both civil (3:1–3) and religious (2:6–11; 3:11) leaders.

However, as with many prophets, Micah's message of judgment is followed with hope in the form of salvation oracles. Among these, 5:1–2 points out that the promises to David are not null and void but will be realized in the future.

Micaiah–The son of Imlah, he was a faithful prophet who contradicted the false prophets and predicted King Ahab's death, for which he was imprisoned (1 Kings 22; 2 Chron. 18). His commissioning and vision of God's throne room are similar to Isa. 6.

Michael–One of the few angelic beings whose names are identified in the Bible. Scripture refers to Michael as "one of the chief princes" (Dan. 10:13), a "great prince" (Dan. 12:1), and an "archangel" (Jude 1:9), indicating that Michael is a high-ranking leader of other angels (Rev. 12:7).

Michal–The younger daughter of Saul (1 Sam. 14:49) and a wife of David.

Midian, Midianites–Midian was one of the sons of Abraham by his wife Keturah (Gen. 25:1–2). Just before dying, Abraham leaves everything to Isaac and sends Midian and his brothers away "to the land of the east" (25:5–6). The biblical narrative regards him as the progenitor of the Midianites, who inhabited what is now southern Jordan and northern Saudi Arabia. The relations between the Israelites and the Midianites over the next centuries are generally adversarial. Moses' experience is the exception: after fleeing Egypt, Moses arrives in Midian, marries a Midianite woman, and has an amicable relationship with Jethro, her father (also named Reuel), who was also a priest (Exod. 2–3). Jethro even accompanies the Israelites during part of their wilderness wanderings and gives Moses advice on leading the people (Exod. 18).

Mikmash–This city (modern Mukhmas) and its sister city, Geba, were located on one of the routes from the Jordan Valley to the central Benjamin plateau. Although a branch of the Wadi Qilt separates the two towns, there was a "pass" across the deep valley (1 Sam. 13:23). As Isaiah describes the advance of the Assyrians toward Jerusalem, this geographical feature emerges (Isa. 10:28–29). It is also evident in a narrative about the Philistine incursion deep into Israelite territory in the early days of Saul's monarchy. The Philistines held a forward outpost at Geba; Saul commanded the Israelite forces at Mikmash, across the pass to the northeast; and Jonathan was at Gibeah of Benjamin, south of Geba (1 Sam. 13:2–3). Saul did not attack the Philistines from Mikmash, since crossing the pass below Geba would have made his forces vulnerable. Instead, Jonathan's attack drove the Philistines out of Geba. They regrouped at Mikmash, however, dislodged the forces of Saul, and dispatched raiding parties (1 Sam. 13:16–18). In order to retake this critical location, Jonathan and his armor-bearer set out from Geba, descended into the wadi, climbed up the other side, and attacked, conquering the outpost and routing the Philistines (1 Sam. 14:1–23).

Miletus–*See* Asia Minor, Cities of.

M

MILL, MILLSTONE–One of several different types of stone implements used to grind grain, usually by hand. This chore was often performed daily, so the sound of mills grinding grain became a symbol of normal life (Jer. 25:10; Rev. 18:22). Women (Matt. 24:41) or servants (Exod. 11:5) typically used mills, or prisoners, like Samson (Judg. 16:21), might be made to perform the mundane task.

MILLO–This name, meaning "fill" in Hebrew, refers to several places or structures in the OT. **(1)** A part of the defensive fortifications of Jerusalem, the construction of which apparently was begun after David conquered the city (2 Sam. 5:9; 1 Chron. 11:8 [NIV: "terraces," but see NIV mg.]). Its exact nature and location in Jerusalem are disputed. It has been proposed that it was a terraced structure upon which houses were built, or that it was a platform that connected the Temple Mount and David's citadel by filling in the valley between them.

The completion or rebuilding of the Millo was one of Solomon's building projects, although it is also possible that Solomon's Millo was a separate structure altogether (1 Kings 9:15, 24; 11:27). Solomon put Jeroboam, who later became the first king of the northern kingdom, in charge of this project (1 Kings 11:27–28). In addition to repairing broken walls and building towers, Hezekiah included the strengthening of the Millo in his preparations for the siege of Sennacherib (2 Chron. 32:5).

(2) The house of Millo, where Joash of Judah was assassinated, may be a part of the structure in Jerusalem (2 Kings 12:20 [NIV: "Beth Millo"]), but this is not certain.

(3) Beth Millo ("house of Millo") was a fortress or city near or a part of Shechem (Judg. 9:6, 20). Although the Hebrew name is almost identical to the one in 2 Kings 12:20, it is likely that they are distinct places.

MINA–*See* Weights and Measures.

MINERALS AND METALS–The Bible contains many references to minerals and metals. Minerals can encompass a wide array of topics, thus the focus here is on valuable minerals such as ornamental stones as well as precious and useful metals.

Copper. References to copper within the Bible are few. Several passages discuss the basic origins of copper, such as the gathering of ore or the smelting process (Deut. 8:9; Job 28:2; Ezek. 22:18, 20; 24:11). Several NT passages acknowledge the presence of minted copper coins as currency (Matt. 10:9; Mark 12:42; Luke 21:2). Pure copper, however, was hard to use, although it could be combined with tin to make the alloy bronze.

Bronze. The first biblical reference to bronze is found in Gen. 4:22, in which we are told that Tubal-Cain forged tools out of bronze and iron. Next, bronze is mentioned in its use in the tabernacle built in the desert. Among the bronze items included were the many bronze clasps and bases for the tent construction (Exod. 26:11, 37; 27:10–11, 17–19). The altar and all its utensils were made of, or overlaid with, bronze (27:1–8). God also instructed Moses to make a bronze basin for washing (30:18). Moses also made a snake out of bronze and placed it on top of his staff when the Israelites were struck with an abundance of venomous snakes (Num. 21:9). Samson was bound with shackles of bronze (Judg. 16:21), and Goliath wore armor and carried weapons of bronze (1 Sam. 17:5–6). Solomon used an extensive amount of bronze in his building of the temple (2 Kings 25:16), and there was bronze in the statue that Daniel dreamed of (Dan. 2:32, 35). Many of the prophets used bronze as a way to discuss something that was to be strong or strengthened by God (Isa. 45:2; Jer. 1:18; Ezek. 40:3).

Iron and steel. One of the earliest references to iron in Scripture is its use by the Canaanites to make chariots (Josh. 17:16, 18). This would have been an early use of the metal in the Iron Age I period (1200–1000 BC). Also, Goliath's spear, which was as big as a weaver's rod, is said to have had a head made of iron (1 Sam. 17:7). Elisha's miracle of making a borrowed ax head float (2 Kings 6:6) shows the continued value of the metal. In his latter days, David amassed iron among the goods to give Solomon to use in building the temple (1 Chron. 22:14; 29:2); Solomon later used these materials with the help of Huram-Abi (2 Chron. 2:13–14). Ezekiel discusses the economic value of iron in the context of trading (Ezek. 27:12, 19), and Daniel uses it as a metaphor for discussing strength (Dan. 2:40–41). The NT recognizes the strength of iron when discussing Christ's iron scepter (Rev. 2:27; 19:15).

Tin. Tin was initially used mainly to produce the copper alloy bronze. Tin was not used in its pure form until well into the Roman period,

M

and even then seldom by itself. The sources of tin in the ancient world are currently debated. The tin from large deposits in Tarshish in southern Spain (Ezek. 27:12) was available through Phoenician traders. Tin is also found in large deposits in Anatolia, but it is currently unknown whether these deposits had been discovered and used during biblical times. A third option is modern-day Afghanistan. Archaeologists have discovered in modern Turkey the remains of a wrecked ship, dated to around 1350 BC, that was carrying ten tons of copper ingots and about one ton of tin ingots. These ingots possibly originated in the area of modern-day Afghanistan and were bound for the Mediterranean trade routes. Tin is mentioned only four times in Scripture, always within a list of other metals (Num. 31:22; Ezek. 22:18, 20; 27:12).

Lead. Lead was used early in human history, but its applications were few. It would have been mined with copper and silver ore and then extracted as a by-product. The Romans used it for various implements, most notably wine vessels. It is referenced nine times within Scripture, either in a list or in reference to its weight. The only two times it is referenced as an object is when Job mentions a lead writing implement (Job 19:24), and when Zechariah has the vision of a woman sitting in the basket with a lead cover (Zech. 5:7, 8).

Gold and silver. Sought after for much of human history, gold and silver have been worked by humans for their ornamental value. The practical uses of these metals within the biblical setting were constrained mainly to their economic and ornamental value. Gold and silver jewelry were used as a form of payment and were minted into coins during the Greco-Roman era. Gold objects are relatively scarce in archaeological finds, mainly because most gold items would have been part of a large treasury carried off as tribute or plunder. Silver appears in the archaeological record more frequently; a remarkable hoard of silver in lump form was found at Eshtemoa (see 1 Sam. 30:26–28). This silver has been dated to the time of the kingdom of Judah, after the northern kingdom of Israel had fallen. The silver in raw lump form was most likely used as a monetary payment, even though it had not yet been minted into coins.

Gold in the ancient world came largely from Egypt and northern Africa. The Bible mentions Havilah as a land of gold (Gen. 2:11), as well as Ophir (1 Kings 9:28), but the exact location of both places is unknown. Silver was mined in southern Spain, along with other metals, and brought to the area through sea trading. The Athenians of the Classical period were also known for their vast silver-mining operations.

Silver and gold are mentioned repeatedly in the OT in reference to their uses in trading and their economic value. Most notably, the Israelites asked their Egyptian neighbors to give them gold and silver items just before they left Egypt (Exod. 3:22). The tabernacle was highly ornamented with these two metals, as was the temple built by Solomon. It is said that Solomon made the nation so wealthy that silver was considered as plentiful as stone (1 Kings 10:27). Perhaps the most notorious articles of silver within Scripture are those paid to Judas for his betrayal of Jesus (Matt. 26:15).

Precious stones. Stones of various origins were used in and around Palestine. The Bible makes few references to their use. Like gold and silver, they were used mainly for their ornamental value. Their scarcity made them highly prized. One notable exception is turquoise. The Egyptian pharaohs were fascinated with turquoise, and they mined extensively for it on the Sinai Peninsula. The remains of several turquoise mines have been found with Canaanite markings, indicating the presence of Canaanite slaves working the Egyptian mines. There was also a line of forts along the northern edge of the Egyptian Empire, used presumably to protect the pharaohs' turquoise interests. Precious stones were also found in Syria, where Phoenician traders would have been able to bring them from other parts of the known world.

Exodus 28:17–21 describes twelve stones set in the breastpiece worn by the Israelite high priest. Twelve stones likewise appear in the foundations of the new Jerusalem (Rev. 21:19–20). Ezekiel uses nine of these same twelve stones to discuss the adornment of the king of Tyre (Ezek. 28:13).

The Bible uses the blanket term "precious stones" to denote a hoard of riches, such as that owned by Solomon (1 Kings 10:10).

MINISTER, MINISTRY–In the NT the most common word used for "minister" is *diakonos* (e.g., 2 Cor. 3:6), and for "ministry," *diakonia* (e.g., 1 Cor. 16:15 [NIV: "service"]). These words function as umbrella terms for NT writers to describe the whole range of ministries performed by the church. They can describe either a special ministry performed by an official functionary (1 Cor. 3:5) or one performed by any believer (Rev. 2:19). In the early church, ministry was based not on institutional hierarchies but on services performed (1 Tim. 3:1–13).

The ministry of Jesus. The church's mind-set flows out of the way in which Jesus understood his ministry. He described his ministry pattern as that of serving (Matt. 20:28; Mark 10:45; John 13:4–17). Thus, he called his disciples to follow a model of leadership in the new community that did not elevate them above others (Matt. 20:20–28; 23:8–12; cf. 1 Pet. 5:3).

Jesus' ministry provides the paradigm for the ministry of the church. The NT writers describe the threefold ministry of Jesus as preaching, teaching, and healing (Matt. 4:23; 9:35; Mark 1:14, 21–22, 39; Acts 10:36–38). The disciples carried on the earthly ministry of Jesus by the power of the Spirit. They too engaged in preaching, teaching, and healing (Matt. 10:7–8; 28:19–20).

The ministry of the church. The church, because it is the body of Christ, continues these ministry responsibilities. In 1 Pet. 4:10–11 is a summary of the overarching ministries of the church, which include speaking the words of God and serving. As a priesthood of believers (Exod. 19:4–6; 1 Pet. 2:5, 9; Rev. 1:5–6), individual members took responsibility for fulfilling the various tasks of service. Thus, all Christians are called to minister (Rom. 15:27; Philem. 13; 1 Pet. 2:16). Even when a member strayed, it was another believer's responsibility to confront that wayward person and, if necessary, involve others in the body to help (Matt. 18:15–20).

Although ministry was the responsibility of all believers, there were those with special expertise whom Christ and the church set apart for particular leadership roles (Eph. 4:11–12). Christ set apart Apollos and Paul for special ministries (1 Cor. 3:5; Eph. 3:7). The church called on special functionaries to carry out specific ministries. For example, the early church appointed seven individuals to serve tables (Acts 6:2). They appointed certain ones to carry the relief fund collected for the Jerusalem Christians (2 Cor. 8:19, 23). As special functionaries, Paul, Apollos, Timothy, Titus, the elders, as well as others accepted the responsibility of teaching and preaching and healing for the whole church.

All the ministries of the church, whether performed by believers in general or by some specially appointed functionary, were based on gifts received from God (Rom. 12:1–8; 1 Cor. 12:4–26). God gave individuals the abilities necessary to perform works of service (Acts 20:24; Eph. 4:11; Col. 4:17; 1 Tim. 1:12; 1 Pet. 4:11). The NT, however, makes it clear that when it comes to one's relationship and spiritual status before God, all Christians are equal. Yet in equality there is diversity of gifts and talents. Paul identifies some gifts given to individuals for special positions: apostles, prophets, evangelists, pastors, and teachers (Eph. 4:11). The description here is of special ministry roles that Christ calls certain individuals to fulfill based on the gifts given to them. The ones fulfilling these roles did not do all the ministry of the church but rather equipped the rest of the body to do ministry (Eph. 4:12–13). No one can boast in the gifts given to him or her because those gifts were given for ministry to others (1 Cor. 4:7). Thus, gifts lead to service, and in turn service results in leadership.

It becomes the responsibility of those who lead to equip others for ministry. When others are equipped for ministry, they in turn minister and edify the whole body (Eph. 4:15–16; 2 Tim. 2:1–2). The goal of all ministry, according to Paul, is to build up a community of believers until all reach maturity in Christ (Rom. 15:15–17; 1 Cor. 3:5–4:5; Eph. 4:12–16; 1 Thess. 2:19–20).

Miracles–Because Scripture sees all things as providentially arranged and sustained by God's sovereign power at all times (Heb. 1:3), miracles are not aberrations in an otherwise closed and mechanical universe. Nor are miracles raw demonstrations of divinity designed to overcome prejudice or unbelief and to convince people of the existence of God (Mark 8:11–12). Still less are they clever conjuring tricks involving some kind of deception that can be otherwise explained on a purely scientific basis. Rather, God in his infinite wisdom sometimes does unusual and extraordinary things to call attention to himself and his activity. Miracles are divinely ordained acts of God that dramatically alert us to the presence of his glory and power and advance his saving purposes in redemptive history.

In the OT, miracles are not evenly distributed but rather are found in greater number during times of great redemptive significance, such as the exodus and the conquest of Canaan. Miracles were performed also during periods of apostasy, such as in the days of the ninth-century prophets Elijah and Elisha. Common to both of these eras is the powerful demonstration of the superiority of God over pagan deities (Exod. 7–12; 1 Kings 18:20–40).

In the NT, miracles often are acts of compassion, but more significantly they attest the exalted status of Jesus of Nazareth (Acts 2:22) and the saving power of his word (Heb. 2:3–4). In the Synoptic Gospels, they reveal the coming of God's kingdom and the conquest of Satan's dominion (Matt. 8:16–17; 12:22–30; Mark 3:27). They point to the person of Jesus as the promised Messiah of OT Scripture (Matt. 4:23; 11:4–6). John shows a preference for the word "signs," and his Gospel is structured around them (John 20:30–31). According to John, the signs that Jesus performed were such that only the one who stood in a unique relationship to the Father as the Son of God could do them.

Just as entrenched skepticism is injurious to faith, so too is naive credulity, for although signs and wonders witness to God, false prophets also perform them "to deceive, if possible, even the elect" (Matt. 24:24). Christians are to exercise discernment and not be led astray by such impostors (Matt. 7:15–20).

The relationship between miracles and faith is not as straightforward as sometimes supposed. Miracles do not necessarily produce faith, nor does faith necessarily produce miracles. Miracles were intended to bring about the faith that leads to eternal life (John 20:31), but not all who witnessed them believed (John 10:32). Additionally, Jesus regarded a faith that rested only on the miracle itself as precarious (Mark 8:11–13; John 2:23–25; 4:48), though better than no faith at all (John 10:38). Faith that saves must ultimately find its grounding in the person of Jesus as the Son of God.

It is also clear that although Jesus always encouraged faith in those who came to him for help (Mark 9:23), and that he deliberately limited his miraculous powers in the presence of unbelief (Mark 6:5), many of his miracles were performed on those who did not or could not exercise faith (Matt. 12:22; Mark 1:23–28; 5:1–20; Luke 14:1–4).

The fact that Jesus performed miracles was never an issue; rather, his opponents disputed the source of his power (Mark 3:22). Arguments about his identity were to be settled by appeal not to miracles but to the word of God (Matt. 22:41–46).

MIRIAM–The sister of Moses and Aaron, and the only known daughter of Amram and Jochebed (Num. 26:59). After Jochebed laid the infant Moses in a basket and placed it in the Nile River, Miriam followed the basket until Pharaoh's daughter discovered it, and she promptly volunteered her mother to assist in caring for the child (Exod. 2:4–10). Miriam, referred to as a "prophet" (Exod. 15:20), led the Israelite women in celebration and worship after the successful crossing of the Red Sea as the Israelites fled Egypt (15:20–21). She is remembered as a central figure in Moses' leadership team during the exodus (Mic. 6:4).

Along with Aaron, she came to oppose the leadership of Moses, apparently because of his interracial marriage to a Cushite woman (Num. 12:1). The end result was that God caused her to become leprous, for which she had to be cast out of the camp for seven days. She was healed because of Moses' interceding prayer. She died and was buried in Kadesh (Num. 20:1).

MIZPAH/MIZPEH–Meaning "watchtower," this is the name of several sites in the Bible. **(1)** Along with "Galeed," a name given to the heap of stones that memorialized the covenant made between Jacob and Laban (Gen. 31:48–49). **(2)** The place where the Israelites assembled in response to the military threat from Ammon and made Jephthah their leader (Judg. 10:17; 11:11). It may have been the home of Jephthah and may be the same place mentioned in Gen. 31:49. From Mizpah, Jephthah and Israel attacked the Ammonites. Mizpah became the place where Jephthah fulfilled his ill-conceived vow (Judg. 11:34–39). This location is most likely synonymous with the Ramath Mizpah in the territory of Gad (Josh. 13:26). **(3)** A city in the tribal allotment of Benjamin. It is listed between Beeroth and Kephirah and seems to have been close to Gibeon and Ramah (Josh. 18:26; 1 Kings 15:22; Neh. 3:7). Of the various places to bear the name "Mizpah," the Benjamite location has the most biblical significance. The men of Israel gathered here to decide how to deal with the Benjamites' behavior toward the Levite's concubine (Judg. 20:1–3; 21:1–8). It was also here that Samuel called the people of Israel together to pray and renew their relationship with God after the ark of the covenant had been sent back by the Philistines (1 Sam. 7:5–6). As a result, when the Philistines attacked, God caused them to panic, and Israel had the victory. Samuel regularly visited Mizpah to render judgment for the Israelites (1 Sam. 7:16). Also, Saul was presented to Israel as its king at Mizpah (1 Sam. 10:17).

Taken collectively, these references show the religious and civic importance of the site for the fledgling nation. After the division of the kingdom, Mizpah became part of the southern kingdom of Judah. King Asa of Judah fortified Mizpah against King Baasha of Israel with materials used from Baasha's fortification at Ramah (1 Kings 15:16–22). Mizpah became an important civic center once again after the destruction of Jerusalem by Nebuchadnezzar and the Babylonians in 587/586 BC. Gedaliah, the Babylonian-appointed governor of the conquered region, set up his government center at Mizpah (2 Kings 25:23–25). The importance of Mizpah is commemorated by Judas Maccabeus in the intertestamental period (1 Macc. 3:46).

Moab–Moab proper lies between the Arnon and the Zered valleys east of the Dead Sea. The Arnon is the deepest gorge in Jordan (seventeen hundred feet) and is two miles wide at the upper edge. It served as a natural northern boundary for geopolitical Moab, even though the nation frequently expanded its control farther north.

After the destruction of Sodom and Gomorrah, Lot's daughters determined to carry on the family line by sleeping with their father (Gen. 19:30–38). The son of the elder daughter was named "Moab." According to an etymology in the LXX, the name in Hebrew means "from my father" (Gen. 19:37).

Moses' song refers to leaders of Moab among those whom Israel would encounter (Exod. 15:15). As the Israelites made their way past Edom (Num. 20:14–21), they may also have given a wide berth to geopolitical Moab, moving instead along the desert highway to the east (Num. 21:10–20; Deut. 2:8–9; Judg. 11:18; but see also Deut. 2:29) until they arrived at the territory that Sihon, king of the Amorites, had previously captured from the Moabites (Num. 21:21–26). This is the plateau (Heb. *mishor*) north of the Arnon (Deut. 2:36) stretching to Ammon (Josh. 13:10). The capital city of Sihon was Heshbon on the plateau (*mishor*) (Josh. 13:21). After defeating the Amorites, the Israelites camped on the "plains of Moab" (Num. 22:1; 33:48–50), where they remained until crossing the Jordan River. Most likely they did not jeopardize their security by moving down into the Jordan Valley.

Frightened by this multitude, the king of Moab and the elders of Midian sent for Balaam to curse the Israelites (Num. 21–24). Instead, Balaam pronounced four sets of blessings on Israel, and in the final one Balaam spoke of a "star . . . out of Jacob" who would "crush the foreheads of Moab" (Num. 24:17). Because the Moabites refused to welcome the Israelites and hired Balaam, the Moabites, along with the Ammonites, were excluded from the assembly of the Lord for ten generations (Deut. 23:3–6). The verse immediately prior to this passage excludes those born of forbidden marriages, which might be the reason for specifying Moab and Ammon.

The plateau (*mishor*) was allocated to the tribes of Reuben and Gad (Num. 32:34–38; Josh. 13:8–9). Their presence enabled the Israelites to maintain a hold in the region, a fact that would be significant some three centuries later (Judg. 11:26). As the Israelites prepared to enter the land, Moses restated the covenant on the plains of Moab (Num. 36:13; Deut. 29:1). When it came time for Moses to die, he climbed Mount Nebo from the plains of Moab to the top of Pisgah, and after his death the Israelites mourned him there for thirty days (Deut. 34:1–8).

During the period of the judges, the Moabites pushed north across the Arnon and as far as Jericho. When Ehud killed Eglon, the Moabites were driven back and subjected to Israel for eighty years (Judg. 3). The respite was temporary, however, due to repeated apostasy on the part of the Israelites. They turned to worship the gods of the peoples around them, among them the gods of the Moabites (Judg. 10:6).

The book of Ruth is set during the period of Judges and Ruth herself was a Moabite women, who allied herself with Israel. Ruth's son was Obed, the father of Jesse, the father of David (Ruth 4:21). This family link with Moab may explain why David sought refuge for his father and mother in Moab in the dark days when he was fleeing from Saul (1 Sam. 22:1–4). David was appealing to a national enemy in doing this since Saul had been fighting against the Moabites along with the Ammonites, the Edomites, and the Philistines since he became king (1 Sam. 14:47). The complexity created for David by this combination of family allegiances and ongoing national concerns is evident in his later actions as king. When he defeated the Moabites, he brutally subdued them, reducing them to a vassal kingdom (2 Sam. 8:2–12). The united kingdom continued to control the plateau of Moab, evident in the towns noted in David's census; it reached through the tribe of Gad to the city of Aroer in the Arnon Gorge (2 Sam. 24:5).

Moab is the object of stinging rebuke from several prophets (Isa. 15–16; 25:10; Jer. 48; Ezek. 25:8–11; Amos 2:1–3). Moab's forthcoming judgment is described in grim terms, equating Moab's end to that of Sodom and Gomorrah (Zeph. 2:9). Even so, God declares, "I will restore the fortunes of Moab in days to come" (Jer. 48:47). Moab will be humbled along with Edom and the Philistines at the word of the Lord (Pss. 60:8; 108:9). After the return from exile, Moabites were among those with whom the Israelites intermarried (Ezra 9:1; Neh. 13:1; cf. Deut. 23:3–6).

Molek–Generally, it has been believed that Molek was a god of the Ammonites (1 Kings 11:5). Molek has long been associated with the practice of child sacrifice, based on several references to the god within the Bible. For example, Leviticus associates child sacrifice with the worship of Molek and prescribes capital punishment for any practitioner of such (18:21; 20:2–5). Josiah is credited with destroying the altar (Topheth) to Molek in the Valley of Ben Hinnom, so that no one could sacrifice a child to Molek there (2 Kings 23:10–13).

Moon–The ancient Jewish calendar was tied to the phases of the moon, with the months beginning with each new moon. The new moon was celebrated with multiple offerings (Num. 28:11–15). Festival days were calculated from the new moon.

The moon figures prominently in prophecy. At the day of the Lord, the sun and the moon will be darkened (e.g., Joel 2:10). While most ancient Near Eastern cultures worshiped the moon, Israel was forbidden such worship (Deut. 4:19).

The account of the moon's creation recorded in Gen. 1:16 does not mention the moon by name. This is in keeping with the general tone of the creation story, wherein God, almost incidentally, creates the things that were worshiped by contemporary cultures.

Mordecai–Esther's Benjamite cousin, he lived in the Persian province of Susa due to the Jewish deportation in the Babylonian exile (Esther 2:5–7). After Esther's parents died, Mordecai assumed a fatherly role in raising the child, and in time he played an influential role in Esther's initial rise to prominence and in the deliverance of the Jews from imminent death at the hand of Haman. Mordecai also alerted King Xerxes (Ahasuerus) to a potential threat on his life, resulting in his own exaltation.

Moriah–The mountain to which God commanded Abraham to go and sacrifice Isaac (Gen. 22:2). The only other time a mountain of this name is mentioned is 2 Chron. 3:1, as the location of the future temple.

Moses–Moses played a leadership role in the founding of Israel as a "kingdom of priests and a holy nation" (Exod. 19:6). Indeed, the narrative of Exodus through Deuteronomy is the story of God using Moses to found the nation of Israel. It begins with an account of his birth (Exod. 2) and ends with an account of his death (Deut. 34). Moses' influence and importance extend well beyond his lifetime, as later Scripture demonstrates.

Moses was born in a dangerous time, and according to Pharaoh's decree, he should not have survived long after his birth. He was born to Amram and Jochebed (Exod. 6:20). Circumventing Pharaoh's decree, Jochebed placed the infant Moses in a reed basket and floated him down the river. God guided the basket down the river and into the presence of none other than Pharaoh's daughter (Exod. 2:5–6), who, at the urging of Moses' sister, hired Jochebed to take care of the child.

The next major episode in the life of Moses concerns his defense of an Israelite worker who was being beaten by an Egyptian (Exod. 2:11–25). In the process of rescuing the Israelite, Moses killed the Egyptian. When it became clear that he was known to be the killer, he fled Egypt and ended up in Midian, where he became a member of the family of a Midianite priest-chief, Jethro, by marrying his daughter Zipporah.

Although Moses was not looking for a way back into Egypt, God had different plans. One day, while Moses was tending his sheep, God appeared to him in the form of a burning bush and commissioned him to go back to Egypt and lead his people to freedom. Moses expressed reluctance, and so God grudgingly enlisted his older brother, Aaron, to accompany him as his spokesperson.

Upon Moses' return to Egypt, Pharaoh stubbornly refused to allow the Israelites to leave

M

Egypt. God directed Moses to announce a series of plagues that ultimately induced Pharaoh to allow the Israelites to depart. After they left, Pharaoh had a change of mind and cornered them on the shores of the Red Sea (Sea of Reeds). It was at the Red Sea that God demonstrated his great power by splitting the sea and allowing the Israelites to escape before closing it again in judgment on the Egyptians. Moses signaled the presence of God by lifting his rod high in the air (Exod. 14:16). This event was long remembered as the defining moment when God released Israel from Egyptian slavery (Pss. 77; 114), and it even became the paradigm for future divine rescues (Isa. 40:3–5; Hos. 2:14–15).

After the crossing of the Red Sea, Moses led Israel back to Mount Sinai, the location of his divine commissioning. At this time, Moses went up the mountain as a prophetic mediator for the people (Deut. 18:16). He received the Ten Commandments, the rest of the law, and instructions to build the tabernacle (Exod. 19–24). All these were part of a new covenantal arrangement that today we refer to as the Mosaic or Sinaitic covenant.

However, as Moses came down the mountain with the law, he saw that the people, who had grown tired of waiting, were worshiping a false god that they had created in the form of a golden calf (Exod. 32). With the aid of the Levites, who that day assured their role as Israel's priestly helpers, he brought God's judgment against the offenders and also interceded in prayer with God to prevent the total destruction of Israel.

Thus began Israel's long story of rebellion against God. God was particularly upset with the lack of confidence that the Israelites had shown when the spies from the twelve tribes gave their report (Num. 13). They did not believe that God could handle the fearsome warriors who lived in the land, and so God doomed them to forty years of wandering in the wilderness, enough time for the first generation to die. Not even Moses escaped this fate, since he had shown anger against God and attributed a miracle to his own power and not to God when he struck a rock in order to get water (Num. 20:1–13).

Thus, Moses was not permitted to enter the land of promise, though he had led the Israelites to the very brink of entry on the plains of Moab. There he gave his last sermon, which we know as the book of Deuteronomy. The purpose of his sermon was to tell the second generation of Israelites who were going to enter the land that they must obey God's law or suffer the consequences. The form of the sermon was that of a covenant renewal, and so Israel on this occasion reaffirmed its loyalty to God.

After this, Moses went up on Mount Nebo, from which he could see the promised land, and died. Deuteronomy concludes with the following statements: "Since then, no prophet has risen in Israel like Moses, whom the Lord knew face to face. . . . For no one has ever shown the mighty power or performed the awesome deeds that Moses did in the sight of all Israel" (Deut. 34:10, 12).

The NT honors Moses as God's servant but also makes the point that Jesus is one who far surpasses Moses as a mediator between God and people (Acts 3:17–26; Heb. 3).

The date of Moses is a matter of controversy because the biblical text does not name the pharaohs of the story. Many date him to the thirteenth century BC and associate him with Ramesses II, but others take 1 Kings 6:1 at face value and date him to the end of the fifteenth century BC, perhaps during the reign of Thutmose III.

Mount of Olives–A ridge of peaks about two miles long running north-south to the east of Jerusalem. It may also refer to the middle two of these peaks directly east of the temple. Kidron and Gethsemane lie at the foot of the mount. It was so named for the large number of olive trees there in ancient times.

David wept here because of Absalom's betrayal (2 Sam. 15:30). Here the glory of the Lord rested after withdrawal from Jerusalem (Ezek. 11:23). The Lord will return to the Mount of Olives (Zech. 14:4).

Sometimes Jesus spent the night here (Luke 21:37). He customarily withdrew to Gethsemane at the foot of this mount (John 18:2). Thus, on the evening before his trial Jesus and the disciples went to the Mount of Olives (specifically Gethsemane) after leaving the upper room (Matt. 26:30), and it was there that the betrayal by Judas took place.

Jesus' triumphal entry began on the Mount of Olives (Matt. 21:1), and he discoursed about the future there (Matt. 24:3). After his resurrection, Jesus gathered and instructed his disciples on the Mount of Olives before ascending to heaven (Acts 1:12).

M

Music, Instruments, Dancing–The Bible often refers to songs, music, musical sounds and instruments, and dancing.

Instruments

Strings. The most frequently mentioned instrument is the *kinnor*, a lyre, also often referred to as a harp. The sound box of the harp is at the base, from which a straight or curved neck rises at a sharp angle so that the strings going from the box to the neck are of different length. The lyre has two uprights and a crosspiece on top, from which the strings of similar length stretch down to the sound box. The *kinnor*-lyre had eight to ten strings (based on Akkadian and Ugaritic findings and Jewish descriptions) and could be played with a pick or by hand. David's "harp" was such a lyre. The "harp" mentioned in the NT (1 Cor. 14:7; Rev. 5:8; 14:2; 15:2) probably was also a lyre. Another OT lyre, or perhaps a harp, the *nebel*, complemented the *kinnor*-lyre. Jewish tradition about the strings implies that it produced a lower sound. The *nebel*-lyre is most often mentioned with other instruments, though occasionally alone. Another stringed instrument mentioned three times, the *'asor*, may have been a harp or a lyre with ten strings (Pss. 33:2; 92:3; 144:9). In Pss. 45:8; 150:4 there is mention of "the strings," which may refer to more than just the stringed instruments specifically mentioned in the Bible. The ancient world also had lutes, an instrument with a long, straight neck, fretted like a guitar or ukulele, proceeding from a small sound box.

Percussion. Timbrels, cymbals, and castanets or rattles are percussion instruments mentioned in the Bible. The timbrel was a hand drum, like a tambourine but without metal jingles. The timbrel accompanies dancing and may have been used by the dancers (Exod. 15:20; Judg. 11:34; 1 Sam. 18:6). Cymbals may have been paired or individual, but it is not certain whether these latter were suspended cymbals or finger cymbals, being four to six inches in diameter. In 2 Sam. 6:5 there is mention of another percussion instrument, *mena'an'im* (the root of this word means "to shake"), perhaps "sistrums" (NIV) or "castanets" (NASB) (although the KJV renders it as "cornets"). Castanets were small hand-clappers joined with a string. Israel likely had all of these, though it is hard to know which is referred to in 2 Sam. 6:5. The cymbal is mentioned once in the NT (1 Cor. 13:1), though not as musically pleasing in that context.

Woodwinds and horns. The OT attests to both an animal horn, most frequently called a *shopar*, and a metal trumpet, the *khatsotserah* (Num. 10:2–10). The NT refers to a horn with a word used to translate both OT terms (*salpinx*). The ancient world had both flutes and shawms. Shawms have a bell-like flare at the end, while the shaft of a flute is straight to the end. What is likely a double-reed shawm is frequently translated "flute" (1 Sam. 10:5; 1 Kings 1:40; Isa. 5:12; 30:29; Jer. 48:36 [NIV: "pipes"]). It is unclear whether the instrument mentioned in Gen. 4:21; Ps. 150:4 commonly translated as "flute" is a woodwind or a stringed instrument. The NT also mentions a flute or reed instrument (Matt. 11:17; 9:23; 1 Cor. 14:7; Rev. 18:22) that could be played for dancing or mourning.

Dancing

The dancing mentioned in the Bible is usually celebratory and positive and is combined with singing or the playing of musical instruments. Such dancing may occur at any happy occasion but is mentioned most often in connection with victory or worship (e.g., Exod. 15:20; Judg. 11:34; 1 Sam. 18:6). The women of Shiloh "join in the dancing" (Judg. 21:21) at an annual festival, which implies some manner of folk dancing. The dancing of Herodias's daughter probably was erotic (Matt. 14:6; Mark 6:22), and the dancing of the Israelites around the golden calf probably was laden with sensuality as well (Exod. 32:19).

Mustard–A plant cultivated for its seeds (ground for spices and pressed for oil). The variety in Palestine, while fast-growing and able to reach ten feet in height, had the smallest seeds of plants then known. Jesus used the mustard plant in a parable to symbolize the growth of the kingdom of God (Matt. 13:31–32) and the seed to symbolize faith (17:20).

Muteness–The inability or choice not to speak (Ps. 38:13; Isa. 56:10). Mosaic law claims that God either makes people mute or allows them to speak (Exod. 4:11). Muteness can be a divine judgment, as when Zechariah is unable to speak after he questions the message of the angel (Luke 1:20). The prophets anticipate a time of reversal, when "the mute tongue [will] shout for joy" (Isa. 35:6). Jesus heals at least two mute people (Matt. 9:32–34; 12:22–24). In both cases the condition is caused by demon possession. Ironically, as

M

the Suffering Servant, one who bears God's judgment, he becomes mute before his accusers (Isa. 53:7; Matt. 26:63; 27:12, 14; Acts 8:26–35). Paul claims that idols are "mute," whereas God's Spirit speaks through believers (1 Cor. 12:2–3).

Myra–*See* Asia Minor, Cities of.

Myrrh–*See* Spices.

Mysia–A northern region of the Roman province of Asia in northwest Asia Minor, now Turkey. Paul entered Mysia from Galatia on his second missionary journey. When the Holy Spirit prevented his access northward into Bithynia, he proceeded through Mysia to the port city of Troas, where a vision instructed him to sail to Macedonia (Acts 16:6–10). He returned to Troas (Acts 20:6; cf. 2 Cor. 2:12; 2 Tim. 4:13) and Assos, another port city of Mysia (Acts 20:13–14). Its third seaport, Adramyttium, was the origin of the ship used on the first leg of Paul's journey to Rome (Acts 27:2). The apostle John writes a letter to the church of Pergamum in Mysia, instructing them to repent from their adherence to false teaching (Rev. 1:11; 2:12–17).

Mystery–A mystery entails knowledge that is disclosed to some but withheld from others. Nothing is mysterious to God (Heb. 4:13), and he alone understands the full purpose of his will (Job 38:1–40:24; Isa. 46:10), but he also condescends to reveal portions of his will to those whom he chooses (John 16:15).

Jesus' parables make known the character and future of God's coming kingdom to his chosen servants, while also concealing it from those outside the circle (Matt. 13:18–23). Paul, by contrast, used "mystery" to refer to the disclosure of God's plan for the redemption of humanity—namely, the inclusion of Gentiles within "Israel" (Rom. 11:25). This plan, foreshadowed in the OT but nevertheless hidden in essentials, had only recently been fully revealed in the death and resurrection of Jesus Christ (Rom. 16:25; Eph. 1:9; 1 Tim. 3:16; cf. 1 Pet. 1:10–12). The gospel message is therefore the revelation of this mystery, the proclamation of the truth about Jesus Christ, now made public to the world (Eph. 3:3–9).

N

Naaman–A Syrian military commander healed of leprosy after reluctantly following Elisha's command to dip himself seven times in the Jordan River (2 Kings 5). Jesus referred to Naaman as a model of faith (Luke 4:27).

Nabal–A wealthy landowner in Carmel, Nabal, gruff and hard, was married to the beautiful and intelligent Abigail. Nabal treated David contemptuously, even though David had protected Nabal's shepherds and possessions. Abigail interceded to keep David from avenging the insult. When Nabal heard, he apparently died of shock, so David took the virtuous Abigail as his wife (1 Sam. 25:2–42).

Nabateans–A Semitic people group inhabiting territory south of the Dead Sea, bordering Judea. The terrain and climate forced them to become experts in water control in agriculture. The probable first mention of this group is from 312 BC in conjunction with Antigonus, who oppressed the Nabatean capital, Petra. The book of 2 Maccabees chronicles the kings of the Nabateans (Arabians) and references Aretas I (2 Macc. 5:8). In 40 BC Herod the Great, whose mother was Nabatean, escaped to Petra because the Parthians attacked Jerusalem. Later, Herod Antipas married the daughter of Aretas IV but subsequently divorced her to marry Herodias. It is this Aretas IV whom Paul references when he describes his escape over the wall in a basket in Damascus (2 Cor. 11:32).

Naboth–A Jezreelite of Samaria, he owned a vineyard near the palace of King Ahab in Jezreel. Since Ahab desired to have this vineyard, he asked Naboth to sell or trade it. Naboth refused, in keeping with the law of inheritance (Lev. 25:23). The sullen Ahab reported this to his wife, Jezebel, who succeeded in having Naboth killed by the slander of false witnesses. After Naboth's death, Ahab took possession of the vineyard. The prophet Elijah predicted the judgment of Ahab and Jezebel for this action, the fulfillment of which came as Ahab's blood was licked by dogs in Jezreel, as Ahab's descendant Joram was left for dead in this same vineyard (2 Kings 9:22–26), and as Jezebel met a violent end so that the dogs licked her blood (2 Kings 9:33–37).

Nadab–**(1)** The firstborn son of Aaron (Exod. 6:23). He served in the priesthood with his father and his brother Abihu (Exod. 24:1). Leviticus 10 notes that Nadab and Abihu offered forbidden fire with the incense. God subsequently destroyed them with fire. Since Nadab and Abihu had no sons, Eleazar and Ithamar, the other two sons of Aaron, served in their stead (1 Chron. 24:1–2). **(2)** The son of Jeroboam, he became king of Israel upon his father's death in the second year of King Asa of Judah (1 Kings 14:20; 15:25). Nadab did evil, as did his father, in his two-year reign. Baasha of the tribe of Issachar assassinated him and reigned in his stead (1 Kings 15:25–28).

Nahash–The Ammonite king who attacked the Israelite city of Jabesh Gilead early in Saul's reign and was subsequently defeated by the new Israelite king (1 Sam. 11). Nahash (lit., "snake") advanced against Jabesh Gilead and demanded to humiliate Israel by gouging out the right eye of everyone in the city as a condition to end the siege. Fortunately for them, Saul responded by raising an army and defeating Nahash and the Ammonites. The Nahash who is in league with David in later texts (2 Sam. 10:2; 17:27) may well be the same king.

N

Nahor–The son of Terah and the brother of Abraham and Haran (Gen. 11:26). Nahor married Milkah, the daughter of his deceased brother, Haran (Gen. 11:28–32). When Abraham headed west for the land of Canaan (Gen. 12:1, 4), Nahor remained in the city of Harran. Through his wife, Milkah, Nahor fathered eight sons, and he fathered another four through his concubine, Reumah (Gen. 22:20–24). Bethuel, one of Nahor's sons through Milkah, fathered Rebekah, who became the wife of Isaac, Abraham's son (Gen. 24:15, 67). Relations between Nahor's eastern branch of the family and Abraham's western branch apparently ceased when Laban, Nahor's grandson, had a falling out with Jacob, Abraham's grandson, in which Laban called on the Lord (Abraham's God) and on Nahor's god to judge between the two parties (Gen. 31:53).

Nahum, Book of–The seventh of the Minor Prophets, Nahum is striking for its powerful poetry and its hard-hitting message. The prophet glories in God's coming judgment on Assyria. After all, Assyria's downfall will bring relief for Judah.

Nahum prophetically anticipates the fall of Nineveh. Historically, the city was defeated by a coalition of Babylonians and Medes. Nahum, however, understands that the real cause of Nineveh's demise and Judah's relief is none other than God. The book begins with a hymn that praises God as warrior who "takes vengeance on his foes" (1:2–8). The remainder of the book specifies that the warrior is coming against Nineveh.

Nain–Just north of Mount Moreh lies Nain; to the southwest was Shunem. When Jesus brought a widow's son back to life, the crowd declared that a prophet had arisen (Luke 7:11–17), remembering Elisha's restoration of the Shunammite woman's son (2 Kings 4).

Names of God–*See* God.

Naomi–A woman of Judah whose family fortunes are the focus of the book of Ruth. Her name means "pleasant," though when her circumstances turned difficult, she asked to be called Mara ("bitter") instead. When her family lived in Moab for a time to escape a famine, she eventually became the mother-in-law of Ruth. She and Ruth returned to her hometown of Bethlehem after the deaths of her husband and sons. Naomi arranged for Ruth's eventual marriage to Boaz, which provided redemption for her family property.

Naphtali–*See* Naphtali, Tribe of.

Naphtali, Tribe of–The tribe descended from Naphtali, son of Jacob and Bilhah. This tribe settled in northern Israel, east of Asher and south of Dan, not far from the Sea of Kinnereth (Sea of Galilee). It is noted that, like other tribes, it failed to completely drive out the Canaanites in its designated territory, which contributed to the difficulties that the nation experienced after the passing of Joshua's generation (Judg. 1:33). Naphtali has a quiet history in Scripture but is mentioned in the prophecy of Isa. 9:1–7, which Matthew cites in connection with Jesus' ministry in Galilee (Matt. 4:12–17). Ezekiel also describes an assigned land area for Naphtali in his temple vision (Ezek. 48:3–4).

Nard–*See* Spices.

Nathan–The prophet Nathan was consulted by David when he contemplated building a temple to house the ark (2 Sam. 7). Without consulting God, Nathan encouraged David in this laudable project, suggesting that in the prophet's mind the project was so obviously right (acknowledging as it did God's supreme kingship over the nation) that there was no need to ask God. However, an unexpected divine refusal came that same night. A divine speech, long by biblical narrative standards (twelve verses), was required to explain the baffling divine refusal. The problem with the project was that the time was not ripe (2 Sam. 7:11; cf. 7:1), for David still had battles to fight.

Nathan reappears in biblical narrative in 2 Sam. 12, sent by God to rebuke David for taking Bathsheba (this confrontation is alluded to in the superscription of Ps. 51). These interventions of Nathan came at David's high point and low point.

Nathanael–One of Jesus' disciples, mentioned by name only in John 1:45–49; 21:2. He was from Cana in Galilee (21:2), where Jesus changed water into wine. Nathanael was initially skeptical of Philip's claims about Jesus because Jesus was from Nazareth (1:45–46), but his skepticism turned to belief when Jesus, who called Nathanael "truly . . . an Israelite in whom there is no deceit," demonstrated miraculous knowledge of where Nathanael had been sitting before he met Jesus (1:47–49).

Nazareth, Nazarene–In the first century, Nazareth was a small village in the extreme southerly part of lower Galilee, midway between the Sea of Galilee and the Mediterranean Sea. It was near Gath Hepher, the birthplace of Jonah the prophet to the Gentiles (2 Kings 14:25), and Sepphoris, one of the three largest cities in the region. Not far was the Via Maris, the great highway joining Mesopotamia to Egypt and ultimately the trading network that linked India, China, central Asia, the Near East, and the Mediterranean. The community, whose population may have averaged around five hundred, subsisted from agriculture. Capital resources included almonds, pomegranates, dates, oil, and wine. (Excavations have located vaulted cells for wine and oil storage, as well as wine presses and storage jar vessels.) Nazareth appears to have been uninhabited from the eighth to the second centuries BC, until it was resettled during the reign of John Hyrcanus (134–104 BC), probably by a Davidic clan of army veterans. The claim that Jesus' adoptive father, Joseph, was a descendant of David and a resident of Nazareth is therefore plausible (Matt. 1:20; Luke 2:4–5). Today, Nazareth is the largest Arab city in Israel.

Although Jesus' ministry was unsuccessful in Nazareth, he and his followers were called "Nazarenes" (Mark 1:24; 10:47; John 18:5, 7; Acts 2:22; 3:6; 24:5). Descendants of Jesus' family continued to live in the area for centuries. The epithet "Nazarene" probably was intended as a slur. Nathanael is unimpressed by Jesus' origin in Nazareth (John 1:46). The village is not mentioned in the OT. Some even doubted its existence, until 1962, when the place name "Nazareth" was discovered on a synagogue inscription in Caesarea Maritima.

Nazirite–Both men and women could take the Nazirite vow (Num. 6:1–21), consecrating themselves to God and abstaining from all grapevine products, avoiding contact with corpses, and allowing their hair to grow long. The first two stipulations mandate separation from conditions reflective of decay and corruption, clearly an affront to God's holiness (cf. Amos 2:11–12). Long hair was the sign of the vow, symbolic of the power of God (Judg. 16:17).

Inadvertently touching a corpse interrupted the vow. Rededication necessitated shaving the head and sacrificing sin and burnt offerings, along with a guilt offering for having defiled something holy (Lev. 5:14–19). The vow could last one's entire life, as was intended for Samson (Judg. 13:7) and Samuel (1 Sam. 1:11), or it could simply be for a period of time (Acts 18:18; 21:24). In the latter case, the vow was terminated with the presentation of sin, burnt, and fellowship offerings and shaving and burning the hair at the tabernacle.

An individual could take the vow by personal volition, or it could be imposed by others. Most of the biblical examples fall into the latter category. The angel of the Lord declared that Samson would be a Nazirite for his entire life, although Samson despised the sanctity of the vow in just about every way (Judg. 13–16). Hannah dedicated Samuel for his life (1 Sam. 1:11). John the Baptist was also apparently given over to these conditions by the word of the angel Gabriel (Luke 1:15).

Nebo–**(1)** Mount Nebo is located in Abarim, a mountain range in northwest Moab separating the Transjordan Plain from the Jordan Valley. Nebo is usually identified with a mountain of the same modern name that is five miles northwest of Madaba and is well over four thousand feet in elevation. This was the mountain that God commanded Moses to ascend to get a glimpse of the promised land before he died (Deut. 32:48–52; 34:1). **(2)** The god Nebo was considered the son of the Babylonian chief god, Marduk, and was himself the god of wisdom and writing. He was thus the patron god of scribes (Isa. 46:1).

Nebo-Sarsekim–A Babylonian official identified in Jer. 39:3. The division and significance of the names in the list is disputed. Some versions treat "Nebo" (Heb. *nebu*) as the second half of Samgar's name, and read this part of the list as "Nergal-sharezer, Samgar-nebo, Sarsechim the Rab-saris" (NRSV, HCSB; similarly, NASB). The NIV and others (see NLT, REB, NET) instead read the Hebrew as two names, with a place name and a title: "Nergal-Sharezer of Samgar, Nebo-Sarsekim a chief officer."

Nebuchadnezzar–The king of Babylon from 605 to 562 BC. Nebuchadnezzar's father, Nabopolassar, was a Chaldean (Aramaic-speaking) tribal chief from the extreme south of Babylon (near what is today the Persian Gulf). In 626 BC he rebelled against Assyria, which for many years had subjugated Babylon to vassal status. In 612 BC the Babylonians, along with the Medes, defeated the Assyrian capital, Nineveh. Remnants of the Assyrian army fled to the region around Harran in northern Syria under the leadership of Ashur-uballit. In 609 BC Pharaoh Necho of Egypt attempted to bolster the Assyrian army, but the Babylonians soundly defeated them at the battle of Carchemish. At this point, Babylon inherited what was the Assyrian Empire, which included Syria and the northern kingdom of Israel. In 605 BC Nabopolassar died of natural causes, and his son Nebuchadnezzar succeeded him as king.

In the same year, according to Dan. 1:1–3, Nebuchadnezzar besieged Jerusalem. In any case, the pro-Egyptian Judean king, Jehoiakim, had no recourse but to submit, turning over to the Babylonian king the temple vessels and also political hostages from the royal family, including Daniel and his three friends.

In 597 BC Jehoiakim revolted against Nebuchadnezzar. By the time the Babylonian army mobilized and made the long march to Jerusalem, Jehoiakim had been replaced by his son Jehoiachin. The city of Jerusalem was then taken. Jehoiachin, along with many leaders, including the priest Ezekiel, were taken into exile in Babylon. Nebuchadnezzar then placed on the throne Jehoiachin's uncle, who took the name "Zedekiah."

Yet, in 586 BC even Zedekiah presumed to rebel against Nebuchadnezzar. This time Nebuchadnezzar defeated Jerusalem, and he killed Zedekiah's sons, gouged out his eyes, and carted him off to Babylon. He also destroyed much of the city, including the palace, walls, and temple. He exiled many of the leading citizens, but he left most of the people in the land under the leadership of Gedaliah, a Judean-born governor. Jeremiah records the account of later atrocities of an insurgent, Ishmael (Jer. 40:7–41:15). Ishmael's assassination of Gedaliah and murder of the Babylonian soldiers in Jerusalem led to yet another Babylonian incursion into Judah in 582 BC.

Nebuchadnezzar died in 562 BC. He was succeeded by his son Amel-Marduk (known in the Bible as Awel-Marduk [2 Kings 25:27]). It is doubtful that Nebuchadnezzar ever worshiped the true God exclusively but he came to recognize Yahweh's great power and wisdom.

Nebushazban–The chief officer of King Nebuchadnezzar of Babylon (r. 605–562 BC), he was one of several Babylonian officials who ordered Jeremiah's removal from the courtyard during the fall of Jerusalem in 586 BC (Jer. 39:13 [KJV: "Nebushasban"]).

Nebuzaradan–A Babylonian official, "the commander of the guard" (2 Kings 25:11), who appears in the biblical text at the fall of the city of Jerusalem in 586 BC. Nebuzaradan is credited with the complete razing of the temple, city structures, and defenses of Jerusalem (2 Kings 25:8–10). He also took many of the notable citizens into exile and left the poor behind (2 Kings 25:11–12). On instructions from Nebuchadnezzar, Nebuzaradan treated Jeremiah well (Jer. 39:11–14). Nebuzaradan returned to the land of Judah a few years later and took another 745 captives into exile (Jer. 52:30).

Necho–Necho II was the third pharaoh of the Twenty-sixth Dynasty of Egypt (r. 610–595 BC). In 609 BC Necho led the Egyptian army through Syria-Palestine to help support the crumbling Assyrian Empire at Harran against the encroaching Babylonians. Necho's goal was to consolidate Egyptian power over the region from Egypt to the Euphrates. While Necho was traveling through Israelite territory, King Josiah of Judah led his army to confront Necho and forced a battle near Megiddo (2 Kings 23:29–35; 2 Chron. 35:20–36:4; cf. Jer. 46:2). Necho had warned Josiah that he was only passing through, but the battle went forward, and Josiah was killed. Three months later, after the Egyptian and Assyrian armies were unsuccessful in battle, Necho summoned Josiah's son Jehoahaz to Riblah in Syria and deposed him, taking him into exile in Egypt. In his stead, Necho renamed Josiah's older son Eliakim, calling him "Jehoiakim," and placed him on the throne of Judah. This made Judah a vassal of Egypt, and Necho required a heavy tribute of gold and silver from Jehoiakim. Four years later, Necho again led the Egyptian army in battle against Babylon at Carchemish and shortly thereafter at Hamath, both serious defeats for Necho. Soon Nebuchadnezzar was campaigning in Palestine, and Jehoiakim switched his allegiance (and vassal loyalty) from Egypt to Babylon. Necho II was able to prevent Nebuchadnezzar and the Babylonian army from invading Egypt, but he never came farther east than Gaza from that time forward.

Needle–The only mention of the word "needle" in the Bible is in the reference to the "eye of a needle" in the Synoptic Gospels (Matt. 19:24; Mark 10:25; Luke 18:25). The purpose here is to contrast one of the smallest openings common to the household with one of Palestine's largest animals. This comparison is an example of hyperbole, expressing the great difficulty that the rich would encounter in abandoning all to follow Christ.

Negev–*See* Wilderness.

Nehemiah–*See* Nehemiah, Book of.

Nehemiah, Book of–Nehemiah son of Hakaliah is one of the most colorful figures in OT history. He is passionate and aggressive; he works hard to achieve the goals that God has set for him. He does not tolerate the sins of others and fights his way through the obstacles that people set in his path. In many ways, he is a study in contrasts with Ezra, his near contemporary. When Ezra discovers sin among his fellow Judeans, he pulls his hair out. When Nehemiah encounters the same problem, he pulls out the hair of the sinners.

The books of Ezra and Nehemiah were originally a single composition, not broken into two parts until the Middle Ages. The book of Nehemiah begins with Nehemiah serving as the cupbearer of King Artaxerxes of Persia. Nehemiah hears a distressing report from his ancestral homeland in Judah and feels called to return to Jerusalem. Receiving permission from Artaxerxes to go back to Judah, he arrives intent on building the walls of the city, thus completing the physical reconstruction of the city. In spite of the efforts of neighboring groups and provinces to block their efforts, the Jews under Nehemiah's leadership are remarkably successful at accomplishing their task. In this, the postexilic people of God surely must have recognized that the prophecies of salvation in Isaiah, Jeremiah, and Ezekiel were coming to fulfillment.

The book of Nehemiah also records Ezra's leadership in guiding the people to reaffirm their commitment to Yahweh and his law. They confess their sin. One might think of the physical wall that Nehemiah built not only as protection but also as a means of physical separation from the Gentiles. Also, then, Ezra's reestablishment of the law of God would serve as a spiritual separation from the lawless Gentiles.

Even with all the success, the book of Nehemiah ends in chapter 13 on a note of disappointment. Nehemiah recounts the strenuous efforts that the faithful under his leadership have made to get right with God, but many people persisted in their sin.

Nehushtan–In 2 Kings 18:4 the name given to the bronze snake that Moses made during the wilderness journey. In one of many incidents in which the Israelites grumbled against Moses, God sent poisonous snakes against the people (Num. 21:4–9). When they confessed their sin and cried out to Moses for relief, God directed him to make the bronze snake and erect it on a pole. Anyone who looked at it would live. Apparently, this object was kept and preserved over the centuries, for it still existed in King Hezekiah's time. Being a sacred relic, it had become an object of idolatry. The king destroyed it as part of his spiritual reforms.

Nephilim–The Hebrew word *nepilim* occurs only in Gen. 6:4; Num. 13:33. Some translations render the word as "giants." Literally, it means "fallen ones." Some scholars have considered the Nephilim to be offspring from the unions between the "sons of God" and the "daughters of humans," but it is also possible that the writer was distinguishing between the Nephilim and the children of those unions who became the "heroes of old" and "men of renown" (Gen. 6:4). Descendants of the Nephilim were purported to have also lived after the flood (Deut. 2:10–11, 20–23; Josh. 14:15; 15:13–14; 2 Sam. 21:16–22; 1 Chron. 20:6–8). Since the entire human race, except for Noah and his family, was destroyed in the deluge, these descendants who lived in Canaan at the time of the exodus most likely descended through Ham, one of Noah's sons (Gen. 10:8–20).

Nergal-Sharezer–A Hebrew rendering of the name of the Babylonian official Nergal-shar-usur ("may Nergal protect the king"), who sat in the Jerusalem gate (Jer. 39:3, 13), married the daughter of Nebuchadnezzar, and later assassinated his brother-in-law, assuming the Babylonian throne in the years 559–556 BC.

New Birth–One of the many pictures of salvation that the Bible uses is new birth. Peter praises God because "he has given us new birth into a living hope through the resurrection of Jesus Christ from the dead" (1 Pet. 1:3). In his conversation with Nicodemus, Jesus states, "No one can see the kingdom of God unless they are born again" (John 3:3). He goes on to explain further that this act of new birth is the work of the Spirit (John 3:5–8). What Jesus speaks of, God had promised in the OT (Ezek. 36:25–27). Paul uses similar language when he asserts that God "made us alive with Christ even when we were dead in transgressions" (Eph. 2:5). Because of our sinful rebellion against God, humanity is spiritually dead. God the Father makes alive those who are spiritually dead by the work of the Spirit through the resurrection of Jesus. This new birth is the starting point for the believer's moral transformation.

New Jerusalem–Both Ezekiel and Revelation envision a new Jerusalem and use similar imagery to describe it and to emphasize God's presence in the city (Ezek. 48:30–35; Rev. 21:1–22:5). According to Revelation, the throne of God, the Lamb, and the river of life are present in the new Jerusalem, which comes down from heaven, is made of gold and glass, is adorned with jewels, and is in the shape of a cube. Only those with names in the Lamb's book of life will dwell in the city (Rev. 21:27). The city represents a new, spiritual order (Gal. 4:25–26; Heb. 12:22).

Nicodemus–Nicodemus is mentioned by name five times in Scripture, only in the Gospel of John. He was a Pharisee and a member of the ruling council of the Jews (the Sanhedrin), and most of what we know about him comes from John 3. He came for discussion with Jesus at night, presumably to avoid being detected while having an amicable interaction with Jesus. Unlike his colleagues, Nicodemus recognized the authority of God in Jesus because of the miracles. Yet Nicodemus failed to understand the true nature of spiritual things (3:4–9) that Jesus subsequently explained to him (3:11–21). Jesus noted that since Nicodemus was a teacher in Israel, he should have understood such things (3:10).

Later, Nicodemus showed a sympathetic disposition toward Jesus when the rulers of the Pharisees aligned themselves against Jesus. Nicodemus noted that the law forbade condemnation before examination, and the other leaders reproached him for his defense of Jesus (John 7:50–52).

Then, after Jesus' crucifixion, Nicodemus helped Joseph of Arimathea with the preparation and entombment of the body of Jesus (John 19:38–42). The testimony of Nicodemus prior to this time had been silent or less overt in front of the council, and this more overt act at the burial may testify to his conversion to discipleship of Jesus.

Nicolaitans–Christ commends the Ephesian church for hating the practices of the Nicolaitans as he does (Rev. 2:6). In Rev. 2:15, Christ calls the church in Pergamum to repent for tolerating some among them who hold to Nicolaitan teaching. There, he compares the Nicolaitans to the Balaam/Balak group, which urged people toward the unholy combination of eating meat sacrificed to idols and sexual immorality. We know little else about this group.

Niger–The second name of Simeon, a church leader at Antioch (Acts 13:1). Literally translated from Latin as "black," it probably means that Simeon was of North African descent and designated "Niger" for his dark skin. His inclusion as one of the "prophets and teachers" of the Antiochian church indicates that the church had a multinational and multiethnic identity. Perhaps the conscious awareness of the nations coming together in worship of Christ motivated their encouragement of Paul's continued missionary activities. Some scholars have suggested that this individual and the Simon of Cyrene mentioned in Mark 15:21 are the same person.

Nile–*See* Rivers and Waterways.

Nimrod–Nimrod is described in more detail than any other individual in the Table of Nations in Gen. 10. One of the sons of Cush, he was a warrior and proverbial as a "mighty hunter" (Gen. 10:8–9; 1 Chron. 1:10). He also founded eight cities in Babylonia and Assyria, regions whose inhabitants became Israel's archenemies (Gen. 10:10–11). At the time of the exile, the Assyrians destroyed Israel, and the Babylonians destroyed Judah, but Micah promised redemption from Assyria and "the land of Nimrod" (Mic. 5:6).

Nineveh–An Assyrian city near modern-day Mosul in Iraq, it is first mentioned in the Bible in Gen. 10:11–12. It became the capital of the Assyrian Empire during the reign of Sennacherib (705–681 BC). Because of Assyria's threat during the late eighth and seventh centuries BC, Nineveh was the target of prophetic oracles that predicted its downfall (Nahum; Zeph. 2:13) and is the setting for the prophetic story of Jonah. The city was sacked and destroyed by the Medes and the Babylonians in 612 BC.

No, No-Amon–The ancient name for the Egyptian city identified by the Greeks as "Thebes." "No" means "city," so the name means "City of [the god] Amon." The full Hebrew name, "No-amon," appears only at Nah. 3:8. Elsewhere the city is called "No" (Jer. 46:25; Ezek. 30:14–16).

Located on the Nile about four hundred miles south of the Mediterranean, Thebes rose to its greatest glory during the New Kingdom (1550–1070 BC) and the rise of Egypt's Eighteenth Dynasty, which originated in Thebes. Magnificent royal tombs and temples were built throughout the city. After the death of Ramesses IX (c. 1070 BC), Thebes was no longer directly connected to the royal family, and its prominence diminished. A revival of the city's prominence and considerable growth occurred during the Twenty-fifth Dynasty (760–656 BC), when Thebes was revered by the Amon-worshiping Sudanese kings of the Kushite Dynasty.

Thebes was sacked by the Assyrian army in 663 BC and suffered raids by the Persians in 525 and 343 BC. The prophets Jeremiah (46:25), Ezekiel (30:14–16), and Nahum (3:8) pronounced judgment against Thebes, a city that epitomized Egypt's pride and defiance of God. *See also* Thebes.

Noah–The eighth descendant listed in the line of Seth and the grandson of Methuselah, Noah was used by God to preserve the human race through the flood. His name means "rest," chosen because his father, Lamech, believed that God would use his son to bring rest from the toil of life resulting from the fall (Gen. 5:29). Enoch was his great-grandfather, and like him, Noah is described as one who "walked faithfully with God" (Gen. 6:9; cf. 5:22, 24). He was the father of Shem, Ham, and Japheth.

Noah is mentioned two other times in the OT. God cites his promise that the "waters of Noah" never again would destroy the earth to affirm his covenant faithfulness to Israel (Isa. 54:9), and in another text groups Noah together with Job and Daniel as those who could deliver themselves by their righteousness, but not disobedient Israel (Ezek. 14:14, 20). In the NT, Jesus cites the conditions in Noah's day as being representative of conditions at the time of his coming (Matt. 24:37–38; Luke 17:26–27). Peter mentions Noah twice, once to refer to the spirits of those who perished in the flood (1 Pet. 3:20) and once to use Noah as an example of God's ability to deliver his people (2 Pet. 2:5). Hebrews 11:7 lists Noah as a hero of faith.

N

Nod–After killing Abel, Cain is banished to the land of Nod, the name of which creates a pun on *nwd*, the Hebrew verb for "wander" (Gen. 4:16). Nod is more a fate than a location (cf. 4:12, 14). Like Adam before him (3:24), Cain is denied the security of place and is exiled "east of Eden"—a phrase symbolizing banishment from God. Israel understood land eviction to be the most severe punishment (cf. Lev. 26:27–32). The LXX mistakenly translates the name as "Naid," a corruption of Hebrew letters.

Nubia–*See* Cush, Cushites.

Numbers, Book of–Numbers gets its name from two pivotal chapters (1; 26), which give a census—more accurately, a military registration—of the Israelites as they travel through the wilderness. But there is much more to Numbers. It is part four of the five-part Torah and, like Exodus and Leviticus before it, presents law in the context of a narrative of the travels in the wilderness. It is in Numbers that we read the account of one of the most devastating of all events in the travel narrative, the episode of the spies sent to the promised land, but this story is just the apex of a theme of grumbling that seems a constant reaction from the people of Israel in the wilderness period.

The book begins with a military registration of all the men of Israel who are twenty years of age and older. There is also a description of the wilderness camp, whose very structure resembles that of a war camp. The tabernacle, God's symbolic home on earth, is placed in the middle of the camp, similar to the position of the war leader. The tabernacle, God's tent, is immediately surrounded by his most loyal troops, the Levites, and then the rest of the army, the other tribes of Israel. The militaristic words that Moses speaks on the mornings of the march as the ark of the covenant takes the lead confirm that the wilderness wandering is envisioned as a long march into battle (Num. 10:35).

Although led by a column of smoke during the day and a pillar of fire at night, the Israelites continually rebel and doubt the power and concern of their God. Thus, the first part of the book (chaps. 1–25) is a story of sin and judgment. The people are constantly grumbling against God's provision in the wilderness (e.g., chap. 11). Lay and priestly leaders rebel against Moses, God's appointed leader (chaps. 12; 16–17). The apex of this rebellion is found in the spy story in chapters 13–14. Here, twelve spies, one from each tribe, are sent to the land in advance of the rest of the people. When they return, they come with good news and bad news. The good news is that the land is beautiful and rich in resources; the bad news is that it is populated by nations "stronger than we are" (13:31). The latter news sends the people into a panic, showing their doubt of God's ability to give them the land in spite of this human obstacle. For this rebellion, God dooms them to forty years in the wilderness. Of that original generation, only Joshua and Caleb, the two faithful spies, will be allowed to enter the land, for even Moses on a different occasion has demonstrated his impatience with his divine master (20:1–13).

Forty years was long enough for the original generation to die off and the next generation to mature. The story of the second generation begins with the giving of their military registration in chapter 26. From this point onward, preparations are under way for the entry into the land. Preliminary battles are met with victory, and laws anticipating the Israelites' entry into a new situation are proclaimed. With hope, however, come questions. Will this new generation really be more faithful than the previous one?

In Numbers the reader learns of God's continued involvement with his sinful people. God does not leave them to die there. Indeed, even after the transgression narrated in the spy episode, God remains faithful and protects his people from threats, including that from King Balak of Moab, who hires the prophet Balaam to curse them (chaps. 22–24).

Oak of Tabor–A recognizable landmark in the territory of Benjamin (NIV: "great tree of Tabor"; KJV: "plain of Tabor"). It was the second of three stops that Samuel instructed Saul to make on a journey to Gilgal confirming his selection by God as king of Israel (1 Sam. 10:1–8). There, Saul met three men traveling to Bethel, confirming Samuel's prophecy.

Oaths–The obligations of relationships within ancient societies and between social groups were frequently reinforced by means of oaths, and the practice of oath making (by both God and people) is witnessed to in the pages of the Bible. The name of God was frequently invoked (Judg. 8:19; 2 Kings 2:2), but oaths were not to be made using the names of foreign deities (Ps. 16:4). For this reason, when an oath was broken, God's name was profaned (Lev. 19:12). To take an oath was to ask God to witness what was promised, and it invited him to act as avenger if the promise was broken (Gen. 31:50; 1 Sam. 12:3). This made oath taking a religious act, and so oaths often were made at sanctuaries and under the supervision of cultic officials (Num. 5:11–31; Judg. 11:11; Hos. 4:15).

In the Bible, God is portrayed as binding himself by oaths, most notably his sworn promises to Abraham (Gen. 22:16–18; 50:24). This fact is used by the author of Hebrews in an argument designed to assure readers that God meant what he said when he made promises to his people (Heb. 6:13–18). The coming of Jesus fulfilled the terms of that oath (Luke 1:73). So too the Davidic covenant was supported by a divine oath (Pss. 89:35, 49; 110:4; 132:11), and this was fulfilled by the enthronement of Christ at his resurrection and ascension (Acts 2:30–33).

Jesus' teaching on oaths (Matt. 5:33–37) does not necessarily contradict OT legislation (cf. Lev. 19:12; Num. 30:2; Deut. 23:21–23) but rather brings out the true heart of God behind the legislation. Oaths are unnecessary, Jesus said, for those who habitually tell the truth. An emphatic yes or no is all that is needed. The teaching of James 5:12 reflects what is found in Jesus' teaching on this subject. This may not outlaw all oath taking, and certainly the apostle Paul did not understand there to be a blanket prohibition of oaths, for in his letters he is on record as making oaths (Gal. 1:20; Phil. 1:8).

Obadiah–**(1)** The palace keeper for King Ahab of Israel. Obadiah hid one hundred prophets from persecution under Jezebel. In 1 Kings 18:1–16 he is caught in the middle of Ahab's hunt for Elijah when the prophet asks him to summon Ahab. **(2)** The fourth of the twelve Minor Prophets (Obad. 1:1). *See* Obadiah, Book of.

Obadiah, Book of–Obadiah is the shortest book in the OT (twenty-one verses). It is a prophecy against one of ancient Israel's most persistent enemies, the Edomites. Many other oracles against Edom occur in the OT, but Obadiah is the only case where an entire book is dedicated to this purpose. Conflict between Edom and Israel goes back all the way to the patriarchal period, when their respective ancestors, the brothers Esau and Jacob, experienced conflict.

But ultimately, Obadiah is more than a book that is against Edom. The book proclaims that God is over all the nations, and though the enemies of God's people may have momentary moments of glory, ultimately they will give way to those whom God has chosen. Indeed, the book ends with the triumphant statement "And the kingdom will be the LORD's" (v. 21).

OBED–The son of Boaz and Ruth (Ruth 4:13–17), grandfather of King David, and ancestor of Jesus Christ (Matt. 1:5; Luke 3:32).

OBED-EDOM–"Obed-Edom the Gittite," in whose house David deposited the ark for three months after the death of Uzzah caused David to fear bringing it to Jerusalem. The blessing of Obed-Edom's household prompted David to reconsider (2 Sam. 6:10–12; 1 Chron. 13:13–14; 15:25). Some scholars suggest that he was one of the many Philistines in David's service (the Gittites in 2 Sam. 15:18–19 certainly are foreigners). "Gittite" is, however, a term for anyone from a village called Gath, and the hometown of Obed-Edom may not be Gath in Philistia (e.g., Gath Rimmon [Josh. 21:24–25]).

OBEDIENCE–A central concept in both Testaments for understanding the way in which God's people are to respond to him. God desires obedience from his people, in contrast to mere lip service (Isa. 29:13; Matt. 15:8; Mark 7:6) or conformity to religious ritual (Hos. 6:6; Mic. 6:6–8). When Saul disobeyed God by sacrificing some of the spoil from his victory over the Amalekites, Samuel the prophet responded, "To obey is better than sacrifice, and to heed is better than the fat of rams" (1 Sam. 15:22).

In the NT, focus shifts from obedience to the Mosaic law to obedience to Jesus Christ. The Great Commission contains Jesus' instructions for his own disciples to make disciples, teaching them to "obey" (Gk. *tēreō*) that which Christ had commanded (Matt. 28:19–20). Jesus' disciples' love for him would lead them to obey his commands (John 14:15, 21–24; 1 John 5:3; 2 John 6), and the disciples' obedience, in turn, would cause them to remain in Jesus' love (John 15:10). Paul instructs children to obey their parents and slaves to "obey" (Gk. *hypakouō*) their masters in obedience to Christ (Eph. 6:1, 5–6; Col. 3:20, 22).

The NT also discusses Christ's perfect obedience to God the Father as a quality to imitate (Phil. 2:5–13) and as the basis for salvation (Rom. 5:19). Since it is only "those who obey the law who will be declared righteous" (Rom. 2:13), and all have sinned (Rom. 3:23), "God made him who had no sin to be sin for us, so that in him we might become the righteousness of God" (2 Cor. 5:21).

ODED–**(1)** The father of the prophet Azariah, who ministered to King Asa of Judah (2 Chron. 15:1). Oded is identified as the prophet in the Hebrew text of 2 Chron. 15:8, which apparently omitted Azariah's name, but it is reinserted in some translations. **(2)** A prophet in the time of King Pekah of Israel and King Ahaz of Judah, he helped to persuade the army of Israel to return prisoners and plunder taken from Judah (2 Chron. 28:9–15).

OFFICES IN THE NEW TESTAMENT–These church offices are God-given positions of leadership within the early church designed to give it structure and direction. Some of these positions have ongoing application for today; others are important primarily for understanding the historical development of the church. The more significant offices in the NT church include the following:

Apostle. Apostles formed the earliest and most important leadership structure. Jesus, early in his ministry, "called his disciples to him and chose twelve of them, whom he also designated apostles" (Luke 6:13). The word "disciple" (*mathētēs*) means "student" or "learner" and indicates the role of these original twelve during Jesus' earthly ministry. Following Jesus' death and resurrection, these same individuals (now minus Judas Iscariot) were typically called "apostles" (*apostolos* [lit., "sent-out one"]), who were then entrusted with Christ's power and authority as his official representatives. Paul describes the foundational role of this office in Eph. 2:20. Their power and authority were without parallel in the historical development of the church.

Prophet. The office of prophet (*prophētēs*) is another foundational one at the time of the establishment of the church (Eph. 2:20). Agabus is described as a prophet (Acts 21:10), and Paul assumes that there were prophets in the church in Corinth (1 Cor. 12:29). Although this is a controversial topic, many believe that this office no longer continues today.

Elder/presbyter. The office of elder or presbyter (*presbyteros*) is one of the most common in the church. This office is based on the model of elders in the Jewish synagogue. Paul and Barnabas appointed elders in every church as early as their first missionary journey (Acts 14:23). James instructs the sick to call on the elders of the church to pray over them (James 5:14). The best job description for elders is 1 Tim. 5:17, where there are two major emphases: first, directing the affairs of the church, and second, preaching and teaching. Elders apparently always functioned in a plurality in Scripture, never as solo leaders.

Overseer/bishop. The office of overseer or bishop (*episkopos*) is mentioned in Phil. 1:1 as well as in 1 Tim. 3:2; Titus 1:7 in the lists of qualifications. Although by the second or third century the office of overseer/bishop had evolved into a singular office of one overseer presiding over a number of elders, this was not true in the NT, where these two titles apparently were different names for the same office.

Deacon. Deacons provide practical, hands-on ministry in the local church. Interestingly, the classic passage on this office, Acts 6:1–6, never uses the actual noun "deacon" (*diakonos*). Instead, other forms of this word are used: "to wait on tables" (*diakoneō* [v. 2]) and "the ministry [lit., 'service'] of the word" (*diakonia* [v. 4]). This word group is used frequently to refer to nonreligious service, such as Martha's meal preparation (Luke 10:40) or in reference to a servant or attendant in one of Jesus' parables (e.g., Matt. 22:13). Originally, the term "deacon" simply meant "servant." In the development of the NT church, it gradually became a technical term used to refer to a specific office, such as in Paul's greeting in Phil. 1:1 and in the list of qualifications in 1 Tim. 3:8–13. The standard understanding of the deacons in the NT church structure is that they assisted the elders/overseers in practical ways (probably on the model of the seven men in Acts 6).

Pastor. Pastors, surprisingly, show up only a single time in most English translations, in Eph. 4:11, where Paul describes how Christ "gave . . . pastors and teachers." "Pastor" (*poimēn*) means "shepherd," and although the noun appears in this sense of a church leader only here, the verb "to shepherd" (*poimainō*) occurs also in Acts 20:28; 1 Pet. 5:2. This shepherding role is associated with the elders/overseers. We see this in Paul's address to the Ephesian elders in Acts 20, where he calls them "elders" (v. 17) and "overseers" (v. 28) and tells them how they are to "be shepherds of the church of God" (v. 28). Peter does the same thing in 1 Pet. 5:1–2, where he calls them "elders" (v. 1) and then calls them "overseers" and tells them to "be shepherds of God's flock" (v. 2).

Teacher. Teachers are mentioned among those with various spiritual gifts in 1 Cor. 12:28–29 and are connected with pastors in Eph. 4:11, apparently as a single combined office.

Evangelist. Evangelists are mentioned in the list of specially gifted individuals in Eph. 4:11, in relationship to Philip the evangelist in Acts 21:8, and as part of the job description for Timothy in 2 Tim. 4:5 ("do the work of an evangelist").

OG–An Amorite king of Bashan, an area northeast of the Sea of Galilee (Deut. 4:47). Og was one of the last of the Rephaites, a gigantic people (Deut. 3:11; 4:47). As the Israelites prepared to enter the promised land, Og attacked them at Edrei, but the Israelites defeated him and seized his land (Num. 21:33–35), which ultimately was allotted to the half-tribe of Manasseh (Deut. 3:13). Israel's defeats of Og and the neighboring Amorite king Sihon were cited as evidences of God's faithfulness (Neh. 9:22; Ps. 136:19–20).

OHOLAH AND OHOLIBAH–Names that Ezekiel assigns to the northern kingdom of Israel (Oholah) and the southern kingdom of Judah (Oholibah) in his graphically sexual extended allegory about their unfaithfulness to God (Ezek. 23). The metaphor involves two sisters, Oholah and Oholibah, who are married to Yahweh. But the sisters are repeatedly unfaithful, going after other gods and making political alliances. Oholah's lover was Assyria, by whom she was condemned to defeat and exile.

OHOLIAB–The son of Ahisamak, of the tribe of Dan, he was a craftsman extraordinaire. He is called an "engraver" who might work on wood or stone, a "designer," and an "embroiderer" (Exod. 38:23). He was appointed by Moses to work with Bezalel in construction of the tabernacle (35:30–34).

OIL–Almost all the oil to which the Bible refers is olive oil. Oil was used primarily for cooking, but also for medicinal purposes, cosmetics, lighting, and religious ceremonies.

Oil was one of the major export products of Palestine, with huge economic impact on Israel and Judah. Oil often was used as currency for other needed materials (Deut. 7:13; Neh. 5:11; Luke 16:6). For example, Elisha performed a miracle with oil to help a widow pay her debts (2 Kings 4:7). Oil was kept as part of the royal stores (2 Kings 20:13; 2 Chron. 32:28). There are dozens of ostraca that detail the trading, bartering, and selling of oil.

Oil was one of the main ingredients for cooking. A typical meal consisted of flour pressed together with oil and fried with oil on a griddle (1 Kings 17:12–16). This was also the typical way in which grain offerings were made at the tabernacle and temple (Lev. 2:1, 4–7). Oil was also used in lamps because it burned cleanly and produced bright light (2 Kings 4:10; Matt. 25:3–8). Lamps were used throughout the house. Small lamps, often no larger than a hand, were used to give people light when they were walking and traveling at night. In such instances, extra oil usually was carried as a reserve (Matt. 25:1–13). Both the tabernacle and the temple used olive oil to light their lamps. The finest oil was also used for sacrifices at the tabernacle (Exod. 27:20; 29:40; Lev. 24:2; Num. 28:5).

Oil was used cosmetically as well. For instance, oil was put in the hair for beauty (Eccles. 9:8). Oil was also the normal base for perfumes, mixed with a variety of spices (Esther 2:12). The tabernacle had special anointing oil that was mixed to make a perfume (Exod. 30:25). Oil was also used medicinally to help heal wounds, either by mixing it with other substances or by itself to help seal a wound (Luke 10:34). The elders of the church were commissioned to pray for and anoint the sick with oil (James 5:14).

Olivet Discourse–The Olivet Discourse is Jesus' sermon predicting the Jewish War, the destruction of the temple, the fall of Jerusalem in AD 70, and the coming of the Son of Man to judge and to save. It is found in the Synoptic Gospels (Matt. 24:1–25:46; Mark 13:1–37; Luke 21:5–36). The name derives from the Mount of Olives, overlooking Jerusalem and the temple, the place where Jesus taught his disciples this material.

Omen–A sign that is read or interpreted to ascertain a divine message, usually to avert some evil or predict the future. Reading omens was a very common practice in Mesopotamia and is known in different forms. One such practice was extispicy: reading the entrails of a sacrificial animal. Other forms included astrology, the observation of freak births (teratoscopy), and observing the behavior of water when poured onto oil (lecanomancy). Ezekiel 21:21 makes note of some of these practices. Generally, the biblical authors outlaw omen reading because God used the institution of the prophet to make his purposes known (Amos 3:7). While most were outlawed, some forms do seem to be present in the Bible. Jacob used the cup for divining (Gen. 44:5) and seems to have been practicing lecanomancy. The Urim and Thummim also had a similar purpose (1 Sam. 14:41).

Omer–*See* Weights and Measures.

Omnipotence–An attribute of God related to his infinity, omnipotence is the attribute of having all power. This attribute is expressed every time Scripture notes God as "almighty" (Heb. *shadday*). In Scripture, God as omnipotent is related to God as eternal, God as the creator of all things, and God as the sustainer of all creation and life.

Nothing is beyond the power of God to act and perform, and what God does is in conformity with his own nature and will. In the NT, omnipotence is noted with the word "almighty" (*pantokratōr*) in 2 Cor. 6:18; Rev. 1:8; 4:8; 11:17; 15:3; 16:7, 14; 19:6, 15; 21:22. These contexts note God as sovereign and eternal, frequently noted with the Johannine expression of God as the one "who is, and who was, and who is to come" (Rev. 1:8).

Omnipresence–The English word derives from the Latin *omnis* ("all") and *praesens* ("present"). Though not found in Scripture, the term accurately describes a divine perfection. God is always in his totality everywhere present, yet separate from his creation (Gen. 1; 1 Kings 8:27; Ps. 139:7–12; Jer. 23:23–24; Heb. 4:13).

Omniscience–The English word derives from the Latin *omnis* ("all") and *sciens* ("knowing"). Though not found in Scripture, the term accurately describes an exclusively divine attribute. God has perfect infinite knowledge of himself and everything actual and possible (1 Sam. 23:8–13; Job 37:16; Pss. 33:13–15; 139:2–6, 11–12; 147:5; Prov. 15:3; Isa. 40:14; 46:10; Dan. 2:22; Matt. 11:21–23; John 21:17; Acts 15:18; 1 Cor. 2:10–11; Heb. 4:13; 1 John 3:20).

Omri–Omri's history is found in 1 Kings 16:16–17, 21–28. Not counting his rival Tibni (who never was king), Omri was the sixth king of Israel (r. 882–871 BC), making his son Ahab the seventh. Omri ruled for six years in Tirzah and then built the city of Samaria and moved the capital there. His kingdom was stable and prosperous. He married Ahab to Jezebel, a princess of Tyre, forging a marriage alliance with Phoenicia.

On–**(1)** The son of Peleth from the tribe of Reuben (Num. 16:1). He was one of the Israelite leaders who rebelled against Moses and Aaron by questioning their leadership role. Numbers 16 does not mention his name again even though the other rebels are mentioned repeatedly; thus it is not clear if he was consumed by fire (as a punishment from God) along with the other leaders who rebelled. Interestingly, in the genealogy of Reuben his name does not appear (Num. 26:5–9). **(2)** A city in Egypt near modern-day Cairo. "On," which is the Greek and Hebrew name of the city, more often goes by its other name, "Heliopolis." On is mentioned in connection with Joseph's wife, Asenath, who was the daughter of Potiphera, the priest of On (Gen. 41:45; 46:20). In a lament against Egypt, Ezekiel names On as one of the cities that will be taken into captivity (Ezek. 30:17).

Onan–One of the sons of the patriarch Judah. He was obligated to father a son through his brother's widow, Tamar, according to the custom of levirate marriage (Gen. 38:8). By practicing what appears to be a form of birth control, Onan refrained from impregnating Tamar by spilling "his semen on the ground," and so Yahweh put him to death for his failure to fulfill his obligation to his dead brother (Gen. 38:9–10).

Onesimus–A runaway slave who belonged to the apostle Paul's friend and convert Philemon. A man of importance, Philemon hosted a church in his Colossian home. While possibly attempting to blend in with the large population of Rome, Onesimus connected with Paul during Paul's imprisonment and was converted to the faith (Philem. 10). Though he was helpful to Paul, the apostle sent him back to Philemon to make things right. Paul pleaded with Philemon to accept Onesimus back as a brother in Christ. Onesimus accompanied Tychicus to Colossae to deliver Paul's letter to that church (Col. 4:9) and to present himself and Paul's personal letter to Philemon. Though the outcome of this request is not known for certain, tradition suggests that Onesimus became a bishop in the early church.

Onesiphorus–An early Christian disciple who, in the context of Paul's exhortation to Timothy not to be ashamed of the gospel or of his "chains" (2 Tim. 1:8, 16), is praised as an example worthy of imitation (1:16–18). Onesiphorus (his name means "profit bringer") is commended for diligently and courageously seeking out Paul in prison and for his many acts of kindness to Paul and the church at Ephesus. Paul's prayer for God's mercy is directed not to Onesiphorus but to his household, suggesting that he was not with them at the time of writing (1:16; 4:19).

Ophel–All or part of the City of David south of the temple location. In Hebrew, this name always appears with the definite article ("the Ophel"), generally in conjunction with a fortifying wall. Jotham built the wall of the Ophel (2 Chron. 27:3). When Manasseh rebuilt the outer wall of the City of David, west of the Gihon spring, it encircled the Ophel (2 Chron. 33:14). Temple servants living on the Ophel (Neh. 3:26; 11:21) repaired the wall opposite the Water Gate to the east and the projecting tower, and the men of Tekoa worked from the projecting tower to the wall of the Ophel (Neh. 3:27).

Ophir–A land most often mentioned in regard to the economic enterprises of different kings, especially involving gold. Together, King Solomon and King Hiram of Tyre in Phoenicia sent ships from the Red Sea port of Ezion Geber to Ophir and brought back 420 (2 Chronicles reports 450 talents) talents of gold (1 Kings 9:26–28; 2 Chron. 8:18). The report about the Queen of Sheba's visit to Solomon says that Solomon and Hiram's ships brought gold from Ophir along with silver, ivory, apes, and peacocks every three years (1 Kings 10:11; 2 Chron. 9:10). Jehoshaphat also built a fleet of trading ships that he intended to send to Ophir, but they were wrecked in harbor and never set sail (1 Kings 22:48–49). David's contribution to the building of the temple (which his son Solomon was to build) included three thousand talents of gold from Ophir (1 Chron. 29:4).

Oracles–Divine pronouncements given to humankind that are either unsolicited (Isa. 7:3–9; Hag. 1:2–11; Zech. 12:1) or a response to an inquiry (2 Kings 8:8). It was common practice throughout the ancient Near East to seek pronouncements from deities and to identify holy sites where sacred individuals could query the deities (e.g., the shrine of Apollo at Delphi). How much time elapsed between the transmission of an oracle and its inscription is uncertain. Inscriptions from the surrounding Near Eastern milieu attest that messages received from a deity often were transcribed immediately upon reception, with the prophet's name attached.

Oreb and Zeeb–Midianite leaders whom the Ephraimites killed. After Gideon and his three hundred soldiers had miraculously routed the Midianite army, Gideon directed the Ephraimites to cut off the fleeing Midianites at the Jordan River. The Ephraimites were successful and captured Oreb and Zeeb, whom they put to death at the rock of Oreb and the winepress of Zeeb respectively (Judg. 7:19–25). Gideon later claimed that the Ephraimites' killing of Oreb and Zeeb was greater than his own accomplishments in the battle (Judg. 8:1–3). See also Ps. 83:11; Isa. 10:26.

Ornan–*See* Araunah.

Orontes River–*See* Rivers and Waterways.

Orpah–The widow of Kilion (see Ruth 4:10). Along with Ruth, she was a Moabite daughter-in-law of Naomi. After Naomi's husband and sons died, Naomi convinced Orpah to remain in Moab rather than return with her to Bethlehem. Orpah thus provides a foil to Ruth, who resolved to stay with Naomi.

Orphans–*See* Poor, Orphan, Widow.

Osnappar–*See* Ashurbanipal.

Othniel–The son of Kenaz and a nephew of Caleb (or possibly Caleb's brother). At Caleb's request, Othniel defeated the inhabitants of Kiriath Sepher, and as a result he received Caleb's daughter Aksah as a bride (Josh. 15:16–19; Judg. 1:13–15). Othniel also served as the first judge of Israel, delivering the people from the hands of Cushan-Rishathaim, the king of Aram Naharaim (Judg. 3:7–11). Israel experienced peace for forty years, which ended with the death of Othniel.

P

Paddan Aram–The "field" or "plain" of Aram was a region of northwestern Mesopotamia. In Genesis it is associated with Aram Naharaim (24:10 [meaning "Aram of the two rivers"]), "the town of Nahor" (24:10), Arameans (25:20), Harran (27:43), and "the land of the eastern peoples" (29:1). Paddan Aram was the home of Bethuel, his children Laban and Rebekah (Isaac's wife), and Laban's daughters Leah and Rachel (Jacob's wives), and it was the birthplace of all of Jacob's children except Benjamin (Gen. 25:20; 28:2–7; 35:26; 46:15).

Palestine–The word "Palestine" is derived from the name of one of the Sea Peoples who migrated to the southern coastal region of the Fertile Crescent from one or more of the coastal regions of the Mediterranean (*see* Philistines).

Palestine is in the southwestern portion of the Fertile Crescent (i.e., western Iraq, Syria, Lebanon, Jordan, and Israel). It is located northeast of the Nile River basin and west-southwest of the basins of the Tigris and Euphrates rivers.

Because of fluidity in the use of the term "Palestine," it is difficult to speak precisely of the land area designated by it. Palestine west of the Jordan River is about six thousand square miles, similar to the land area of the state of Hawaii.

Palms, City of–*See* Jericho.

Pamphylia–A small Roman province on the south coast of central Asia Minor (modern Turkey). Pamphylia was a flat plain of approximately eighty by twenty miles. Jews from this region were present at Pentecost (Acts 2:10). Its capital city of Perga was Paul's first entry into Asia Minor on his first missionary journey with Barnabas (13:13). After traveling northward to preach the gospel in the cities of Lycaonia, they returned to Pamphylia, preaching in Perga and sailing from the port city of Attalia (14:25). Paul and Barnabas split over their disagreement about John Mark, who had deserted them in Pamphylia (15:38). See also Acts 27:5.

Paphos–A Roman city rebuilt by Augustus and located on the southwest coast of the island of Cyprus. Paul and Barnabas traveled to the new Paphos, where they encountered the Jewish magician Elymas (Bar-Jesus) and converted the Roman official Sergius Paulus to faith in Jesus (Acts 13:6–13).

Parables–The word "parable" is used to speak of a particular literary form that communicates indirectly by means of comparative language, often for the purpose of challenging the listener to accept or reject a new way of thinking about a particular matter. Parables regularly incorporate concrete and accessible images from the daily life of the audience, and often they are terse and pointed, mentioning only the details relevant for an effective comparison. However, any attempt to define the term "parable" in a clear and concise way is complicated by the fact that both the Hebrew (*mashal*) and the Greek (*parabolē*) words regularly translated by the English word "parable" have much broader connotations. For instance, in the OT *mashal* can designate proverbs (Prov. 1:1), riddles (Ezek. 17:2), prophetic utterances (Num. 23:7, 18; 24:3, 15, 20, 21, 23), and sayings (1 Sam. 10:12); similarly, in the NT *parabolē* denotes proverbs (Luke 4:23), riddles (Mark 3:23), analogies (Mark 7:17), and more. Therefore, no comprehensive definition of parables is agreed upon by biblical scholars, and very little said about parables in general will apply to every parable.

Paran–The desert to which the Israelites journeyed after leaving the Desert of Sinai (Num. 10:11–12). The location is never explicitly mentioned, but it can be inferred from some of the descriptions of the Israelites' wilderness journey. It is a desert region south of Judah, west of Edom, and north of Sinai, within the region known as the Negev. This is the location from which Moses sent spies to explore the promised land (Num. 13:3). They subsequently returned to the Desert of Paran at Kadesh (Num. 13:26), giving us a geographical reference near Kadesh. Other references to the Desert of Paran confirm this location. Genesis 21:21 specifies the Desert of Paran as the place to which Abraham banished Ishmael, and specific references to Egypt and Beersheba clarify its location between them. See also 1 Kings 11:18.

Parthians–The descendants of the Parni tribe. They claimed independence from Seleucid dominance and rose to power under King Mithridates I (r. 171–138 BC). At its height, the Parthian Empire extended from the Euphrates River to the Indus Valley. The Romans never conquered them, but the Sasanian Persians overthrew the Parthian Empire in AD 224. In Acts 2:9 Parthian Jews are mentioned as present in Jerusalem on the day of Pentecost.

Parties, Jewish–*See* Jewish Parties.

Paschal–Formed from "Pascha" (a Latinized version of *Pesach*, the Hebrew term for "Passover"), this adjective pertains to the Feast of Passover. *See* Festivals.

Pashhur–**(1)** A priest, the son of Immer, during the time of Jeremiah. As the "official in charge of the temple," he put the prophet in stocks (Jer. 20:1–6). Jeremiah delivered a prophecy against him and renamed him "Magor-Missabib" ("Terror on Every Side"). **(2)** Jeremiah also mentions a Pashhur son of Malkijah who is not identified as a priest when he is introduced in Jer. 21:1. He was sent by King Zedekiah to encourage the prophet to beseech God for help during the Babylonian siege. In Jer. 38:1 he is part of a group that gets Jeremiah arrested. **(3)** Jeremiah 38:1 also mentions Pashhur as the father of Gedaliah. Gedaliah is not the governor of the same name. Pashhur here could conceivably be one of the previous two men, but we are uncertain.

Passover–*See* Festivals.

Pastor–*See* Offices in the New Testament.

Pastorals, Pastoral Letters–The letters of 1 Timothy, 2 Timothy, and Titus are referred to as the Pastoral Letters (or Pastoral Epistles). This name reflects that these letters are directed to persons serving with pastoral responsibilities. They might be better called "missionary letters," since Timothy and Titus were serving in missionary settings. But the traditional name "Pastorals" has been used since the eighteenth century.

Pathros–A region associated with Mizraim (Egypt) in Isa. 11:11; Jer. 44:1, 15; Ezek. 29:14; 30:14. Most likely it is Upper Egypt (so the NIV), the region just south of Mizraim (Lower Egypt). The Egyptian name for the "south land" refers to the area between Memphis and Aswan and is philologically similar to "Pathros."

Patmos–A small island in the Aegean Sea, thirty-seven miles from Miletus. While under Roman rule, it was used as a place of political exile. Around AD 95–97 John the Seer was exiled to the island, where he wrote the book of Revelation: "I, John . . . was on the island of Patmos because of the word of God and the testimony of Jesus" (Rev. 1:9). According to tradition, John communicated with God while in a cave, which exists until today and is called the "Holy Cave of Revelation."

Patriarch–The male head of a family. The OT describes the Israelite nation as an extended family descended from a line of common ancestors, the patriarchs Abraham, Isaac, and Jacob (also called "Israel" [see Gen. 32:28]). Each of Jacob's sons (or his grandsons Ephraim and Manasseh) traditionally gave his name to one of the tribes that made up the Israelite people. The NT applies the term "patriarch" to individuals of the generations from Abraham (Heb. 7:4) to his twelve great-grandsons (Acts 7:8) and, in one case, to the tenth-century king David (Acts 2:29). In the OT the term "patriarch" is not used, though the concept of Abraham, Isaac, and Jacob as national fathers is frequently expressed, as in Exod. 3:15, which refers to Israel's God as "the

Lord, the God of your fathers—the God of Abraham, the God of Isaac and the God of Jacob."

Paul–A Pharisee commissioned by Jesus Christ to preach the gospel to Gentiles. His Jewish name was "Saul" (Acts 9:4; 13:9), but he preferred using his Roman name, especially when he signed his letters.

By our best estimates, Paul spent about thirty years preaching the gospel of Jesus Christ (AD 34–67)—a ministry that can be divided roughly into three decades. The first decade of his ministry (AD 34–46) has been called the "silent years," as we have few details from Acts or the Pauline Epistles about his activities. For example, we know that he preached in Damascus for a while and spent some time in Arabia (a total of three years [Gal. 1:17–18]). He made a quick trip to Jerusalem to meet Peter and James the brother of Jesus. Then he returned home to Tarsus, evidently preaching there for several years, until Barnabas brought him to Antioch in Syria to help with the ministry of this mixed congregation of Jews and Gentiles (Acts 9:26–30; 11:25–26). In the second decade of his ministry (AD 46–59), Paul spent most of his life on the road, an itinerant ministry of preaching the gospel and planting churches from Cyprus to Corinth. For most of the third decade (AD 59–67), Paul ministered the gospel from prison, spending over two years imprisoned in Caesarea, another two to three years in a Roman prison (Acts ends here), released for a brief time (two years?) before his final arrest and imprisonment in Rome, where, according to church tradition, he was executed.

During his itinerant ministry, Paul traveled Roman roads that led him to free cities (Ephesus, Thessalonica, Athens) and Roman colonies (Pisidian Antioch, Iconium, Lystra, Derbe, Troas, Philippi, Corinth). Founding churches in urban centers afforded Paul more opportunities for ministry and for his work of making and repairing tents. Traveling within the borders of the Roman Empire also provided a better chance of protection as a citizen. At first, Paul and Barnabas covered familiar territory: Cyprus (Barnabas's home region) and Anatolia (Paul's home region). Then, with successive journeys Paul and other missionary companions branched out to Asia Minor, Macedonia, and Achaia. Some of the towns that Paul visited were small and provincial (Derbe, Lystra); others were major cities of great economic and intellectual commerce (Ephesus, Corinth, Athens). In the midst of such cultural diversity, Paul found receptive ears among a variety of ethnic groups: Gauls, Phrygians and Lycaonians, Greeks, Romans, and Jews. Previously, Paul's Gentile converts had worshiped many gods (local, ethnic, and imperial), offered sacrifices at many shrines and temples, and joined in all the religious festivals (often involving immoral and ungodly practices). After believing the gospel, Paul's predominantly Gentile churches turned from their idolatrous ways to serve "the living and true God" (1 Thess. 1:9). Their exclusive devotion to one God quickly led to economic and political problems, for both Paul's converts and the cities of their residence. No more offerings for patron gods, no more support for local synagogues or the imperial cult—Paul's converts were often persecuted for their newly found faith by local religious guilds (idol makers!) and civic leaders courting Roman favor (Acts 17:6–9; 19:23–41; Phil. 1:27–30; 1 Thess. 2:14–16). Indeed, Paul often was run out of town as a troublemaker who preached a message that threatened both the Jewish and the Roman ways of life (Acts 16:19–24; Phil. 3:17–4:1). It is no wonder that Paul's activities eventually landed him in a Roman prison. It was only a matter of time before his reputation as a "lawbreaker" caught up with him (Acts 21:21). But that did not stop Paul. Whether as a prisoner or a free man, Paul proclaimed the gospel of Jesus Christ until the day he died.

Paul was a tentmaker, a missionary, a writer, a preacher, a teacher, a theologian, an evangelist, a mentor, a prophet, a miracle worker, a prisoner, and a martyr. His life story reads like the tale of three different men: a devout Pharisee, a tireless traveler, an ambitious writer. He knew the Scriptures better than did most people. He saw more of the world than did most merchants. He wrote some of the longest letters known at that time. To his converts, he was a faithful friend. To his opponents, he was an irrepressible troublemaker. But, according to Paul, he was nothing more or less than the man whom God had called through Jesus Christ to take the gospel to the ends of the earth.

Paulus, Sergius–*See* Sergius Paulus.

Pekah–The eighteenth king of Israel. He came to power by assassinating Pekahiah and was assassinated by Hoshea. Since he is assigned twenty years of rule (2 Kings 15:27), it is possible that he actually began ruling part of Israel as a rival to Menahem before consolidating his power by murdering Pekahiah, since his sole rule of Israel was from 735 to 733 BC.

After gaining power over all of Israel, Pekah formed a coalition with King Rezin of Syria, and they attacked Judah (2 Kings 15:37). Isaiah prophesied to Ahaz of Judah that the threat of Rezin and Pekah would be averted, and that both Syria and Israel (Ephraim) would be conquered by Assyria (Isa. 7). This was fulfilled when Tiglath-pileser III conquered Syria and invaded part of Israel (2 Kings 15:29).

Pekahiah–King of Israel (r. 737–735 BC) after his father, Menahem, during the divided monarchy. He reigned over Israel for two years from Samaria beginning in the fiftieth year of the reign of King Azariah of Judah (2 Kings 15:22–23). Pekahiah is noted as having done evil in the eyes of the Lord in the pattern of Jeroboam (2 Kings 15:24). He was assassinated in the royal palace in Samaria by one of his chief officers, Pekah, who then reigned in his stead (2 Kings 15:25).

Peleg–A son of Eber, the brother of Joktan, and the father of Reu, he lived 239 years (Gen. 10:25; 11:16–19; 1 Chron. 1:19). He was a direct descendant of Noah through Shem and an ancestor of the patriarch Abraham (1 Chron. 1:25). He is included in the Lukan genealogy of Jesus (Luke 3:35).

It is noted that the earth was divided in Peleg's time (Gen. 10:25; 1 Chron. 1:19). The Hebrew word translated as "divided" is a play on the name "Peleg," both having the same Hebrew root. This interesting statement has been variously interpreted. It may be a reference to the division of languages at the tower of Babel (Gen. 11:1–9), the spreading of Noah's descendants after the flood ("from these the nations spread out over the earth after the flood" [Gen. 10:32]), or something else of unknown referent. This is probably a reference to the outcome of the tower of Babel, noted as a significant event in the Genesis record.

Pelethites–A group, possibly of Philistine origin, that served as troops attached to David and separate from the main army (2 Sam. 20:7). They are always mentioned in company with the Kerethites. They may have originated in the band that David built around himself in Ziklag (1 Sam. 27:8), as they are associated with men from Gath in 2 Sam. 15:18. As a special unit, they were under the command of Benaiah (2 Sam. 8:18; 20:23). Their loyalty to David is evident from their service in putting down the rebellions of Absalom (2 Sam. 15:18) and Sheba (2 Sam. 20:7) and later in ensuring Solomon's succession to the throne (1 Kings 1:38, 44).

Peninnah–One of Elkanah's two wives (1 Sam. 1:2, 4). When the family went to God's house for the annual sacrifices, she provoked her rival, Hannah, who had no children. In her sadness, Hannah prayed for a son, and when "the Lord remembered her," Samuel was born (1 Sam. 1:1–20).

Pentapolis–The five main Philistine cities of Gaza, Ashkelon, Ashdod, Ekron, and Gath, which were the locus for Philistine power and culture. These cities were located along the coast of the Mediterranean and slightly inland and controlled major trade routes.

Pentateuch–The biblical corpus known as the Pentateuch consists of the first five books of the OT: Genesis, Exodus, Leviticus, Numbers, and Deuteronomy. The word "Pentateuch" comes from two Greek words (*penta* ["five"] and *teuchos* ["scroll case, book"]) and is a designation attested in the early church fathers. The collection is also commonly known as the "Five Books of Moses," the "Law of Moses," or simply the "Law," reflecting the traditional Jewish name "Torah," meaning "law" or "instruction." The Torah is the first of three major sections that compose the Hebrew Bible (*Torah, Nebiim, Ketubim* [Law, Prophets, Writings]); thus for both Jewish and Christian traditions it represents the introduction to the Bible as a whole as well as its interpretive foundation.

Pentecost–Greek parlance for the OT Festival of Weeks described in Lev. 23:15–22. It gets this name because it is celebrated fifty days after the Passover (Gk. *pentēkostē* means "fiftieth"). The Festival of Weeks was an important pilgrimage feast commemorating the end of the grain harvest. Usually the harvest season began the week of Passover and continued for fifty days until the Festival of Weeks. The first NT use of the word occurs in Acts 2:1. There is little doubt that Luke's use of "Pentecost" refers to the Festival of Weeks. Paul mentions in 1 Cor. 16:8 that he intends to stay in Ephesus until Pentecost but gives no explanation of what he means by "Pentecost." This early

Pauline document suggests that for Christians, Pentecost was an established date that needed no explanation.

Penuel–A place, and later a town, on the Jabbok River about eight miles west of the Jordan. The name "Penuel" (NIV: "Peniel"), meaning "face of God," was given to this place by Jacob after he wrestled there with "a man" and then said that he had seen God "face to face" (Gen. 32:22–32). When Gideon was pursuing the Midianites, the people of Penuel refused to provide food for his men, and so when he returned, he destroyed their tower and killed the men (Judg. 8:8–9, 17). The fortifying of this town was one of Jeroboam's first acts as king of Israel (1 Kings 12:25).

Peor–A mountain in Moab, in the area of Mount Nebo. This location is derived from Num. 24:2, which mentions that the view from Peor affords a glimpse of the plains of Moab. No precise location has been identified. In Num. 23 Peor is the site of Balaam's pronouncements of blessing upon Israel, inspired by God. Elsewhere (Num. 23:3, 5, 18; Ps. 106:28), Peor is associated with apostasy and illicit religious practice (the worship of Baal of Peor).

Perea–The region east of the Jordan River and Samaria, south of the Decapolis (modern Jordan). In the NT it is referred to as *peran tou Iordanou* ("beyond the Jordan" or "the region across the Jordan") (Matt. 4:25; 19:1; Mark 3:8; 10:1). It was part of the kingdom of Herod the Great, apportioned to his son Herod Antipas, who also ruled Galilee as a client king of the Roman Empire in Jesus' time. Herod's fortress in Machaerus (southern Perea) is the probable location of John the Baptist's imprisonment and beheading (Mark 6:17–28). Jesus traveled through Perea (Matt. 19–20) to arrive in Jerusalem for his Passion Week.

Perez–A grandson of Jacob, a son of Judah by Tamar, and the father of Hezron listed in the ancestry of David and Jesus (Gen. 46:12; Ruth 4:18; 1 Chron. 2:4–5; 4:1; Matt. 1:3; Luke 3:33). His was a key ancestral touchstone name (Num. 26:20–21; Ruth 4:12; 1 Chron. 9:4; 27:3; Neh. 11:4–6), meaning "breach" or "breaking out," as he broke out of the womb ahead of his firstborn twin brother, Zerah (Gen. 38:29).

Perga–A chief Greco-Roman city of Pamphylia eight miles from the southern coast of Asia Minor near the Cestrus River, with a port city of Attalia. Surviving architectural ruins testify to Perga's beauty and wealth. Its patron deity was Artemis (Diana). On his first missionary campaign, Paul passed through Perga on his way out (Acts 13:13–14 [at which time John Mark left the party]) and preached there on the return leg (14:25).

Pergamum–*See* Asia Minor, Cities of.

Perizzites–One of the Canaanite nations at the time of Abraham whose land Yahweh promised to Abraham's descendants (Gen. 13:7; 15:20).

Persia–The history of the Persians and their rulers prior to their emergence in biblical, Greek, and Mesopotamian history remains poorly understood, but probably they had come to the Iranian plateau from central Asia around 1000 BC, roughly the time of the emergence of monarchic Israel in the Levant.

As a political entity, the Persians appear in ancient Near Eastern history around 550 BC, when the Persian leader Cyrus II ("the Great") defeated the Medes (another Iranian people to whom the Persians had been subject) and seized their capital at Ecbatana, along with their royal treasure. Cyrus claimed descent from a line of Achaemenid kings going back to the second half of the seventh century BC and founded by Cyrus I ("of Anshan"). The term "Achaemenid" refers to a yet more distant, and possibly legendary, ancestor Achaemenes, who putatively lived around 700 BC. Cyrus then turned toward the territory of the Lydian (Greek) king Croesus in modern western Turkey, which he conquered with the fall of Sardis and the defeat of Croesus around 546 BC. Cyrus's territorial gains in Anatolia would remain a part of the Persian Empire until the time of Alexander the Great.

Following this western campaign, which would set the stage for two centuries of Greco-Persian rivalry, Cyrus returned to Mesopotamia, where he marched against the Neo-Babylonian Empire of Nabonidus, taking advantage of a falling out between Nabonidus and the inhabitants of Babylon (Nabonidus had controversially removed images of Marduk from their rightful place in Babylon). It is at this point that the history of the Persian Empire intersects dramatically with biblical history, for Cyrus's capture of the capital Babylon in the fall of 539 BC came only half a century after the Neo-Babylonian king Nebuchadnezzar II had sacked Jerusalem and exiled the elite inhabitants of the southern kingdom of Judah to Mesopotamia, including a group that was brought to Babylon itself. Like the priests of Marduk (the chief Babylonian deity), who in the Cyrus Cylinder inscription lauded Cyrus for delivering them from the impious Nabonidus and restoring the proper worship of Marduk in Babylon, the Hebrew Bible speaks fondly of Cyrus as the restorer of the Jewish people from exile. It was Cyrus, according to 2 Chron. 36:23; Ezra 1:2–4, who mandated that a group of Judeans return to their homeland and reestablish their capital Jerusalem and the temple of their deity, Yahweh. Isaiah 45:1 speaks of Cyrus as Yahweh's "anointed" and suggests a personal and intimate relationship between the king and the God of Israel. In terms of the biblical periodization of Israelite history, the edict of Cyrus marked the end of the exilic period and the beginning of what modern scholars term the "Persian period" of Israelite and Jewish history.

Cyrus was succeeded by his son Cambyses II, who conquered Egypt before his death in 522 BC. Darius succeeded Cambyses through a palace intrigue in which he emerged over Cyrus's son Bardiya (also known as Smerdis or Gaumata). The circumstances of Darius's succession remain unclear in several respects. He was not in the royal line, yet in his own monuments he insists that it was his rivals who were usurpers and that he was the rightful claimant of the throne. Under Darius ("the Great"), the Achaemenid Empire reached its greatest geographical extent. He organized the empire into twenty-two administrative districts, or "satrapies," and built up a vast network of roads and cities. The lands of biblical Israel fell into a large satrapy known as "Beyond the River," or "Trans-Euphrates" (see, e.g., Ezra 4:10). Darius is remembered in the Bible as renewing Cyrus's order for the rebuilding of the Jerusalem temple. The decree of Darius is represented in Ezra 6:1–15. As a result of his attention to the matter, the temple was completed during his reign, in 515 BC (Ezra 6:15). Daniel 5:31 portrays Darius ("the Mede," not "the Persian"; see also Dan. 9:1, which reaffirms Darius's Median ethnicity while making him the son, not the father, of Ahasuerus/Xerxes), not Cyrus, as the conqueror of Babylon (though it is Belshazzar, not Nabonidus, who loses his kingdom).

Darius was succeeded by his son Xerxes, who in 481 BC led a vast army across the Bosphorus into Greece. He was turned back by a series of defeats and was assassinated in 465 BC. Neither Xerxes nor his successors managed to expand the empire beyond the achievement of Darius. The Bible mentions Xerxes (Ahasuerus) at Ezra 4:5–6 and alludes to him at Dan. 11:2. Artaxerxes appears in the books of Ezra and Nehemiah (e.g., Ezra 4:7; Neh. 2:1); however, the identification of this figure is controversial, whether he is Artaxerxes I (r. 464–424 BC), Artaxerxes II (r. 405–359 BC), or even Artaxerxes III (r. 359–338 BC). Moreover, it is debated whether Ezra and Nehemiah were contemporaries (i.e., living under the same king Artaxerxes), and which one of them preceded the other in his mission. Moreover, it is unclear from ancient versions whether the king in the book of Esther is meant to be Xerxes (Ahasuerus) or Artaxerxes I (so the LXX).

The Achaemenid Empire fell in 330 BC, during the reign of Darius III, whom Alexander the Great defeated decisively at Gaugamela in 331 BC.

Peter–Simon Peter is the best-known and the most colorful of Jesus' twelve disciples. The name "Peter" means "rock" in Greek. In some biblical texts, he is also called "Cephas," which is the Aramaic word for "rock" (see esp. John 1:42). Despite the ups and downs of Peter's spiritual life, God was able to use him as the foundational apostle for the establishment of the NT church.

Peter, First Letter of–First Peter is a concise handbook designed to prepare the Christian community to live faithfully and wisely as a minority facing an increasingly hostile community and government.

Peter states that it is all about grace (5:12). The Christian's identity is grounded in the person and work of Jesus (1:2). His sufferings are a model of what Christians are expected to endure (1:11, 19; 2:21–25; 3:1–18; 4:12–17; 5:1), so his readers should see this as normal. This suffering is also a refining and testing process (1:6–7; 5:8–10). It fulfills God's plan as revealed in the Scriptures (1:10–12, 23–25); thus one can be sure that behind all such experiences stand the purposes of God (1:2–3, 20–21; 3:18–22; 4:19; 5:6–7). Things are not out of control but rather are leading to the accomplishment of salvation for many (1:5, 9). Jesus has triumphed over all powers and authorities that might be fearfully ranged against his people (3:18–22). Like Noah and those on the ark, Christ's people will be delivered through all events to an outcome of joy (1:6, 8).

A knowledge of the Scriptures (1:10–12, 23–25) equips those who are being sanctified to rightly understand what is happening and so fear God, whose judgment approaches (1:17; 3:6; 5:5, 7), rather than people. The believer should look first to God's approval while being aware of the watching eye of those who would seek a basis for a charge (2:12; 3:1, 17; 4:14–19). This involves putting off the pagan lifestyle (2:1, 11) and putting on obedience (1:2, 14–16; 3:1–17). Peter surveys the behaviors most in need of attention: self-control, particularly in the way Christians speak when provoked (2:22–23; 3:4, 9–11), and family life, particularly when a woman is married to a threatening, unbelieving husband (3:1–6). Christian husbands are admonished to set a counterexample by knowing and honoring their wives (3:7). It is especially important that believers are seen to be submissive to government authorities (2:13–17) and to their masters (2:18–20). Within the church, sound leadership (5:1–4) supported by a new generation of respectful young men (5:5) is essential. Throughout all of this, Peter points the reader to the sanctifying work of the Holy Spirit (1:2).

Peter strongly argues that the appropriate response to injustice and persecution is grace given as received from Jesus. The Christian's defense is the gospel. Like Job, the believer's mode of resistance is to present the integrity of a holy, redeemed, priestly lifestyle (3:15–16). One endures through informed belief in the gospel and through faithfulness to the triune God, who keeps his promises (1:9; cf. Hab. 2:4). The outcome is left in God's hands (5:6–7).

Peter, Second Letter of–Second Peter is a model of the Christian approach to those who are tempted to follow another gospel.

Second Peter focuses first on the work of God in Christ, which saves those who believe in Jesus (1:3). This faith is based on the knowledge of God and of Jesus (1:2) and is a response to the gospel call. God has given to the believer everything needed to live in a godly way, to endure, and to discern truth from error so as to die assured of not having been deceived (1:4).

Peter grounds that assurance in the Scriptures (1:19–21), in the testimony of the eyewitnesses of Jesus (1:12–16), including himself, and in the writings of the apostle Paul, to whom Jesus had given wisdom for this purpose (3:15–16). One develops certainty in the faith not only by referring to these sources but also by putting the faith into practice (1:5, 10, 15). The faith, then, is rooted in history, not in "cleverly invented stories" (1:16). Consequently, Peter expresses his passion to see that his eyewitness account will be accessible to the next generation (1:14–15).

He speaks plainly of "Scripture" as an identifiable body of texts written at the instigation of the Holy Spirit (1:20–21) and places the writings of Paul on the same level (3:16). By this, Peter implies that his letter is to be received as carrying the same authority and usefulness.

False teachers are a permanent challenge to God's people. Doctrine and behavior are products of each other (2:1–3).

Peter is particularly concerned that his readers not think that Jesus' delay in appearing is proof that the apostolic witnesses were wrong (3:3–4). Jesus has not returned because were he to do so, it would end all opportunity for unbelievers to hear the gospel and be saved (3:9). God is gracious and long-suffering and is calling his people to reflect his character by giving people the opportunity to be saved. His patience is salvation (3:15). The gospel mission, then, provides the second motivation for the believer to practice the faith (3:11–16) and not waver.

Second Peter ends by challenging believers to constantly grow in the knowledge and grace of Christ (3:17–18).

Pharaoh–From an Egyptian term meaning "great house," "Pharaoh" refers to Egypt's supreme leader. The Pentateuch refers to the pharaohs by title only. (The omission of the personal name of the pharaoh may reflect the Egyptian practice of not naming their enemies.)

Beyond the Pentateuch, six other pharaohs are mentioned, some by name. **(1)** Solomon married the daughter of a pharaoh who led him to betray God (1 Kings 3:1). **(2)** Jeroboam rebelled against Solomon and received sanctuary from Pharaoh Shishak, who later raided Judah under Rehoboam (1 Kings 11:18, 40). **(3)** Hoshea, the last king of the northern kingdom, sought help from Pharaoh So (Osorkon), bringing on him the wrath of King Shalmaneser of Assyria (2 Kings 17:4). **(4)** The Assyrian king Sennacherib sent an envoy to Jerusalem who chided Hezekiah for depending on an unnamed and unreliable pharaoh (2 Kings 18:21; Isa. 36:6). **(5)** Pharaoh Necho meddled in the affairs of Judah when he killed Josiah and deposed his son Jehoahaz, replacing him with Jehoiakim (2 Kings 23:29–35). **(6)** Pharaoh Hophra was the Egyptian leader upon whom Zedekiah vainly depended against the Babylonians (Jer. 44:30).

P

PHARISEES–*See* Jewish Parties.

PHARPAR–A river in the region of Damascus mentioned by the Syrian general Naaman as being superior to the Jordan River (2 Kings 5:12). Its exact identity is uncertain, but often it is identified with the Wadi el-Awaj, which flows just south of Damascus.

PHICOL–The commander of Abimelek's army, referred to in conjunction with the establishment of covenants with Abraham (Gen. 21:22, 32) and Isaac (Gen. 26:26). The two accounts are possibly discussing two different people, since sixty to seventy years separate the events. Therefore, this may be a reference to a family title, which could serve to connect them.

PHILADELPHIA–*See* Asia Minor, Cities of.

PHILEMON–*See* Philemon, Letter to.

PHILEMON, LETTER TO–Late in life, while in prison, Paul wrote this letter to the slave owner Philemon concerning his runaway slave Onesimus. The main purpose of the letter was to straighten out problems between Philemon and Onesimus. Besides an implicit theology describing the relationships that fellow Christians have with one another, the book focuses on the changed relationship that a Christian slave had with his Christian master.

Somehow Onesimus (whose name means "useful") had become "useless" to Philemon (v. 11), having wronged his master and incurred a debt (v. 18). Subsequently, Onesimus had become a Christian due to Paul's ministry in prison, whereby the apostle sends Onesimus back to Philemon with this letter, asking him to receive his slave as a brother in Christ (v. 16). Paul even requests that Philemon return Onesimus to him because the slave has proved "useful" to the imprisoned Paul (vv. 12–14). Paul offers to pay the debt owed by Onesimus, perhaps even hinting at his manumission (vv. 15–21). (It was customary at that time for masters to free their slaves at the age of thirty. Some slaves were required to purchase their freedom; others received it as a gift from their masters.)

We are not told how Onesimus had come into contact with Paul, but it appears that Onesimus has worked with Paul for some time (cf. Col. 4:9). Was Onesimus a runaway slave who happened to meet Paul in prison? Or did Onesimus seek out Paul, hoping that the apostle would act as mediator in regard to a grievance between him and his master? If the former is true, then Paul sends his letter in order to encourage Philemon not to punish the slave as a runaway—a crime punishable by death. If the latter is the case, then Onesimus is taking advantage of a Roman law that allowed slaves to appeal to a friend of their master when they had a grievance against the slave owner. Both scenarios are possible, but the latter seems more likely because Paul sends the letter to the entire congregation that meets in Philemon's house, hoping to add social pressure to Philemon's decision. Either way, Paul is convinced that Onesimus's conversion has changed everything, turning a master, a slave, and an apostle into equal brothers in Christ.

PHILIP–**(1)** The tetrarch of Iturea and Traconitis, regions northeast of Palestine, at the time when John the Baptist's public ministry began (Luke 3:1). **(2)** One of Jesus' twelve apostles (Matt. 10:3; Mark 3:18; Luke 6:14; John 1:43). Philip, like Andrew and Peter, was from Bethsaida (John 1:44). It was Philip who introduced Nathanael to Jesus (John 1:45–48). John's Gospel mentions Philip three times subsequent to chapter 1 (6:5–7; 12:20–22; 14:6–10), in the last instance recording Philip's shortsighted request for Jesus to show the Father to the apostles. **(3)** One of seven men selected by the Jerusalem church to care for the distribution of food to its widows (Acts 6:1–6). This man, also known as Philip the evangelist (21:8), shared the message of Jesus Christ in a city of Samaria, performing great miracles (8:5–13). Philip later explained the good news of Jesus to an Ethiopian eunuch whom he encountered (8:26–38). After Philip baptized the eunuch, "the Spirit of the Lord suddenly took Philip away" (8:39). Philip then preached in several towns, finally arriving at Caesarea, where he settled (8:40). Years later,

Paul stayed in Caesarea with Philip and his four prophesying daughters (21:8–9).

Philip, Herod–*See* Herod.

Philippi–A city in northeastern Macedonia, approximately ten miles from the Aegean coast. The city had its share of trade, being on the Via Egnatia, the main east-west route from the Adriatic through Thrace. The city lay on the plain between the mountains in the north and the sea to the south.

Luke identifies Philippi as the chief city of its division in Macedonia and as a Roman colony (Acts 16:12). Paul arrived in Philippi around AD 50–52 after receiving a divine injunction to spread the gospel there (16:9–10). There was a small Jewish population, but not enough for a synagogue (16:13), so the Jewish women of the city would go to a place beside the river to worship Yahweh. Paul brought the gospel to them there, and the first convert was a God-fearing woman, Lydia (16:14). The church established there was predominantly Gentile.

Paul came through the city again on his third missionary journey (Acts 20:6). As far as we know, this was the last time he saw the church, though he wrote back with thanks and instruction in his letter to the Philippian church.

Philippians, Letter to the–One of the "prison epistles" of Paul (along with Ephesians, Colossians, and Philemon). These are traditionally viewed as having been written during Paul's first Roman imprisonment (AD 60–62), though some maintain that they were written either from Caesarea or Ephesus at an earlier date. In Philippians, Paul is writing to the church that he established on his second missionary journey (likely between AD 49 and 52), probably the first Christian church founded in Europe.

The broad occasion for the letter is the return of Epaphroditus, a member of the Philippian church who had brought a financial gift to Paul (2:25–30). Epaphroditus had fallen ill while in Paul's service, and the news had reached Philippi. Paul sends him home to be reunited with his loved ones and sends this letter along with him. Paul lauds the work of Epaphroditus in the ministry (2:29–30) and thanks the Philippians for their generous gift (4:10–20) and their partnership in his ministry for the gospel (1:5).

Paul also takes this opportunity to reassure his friends about his circumstances in prison. His imprisonment is serving to advance the gospel (1:12–14), both among the palace guard, whom Paul evangelizes, and among other Christians who are emboldened by Paul's courage. It is the pastoral spirit in Paul that moves him to comfort his audience, though it is he who is in distress (1:19). Paul is not fearful for his future, whether it holds eventual freedom or death; either is acceptable to him (1:21–24).

Paul then tells his readers that the most important thing is to live their lives in a way worthy of the gospel (1:27). This will be evidenced by their standing firmly together as one, unafraid of any opposition. Whatever suffering comes their way is a gift from God, as is also the gift of belief in Christ (1:29).

The report from Epaphroditus must have reflected some troubles brewing in the church at Philippi. A quarrel between two women was spreading throughout the church (4:2), and Judaizers (Jewish Christian missionaries) were at work there, insisting that Gentile Christians must be circumcised (3:2).

Paul addresses the first concern with the beloved "Christ hymn" (2:1–11). From the Christian's unity with Christ should flow unity with one another. Every believer should adopt the humble, unassuming attitude of Jesus, who emptied himself first of his divine prerogatives, then of his human dignity, then of his life. Rather than taking their salvation for granted, Christians must consider their position before God with fear and trembling (2:12).

Concerning the Judaizers, Paul gives a threefold warning: "Watch out for those dogs, those evildoers, those mutilators of the flesh" (3:2). These three insults are deliberately ironic. The Judaizers considered themselves defenders of the traditions of Moses and the Scriptures, yet Paul calls them "dogs," an animal associated with uncleanness and Gentiles. They promote the "good work" of circumcision, but they are actually promoting the harmful work of confidence in worldly acts. "Mutilators of the flesh" refers to the insistence that Gentile Christians be circumcised. Paul mocks this idea, as circumcision is irrelevant in the new covenant. In fact, it is Christians, not Judaizers, who are the true circumcision—that is, the people of God.

The real problem with the Judaizers is that they put their confidence in the flesh—that is, in the tangible elements of religion, such as circumcision. But Paul explains that he has more reason than most to trust in these religious credentials. His are flawless: he had been circumcised on the eighth day, a learned Hebrew, even a Pharisee. Yet this "advantage" he disdains, knowing that Christ is worth far more. He rejects his previous religious standing, counting it as "garbage" or "dung" for the righteousness that comes from God based on faith (3:7–9). Paul offers himself as a model for the Philippians to follow (3:17).

To correct the contentious atmosphere in their church, the Philippians should focus on the positive aspects of their fellow believers: things they see that are noble, right, pure, lovely, and admirable. This and practicing their faith as they have learned from Paul will guarantee them peace from God.

Philistines–The Philistines inhabited the southern coastal plain of Palestine as early as the time of Abraham (Gen. 21:32, 34; 26:1, 8, 14–15, 18) and of Moses (Exod. 13:17; 15:14; 23:31), and as late as the exilic (Ezek. 16:27, 57; 25:15–16) and postexilic (Zech. 9:6) periods.

The mention of Philistines in Gen. 21 and 26 refers either to early inhabitants of the territory that later would be inhabited by Philistines or to peoples who later would become part of the Philistine nation. The Philistines mentioned in the Bible may constitute diverse peoples who migrated by land or by sea to the southern coastal region of Palestine over several centuries.

Prior to the influx of at least some of the Philistines from eastern Mediterranean islands, the southern coastal region was, at various times, inhabited by Canaanites (Num. 13:29; Deut. 1:7; Josh. 5:1; cf. Josh. 13:4); Anakites, who fled to Gaza, Gath, and Ashdod after being defeated by Joshua (Josh. 11:21–22); and Avvites, who were replaced by the victorious Caphtorites (Deut. 2:23; Josh. 13:3).

The migration of Judah and other tribes of Israel into Canaan resulted in several centuries of hostility with the Philistines. Judah's allotment of land included the cities and surrounding areas of Ekron, Ashdod, and Gaza, as well as "the coastline of the Mediterranean Sea" (Josh. 15:45–47). The soldiers of Judah subsequently conquered at least part of this area (Judg. 1:18).

During the time of the judges, Shamgar "struck down six hundred Philistines with an oxgoad" (Judg. 3:31). Samson burned the grain, vineyards, and olive groves of the Philistines when he fastened torches to the tails of foxes (15:4–5). He killed a thousand Philistines with the jawbone of a donkey (15:15) and, after they had gouged out his eyes, killed many Philistine leaders when he pushed over the pillars supporting one of their temples (16:21, 29–30).

In one of their many victories over Israel (cf. Judg. 10:7; 13:1; 15:11; 1 Sam. 4:2, 10; 12:9), the Philistines captured the ark of God and placed it in the temple of Dagon in Ashdod (1 Sam. 5:1). The next day the god was found lying on his face before the ark of God.

Saul's reign as Israel's king was characterized by war with the Philistines (1 Sam. 9:16; 14:52; cf. 7:13) and included both defeat (13:6–7; 23:27; 31:1) and victory (14:13, 22, 31, 47; 17:52–53; 24:1).

The military dominance of the Philistines over Israel during the time of Saul is attributed to their control of blacksmithing and ironwork (1 Sam. 13:19–22). This superiority in weapons allowed the Philistines to extend their influence beyond the region of the five cities into Judean territory (1 Sam. 4:1; 7:7; 10:5; 13:3, 16–18, 23; 17:1; 29:1, 11; 31:7–8, 10; 2 Sam. 5:18, 22; 23:14).

Saul became jealous of David after his defeat of the Philistine champion Goliath (1 Sam. 17:4, 50; 18:7–9). To win the hand of Saul's daughter Michal, David and his men killed two hundred Philistines and presented their foreskins to Saul (18:27). When Saul later attempted to kill David, David sought refuge with the Philistines and lived with them for sixteen months (27:1, 7).

When the Philistines gathered to fight against Israel, David's host, Achish, invited him to participate in the battle against his enemy Saul (1 Sam. 28:1). David was spared the dilemma of fighting against his own people when, fearing his betrayal, the other Philistine rulers refused to let David accompany them (29:4). In the ensuing battle between Israel and the Philistines, Saul's sons were killed, and Saul took his own life after being critically injured by a Philistine archer (31:2–4).

David's early success in battle against the Philistines (1 Sam. 17:50; 19:8; 23:5) continued upon his accession to kingship after the death of Saul (2 Sam. 5:20, 25; 8:1, 12), though in his old age David was too tired to fight well against the Philistines (2 Sam. 21:15).

Later battles between Judah and the Philistines took place during the reigns of Jehoram

(2 Chron. 21:16–17), Uzziah (2 Chron. 26:6–7), Ahaz (2 Chron. 28:18), and Hezekiah (2 Kings 18:8). Jehoshaphat received tribute from the Philistines (2 Chron. 17:11).

Phinehas–**(1)** The son of Eleazar and a grandson of Aaron the high priest. At Baal Peor Phinehas killed Zimri and a Midianite woman for their idolatry and sexual immorality. Because of Phinehas's zeal, God ended the plague and granted him the high priesthood (Num. 25:1–13). Phinehas defeated the Midianites and killed Balaam (Num. 31:1–12). Phinehas averted war against the eastern tribes by listening to their explanation for building an altar (Josh. 22:1–34). Phinehas's zeal is cited to justify the Maccabean revolt and high priesthood (1 Macc. 2:54). **(2)** One of the two sons of Eli the high priest at Shiloh. Phinehas and his brother, Hophni, were corrupt priests (1 Sam. 2:12–17, 22). Their judgment was announced in 1 Sam. 2:27–36, which was fulfilled when they were killed by the Philistines and lost the ark of the covenant (4:17). In addition, Phinehas's wife died in childbirth (4:19–22).

Phoebe–A woman whom Paul commends to the church in Rome in the final greetings of his letter to the Romans (16:1). The church is told to welcome her in the Lord and to assist her, since she has served as a benefactor to Paul and others. She is identified as a *diakonos* of the church in Cenchreae (near Corinth), which may mean "deacon," "minister," or "servant." It is not clear whether this is a leadership position or a general description of her service. In either case, Phoebe appears to have served as the courier for the letter.

Phoenicia–The name "Phoenicia" probably comes from the Greek word *phoinix*, meaning "purple red." This name derived from the famous purple-red dye made from the murex snail that was produced in this region. The evidence shows that the Phoenicians were primarily sea traders and artists.

The geographical and chronological boundaries for Phoenicia are imprecise, in part because the term "Phoenician" is not mentioned before Homer. In Homer the inhabitants of Sidon are called "Phoenicians," but it is possible that the term may first occur in Mycenaean Linear B texts of the thirteenth century BC. Based on the written records, it is safe to assume that the heartland of Phoenicia was along the coastal regions of modern-day Lebanon, extending to parts of Syria and Israel.

In OT times the territory occupied by the Phoenicians was called "Canaan" by the Israelites (Isa. 23:11), "Canaanite" (Heb. *kena'an* means "merchant") being the name applied by the inhabitants to themselves (Gen. 10:18). It is important to note that this self-designation is found as late as the second century BC on coins minted in Beirut ("Laodicea, which is in Canaan"). However, since Phoenicia was usually formed of independent city-states, it was common practice in all periods to refer to Phoenicia by the name of one of its principal cities (Gubla/Byblos, Tyre, Sidon).

By the time of David, Tyre was ruled by Hiram I, whose reign began a golden age. Phoenicia became allied commercially with David (2 Sam. 5:11; 1 Kings 5:1), and Hiram supplied Solomon with wood, stone, and craftsmen for the construction of the temple and Solomon's palace (1 Kings 5:1–12; 2 Chron. 2:3–16). Ships and navigators from Phoenicia were sent to assist the Judean fleet and to develop the port of Ezion Geber as a base for commerce (1 Kings 9:27). Phoenicia, itself long influenced by Egyptian art, motifs, and methods, was now in a position to influence Israelite art.

During the ninth and eighth centuries BC, the Phoenicians expanded into the western Mediterranean and founded colonies in Sardinia, Sicily, North Africa, and Iberia. Alexander the Great captured Tyre in the fourth century BC, and the slaughter and destruction were extreme, but the city recovered and, like Sidon, was still prosperous in Hellenistic and Roman times (see, e.g., Matt. 11:21–22; Acts 12:20).

Phoenician religion had a pantheon that differed from city to city and from one age to the next. Nature and fertility deities predominated. The following were their chief deities: Baal, Astarte, Eshmun, Adonis, Melqart, and Tanit (more popular in North Africa). Baal, the chief god of Tyre and Sidon, was at times the leading rival to Yahweh worship in Israel (1 Kings 16:29–22:18), and his consort was Astarte.

The Phoenicians spoke a Northwest Semitic language closely related to Hebrew and Aramaic, and according to Herodotus, the Phoenicians introduced the alphabet to Greece. The Phoenician alphabetic script is similar to early Hebrew and Aramaic scripts from the first millennium BC.

Phoenix–A safe harbor on the southern shore of western Crete proposed as a winter port for the ship transporting Paul to Rome (Acts 27:12). In Greek, the name designates date palms and a mythical bird from Egypt. Modern Loutro is a candidate for the location, but it is disputed whether this fits the description in Acts: "facing both southwest and northwest." Finikas Bay, about one mile west of Loutro, is another candidate.

Phrygia–An inland territory in west-central Anatolia (modern-day Turkey). Biblical mention of Phrygia occurs primarily in the book of Acts. Such occurrences include the presence of Phrygian Jews in Jerusalem at the first Pentecost (2:10), the evangelism of Paul and Barnabas at the Phrygian cities of Pisidian Antioch and Iconium (13:14–14:4), the passing through Phrygia by Paul, Silas, and Timothy on their way west through Asia Minor (16:6), and the travels of Paul through "the region of Galatia and Phrygia" (18:23). Other biblical accounts include Col. 1:7; 4:12–13, which cites the work of Epaphras in three Phrygian cities, and Rev. 1:11; 3:14–22, which addresses the Phrygian church at Laodicea as one of the seven churches of Asia.

Phylactery–*See* Frontlets.

Pilate, Pontius–Pontius Pilate was the fifth Roman governor of Judea. He presided at the trial of Jesus, ultimately sentencing him to death. Based on the account of Josephus, he was appointed to his post in AD 26 or 27 and was removed from it ten years later (c. AD 37) by the governor of the neighboring province of Syria after he mishandled a confrontation with a group of religious fanatics in Samaria.

Pilate is known not only from the NT, but also from Josephus, Philo, the Roman historian Tacitus, and from an inscription discovered in 1961 in Caesarea identifying Pilate as "prefect" of Judea. This technical term has connotations of military authority and is more specific than the NT's broader term "governor" (Gk. *hēgemōn*).

Pillar–In ancient Israel and surrounding cultures, pillars were used in every kind of architectural construction, from simple houses (Prov. 9:1) to palaces (Ps. 144:12) and temples (Judg. 16:29; 1 Kings 7:15–22). One of the distinctive features of Israelite domestic architecture was the division of the ground floor of the house into two, three, or four rooms divided by rows of pillars. Such pillars rested on stone foundations that often survived even when the rest of the building had been destroyed, thus allowing modern archaeologists to identify many remains of pillared houses.

Stone pillars (obelisks) were used in religious worship in ancient Israel, such as those erected by Jacob (Gen. 28:18, 22; 35:14). A pillar could also commemorate a covenant (Gen. 31:45; Exod. 24:4; Josh. 24:26; 2 Chron. 34:31) or a tomb (Gen. 35:20). In later stories, pillars are viewed negatively, as in 2 Kings 18:4, where Hezekiah is credited with destroying Asherah pillars as part of a broad religious reform (see also Jer. 43:13). Archaeologists have discovered cultic pillars in the temple at Tell Arad, among other places.

The temple of Solomon at Jerusalem incorporated two highly decorated pillars, Jakin and Boaz (1 Kings 7:21), made of bronze and reported to be 18 cubits (27 feet) high and 12 cubits (18 feet) in circumference, with an additional height of 5 cubits (7.5 feet) including the capital (1 Kings 7:16; cf. 2 Kings 25:17). When Jerusalem fell to the Babylonians in 586 BC, the bronze pillars were destroyed, and their bronze was taken to Babylon (2 Kings 25:13).

In ancient cosmology, the earth and the heavens were thought to be supported by pillars (Job 9:6; 26:11; Ps. 75:3).

In the NT, the pillar is used as a metaphor for leaders in the church (Gal. 2:9) or the church itself (1 Tim. 3:15).

Pillar of Fire and Cloud–As Moses and the Israelites traveled through the desert, God guided them by going ahead of them, appearing as a pillar of cloud by day and a pillar of fire by night (Exod. 13:21–22). Prior to the miraculous crossing of the Red Sea, the pillar of cloud separated the Israelites from the Egyptian army, protecting them and giving them light (Exod. 14:19–20). The pillar lit the way for the Israelites (Neh. 9:12).

When the tabernacle was set up, the pillar of cloud or fire settled upon it (Exod. 40:34–38), so that the pillar was always in the sight of the Israelites. The Israelites moved whenever the cloud moved from above the tabernacle (Exod. 40:36–37; Num. 9:17). While Moses was meeting with God, the cloud stayed at the entrance to the tent of meeting (Exod. 33:9; Num. 12:5; Deut. 31:15; see also Ps. 99:7).

Pillar of Salt–When Lot's wife looked back while fleeing from the destruction of Sodom and Gomorrah, thus failing to obey the instructions of the angels, she became a pillar of salt (Gen. 19:17, 26). This story has long been associated in local lore with natural salt formations in the environs of the Dead Sea.

Pim–*See* Weights and Measures.

Pishon–One of four rivers (with Gihon, Tigris, and Euphrates) that branched off from the river flowing from Eden (Gen. 2:10–11). The Pishon flowed through Havilah. Neither name can be identified with a location known today. However, Pishon may have referred to a river known to the Israelites, since the context contains names of several other identifiable places.

Pisidia–A mountainous region in central Asia Minor (modern Turkey). Paul passed through Pisidia on his first missionary journey, on his way to Pisidian Antioch (Acts 13:14). This Antioch was not actually in Pisidia, but was so named because of its proximity and to distinguish it from other cities of the same name. Paul passed again through Pisidia on the return leg of his first journey (Acts 14:24). Because of its mountainous terrain, the limited extent to which the region had been Hellenized and later Romanized, and the reputation of the inhabitants in antiquity for robbery, many commentators have suggested that Paul is referring to his travels in Pisidia in 2 Cor. 11:26, where he says, "I have been in danger from rivers, in danger from bandits."

Pithom and Rameses–Supply cities built by the Israelites during their Egyptian enslavement (Exod. 1:11). Several archaeological sites in the Nile Delta have been proposed. Rameses is identified as an Israelite settlement (Gen. 47:11) or starting point of the exodus from Egypt (Num. 33:3).

Plagues–The plagues unleashed against Egypt (Exod. 7:1–11:10) demonstrated to Pharaoh (Exod. 9:14), to the Israelites (Exod. 10:2), and to "all the earth" (Exod. 9:16; Rom. 9:17) God's sovereign control over nature on behalf of his covenant people. Both the timing and the intensity of the plagues indicate that these were not random natural phenomena. The unfolding of the whole series of plagues would have taken at least nine months.

Plow–An instrument and process used by farmers to break up ground in preparation for planting (Isa. 28:24; Hos. 10:11). The plow was made of wood (1 Kings 19:21), and the point was covered with a metal plowshare (Isa. 2:4; Joel 3:10) that required occasional sharpening (1 Sam. 13:20–21). Usually, plowmen used pairs of oxen (1 Kings 19:19; Job 1:14) to pull the plow, although one might harness single animals or other animals such as donkeys (Deut. 22:10), depending on the situation and resources. The busy time of plowing at the beginning of the rainy season (around November) required hard work (Exod. 34:21; Prov. 20:4) and commitment (Luke 9:62). One also finds the term "plow" used figuratively for creating or doing something (making trouble [Job 4:8]), often with the negative ideas of destruction (Jer. 26:18) or punishment (Ps. 129:3).

Plumb Line–A cord with a weight attached to one end, to measure verticality, used in ancient construction. Appearing in five OT passages, a plumb line measures righteousness and signals God's commitment for renewal. In Amos 7:7–9 a plumb line in the hand of God communicates his judgment. In Zech. 4:10 a plumb line in the hand of Zerubbabel brings rejoicing (NIV: "capstone"). A plumb line signals God's act of washing in 2 Kings 21:13. A plumb line in Isa. 28:17; 34:11 is righteousness and justice as well as desolation and chaos. While signaling an end, a plumb line also indicates a new beginning.

Pontius Pilate–*See* Pilate, Pontius.

Pontus–The eastern half of the dual Roman province of Pontus and Bithynia. Pontus was the northeast region of Asia Minor (modern Turkey), north of the province of Galatia, on the south shore of the Black Sea. Its Persian dynasty under Mithridates VI ended with the Roman conquest by Pompey in 63 BC. Christianity spread to Pontus early: Jews from Pontus were present at Pentecost (Acts 2:9); Peter's first letter addresses believers in Pontus (1 Pet. 1:1). Paul worked and traveled with Aquila (husband of Priscilla), a native of Pontus (Acts 18:2). The location and terrain of Pontus favored its prosperous trade economy.

Poor, Orphan, Widow–Taken together "poor," "orphan," and "widow" are mentioned in the NIV 280 times, evidence of God's particular concern for those in need. "Poor" is an umbrella term for those who are physically impoverished or of diminished spirit. In biblical terms, "poor" would include most orphans and widows, though not every poor person was an orphan or widow.

The NT advances the atmosphere of kindness and nonoppression toward the poor and those in need found in the OT. The NT church was marked by such a real and selfless generosity that its members sold their own possessions and gave to "anyone who had need" (Acts 2:45). The poor were to be treated with generosity, and needs were to be addressed whenever they were discovered (Matt. 19:21; Luke 3:11; 11:41; 12:33; 14:13; 19:8; Acts 6:1; 9:36; Rom. 15:26; Gal. 2:10).

Furthermore, because of the incarnation of Christ, in which the almighty God chose to dwell with humanity, distinctions between believers on the basis of material wealth and, more specifically, favoritism toward the rich were expressly forbidden by the NT writers (1 Cor. 11:20–22; Phil. 2:1–8; James 2:1–4).

Other specific biblical instructions regarding people in need concern those without parents and especially those without a father. Such individuals are referred to as "fatherless." As with the provisions made for the poor, oppression of orphans or the fatherless was strictly forbidden (Exod. 22:22; Deut. 24:17; 27:19; Isa. 1:17; 10:1–2; Zech. 7:10). Furthermore, God is often referred to as the provider and helper of the orphan or fatherless (Deut. 10:18; Pss. 10:14, 18; 68:5; 146:9; Jer. 49:11). Jesus promised not to leave his followers as "orphans," implying that he would not leave them unprotected (John 14:18). In one of the clearest statements of how Christian belief is to manifest itself, James states, "Religion that God our Father accepts as pure and faultless is this: to look after orphans and widows in their distress and to keep oneself from being polluted by the world" (James 1:27).

Since widows are bereft of their husbands and thus similar to orphans in vulnerability and need, they are the beneficiaries of special provisions in both Testaments. Oppression was forbidden (Exod. 22:22), provisions were to be given in similar fashion to that of the poor and orphans (Deut. 24:19–21), and ample warnings were given to those who would deny justice to widows (Deut. 27:19). Jesus raised a widow's son from death (Luke 7:14–15), a miracle especially needed because she lacked provision after her only son's death. The apostle Paul gave specific rules to Timothy regarding who should be placed on the list of widows to receive daily food: they must be over sixty years old and must have been faithful to their husbands (1 Tim. 5:9). In the book of Revelation, a desolate city without inhabitants is aptly described as a "widow" (18:7).

Porcius Festus–*See* Festus.

Postexilic–This term means "after the exile." The postexilic period began with the decree of the Persian emperor Cyrus in 539 BC allowing the Jews to return to their land from the Babylonian captivity (Ezra 1:1–4). The returnees are referred to as the postexilic community and the period as the Second Temple period, for it was at this time that the temple was rebuilt.

Potiphar–The royal official of Pharaoh who purchased Joseph as a slave from Ishmaelite traders (Gen. 37:36). When Potiphar saw that God was giving Joseph great success in his endeavors, he entrusted Joseph with managing all his possessions. Potiphar's wife took advantage of Joseph's independence and made repeated sexual advances toward him, but Joseph remained faithful to his master, even to the point of running away from Potiphar's wife (Gen. 39:12). Potiphar threw Joseph into prison when his wife lied and said that it was Joseph, not she, who had been the aggressor (Gen. 39:16–20).

Potiphera–A priest in the Egyptian city of On (better known as Heliopolis, "city of the sun" [cf. Jer. 43:13]), his name means "he whom Re [the sun god] has given." He became Joseph's father-in-law when his daughter, Asenath, was given in marriage to Joseph by Pharaoh (Gen. 41:45), and then he was the grandfather of their sons, Manasseh and Ephraim (Gen. 41:45; 46:20).

Potsherd–A broken piece of pottery that is essentially useless. Because of the easy availability and cheap cost of pottery in the ancient Near East and pottery's relative fragility, broken pottery was common. Potsherds are mentioned a few times in the Bible. Job used a potsherd to scrape his skin when he was infected with skin sores (Job 2:8). The gate near the Valley of Ben Hinnom was called the "Potsherd Gate" (Jer. 19:2). It is at this place that Jeremiah smashed a clay pot into potsherds to warn the people of God's wrath.

Potter's Field–A burial ground for foreigners outside Jerusalem. The land was purchased with the thirty pieces of silver that Judas received for betraying Jesus (Matt. 27:3–10; Acts 1:18–19), though it is unclear whether it was the priests or Judas who made the purchase. The silver was "blood money" because it had been used to arrange for Jesus' death, and so it could not go back into the temple treasury. Therefore, it was used to purchase the plot of land, most likely from a potter. It is identified with the "Field of Blood" (Matt. 27:8; Acts 1:19 [Aram. "Akeldama"]).

Praetorian Guard–The elite bodyguard maintained at Rome by the emperors, starting with Augustus. When Paul was placed under house arrest in Rome after having appealed to Caesar, he had a soldier guarding him (Acts 28:16). It was often the praetorians who were given the duty of guarding prisoners. Paul relates in the Letter to the Philippians that because of his imprisonment, the cause of Christ had become known throughout "the whole praetorian guard" (Phil. 1:13 NASB [NIV: "palace guard"]).

Praetorium–The official residence of a Roman governor, military commander, or official. In the Gospel accounts, the praetorium of Pontius Pilate in Jerusalem is the location of some of the beatings, mockings, and trials of Jesus (Matt. 27:27–31; Mark 15:16–20; John 18:28–19:15). The term could also be used of the praetorian guard, Caesar's personal troops. This seems to be the meaning in Phil. 1:12–13, where Paul (probably writing from imprisonment in Rome) says, "It has become clear throughout the whole palace guard [*praitōrion*] and to everyone else that I am in chains for Christ."

Prayer–In the OT there is no language or understanding comparable to modern ways of talking about prayer as conversational or dialogical. Prayer does not involve mutuality. Prayer is something that humans offer to God, and the situation is never reversed; God does not pray to humans. Understanding this preserves the proper distinction between the sovereign God and the praying subject. Therefore, prayers in the OT are reverential. Some OT prayers have extended introductions, such as that found in Neh. 1:5, that seem to pile up names for God. These should be seen as instances not of stiltedness or ostentation, but rather as setting up a kind of "buffer zone" in recognition of the distance between the Creator and the creature. In the NT, compare the same phenomenon in Eph. 1:17.

A presupposition of prayer in the OT is that God hears prayer and may indeed answer and effect the change being requested. Prayer is not primarily about changing the psychological state or the heart of the one praying, but rather about God changing the circumstances of the one praying.

The depiction of prayer in the NT is largely consistent with that of the OT, but there are important developments.

Jesus tells his disciples to address God as "Father" (Matt. 6:9; cf. Rom. 8:15; Gal. 4:6). Prayer to God is now to be made in the name of Jesus (Matt. 18:19–20; John 14:13; 15:16; 16:23–26).

Prayer can also be made to Jesus (John 14:14), and such devotion to him in the early church is evidence of his being regarded as deity. Unlike anything prior in the OT, Jesus tells his followers to pray for their enemies (Matt. 5:44). Jesus and his followers serve as examples (Luke 23:34; Acts 7:60).

The Holy Spirit plays a vital role in prayers. It is by him that we are able to call out, "Abba, Father" (Rom. 8:15; Gal. 4:6). The Spirit himself intercedes for us (Rom. 8:26). Our praying is to be done in the Spirit (Eph. 6:18; Jude 20; possibly 1 Cor. 14:15).

Jesus encourages fervent and even continual or repeated prayer (Luke 18:1–8), but not showy or repetitive prayer (Matt. 6:5–8).

Jesus becomes the model of prayer. He prays before important decisions (Luke 6:12–13) and in connection with significant crisis points (Matt. 14:23; 26:36–44; Luke 3:21; 9:29; John 12:27). He offers prayers that are not answered (Luke 22:41–44) and prayers that are (Heb. 5:7). Even as he tells his disciples to always pray and not give up (Luke 18:1 [which is also the meaning of the sometimes overly literalized "pray without ceasing" in 1 Thess. 5:17 NRSV]), so he himself wrestles in prayer (Luke 22:41–44; Heb. 5:7). He has prayed for his disciples (John 17; Luke 22:32), and even now, in heaven, he still intercedes for us (Heb. 7:25). Indeed, our intercession before God's throne is valid because his is (Heb. 4:14–16).

Predestination–The term "predestination" means "to determine or decide something beforehand." Some form of the Greek verb *proorizō* ("to determine beforehand") occurs six times in the NT (Acts 4:28; Rom. 8:29, 30; 1 Cor. 2:7; Eph. 1:5, 11). It is practically synonymous with the concept of foreordination and is closely related to divine foreknowledge (Acts 2:23; Rom. 8:29; 1 Pet. 1:1–2, 20). Various Scriptures indicate that God the Father is the one who predestines (John 17:6–10; Rom. 8:29; Eph. 1:3–5; 1 Pet. 1:2).

Preexilic–This adjective denotes Israel's history prior to the Babylonian exile (587/586 BC), especially the prophets and the events of the ninth, eighth, and seventh centuries BC.

Preparation Day–All four Gospels refer to Preparation Day (*paraskeuē*) as the day of Jesus' crucifixion. According to Mark 15:42, Preparation Day was "the day before the Sabbath," meaning Friday (cf. Luke 23:54). By the end of the first century, *paraskeuē* had become a technical term meaning "Friday" (*Did.* 8.1; cf. *Mart. Pol.* 7.1). The precise referent of Preparation Day in John 19:14 is disputed, as the Greek phrase *paraskeuē tou pascha* has been translated as "the day of Preparation of the Passover" (NIV, ESV). John 19:31 states that Preparation Day was immediately followed by the Sabbath, which would place Jesus' crucifixion on Friday and his final supper (John 13:2) on Passover Thursday (cf. Matt. 26:18). However, John 18:28 states that the Jewish leaders "wanted to be able to eat the Passover," suggesting that Jesus was crucified on Passover. In this verse, "the Passover" (*pascha*) may refer to the continuing Feast of Unleavened Bread, or it may be that the Jews had prepared but not eaten the Passover by early the next morning. Regardless, the Gospels clearly record that Jesus was crucified on Friday, Preparation Day.

Presbyter, Presbytery–*See* Offices in the New Testament.

Priests–A priest is a minister of sacred things who represents God to the people and the people to God. The OT identifies priests of Yahweh and priests of other gods and idols. The only pagan priest that the NT mentions is the priest of Zeus from Lystra who wanted to offer sacrifices to Paul and Barnabas, whom the crowd mistook for deities (Acts 14:13). All other NT references build upon OT teaching about priests of Yahweh.

Early biblical history records clan heads offering sacrifices for their families (Gen. 12:7–8; 13:18; 22; 31:54; 46:1). Although the patriarchs performed these duties, they are never called "priests"; the only priests mentioned from this time are foreigners such as Melchizedek, the Egyptian priest of On, and Moses' father-in-law Jethro (Gen. 14:18; 41:45, 50; 46:20; Exod. 3:1; 18:1). Whereas all Israelites could be called "a kingdom of priests and a holy nation" (Exod. 19:6), a distinctive priesthood came to light when God instructed Moses to prepare special priestly clothes for Aaron and his sons (Exod. 28). The high priest was distinguished from the others by more magnificent clothes. By failing to wear their special clothes while serving at the tabernacle, the priests would incur guilt and die (Exod. 28:43).

In NT times many priests exerted religious and civil power as leaders of the Sadducees and the Essenes. Some priests, such as Zechariah, were portrayed as righteous men (Luke 1:5–6). Others were said to have come to faith in Jesus (Acts 6:7). Supporting the role assigned by Moses, Jesus regularly required those whom he healed to show themselves to the priest. Even so, most Gospel references to priests underscore their opposition to Jesus' ministry and the role they played in his trial and crucifixion. This opposition continued after the resurrection, as priests challenged the witness of the apostles. When Peter and John proclaimed that a crippled beggar had been healed by Jesus' power, the priests and others jailed, interrogated, and forbade them from speaking in Jesus' name (Acts 4:1–20). The Sanhedrin questioned Stephen about charges of blasphemy and speaking against the temple and the Mosaic law (6:11–7:1). Saul (Paul) received a letter of authority from the high priest to arrest Christians (9:1–2). Later, as a follower of Jesus, he stood trial before Ananias, who charged him before Felix (24:1), and a wider group of chief priests who charged him before Festus (25:1–3).

Hebrews uniquely highlights how the priesthood of Jesus surpassed the OT priesthood. The OT priests presented sin offerings, but their sacrifices needed to be repeated regularly, whereas Jesus, the faithful and merciful high priest, offered a sacrifice that never needed repeating and was available to everyone at all times. Jesus also surpassed the Aaronic priests because they first needed to offer sacrifices for their own sins, but he never sinned. Furthermore, since he offered the perfect sacrifice of himself, all people, not just priests, could draw near to God.

The NT develops the idea of a priesthood of all believers by taking the concept that Israel would be a kingdom of priests and transferring it to the church (1 Pet. 2:4–9; cf. Exod. 19:6). Reflecting the general biblical view of priesthood, believers offer spiritual sacrifices to God, represent God to the world by revealing his works of salvation, and represent the world to God through prayer. In the NT, the priesthood of believers is corporate; a priestly office in the church is never expressly mentioned.

Principalities–One of the names given to spiritual realities that were created by God in Christ but are now corrupted. Paul says that it is these "principalities" (Gk. *archē*), not "flesh and blood," that form the real opposition for Christians (Eph. 6:12 KJV). Synonyms that appear in various Bible translations are "rulers," "authorities," "powers," "spiritual forces," and "thrones" (Rom. 8:38; Eph. 3:10; 6:12; Col. 1:16).

Prison, Prisoner–In comparing modern society to that of biblical times, it is important to acknowledge what is distinctive about prisons in many modern societies. Prisons serve multiple functions, including imposing incarceration as punishment for crimes committed, segregating dangerous criminals from the larger population, deterring crime by imposing a negative incentive, and rehabilitating offenders so that they can eventually return to society. In many cases where modern law imposes incarceration as the penalty for crime, ancient and biblical law imposed economic penalties (such as fines), corporal punishment (beatings), and capital punishment (death). In addition, many of the biblical references to prisons and prisoners involve what in modern society would be considered political rather than criminal incarceration.

The story of Joseph prominently features an Egyptian prison. Joseph was falsely put in prison for the crime of molesting his master's wife (Gen. 39:19–20), while his companions were imprisoned for the otherwise unspecified crime of causing offense to the king (40:1). As this story illustrates, the sentences were not of a predetermined duration, and release depended on the goodwill of the king (Gen. 40:13), a situation in which Paul also found himself hundreds of years later during Roman times (Acts 24:27). When Joseph imprisoned his brothers, it was on a presumption of guilt for the crime of espionage (Gen. 42:16). In Roman times, in contrast, certain prisoners had a right to be put on trial eventually, if not quickly (Acts 25:27; see also 16:37). Imprisonment could also be imposed for failure to pay a debt (Matt. 18:30). Joseph kept Simeon in prison as a guarantee that his brothers would fulfill a prior agreement (Gen. 42:19, 24). In addition to specialized dungeons, prisoners could also be confined in houses (Jer. 37:15; Acts 28:16) and pits (Zech. 9:11).

In both Testaments, release from prison is a symbol of God's salvation. The theme is prominent in the psalms, as in Ps. 146:7: "The Lord sets prisoners free" (see also Pss. 68:6; 107:10; 142:7). In Acts 12:7 Peter is freed from prison by a divinely sent messenger. Paul wrote a number of letters from prison and identified himself as a prisoner of Christ (Eph. 3:1; Col. 4:10; 2 Tim. 1:8; Philem. 1). Some texts refer in mythological terms to a prison that confines spirits or Satan (1 Pet. 3:19; Rev. 20:7).

Prison Letters, Prison Epistles–Paul's prison letters include Ephesians, Philippians, Colossians, and Philemon. Traditionally they have been considered to have been written by Paul during his first Roman imprisonment (c. AD 60–62), though some scholars think they may have been written during a time of incarceration in Caesarea, Ephesus, or elsewhere. *See also* Paul.

Proconsul–The senate-appointed governor of a Roman province (KJV: "deputy"). The proconsul oversaw civil, judicial, and military affairs in the province. Sergius Paulus was proconsul of Cyprus (Acts 13:7), and Gallio of Achaia (Acts 18:12). The city clerk in Ephesus calmed a disturbance before it escalated to the jurisdiction of the court and the proconsul (Acts 19:38).

Procurator–The governor of a Roman imperial province, also called "prefect." The prefect or procurator collected taxes, oversaw judicial matters, and commanded auxiliary military troops. Pontius Pilate was prefect of the province of Judea from about AD 26 to 36 (Matt. 27:2). The title was changed to "procurator" in the mid-first century. Paul was imprisoned in Caesarea under Felix, procurator of Judea in AD 52–60 (Acts 23:24–24:26). Felix was succeeded by Porcius Festus (Acts 24:27), who approved Paul's request to appeal to Caesar (25:12).

Prodigal Son–The parable of the prodigal (or "wasteful") son is told by Jesus following the parables of the lost sheep and the lost coin, in which the owner figure loses something of value and rejoices upon finding it again (Luke 15). Similarly, the parable of the prodigal son is focused primarily upon the mercy and forgiveness of the father. In this parable, the younger of two sons requests his share of what the father will leave them as an inheritance. The father grants it, and the son, after relocating to a distant country, squanders it on the pleasures of this world. With his inheritance exhausted and the land suffering a severe famine, the son's livelihood becomes dependent upon his new job, feeding pigs. In despair at being in this lowly position, the son decides to come home and face his father, who, in an amazing turn of events, is overjoyed at the return of his lost son. During the feast celebrating his return, however, the older brother becomes envious because he has been faithful yet has never received such an honor.

The parable is an allegory about Jesus' ministry, with the father representing God himself, the younger brother representing the sinners and tax collectors to whom Jesus is ministering, and the older brother representing the religious leaders who are rejecting God's offer of free grace to sinners who will repent and return to God. It is significant that the parable is open ended, with no response recorded from the older brother. The father states his love for both sons and affirms to the older one that "everything I have is yours." It remains to be seen whether he will now choose to welcome the prodigal and join in the feast in the kingdom of God. God's offer of salvation remains an open invitation.

Promise–A technical term for "promise" does not appear in the OT, but its concept is present throughout Scripture. God unfolds the history of redemption by employing the idea of promises. The writers of the NT repeatedly assert that Jesus Christ has fulfilled God's promises in the OT (e.g., Luke 24:44–48; 1 Cor. 15:3–8).

Most remarkable is the promise that God made to Abraham, Isaac, and Jacob (Gen. 12:1–3; 13:14–17; 17:4–8; 22:17–18; 26:1–5; 28:13–15). God called Abraham in order to give him three specific blessings: the land, descendants, and the channel of blessing among the nations. As a sign of his promise, God made a covenant of circumcision with Abraham and his descendants (17:10–14). With Isaac (26:1–5) and Jacob (28:13–15), God repeatedly reconfirmed the promise made to Abraham. At the time of the exodus and later the settlement in Canaan, God's promise to Abraham was partially fulfilled by multiplying his descendants into millions and by giving them the promised land.

The central message of the NT is that God's promises in the OT are fulfilled with the coming of Jesus Christ. Matthew's numerous citation formulas are evidence of this theme. In Luke 4:16–21 Jesus pronounces the fulfillment of Isaiah's promise (about the Messiah's ministry [Isa. 61:1–3]) in his own life. The book of Acts specifically states that Jesus' suffering and resurrection and the coming of the Holy Spirit are the fulfillment of the OT promises (2:29–31; 13:32–34). Jesus' identity both as the descendant of David (Acts 13:23) and as the prophet like Moses (Acts 3:21–26; cf. Deut. 18:15–18) is also regarded as the fulfillment of the OT.

Paul's view of God's promises is summarized in this statement: "For no matter how many promises God has made, they are 'Yes' in Christ" (2 Cor. 1:20). According to Rom. 1:2–3, Paul regards the gospel as the message that God "promised beforehand through his prophets in the Holy Scriptures regarding his Son." In Rom. 4 Abraham's faith is described in terms of his trust in God's promises, which leads to his righteousness. He is presented as our model of faith in God's promises. The famous phrase "according to the Scriptures" in 1 Cor. 15:3–4 is, in a sense, understood by Paul as the fulfillment of God's promises regarding Christ's death and resurrection.

In the NT, God makes new promises based on the work of Christ, including the final resurrection and the second coming of Christ (John 5:29; 11:25–26; 1 Cor. 15:48–57; 2 Cor. 4:14; 1 Thess. 4:13–18). Furthermore, the message of the gospel is presented as multiple promises, including eternal life, the fullness of life in Christ, the forgiveness of sins, the indwelling of the Holy Spirit, the peace of God, the knowledge of God, and the joy of God (Matt. 28:18–20; John 3:16; 10:10;

14:16, 27; 16:20–24; 17:25–26; Phil. 4:4–9; 1 John 1:9).

Prophecy, Prophets, Prophetess–A prophet is a messenger of God, a person to whom God entrusts his message to an individual or to a nation. Indeed, the last book in the OT is named "Malachi," which means "my messenger." Isaiah heard God ask, "Whom shall I send?" and he cried out, "Send me!" (Isa. 6:8). A good template for understanding the phenomenon is Moses and Aaron. Moses was to tell Aaron what to say, and Aaron would say it. "Then the Lord said to Moses, 'See, I have made you like God to Pharaoh, and your brother Aaron will be your prophet'" (Exod. 7:1).

In the NT period there were a number of prophets. John the Baptist could point to Jesus and proclaim him to be the Lamb of God, who takes away the sins of the world (John 1:29). Agabus the prophet predicted a famine and, later, Paul's arrest (Acts 11:28; 21:10–11).

Paul lists "gifts of the Spirit" (1 Cor. 12:4–11), including prophecy and various phenomena reminiscent of the OT prophets' ecstatic state. Paul warns the Corinthians not to overdo this sort of thing and so to be mature (1 Cor. 14:19–20). Near the end of his life, in one of his last letters, he speaks of prophecy as normative in the church, particularly in establishing an authoritative body of elders to rule and especially to preach the gospel (1 Tim. 1:18; 4:14). Peter draws a connection between the ministry of the OT prophets and the proclamation of the gospel of Jesus Christ (1 Pet. 1:10–12). Evangelism seems to be the normative mode for prophecy today: forthtelling by calling people to turn from their sins to Jesus, and foretelling by speaking of his return and the final judgment.

Thus, all Christians hold the office of prophet, even if they never participate in the ecstatic state experienced by the Corinthians. The greatness of a prophet is in how clearly the prophet points to Jesus. John the Baptist was the greatest of the OT prophets by that measure, but any Christian on this side of the cross and resurrection can proclaim the gospel even more clearly. Thus, the prophetic ministry of any Christian is greater than John's (Matt. 11:11).

Five prophetesses are mentioned in the OT: Miriam (Exod. 15:20), Deborah (Judg. 4–5), Huldah (2 Kings 22:14–20; 2 Chron. 34:22–28), Isaiah's wife (Isa. 8:3), and Noadiah (Neh. 6:14).

Similarly in the NT, Peter recognizes God's promise through Joel being fulfilled in the gift of prophetic speech to women as well as men at Pentecost (Acts 2:18); and Paul, acknowledging that women prophesy publicly in the congregation, is concerned only with the manner of their doing so (1 Cor. 11:5). The prophetess Anna proclaims the baby Jesus as the Messiah (Luke 2:36–38), Luke reports that the four unmarried daughters of Philip the evangelist also prophesy (Acts 21:8–9). The only false prophetess in the NT is the apocalyptic figure of Jezebel in Rev. 2:20.

Proverbs, Book of–The preface to the book of Proverbs (1:1–7) introduces its intent to make its reader wise. Although the discourses of the book (chaps. 1–9) are the instructions of a father to his son, the preface widens the audience to include both the "simple" (1:4) and the "wise" (1:5). The preface also informs the reader that wisdom begins with the fear of the Lord, thus indicating that wisdom is more than practical advice. Wisdom is a theological truth.

Fear of the Lord. According to Proverbs, no one can be wise without having the proper relationship with God (1:7). This relationship is characterized by "fear." This fear is not horror, but it is more than respect. The point is that the wise person must understand that God, and no one else, is at the center of the universe, that God is more important than any human being. After all, God created the world (3:19–20; 8:22–31), so it is important to know one's place before the Creator in order to understand how the world works.

Wisdom and folly. The relational nature of wisdom as "fear of the Lord" is taught in yet another intriguing way. In 1:20–33; 8:1–36; 9:1–6 the reader encounters a woman, Wisdom, who invites all the young men (the readers) to dinner. Such an invitation presumes an intimate relationship. The location of Wisdom's home on "the highest point of the city" (9:3) reflects the location of the temple and indicates that Wisdom stands for Yahweh's wisdom, even Yahweh himself. On the other hand, in 9:13–18 another woman, Folly, issues a rival invitation. Her home too is on "the highest point of the city" (9:14), indicating that she stands for a god as well, but in her case the false gods of the nations. In chapter 9, the reader must decide with whom to dine, Wisdom (Yahweh) or Folly (false gods). Thus, wisdom and folly are not only practical, but also theological categories.

Someone who acts wisely is behaving like a proper worshiper of the true God, whereas someone who acts foolishly is behaving like an idolater.

Providence–The word "providence" comes from the Latin word *providentia*, which means "foresight." However, the modern theological use of the term refers not to foresight or foreknowledge per se but rather to how God continues to sustain and guide his creation. There is no single term in either the OT or the NT that translates as "providence." The one time the word occurs in the NIV (Job 10:12), the Hebrew word (*peqqudah*) is one that the NIV in other places usually translates with words such as "care," "charge," or "oversight." The concept of divine providence comes not from any one word but rather from numerous statements in the Bible that speak of God's continuing supervision of his world.

Psalms, Book of–A collection of 150 poems. They are the hymnbook of the OT period, used in public worship. Psalms contains songs of different lengths, types, and dates. The earliest psalm (Ps. 90) is attributed to Moses (mid-second millennium BC), while the content of Ps. 126 and Ps. 137 points to the latest periods of the OT (mid-first millennium BC). They continue to be used as a source of public worship and private devotion.

Although the psalms are not theological essays, readers can learn about God and their relationship with God from these poems. The book of Psalms is a bit like a portrait gallery of God, using images to describe who he is and the nature of our relationship with him. Some examples include God as shepherd (Ps. 23), king (Ps. 47), warrior (Ps. 98), and mother (Ps. 131), and the list could be greatly expanded. Each one of these picture images casts light on the nature of God and also the nature of our relationship with God. After all, the aforementioned psalms explicitly or implicitly describe God's people as sheep, subjects, soldiers, and children.

Puah–One of the Hebrew midwives blessed by God for refusing to heed Pharaoh's command to execute all newborn Hebrew males (Exod. 1:15–22).

Pul–The biblical record and cuneiform documents agree that this was an alternate appellation for the Assyrian king Tiglath-pileser III (r. 744–727 BC). Pul is first mentioned as campaigning in Samaria during the reign of Menahem and subsequently exacting tribute from him (2 Kings 15:19; 1 Chron. 5:26). *See also* Tiglath-pileser III.

Purim–*See* Festivals.

Purity, Purification–The concepts of purity and purification are largely unfamiliar to modern Western readers of the Bible. These terms often appear in cultic contexts and are used to refer to physical, ritual, and ethical purity. They are most frequently applied to the process needed to restore someone to a state of purity so that he or she could participate in ritual activities once again (Lev. 22:4–7). These terms are cultural and theological, serving to constrain actions and behaviors through definite boundaries; thus, in their ancient use they have little to do with modern notions of hygiene (e.g., diseases that may be caught from a pig [Lev. 13]; the medical advantages of washing [Lev. 15]; quarantining a leper [Lev. 13]). Although some have attempted to relate the rules of purity to simple physical events, such modern medical rationale cannot account for the range of prohibitions or find explicit support in the text.

In the NT, the idea of ceremonial purity as an important element in Jewish life appears in John 11:55; Acts 21:23; 24:18. But just as in the prophets, the notion of purity is applied to a life lived in wholehearted devotion to God. An individual is purified when obeying the truth (1 Pet. 1:22). James describes repentance in terms of purity: "Wash your hands, you sinners, and purify your hearts, you double-minded" (James 4:8); and he describes helping those in distress as the kind of genuine piety that "God our Father accepts as pure and faultless" (James 1:27).

Purple–Because purple dye was expensive, purple cloth represented wealth (Prov. 31:22; Luke 16:19; Acts 16:14; Rev. 18:16) and authority (Judg. 8:26; Dan. 5:7), especially royalty (Lam. 4:5; cf. Mark 15:20; John 19:2–5). In the tabernacle, temple, and the priestly garments, purple was often combined with blue and scarlet or crimson, themselves symbols of wealth and power (Exod. 26:1; 28:4–15, 33; Num. 4:6–12; 2 Chron. 3:14).

Put–A grandson of Noah, a son of Ham, and brother of Cush (Ethiopia), Mizraim (Egypt), and Canaan in the Table of Nations (Gen. 10:6; 1 Chron. 1:8). "Put" appears as a geographic designation that can be identified with Libya, based on Old Persian *putiya* and Babylonian *puṭa,* and is the source of soldiers in passages in Ezekiel (27:10; 30:5; 38:5), Jeremiah (46:9), and Nahum (3:9). Another Hebrew word for Libya, "Lub," always occurs in the plural and likely refers to the population, "the Libyans." *See also* Libya.

Q

Quartus–A believer in Corinth whom Paul refers to as "our brother" as he conveys greetings from Erastus and Quartus to the church in Rome (Rom. 16:23).

Queen–The highest-ranking female member of a royal household. In the book of Esther the position of queen, though tenuous, is shown to be one of influence over the king (chap. 7) and over the nation (1:16–20). A queen may also be associated with great beauty (Esther 2:2–17; Song 6:8–9; Ezek. 16:13). A queen's participation in governing with the king varies in different passages. Queen Esther is expected to come before the king only when summoned (Esther 4:11), while the queen of King Belshazzar enters the banquet hall freely to counsel the king (Dan. 5:10–12). In Neh. 2:6 the queen of Persia sits enthroned beside the king.

In some passages the title of queen is bestowed not on the wife but on the mother of the king, who is called the "queen mother" (1 Kings 15:13; 2 Kings 10:13; 2 Chron. 15:16; Jer. 13:18; 29:2). Hence, Jezebel is referred to not as queen but only by name or as the wife of the king (e.g., 1 Kings 16:31; 21:5–7; cf. Herodias in Matt. 14:3).

The term "queen" also appears in prophetic texts in reference to other gods (the "Queen of Heaven" in Jer. 7:18; 44:15–24) and to the city of Babylon (Isa. 47:5–7).

Queen of Heaven–The title that Jeremiah uses in reference to a goddess being worshiped in Judah (Jer. 7:18; 44:17–19, 25). This title was bestowed on several major goddesses in the ancient Near East, and since Jeremiah avoids using her name, the precise identity of the goddess is uncertain.

Queen of Sheba–*See* Sheba, Queen of.

Quirinius–Publius Sulpicius Quirinius (c. 50 BC–AD 21) was a successful Roman military commander and politician best known for conducting a census mentioned at the beginning of Christ's birth narrative in Luke 2:2. Ancient historians, including Tacitus, Strabo, and Josephus, wrote about Quirinius, so a fair bit is known about his career. However, all this information lends to a historical problem when compared to the Gospel accounts. Jesus' birth takes place during the time of Herod the Great (Matt. 2:1; Luke 1:5), but only Luke's account mentions Quirinius conducting a census as the governor of Syria before Herod's death. Every other known account places this census in AD 6/7, some ten years after Herod's death. For centuries a number of attempts have been made to solve the problem, but without more evidence each solution remains inconclusive.

Qumran–*See* Dead Sea Scrolls.

R

Raamses–*See* Rameses.

Rabbah–The capital city of the Ammonites, located about twenty-three miles east of the Jordan River at the site of the modern city of Amman. A wealthy city due to its prominent position on the major trade route from Arabia in the south to Damascus in the north, Rabbah was the site of the magnificent bed of King Og (Deut. 3:11). The city was composed of two parts: the "city of waters" and the "royal city" (2 Sam. 12:26–27 KJV). Under the leadership of David, the Israelites took possession of Rabbah. It was during this siege that Uriah the Hittite was killed (2 Sam. 12:29–31). Soon after the division of the kingdom, Rabbah regained its independence. Both Jeremiah and Amos prophesied the destruction of Rabbah, but Jeremiah's prophecy also includes a promise of its restoration (Jer. 49:2–6; Amos 1:13–15).

Rabbi–A title applied to teachers and others in respected positions, literally meaning "my master." By the NT era, the term was used in a more specific sense to refer to teachers of the Mosaic law.

In the NT, the title occurs only in the Gospels of Matthew, Mark, and John, and it is most commonly used to address Jesus (Mark 9:5; 11:21; 14:45; Matt. 26:25, 49). The title is used more widely in John's Gospel by individuals such as Nathanael and Nicodemus, as well as the group of disciples (John 1:38, 49; 3:2; 4:31; 6:25; 9:2; 11:8). The title conveys the respect of pupil for master and indicates the nature of the relationship that Jesus had with his followers.

Others were also called "Rabbi," including John the Baptist and some of the Pharisees (John 3:26; Matt. 23:7). Although the Pharisees considered the title an honor, Jesus instructed his disciples not to allow themselves to be addressed as "Rabbi" and to acknowledge only one teacher, Christ (Matt. 23:8, 10).

Rabboni–An Aramaic form of the more commonly found title "rabbi," meaning "my master" or "my teacher" (Mark 10:51 [NASB, NKJV]; John 20:16). *See also* Rabbi.

Rab-saris–A high-ranking official associated with Assyrian and Babylonian courts. A Rab-saris was sent with the Assyrian delegation to King Hezekiah (2 Kings 18:17), another was included with the Babylonian court in the gate of Jerusalem (Jer. 39:3), and a third helped with the release of Jeremiah from prison (Jer. 39:13). In Dan. 1 Ashpenaz, the Rab-saris at Nebuchadnezzar's court (NIV: "chief of his court officials"), was responsible for bringing Daniel and his companions into the king's palace and for assigning their Babylonian names.

Rabshakeh–An Assyrian loanword in Hebrew, it designates one of the three officers sent by King Sennacherib of Assyria to King Hezekiah of Judah when the Assyrians invaded Jerusalem in 701 BC (2 Kings 18–20; cf. Isa. 36–37). Besides the other two officers—the Tartan (lit., "commander in chief"; NIV: "supreme commander") and the Rab-saris (lit., "chief eunuch"; NIV: "chief officer")—the Rabshakeh (lit., "chief cupbearer"; NIV: "field commander"), who could communicate effectively in the Judean language, openly challenged Hezekiah (2 Kings 18:23–25) and humiliated the people (18:27–37).

Raca–A term of abuse that probably derives from an Aramaic word meaning "empty" or "worthless" and has the sense of "fool" or "good-for-nothing." In Matt. 5:22 Jesus condemns those who call their brother or sister "Raca," comparing this verbal abuse with the act of murder.

Rachel–A daughter of Laban (Gen. 29:6); a wife of Jacob (29:28); mother of Joseph and Benjamin (35:24). Rachel is best known for her tumultuous relationship with her husband, Jacob, who, after meeting the beautiful shepherdess, agrees to work seven years for her father, Laban, in order to marry her. Jacob, however, receives Laban's oldest daughter, Leah, on his wedding night and must serve Laban an additional seven years for Rachel. Genesis 29–30 records the tension between Jacob's two wives as they engage in a childbearing competition for their husband's love. Clearly the object of Jacob's affection, Rachel bears only two of his twelve sons, Joseph and Benjamin. Outside Genesis, Rachel is mentioned in Ruth 4:11 and 1 Sam. 10:2, and in Jer. 31:15 and its NT quotation in Matt. 2:18.

Rahab–**(1)** A woman associated with the conquest whose history is recounted in Josh. 2. Two Israelite soldiers entered Jericho and headed straight for the nearest brothel (Josh. 2:1). There, they "lay down" (the literal meaning of *shakab*, which the NIV translates as "stayed there") with Rahab. They were on a reconnaissance mission under Joshua's command, as a precursor to invasion. The king of Jericho demanded that Rahab hand over the spies to him. She lied and sent the pursuers away on a false path, enabling the Israelites to escape. Her justification for this action was that she, and all of Canaan, knew that Israel's God was with Israel and surely would destroy Jericho. She asked the spies to spare her family. This they promised to do if she would mark her window with a red cord, which she did.

These acts identified Rahab with Israel and Israel's God, making her, as it were, a de facto Israelite. Thus, her works justified her to Joshua and saved her family (James 2:25). Although the citizens of Jericho believed in the coming judgment, only Rahab's faith moved her to switch loyalties. Thus, her faith saved her (Heb. 11:31). The red cord in the window connects her story with Passover, where the angel of death passed over Israelite houses marked with lamb's blood. Joshua's forces passed over Rahab's house, since it bore this mark. She is found in the genealogy of Jesus (Matt. 1:5).

(2) A mythological monster especially associated with the ocean that represented the natural forces of chaos in the world. Many scholars believe that Rahab is identical to the Canaanite Leviathan. In the OT Yahweh fights Rahab in the process of ending chaos and creating the world. Rahab is depicted as a poor opponent (Job 9:13; 26:12; Ps. 89:10; Isa. 51:9). Later, Egypt is sometimes equated with the monster Rahab (Ps. 87:4; Isa. 30:7), although there is no historic relationship between the two. The NKJV transliterates the Hebrew in Isa. 30:7 as though a proper name, Rahab-Hem-Shebeth, but most versions translate it with a phrase such as "Rahab the Do-Nothing" (NIV) or "Rahab who sits still" (ESV, NRSV).

Rain–In an agrarian society with an unpredictable climate, such as Israel, rainfall was of the utmost importance. Two rainy periods could be hoped for each year, in February/March and in October/November, and these seasons were critical in producing a good crop. Regular rainfall thus formed a significant part of God's promise of a good and fruitful land for his people (Lev. 26:4). Solomon's prayer acknowledges the conditional nature of this promise: rain would be withheld from a sinful nation but would be given to a forgiven and obedient people (1 Kings 8:35–36).

Rain could also be sent in judgment, most notably in the flood narratives, where God sent rain in order to destroy all living things on the face of the earth (Gen. 7:4), and in the exodus narrative, where rain accompanied hail and thunder in the seventh plague (Exod. 9:23).

Since rain is completely beyond human control, it naturally became a symbol of God's sovereignty in both blessing and curse. A striking example of this is in 1 Kings 17–18, when for three years the rains were withheld, until finally Elijah's trust in God was vindicated above the prophets of Baal, and the rain followed. The effectiveness of Elijah's prayers, first for drought and later for rain, is held up in the NT as an example for all believers (James 5:17–18).

Rainbow–The great beauty of rainbows results from their containing the full spectrum of visible light. In Scripture rainbows have a special significance and symbolism. A rainbow is a sign of God's covenant with the earth to never again destroy all life with a flood as he did in the time of Noah (Gen. 9:13–14, 16). The power of this particular image comes from the transformation of a bow—typically a symbol of warfare, destruction, and death—into a colorful symbol of heavenly mercy, grace, and peace. The rainbow thus became a sign of God's kindness and mercy and is found in descriptions of God in the heavenly visions of both Ezekiel and John (Ezek. 1:28; Rev. 4:3; 10:1).

Raisins–Raisins, or dried grapes, were among the foods forbidden to Nazirites (Num. 6:3). The reference to raisins in Song 2:5 indicates a belief in their aphrodisiac quality. Elsewhere, raisins frequently appear as a staple food, often pressed into cakes or patties that were easily transported (1 Sam. 25:18) and supplied quick energy (1 Sam. 30:12). Raisin cakes were also used as cultic offerings to other gods (Hos. 3:1).

Ramah–**(1)** A town in Benjamin (Josh. 18:25), possibly located on the site of the modern city of Er-Ram, five miles north of Jerusalem, or three miles further north at Ramallah. Ramah was located near the cities of Gibeon and Mizpah and close to the eventual border between Israel and Judah. It was a resting place on the road to the north (Judg. 19:13). The judge Deborah held court near Ramah on the road to Bethel (Judg. 4:5).

When King Baasha of Israel invaded Judah, he made Ramah his base, fortifying the city in order to control northern access to Jerusalem (1 Kings 15:17). After Baasha was forced to abandon his position, King Asa of Judah dismantled the fortifications and used the materials to strengthen the cities of Geba and Mizpah (15:22). Following the return from exile, some of the Benjamites resettled in the city of Ramah (Neh. 11:33). Rachel's tomb was said to be near Ramah, and the place is associated with her mourning for her children in Jeremiah's prophecy (Jer. 31:15). Some scholars believe that Ramah of Benjamin was also the birthplace of Samuel (see #2).

(2) The birthplace and burial site of Samuel (1 Sam. 1:19; 25:1), also known as Ramathaim, or possibly Ramathaim Zuphim (1:1 NIV mg.), situated in the hill country of Ephraim. Ramah was Samuel's home throughout his time as judge over Israel, and he built an altar to God there (7:17). It was at Ramah that the Israelite elders came to Samuel to demand a king (8:4–5). Later, when David fled from Saul's house, he went to Ramah to take counsel from Samuel and find refuge from the king.

Rameses–The Egyptian city and region settled by Joseph and his family, "the best part of the land" (Gen. 47:11). This was later the point of departure for the Israelites leaving Egypt (Exod. 12:37; Num. 33:3, 5). It is also the name of one of the two store cities that the Israelites were forced to build in Egypt (Exod. 1:11).

Ramoth Gilead–A city of refuge located in the Transjordan territory of Gad (Deut. 4:43; Josh. 20:8; 21:38). King Ahab of Israel invited King Jehoshaphat of Judah to ally with him to retake Ramoth Gilead from the Arameans. In the ensuing battle Ahab was fatally wounded (1 Kings 22; 2 Chron. 18). After Ahab's son Joram was injured at Ramoth Gilead, Elisha's representative traveled there to anoint Jehu as king of Israel (2 Kings 8:25–9:13). Ramoth Gilead is commonly identified with Tell er-Rumeith, a small fortification about three miles south of Ramtha in northern Jordan, near the Syrian border.

Ram's Horn–*See* Shofar.

Ransom–A payment made to redeem a slave, release a captive, or free a criminal from punishment.

In the OT, slaves could be set free by ransom (Lev. 19:20), and certain kinds of criminals are excluded from ransom (Num. 35:31–32), implying that others could be ransomed to escape their punishment. Ransom is also used more broadly to include notions of atonement (Exod. 30:12) and as a near synonym for "redemption" (Jer. 31:11 NASB, NRSV, KJV). "Ransom" is frequently used metaphorically to describe God's saving actions on behalf of the nation (Isa. 43:3; 50:2; Jer. 31:11; Hos. 13:14), saving them from their enemies, or of individuals (Job 5:20; Ps. 55:18), saving them from death. In these cases, the emphasis is on the rescue effected, not the price paid.

In the NT, "ransom" is used to describe the atoning work of Christ. Jesus describes his own purpose: "The Son of Man did not come to be served, but to serve, and to give his life as a ransom for many" (Mark 10:45 // Matt. 20:28). Paul uses the same language: "Christ Jesus, who gave himself as a ransom for all people" (1 Tim. 2:5–6). The author of Hebrews describes the effect of this ransom: "He has died as a ransom to set them free from the sins committed under the first covenant" (Heb. 9:15). All three references indicate that the price paid for the ransom is

R

Jesus' life, given up to death on the cross. Each of the literal meanings of "ransom" has its metaphorical equivalent: Christ's death frees us from our slavery to sin and death (Rom. 6:6), releases us from our captivity to the law (7:4–6), and pays the price of the punishment that our sins deserved (3:25–26). The ransom was not paid to the devil, and it is best understood as the satisfaction of God's own justice (Rom. 6:23).

Rape–Nonconsensual sexual intercourse imposed on a person by force or trickery. The rape of a betrothed woman was considered a capital offense under OT law (Deut. 22:25–27), and a woman who had been the victim of this crime was not dishonored by it. A man who raped an unattached woman was required to pay her bride-price and marry her in order to preserve her honor. Such a man was not permitted to later divorce his wife. The OT contains a number of stories describing rape and its consequences (see Gen. 19:30–35; 34; 2 Sam. 13:1–22 for examples).

Rapture–The word "rapture" (from Lat. *raptura*) describes Christians being "caught up" to meet the Lord at the second coming (1 Thess. 4:17). This seems to immediately follow the resurrection of the dead. Paul claims those who have "fallen asleep" will rise first (4:15), then the living will be caught up with them in the clouds and meet the Lord in the air.

Futurists disagree as to the timing of the rapture. Pretribulationists hold that the rapture happens before the great tribulation begins, sparing the church the trauma of that period. Midtribulationists place it at the midpoint of the tribulation. Both of these views see a two-part second coming: first, Christ returns secretly to remove his church; then, he returns visibly at the end of the tribulation. Posttribulationists see the church remaining throughout the entire period, protected from the wrath of God but experiencing intense persecution from the world.

Raven–An omnivorous member of the crow family, the raven is listed among the unclean birds in Lev. 11:15 because it is a scavenger that feeds on live prey and carrion. Despite this, the raven is used as an example of God's care for his creation (Job 38:41; Ps. 147:9; Luke 12:24). God uses ravens to bring food to Elijah while he is hiding in the wilderness (1 Kings 17:4–6). A raven is the first bird sent out by Noah at the end of the flood (Gen. 8:6–7). It does not return, presumably because it was able to find its own source of food. As part of God's vengeance against Edom, ravens and other birds of prey will nest in the city (Isa. 34:11). Together with the vulture, the raven is used as a metaphor for vicious destruction (Prov. 30:17).

Rebekah–The daughter of Abraham's nephew Bethuel (Gen. 24:15); Isaac's wife (24:67); the mother of Esau and Jacob (25:25–26). Rebekah is introduced as a beautiful virgin who is willing to serve others (Abraham's servant) and to follow God's plan (to marry Isaac). Like Isaac's mother, Rebekah is barren, but following Isaac's intercessory prayers, she becomes pregnant with twins twenty years after her wedding (25:20–21, 24–26). According to Gen. 25, Rebekah loves the younger son, Jacob, while Isaac loves the elder, Esau. Rebekah schemes to provide Jacob with the fatherly blessing due the elder son by disguising Jacob as Esau so that Isaac will unknowingly bless his younger son (27:5–17). In response, Esau plots to kill Jacob, and Rebekah is forced to send Jacob away to the home of her brother, Laban (27:42–28:5).

Reconciliation–The restoration of a relationship from a state of hostility to one of peace.

The need for reconciliation between God and humanity begins when Adam and Eve rebel against God. What has been a relationship of intimate fellowship becomes one of fear and mistrust as Adam and Eve's sin brings God's judgment (Gen. 3:14–19). But in the midst of judgment is the cryptic promise of a descendant of the woman who will crush the serpent and end the estrangement between God and humanity (3:15). The rest of the OT gives glimpses of what reconciliation will be like. God gives the sacrificial system as a means to deal with sin and restore fellowship with him (Lev. 1–7; 16). Despite Israel's sin, God pursues reconciliation with Israel like a husband chases after a wayward wife (Hos. 1–3). Israel's hope for reconciliation is often expressed in terms of a desire for peace. Although Aaron's benediction asks God to give peace to his people in the present (Num. 6:24–26), God's people look forward to the day when a covenant of peace will be established through the Suffering Servant and announced to the ends of the earth (Isa. 52–54).

What is largely hinted at in the OT is stated explicitly in the NT. Paul in particular explains how believers are reconciled to God and the consequences of that reconciliation. God, not humanity, has taken the initiative. Even though we were sinners subject to God's wrath, alienated from God and enemies in thought and act, Christ died for us (Rom. 5:6–11; Col. 1:21). As the last Adam, Christ has removed the barrier that our sinful rebellion had created between God and humanity by taking the punishment for our sin. Thus reconciliation is a gift that God offers to humanity (Rom. 5:11), not something that we do to appease God. Because God has reconciled us to himself through Christ, he has entrusted us with the ministry of reconciliation (2 Cor. 5:19). Using his people as ambassadors, God appeals to humanity to be reconciled through the work of Christ, whom, though sinless, God made sin for us "so that in him we might become the righteousness of God" (2 Cor. 5:20–21). God's purpose in reconciliation is to present the believer "holy in his sight, without blemish and free from accusation" (Col. 1:22). The result of reconciliation is the joy that comes from being at peace with God (Rom. 5:1–2, 11). In view of this, Paul's frequent greeting "grace and peace" in his letters takes on new light as his desire for believers to experience the reality of their reconciliation to God.

Reconciliation between God and humanity makes it possible for people truly to be reconciled to one another. Even the natural hostility between Jew and Gentile has been overcome by the work of Christ. Through the cross, Christ "destroyed the barrier, the dividing wall of hostility, by setting aside in his flesh the law with its commands and regulations" (Eph. 2:14–15). As a result, Jew and Gentile have been brought together in one body as fellow citizens of God's kingdom who stand on equal footing before God (Eph. 2:16–22).

Drawing upon the prophetic hope of the OT, the NT also speaks of a cosmic reconciliation. Through Christ, God is pleased "to reconcile to himself all things, whether things on earth or things in heaven, by making peace through his blood, shed on the cross" (Col. 1:20). By this Paul does not mean the salvation of everyone, but rather that the reconciling work of Jesus is the means by which God restores the created order to peace. Whereas the first Adam's sin brought a curse upon creation, Christ, as the last Adam, has brought peace that will culminate in new heavens and a new earth free from the effects of sin and death (Isa. 65:17; Rev. 21–22). It is there that God will dwell with his people forever in perfect harmony (Rev. 21:2–5).

Recorder–An Israelite court official who could represent the king in political and financial matters (2 Kings 18:18–37; 2 Chron. 34:8; Isa. 36:3–22).

Redemption, Redeemer–More than a simple notion of deliverance, redemption spoke as much of the grace of the redeemer as of the deliverance of the redeemed. Classical texts use the Greek word *apolytrōsis* ("redemption") to articulate the ransom payment given to release a slave, a captive of war, or someone sentenced to death. The group of words based on the Greek term *lytron* ("ransom") conveys the idea of payment for release. The corresponding Hebrew word *padah* is a commercial term rooted in the idea of the transfer of ownership.

The experience of the exodus gave the idea of redemption religious significance. The commemoration of this redemptive event included the dedication of the firstborn to Yahweh (Exod. 13:12–13). Moreover, Israel itself, God's own firstborn (Exod. 4:22), was redeemed by Yahweh—language that Isaiah later picked up to describe Abraham (Isa. 29:22). As the theme of redemption continued to broaden, God's redemption came to include deliverance from all Israel's troubles (Ps. 25:22). Redemption included the whole of the human situation, not just the eternal destiny (or the new age to come).

The NT champions the theme of redemption (see Luke 4:18–19). When Jesus came, teaching that he would redeem his people from the slavery of sin (John 8:34–36), he spoke of himself as a ransom for many (Matt. 20:28 // Mark 10:45). Paul's theology of the cross accentuated the same connection between sin, slavery, and Jesus' ransom. He saw people as sold into slavery under sin (Rom. 6:17; 7:14) and redeemed by Jesus' sacrifice (3:24). The Christian idea of ransom followed the accepted contemporary idea that people who are sentenced to death (Rom. 6:23) can gain their life back if a redeemer buys it with a ransom (Col. 1:13–14).

Although redemption is present, the fullness of it still awaits the future (Rom. 8:18–23), when the redeemer will fill all in all (1 Cor.

R

15:28; Col. 1:19–20). Contrary to Hellenistic conceptions of redemption, which expect redemption *from* the body, Paul expects redemption *of* the body. God's eschatological redemption is universal; it restores the relationship between creation and the Creator (Col. 1:21–23; Eph. 1:7–10).

Red Heifer–In Num. 19 the red heifer is designated for sacrifice as part of the disposal of impurity from within the Israelite camp. The red heifer was to be burned along with cedar, hyssop, and scarlet wool, and the ashes thus produced were to be stored in a ceremonially clean place and preserved as "water of cleansing." Specifically, the procedure under consideration in Num. 19 concerns the disposal of impurity resulting from direct or indirect contact with a corpse, which was removed from the impure person by washing with the "water of cleansing." It is unclear why a red heifer is specified, although most commentators agree that the color probably was understood as representative of blood. Hebrews 9:13–14 indicates that the significance and efficacy of this procedure are fulfilled by the sacrifice of Christ.

Red Sea, Reed Sea–The Red Sea separates the Arabian Peninsula (to the north and east) from the African continent along its approximately fourteen-hundred-mile length. At its southern end, the Red Sea is connected to the Indian Ocean through the Gulf of Aden. At its northern end, the Red Sea divides into the gulfs of Suez and Aqaba, which surround the Sinai Peninsula on two sides.

Perhaps the best-known appearance of the Red Sea (Heb. *yam sup*) in the Bible is the story of the exodus from Egypt and the miraculous crossing of the Red Sea by the Israelites (Exod. 14:17–15:21).

Refine–In metallurgy, to separate pure metal from impurities. The process of refining is used figuratively in the Bible in reference to God purifying his people from their sin (Jer. 9:7; Zech. 13:9; Mal. 3:3).

Regem-Melek–Probably the name, though possibly the title, of an emissary sent by the people of Bethel to the priests and prophets to determine whether fasting in the fifth month, likely to commemorate the destruction of the temple and Jerusalem by the Babylonians, was still required as the new temple neared completion seventy years later (Zech. 7:2–3).

Regeneration–In the most basic sense, regeneration refers to God giving new life to someone or something. Although the word "regeneration" does not appear in the NIV, the concept is abundantly present in a variety of terms and images, especially those of new birth, new life, new self, new heart, and new creation. The biblical concept of regeneration is applied to both individuals (John 3:1–21; 2 Cor. 5:17; Titus 3:5–7) and creation (Matt. 19:28; 27:51–53; 1 Cor. 15:20–23).

The regeneration of the individual and creation are inseparable. God imparts new spiritual life to his chosen people so that they respond in faith and obedience to him. The same regenerating power that brings the believer alive will one day renew all creation to make a suitable place for God's regenerate people to dwell. *See also* New Birth.

Rehoboam–A son of Solomon, he was the first king of Judah (928–911 BC) after the ten northern tribes broke away to form a separate kingdom.

After Solomon's death, the tribe of Judah immediately proclaimed Rehoboam king, but the ten northern tribes imposed conditions on their acceptance of his leadership. Solomon had wrongly oppressed the northern tribes, and they wanted relief from his son. Listening to the counsel of his contemporaries rather than the wiser, older advisers, Rehoboam refused and even boasted that he would increase their work and taxation. They thus rejected him as king and appointed Jeroboam as their king (1 Kings 12:1–24). At first, Rehoboam waged war against the north, but he stopped when the prophet Shemaiah told him that he would fail because of God's judgment (2 Chron. 11:1–4). He returned south and fortified the border (2 Chron. 11:5–12). Rehoboam, like his father, engaged in false worship, and so God allowed him to be defeated and the temple plundered by King Shishak of Egypt. However, he repented and thus was not completely destroyed (2 Chron. 12).

Rehoboth–The name "Rehoboth" can mean either "plazas" or "spacious place." **(1)** In the Table of Nations, Rehoboth Ir is named as one of four cities built by Nimrod (Gen. 10:11), who "was a mighty hunter before the Lord" (Gen. 10:9). It may refer to a district of Nineveh rather than an independent city. **(2)** One of the wells that Isaac dug. Isaac previously dug two other wells in the Negev but lost both to the "herders of Gerar" (Gen. 26:20), who claimed that the water was theirs. His third well in the region he named "Rehoboth," saying, "Now the LORD has given us room" (Gen. 26:22).

REKAB–**(1)** One of Saul's commanders, a son of Rimmon, he and his brother Baanah murdered Saul's son Ish-Bosheth and brought his head to David. Contrary to their expectations in carrying out the act, David had the brothers executed (2 Sam. 4). **(2)** The father or ancestor of Jehonadab (Jonadab), who accompanied Jehu to Samaria when he destroyed the house of Ahab and assisted him in slaughtering the worshipers of Baal (2 Kings 10). *See also* Rekabites.

REKABITES–A family, or perhaps an order, who traced their lineage back to Jehonadab (2 Kings 10; called "Jonadab" in Jer. 35 [NASB, NRSV, KJV]), a Kenite son or descendant of Rekab (see 1 Chron. 2:55), and were, like Jehonadab, zealous for the Lord. When Nebuchadnezzar invaded Judah, the Rekabites fled to Jerusalem to escape. According to their tradition, Jehonadab ordered the family to live in tents, avoid agriculture, and abstain from alcohol. Jeremiah tested their commitment by commanding them to drink wine, which they refused to do. Jeremiah used their obedience to their forefather as an object lesson for the unfaithful Judah (Jer. 35). *See also* Rekab.

RELEASE, YEAR OF–Refers to the seventh year, wherein the law was read at the Feast of Tabernacles and debts were canceled (Deut. 15:1–9; 31:10–13). Jubilee was another year of release because slaves were set free and property that had been sold reverted to its original owner (Lev. 25:25–33, 54; 27:24). The NT uses language reminiscent of the year of release and Jubilee to speak about Jesus' redemptive work (Rom. 6:17–23; 8:1–4; Col. 2:13–14; Heb. 2:14–15).

REMALIAH–The father of Pekah, who was the chief officer of King Pekahiah and assassinated him in order to become king of Israel (2 Kings 15:25–16:5).

REMISSION–A word used in the KJV to describe the removal of the guilt or penalty of sin acquired through belief in Christ (Acts 10:43) and effected through his shed blood (Matt. 26:28; Heb. 9:22), bringing about salvation (Luke 1:77).

REMNANT–The central idea of the remnant concept or remnant theology is that in the midst of seemingly total apostasy and the consequential terrible judgment and/or destruction, God always has a small, faithful group that he delivers and works through to bring blessing.

Early allusions to the idea of a remnant are introduced in the book of Genesis. Noah and his family (Gen. 6–9) are the remnant that is saved during the flood, when all other people are destroyed in judgment. The remnant theme surfaces in several other places in the OT. For example, when Elijah complains to God that he is the only faithful one left, God corrects him by pointing out that he has maintained a remnant of seven thousand faithful ones in the midst of national apostasy (1 Kings 19:10–18).

However, it is in the OT prophets that the remnant theme flowers into full blossom. The Hebrew words for "remnant" (*she'ar, she'erit*) occur over one hundred times in the prophetic books. The prophets proclaim that since Israel/Judah has broken the covenant and refuses to repent and turn back to God, judgment is coming. This judgment takes the form of terrible foreign invasions and destruction, followed by exile from the land. Thus, the northern kingdom, Israel, is destroyed and exiled by the Assyrians in 722 BC, and the southern kingdom, Judah, is destroyed and exiled by the Babylonians in 587/586 BC. Yet the prophets also prophesy hope and restoration beyond the judgment. They declare that many will be destroyed in the judgment, but not all. They prophesy that a remnant will survive, and that God will work through the remnant to bring blessings and restoration. Usually the remnant is identified as those who go into exile but who likewise hope to return to the land. The reestablishment of the remnant is often connected with the inauguration of the messianic age.

The remnant theme continues into the NT, but it is not nearly as prominent in the NT as it is in the OT prophets. The term "remnant" does not occur in the Gospels, although the idea is implied in several texts. Thus, in Matt. 7:13–14 Jesus states, "For wide is the gate and broad is the road that leads to destruction, and many enter through it. But small is the gate and narrow the road that leads to life, and only a few find it." Likewise, in Matt. 22:14 Jesus summarizes his preceding parable by stating, "Many are invited, but few are chosen."

R

Repentance–The act of repudiating sin and returning to God. Implicit in this is sorrow over the evil that one has committed and a complete turnabout in one's spiritual direction: turning from idols—anything that wrests away the affection that we owe God—to God (1 Sam. 7:3; 2 Chron. 7:14; Isa. 55:6; 1 Thess. 1:9; James 4:8–10).

Rephaim–*See* Rephaites.

Rephaim, Valley of–A valley southwest of Jerusalem, marking part of the border between Judah and Benjamin (Josh. 15:5; 18:16). After David became king and took Jerusalem, the Philistines twice encamped in the Valley of Rephaim to attack the city; both times David defeated them (2 Sam. 5:18, 22; cf. 2 Sam. 23:13; 1 Chron. 11:15; 14:9). Isaiah 17:5 refers to gleaning heads of grain in this valley.

Rephaites–A people group also called the "Anakites" (Deut. 2:11 [NRSV: "Anakim"]). They are described as giants (Deut. 3:11) who made Moses' spies feel like grasshoppers in comparison, and they are associated with the antediluvian Nephilim (Gen. 6:4; Num. 13:33). Thus, the KJV often translates the term as "giants" (e.g., Deut. 2:11; Josh. 12:4).

Rephidim–The location of the final Israelite encampment in their exodus from Egypt before they reached Mount Sinai (Exod. 17:1, 8; 19:2; Num. 33:14–15). Here the Israelites' complaints of thirst resulted in the miraculous provision of water from a rock after Moses struck it with his staff. That grumbling led Moses to call the place "Massah" ("testing") and "Meribah" ("contention"). At Rephidim the Israelites under Joshua also repelled an Amalekite attack, with success dependent on Moses' raised hands supported by Aaron and Hur (Exod. 17:8–16).

Restitution–An act of restoration in which compensation is given to account for a loss by the person responsible for that loss. As an integral part of community life, restitution protects against the loss of one's property due to a neighbor's carelessness or treachery.

As a part of economic life, restitution is prescribed for directly or indirectly causing someone else to lose his or her possessions. A thief must make restitution (Exod. 22:3). Restitution aims to restore what was lost through equal replacement (an ox for an ox in Exod. 21:36) and can involve matching value monetarily (21:34). However, in the case of theft, restitution is to be higher than equal value. Such cases may involve giving back double, quadruple, or sometimes quintuple of what was taken (22:1, 7), even to the point of selling oneself to pay the debt (22:3). In this way, restitution may also function as a deterrent, especially against theft.

In Num. 5:5–8 and Lev. 6:1–7, acts against one's neighbor are counted as acts against God, thus requiring an additional restitution, one-fifth of the value of the lost property, to be given to the priest along with a guilt offering. In this way, restitution operates not only to restore the owner of lost property, but also to restore the guilty party before God.

Resurrection–Christ's resurrection is *the* foundational event for the Christian faith. Paul goes so far as to say that if Christ did not rise, then the Christian faith is futile and Christians are to be pitied more than all others (1 Cor. 15:17–19). Resurrection's climaxing position in all four Gospel narratives yields the same understanding. Christ came not merely to die, as some claim, but to conquer death. Resurrection gives everything that Christ did before his death an "of God" significance, and it establishes everything that follows as a guarantee of God's eschatological promises. Without the resurrection, Jesus would have been just another "prophet hopeful" who died a tragic peasant death in Jerusalem. However, as it is, evidenced by the resurrection, he is the Son of God. According to the NT, the resurrection is the triumphant cry that God indeed did come to visit his creation and conquer the power of sin and death.

Although the Gospels' presentations of Jesus' resurrection vary in some detail (probably due to purpose and audience), all of them treat the event as *the* theological centerpiece of the Gospel narrative. The resurrection story launches God's eschatological work and opens the door, as the postresurrection appearances show, for a connection between the Jesus story and the church story. It is the foundation both for the Great Commission (Matt. 28:18–20) and for Pentecost (Luke 24:49). All people of all nations can now meet the living Christ.

Reuben–Reuben was the eldest son of Jacob and Leah. In Hebrew his name is a wordplay on "the Lord has seen my misery" (Gen. 29:32), referring to the troubles that Leah felt at not being loved by her husband. Jacob removed his privileges as firstborn son because Reuben slept with Rachel's maidservant Bilhah (Gen. 35:22; 49:3–4). When Jacob's ten sons conspired to kill their brother Joseph, Reuben tried to protect Joseph by suggesting that he be placed in a cistern. Reuben was greatly upset when his brothers sold Joseph to Midianite merchants (Gen. 37:22, 29).

Reuben, Tribe of–The tribe descended from Reuben, eldest son of Jacob and Leah. Moses gave permission for the Reubenites, the Gadites, and the half-tribe of Manasseh to take as their inheritance the land east of the Jordan River, as long as they assisted the other tribes in conquering Canaan (Num. 32). When these three groups built an altar, the rest of Israel approached them to do battle, until it became clear that they were setting up not an alternative place of worship but rather a place of remembrance (Josh. 22).

Revelation, Book of–The final book of the Bible is known by its opening line: "The revelation of Jesus Christ" (1:1 ESV, NRSV, KJV).

In powerful language and vivid imagery, Revelation presents the conclusion to God's grand story of salvation, in which he defeats evil, reverses the curse of sin, restores creation, and lives forever among his people. Although the details are often difficult to understand, the main idea of Revelation is clear: God is in control and will successfully accomplish his purposes. In the end, God wins. As a transformative vision, Revelation empowers its readers/listeners to persevere faithfully in a fallen world until their Lord returns.

The overall purpose of Revelation is to comfort those who are facing persecution and to warn those who are compromising with the world system. During times of oppression, the righteous suffer and the wicked seem to prosper. This raises the question "Who is Lord?" Revelation says that Jesus is Lord in spite of how things appear, and he will return soon to establish his eternal kingdom. Those facing persecution find hope through a renewed perspective, and those who are compromising are warned to repent. Revelation's goal is to transform the audience to follow Jesus faithfully.

Introduction (1:1–20). Chapter 1 includes both a prologue (1:1–8) and John's commission to write what he sees (1:9–20). John's vision focuses on the risen, glorified Christ and his continued presence among the seven churches.

Messages to the seven churches (2:1–3:22). Chapters 2–3 contain messages to seven churches of Asia Minor: Ephesus, Smyrna, Pergamum, Thyatira, Sardis, Philadelphia, and Laodicea. The seven messages follow a similar literary pattern: a description of Jesus, a commendation, an accusation, an exhortation coupled with either warning or encouragement, an admonition to listen, and a promise to those who overcome. These messages reflect the twin dangers faced by the church: persecution and compromise.

Vision of the heavenly throne room (4:1–5:14). In chapters 4–5 the scene shifts to the heavenly throne room, where God reigns in majestic power. All of heaven worships the Creator and the Lion-Lamb (Jesus), who alone is qualified to open the scroll because of his sacrificial death.

Opening of the seven seals (6:1–8:1). The unveiling of God's ultimate victory formally begins here. This section begins the first of a series of three judgment visions (seals, trumpets, and bowls), with seven elements each. When the sixth seal is opened, the question is asked, "Who can withstand it?" Chapter 7 provides the answer with its two visions of God's people; only those belonging to God can withstand the outpouring of the Lamb's wrath.

Sounding of the seven trumpets (8:2–11:19). The trumpet judgments, patterned after the plagues of Egypt, reveal God's judgment upon a wicked world. Again, before the seventh element in the series, there is an interval with two visions (10:1–11; 11:1–14) that instruct and encourage God's people.

The people of God versus the powers of evil (12:1–14:20). Chapter 12 offers the main reason why God's people face hostility in this world. They are caught up in the larger conflict between God and Satan (the dragon). Although Satan was defeated by the death and resurrection of Christ, he continues to oppose the people of God. Chapter 13 introduces Satan's two agents: the beast from the sea and the beast from the earth. The dragon and the two beasts constitute an unholy trinity bent on seducing and destroying God's people. As another interval, chapter 14 offers a glimpse of the final future that God has in store for his people. One day the Lamb and his followers

R

will stand on Mount Zion and sing a new song of redemption.

Pouring out of the seven bowls (15:1–16:21). The seven golden bowls follow the trumpets and seals as the final series of seven judgments. As the bowls of God's wrath are poured out on an unrepentant world, the plagues are devastating indicators of God's anger toward sin and evil. The only response from the "earth dwellers" (MSG; NIV: "inhabitants of the earth" [17:2, 8]; this is a common term in Revelation for unbelievers) is to curse God rather than repent (16:9, 11, 21).

Judgment and fall of Babylon (17:1–19:5). This section depicts the death of Babylon, a pagan power said to be "drunk with the blood of God's holy people, the blood of those who bore testimony to Jesus" (17:6). The funeral laments for the deceased Babylon of chapter 18 give way to a celebration as God's people rejoice over Babylon's downfall (19:1–5).

God's ultimate victory (19:6–22:5). This climactic section describes God's ultimate victory over evil and the final reward for the people of God. This scene includes the return of Christ for his bride (19:6–16), Christ's defeat of the two beasts and their allies (19:17–21), the binding of Satan and the millennial reign (20:1–6), the final defeat of Satan (20:7–10), and the final judgment and the death of death itself (20:11–15). Chapter 21 features a description of the new heaven and new earth, where God's long-standing promise to live among his people is fully realized.

Conclusion (22:6–21). Revelation closes with final blessings for those who heed the message of the book and warnings for those who do not. Jesus' promise to return soon is met with John's prayer, "Come, Lord Jesus" (22:20).

Revelation of God–God is the all-powerful, all-knowing, morally perfect creator of the universe; and we are his creatures—no less, but also no more. Thus, an unimaginable distance must exist between God and us. The biblical writers note our creaturely limitations and God's transcendence. But God has made himself known in two general ways, according to Scripture.

First, the biblical writers expect each of us to grasp something of God's nature, based on what is called "general revelation." General revelation operates in a broadcasted way, so to speak, relying upon commonplace experience and the latter's God-given ability to make us aware of his existence and nature. We all see the heavens that "declare the glory of God" (Ps. 19:1). Paul argues that every person can detect the "invisible qualities" of God, his "eternal power and divine nature," in what he has created, so that we have no excuse for decadent theology and behavior (Rom. 1:20). The law of God is "written on [our] hearts" (Rom. 2:15), so that we grasp what we owe to him and each other. Even though God has not spoken directly to every nation, "he has not left himself without testimony"; he has shown all people "kindness by giving [them] rain from heaven and crops in their seasons" (Acts 14:17). We can learn some things about God from these sources given to us, and thus we are accountable for right conduct in relationship to them. However, general revelation lacks the detail and assurance of what is called "special revelation."

Special revelation differs from general revelation in having a target audience. It conveys information about God, human beings, and our world that cannot be deduced from everyday, highly accessible experience. Jesus suffered for our sins. Our trust in his death on the cross will save us. God is a Trinity of Father, Son, and Holy Spirit, though there is one God. Christ will return in power and glory to judge all nations. We can think of God as our heavenly Father, a morally perfect deity who cares about the individual person. The Holy Spirit helps us in our weakness as we wonder how to pray. God is always sovereign, even over the wicked deeds of human beings and the suffering that they cause. These are essential points of Christian doctrine. Yet we cannot substantiate any of them by carefully observing ourselves, our world, or the facts of history. Indeed, sometimes our own thoughts lead us to resist these claims because they entail great mysteries. One can easily (but wrongly) equate "I do not understand this" with "This is false." Thus, our knowledge of these doctrines rests upon God's willingness to speak and our readiness to hear what he says with humility and trust, without having all our questions answered. The vehicle for this latter kind of knowledge is called "special revelation."

Revenge, Revenger–*See* Avenger.

Reverence–Closely related to honor and respect and often translating the Hebrew and Greek words for "fear," reverence is directed primarily toward the sacred or divine, such as God's sanctuary (Lev. 19:30; 26:2), the temple (Ps. 5:7), God's name (Rev. 11:18), God himself (Dan. 6:26; Mal. 2:5), and his messengers, the angel of the Lord (Josh. 5:14), and Peter (Acts 10:25). Reverence for God motivates behavior that honors him, such as just governance (Neh. 5:15), mutual submission (Eph. 5:21), purity (2 Cor. 7:1), and obedience (Col. 3:22). It is an attitude of acceptable worship (Heb. 12:28), connected with humility (Jer. 44:10), which may win over unbelievers (1 Pet. 3:2).

Rezin–The king of Aram who in 733 BC, accompanied by King Pekah of Israel, invaded Judah and threatened Jerusalem during the reign of King Ahaz of Judah. Ignoring the advice of the prophet Isaiah, Ahaz enlisted the support of King Tiglath-pileser III of Assyria. See 2 Kings 15:37–16:9; Isa. 7:1–9.

Rhegium–A port city of Greek influence on the Strait of Messina at the southern tip of Italy, across from Sicily (modern Reggio di Calabria). Paul's ship docked there overnight en route to Rome (Acts 28:13). It was the last stop before docking at Puteoli and embarking by land to Rome.

Rhodes–A Mediterranean island of over five hundred square miles, with a capital city also named "Rhodes" at the northeast point. In Ezekiel's lament for Tyre, Rhodes is mentioned as its trading partner (Ezek. 27:15). Rhodes became a leading Greek republic after Alexander and built the Colossus of Rhodes (completed in 292 BC), a statue of Apollos (Helios), the sun god, whose cult was centered there. Due to disloyalty, the Romans advanced Delos to hinder the rise of Rhodes, leaving the island as a resort for learning and leisure by the time Paul stopped there on his last journey (Acts 21:1).

Riblah–A Syrian city located on the eastern border of the Orontes River. The modern city of Riblah is in the same location. Riblah was the site for the deposing of two kings of Judah. After reigning only three months upon the death of his father, Josiah, Jehoahaz was taken captive by Pharaoh Necho, bound in chains at Riblah, and deported to Egypt (2 Kings 23:29–34). Twelve years later, Zedekiah was punished by King Nebuchadnezzar for rebellion, and his sons along with the chief priest and other officials were executed in Riblah, which the Babylonian king was using as a staging area (2 Kings 25:6–7, 18–21; Jer. 39:5–6; 52:9–10, 26).

Riddle–A word puzzle, often involving a pun, in which the true meaning of a word or phrase is hidden and must be discovered. To solve a riddle requires an understanding of the mind-set of the person who crafted it. Although often associated with wisdom sayings, the most famous riddle in the Bible is that presented by Samson, a man known more for his brawn than his brain. Samson's riddle functions both as an entertaining brainteaser and as the object of a bet with his bridegrooms (see Judg. 14). A riddle can be performed with a harp (Ps. 49:4) and is listed alongside proverbs, parables, and the sayings of the wise (Prov. 1:6). The ability to explain riddles is a talent attributed to Daniel along with interpreting dreams and solving difficult problems (Dan. 5:12). God may communicate with riddles (Dan. 5), or he may purposely avoid them (Num. 12:8).

Righteousness–Righteousness is an important theme in both Testaments of the Bible. The concept includes faithfulness, justice, uprightness, correctness, loyalty, blamelessness, purity, salvation, and innocence. Because the theme is related to justification, it has important implications for the doctrine of salvation.

Being careful to avoid imposing Western philosophical categories onto OT texts, we may say that the core idea of righteousness is conformity to God's person and will in moral uprightness, justness, justice, integrity, and faithfulness. Behind the many and varied uses of righteousness language in the OT stands the presupposition that God himself is righteous in the ultimate sense (e.g., Ezra 9:15; Isa. 45:21; Zeph. 3:5). Righteousness is the expression of his holiness in relationship to others (Isa. 5:16), and all other nuances of righteousness in the biblical texts are derived from this.

Related to humans, righteousness is often found as the opposite of wickedness. Righteousness often occurs in evaluative contexts, where it relates to proper conduct with respect to God, the order of the world as he created it, the covenant, or law (e.g., Deut. 6:25). God reigns in righteousness and justice (e.g., Ps. 97:2), and humans should align their conduct with this righteous reign. Righteousness can be expressed as personal integrity with phrases such as "my righteousness" (2 Sam. 22:21, 25; Ps. 7:8) and "their righteousness" (1 Sam. 26:23). Unrighteousness is found in poetic parallel to injustice (e.g., Jer. 22:13); the unjust are parallel with the wicked (Ps. 82:2).

Righteousness language is more rare in the Gospels than one might expect in light of OT and Jewish intertestamental usage. These references fit with the Jewish setting: righteousness is required of God's people, and unrighteousness is to be avoided. Righteousness is proper conduct with respect to God or Torah (Matt. 21:32) in contrast to wickedness (Matt. 13:49). Righteousness could be conceived as one's own (e.g., Luke 18:9) and has its reward (Matt. 10:41). While the specific terms related to righteousness are infrequent in the Gospels, the broader concept of conformity to God's will is widely apparent in calls for repentance, personal moral uprightness, mercy, and concern for the marginalized. The NT Epistles continue these general strands of the concept. Righteousness is related to personal conduct (1 Thess. 2:10; 1 Tim. 6:11; 2 Tim. 2:22; 1 Pet. 2:24) and is contrasted with wickedness (2 Cor. 6:14); it is a matter of doing, not knowing (Rom. 2:13). An example of righteousness in doing is the kindness shown by the prostitute Rahab, who hid the Israelite spies (James 2:25).

The NT does signal some new dimensions related to righteousness. In the Sermon on the Mount (Matt. 5–7), Jesus extends the requirements of righteousness to conformity to his own teaching and directives, a shocking display of authority. In his mission to call sinners rather than the "righteous" (e.g., Mark 2:17), Jesus implicitly questions the righteousness of the "righteous." In similar manner, personal righteousness in terms of a righteousness of one's own is negative in the NT (Rom. 10:3; Phil. 3:6; cf. Luke 18:9).

The NT continues the OT theme of righteousness as it relates to God himself. God is righteous (John 17:25; Rom. 3:5; 9:14; Heb. 6:10; cf. Matt. 6:33). His judgments are righteous (Rom. 2:5), and his commands and laws are righteous (Rom. 7:12; 8:4). God is a righteous judge (2 Tim. 4:8). His saving activity is righteous; he does not compromise his own justice in justifying the ungodly (Rom. 3:24–26). The righteousness of God is contrasted with human unrighteousness and wickedness (Rom. 3:5; James 1:20). Since God reigns over creation in righteousness, human conduct should conform to that standard (e.g., Rom. 14:17). Jesus is also noted as righteous (Acts 3:14; 7:52; 22:14; 1 Pet. 3:18; 1 John 2:1, 29). He fulfilled righteousness in the absolute sense of demonstrating complete conformity to the nature and will of God (e.g., 1 Pet. 3:18). He also fulfilled God's righteousness in the sense of his saving activity toward humans (e.g., 2 Pet. 1:1).

Rishathaim–Meaning "double wickedness," this appellation is attached to the name of Cushan, king of Mesopotamia (Aram-Naharaim). The people of Israel served him eight years before Othniel son of Kenaz, first of the judges, delivered them (Judg. 3:8–9). *See also* Cushan-Rishathaim.

Ritual–*See* Sacrifice and Offering; Worship.

Rivers and Waterways–***Eden's rivers.*** Genesis 2:10–14 describes the garden in Eden as the source of an unnamed river that subsequently divided into four "headwaters": the Pishon, the Gihon, the Tigris, and the Euphrates. This description defies any attempt to locate the purported site of Eden in terms of historical geography. The Tigris and the Euphrates do not diverge from a common source, but instead converge before emptying into the Persian Gulf. Moreover, the Gihon, if it is to be identified with the sacred spring of the same name in Jerusalem (1 Kings 1:45), is several hundred miles away from the Tigris and the Euphrates. The Pishon is otherwise unknown. If, as various commentators since antiquity have suggested, the Gihon and the Pishon are to be identified with other great rivers in the same class of importance as the Tigris and the Euphrates (the Nile, the Ganges, etc.), then this would further confound any attempt to understand Gen. 2:10–14 in terms of historical geography.

The Nile River. The Nile (Heb. *ye'or*) is fed by two major tributaries: the White Nile, which begins at Lake Victoria, and the Blue Nile, which begins in Ethiopia. At over four thousand miles, the Nile is the longest river in the world. The ancient civilization of Egypt depended entirely on the flow of the Nile and upon its annual flood (the "gift of the Nile") for irrigation of crops. Even today, arable land along the Nile is confined in some places to an area no more than a few miles from its banks.

Two of the plagues sent by God upon the Egyptians took place at the Nile, an appropriate setting for a confrontation between the God of Israel and the Egyptian pharaoh, himself a living representation of the Egyptian pantheon.

God told Moses to confront Pharaoh at the Nile (Exod. 7:15), and the first plague with which God afflicted the Egyptians consisted of turning the Nile into blood, causing its fish to die and rendering its water unsuitable for drinking. The Egyptians were forced to dig wells along its banks (7:20–21). The second plague involved the multiplication of frogs in the Nile, to the point of great inconvenience (8:3).

Isaiah continues the theme of God punishing the Egyptians by attacking the Nile: "The waters of the river will dry up, and the riverbed will be parched and dry. The canals will stink; the streams of Egypt will dwindle and dry up. The reeds and rushes will wither, also the plants along the Nile" (Isa. 19:5–7).

The Euphrates River. The Euphrates is the westernmost of the two great rivers of Mesopotamia (along with the Tigris [see below]), the land "between the rivers." As mentioned above, the Euphrates was one of the four rivers flowing from the garden of Eden, according to Gen. 2:14. Along the Euphrates were located the ancient cities of Carchemish, Emar (Tell Meskeneh), Mari, Babylon, and Ur. The Euphrates runs over seventeen hundred miles from northwest to southeast, beginning in the mountains of eastern Turkey before joining with the Tigris and entering the Persian Gulf.

In the Bible, the Euphrates represents the northern boundary of the territory granted to Abraham (Gen. 15:18; see also Exod. 23:31). David extended his territory as far as the Euphrates when he fought the Aramean king Hadadezer (2 Sam. 8:3), and so the dimensions of Israel at its apex under Solomon are described as controlling all the kingdoms "from the Euphrates River to the land of the Philistines, as far as the border of Egypt [i.e., the southern limit of his realm]" (1 Kings 4:21).

The Tigris River. Along with the Euphrates, the Tigris (Heb. *khiddeqel*) was one of the two rivers of ancient Mesopotamia. The Tigris lies east of the Euphrates and runs over a course of approximately 1,150 miles from northwest to southeast, finally joining with the Euphrates and emptying into the Persian Gulf. In antiquity, the cities of Calah, Nineveh, and Asshur lay along the Tigris. The Tigris is mentioned twice in the Bible: first, as one of the four headwaters emanating from the garden of Eden (Gen. 2:14) and, second, as the location of Daniel's visionary experience (Dan. 10:4).

The Jordan River. The Jordan (Heb. *yarden*) runs southward from the Hula Valley into the Sea of Galilee (also known as the Sea of Tiberias; modern Lake Kinneret) and from there through a river valley (the "plain of the Jordan" [see Gen. 13:10]) to the Dead Sea.

In the OT, several memorable stories are set near the Jordan. In addition to Joshua's dramatic crossing of the Jordan (Josh. 3:1–17), the "fords of the Jordan" were strategic locations, and it was there that the Gileadites slaughtered forty-two thousand Ephraimites as they attempted to return to their territory on the western side of the Jordan (Judg. 12:5). Elisha instructed Naaman, the leprous Aramean general, to bathe seven times in the Jordan for the healing of his condition (2 Kings 5:10). When Elisha's companions wished to build shelters for themselves, they went to the Jordan, where they knew they would find abundant vegetation and poles (2 Kings 6:2; cf. Zech. 11:3). When one of them dropped an iron ax head into the water, Elisha caused it to float to the surface (2 Kings 6:6–7).

In the NT, the Jordan was the site of much of John the Baptist's ministry (Matt. 3:5–6; Mark 1:5; Luke 3:3). John 1:28 specifies that John was on the eastern bank (also John 3:26; 10:40). It was in the waters of the Jordan that he baptized those who came to him, including Jesus (Matt. 3:13; Mark 1:9; Luke 3:21).

The wadi of Egypt. In a number of texts the "wadi of Egypt" (or "brook of Egypt") represents the far southern limit of Israelite territory. Some ancient interpreters understood this as referring to the Pelusian branch of the Nile River delta, while most modern scholars favor the Besor River, farther east, in present-day Israel. Several biblical passages refer to the Shihor River as marking a boundary between Egypt and Israelite territory (Josh. 13:3; 19:26; 1 Chron. 13:5; Isa. 23:3; Jer. 2:18).

The Orontes River. Although it is not mentioned in the Bible, the Orontes marked an important international boundary in the biblical world. The Orontes begins in the Bekaa Valley in present-day Lebanon, then flows northward between the Lebanon and the Anti-Lebanon mountain ranges before turning sharply westward to empty into the Mediterranean Sea. Along the Orontes lay the kingdom of Hamath (see, e.g., 2 Sam. 8:9; 2 Chron. 8:3; Jer. 39:5).

Rizpah–King Saul's concubine, with whom he fathered two sons, Armoni and Mephibosheth. She first appears when Saul's son

R

Ish-Bosheth accuses Abner of having sexual intercourse with her—an innuendo for royal pretensions—which Abner denies (2 Sam. 3:7–10). She reappears in the episode relating to the sacrifice of her sons and their five nephews in Gibeon as atonement for Saul's alleged brutality against the Gibeonites—David's remedy for a three-year famine (2 Sam. 21:1–14).

Rock–In the OT, the "rock" (*sela', tsur*) is an image of inaccessibility and so of refuge from danger (Isa. 7:19), but rocks will not provide refuge on the day of God's wrath (Isa. 2:10, 19, 21; cf. Rev. 6:15–16). A great rock providing needed shade (Isa. 32:2) is a variation on this theme of protection. By extension, the image is applied to God himself in poetry (e.g., 2 Sam. 22:2; Ps. 31:3, in both cases parallel with "fortress"). God as the "Rock" is the object of trust (2 Sam. 22:3). This quality is an aspect of his incomparability: "And who is the Rock except our God?" (2 Sam. 22:32).

Rod, Staff–A wooden walking stick that could have various functions. In ancient times, people did considerable amounts of walking. The ground in Israel is very uneven and rocky, making a walking stick a useful item (Gen. 32:10; Matt. 10:10). It is likely that walking sticks were customized so that they could serve as identification (Gen. 38:25).

Besides their utilitarian purpose, a rod or staff also came to denote an office and/or one's authority. Military figures carried staffs that indicated their status (Judg. 5:14), and Gen. 49:10 predicts that the ruler's staff will not depart from the tribe of Judah. Shepherds also carried a staff (Ps. 23:4; Mic. 7:14).

Sometimes a staff signified the presence of God with an individual. It was symbolic of the tree from which it was made, and a tree sometimes symbolically represented God. For this reason, some divine signs are associated with a raised staff. This was the case of Aaron's staff. The Red Sea split after Moses extended his rod, and the Israelites had the better of the Amalekites on the battlefield as long as Moses kept the rod above his head. *See also* Aaron's Rod.

Roman Empire–*See* Rome, Roman Empire.

Romans, Letter to the–Romans is a letter sent by Paul from Corinth to the house churches in Rome. Romans is one of the last letters Paul wrote while he was a free man. Shortly after sending it, Paul traveled to Jerusalem, where he was arrested, and subsequently spent several years in prison in Caesarea and Rome.

The main point of Paul's letter to the Romans is that the righteousness of God has been fully revealed in Christ Jesus. According to Paul, this is "good news" (gospel) for Jews and Gentiles. In fact, the entire letter is Paul's explanation of why he believes that this new revelation of God's righteousness in Christ is good news for all people, even his own kin.

Judgment of God against ungodliness and unrighteousness (1:18–3:20). What are we to make of Paul's view of the law and how it functions in the first part of Romans (1:18–3:20)? Some take 3:20 as the climax of this part of the argument, where Paul assigns one purpose to the law: to define sin. So according to this line of interpretation, Paul believes that God gave the law in order to show humanity's need of Christ. Since no one is able to keep the whole law, especially those to whom it has been given, the Jews, then "all have sinned and fall short of the glory of God" (3:23). The implication, of course, is that God gave the law in order to reveal to people Israel's failure so that Israel would recognize their need for a righteousness that depends not on obedience but on God's free gift through Christ. But there are two problems with this approach: Paul is offended by the idea that God gave the law to the Israelites in order to cause them to "stumble so as to fall" (11:11–12), and he also maintains that there were some who kept the law (Gentiles!), proving that "doers of the law will be justified" (2:13–14 NASB, NKJV). In other words, the law is God's gift to Israel that is supposed to give it an advantage when it comes to righteousness (3:1–2). But the Jews had disobeyed God (2:17–24), incurring his wrath (just like the Gentiles [1:18–32]). So Paul makes the argument that God is right to punish Israelites (as well as the Gentiles) for their disobedience (2:1–12): "There will be trouble and distress for every human being who does evil: first for the Jew, then for the Gentile" (2:9). In other words, 1:18–3:20 is not only an argument for the universality of sin (which neither Jew nor Gentile would deny) but also a justification of the revelation of God's righteous wrath against *all* ungodliness and disobedience, even for the Jewish people. Paul is pointing out the justice of God by emphasizing his impartial punishment of sin.

But this is where an interlocutor (a hypothetical opponent of Paul) could raise an objection: "But we Jews have the covenant with God, consisting of laws and promises from God. God promised to bless the sons of Abraham and gave us the law—with all the prescriptions for sacrifices and atonement—to deal with sin. We will escape God's wrath because God is faithful even though we are not." Even though Paul's interlocutor does not use these words, this is the basis of the argument that Paul puts into the mouth of his imaginary opponent in 3:1–8. The interlocutor essentially says, "If our sin reveals the righteous wrath of God, then Paul is saying that our disobedience serves his purpose. Why should we be judged as sinners?" In other words, what is the point of the covenant if God's chosen people are no better off than pagans on the day of judgment? But this is the very point that Paul will contend with on two counts. First, who says that God's chosen people do not have an advantage in preparing for the day of judgment (an argument that he will come back to in 9:1–11:32)? Second, who says that the law is God's only requirement of the covenant (a question that he answers in 3:21–5:21)? Throughout the entire Roman letter Paul holds two seemingly contradictory ideas in tension: the fulfillment of God's covenant promises to Abraham is not contingent upon Israel's obedience (God is faithful), and not every descendant of Abraham will realize the covenant promises of God (only those who have faith like Abraham). The reason for the tension is that a new kind of righteousness has been revealed apart from the law (although predicted by the Law and the Prophets), fulfilling the salient requirement of the covenant. Those who believe that the righteousness of God is found *in Christ* will inherit the promises of God to Abraham, whether Jew or Gentile. Therefore, Christ's followers are the sons of Abraham, the children of the covenant, justified by faith, not by law. All of this is by divine design—what Paul calls "predestination."

Righteousness of God in Christ by faith (3:21–5:11). According to Paul, sacrifices prescribed by the law only deferred the wrath of God. "In his forbearance he had left the sins committed beforehand unpunished" (3:25). On the other hand, Jesus' sacrificial death, a public display of God's righteousness, atones for the sins of Jews *and* Gentiles "at the present time" (3:25–30). To describe the justification of Christ's death as an act of redemption, Paul uses a technical word, "propitiation" (v. 25 [NIV: "sacrifice of atonement"]), which has two meanings: either God's righteous requirement was "satisfied" by the blood of Christ, or God's wrath was "appeased" by the blood of Christ. Either way, at this point we might have expected Paul to explain how Christ's death satisfied the requirements of the law by offering the perfect sacrifice (much like the argument of Hebrews). Instead, he emphasizes the role of faith in this new revelation of God's righteousness: both the faith(fulness) of Jesus and the faith of those who believe in him (the phrase often translated "faith in Jesus Christ" might also mean "faithfulness of Jesus Christ" [3:22, 26]). This does two things at once: it makes the righteousness of God available to Gentiles as well as Jews because it is based on faith ("Is God the God of Jews only? Is he not the God of Gentiles too? Yes, of Gentiles too" [3:29]), and it elevates the role of faith above works of the law in the story of God's covenant with Israel ("For we maintain that a person is justified by faith apart from the works of the law" [3:28]). In other words, by privileging faith over works of law, Paul has made a way for Gentiles to realize the promises God made to Abraham and has established the supreme requirement of the Abrahamic covenant for Jews. This is why scholars say that 4:1–25 (Paul's interpretation of God's covenant with Abraham) is crucial to his argument for the righteousness of God in Christ.

Abraham was God's first Gentile convert. That is to say, Abraham was an uncircumcised Chaldean when God established his covenant with the father of Israel. For Paul, the sequence of the story is pivotal to his argument. In 4:3 he quotes Gen. 15:6, "Abraham believed God, and it was credited to him as righteousness," and points out that God's righteousness was "credited" or "reckoned" to the patriarch because of his faith while he was still uncircumcised (Rom. 4:10–12). Abraham believed God's promise of making him the father of many nations even though he had no son. Faith in God's promise is what made this uncircumcised man righteous. Furthermore, because of his faith, the promise of God was fulfilled: Abraham not only became the father of Israel; he became the father of *all* nations (Gentiles) who have faith like Abraham. And what kind of faith is that? It is a resurrection faith—one who believes that God gives life to the dead, not only dead loins and a dead womb, but also

R

a dead man (4:16–25). So the righteousness of God is "reckoned" for "us who believe in him who raised Jesus our Lord from the dead. He was delivered over to death for our sins and was raised to life for our justification" (4:24–25). Faith in the promise of God is the requisite of covenant blessing. If the covenant were based on works of law, then Israel would be the only beneficiary of God's grace, and the promises God made to Abraham—that he would be the father of many nations—would be made void (4:13–15). "Therefore, the promise comes by faith, so that it may be by grace and may be guaranteed to all Abraham's offspring—not only to those who are of the law but also to those who are of the faith of Abraham. He is the father of us all" (4:16).

The death and resurrection of Jesus changed everything. It turned God's enemies into friends. It brought peace to those who deserved God's wrath. In Christ's death, God loves the ungodly. In Christ's resurrection, hope befriends the helpless. When Paul spells out the advantages of the righteousness of God in Christ in 5:1–11, it reads like a condensed version of all that is right with the gospel according to Paul. His favorite triad is there: faith, hope, love. He employs his favorite metaphors to explain the meaning of the sacrifice of Christ: justification and reconciliation. He writes of salvation in every tense: past, present, and future. In fact, the rest of the argument in 5:12–8:39 is Paul's explanation of what he means in these few verses, gathering up issues raised at the beginning of the letter—the problem of sin, the law, and the righteousness of God.

Questions regarding the righteousness of God in Christ by faith (5:12–8:39). Paul once again begins with the human condition: the law of sin and death reigns in the world because of Adam. But where the first Adam failed, the second Adam (Christ) has succeeded: because of his obedience, grace reigns eternally through his righteousness (5:12–21). How does this righteousness apply to Christ believers, especially Gentiles without law? Sin was crucified with Christ so that believers can be slaves of righteousness, freed from the bondage of sin (6:1–23). Furthermore, believers have been freed from the law, a spiritual and holy gift that sin used to arouse the flesh, effecting death (7:1–25). What the law could not do (bring life) because of the weakness of the flesh, God did by sending his Son in human flesh in order to condemn sin, bring about justice/righteousness required by the law, and provide his Spirit to enable believers to have resurrection life (8:1–27). This has been God's plan from the beginning (predestination): he will have a people (election) like Jesus Christ (justification), who will share in his resurrection (glorification). And what God starts, he finishes. Nothing can frustrate the plans of God. His love is too great; his power is irrepressible (8:28–39). Since God is the one who justifies the "elect," no charge can be brought against them (8:33).

Paul's advice (chapters 9–16). The conclusion to Paul's argument—believers in Christ can do nothing to jeopardize God's love for them as his "elect"—brings to mind the problem of Israel's rejection of the gospel (9:1–11:32). If Paul believes that God's promises are irrevocable, should not the same apply to Israel? If the righteousness of God is found in Christ, what does this mean for Jews who do not believe in Jesus? Does their unbelief undermine God's faithfulness? This was more than a theological problem for Paul. Ethnic issues threatened to divide the church in Rome. Evidently, Gentile believers were displaying an arrogant attitude toward Jewish members of the church (11:13–24), contemptuous of their dietary restrictions and Sabbath observances (14:3–6). Perhaps Paul's notorious reputation as a lawbreaker (3:8) added fuel to the fire of ethnic strife and emboldened Gentile believers to disregard Jewish sensibilities with smug confidence, especially in a place such as Rome, where tensions between Jews and Gentiles were prevalent. Or, maybe Paul had nothing to do with it; Gentile contempt for Jewish people and their ways was an unfortunate by-product of the argument for Gentile inclusion: the law no longer defined righteousness ("Who needs the Jews and their law?"). Whatever the cause, Israel's rejection of the gospel coupled with the historical problem of Jew versus Gentile was a delicate issue that required a carefully nuanced answer from Paul (9:1–11:32), setting up his advice for house churches that needed to learn how to get along with one another (12:1–15:13).

ROME, ROMAN EMPIRE–Rome began as a city-state but soon became a transcontinental empire reaching over parts of Europe, Africa, and Asia. Rome emerged as the most dominant force in the Mediterranean after it defeated Carthage in the Second Punic War (218–201 BC). Thereafter, Rome began to expand its control and power over the various Hellenistic city-states in the east, including Macedonia, Illyria, and Asia Minor. By the mid-first century AD, Rome had also conquered or annexed Syria, Palestine, Egypt, Cyrene, Gaul, Spain, North Africa, and Armenia.

The transition from the Roman Republic to the Roman Empire took place under the Roman emperors beginning with Julius Caesar (100–44 BC), who, after crossing the Rubicon and defeating Pompey, was proclaimed *dictator perpetuus* ("dictator for life"). The period after Julius Caesar's assassination (44 BC) was a time of political upheaval as Rome was marred by a series of civil wars. The first was between Octavius and Antony against Caesar's assassins Brutus and Cassius. This climaxed in the Battle of Philippi (42 BC), which the former allies of Julius Caesar won. The second was between Octavius and Antony, where Antony and Cleopatra were defeated at the Battle of Actium in 31 BC, leaving Octavius as the undisputed leader of Rome.

Octavius was given the honorific name "Augustus" by the senate. His reign (31 BC–AD 14) marked a period of consolidation, reorganization, and renewal of the Roman Empire. Augustus embarked on an empire-wide policy of fiscal rationalization, developed a constitutional settlement for Rome, centralized his military authority over the various provinces, and had Julius Caesar deified. What is most significant about Augustus is that it is with his reign that the Roman Empire essentially began. He was the emperor at the time of Jesus' birth (Luke 2:1).

Tiberius, Augustus's adopted heir, reigned in the years AD 14–37. He was a highly successful military general, but as emperor he was remembered as being gloomy and melancholic. It was during the reign of Tiberius that Jesus conducted his ministry in Palestine.

Tiberius was succeeded by his adopted grandson Caligula, who reigned in the years AD 37–41. Caligula was the son of the popular Roman general Germanicus, who died in Antioch in AD 19. Historical sources are not favorably disposed toward Caligula, who was remembered as a malevolent tyrant given to self-aggrandizement and sexual perversity. In AD 39/40 Caligula departed from imperial policy that permitted emperor worship in the east and veneration of deceased emperors in Rome, and he often appeared dressed as a god in public and demanded worship as a living god. During this time he deposed Herod Antipas, the tetrarch of Galilee and Perea, on suspicion of consorting with Parthia (Josephus, *Ant.* 18.7). Caligula also ordered that his statue be placed in the holy of holies in the Jerusalem temple (Philo, *Embassy* 203). Petronius, the governor of Syria, knowing that such an act would lead to civil war, refused to comply and appealed to Caligula to reverse the order. In response, Caligula sent an order to Petronius that he commit suicide. Fortunately, news of Caligula's assassination by a conspiracy involving the praetorian guard and senators reached Petronius first.

Claudius, Caligula's uncle, reigned in the years AD 41–54, and his rule was defined by numerous public works, a reordering of the judicial system, a torrid series of marriages, the conquest of Britain, and a number of attempted coups by the Roman senate. In AD 49 he expelled the Jews from Rome because of disputes about a certain "Chrestus," probably Christ (cf. Acts 18:2). No one is sure whether Claudius was murdered or died of old age, but he remained a sharp contrast to the brutal excesses of Caligula and Nero.

Nero, the stepson of Claudius, reigned in the years AD 54–68. The early period of his rule was marked by cultural endeavors and diplomatic efforts. The later years were, in contrast, distinguished by tyranny and self-aggrandizement. There was a Jewish revolt against Rome in Judea (AD 66–70) during Nero's reign, and Vespasian was sent to pacify the territory. According to ancient sources, Nero accused Christians of starting the fire of Rome in AD 64 and subjected them to the cruelest of punishments, including crucifixion, being thrown to wild animals, and even being burned alive. It probably was during this time that the apostles Peter and Paul were martyred in Rome. Nero eventually was declared a public enemy by the Roman senate, and he committed suicide before he could be captured in AD 68. There arose a "Nero redivivus" legend, whereby many hoped or feared that Nero had not died in AD 68 but had fled to Parthia and would return to Rome in order to destroy it (*Sib. Or.* 4.119–24; 5.137–41, 361–96), and this arguably stands behind the imagery of Rev. 13:3; 17:8–11.

The suicide of Nero left a power vacuum in Rome, and AD 69 saw no less than four emperors ascend the throne: Galba, Otho, Vitellius, and finally Vespasian. Galba was governor of

Hispania Tarraconensis and was invited to become emperor by the senate, but he was killed by the praetorian guard after they were bribed by the praetor Otho. Otho himself committed suicide after his forces were defeated by Vitellius, the commander of the legions on the Rhine. Vitellius became emperor, but he was fiscally irresponsible and murdered many of his rivals. The legions in the Danube, Egypt, Syria, and Judea had declared Vespasian emperor and marched on Rome. Vespasian controlled the grain supplies to Rome from Egypt and had a superior force. Vitellius's forces were defeated at Bedriacum, and Vitellius went into hiding but eventually was killed in Rome. Vespasian was declared emperor by the senate, and so began the Flavian dynasty, which restored order after the chaos of civil war.

The Flavians ruled in the years AD 69–96. Vespasian (r. AD 69–79) consolidated the empire after its year of strife and instituted new taxes, such as the *fiscus judaicus*, a war reparation tax placed on all Jews and paid to the temple of Jupiter in lieu of the Jerusalem temple tax. Vespasian was succeeded by his sons Titus (r. AD 79–81) and Domitian (r. AD 81–96). When Vespasian sailed to Rome from Judea, Titus was left in charge of the siege of Jerusalem, which he completed and celebrated in a triumph in Rome in AD 72. This triumph is memorialized in the Arch of Titus, which depicts Roman soldiers bringing the vessels of the temple to Rome as part of the booty taken. Later Roman writers regarded Domitian as a malevolent and malicious tyrant (e.g., Tacitus, Suetonius), but this probably is an exaggeration caused partly by a desire to highlight the greatness of succeeding emperors such as Nerva and Trajan. It probably was during the reign of Domitian that some Christians in Asia Minor were being persecuted for their failure to worship the emperor, as depicted in the book of Revelation.

The birth of the church and the growth of Christianity took place within the wider social, religious, and cultural context of the Greco-Roman world. The politics and power of the Roman Empire provide the backdrop for the birth of Jesus (Luke 2:1), and since Rome was considered to be the center of the world, it was necessary that Paul himself testify to Jesus Christ there (Acts 19:21). The history, literature, and cultural background of Rome form an important background to the NT and should be studied along with the history and literature of Judaism during the time of Jesus and the apostles. Although the Romans were the primary threat to the survival of Christians in the ancient world, after the conversion of Constantine in the fourth century AD, they became the primary means by which Christianity spread to the rest of Europe and western Asia.

Rooster–A rooster marks the passage of time in the story of Peter's denial of Jesus in all four Gospels (Matt. 26:34, 74–75; Mark 14:30, 72; Luke 22:34, 60, 61; John 13:38; 18:27). In the story, Jesus predicts that Peter will deny him three times before the rooster crows. The event takes place in the Sanhedrin courtyard in the presence of the high priest's servants (the high priest was one of the people trying Jesus). In Mark 13:35 Jesus warns that the coming apocalypse will take people by surprise if they are not watching during the different times of night, including "when the rooster crows."

Rufus–One of the two sons of Simon of Cyrene, who was conscripted to carry Jesus' cross (Mark 15:21). A man named "Rufus" is sent greetings by Paul in Rom. 16:13, and he may be the same person. The equation of the two is made more likely if Mark's Gospel was written for a Roman audience.

Ruhamah–*See* Lo-Ruhamah.

Ruth–*See* Ruth, Book of.

Ruth, Book of–The book of Ruth is set during the time of the judges. The book of Judges selects stories that illustrate the difficulties of the time between Joshua and the rise of kingship, particularly in the period before the rise of David. Ruth, however, gives a story of hope in the midst of suffering.

Although no supernatural events or miracles punctuate the book of Ruth, the attentive reader finishes it knowing that God's hand guided the events of this story as directly as those of the story of the exodus from Egypt. The book of Ruth is a story of God's providence narrated in an extremely subtle manner. When the narrator says, "As it turned out, [Ruth] was working in a field belonging to Boaz" (2:3), the meaning is that Ruth herself did not know the significance of her action. God was guiding her toward deliverance.

The book also tells a story of a non-Israelite (Gentile), Ruth herself, who joins the people of faith. In this, we are to see a preview of the fulfillment of God's promise to Abraham that his descendants will be a blessing to all peoples on earth (Gen. 12:3).

Finally, Ruth's story may be a family story, but this family leads to great things in Israel. Ruth's survival leads ultimately to the birth of David, one of the greatest figures in biblical history. In this way, the author says that David was a divine gift to Israel. Of course, Christian readers further recognize that Ruth is named later in the genealogy of the one who is David's greater son, Jesus Christ (Matt. 1:5).

S

Sabbath–God's people were to observe the Sabbath on the seventh day of each week by resting from normal daily work. It is first explicitly introduced in Exod. 16:23–30, where God provides twice as much manna for the Israelites in the desert on the sixth day so that they might enjoy his provision for them on the seventh day without having to gather it on that day.

The Sabbath command is incorporated into the Ten Commandments (Exod. 20:8–11). The motivation given in Exodus for keeping the Sabbath is the fact that God made the world in six days and rested on the seventh (cf. Gen. 2:2–3)—hence sometimes it is considered a "creation ordinance." God's rest was his enjoyment of a world that met his expectations, and thus the weekly celebration might look to a time when the world would once again truly enjoy such "rest." In Deut. 5:12–15 the motivation is given as the new creation event, the redemption of Israel from slavery in Egypt.

Although religious worship is not prominent in the Sabbath injunctions in the OT, there was to be a gathering of God's people on that day with special offerings (Lev. 23:3; Ezek. 46:3–5), and it was a day when a visit to a prophet might be more likely (2 Kings 4:23). Psalm 92 is identified as a psalm for the Sabbath.

The terms "Sabbath" or "Sabbath rest" could also be applied to special days, such as the Day of Atonement, which did not fall on the seventh day (Lev. 16:31). In an extension of the sabbatical system, the land was to enjoy a Sabbath of rest every seven years (Lev. 25:4–7).

By NT times, regular gatherings were held at local synagogues on the Sabbath wherever a sufficient number of observant Jews resided. Jesus offended Pharisaic sensitivities with regard to Sabbath observance, using it to alleviate human suffering and presenting himself as the true representative of humanity, for whom the Sabbath was designed (Matt. 12:1–13; John 5:9–10). The healings on the Sabbath day draw attention to the realization of God's creative and redemptive purposes for the world.

The writer to the Hebrews treats the Sabbath as a foretaste of the ultimate rest God provides for those who persevere in faith and obedience (Heb. 4:1–11).

Paul regards the victory of Christ as bringing a freedom "with regard to a religious festival, a New Moon celebration or a Sabbath day" (Col. 2:16 [cf. Gal. 4:10]). Some Christians understand this as denying continuity of the Sabbath principle of a weekly day of rest. Others understand it in a way similar to Jesus' remarks on Pharisaic restrictions imposed on the day and see a continuity of Sabbath observance, perhaps with a change of day, to make it a celebration of the Lord's resurrection on the first day of the week (the Lord's Day).

Sabbatical Year–*See* Festivals.

Sackcloth–Made of goat or camel hair, a material that was made into sacks for grain and into clothes generally worn to express grief or repentance (Gen. 37:34; 2 Sam. 3:31). Occasionally sackcloth was worn to express social protest (Esther 4:1; Dan. 9:3). It was generally black or dark in color (Rev. 6:12), rough in texture, and worn close to the body, even next to the skin in extreme cases (1 Kings 21:27; 2 Kings 6:30; Job 16:15).

Sacrifice and Offering–The words "sacrifice" and "offering" often are used interchangeably, but "offering" refers to a gift more generally, while "sacrifice" indicates a gift consecrated for a divine being. Sacrifices were offered to honor God, thanking him for his goodness. More important, they enabled persons to be made right with God by atoning for their sins. Whereas sin upset the fellowship God desired to have with people and kindled his wrath, sacrifice restored the relationship.

Leviticus introduced five main sacrifices: the *'olah* (1:1–17; 6:8–18), the *minkhah* (2:1–16; 6:14–23), the *shelamim* (3:1–17; 7:11–36), the *khatta't* (4:1–5:13), and the *'asham* (5:14–6:7). Most of these focused on uncleanness or sin. The worshiper who brought such an offering was not allowed to eat any of it, as it was wholly given to God. Even when priests were allowed to eat part of a sacrifice, their portion was "waved" before God, indicating that it belonged to him.

1. The *'olah*, or burnt offering, is the basic OT sacrifice connected with atonement for sin (Lev. 1:4). When rightly offered, it was accepted as "an aroma pleasing to the LORD." The worshiper brought a male animal (young bull, sheep, goat, dove, or young pigeon) without blemish, laid a hand upon it, and then killed it. After the priest sprinkled some of the blood on the altar, the rest was burned up.

2. The *minkhah* is simply a gift or offering. The Hebrew word is often used for a present given to another person or tribute to a ruler. When used of sacrifice, it is usually rendered as "grain offering" or "meal offering." A *minkhah* can, on occasion, include flesh or fat (Gen. 4:4; Judg. 6:18–21). Considered "an aroma pleasing to the LORD," it consisted of unground grain or fine flour mixed with oil and incense and was presented either cooked or uncooked. Part of the offering was burned as a "memorial portion," the rest being given to the priests (Lev. 2:1–3). It usually was accompanied by a drink offering—wine poured out on the altar. Grain offerings frequently complemented burnt offerings or fellowship offerings. The showbread may have been considered a grain offering.

3. The *shelamim* (NIV: "fellowship offering") has traditionally been called the "peace offering," as the term is related to *shalom*. This offering most likely indicated that the worshiper was at peace with God and others; all the worshiper's relationships were whole. Classified into three types, it could be used to express thanksgiving, to signify the fulfillment of a vow, or simply to denote one's desire to bring an offering to God out of free will. Only those who made a vow were required to offer a *shelamim*; the other forms were wholly optional. The worshiper brought a male or female animal (ox, sheep, or goat) without blemish, laid a hand on its head, and slaughtered it. The priest sprinkled its blood on the sides of the altar and burned the fat surrounding the major organs. It is described as "an aroma pleasing to the LORD."

This offering significantly recognized the covenant relationship existing between those who shared in it. God received the fatty portions, the officiating priest received the right thigh, the other priests the breast, and the remainder was shared among members of a family, clan, tribe, or some other group.

4. The *khatta't*, or sin offering, atoned for the sin of an individual or of the nation and cleansed the sacred items in the tabernacle that had been corrupted by sin. Since a sin offering could purify ceremonial as well as moral uncleanness, people who were unclean due to childbirth, skin diseases, bodily discharges, and so forth also brought them (Lev. 12–15).

5. The *'asham*, or guilt offering, provided compensation for sins. A ram without blemish was sacrificed, its blood was sprinkled on the altar, and its fatty portions, kidneys, and liver were burned. The rest was given to the priest. In addition, the value of what was misappropriated plus one-fifth of its value was given to the person wronged or to the priests.

Christians quickly came to understand Christ's death as the final sacrifice that completed the OT system. Various NT authors consider the nature of Christ's death and metaphorically relate it to OT sacrifices, but the writer of Hebrews develops this in the most detail. According to Hebrews, the sacrificial system was merely the shadow that pointed to Jesus. Although the blood of animals could not adequately deal with sins, Jesus' sacrifice could (Heb. 10:1–10). Jesus is regularly identified as the sacrificial lamb whose blood purifies humanity from sin (John 1:29, 36; Rom. 8:3; 1 Cor. 5:7; Eph. 5:2; 1 Pet. 1:19; 1 John 1:7; Rev. 5:6, 12; 7:14; 12:11; 13:8). His sacrifice is considered a propitiation that turns away God's wrath (Rom. 3:25; 1 John 2:2).

SADDUCEES–*See* Jewish Parties.

SALAMIS–The first stop on Paul and Barnabas's journey to the island of Cyprus (Acts 13:5). Located on the east coast of Cyprus, Salamis was an important Greco-Roman commercial city with a notable Jewish population.

S

SALEM–A shortened and probably archaic form of "Jerusalem." Melchizedek was the king of Salem (Gen. 14:18; Heb. 7:1–2). The name "Salem" means "peace."

SALIM–A place mentioned only in reference to Aenon, where John conducted his last baptisms (John 3:23). Its location is debated.

SALMONE–Modern Cape Sidero, the northward-pointing promontory on the eastern end of the island of Crete, past which Paul sailed en route to Rome in an attempt to avoid unfavorable winds (Acts 27:7).

SALOME–Mark lists Salome among the women who observed Jesus' crucifixion (Mark 15:40), who followed and cared for Jesus in Galilee (15:41), and who attempted to anoint Jesus' body (16:1). Matthew 27:56 may speak of her as "the mother of Zebedee's sons," who asked Jesus to honor her sons (Matt. 20:20–21). Although of doubtful accuracy, several extrabiblical sources relate Salome to Mary, Joseph, or Zachariah. Additionally, Josephus identifies the daughter of Herodias (Matt. 14:6–11; Mark 6:22–28) by this name.

SALT–A crystallized mineral compound, often harvested from the Dead Sea, used with food for flavor and preservation (Job 6:6) and medicinally rubbed on infants (Ezek. 16:4). Salt was to be added to the grain offering to represent the covenant (Lev. 2:13). Just as salt survives the sacrificial fires, so does the covenant survive the difficulties of life. In the first century, salt was known as a preservative, seasoning, and fertilizer. All these uses may be behind Jesus' statement that his disciples were "the salt of the earth" (Matt. 5:13), indicating that they were important for the welfare of the world.

SALT, COVENANT OF–*See* Covenant; Covenant of Salt.

SALVATION–"Salvation" is the broadest term used to refer to God's actions to solve the plight brought about by humankind's sinful rebellion and its consequences. It is one of the central themes of the entire Bible, running from Genesis through Revelation.

In many places in the OT, salvation refers to being rescued from physical rather than spiritual trouble. Fearing the possibility of retribution from his brother Esau, Jacob prays, "Save me, I pray, from the hand of my brother Esau" (Gen. 32:11). The actions of Joseph in Egypt saved many from famine (45:5–7; 47:25; 50:20). Frequently in the psalms, individuals pray for salvation from enemies that threaten one's safety or life (Pss. 17:14; 18:3; 70:1–3; 71:1–4; 91:1–3).

Related to this usage are places where the nation of Israel and/or its king were saved from enemies. The defining example of this is the exodus, whereby God delivered his people from their enslavement to the Egyptians, culminating in the destruction of Pharaoh and his army (Exod. 14:1–23). From that point forward in the history of Israel, God repeatedly saved Israel from its enemies, whether through a judge (e.g., Judg. 2:16; 3:9), a king (2 Kings 14:27), or even a shepherd boy (1 Sam. 17:1–58).

But these examples of national deliverance had a profound spiritual component as well. God did not save his people from physical danger as an end in itself; it was the necessary means for his plan to save them from their sins. The OT recognizes the need for salvation from sin (Pss. 39:8; 51:14; 120:2) but, as the NT makes evident, does not provide a final solution (Heb. 9:1–10:18). One of the clearest places that physical and spiritual salvation come together is Isa. 40–55, where Judah's exile from the land and prophesied return are seen as the physical manifestation of the much more fundamental spiritual exile that resulted from sin. To address that far greater reality, God announces the day when the Suffering Servant would once and for all take away the sins of his people (Isa. 52:13–53:12).

As in the OT, the NT has places where salvation refers to being rescued from physical difficulty. Paul, for example, speaks of being saved from various physical dangers, including execution (2 Cor. 1:8–10; Phil. 1:19; 2 Tim. 4:17). In the midst of a fierce storm, Jesus' disciples cry out, "Lord, save us! We're going to drown!" (Matt. 8:25). But far more prominent are the places in the Gospels and Acts where physical healings are described with the verb *sōzō*, used to speak of salvation from sin. The healing of the woman with the hemorrhage (Mark 5:25–34), the blind man along the road (Luke 18:35–43), and even the man possessed by a demon (Luke 8:26–39), just to name a few, are described with the verb *sōzō*. The same verb, however, is also used to refer to Jesus forgiving someone's sins (Luke 7:36–50) and to his mission to save the lost from their sins (Luke 19:10). Such overlap is a foretaste of the holistic salvation (physical and spiritual) that will be completed in the new heaven and earth (Rev. 21–22). The NT Epistles give extensive descriptions of how the work of Jesus Christ saves his people from their sins.

Samaria–Samaria was the capital city of the northern kingdom of Israel. After the fall of Jeroboam I's dynasty, and the rules of Baasha, Elah, and Zimri, the ruling center of the northern kingdom moved from Tirzah to Samaria during the rule of Omri (r. 882–871 BC), the first king of northern Israel's third dynasty.

Samaria remained the capital of the northern kingdom of Israel until it fell to the Assyrians under Sargon II in 721 BC, when he deported most of the population to other areas of the Assyrian Empire (2 Kings 17:6). According to Sargon's annals, he improved the city and populated it with peoples deported from other countries that he had conquered. The report of the fall of Samaria in 2 Kings 17:24 generally agrees with this. The populace of Samaria worshiped its own gods and the God of Israel as well.

Besides being the name of the capital city of the northern kingdom of Israel, "Samaria" was a name for the northern kingdom itself. The northern kingdom was always politically and economically more prosperous than Judah.

In the NT, Samaria is the region between Galilee and Judea through which Jews avoided traveling. By this time, there had been great animosity between the Jews and Samaritans for centuries. Luke lists Samaria as one of the regions to which Jesus' disciples would be witnesses (Acts 1:8). The archaeological ruins of Samaria lie eight miles northwest of the modern city of Nablus. The town of Sabastia is located there today. *See also* Samaritans.

Samaritans–According to the Bible, the Samaritans are the descendants of the peoples whom Sargon II settled in Samaria after he conquered it and the northern Israelites (*see also* Samaria). As such, they were not quite Jewish, not quite Gentile.

The NT mentions the Samaritans. The story of the woman at the well in John 4 depicts Jesus ministering to a Samaritan. We learn in this passage (John 4:9) that Jews like Jesus did not eat or drink from the same vessel as a Samaritan since they believed it would render them ritually unclean (see NET: "For Jews use nothing in common with Samaritans"). One of the chief points of contention between Jews and Samaritans is highlighted in this passage: Samaritans believe that Mount Gerizim is God's chosen worship site, not Zion. Also alluded to here is the Samaritans' belief in a "returning one" (Aram. *taheb*), who will guide the Samaritans to repentance and reestablish proper worship. In John 8:48 Jesus' opponents level a charge against him, asking him if he is not indeed a Samaritan and possessed by a demon.

Samgar-Nebo–Possibly an official of the Babylonian king Nebuchadnezzar. According to the Hebrew text, he, along with other Babylonian officials, took his seat in Jerusalem's middle gate during the siege (Jer. 39:3 NRSV).

Samos–An important mountainous island, with a capital city by the same name (meaning "height" or "mountain"), in the Aegean Sea to the southwest of Ephesus. A naval and cultural center (and the birthplace of Pythagoras), Samos apparently had a large population of Jews by the second century BC (cf. 1 Macc. 15:15–24). At the end of his third missionary campaign, Paul's ship either came near or stopped at (Gk. *paraballō*, a nautical term meaning "to approach, arrive at, sail to") Samos en route to Miletus (Acts 20:15).

Samothrace–A small island in the northeast of the Aegean Sea, south of Thrace. With a peak over a mile above sea level, Samothrace ("the height/mountain of Thrace") is the highest of all the Aegean islands and a conspicuous navigational landmark. On his second missionary campaign, Paul's ship overnighted at Samothrace en route to Neapolis (Acts 16:11), and he may have stopped there on the third missionary campaign (see Acts 20:6).

Samson–The last judge of Israel whose story is found in the book of Judges (chaps. 13–16). The period of judges was a time of spiritual confusion, moral depravity, and political fragmentation. The situation became increasingly worse as time wore on in Judges, and the time of Samson was the worst of all. Samson did nothing except to satisfy his own desires and lusts. He did not care about God, his family, or his nation. Even so, God used him to deliver Israel in spite of his sin.

Samuel–Samuel oversaw the transition from the period of judges to the time of the monarchy. He was the final judge (1 Sam. 7:6, 15–16;

cf. 8:1 NIV mg.). He also was a priest (2:18) and functioned as a prophet (3:20).

Samuel was remembered as an important and faithful spiritual leader, compared favorably even to Moses (Jer. 15:1; Acts 13:20; Heb. 11:32). He is honored as a prophet whose words anticipated the coming of Jesus Christ (Acts 3:24).

Samuel, Books of–The books of Samuel tell the story of how kingship began in Israel and was subsequently secured under David. Almost all of David's own story is recounted in Samuel, including God's promise to him of a dynasty. This promise became a key seedbed for the messianic hope within the OT, which finds its fulfillment in Jesus as David's son (Matt. 1:1).

Kingship lies at the heart of Samuel. But although it is concerned with the story of Israel's first two kings, it places their story within the framework of God's reign. No matter what authority a king in Israel might claim, it was always subject to God's greater authority. Indeed, Samuel makes clear that God did not need a king but rather chose the monarchy as the means by which his own reign might be demonstrated.

An important way in which God's reign is demonstrated is through the motif of the reversal of fortunes, in which the powerful are brought down and the weak raised. This is announced in Hannah's Song (1 Sam. 2:4–8) and is then demonstrated when God removed the corrupt family of Eli from their position of power in the sanctuary at Shiloh (2:27–36; 4:1–18). On the other hand, Samuel himself came to prominence even though he had no position of power. Saul, likewise, although a member of a relatively wealthy family (9:1–2), knew that he was not someone who had automatic power (9:21) but still was raised up to be king by God. Yet when he, like Eli before him, became corrupt and clung to power rather than submit to God, he too was removed so that he could be replaced (15:28–29).

David also came from a humble position as the youngest son in his family (1 Sam. 16:11), but unlike Eli and Saul, he would not grasp power for himself. Indeed, he twice refused to kill Saul when he had the chance (1 Sam. 24; 26) and punished those who claimed that they could exercise violence on his behalf (2 Sam. 1:11–16; 4:9–12). Even when it seemed that David had later lost all to Absalom, he held to the fact that he could reign only as long as he had God's support (2 Sam. 15:25–26). This, in fact, is a central theme in 2 Sam. 7 when David wanted to build a temple for God, for there it is made clear that David cannot act without God's authority, and that his descendants will have authority as long as they too submit to God (7:11b–15). David's closing songs (22:1–23:7) make clear that the king has no authority apart from God.

Kingship in Israel is closely related to the theme of God's reign. The possibility of kingship first arises in Hannah's Song (1 Sam. 2:10) and is confirmed by the man of God who announces the judgment against Eli's family (2:34). Both references occur before Israel's elders requested a king because of the failure of Samuel's sons (8:1–9), indicating that the request for a king did not take God by surprise. In addition, it indicates that authentic kingship in Israel could only be that which was initiated by God.

The story of Saul's rise to the throne needs to be read in light of this. Although the human move to kingship stemmed from the request of the elders for a king (1 Sam. 8:4–9), it was still the case that Saul could become king only because of God's decision. Although 1 Sam. 8–12 often has been broken down into supposedly conflicting sources, it is better to read it as a unified text but to note that the narrator's voice is not equivalent to any of the characters that speak through it. When the text is understood in this way, it is possible to appreciate that kingship was part of God's purposes for Israel, but it needed to follow his model. Kings in Israel could prosper only when they submitted to the greater reign of God. It was Saul's mistake that he did not recognize this. David, although he made some terrible mistakes, always understood this truth, and his closing songs (2 Sam. 22:1–23:7) reflect on it. David learned what Saul never did: power is never something to be grasped; rather, it can only be accepted as a gracious gift from God to be used for his purposes.

Sanballat–The governor of Samaria who resisted Nehemiah's efforts to rebuild Jerusalem's walls. He and his associates (Tobiah and Geshem) appealed to the Persian king but were ultimately unsuccessful (see Neh. 2:10, 19; 4:1–7; 6:1, 2, 5, 12, 14). Even later, Nehemiah deposed one of the sons of the priest Joiada for being the son-in-law of Sanballat (13:28).

Sanctification–In the biblical sense, the word "sanctification" relates directly to the Hebrew and Greek words for "holy." One may even argue that "holyfication" would be preferable to "sanctification" to underscore the intertwined nature of these terms.

Despite continued emphasis by many writers that "holy" speaks to separation and that "to be holy" means "to be set apart," the biblical terms are relational and speak primarily of belonging. "To be holy" (sanctified) means "to belong to God"; separation follows only as the exclusivity of this relationship demands it.

The gradation of the OT priesthood into levels of holiness that enabled entrance and service in weaker or stronger intensities of God's presence underscores further this dynamic quality of holiness. Although all the people of Israel were holy (belonging to God), the priests enjoyed a higher degree of holiness than the ordinary Israelite. Within the ranks of the priests, the high priest went through stricter rituals of consecration (Exod. 29:1–8, 20–21; Lev. 8:7–24; 21:13–15), since he alone could minister in the most intensive presence of God (Lev. 16:1–17). Less holy were those of the Aaronic lineage born with physical defects. Although sufficiently holy to eat from the most holy offerings, they could not serve at the altar (Lev. 21:16–23).

Average Israelites possessed a lower level of holiness than Levites and priests but could, as individuals, acquire greater levels of holiness through obedience (Lev. 11:44–45; Num. 15:40–41). Moreover, special vows, like that of the Nazirite, enhanced the average Israelite's quality as holy. The Nazirite vow (Num. 6:1–21) did not transfer priestly status to any person, but it did elevate one's holiness to a comparable level during the period of dedication.

This dynamic relationship between divine presence and holiness translates directly to the NT use of *hagiasmos* (and cognates). Although the Gospels rarely use "sanctification" vocabulary, Jesus' ongoing polemic against the Pharisees, who had turned their piety (holiness) into a question of mere conspicuous behavior, makes the same point. John's correlation of Jesus' sanctification as God's Son with the disciples' experience of the Spirit's empowerment (John 10:34–38; 17:17–19) indicates the same. Sanctification could not be separated from purpose and sending (20:21–23) and could not be reduced to a process of learning specified "Christian" behaviors. This, again, follows the pattern outlined in Acts; it was the outpouring of the Spirit that enabled the disciples to live the Christian life, which required the dynamic, creative power of God's presence (Acts 1:8; 2:1–21).

Paul's conversion exemplifies this tight connection between divine presence and sanctification (holiness). Not attaining the experience of God that he expected from keeping the law, Paul found the law-promised access to God in Christ. This turned him into a theologian of the Spirit who focused on the relational quality of God's presence. In Paul's vernacular, "divine presence," as expressed through the language of holiness or sanctification, stems from the relational work of the Holy Spirit. Accordingly, sanctification centers on deepening the relationship between God and the Spirit-filled Christian. Sanctification as a process of "learning" ethics surfaces only as a derivative; ethics is a by-product of divine presence, not vice versa. The antidote to the vices of the flesh (Gal. 5:18–21) is not a contrasting list of virtues of the Spirit but rather a fruit, the product or result, of living in God's presence (5:22–23).

For Paul, Spirit possession was synonymous with being a Christian (Rom. 8:9). His concern involved the intensity of the Spirit's presence. The Spirit could be grieved and his presence quenched—a devastating situation to the Christian's power and sanctity (Eph. 4:30; 1 Thess. 5:19).

Sanhedrin–The Jewish ruling body in Jerusalem that played a part in Jesus' execution and the persecution of the early church. In the NT the word refers to the council in Jerusalem headed by the high priest that was charged by the Roman authorities with maintaining order among the Jewish people.

In the first century AD, the Sanhedrin functioned as the highest judicial authority of the nation of Israel (which sheds light on Matt. 5:22). The Sanhedrin contained members from the Sadducees and the Pharisees, along with other prominent members of the Jewish establishment. As the highest authority representing the religious establishment of Israel, the Sanhedrin under the high priest Caiaphas played a prominent role in the final conflict that led to Jesus' crucifixion.

After Jesus was taken from the garden of Gethsemane, the Sanhedrin tried him on a charge of blasphemy using false testimony, and some of the Gospels also have the accusers claim that Jesus promised to destroy the temple and raise it in three days, taking his words as a literal threat against the temple (Matt. 26:58–68; Mark 14:53–65; Luke 22:63–71; see also John 18:13–27). The Sanhedrin was unable to carry out a sentence of death that the charge of blasphemy called for, however, and so they were forced to bring Jesus to the Roman authorities to achieve their desired result.

Following the death and resurrection of Jesus, the Sanhedrin attempted to suppress the budding Christian movement by arresting Peter and John and having them beaten for preaching about Jesus (Acts 4:1–21). The Sanhedrin also ordered the apostles "not to speak in the name of Jesus" (5:40). Paul, after being arrested, was brought before the Sanhedrin so that they might determine his crime, and he cleverly used the disagreement between the Sadducees and the Pharisees regarding the resurrection of the dead to disrupt the assembly (23:1–9). They then plotted to kill him (23:12–22).

Sapphira–Sapphira and her husband, Ananias, died as a result of withholding part of the proceeds of a property sale from the early community of believers (Acts 5:1).

Sarah–The wife of Abraham, the father of Israel and God's chosen people. Thus, Sarah is a matriarch (mother) of Israel along with Rebekah and Rachel.

According to Gen. 11:29–30, Sarai was married to Abram before they entered the promised land. The passage also announces that she was barren. Since an essential part of the divine promises to Abram is that he will be father to a great nation, the lack of offspring is a considerable problem and propels much of the plot of the narrative (esp. Gen. 12–26).

In brief, Sarai's inability to conceive is an obstacle to the fulfillment of the promise and is a threat to Abram's faith. Thus, when a famine forces them to go to Egypt to survive, he tells his wife to lie about her status by saying that she is his sister. Although it is true that she is his half sister, the statement is a lie because he hides the most relevant part of his relationship with her and puts the matriarch in danger (Gen. 12:10–20; 20:12). Abraham's faith (the narrative does not reveal Sarah's thinking except perhaps in Gen. 18:10–15, when she laughs at the thought of giving birth in her old age) in God's ability to fulfill the promise fluctuates, and he certainly has not come to a consistent position of trust even just before the birth of Isaac (Gen. 20). As a matter of fact, acting on fear and trying to produce an heir, Abraham takes a concubine, Hagar, who gives birth to Ishmael. Sarah's relationship with Hagar is troubled (Gen. 16), and Sarah treats her harshly and eventually has Hagar and Ishmael expelled from their camp (21:8–21).

Eventually, in advanced old age, Sarah gives birth to Isaac, the child of the promise (Gen. 21:1–7). Sarah is not mentioned in the story of the "binding of Isaac," the focus again being on Abraham's faith.

Later OT literature often looks back on Abraham as patriarch, but only Isa. 51:2 explicitly mentions Sarah in the role of cofounder of the people of God. She is mentioned also in the NT, along with Abraham, as the one through whom God brings the promise of a son to fulfillment (Rom. 4:19; 9:9; Heb. 11:11). In 1 Pet. 3:6 Sarah is put forward as a model of wifely submission because she obeys Abraham and refers to him as her lord (likely a reference to the Greek version of Gen. 18:12).

Sardis–*See* Asia Minor, Cities of.

Sargon–The third ruler of the Neo-Assyrian Empire, Sargon II (r. 721–705 BC), took credit for his predecessor's defeat of Samaria in 722 BC and advanced the policies of Tiglath-pileser III. On Sargon's third campaign, in 712 BC, he captured Ashdod (Isa. 20:1) and other cities in today's Gaza Strip. Subsequently he defeated Babylon in 710 BC and removed Marduk-Baladan, who later rebelled against Sennacherib.

Satan–*See* Devil, Demons.

Satan, Synagogue of–A metaphor used to describe Jewish persecutors of the church in Smyrna (Rev. 2:9) and in Philadelphia (3:9).

Satrap–The official title of a governmental ruler under the sovereignty of the Persian king. These rulers were entrusted with the provinces of the Persian Empire. According to Dan. 6:1, Darius appointed 120 of them over the empire. They appear in the books of Ezra, Esther, and Daniel.

Saul–**(1)** The first king of Israel (1 Sam. 9:1–2 Sam. 1:27; 1 Chron. 9:35–10:14). Out of fear of their enemy the Philistines as well as displeasure over Samuel's wicked sons, the people of Israel asked Samuel for a king like all the other nations had (1 Sam. 8). Though God and Samuel both expressed displeasure with the people's request, God directed Samuel to anoint Saul as king. Saul's initial reluctance to make his role public and also his hesitation to immediately confront the Philistines are not a sign of humility, but rather are an early example of the kind of disobedience to God and his prophet Samuel that eventually would bring God's great anger against him.

Saul's first significant failure, however, occurred before a battle with the Philistines, while he and his army were camped at Gilgal (1 Sam. 13). Before initiating battle, it was necessary to offer sacrifices. Samuel the priest, however, was late in arriving. Saul grew nervous because his troops were deserting, so he sacrificed the animals. When Samuel arrived, he confronted Saul. After all, with God on one's side, large numbers of troops were unnecessary. Saul thus displayed a lack of confidence in God by his actions. For this, Samuel announced that he would not found a dynasty of kings (13:13–14).

Soon thereafter, Saul showed his disobedience in another important aspect of war. Upon victory, the king should immediately offer all the plunder to God. In addition, if the enemy came from within the land, all the captives were to be put to death (*see* Holy War). However, after defeating the hated Amalekites (cf. Exod. 17:8–16; Deut. 25:17–19), Saul kept the sheep and did not personally execute King Agag, their leader (1 Sam. 15). For this, Samuel announced God's decision to remove him from the kingship and anoint another king (15:26).

At this time, Samuel anointed David, but David did not immediately become king (1 Sam. 16:1–13). For a period of time, David entered into Saul's service (16:14–23). It was never David's intention to forcibly remove Saul from the throne (1 Sam. 24; 26), but Saul grew intensely jealous of this popular young man. Indeed, Saul was a man deeply plagued by mental problems, perhaps depression and paranoia, even before the conflict with David. His jealousy also brought him into conflict with his own brave son, Jonathan, who had a deep friendship with David. Saul ejected David from the court and then spent much of his energy trying to track him down and kill him. He was, however, unsuccessful.

Eventually, God abandoned Saul. He was defeated and killed by the Philistines in the battle of Mount Gilboa (1 Sam. 31), and David mourned his death and the death of his friend Jonathan (2 Sam. 1).

(2) Another name for the apostle Paul (*see* Paul).

Scapegoat–A goat that carried away the sins of Israel. Chosen through lot on the Day of Atonement by the high priest, the scapegoat was offered to God alive and then released into the desert (Lev. 16:8, 10). The high priest laid his hands upon the head of the scapegoat, thus symbolically transferring all of Israel's guilt and sin to it. An appointed man then took the goat into the wilderness and released it, where it would "carry on itself all their sins to a remote place" (16:22). The complete removal of Israel's sin provided a powerful demonstration of the purification offered through the sacrifices on the Day of Atonement. The act of releasing the scapegoat caused the chosen man to become unclean. After bathing himself with water, he was able to reenter the camp (16:26).

Scepter–A rod, club, or mace that signified royal authority and power. The king ruled over the nation and enemies with his primary weapon, the scepter (Num. 24:17; Pss. 2:9; 110:2).

Sceva–In Acts 19:14 Sceva is mentioned as a "Jewish chief priest." His seven sons were among a group of itinerant Jewish exorcists in Ephesus who unsuccessfully tried to exorcize demons in the name of Jesus, which Paul was able to do. No such Jewish high priest is known from other sources, nor is one known to have lived in Ephesus. Sceva may have taken the title for himself to impress the Ephesians.

Scribe–An individual with the ability to read and write who uses these skills in a professional manner. The scribe was highly esteemed in ancient Mesopotamia and Egypt. Most scribes were royal secretaries (2 Sam. 8:17; 20:25). Early scribal activities included writing official records, drafting letters, and preparing royal decrees, deeds, and other things (2 Kings 12:10; 25:19; 2 Chron. 26:11). The scribes also read to the king (Jer. 36:21). As a result, scribes often became counselors to the king in matters of state (1 Chron. 27:32). After the exile, scribes became experts in the law of Moses (Ezra 7:6). By NT times, scribes were associated with the Pharisees as professional teachers of the law (Mark 2:16). Along with the chief priests, scribes conspired to kill Jesus (Luke 19:47).

Scripture–The term "Scripture" (*graphē*) appears fifty-one times in the NT, used in reference to the OT. Sometimes the biblical writers cite a specific OT text as Scripture, while at other times they refer to Scripture in a more comprehensive manner.

Scroll–References to "books" in biblical narratives are more properly said to indicate scrolls—that is, book rolls—made from papyrus, tanned hides of sheep and goats (as were most of the DSS), or parchment (hides with the hair removed and rubbed clean) (2 Tim. 4:13). They were unrolled for reading (Luke 4:17, 20) and could be secured with a wax seal (Rev. 5:1). The physical limitations of scroll length probably affected the size of biblical books. Almost invariably, only one side was written on, which makes Ezek. 2:9–10 and Rev. 5:1 exceptional.

Scythians–An ethnic group that inhabited the northern and eastern shores of the Black Sea. The term is also used more generically to refer to a nomadic people who rode on horseback, herded sheep and cattle, and moved from one seasonal pasture to another on the steppes from the Black Sea to what is now southern Russia. They often were employed as military mercenaries by Near Eastern powers.

Some earlier biblical scholars associated Scythians with the horse-riding nation that would bring destruction from the north (Jer. 4:29; 5:15–17; 6:22–26; 50:41–42; Zeph. 1:2–18), although more recent scholars normally identify this foe as the Babylonians.

Seal–In the biblical world, documents were sealed with clay or wax (1 Kings 21:8; Job 38:14; Neh. 9:38; Jer. 32:10; Rev. 5:1). The integrity of the seal was assured by impressing an image into the soft substance, which would then harden and retain the unique image of the sender's seal. The archaeological record attests this practice in the form of bullae (the impressions themselves, which survive long after the documents have disintegrated) as well as a large number of seals, which often were carved (Exod. 28:11; 39:6; Sir. 38:27; 45:11) into semiprecious stones or stone cylinders.

A person's unique seal was closely identified with the owner and could be worn as a ring or pendant (see Gen. 38:18; Esther 8:8; Song 8:6). Besides documents, we have records of the sealing of caves (Matt. 27:66; cf. Dan. 6:17; 2 Macc. 2:5) and bags (Job 14:17; Tob. 9:5). In apocalyptic literature, seals are used to conceal prophecies of the future (Dan. 12:4) and to mark humans as belonging to God (Rev. 7:3–8).

Sea of Galilee–A large, freshwater lake in the northern, Galilee region of Israel measuring thirteen miles long, eight miles wide, and between 80 and 150 feet deep. Because it is shaped like a harp, the OT refers to it as the "Sea of Kinnereth," which comes from the Hebrew word for "harp" (Num. 34:11; Deut. 3:17; Josh. 13:27; 19:35). It is also called "Lake of Gennesaret," which derives from the lush Plain of Gennesaret nearby (Matt. 14:34), and the "Sea of Tiberias," which comes from the name of the most prominent city on its banks (John 6:1; 21:1).

The Sea of Galilee is located about sixty miles north of Jerusalem and is fed by the Jordan River. It is surrounded by mountain peaks and cliffs, except on the southern side, where the Jordan River flows out of it. These peaks form a valley and make for strong, frequent, and unexpected storms as the Mediterranean winds blow down the western slopes and swirl across the sea. Jesus demonstrated his power over nature as he calmed such violent storms (Matt. 14:22–33; Mark 6:45–51; John 6:16–21).

The Sea of Galilee boasted a large fishing industry, which provided the ideal location for Jesus to call his first disciples—Peter, Andrew, James, and John, who were fishermen (Mark 1:16–20). Much of Jesus' ministry in the Synoptic Gospels took place in the towns around the Sea of Galilee. The Sea of Galilee provided an abundance of fishing illustrations (Matt. 13:48) and lessons on discipleship. Its shore may have provided a convenient location for the feeding of the five thousand (Matt. 14:13–21; Mark 6:35–44; Luke 9:10–17; John 6:1–13). After Jesus' resurrection, his disciples briefly returned to their fishing nets on this lake, resulting in the miraculous catch of 153 fish (John 21:11).

Sea of Reeds–*See* Red Sea, Reed Sea.

Secundus–One of several travel companions of Paul on his third missionary campaign, mentioned only in Acts 20:4. Secundus (along with Aristarchus), from Thessalonica, may have been among the "representatives of the churches" accompanying the collected gifts for Jerusalem (2 Cor. 8:16–24; see also Acts 24:17; Rom. 15:25–26).

Seer–*See* Prophecy, Prophets, Prophetess.

Seir, Mount–"Seir" means "hairy" and derives from Esau's hairiness (Gen. 25:25) or the woody nature of the mountain. It is located south of the Dead Sea. Although it was once occupied by the Horites (Gen. 14:6), Yahweh gave Mount Seir to Esau's descendants (Deut. 2:4–12). Thus, it is used in both biblical and extrabiblical literature to refer to Edom (2 Chron. 20:10–33). The Edomites' sense of security, arising from the height and ruggedness of Mount Seir, coupled with their hostility against Judah made them a constant object of prophetic diatribes (Isa. 63:1–7; Jer. 49; Ezek. 35:2–15; Obad. 1).

Selah–Although the Hebrew word *selah* appears seventy-one times in Psalms and three times in the book of Habakkuk, its meaning remains obscure. Most, however, agree that it represents some sort of instruction for worshipers. Those who seek the word's meaning in its etymology suggest that it directs worshipers to sing or play louder or to pray.

Seleucia–*See* Asia Minor, Cities of.

Sennacherib–A king of Assyria (r. 705–681 BC), he came to the throne upon the death of his powerful father, Sargon II, who had solidified Assyria's empire, including incorporating the northern kingdom of Israel (722 BC). Many vassal states chose this moment of transition to rebel against Assyria, including Hezekiah of Judah, who stopped paying tribute. Sennacherib responded by moving his army to Judah in 701 BC, a moment of crisis recorded in 2 Kings 18:13–19:37; 2 Chron. 32:1–23; Isa. 35:1–37:38.

Seraphim–Seraphim appear in Isa. 6:2, 6. The prophet sees God on his throne, and over him fly the seraphim. They have six wings: with two they cover their faces, with two they cover their feet, and with two they fly. The Hebrew word *sarap* means "to burn"; thus, the *serapim* are "burning ones" (cf. *sarap* in Num. 21:6, 8; Deut. 8:15; Isa. 14:29; 30:6 in reference to venomous serpents). They are living bolts of lightning, and their cries of "Holy, holy, holy," are peals of thunder, which shake the heavenly temple and fill it with smoke.

Sergius Paulus–A Roman proconsul on the island of Cyprus at the time of Paul's first missionary journey (Acts 13:7). Described as an intelligent man and interested in the Christian faith, he summoned Paul and Barnabas in order to hear their message. One of his attendants, Elymas, tried to dissuade him from believing and was subsequently cursed by Paul and blinded by God as punishment (13:8–11). This highly placed Roman official became the first recorded convert from Paul's first missionary journey when he saw the miracle of judgment. Luke, however, stresses the role of the apostles' teaching in his conversion (13:12).

Sermon on the Mount–The Sermon on the Mount is the inaugural sermon of Jesus in Matthew's Gospel (5:1–7:29), which sets out Jesus' kingdom program for the people of God. Whether this was a single sermon delivered on one occasion or Matthew's compilation of Jesus' teaching is uncertain. Luke's Gospel has a similar sermon (6:17–49), which may or may not be the same event (sometimes called the "Sermon on the Plain" because of v. 17, although this may simply be a "level place" on the same hill that Matthew describes). *See* Beatitudes.

Serpent–The serpent initially appears in Gen. 3:1, endowed with wisdom and the capacity to speak. In addressing Eve, it intentionally changes God's positive command to eat from all trees of the garden, with one exception, to a comprehensive prohibition and then goes on to contradict God and promise that eating will make Adam and Eve "like God, knowing good and evil" (3:5). While an explicit identity for the serpent is not given at this point, the curse pronounced against the creature (3:14–15) has transcendent implications (cf. Rom. 16:20). By the first centuries BC and AD, the serpent became linked with the malevolent figure of Satan, the devil, the great dragon. This connection is most comprehensively articulated for the Christian community in Rev. 12:9–15; 20:2. Eve acknowledged its deceptive wiles (Gen. 3:13), a point that both Jesus (John 8:44) and Paul (2 Cor. 11:3) reinforce.

For the Christian community receiving the Revelation of John, "the great dragon, that ancient serpent" (20:2), presented a powerful metaphor. Wise, shrewd, quick, beguiling, and terrifying, it had been in opposition to God in the age-old conflict between good and evil, the reality of which was expressed across cultural boundaries and a part of which was enveloping the church in the Roman Empire of late antiquity. Even its defeat was not instantaneous; the "head" of the serpent, struck by the death and resurrection of Jesus Christ, would bear one final blow; the cosmic evil would be ultimately and completely defeated to accomplish the purposes of God. *See also* Venomous Serpent.

Servant of the Lord–One of the most important themes in Isaiah is the messianic promise of a Davidic king. Yet intertwined throughout Isa. 42–53 are several passages that also identify the coming messianic personage as a servant, or more specifically, the Servant of the Lord. Often called the "Servant Songs," four passages in Isaiah focus particularly on the coming Servant of the Lord (42:1–7; 49:1–6; 50:4–9; 52:13–53:12). These texts present several important aspects of the coming Servant. First, God declares that he delights in his Servant and that he will put his Spirit on him. Furthermore, the Servant will establish justice and righteousness, two dominating themes of the prophetic literature associated with the coming Messiah. The Servant will regather the people of Israel, but he will also be a light and a covenant to the nations/Gentiles and thus will provide life for all of God's people. Ironically, however, and in contrast to the Davidic kingly images of the Messiah, Isaiah declares that the Servant will come quietly and humbly. Shockingly, the Servant of the Lord will be mocked and rejected by his people, even though he bears their sin and suffers for their iniquities. In fact, Isaiah declares, it is through the suffering of the Servant that righteousness is to be found (thus, the Servant is often referred to as the Suffering Servant). Even though the Servant will suffer greatly and be humiliated, ultimately he will be lifted up and exalted.

Throughout the Gospels there are quotes from and allusions to the Servant Songs, especially Isa. 53, thus establishing clearly that Jesus is the promised Servant of the Lord. Paul makes numerous allusions to Isa. 53 as he discusses the redemptive work of Christ, and Peter includes the Servant theme as part of his foundational understanding of Jesus' work and mission.

Yet, although the NT bears strong testimony that Isaiah's prophecies concerning the Servant of the Lord are fulfilled by the Messiah, Jesus Christ, there is still a sense in which Jesus also represents the ideal Israel. Unlike Israel, however, Jesus (the true Israel) is completely obedient, thus fulfilling many of the things that the nation itself had failed to complete. In this sense, as we find in Isaiah, the nation Israel can be called "the Servant." On the other hand, only Jesus Christ, as the perfect and ideal Servant of the Lord, fulfills all that Isaiah prophesies of the coming one in the Servant Songs.

Seth–The third son of Adam and Eve, Seth was viewed as a God-given replacement for the murdered Abel (Gen. 4:25–26). His name (Heb. *shet*) is a wordplay on "God has granted [*shat*] me another child," suggesting that he will be a new foundation for humanity.

Seven Churches of Asia–The addressees of the book of Revelation: Ephesus, Smyrna, Pergamum, Thyatira, Sardis, Philadelphia, and Laodicea. All seven were located in the Roman province of Asia, present-day western Turkey.

Sex, Sexuality–When God creates humans, he pronounces them "very good/beautiful" (Gen. 1:31). They are designed to be magnificent visual displays of God's character (1:26–27). Human sexuality originally is set in a context of overwhelming beauty. God's first command is to reproduce and extend this paradise throughout the earth (1:28). Human sexuality is not simply a mechanism for reproduction. From the outset it has been about completion, without which there is loneliness (2:18).

Although the Bible does not define the distinctives of masculinity and femininity in any detail, it does defend that there are distinctions between the genders. Behaviors that confuse the genders are explicitly condemned (Deut. 22:5; 1 Cor. 6:9; 11:4–16).

Homosexual intercourse (Lev. 18:22; 20:13; Rom. 1:24–27; 1 Cor. 6:9; 1 Tim. 1:10) and intercourse with an animal (Exod. 22:19; Lev. 18:23; 20:15–16; Deut. 27:21) are violations of God's created order.

Although damaged by sin, marriage continues to be the ultimate human relationship involving intimacy, privacy, and liberty. Marriage is defined by a covenant—a contract witnessed and enforceable, not just a promise made in private. The couple separate from their parents to become "one flesh" (Gen. 2:24).

Once the marriage contract is agreed upon, the couple are married. They cannot consummate the marriage until the economic commitments of the contract have been delivered (Matt. 1:18; 25:1–13). This is celebrated with a feast. Jesus uses this custom as an analogy for his departure and return (John 14:1–3).

Paul commands husbands to love their wives (Eph. 5:25–33; cf. Gen. 24:67; 29:20; 1 Sam. 1:5; Eccles. 9:9; Song 8:6–7). Nowhere in the Bible is a wife commanded to love her husband, though older women should teach younger women to do so (Titus 2:3–4). Love is the husband's responsibility. Love is a command that can be obeyed, not just a pleasurable feeling over which one has no control. The model of husbandly love is Jesus laying down his life for his people.

The ecstasy of making love is celebrated in the erotic Song of Songs, which holds out the hope of such marital delight even now. The axiom of marriage is a righteous jealousy (cf. Exod. 20:5; 34:14; Num. 5:14, 30; Prov. 6:34).

The first year of marriage is especially important and is protected by exemption from military service (Deut. 20:7; 24:5).

When a man dies without a male heir, his widow's possession of that part of the family estate can result in her marrying a man from another family and so alienating that land. This can be resolved either by the injustice of eviction or by the device of levirate marriage. The nearest male relative of the deceased husband marries the widow, and their son then inherits the deceased husband's name and title to the land (Deut. 25:5–10; cf. Gen. 38; Ruth).

Concubines are wives from poor families, slaves, or captives, and their marriages are protected (Exod. 21:7–9; Deut. 21:11–14).

Rape of a married woman constitutes adultery by the rapist, not the victim. Consensual sex with a married woman is adultery by both parties. Rape of a single woman is treated as fornication, with no blame attached to the woman. Her father has the option of letting her marry the man or receiving significant financial compensation (Exod. 22:16–17; Deut. 22:23–27). Her father has the right to take the money and refuse the marriage. To falsely accuse a woman of adultery is a crime (Deut. 22:13–21).

Prostitution is an extreme form of adultery or fornication and totally forbidden (Lev. 19:29; Deut. 23:17). Under the new covenant, this warning is heightened by the reality of the gift of the Holy Spirit transforming each believer into the temple of the Lord (1 Cor. 6:15–20).

Originally, marriage between siblings is implied (Gen. 4:17, 26; 5:4). Abram married his half sister, Sarai (Gen. 20:12; cf. Gen. 11:29; Num. 26:59). The Mosaic covenant at Sinai bans marriage to blood relationships closer than first cousins and to in-laws (Lev. 18:6–30; cf. 2 Sam. 13; 1 Cor. 5:1).

Polygamy occurs soon after the fall (Gen. 4:19–24). It is never explicitly forbidden in the Bible, but it is managed by OT law so as to restrain further injustice and damage. It is always seen as less than satisfactory (cf. Gen. 29–30; 1 Sam. 1:6; 2 Sam. 13; 1 Kings 1–2; 11). In the NT, monogamy is mandatory for those who would lead the church (1 Tim. 3:2, 12; Titus 1:6).

Shackles–*See* Bond.

Shaddai–A transliteration of part of the Hebrew expression *'el shadday* (Gen. 17:1; 28:3; 35:11; 43:14; 48:3; Exod. 6:3; Ezek. 10:5), translated as "God Almighty," following the Vulgate translation. There is no scholarly consensus on the translation or its precise meaning.

Shadrach–The Babylonian name given to Hananiah ("Yahweh is gracious to me") by Nebuchadnezzar's chief official, Ashpenaz, as part of an attempt to turn him into a Babylonian official (Dan. 1:7). He is one of Daniel's Judahite companions, along with Abednego and Meshach. The three later are appointed as administrators over the province of Babylon (2:49). After being accused of failing to worship one of Nebuchadnezzar's gods, the men are cast into the fiery furnace. They are kept safe by a fourth "man," who looks like a "son of the gods" (3:25). Afterward, all three are promoted (3:8–30). "Shadrach" likely means "command of Aku" (moon god).

Shallum–A son of King Josiah (1 Chron. 3:15), he ruled by the name "Jehoahaz" for three months until deposed by Pharaoh Necho (2 Kings 23:31–34). Jeremiah prophesied that Shallum would die in exile because he failed to uphold the cause of the needy and to continue his father's reforms (Jer. 22:11–17). *See also* Jehoahaz.

Shalmaneser–The name of a number of Assyrian kings, only two of whom seem to have direct biblical significance. Shalmaneser III fought against a coalition of Syrian kings who supposedly were backed by Ahab of Israel, at the battle of Qarqar in 853 BC. Shalmaneser III later exacted tribute from Jehu, an Israelite king, around 841 BC. Jehu's submission to Assyria is recorded in Shalmaneser III's Black Obelisk inscription. Shalmaneser V was a son of the Assyrian king Tiglath-pileser III. In 721 BC, Shalmaneser V conquered Samaria, the capital of Israel's northern kingdom, because Hoshea failed to pay tribute to Assyria (2 Kings 17:3–6). Shalmaneser V's reign was likely brought to an end in a violent coup led by Sargon II.

Shamgar–A judge of Israel (Judg. 3:31; 5:6), apparently a foreigner (cf. Jael [Judg. 4:17; 5:6]). His name is perhaps Hurrian and occurs in texts from Nuzi. His appellation "son of Anath" may either indicate his hometown (Beth Anath in Galilee [Josh. 19:38]) or be a title connected to the Canaanite deity Anath, perhaps with military connotations.

Shaphan–The son of Azaliah, he was secretary to King Josiah. Shaphan's reading of the Book of the Law, which Hilkiah the high priest had recently found, to King Josiah ultimately led to sweeping religious reform in Judah (2 Kings 22:3–20; 2 Chron. 34:8–28). Shaphan's sons Ahikam (2 Kings 22:12; Jer. 26:24), Elasah (Jer. 29:3), and Gemariah (Jer. 36:10–12), as well as his grandson through Ahikam, Gedaliah (Jer. 39:14; 40:11; 41:2), appear prominently in the book of Jeremiah.

Sharon–"Sharon" refers to the Sharon Plain (e.g., Acts 9:35). The coastal plain, one of the north-south sections into which Palestine can be divided north of the Negev, is the westernmost geographical feature of these strips. The Mediterranean Sea is to the west of the coastal plain and the foothills of the Shephelah to the east. The coastal plain is called the Sharon Plain once it extends north of the Yarkon River. The Sharon Plain is divided by two kurkar (local sandstone) ridges running north to south. North, toward the Carmel Mountains, the plain narrows and virtually disappears at the promontory at Haifa. It widens farther north past Akko and into Lebanon.

Shear-Jashub–The son of Isaiah, whom God commanded the prophet to take with him to meet King Ahaz (Isa. 7:3). "Shear-Jashub" is a sign-name and message to the fearful king. It means "[only] a remnant will return." There is ambiguity in "return," which could indicate either a physical return or repentance. The name is an assurance to Ahaz that he has nothing to fear from the foreign alliance: only a remnant of the armies of Aram and Israel will return home. Or it could mean that only a remnant will turn to God in faith.

Sheba–**(1)** A Benjamite, son of Bikri, who led a revolt against David (2 Sam. 20) in the aftermath of Absalom's rebellion. Joab pursued Sheba to the city of Abel Beth Maakah, where he was killed by the inhabitants, and thus the city was spared a siege. **(2)** The region made famous by the queen who visited Solomon in order to test his wisdom (1 Kings 10:1–13; 2 Chron. 9:1–12; see also Job 6:19; Ps. 72:10, 15; Isa. 60:6; Jer. 6:20; Ezek. 27:22, 23; 38:13); the region is located in southwestern Arabia (modern Yemen).

Sheba, Queen of–A queen who came to Jerusalem to visit Solomon (1 Kings 10; 2 Chron. 9; cf. Matt. 12:42). Sheba probably is located in southwestern Arabia (modern Yemen).

Shebat–The eleventh month of the year according to the Babylonian calendar (roughly February/March). See Zech. 1:7.

Shebna–Shebna (or "Shebnah," a variant Hebrew spelling) served as a royal officer of King Hezekiah and as one of his intermediaries (2 Kings 18:18; 19:2; Isa. 36:3; 37:2). He was criticized by Isaiah (Isa. 22:15–25).

Shechem–**(1)** The son of Hamor the Hivite, who was the head of the town and environs of Shechem (Gen. 34:2; cf. Josh. 24:32; Judg. 9:28). He raped Jacob and Leah's daughter Dinah, whose brothers killed him, Hamor, and the men of their town and plundered it in revenge.

(2) A crucial town in the hill country on the border of the tribal allotment of Ephraim (Josh. 20:7). Shechem is the first Canaanite town to be mentioned in the book of Genesis (12:6). Abraham camped at the site near the oak tree of Moreh, and God revealed himself to Abraham there, giving the first indication of the importance of the place. In response to God's revelation, Abraham built an altar at Shechem. Later, Jacob settled in the region of Shechem and purchased land from Hamor the Hivite (33:18–19). When Hamor's son Shechem raped Jacob's daughter Dinah, her brothers Simeon and Levi killed the men of the region, and Jacob's other sons pillaged the town of Shechem. Jacob buried his foreign gods at Shechem under the aforementioned oak tree in response to the revelation of God (35:1–4). It was in the general region of Shechem that Joseph later would seek his brothers and their flocks (Gen. 37). Israel would bury the bones of Joseph there in accordance with his wishes (50:25; Josh. 24:32).

Due to the revelation of God and its significance to the patriarchs, Joshua gathered the Israelites to Shechem after the conquest of Canaan and just prior to his death in order to renew the covenant (Josh. 8:30–35; 24). After the conquest the town was allotted to the Kohathite Levites and was one of the cities of refuge (Josh. 20:7; 21:21; 1 Chron. 6:67). However, in the period of the judges Shechem apparently was still under the cultural and religious influence of the Canaanites, as evidenced by the presence of the temple of Baal-Berith (Judg. 9:4). Abimelek, whose mother was a Shechemite, convinced the people of the town to make him their king. After three years, the Shechemites rejected Abimelek, and he killed many of them and destroyed the town (Judg. 9). It was at Shechem that the ten northern tribes made the decision to reject Solomon's son Rehoboam and make Jeroboam their king. Jeroboam subsequently made Shechem his capital for a period (1 Kings 12).

Sheepfold–A sheepfold is an enclosure used to confine livestock, either near inhabited areas (Num. 32:16) or in the open country (1 Sam. 24:3). Referring to the protective function of sheepfolds, Jesus refers to himself as the gate of a sheepfold (John 10:1, 9, 16), who keeps his flock from bandits.

Sheep Gate–*See* Gates of Jerusalem and the Temple.

Shekel–*See* Weights and Measures.

Shem–The eldest son of Noah (Gen. 9:24; 10:21) and the brother of Ham and Japheth. He and his wife were among the eight survivors of the flood (6:6–9). He was the father of the Semites, ancestor of the Hebrews (Gen. 11:10–14), and in the lineage of the Messiah (Luke 3:36).

Shema, The–*Shema* is the transliteration of a Hebrew word meaning "hear" (*shema'*), the first word of Deut. 6:4: "Hear, O Israel: The Lord our God, the Lord is one." The text that begins with this verse is therefore referred to as the Shema.

Jesus called the Shema the greatest commandment (Mark 12:29–30; Matt. 22:37–38; Luke 10:27) and invoked it in teaching his oneness with the Father (John 10:30). Paul later expanded the Shema to include Jesus (1 Cor. 8:6).

Shemaiah–A prophet who delivered God's word to King Rehoboam regarding Jeroboam (1 Kings 12:22–24; 2 Chron. 11:2–4) and the cause of the invasion by King Shishak of Egypt (2 Chron. 12:5, 7). He also recorded the events of Rehoboam's reign (2 Chron. 12:15).

Sheol–In the OT, an underworld place to which all were destined after death. The Hebrew word *she'ol* is generally translated as "the grave" in modern versions of the Bible, including the NIV. Sheol appears in the OT most frequently in songs and prayers (David's song [2 Sam. 22:6]; Hannah's prayer [1 Sam. 2:6]; many references in Psalms), as well as in the wisdom books of Job and Proverbs. The ancient Israelites visualized the cosmos as composed of three distinct realms: heaven, the realm of the divine; earth, the realm of humanity and God's creation; and Sheol, a place underneath the earth and the seas, the realm of the dead (Job 11:8; 26:5–7).

When the OT was translated into Greek for Hellenized Jewish readers, "Sheol" was translated as "Hades," importing a similar Greek concept of the underworld into the biblical text. The NT uses the words "Hades" and "hell" interchangeably; however, the distinction between the grave and hell is maintained.

Shephelah–The Hebrew word *shepelah,* translated "lowland" or "foothills," generally refers to the low hills immediately west of the Judean hill country, although on two occasions it indicates similar topographical features in proximity to the hills of western Galilee (Josh. 11:2, 16). The region functioned as a buffer zone between the secure location in the hill country and the foreign powers on the coastal plain.

Shepherd–Shepherds were pastoralists who herded sheep and goats for meat, milk, clothing, and sacrifices. Shepherding was an integral part of life and a potent symbol in Israelite culture, reflected in biblical portrayals of Abel (Gen. 4:2), Moses (Exod. 3:1), David (1 Sam. 16:11), and Jesus (Luke 2:8–20; John 10:11, 14).

A shepherd could herd his or her own flock (Gen. 30:37–43). Sons (Gen. 37:2), daughters (Gen. 29:6, 9), or hirelings (Gen. 13:7; 1 Sam. 25:7; Luke 17:7) could assume the task. As agriculture developed and crops were cultivated, shepherds became marginalized (note that it was the youngest son of Jesse, David, who tended the sheep [1 Sam. 16:11–13]) and even despised (Gen. 46:34). Shepherds could live in villages, daily herding their flock to and from nearby arable land (Gen. 29:7–14). Once all the grazing land had been consumed, shepherds led the flock to pastureland far enough from town to prohibit daily returns. They would then live a seminomadic existence, wandering when new grazing land and water were needed (Gen. 37:12; cf. Isa. 13:20). Shepherds constructed makeshift enclosures out of available materials (stones, brush) or used a cave and remained with the flock throughout the night (Gen. 31:40; Song 1:8; Luke 2:8)

The vital role of shepherding in ancient Near Eastern culture naturally led to the metaphorical use of the term to refer to both civil authorities (Num. 27:17; 1 Kings 22:17; Isa. 44:28; Ezek. 34:1–19) and deity (Gen. 48:15; 49:24; Pss. 23:1; 78:52), both in Israel and among its neighbors. Both the exodus (Exod. 15:13, 17; Ps. 78:52–55, 71–72) and the return from Babylonian exile (Ps. 44:11–23; Jer. 23:1–8; 31:8–14) are portrayed in pastoral terms as Yahweh shepherding his people to safe pasture. In the NT, Jesus called himself the "good shepherd" (John 10:1–16), and the metaphor is extended to church leaders who are to imitate the good shepherd in their provision and protection of God's people (Acts 20:28; 1 Pet. 5:1–3).

Sheshbazzar–An early leader of the postexilic community who returned from Babylonian captivity to Jerusalem soon after Cyrus the Persian issued a decree that allowed them to go back (c. 539 BC). Though Jewish, he had a Persian name. He was commissioned by Cyrus to bring the temple vessels taken by Nebuchadnezzar (Dan. 1:2) back to Jerusalem and to rebuild the temple (Ezra 1:8, 11). Upon his return, Sheshbazzar oversaw the construction of the foundation of the temple (Ezra 5:16), but then the building stopped for a period of time and the temple was not completely finished until 515 BC.

Shethar-Bozenai–A Persian officer who attempted to hinder the rebuilding of the temple with Tattenai, the Persian governor of the lands east of the Euphrates (Ezra 5:3, 6; 6:6). Later he was mandated to help with the procurement of supplies for the rebuilding process due to Darius's decree (Ezra 6:13).

Shibboleth–The Hebrew word used by Jephthah's forces in Judg. 12:6 to identify escaping Ephraimite troops, who would pronounce it as "Sibboleth." The meaning of the word is uncertain and probably irrelevant to the events recounted in Judg. 12, but it may mean "ear of corn" or "flowing water."

Shiggaion–One of the classifications in the superscriptions of the psalms, appearing only in Ps. 7 (cf. Hab. 3:1). Its meaning is uncertain. The root meaning seems to relate to "wandering" or "ranging." Musically, this could mean that the tune went up and down the scale. It has also been interpreted to mean "fervent," suggesting a passionate lament. *See also* Shigionoth.

Shigionoth–A word found in the heading to Habakkuk's prayer (Hab. 3:1), in the place where a stylistic comment might occur in the title of a psalm. Its meaning is uncertain, but it seems to be a plural of "Shiggaion" (cf. Ps. 7 superscription). It perhaps indicates the literary genre of the prayer or a musical style to be used in singing it. *See also* Shiggaion.

Shihor–*See* Rivers and Waterways (The wadi of Egypt).

Shiloah, Waters of–Probably the Siloam aqueduct, which passed southward from the Gihon spring along the western slope of the Kidron Valley and provided water for irrigation. Preparing for military siege, Hezekiah dug an underground tunnel to redirect parts of it to the Pool of Siloam (2 Kings 20:20). In Isa. 8:6–8 "waters of Shiloah" is a metaphor for God's presence and blessing for his people, which they rejected; as a result, the "mighty floodwaters of the Euphrates," representing Assyria's power, would sweep over and inundate Judah.

Shiloh–Protected in the hill country of Ephraim, Shiloh was a secure location for the tabernacle and the ark of the covenant in the early centuries of Israel's presence in the land. Judges 21:19 gives a remarkably precise location for Shiloh. It was "north of Bethel, east of the road that goes from Bethel to Shechem, and south of Lebonah." This means that it was centrally located in the hill country just off the internal north-south ridge route.

The Israelites established their worship center at Shiloh after the conquest of the land (Josh. 18:1), and it was there that the assembly gathered in order to apportion the rest of the tribal allotments after Judah's apportionment (18:8–10).

Although it is uncertain when the sanctuary at Shiloh was destroyed, it was likely by the Philistines as they later encroached well into Israelite territory (1 Sam. 13). Nevertheless, Shiloh remained a significant location. As the northern kingdom broke away from the south, Ahijah from Shiloh prophesied to Jeroboam son of Nebat (1 Kings 11:29–40) and later addressed Jeroboam's wife (1 Kings 14:2–4). Jeremiah reminded the inhabitants of Jerusalem that God destroyed Shiloh, the first dwelling place for his name in the land, because of the wickedness of Israel and would do the same again to the temple in Jerusalem (Jer. 7:12–14; 26:6–9). Even the psalmist noted the tragedy: "He abandoned the tabernacle of Shiloh" (Ps. 78:60).

Shimei–A Benjamite and the son of Gera, Shimei cursed David in the name of the Lord near Bahurim during David's flight from Jerusalem (2 Sam. 16:5–14). David twice refused to have Shimei executed, first at the time of the curse and then later at David's reinstallment as king (19:23). Although David had promised Shimei with an oath that he would live, in his final days David instructed Solomon to kill Shimei. King Solomon offered Shimei a life sentence in Jerusalem, with death the punishment for leaving. Shimei later left and was killed (1 Kings 2:36–46).

Shinar, Plain of–The Plain of Shinar was the site of the tower of Babel. According to Genesis, people settled here after they moved "eastward" (Gen. 11:2 [or perhaps "from the east" or "in the east"]). The identification of Shinar as Babylonia (so the NIV footnote at 11:2) makes it probable that this phrase is better rendered "eastward" (NIV) or "to the east" (NLT). After the immigrants settled, they began to build a tower that would help them not "be scattered over the face of the whole earth" (11:4). When God confused their language, they were indeed scattered (11:9).

Shiphrah–One of the two Hebrew midwives (the other being Puah) who refused to heed the command of the king of Egypt to execute all male children upon their birth (Exod. 1:15–22). Consequently, the Hebrew population increased, and she was blessed because she feared God.

Shisha–The secretary of David, also known as Seraiah (2 Sam. 8:17), Sheva (2 Sam. 20:25), and Shavsha (1 Chron. 18:16).

Shishak–Shishak was king of Egypt (r. 935–914 BC) during the reigns of Solomon and his son Rehoboam. He gave sanctuary to Solomon's rebellious servant Jeroboam, who, upon Solomon's death, became king of the northern tribes (1 Kings 11:40). Not only was Shishak instrumental in stripping away the ten northern tribes from Solomon's son, but also he stripped away from Rehoboam much of Solomon's glorious gold and treasure (1 Kings 14:25–26). This was understood by the Chronicler as a direct judgment on Rehoboam because he had forsaken God's law (2 Chron. 12:2–9). Shishak is there presented as being in command of a vast international force, including Libyans and Ethiopians.

Shofar–An instrument made out of an animal's horn (most commonly a ram) that had at most three notes. The Hebrew word *shopar* most often is translated as "trumpet" or "horn." It had many uses and was most often used to signal troops during times of war (Josh. 6:4; Judg. 3:27) and to gather people for religious or civic ceremonies (Exod. 19:13; 2 Sam. 15:10). It also has eschatological connotations in relationship to the day of the Lord (Joel 2:1).

Shulammite–The Shulammite (KJV: "Shulamite") is found only in Song 6:13. Some connect the name with Shulmanitu, a Mesopotamian goddess of love, but such a view depends on identifying the Song of Solomon as connected to a pagan ritual, which is unlikely. Some others, noting an association between Shulam and the city of Shunem, argue that the title refers to a well-known woman from Shunem, possibly Abishag (1 Kings 1:1–4:15), the woman who kept David warm in his old age. Most likely, the term is a feminine form of the name "Solomon," which as a noun is also *shalom*, meaning "peace."

Shunammite–A person from Shunem. In the Bible, two women are referred to as "the Shunammite." The woman whose son Elisha raises from the dead (2 Kings 4) is known only by this title. Abishag, the young woman who kept warm the elderly King David, is identified as "the Shunammite" as well (1 Kings 1–2). *See also* Shunem.

Shunem–Shunem of Issachar's territory (Josh. 19:18) is important in connection with three women. First, it was at Shunem that Saul, afraid of numerous enemies and having gotten no response to his request to God for guidance (1 Sam. 28:4–7), decided to consult a medium in the nearby town of Endor. The medium conjured Samuel, who in a postmortem rebuke announced Saul's impending death. Second, the beautiful Shunammite Abishag kept David warm in his old age (1 Kings 1:3–4, 15). Later, in an attempt to usurp the kingdom, Solomon's brother Adonijah schemed with Bathsheba to convince Solomon to give him Abishag in marriage, but the shrewd king instead had Adonijah killed (1 Kings 2:16–25). Third, in Shunem a wealthy but barren woman provided for Elisha, who blessed her in return with a miraculous conception. But after her son had grown, he suddenly died. She called upon Elisha after the fact, and he then raised her son from death (2 Kings 4:8–37).

Shur, Wilderness of–A region of desert and perhaps a specific place in the Sinai Peninsula east of what is today known as the Suez Canal. Hagar was traveling to Shur when she met the angel of the Lord (Gen. 16:7). Abraham settled between Kadesh and Shur before he told Abimelek that Sarah was his sister (20:1). Ishmael's descendants also settled in the area (25:18). Moses led the Israelites into the wilderness of Shur (NIV: "Desert of Shur") after they fled Egypt and crossed the Red Sea (Exod. 15:22). Both Saul and David traveled through Shur in pursuit of their Amalekite enemies (1 Sam. 15:7; 27:8).

Sicarii–*See* Jewish Parties (Zealots).

Siddim–In this valley the kings of five allied cities (Sodom, Gomorrah, Admah, Zeboyim, and Bela) awaited the approach of invaders (Gen. 14:3, 8, 10). This term appears to have been assigned to a broad, flattish tract, sometimes of considerable width, enclosed on each side by a definite range of hills.

Sidon–*See* Tyre and Sidon.

Siege–Ancient accounts and remains (e.g., the bas relief from Sennacherib's palace in Nineveh depicting the siege of Lachish) and the biblical record (2 Kings 25:1–2; Ezek. 4:2) reveal the siege techniques of the period. Spies sought any strategic weakness (Judg. 1:22–26). The city's water supply was interrupted (2 Sam. 12:27). People were prevented from entering or leaving. An attempt was made to starve the inhabitants into surrendering. The besieging army might use siege engines, scaling ladders, earthen ramps, and battering rams and make tunnels under walls. Although scholars refer to the Assyrian "siege" of Jerusalem in 701 BC, Isa. 36–37 and 2 Kings 18–19 indicate that the city was only blockaded, and the word used in Isa. 1:8 (*netsurah* [NIV: "under siege"]) means "watched, guarded."

Siege Works–A general war term referring to systematic methods or mechanisms designed to overcome a fortified city. Siege works might include earthen ramps built against city walls (Ezek. 4:2), towers probably designed for use by archers (Isa. 29:3), scaling ladders, and battering rams used to weaken walls and gates (Ezek. 21:22). Wood was the primary material (Deut. 20:20) used in the construction of siege works, often accompanied by metal, particularly on the heads of battering rams for added strength and weight. Nebuchadnezzar used siege works to overcome Jerusalem's fortifications during Zedekiah's reign (2 Kings 25:1; Jer. 52:4). Utter destruction often followed once a city's defenses were overcome and the besieging forces had gained entry into the city (Jer. 52:10, 13).

Sign–Signs are visible, typically being an object, a mark, an event, or a custom. In addition, signs are symbolic, pointing to things not seen. Signs often reveal or share some quality with the unseen reality to which they point, and so they are a token of that reality. In the Bible, signs typically are caused or instituted by God, and in many cases they are miraculous. However, in a few cases signs are set forth as the work of other gods (as in Deut. 13:1–2) or as being instituted by merely human design (as in Num. 2:2). In summary, a sign may be defined as something seen that points to something unseen, and that is instituted or created to do so by someone's intention.

Several examples support this definition. Keeping the Sabbath is a sign of God's rest after creating the world (Exod. 31:15); the Sabbath rest itself imitates God's rest. Circumcision is a sign of God's promise to both Abraham and his descendants; circumcision is also a physical mark that is related to human fertility (Gen. 17:11). The rainbow is a sign of God's promise not to destroy the world by water and rain; rainbows appear only with rain (Gen. 9:13). (In the original Hebrew text, both the custom of circumcision and the rainbow that appears after the great flood are called "signs.") The early Passover plagues both bring and warn of judgment, while the healing miracles of Jesus both bring and promise blessing. While signs point to unseen realities, these realities do not diminish the value or importance of the visible world. Instead, the unseen realities themselves are ultimately expressed in the visible world.

Signet–A ring with a seal inscribed upon it. A signet ring denoted authority and honor. Set on the front side of the ring was a hard or semiprecious stone with a seal inscription carved in reverse. The seal upon the ring served as an individual's official stamp or signature and could prove authenticity. For instance, a royal document was not considered legitimate unless stamped with the king's seal. Proof of witness to a contract also was confirmed by stamping the seals of the involved parties on a document or object. A seal could also be used to fasten a document by stamping a small, circular lump of clay ("bulla") over the document. A seal might bear the name of its owner and/or various decorations. Some common motifs include Egyptian themes such as scarabs or winged sun discs, animals such as lions and bulls, and plant patterns incorporating important or symbolic plants such as the lotus, papyrus, or pomegranate. For occurrences in the Bible, see Gen. 38:18; 41:42; Exod. 28:36; Esther 3:10.

Sihon–The Amorite king of Heshbon who opposed the passage of the Israelites through his territory on their journey from Egypt to Canaan (Num. 21:21–22; Deut. 2:26–29). Moses informed Sihon that the Israelites would stay on the highway and pay for any food or drink that they needed on the way. But Sihon refused, and he assembled his troops to fight against Israel in the wilderness (Num. 21:23). The Israelites defeated Sihon and took the cities and villages of his kingdom (21:24–25).

Silas–Silas was a Jewish Christian, a Roman citizen (Acts 16:37–38), and a leader of the Jerusalem church (15:22). He was assigned the very important role of emissary of the Jerusalem church to Antioch, carrying the letter related to the Jerusalem council of Acts 15. He was also a prophet (15:32). Paul chose Silas to accompany him on the second missionary journey (15:40–41), yet Silas was a coequal with Paul rather than a subordinate like Timothy. Silas's presence probably was a validation of Paul's gospel, and Silas likely represented the Jerusalem church in the "Pauline" missionary work.

Paul probably refers to Silas as an apostle of Christ in 1 Thess. 2:6. Silas preached the gospel to the Corinthians (2 Cor. 1:19) and is a named cosender of both Thessalonian letters. The same Silas is the secretary who wrote down the letter 1 Peter for the apostle Peter (1 Pet. 5:12–13). "Silas" is the Greek form of the Hebrew or Aramaic name "Saul"; the Latin spelling is "Silvanus" (cf. Gk. *Silouanos* in 2 Cor. 1:19; 1 Thess. 1:1; 2 Thess. 1:1; 1 Pet. 5:12).

Siloam–A Byzantine-era pool on the southwest side of the Ophel Hill, near Jerusalem. Siloam is mentioned three times in the NT (Luke 13:4; John 9:7, 11). The Siloam Tunnel is one of two subterranean channels (along with "Hezekiah's Tunnel") bringing water from the Gihon spring to this location. These tunnels are best known for the discovery (in 1880) of the so-called Siloam Inscription, which describes the completion of work on those tunnels in some detail. The events mentioned in this inscription generally have been associated with 2 Kings 20 and 2 Chronicles 32, which describe the building projects of King Hezekiah, including "how he made the pool and the tunnel by which he brought water into the city" (2 Kings 20:20) and how he "blocked the upper outlet of the Gihon spring and channeled the water down to the west side of the City of David" (2 Chron. 32:30). The inscription has been dated to the late eighth century BC, based on paleographic data, and usually is associated with the preparations for Hezekiah's rebellion against Sennacherib in 701 BC.

Silvanus–*See* Silas.

Silversmith–A metalworker who creates objects out of silver and sometimes gold, brass, or iron (2 Chron. 2:7). The OT references translated "silversmith" are based on the Hebrew word for "smelter, refiner" with "silver" as a modifier (Judg. 17:4; Isa. 40:19) or implied from context (Prov. 25:4; Jer. 10:9). In the NT, the only silversmith is Demetrius of Ephesus (Acts 19:24), a guild leader who made shrines honoring Artemis. Recognizing that the gospel threatened his industry, he incited a riot against Paul.

Simeon–**(1)** Jacob's second son by Leah. Along with Levi, he massacred the men of Shechem for defiling their sister Dinah (Gen. 34). He was imprisoned in Egypt by Joseph when the other brothers returned to Canaan (42:24). He is identified in Jacob's blessing as a violent man whose descendants would be scattered in Israel (49:5–7). **(2)** A righteous and devout man in Jerusalem who had received a vision that he would witness the Messiah's coming (Luke 2:25–35). After seeing Jesus, he offered praise to God. His words are often called the *Nunc Dimittis*, the first two words of his prayer in Latin ("now dismiss [your servant in peace]"). He prophesied that Jesus was "destined to cause the falling and rising of many in Israel, and to be a sign that will be spoken against" (2:34). **(3)** One of the prophets and teachers in Antioch along with Barnabas and Saul (Acts 13:1). He is called "Niger," evidently because he was an African or of dark complexion. **(4)** A variant name for Simon Peter (Acts 15:14; see NIV mg.).

Simeon, Tribe of–In the wilderness, the tribe of Simeon camped between Reuben and Gad. The Simeonites were allotted land within Judah's territory. Their subsequent absorption fulfilled Jacob's prophecy of scattering (Gen. 49:5–7).

Simmagir–*See* Samgar-Nebo.

Simon–**(1)** One of the original twelve apostles (Matt. 10:2), also called "Peter." Simon Peter was the brother of Andrew and a fisherman by trade (Matt. 4:18). (*See also* Peter.) **(2)** The Zealot, one of the original twelve apostles (Matt. 10:4). **(3)** One of the brothers of Jesus, along with James, Joseph, and Judas (Matt. 13:55; Mark 6:3). **(4)** A leper who lived in Bethany. In his house the precious bottle of ointment was poured upon Jesus in preparation for his burial (Matt. 26:6). **(5)** A man from Cyrene who carried Jesus' cross on the way to crucifixion (Matt. 27:32). **(6)** A Pharisee who invited Jesus for a meal (Luke 7:40). Jesus was anointed with ointment in his house. He perhaps is the same individual as in Matt. 26:6. **(7)** The father of Judas Iscariot, who betrayed Jesus (John 6:71). **(8)** A sorcerer who believed the gospel and was baptized. However, he became enamored with the miraculous power of Philip and with the ability of the apostles to impart the Holy Spirit, and he offered them money to give him that ability (Acts 8:9–25). **(9)** A tanner with whom Peter stayed in Joppa before traveling to the house of Cornelius (Acts 9:43).

Simon Peter–*See* Peter.

Sin–Sin enters the biblical story in Gen. 3. Despite God's commandment to the contrary (2:16–17), Eve ate from the tree of the knowledge of good and evil at the prompting of the serpent. When Adam joined Eve in eating the fruit, their rebellion was complete. They attempted to cover their guilt and shame, but the fig leaves were inadequate. God confronted them and was unimpressed with their attempts to shift the blame. Judgment fell heavily on the serpent, Eve, and Adam; even creation itself was affected (3:17–18).

In the midst of judgment, God made it clear in two specific ways that sin did not have the last word. First, God cryptically promised to put hostility between the offspring of the serpent and that of the woman (Gen. 3:15). Although the serpent would inflict a severe blow upon the offspring of the woman, the offspring of the woman would defeat the serpent. Second, God replaced the inadequate covering of the fig leaves with animal skins (3:21). The implication is that the death of the animal functioned as a substitute for Adam and Eve, covering their sin.

In one sense, the rest of the OT hangs on this question: How will a holy God satisfy his wrath against human sin and restore his relationship with human beings without compromising his justice? The short answer is: through Abraham and his offspring (Gen. 12:1–3), who eventually multiplied into the nation of Israel. After God redeemed them from their slavery in Egypt (Exod. 1–15), he brought them to Sinai to make a covenant with them that was predicated on obedience (19:5–6). A central component of this covenant was the sacrificial system (e.g., Lev. 1–7), which God provided as a means of dealing with sin. In addition to the regular sacrifices made for sin throughout the year, God set apart one day a year to atone for Israel's sins (Lev. 16). On this Day of Atonement the high priest took the blood of a goat into the holy of holies and sprinkled it on the mercy seat as a sin offering. Afterward he took a second goat and confessed "all the iniquities of the people of Israel, and all their transgressions, all their sins, putting them on the head of the goat, and sending it away into the wilderness. . . . The goat shall bear on itself all their iniquities to a barren region; and the goat shall be set free in the wilderness" (Lev. 16:21–22 NRSV). In order for the holy God to dwell with sinful people, extensive provisions had to be made to enable fellowship.

During the next four hundred years of prophetic silence, the longing for God to finally put away the sins of his people grew. At last, when the conception and birth of Jesus were announced, it was revealed that he would "save his people from their sins" (Matt. 1:21). In the days before the public ministry of Jesus, John the Baptist prepared the way for him by "preaching a baptism of repentance for the forgiveness of sins" (Luke 3:3). Whereas both Adam and Israel were disobedient sons of God, Jesus proved to be the obedient Son by his faithfulness to God in the face of temptation (Matt. 2:13–15; 4:1–11; 26:36–46; Luke 3:23–4:13; Rom. 5:12–21; Phil. 2:8; Heb. 5:8–10). He was also the Suffering Servant who gave his life as a ransom for many (Mark 10:45; cf. Isa. 52:13–53:12). On the cross Jesus experienced the wrath of God that God's people rightly deserved for their sin. With his justice fully satisfied, God was free to forgive and justify all who are identified with Christ by faith (Rom. 3:21–26). What neither the law nor the blood of bulls and goats could do, Jesus Christ did with his own blood (Rom. 8:3–4; Heb. 9:1–10:18).

After his resurrection and ascension, Jesus' followers began proclaiming the "good news" (gospel) of what Jesus did and calling to people, "Repent and be baptized, every one of you, in the name of Jesus Christ for the forgiveness of your sins" (Acts 2:38). As people began to experience God's forgiveness, they were so transformed that they forgave those who sinned against them (Matt. 6:12; 18:15–20; Col. 3:13). Although believers continue to struggle with sin in this life (Rom. 8:12–13; Gal. 5:16–25), sin is no longer master over them (Rom. 6:1–23). The Holy Spirit empowers them to fight sin as they long for the new heaven and earth, where there will be no sin, no death, and no curse (Rom. 8:12–30; Rev. 21–22).

As even this very brief survey of the biblical story line from Genesis to Revelation shows, sin is a fundamental aspect of the Bible's plot. Sin generates the conflict that drives the biblical narrative; it is the fundamental "problem" that must be solved in order for God's purposes in creation to be completed.

Sin, Desert of–One of the locations of the Israelites' travels when they came out of Egypt. It is located between Elim and Mount Sinai (Exod. 16:1; 17:1; Num. 33:11–12) and should not be confused with the wilderness of Zin. About one month after the exodus, the Israelites came to this place, where they complained of starvation, and God provided manna and quail for them (Exod. 16:4–21). The exact location of the Desert of Sin is unclear, as it depends on the location of Mount Sinai, also unknown.

Sin, Wilderness of–*See* Sin, Desert of.

Sinai, Mount–The mountain where Moses met with God and received the law and instructions for building the tabernacle. It is important to note that Sinai is sometimes referred to as Horeb.

The exact location of the mountain cannot be determined with certainty. Complicating matters is the fact that the desert and the peninsula on which the mountains sit are both called "Sinai." Furthermore, although some have speculated that the mountain must be a volcano, given the description of smoke coming from the mountain and the earthquakes (Exod. 19:16, 18), this suggestion is of little specific help because many of the mountains in this region at one time were active volcanoes. Several locations for the mountain have been suggested.

Sisera–The commander of the army of King Jabin of Canaan. Sisera fled from Deborah and Barak's forces into the tent of Jael. When Sisera fell asleep, Jael killed him by driving a tent peg through his head (Judg. 4:1–22).

S

Sivan–Persian word for the third month of the Jewish year, extending from the new moon in June to the new moon in July (Esther 8:9).

Slave, Servant–There are numerous relationships in the OT that could be characterized as following a servant-master model. These included service to the monarchy (2 Sam. 9:2), within households (Gen. 16:8), in the temple (1 Sam. 2:15), or to God himself (Judg. 2:8). We also see extensive slavery laws in passages such as Exod. 21:1–11; Lev. 25:39–55; Deut. 15:12–18. The slavery laws were concerned with the proper treatment of Hebrew slaves and included guidelines for their eventual release and freedom. For example, Hebrew slaves who had sold themselves to others were to serve for a period of six years. On the seventh year, known also as the Sabbath Year, they were to be released. Once released, they were not to be sent away empty-handed, but rather were to be supported from the owner's "threshing floor" and "winepress." Slaves also had certain rights that gave them special privileges and protection from their masters. Captured slaves, for example, were allowed rest on the Sabbath (Exod. 20:10) and during special holidays (Deut. 16:11, 14). They could also be freed if their master permanently hurt or crippled them (Exod. 21:26–27). Also, severe punishment was imposed on a person who beat a slave to death (Exod. 21:20–21).

Slavery was very common in the first century AD, and there were many different kinds of slaves. For example, slaves might live in an extended household (*oikos*) in which they were born, or they might choose to sell themselves into this situation (1 Pet. 2:18–25). Although slavery was a significant part of society in the first century AD, we never see Jesus or the apostles encourage slavery. Instead, both Paul and Peter encouraged godly character and obedience for slaves within this system (Eph. 6:5–8; Col. 3:22–25; 1 Tim. 6:1–2; Philemon; 1 Pet. 2:18–21). Likewise, masters were encouraged to be kind and fair to their slaves (Eph. 6:9; Col. 4:1). Later in the NT, slave trading was condemned by the apostle Paul as contrary to "sound doctrine" and "the gospel concerning the glory of the blessed God" (1 Tim. 1:10–11).

Jesus embodied the idea of a servant in word and deed. He fulfilled the role of the "Servant of the Lord," the Suffering Servant predicted by the prophet Isaiah (Isa. 42:1–4; 50:4–9; 52:13–53:12). He also took on the role of a servant in the Gospels, identifying himself as the Son of Man who came to serve (Mark 10:45) and washing the disciples' feet (John 13:4–5). Paul says that in the incarnation Jesus took on "the very nature of a servant" (Phil. 2:7).

The special relationship between Jesus and his followers is captured in the servant-master language of the NT Epistles, especially in Paul's letters (Rom. 1:1; Phil. 1:1; Titus 1:1). This language focuses not so much on the societal status of these servants as on the allegiance and honor owed to Christ Jesus.

Smyrna–*See* Asia Minor, Cities of.

Sodom and Gomorrah–After Abram (Abraham) realizes that the land between Bethel and Ai cannot support both him and Lot, he suggests that they part company. Abraham gives Lot first choice, and he decides to settle in the fertile cities of the Jordan plain on the outskirts of Sodom (Gen. 13:1–12). The text then describes Sodom's inhabitants as "wicked" and "sinning greatly against the Lord" (13:13). In Gen. 18 God reveals to Abram his plan to destroy Sodom and Gomorrah because of the "outcry against" these cities and their "grievous" sin. God says, "I will go down and see if what they have done is as bad as the outcry that has reached me" (18:20). Abram pleads on behalf of Sodom and bargains with God to spare the righteous in the city.

Two angels of the Lord then arrive at Sodom to carry out the task of God's investigation, and Lot meets them and invites them to stay the night with him. The men of Sodom then surround the house and demand that the visitors be brought out to them to be raped. Lot refuses and offers his daughters instead, intending to protect the visitors. The angelic messengers strike the wicked men of Sodom with blindness, and Lot, his wife, and his daughters flee the city. God destroys Sodom and Gomorrah with a rain of "burning sulfur" (Gen. 19:24).

In both the OT and the NT, the cities' names become a symbol of warning against violent wickedness and of God's wrathful response of fiery destruction (Deut. 29:23; Isa. 1:9; Rom. 9:29; Jude 7). The ancient site of the cities is disputed, though they likely were located near the Dead Sea.

Sodomite–Those who imitated the wickedness of Sodom, especially males who had sexual intercourse with other males (1 Cor.

6:9; 1 Tim. 1:10 NRSV [NIV: "those practicing homosexuality"]). Initially, the term "sodomite" referred to a citizen of the town of Sodom. Sodom was, along with Gomorrah, one of the cities near the Dead Sea destroyed by God for its wickedness (Gen. 19:24).

Solomon–As the son and successor to David, Solomon reigned forty years over the united kingdom of Israel (c. 971–931 BC). Extensive accounts of his reign are provided in 1 Kings 1–11; 2 Chron. 1–9. Solomon, the second son born to Bathsheba, was marked out at birth as "loved by the Lord" (2 Sam. 12:24–25 NIV mg.). He succeeded his father as king, even though he was not David's oldest living son (1 Kings 2). The building of the temple is the centerpiece of the biblical accounts of Solomon's reign.

It is common to divide Solomon's reign into two unequal halves (1 Kings 1–10; 11), with Solomon only becoming apostate due to the influence of foreign wives (1 Kings 11).

The immediate dissolution of the united kingdom after Solomon's death cannot be simply blamed on the inept handling of the crisis by his son Rehoboam (1 Kings 12). Solomon's policies put an inordinate economic burden on the North (4:7–19). His conscription of forced labor (5:13–18) and sale of twenty cities in Galilee to Hiram of Tyre (9:10–14) were resented. The raising up of a series of adversaries, including Jeroboam, was a divine judgment (11:9–13). The prophet Ahijah favored Jeroboam (11:29–39). The prophet Shemaiah prevented Rehoboam's military invasion of the north (12:21–24). The northern tribes wanted relief from Solomon's harsh policies ("Your father put a heavy yoke on us" [12:4]). Rehoboam was unwilling (or unable?) to compromise. Solomon's death is reported in 1 Kings 11:41–43, but frequent allusions to him follow (e.g., 12:2, 4, 6, 9), for it was his policies that precipitated the split.

Solomon's Porch–A magnificent roofed structure, two hundred yards long, that stood behind the east wall of Herod's temple, similar to a Greek stoa. Jesus taught here during the Feast of Dedication (John 10:22–23). It was also known as Solomon's Colonnade (NIV) or Portico (NRSV) because of the many columns that made up its architecture and the erroneous belief that it dated from the time of Solomon. It figured prominently in the gatherings of the early church (Acts 3:11; 5:12).

Song of Songs, Book of–By its title, Song of Songs claims to be the most sublime song of all. The history of its interpretation also reveals that it may be the most misunderstood song as well. The reader of this book is dazzled by its intensity and honest expression of desire for intimate relationship. No wonder that early theologians who thought that the body was only a temporary casing for the all-important spirit felt that this book could not be talking about what it appeared to be talking about. Thus, for example, when the woman describes the man as a sachet of myrrh lodged between her breasts (1:13), this had to be a reference to Christ spanning the OT and the NT (so Cyril of Alexandria). But over time this book could not be suppressed by such interpretive strategies. Today most scholars and a majority of readers readily acknowledge that Song of Songs is love poetry that articulates human desires as well as our joys and worries.

Song of Songs celebrates love between a man and a woman. It reminds the people of God that intimate relationship is a divine gift that should be enjoyed. Although joy is indeed the dominant note of the book, the reader is warned that love is a powerful emotion that has its disappointments (so begins the poem in 5:2–6:3). Accordingly, the woman makes sure that the young girls who are watching and looking at her understand that it is important not to hurry love (2:7; 3:5; 8:4).

But we must not read Song of Songs in isolation from the rest of the canon. This book describes the man and the woman in the garden as naked and enjoying each other. How can the reader not think of the garden of Eden? God created a man and a woman and established marriage as a source of mutual joy (Gen. 2:23–25). The next chapter, however, narrates the fall, where the rebellion against God results in alienation not only between God and Adam and Eve, but also between Adam and Eve. Their estrangement results in their efforts to cover themselves from the gaze of the other and their ejection from the garden. The poems of Song of Songs, then, may be seen as the story of the "already but not yet" redemption of sexuality.

Last, the broader canon frequently uses marriage as a metaphor of the relationship between God and his creatures (e.g., Ezek. 16; 23; Hos. 1–3). In other words, the more we learn about intimate marital relationships, the more we learn about our intimate relationship with God. Thus, Song of Songs may be read in a way that deepens our understanding of God and his love toward his people (cf. Eph. 5:21–33).

Son of God–In the OT, heavenly beings or angels are sometimes referred to as "sons of God" (Gen. 6:2; Job 1:6; 2:1; 38:7; Pss. 82:6; 89:6). The more important background for the NT, however, is the use of the term with reference to the nation Israel and the messianic king from David's line. Israel was God's son by virtue of God's unique calling, deliverance, and protection. Hosea 11:1 reads, "When Israel was a child, I loved him, and out of Egypt I called my son." Similar references to God as the father of his people appear throughout the OT (Exod. 4:22; Num. 11:12; Deut. 14:1; 32:5, 19; Isa. 43:6; 45:11; Jer. 3:4, 19; 31:9, 20; Hos. 2:1). The king from the line of David is referred to as the son of God by virtue of his special relationship to God and his representative role among the people. In the Davidic covenant, God promises David concerning his descendant, "I will be his father, and he will be my son" (2 Sam. 7:14; cf. Pss. 2:7; 89:26). Later Judaism appears to have taken up these passages and identified the coming Messiah as the "son of God."

Son of Man–In the OT, the phrase "son of man" usually refers to humanity in general or to a specific individual. In Ezekiel, for instance, God addresses the prophet himself as "son of man," possibly indicating his human status compared with God or, alternatively, highlighting his unique status as God's prophet in contrast with the rest of humanity.

One of the most crucial OT "son of man" texts is Dan. 7 because of its influence on the "Son of Man" in the Gospel tradition. The first half of the chapter records Daniel's vision (7:1–14), while the second half contains its interpretation (7:15–27). In the vision Daniel sees "one like a son of man, coming with the clouds of heaven" (7:13). This exalted figure contrasts with the first three beasts, which are "like a lion" (7:4), "like a bear" (7:5), and "like a leopard" (7:6). The fourth beast is so gruesome that it defies comparison with any species of the animal kingdom (7:7). Many agree that the beasts likely refer to ancient world empires; however, the referent of "one like a son of man" has given rise to much debate. The figure may refer to earthly Israel, since at this figure's vindication he is endowed with authority and glory. This is precisely what "the holy people of the Most High" receive in verse 27. In this way, the "one like a son of man" is a symbol for the persecuted, earthly saints. Alternatively, the exalted figure could be a heavenly being such as the archangel Gabriel (9:21) or Michael (10:13; 12:1). Here "one like a son of man" is the heavenly counterpart and leader of suffering Israel and fights a cosmic battle on its behalf.

In the NT the term "Son of Man" occurs mostly in the Gospels and, with the exception of John 12:34 (where the crowd quotes Jesus), is uttered exclusively by Jesus himself. Unlike in Daniel, the epithet occurs in the Gospels with the definite article, likely indicating that the Son of Man was a known figure. In first-century Judaism many Jews believed that the Son of Man would return at the end as savior and judge. The OT provides the most helpful background for understanding the Son of Man in the Gospels.

The Son of Man sayings in the Gospels fall within three categories: earthly, suffering-resurrection, and future-vindication sayings. Starting with the earthly sayings, in Mark 2:10, for example, the Son of Man has "authority on earth to forgive sins," and in 2:28 he exercises dominion over the Sabbath. Although in Daniel the Son of Man does not receive such authority until his appearance in Yahweh's presence at his vindication, the Son of Man in the Gospels exercises such authority during his earthly ministry. Jesus also predicts that the Son of Man will suffer, die, and be raised again. In Mark, these suffering-resurrection predictions occur three times (8:31; 9:31; 10:33–34). Echoing Dan. 7, this plight of Jesus recalls the suffering of the holy ones caused by the little horn (v. 21). If the "one like a son of man" represents the holy ones in their vindication, then it is reasonable that he does so in their suffering as well; however, the text of Daniel is silent on this point. Finally, the clearest reference to Dan. 7 occurs in the future-vindication sayings. In Mark 13:26; 14:62 the Son of Man comes with/on the clouds, which points to his vindication over the Sanhedrin, the dominant adversaries of Jesus in Mark. Matthew appears to develop even more than Mark the judicial responsibilities of the Son of Man (Matt. 13:41–43; 25:31–33). Meanwhile, in Luke the church must stay alert and be prepared for the return of the Son of Man (12:39–40; 17:22–37; 21:34–36).

Finally, the Son of Man in Revelation is in the heavenly temple functioning as both judge and caretaker of the seven churches (Rev. 1:12–20) and reaps the saints while "seated on the cloud" (14:14–16).

Sons of God–*See* Son of God.

Sop–The KJV uses "sop" to refer to a thin bit or morsel of bread torn from a flat loaf and dipped into a common dish of meat with broth (cf. Ruth 2:14). At his last supper with his disciples, Jesus dipped a piece of bread in the common or central dish of the Passover platter and handed it to Judas Iscariot, revealing Jesus' unwillingness to treat his betrayer as an enemy and exposing Judas's hardness of heart (John 13:26–30).

Sorek, Valley of–One of four major valleys draining water runoff from the central hill country watershed westward through the Shephelah to the coastal plains (the other three are Aijalon, Elah, and Guvrin). The ridges between these valleys provide the approach routes to the hill country from the coast. The Philistine city Timnah (the city of Samson's first love escapade with a Philistine woman [Judg. 14]) lay downstream in the Valley of Sorek. It also was the location of Samson's debacle at Delilah's bosom (Judg. 16:4–30). The cow-drawn cart returning the ark of the covenant from Philistine captivity came up the Valley of Sorek from Ekron to Beth Shemesh (1 Sam. 6:10–12).

Sosipater–A "fellow Jew" present with Paul during his writing of his letter to the Romans and whose greetings are conveyed to the church at Rome (Rom. 16:21). He perhaps is the same person as Sopater, who accompanied Paul on his third missionary journey (Acts 20:4).

Sosthenes–**(1)** A synagogue ruler (leader) in Corinth when "the Jews" instigated legal action against Paul (Acts 18:12–17). Gallio, proconsul of Corinth, dismissed it as an internal Jewish matter. "The crowd" (probably the Jews, but perhaps the Greeks) shamed Sosthenes by publicly beating him, apparently believing that he was responsible for their loss (18:17); perhaps he selected or presented the charges. Apparently, Gallio agreed that Sosthenes' actions were shameful, since he did not intervene. **(2)** The cosender of 1 Corinthians (1:1). The fact that Paul names Sosthenes as cosender indicates that he had some role in the letter's composition. It is possible, but not proven, that this is the same person as in Acts 18:12–17. If so, he had become a believer in Jesus Christ, and perhaps he went to Ephesus from Corinth to visit Paul with Stephanas, Fortunatus, and Achaicus (see 1 Cor. 16:17–18).

Soul–The way the word "soul" is used in English does not align well with any single Hebrew or Greek word in the Bible. It is widely accepted that the biblical view (both OT and NT) of humanity does not recognize sharp boundaries between body and soul (bipartite anthropology) or between body, soul, and spirit (tripartite). The human being is, according to biblical teaching, a psychosomatic unity.

Sovereignty of God–Broadly speaking, the Bible describes sovereignty as God's divine authority to rule his creation in general and Israel in particular. He is the Lord of all creation and the King of Israel. He is almighty (sovereign) to accomplish his purpose, which is to restore his kingdom on earth through Christ (1 Tim. 6:14–15), to whom he now has given all authority (Matt. 28:18). Rather than an aloof divinity of perfection, God is presented in the Bible as intensely personal and superbly engaged in the affairs of his creation. He remains outside his creation as its supreme, infinite Creator (transcendence), while allowing his love to instruct both his justice and his power (immanence). He creates not because the necessity of his perfection requires it but rather out of sovereign freedom and love. He is both protective of his position as Lord of creation and concerned for his people's welfare (Deut. 6:13–19). His sovereignty displays his moral character (Exod. 15:11–18) while demanding reciprocal love and relational obedience from his people.

Sower–A farmer or one who plants seeds by scattering them. A very common profession in biblical times, it was frequently used metaphorically to refer to the natural rewards of living lives of holiness or sin, or of reaping what one sows (Prov. 11:18; 2 Cor. 9:6; Gal. 6:7). Jesus contrasted the "sower" with the "reaper" to illustrate different responsibilities that individuals have in participating in God's "harvest" (John 4:36). He also used this example in one of his most famous parables to illustrate various responses of people to the word of God (Matt. 13:1–9 pars.).

Spain–A country on the Iberian Peninsula in southwestern Europe that was conquered by the Romans about 200 BC. Paul expressed a desire to evangelize the area before his death (Rom. 15:24, 28), though there is considerable debate as to whether he fulfilled this desire.

Span–*See* Weights and Measures.

Spices–Spices were in high demand during the biblical period, making food and living more enjoyable, especially for the wealthy. They were used in food (implicit in Ezek. 24:10) and drink (Song 8:2). The spice trade forged the earliest routes from northern India to Sumer, Akkad, and Egypt (cf. Gen. 37:25). Trade led to cultural exchange and, in the time of Solomon, to national wealth from tolls collected on such shipments. Ezekiel 27:22 and Rev. 18:13 show the value associated with this trade, and 2 Kings 20:13 places spices among King Hezekiah's "treasures." The sensual luxury of spices could be erotic (e.g., Esther 2:12; Song 5:1; 6:2; 8:14); indeed, Song of Songs, though short, uses the word *bosem* (NIV: "spice, perfume, fragrance") more than any other book in the OT. Some spices, such as frankincense, were important to worship rituals in ancient Israel, being used in offerings (Lev. 24:7) and in the anointing oil and incense (Exod. 25:6; 30:22–38). Producing the right mixtures required skilled individuals (Exod. 30:25; 1 Chron. 9:29–30).

Spirit–In the world of the Bible, a person was viewed as a unity of being with the pervading breath and thus imprint of the loving and holy God. The divine-human relationship consequently is portrayed in the Bible as predominantly spiritual in nature. God is spirit, and humankind may communicate with him in the spiritual realm. The ancients believed in an invisible world of spirits that held most, if not all, reasons for natural events and human actions in the visible world.

The OT writers used the common Hebrew word *ruakh* ("wind" or "breath") to describe force and even life from the God of the universe. In its most revealing first instance, God's *ruakh* hovered above the waters of the uncreated world (Gen. 1:2). In the next chapter of Genesis a companion word, *neshamah* ("breath"), is used as God breathed into Adam's nostrils "the breath of life" (2:7). God thus breathed his own image into the first human being. Humankind's moral obligations in the remainder of the Bible rest on this breathing act of God.

The OT authors often employ *ruakh* simply to denote air in motion or breath from a person's mouth. However, special instances of the use of *ruakh* include references to the very life of a person (Gen. 7:22; Ps. 104:29), an attitude or emotion (Gen. 41:8; Num. 14:24; Ps. 77:3), the negative traits of pride or temper (Ps. 76:12), a generally good disposition (Prov. 11:13; 18:14), the seat of conversion (Ezek. 18:31; 36:26), and determination given by God (2 Chron. 36:22; Hag. 1:14).

The NT authors used the Greek term *pneuma* to convey the concept of spirit. In the world of the NT, the human spirit was understood as the divine part of human reality as distinct from the material realm. The spirit appears conscious and capable of rejoicing (Luke 1:47). Jesus was described by Luke as growing and becoming "strong in spirit" (1:80). In "spirit" Jesus "knew" what certain teachers of the law were thinking in their hearts (Mark 2:8). Likewise, Jesus "was deeply moved in spirit and troubled" at the sickness of a loved one (John 11:33). At the end of his life, Jesus gave up his spirit (John 19:30).

According to Jesus, the spirit is the place of God's new covenant work of conversion and worship (John 3:5; 4:24). He declared the human spirit's dependence on God and ascribed great virtue to those people who were "poor in spirit" (Matt. 5:3).

Human beings who were possessed by an evil spirit were devalued in Mediterranean society. In various places in the Synoptic Gospels and the book of Acts, either Jesus or the disciples were involved in exorcisms of such spirits (Matt. 8:28–33; Mark 1:21–28; 7:24–30; 9:14–29; 5:1–20; 9:17–29; Luke 8:26–33; 9:37–42; Acts 5:16).

The apostle Paul pointed to the spirit as the seat of conversion (Rom. 7:6; 1 Cor. 5:5). He described believers as facing a struggle between flesh and spirit in regard to living a sanctified life (Rom. 8:2–17; Gal. 5:16–17). A contradiction seems apparent in Pauline thinking as he appears to embrace Greek dualistic understanding of body (flesh) and spirit while likewise commanding that "spirit, soul and body be kept blameless" (1 Thess. 5:23). However, the Christian struggle between flesh and Spirit (the Holy Spirit) centers around the believer's body being dead because of sin but the spirit being alive because of the crucified and resurrected Christ (Rom. 8:10). Believers therefore are encouraged to lead a holistic life, lived in the Spirit.

Spirit, Holy–God's Spirit is described in the opening chapters of Genesis as partaking in creation. His Spirit likewise is seen throughout the OT as an agent in establishing God's people as a nation and a people of his own. Leaders of Israel were chosen and possessed by the Spirit to assist in leading the people into God's will (Deut. 34:9; Judg. 6:34; 15:14; 1 Sam. 11:6; 16:23). Typically, the moment the Spirit of God descended on a leader, miraculous fortitude, wisdom, and power resulted. The Spirit also provided whatever was needed for God's prophets—courage, inspiration, and miracles (Num. 11:25; 1 Sam. 10:10; Isa. 11:2; Ezek. 2:2; Dan. 4:8; Joel 2:28). The office of prophet included prophesying both in the king's court and among the people of the land. As the Spirit came on a prophet of God, the prophet would correct the king's and others' behavior and at times foretell the future or the outcome of possible decisions.

In the Synoptic Gospels, the Holy Spirit functions in much the same way as in the OT. One such function appears in Luke's birth narrative when the angel answers Mary's question as to how she might conceive while a virgin (Luke 1:34): "The Holy Spirit will come on you, and the power of the Most High will overshadow you" (1:35). The Greek verb translated "will overshadow you" is used in the LXX to describe God's protective nature (Pss. 91:4; 140:7). Likewise, the coming of God's Spirit presented empowerment (Acts 1:8). Thus, Mary received both divine empowerment and protection. As the birth narrative continues, Luke records how other characters in the story, Elizabeth and Zechariah, were filled with the Spirit when Mary came to visit while pregnant with Jesus and when John the Baptist, the forerunner of the Messiah, was born (1:41, 67). The evangelists record the Spirit descending on Jesus at the time of his baptism (Matt. 3:16; Mark 1:10; Luke 3:22; John 1:32–34) and describe him as full of the Spirit when he was led by the Spirit into the desert (Luke 4:1). Finally, in John's Gospel the Spirit is the promised comforter whom Jesus will give to his followers. He will testify about Christ (John 15:26).

In the new covenant the Spirit-possession of the OT gave way to believers' reception of the Spirit at conversion. In Acts the Holy Spirit is presented as instrumental in carrying out the mission of the church, providing power and signs as well as moving and motivating missionaries. The apostle Paul attributes to the Holy Spirit the function of imbuing believers and the church with an assortment of virtues (Gal. 5:22), gifts (Rom. 12:7–8; 1 Cor. 12:1–11), and ministers (Eph. 4:7–13). He uses the idea of life in the Spirit as a point of contrast with life in the flesh. In John's letters the Spirit is described as providing discernment of truth (1 John 4:6).

Spiritual Gifts–The Christian faith is the faith of the new covenant promised to Israel's prophets of old (Jer. 31:31–34; Ezek. 36:26–27; Joel 2:28–29). As Jesus came to fulfill these prophecies about God's renewed presence among his people (Mark 1:14–15), powerful acts of God's Spirit gave visible expressions to the presence of God's kingdom (Matt. 12:28; Luke 7:22). According to the NT, God established the new covenant by an outpouring of his Spirit (Acts 2:1–21) that empowered the church to continue the ministry of Jesus. Paul expresses the centrality of this experience when he states that unless a person evidences the presence of God's Spirit, such an individual does not belong to Christ (Rom. 8:9). Put differently, the Spirit seals believers' relationships with Christ (2 Cor. 1:22; Eph. 4:30), making them a part of his body, the church (1 Cor. 12).

Spiritual gifts are understood in light of this. They are seen as the Spirit's enablement of Christians to express their new covenant relationship with God. The Spirit gifts all Christians, empowering them to function as serving members of Christ's body and thereby fulfilling their purpose in God's plan. Divine gifts are therefore indispensable to the Christian life, which without them would fail to bear witness to its supernatural origin.

Although the NT mentions or alludes to individual gifts in various places, Paul gives three lists (Rom. 12:6–8; 1 Cor. 12:4–11, 28–30; Eph. 4:7, 11). They are examples of how the Spirit manifests himself in the Christian community (1 Cor. 12:7). As Spirit manifestations, *charismata* are a permanent and necessary endowment for the church. The individual gifts may vary over time and between specific congregations, but it would be unthinkable for Paul that *charismata* as such would cease. Since their purpose is to empower the church to evidence the presence of God's kingdom, they will not cease until the end, when the kingdom becomes visible to all (1 Cor. 13:8–10).

Stachys–A believer at the church in Rome whom Paul greets as "my dear friend" (Rom. 16:9).

S

Stars–The word "star" is used in the Bible to refer to any bright point of light in the night sky; no linguistic distinction is made between stars and planets (cf. 2 Pet. 1:19; Rev. 2:28; 22:16).

Stars often are used to illustrate the scope of God's promises (Gen. 15:5; 22:17; 26:4; Deut. 10:22). They were used throughout the ancient Near East to represent the king, an association also evident in the OT (Num. 24:17; Isa. 14:12). Stars also were named, and some were objects of worship, a practice condemned in Israel (Amos 5:26; cf. Deut. 4:19). Stars were subject to study by foreign sages who sought to predict the future based on their observations, although their efficacy is denied (Isa. 47:13). Nonetheless, the arrival of the Messiah is heralded by a star in the service of its creator (Matt. 2:2–10). The falling (Rev. 6:13) and the darkening (Joel 2:10; 3:15) of stars are used to depict the coming of the day of the Lord in judgment.

Stephanas–The head of a household in Corinth whose members were the first converts in the region of Achaia (1 Cor. 16:15). They were baptized by Paul (1:16) and became ministers to the Christians in Corinth. They gave themselves to the advance of the gospel and labored diligently (16:16). Paul encouraged the Corinthian Christians to submit to these Christian laborers, including Stephanas himself (16:16, 18). He, along with Fortunatus and Achaicus, probably brought a letter from the Corinthians to Paul (7:1) and may also have carried the letter that we know as 1 Corinthians back to Corinth. The three men refreshed the spirits of both Paul and the congregation there (16:17–18).

Stephen–Because of rapid growth in the early church, the apostles found it necessary to delegate tasks to others. Stephen was first named and chosen by the Jerusalem church as one of seven men whose task was to help distribute food equitably among the widows, especially the Greek-speaking widows, of the church. He is described as "a man full of faith and of the Holy Spirit" (Acts 6:5) and "full of God's grace and power" (6:8).

Stephen became the first known Christian martyr after a strange trial in front of the Sanhedrin. His defense focused on a review of Jewish history, climaxing in the claim that Israel had always opposed and persecuted God's messengers and now had betrayed and murdered their own Messiah, "the Righteous One" (Acts 7:51–53). The Sanhedrin responded in rage and took Stephen out of the city to stone him. As he was being stoned to death, Stephen saw Jesus standing at the right hand of God, asked him to receive his spirit, and then sought forgiveness for his killers in a prayer similar to one that Jesus prayed (Acts 7:59–60; cf. Luke 23:24).

The persecution resulting from Stephen's stoning scattered the Jerusalem church, providing further opportunities for evangelism. Saul of Tarsus is first mentioned in this account, as witnessing and approving Stephen's death (Acts 7:58; 8:1).

Stewardship–The management of available resources in the recognition that God is the owner and provider of all things. The Bible is clear that God is the maker and owner of all things. The psalmist wrote, "The earth is the Lord's, and everything in it, the world, and all who live in it" (Ps. 24:1). God told Job, "Everything under heaven belongs to me" (Job 41:11). In the same way, God says, "The silver is mine and the gold is mine" (Hag. 2:8). Stewardship is based upon the principle that God is the maker of all things. Since God is the creator and owner of all things, God's followers are charged with managing what he has given.

Stocks–A device used for punishment. Stocks are large wooden frames with holes for a person's arms and legs, which are clamped, thus immobilizing the prisoner. Jeremiah was put into stocks (Jer. 20:2–3; 29:26), and Job uses stocks (shackles) to symbolize suffering (Job 13:27; 33:11). In NT times, Roman stocks had a number of holes designed to force the prisoner's legs apart. Paul and Silas were imprisoned and put in stocks (Acts 16:24–26).

Stone–Rocks and stones were found naturally on the ground (Job 8:17; Ps. 91:12; Isa. 5:2; Mark 5:5; Luke 3:8). They could be heaped or piled up as a sign of disgrace (Josh. 7:26; 8:29; 2 Sam. 18:17), as a marker or memorial (Gen. 31:46–50), or as an altar (Exod. 20:25). A single rock or stone could also be used as a place marker (Gen. 28:22; 35:14, 20;

1 Sam. 7:12), especially standing stones (Deut. 27:2–8; Josh. 4:3–9). Large stones could also be used to cover a well (Gen. 29:2–3) or to seal a cave or tomb, such as at the tombs of Lazarus (John 11:38–39) and of Jesus (Matt. 27:60; Mark 16:3–4).

Stone was used as a construction material, particularly for the temple (1 Kings 5:15–18; 1 Chron. 2:22; Ezra 5:8; Hag. 2:15; Mark 13:1–2). Stone was used in a building's foundation and for the cornerstone or capstone (1 Kings 5:17; Jer. 51:26; Isa. 28:16), as well as for the walls (Hab. 2:11). Psalm 118:22 refers metaphorically to the stone rejected by the builders becoming the cornerstone. In the NT, this is interpreted as referring to Jesus (Matt. 21:42; Mark 12:10; Luke 20:17; Acts 4:11; 1 Pet. 2:7; cf. Eph. 2:20). Stone could also function as a writing material (Josh. 8:32), such as the tablets on which the Ten Commandments were inscribed (Exod. 24:12; Deut. 9:9–11; 1 Kings 8:9; cf. 2 Cor. 3:3, 7). Stone was also carved, although at Sinai the Israelites are instructed not to use cut or "dressed" stones when constructing an altar (Exod. 20:25; cf. Josh. 8:31). The phrase "carved stone" refers specifically to idols, since stone was one material used for crafting false gods (Lev. 26:1; cf. Deut. 4:28; 29:17; 2 Kings 19:18; Isa. 37:19; Rev. 9:20); the term "stone" itself can therefore be used to refer to an idol, especially in the phrase "wood and stone" (Jer. 3:9; Ezek. 20:32).

Stones were used as a weapon or instrument of destruction, whether thrown by hand (Num. 35:17, 23) or flung with a sling (Judg. 20:16; 1 Sam. 17:40, 49–50; Prov. 26:8). The verb "to stone" refers to the throwing of stones at an individual, which typically functioned as an official manner of execution (Exod. 19:13; 21:28–29; Deut. 21:20–21; 1 Kings 21:13–15; John 8:5; Acts 7:58–59), although it was at times the action of an angry crowd (Exod. 17:4; 1 Kings 12:18; cf. John 8:59).

The phrases "precious stones" and "costly stones" refer to gems (2 Sam. 12:30; Esther 1:6; Isa. 54:12; 1 Cor. 3:12). Gems were used as a display of wealth or honor (1 Kings 10:2, 10–11; 2 Chron. 32:27; Ezek. 27:22) and for decoration (1 Chron. 3:6; Rev. 17:4; 18:16). The two stones on the high priest's ephod and the twelve precious stones on his breastpiece represented the twelve tribes (Exod. 25:7; 28:9–12, 17–21), a symbolism echoed in the twelve types of precious stones adorning the foundations of the new Jerusalem (Rev. 21:19–20).

Rocks and stones are used often in metaphors or similes (e.g., hard as a rock, still as a stone). They can represent something that is common (1 Kings 10:27; Job 5:23; Matt. 3:9; 4:3), strong (Job 6:12), hard (Job 38:30; 41:24), heavy (Exod. 15:5; Prov. 27:3), motionless (Exod. 15:16), or immovable (Zech. 12:3). A "heart of stone" describes coldheartedness (Ezek. 11:19; 36:26). A "stumbling stone," which is literally a stone that causes one to stumble (Isa. 8:14), is used in the NT as a metaphor for an obstacle to faith in Jesus (Rom. 9:32–33; 1 Pet. 2:8).

Straight Street–After Saul was blinded by light from heaven, he stayed in the house of Judas on Straight Street in Damascus (Acts 9:3–9, 11). There Ananias, sent by the risen Christ, laid his hands on Saul, who regained his sight (9:10–18). The general course of Straight Street is still identifiable in modern Damascus.

Stumbling Block–In the OT, this image is used to convey the concept of a "stumbling block" in a literal (Lev. 19:14) or figurative (Jer. 6:21) sense. In the NT, the image is used as a messianic reference—Christ as a stumbling block (Rom. 9:32–33; 1 Cor. 1:23; 1 Pet. 2:8). This rendition of messianic expectation plays off the Isaianic presentation of God as a stumbling block to his faithless people. The NT Greek words that are translated as "stumbling block" (*skandalon*) or "to cause to stumble" (*skandalizō*) have either a christological or a moral application.

Suffering–While in the OT suffering is regularly an indication of divine displeasure (Lev. 26:16–36; Deut. 28:20–68; Ps. 44:10–12; Isa. 1:25; cf. Heb. 10:26–31), in the NT it becomes the means by which blessing comes to humanity.

The Bible often shows that sinfulness results in suffering (Gen. 2:17; 6:5–7; Exod. 32:33; 2 Sam. 12:13–18; Rom. 1:18; 1 Cor. 11:27–30). Job's friends mistakenly assume that he has suffered because of disobedience (Job 4:7–9; 8:3–4, 20; 11:6). Job passionately defends himself (12:4; 23:10), and in the final chapter of the book God commends Job and condemns his friends for their accusations (42:7–8; cf. 1:1, 22; 2:10). The writer makes clear that suffering is not necessarily evidence of sinfulness. Like Job's friends, Jesus' disciples assume that blindness is an indication of sinfulness (John 9:1–2). Jesus rejects this simplistic notion of retributive suffering (John 9:3, 6–7; cf. Luke 13:1–5).

The NT writers reveal that Jesus' suffering was prophesied in the OT (Mark 9:12; 14:21; Luke 18:31–32; 24:46; Acts 3:18; 17:3; 26:22–23; 1 Pet. 1:11; referring to OT texts such as Ps. 22; Isa. 52:13–53:12; Zech. 13:7). The Lord Jesus is presented as the answer to human suffering: (1) Through the incarnation, God's Son personally experienced human suffering (Phil. 2:6–8; Heb. 2:9; 5:8). (2) Through his suffering, Christ paid the price for sin (Rom. 4:25; 3:25–26), so that believers are set free from sin (Rom. 6:6, 18, 22) and helped in temptation (Heb. 2:18). (3) Christ Jesus intercedes for his suffering followers (Rom. 8:34–35). (4) Christ is the example in suffering (1 Pet. 2:21; 4:1; cf. Phil. 3:10; 2 Cor. 1:5; 4:10; 1 Pet. 4:13), and though he died once for sins (Heb. 10:12), he continues to suffer as his church suffers (Acts 9:4–5). (5) Christ provides hope of resurrection (Rom. 6:5; 1 Cor. 15:20–26; Phil. 3:10–11) and a future life without suffering or death (Rev. 21:4).

The NT writers repeatedly mention the benefits of suffering, for it has become part of God's work of redemption. The suffering of believers accompanies the proclamation and advancement of the gospel (Acts 5:41–42; 9:15–16; 2 Cor. 4:10–11; 6:2–10; Phil. 1:12, 27–29; 1 Thess. 2:14–16; 2 Tim. 1:8; 4:5) and results in salvation (Matt. 10:22; 2 Cor. 1:6; 1 Thess. 2:16; 2 Tim. 2:10; Heb. 10:39), faith (Heb. 10:32–34, 38–39; 1 Pet. 1:7), the kingdom of God (Acts 14:22), resurrection from the dead (Phil. 3:10–11), and the crown of life (Rev. 2:10). It is an essential part of the development toward Christian maturity (Rom. 5:3–4; 2 Cor. 4:11; Heb. 12:4; James 1:3–4; 1 Pet. 1:7; 4:1).

Suffering is associated with knowing Christ (Phil. 3:10); daily inward renewal (2 Cor. 4:16); purity, understanding, patience, kindness, sincere love, truthful speech, the power of God (2 Cor. 4:4–10); comfort and endurance (2 Cor. 1:6); obedience (Heb. 5:8); blessing (1 Pet. 3:14; 4:14); glory (Rom. 8:17; 2 Cor. 4:17); and joy (Matt. 5:12; Acts 5:41; 2 Cor. 6:10; 12:10; James 1:2; 1 Pet. 1:6; 4:13). Other positive results of Christian suffering include perseverance (Rom. 5:3; James 1:3), character and hope (Rom. 5:4), strength (2 Cor. 12:10), and maturity and completeness (James 1:4). Present suffering is light and momentary when compared to future glory (Matt. 5:10–12; Acts 14:22; Rom. 8:18; 2 Cor. 4:17; Heb. 10:34–36; 1 Pet. 1:5–7; 4:12–13).

Throughout the Bible, believers are instructed to help those who suffer. The OT law provides principles for assisting the poor, the disadvantaged, and the oppressed (Exod. 20:10; 21:2; 23:11; Lev. 19:13, 34; 25:10, 35; Deut. 14:28–29; 15:1–2; 24:19–21). Jesus regularly taught his followers to help the poor (Matt. 5:42; 6:3; 19:21; 25:34–36; Luke 4:18; 12:33; 14:13, 21). It is believers' responsibility to show mercy (Matt. 5:7; 9:13), be generous (Rom. 12:8; 2 Cor. 8:7; 1 Tim. 6:18), mourn with mourners (Rom. 12:15), carry other's burdens (Gal. 6:1–2), and visit prisoners (Matt. 25:36, 43). *See also* Servant of the Lord.

Sun–The sun was worshiped as a god or goddess in all the nations around Israel in OT times, and the polemic against sun worship in Deut. 4:19; 17:3; Jer. 8:2; Job 31:26–28 suggests that sun worship also made inroads into Israel. By way of contrast, the OT attests to the sun's created status (Gen. 1:16) and counts it as subject to God's control (e.g., Josh. 10:12–13).

In the OT, the sun often is associated with and symbolic of life (e.g., Eccles. 7:11; cf. Ps. 58:8) or justice (Ps. 19:6; Job 38:13; Mal. 4:2; cf. 2 Sam. 23:3–4). The darkening of the sun is presented as a sign of judgment heralding the day of the Lord (Isa. 13:10; Ezek. 32:7; Joel 2:10, 31; 3:15; Amos 8:9; Matt. 24:29; Mark 13:24; Rev. 6:12; 9:2), which many associate with the darkness that fell during the crucifixion (Matt. 27:45; Mark 15:33; Luke 23:44).

Superscription–A heading applied to the beginning of some psalms. These superscriptions may refer to people, historical circumstances, musical aspects, or classifications. The precise meaning of many of the terms in the superscriptions is unclear.

Sur Gate–A gate in Jerusalem that provided access to the temple precincts from the royal palace. In Hebrew, *sur* means "to turn aside" or "to depart." "Sur Gate" is used in 2 Kings 11:6, whereas 2 Chron. 23:5 prefers "Foundation Gate." At this gate, the priest Jehoiada stationed soldiers as security during Josiah's coronation.

Susa–Occupied as early as 4000 BC, Susa is about two hundred miles east of Babylon.

The Hebrew name for the city, *shushan*, means "lily," but the name's proper origin is in the similar sounding "Shush," which may be traced to In-Shushinak, the high god of the Elamites. Susa is mentioned in Ezra, Nehemiah, Esther, and Daniel. Nehemiah served at Artaxerxes I's palace at Susa (Neh. 1:1, 11; 2:1). A substantial portion of the book of Esther takes place at Susa. Ezra 4:9–10 reports that people from Susa were deported by the Assyrian king Ashurbanipal, and Dan. 8:2 identifies Susa as the setting of Daniel's vision.

Susa first saw fame as the capital of Elam, from which a number of early texts were recovered, including the law code of Hammurabi. After being destroyed by Ashurbanipal of the Assyrians (c. 640 BC), Susa was rebuilt and eventually rose to its apex in the Persian Empire under Darius (521–486 BC). It served as a capital alongside Persepolis, Ecbatana, and Babylon. After surrendering to Alexander the Great (c. 331 BC), who would soon conquer the entire Persian Empire, Susa remained significant but began a slow decline. Part of its site remains occupied by the city of Shush in the Khuzestan province of Iran.

Susanna–A woman healed by Jesus who supports him and his disciples in their ministry, probably both financially and through service (Luke 8:3).

Swaddling Clothes–Newborn infants were wrapped in strips of cloth to keep them clean and warm and to help their limbs grow properly. Mary displayed her maternal care for the infant Jesus by wrapping him in cloths (Luke 2:7, 12). Ezekiel refers to the practice when speaking of God's care for the rescued Israel (Ezek. 16:1–7).

Swine–Pigs were widely domesticated in the ancient Near East, and in biblical times they probably resembled the wild European boar, which still existed in the forests (Ps. 80:13). These animals would have been brown or gray and much hairier than modern domestic breeds, the boars having tusks and the piglets stripes. In Israel, however, pigs were regarded as one of the most unclean of all creatures, both ritually (Lev. 11:7; Deut. 14:8; Isa. 65:4; 66:3, 17) and physically (2 Pet. 2:22). To associate anything of value with swine subjected it to ridicule and rendered it worthless (Prov. 11:22); it was wasteful and abhorrent (Matt. 7:6). The presence of herds of domesticated pigs became a mark of Gentile territory, and when Jesus once cast out some demons in such an area, he allowed them to enter swine, which promptly drowned themselves in the lake (Mark 5:1–20 pars.). Thus, when the prodigal son in Jesus' parable ends up herding pigs, this represents the most degrading occupation an Israelite could imagine (Luke 15:15–16).

Sychar–A town in Samaria where Jesus asked a Samaritan woman for a drink as she drew water from nearby Jacob's Well (John 4:5). Sychar is commonly identified as the modern village of 'Askar on the shoulder of Mount Ebal and opposite Mount Gerizim. Sychar lies about a mile from ancient Shechem. The region is saturated with underground springs, which make it a convenient stopping place for tired and thirsty travelers (John 4:6). Jacob apparently gave this plot of land to his son Joseph (Gen. 48:22; John 4:5), and eventually it became the most important Samaritan city.

Synagogue–In English, the word "synagogue" refers either to a Jewish congregation or to the place where that congregation meets. Synagogues of the biblical era functioned as both religious and civic centers for the Jewish community.

Since synagogues were institutions with a documented history no earlier than the third century BC, they are not mentioned in the OT. The Greek word from which the English one is derived does appear frequently in the LXX, but always with a general reference to a gathering, assembly, or meeting.

Synagogues frequently were locations of the teaching and healing ministry of Jesus. He began preaching the kingdom of God, teaching, and performing healing miracles in Galilean synagogues (Matt. 4:23; 9:35; 12:9; 13:54; Mark 1:21–29, 39; 3:1; 6:2; Luke 4:15–38, 44; 6:6–11; 13:10–17; John 6:59; 18:20). Later, the apostle Paul customarily initiated his mission work in the local synagogue at each of his destinations (Acts 9:19–20; 13:5, 14–15; 14:1; 17:1, 10, 17; 18:1–8; 19:8).

The last (and, from a twenty-first-century perspective, most controversial) use of the word "synagogue" in Scripture is the difficult phrase "synagogue of Satan" (Rev. 2:9; 3:9), which must be read in its context. This was written in response to the significant persecution in Asia Minor of the churches at Smyrna and Philadelphia by Jews who were in collusion with the Roman authorities. They were falsely accusing Jewish and Gentile Christian believers, creating unspeakable suffering for them. This phrase, intended to encourage Christian perseverance, implies that the churches in view represented true Israel, while their accusers were false Jews.

Synoptic Gospels–In NT studies, "Synoptic" refers to the Gospels of Matthew, Mark, and Luke, which, due to their similarities, can be compared side by side (synoptic = seeing together). Although coined earlier, the term "Synoptic" did not become the commonly used reference to the first three Gospels until the nineteenth century.

Syntyche–One of two Christian women residing in Philippi whom Paul identifies as coworkers in the ministry of the gospel (Phil. 4:2–3). In response to an apparent conflict between her and the other woman, Euodia, Paul exhorts them to live in Christian harmony (Phil. 4:2).

Syracuse–A Greek colony on the eastern coast of Sicily that eventually grew to be a rich and powerful city. Captured by Rome in 212 BC, it later became a Roman colony. After Paul's shipwreck and subsequent three-month stay at Malta, he eventually resumed his voyage to Rome, sailing now upon an Alexandrian ship. The ship stopped at Syracuse for three days before continuing the journey (Acts 28:11–13).

Syria–The Syrian-Arabian Desert is located within the hollow of the Fertile Crescent. "Syria" refers to a west Asian Semitic culture along with its distinct language, Syriac. However, Syria also was known as a province of the Roman Empire. Syrian Antioch became an important center of early Christianity. The city was located on the Old Silk Route, the international trade route along the Mediterranean Sea that extended through central Asia to China.

Syrophoenician–This term occurs only in Mark 7:26 (cf. NIV: "born in Syrian Phoenicia") and designates an inhabitant of Syrophoenicia. Mark 7:26 specifies the woman as a Syrophoenician by lineage and also calls her a "Greek." Matthew 15:22 calls the same woman a "Canaanite" (which corresponds to the Phoenicians' definition but may also be understood as a general term including the early inhabitants of Phoenicia; cf. Num. 13:29) in order to highlight a contrast: this descendant of prototypical idolaters (Deut. 7:1–6; Ezra 9:1) exhibited more faith than most of Israel. In light of the two texts, it seems that the woman was a Greek-speaking member of the Phoenician people, still recognized by Jews as Canaanites.

Syrtis–Two large and dangerously shallow bays of the Mediterranean Sea to the north of Africa, into which the sailors were afraid of being blown by the storm on Paul's trip to Rome (Acts 27:17). The larger is today's Gulf of Sirte (or Sidra) near Libya, and the lesser is today's Gulf of Gabes near Tunisia.

T

Taanach–Taanach has been confidently identified as Tell Ta'annek, located in the Jezreel Valley, five miles southeast of Megiddo. The mound is imposing, covering eleven acres and rising well over one hundred feet above the valley floor.

The king of Taanach was one of many defeated by Joshua, though the city itself was not said to have been taken (Josh. 12:21). While at first associated with Asher and Issachar, Josh. 17:11 and 1 Chron. 7:29 say that eventually it was given to Manasseh, and Josh. 21:25 lists it as a city of Manasseh given to the Levites (along with Gath Rimmon).

During the period of the judges, Taanach was the site of a major battle between forces led by Barak and Deborah and those led by the Canaanite Sisera. The former were victorious, and this led to liberation from Canaanite oppression for a period (Judg. 5:19). During the time of Solomon, Taanach became a capital of one of the administrative districts formed by the king in order to provide supplies one month a year to the court (Baana son of Ahilud was the administrator [1 Kings 4:12]).

Tabernacle, Tent of Meeting–"Tabernacle" in Hebrew (*mishkan*) is a general word for a tent or a dwelling. In the Pentateuch particularly, "tabernacle" most often refers to the special dwelling place of God among the Hebrew people during their wandering through the wilderness. The tabernacle was the abode of God's glory before the building of Solomon's temple in Jerusalem. The detailed description of the tabernacle and its construction composes more than one-third of the book of Exodus (chaps. 25–40), signifying its theological importance to the life of God's people before the forming of the nation-state of Israel.

The detailed command of God to build the tabernacle in Exod. 25–30 is part of a larger dramatic narrative. While Moses is on the mountain of God receiving the instructions for the tabernacle, the Hebrews have embarked on a festival of revelry and worship, offering sacrifices to a golden calf, constructed during Moses' absence (32:1–19). Moses is furious and smashes the tablets of the Ten Commandments on the ground, and yet he returns to the mountain to intercede for the people. God punishes the people with a plague but does not destroy or abandon them completely, for "the Lord, the compassionate and gracious God, slow to anger, abounding in love and faithfulness" (34:6) renews his covenant with the people, and Moses again returns from the mountain with the Ten Commandments (34:27–29). Exodus 35–40 then recounts the careful obedience with which the people adhere to God's command to build the tabernacle, assiduously following the instructions given in Exod. 25–30.

The description of the tabernacle given in the text is of an ornate sanctuary within a tent structure situated at the very center of Israel's camp. The tabernacle thus took the place of the tent of meeting described in Exod. 33:7–11, which was pitched outside the camp. However, the terms "tabernacle" and "tent of meeting" appear to be used synonymously in the Pentateuch after the construction of the tabernacle was completed. According to the text, the dimensions of the tabernacle were as follows: 150 feet long, 75 feet wide, and 7.5 feet high (Exod. 27:18). Around the exterior of the tabernacle was an outer courtyard where an altar for burnt offerings stood at the entrance to the tent of meeting, as well as a basin filled with water for the ritual purifications of the priests. Within the outer enclosure of the tabernacle stood a lampstand, an incense altar, and a table where the bread of the Presence was placed. Within the temple was a second enclosure, the holy of holies, where the ark of the covenant was placed beneath the wings of the golden cherubim.

Tabitha–The Aramaic equivalent of the Greek name "Dorcas" (both mean "gazelle"). A Christian who lived in Joppa, she was well known for her good deeds. She became ill and died, and Peter, having heard the news, came and raised her from the dead (Acts 9:36–42).

T

Table of Nations–The genealogy of Noah's sons in Gen. 10:1–32, which includes not only individuals but also names of places and nations.

Tabor–A mountain in Lower Galilee, southwest of the Sea of Galilee and north of the Hill of Moreh and Mount Gilboa. Tabor's strategic location and ease of fortification led to it becoming a location of military note throughout history, including its fortification by Josephus during the Jewish revolt. In Judg. 4:1–15 Deborah tells Barak to go to Mount Tabor and then to lead an attack from Tabor upon Sisera's men, who are then routed. In Judg. 8:18 Mount Tabor is also mentioned when Gideon confronts and kills Zebah and Zalmunna, two kings of Midian. Hosea uses the phrase "a net spread out on Tabor" to illustrate his judgment against Israel (Hos. 5:1).

Tadmor–A city built in the Syrian Desert between Mari and Damascus. It was fortified by Solomon, probably as part of his control of the important trade routes between Palestine and Mesopotamia (2 Chron. 8:4). The site was renamed "Palmyra" during the Hellenistic period and was destroyed by the Romans in the third century AD.

Tahpanhes–A Hebrew transliteration of an Egyptian place name for an outpost bordering Sinai (see Jer. 2:16; 46:14). After the destruction of Jerusalem, a group of Israelites desired to escape to Tahpanhes. Jeremiah counseled against this, warning that Nebuchadnezzar would eventually reach Tahpanhes, and prophesying that if the people remained in the land, God would grant them mercy. However, the Jews did not listen and fled to Egypt, taking Jeremiah with them. It was in Tahpanhes that Jeremiah finished out his prophetic career (Jer. 42:19; 43:7–9; 44:1). Ezekiel also included this city in his oracle against Egypt (Ezek. 30:18 [NRSV, KJV, ESV: "Tehaphnehes"]).

Talent–*See* Weights and Measures.

Talitha Cumi–The KJV and RSV rendering of Jesus' words in Mark 5:41 to Jairus's daughter. The NIV, following a different manuscript tradition, reads "*Talitha koum.*" The underlying Aramaic phrase, *talyetha' koumi*, literally means "Little girl, get up!" Mark's addition of "I say to you" in his paraphrase accurately conveys the sense of the command. Matthew and Luke also record Jesus' healing of Jairus's daughter (Matt. 9:23–26; Luke 8:49–56), but only Mark includes the Aramaic words that Jesus spoke.

Talmai–King of Geshur (a region in the lower Golan Heights), whose daughter Maakah married David. This marriage sealed a political alliance, but David and Maakah's son Absalom fled to Talmai for refuge after he killed David's firstborn son, Amnon (2 Sam. 3:3; 13:37; 1 Chron. 3:2).

Tamar–**(1)** Judah's daughter-in-law who bore him twin sons, Perez and Zerah, thus carrying on the family of Judah (1 Chron. 2:4). In Gen. 38, Tamar, after being married to Judah's first son, Er, and then his second son, Onan (both killed by God for their wickedness), was to marry Judah's third son, Shelah, according to Israelite custom. Afraid that Shelah too would die, Judah resisted this duty and instructed Tamar to live as a widow at her father's house.

When Tamar saw that she would not be allowed to marry Shelah, she disguised herself as a prostitute and was approached by Judah. Providing her with a pledge, Judah impregnated Tamar. Tamar, when found to be pregnant, was accused of acting unscrupulously. But upon revealing Judah's pledge, Tamar was declared by Judah to be "more righteous than I" (Gen. 38:26). Tamar is mentioned later in Scripture in a blessing (Ruth 4:12) and holds a place in the genealogy of Jesus (Matt. 1:3).

(2) The daughter of King David who was raped by her half brother, Amnon. The violence done to Tamar was later avenged by her brother Absalom, who killed Amnon (2 Sam. 13). **(3)** The beautiful daughter of Absalom (2 Sam. 14:27), perhaps named after her aunt. **(4)** A location on the southeastern boundary of Judah (Ezek. 47:18–19; 48:28). This may be

Hazezon Tamar (Gen. 14:7), which became En Gedi (2 Chron. 20:2).

Tamarisk–A small shrub or tree with tiny leaves and slender branches common in desert regions and useful for shade or wood. Abraham planted a tamarisk tree as a sign of his covenant with Abimelek (Gen. 21:33). Tamarisks were also used as landmarks identifying the locations where Saul and his officials met during his pursuit of David (1 Sam. 22:6) and where the bones of Saul and Jonathan were buried at Jabesh (31:13). Tamarisk fruit was the possible source of the manna that the Israelites ate in the wilderness.

Tarshish–The Hebrew word *tarshish* refers to a precious stone (NIV: "topaz"; Exod. 28:20; Ezek. 1:16). The name of the stone probably comes from its place of origin. "Tarshish" is also used as a name, and is frequently mentioned in the OT. Solomon engaged in trade with Tarshish (1 Kings 10:22 NRSV, NASB; 2 Chron. 9:21 NRSV, NASB), and it is described as a source of precious metals such as gold and silver (Jer. 10:9; Ezek. 27:12). Its location is unknown, but it is associated with islands (Ps. 72:10 NRSV, NASB) and with Jonah's flight by ship from Joppa on the Mediterranean (Jon. 1:3). Both Tartessus in southwest Spain and the island of Sardinia have been suggested as possible sites.

The phrase "ships of Tarshish" (Ps. 48:7; Isa. 23:1) may refer to a fleet originating from Tarshish or more generally to a type of seaworthy merchant vessel. It is thus sometimes translated by the NIV as "trading ships" (1 Kings 10:22; 22:48).

Tarsus–*See* Asia Minor, Cities of.

Tartarus–In Greek and Roman mythology, Tartarus is a place in Hades or the underworld where the wicked are sent for punishment. The name "Tartarus" appears in some English versions of 2 Pet. 2:4 (e.g., HCSB; see NIV mg.) based on a transliteration of the Greek term, but most translations render it as "hell." *See also* Hell.

Tattenai–A Persian governor of the lands east of the Euphrates during the reign of Darius I, as attested by a cuneiform text from 502 BC. In 1 Esdras 6–7, he is called "Sisinnes." Together with Shethar-Bozenai and other officials, Tattenai wrote to Darius to inquire whether the Jews had permission to rebuild their temple (Ezra 5:6–17). Darius ordered not only to allow the Jews to rebuild but also to help provide whatever the priests required (6:1–12). Tattenai and his associates dutifully followed Darius's instructions (6:13).

Tax Collector–In the Roman Empire, tax collectors (KJV: "publicans") were employed to help collect taxes in the provinces. People bid for the job of tax collector, and they were compensated by collecting more than the required tax from the people. Tax collectors were despised by Jews as greedy because of the excessive profits they reaped. They also were counted as traitors because they worked for the Romans. In the NT, tax collectors often are associated with Gentiles and sinners (Matt. 5:46–47; 11:19; 21:32).

Jesus was criticized by the Jewish leaders for eating with "tax collectors and sinners" (Matt. 9:11). Jesus welcomed and taught tax collectors (Luke 5:29; 15:1). Matthew, one of Jesus' disciples, was a tax collector (Matt. 10:3). Zacchaeus was a "chief tax collector," which probably indicates that he was contracted with the Romans to collect taxes over a specific area, and he supervised others who did the actual collecting (Luke 19:2).

Tekoa–A town in the territory of Judah about 7.5 miles south of Bethlehem, perhaps at the modern site of Khirbet et Tuqu'. Tekoa is associated with the Hezronites (1 Chron. 2:24; 4:5), as the son of Hezron (who was Judah's grandson) was the leader, or "father," of Tekoa. Jeremiah 6:1 indicates that it was south of Jerusalem. The Greek translation of Josh. 15:59 may refer to Tekoa in association with Bethlehem. Rehoboam included it in a line of defensive fortifications (2 Chron. 11:6).

Tekoa was the birthplace of Ira, one of David's mighty warriors (2 Sam. 23:26). It is better known as the birthplace of Amos, the shepherd and caretaker of sycamore-fig trees turned prophet to the northern kingdom of Israel (Amos 1:1; 7:14). Tekoa also was the origin of a wise, or skilled, woman whom Joab recruited as part of petitioning David to restore Absalom after he had killed Amnon (2 Sam. 14).

Temple of Jerusalem–*See* Jerusalem Temple.

Ten Commandments–The Ten Commandments are also identified as the Decalogue, meaning the "Ten Words." These commands are part of the Bible's legal literature revealed by God to his people Israel. They are the words of the covenant (Exod. 34:28) and define Yahweh's covenant relationship with Israel. Some biblical laws are conditional and written in the style of case law, which employs an "if . . . then" personalized format (most of Exod. 21:2–22:17; Deut. 21:18–19; 22:6–9; 23:21–25; 24:10–12). Other laws are stated in absolute terms: "you shall . . ." or "you shall not . . ." (Exod. 22:18–23:19). The latter, second-person format characterizes the Ten Commandments (Exod. 20:1–17; Deut. 5:6–21).

The Ten Commandments were revealed at Mount Sinai after the exodus from Egypt and prior to the conquest of the land (Exod. 20:1–17). These laws were restated with some variation to a second generation of Israelites approximately thirty-eight years later in Moab, east of the Jordan River (Deut. 5:1–5). Because the postexodus generation refused to believe God and enter the land, they experienced the wrath of God, which brought their demise over a thirty-eight-year period. God then renewed his covenant with the succeeding generation and made preparations for them to enter the promised land (Deut. 2).

The Ten Commandments are prefaced with a staggering manifestation of God (Exod. 19) that accentuates his awesome character. This theophany revealed the transcendent God, who speaks his word to his people from heaven as the Great King. At this point in redemptive history, Israel was established as an independent nation, and the mediatorial role of Moses was confirmed (Exod. 19:9). The declaration of divine law does not mean the absence of grace. The grace of redemption in the exodus preceded the statement of law at Sinai. In both Exodus and Deuteronomy, the Decalogue is prefaced by God's statement: "I am the Lord your God" (Exod. 20:2; Deut. 5:6) to underscore the importance of relationship.

The Decalogue contains mainly negative commands. There are two positive commands, those enjoining remembrance of the Sabbath (Exod. 20:8; Deut. 5:12) and honor for parents (Exod. 20:12; Deut. 5:16). The commands vary in length, style, and content. Some commands include motivational or explanatory statements. The first four commands of the Decalogue refer to humans' relationship with God, and the remaining six refer to humans' relationships with one another, especially with fellow covenant partners.

Terah–The father of Abram (Abraham), Nahor, and Haran (Gen. 11:24–32). After Haran's death in Ur, Terah and family traveled to the city of Harran, where Terah died at the age of 205. He was a pagan (Josh. 24:2), perhaps a moon worshiper, for his name is related to the Hebrew word for "moon," and Ur and Harran are known ancient centers of moon worship. Abram only moved after his father died (Acts 7:4), suggesting that Abram, though listed first among the sons, was not the oldest son, being only seventy-five at the time (Gen. 12:4).

Teraphim–Teraphim are household idols that varied in size and purpose. Rachel hid them from Laban by sitting on them (Gen. 31:19–35). It is clear that Laban valued them highly, possibly because of their perceived powers of divination (30:27). When David fled from Saul's men, Michal put teraphim in his bed with goats' hair at the head (1 Sam. 19:11–16), indicating substantial size and raising the question as to why David possessed teraphim. The details of both incidents suggest that these objects were viewed by the authors with contempt.

Teraphim were associated with false worship and divination (2 Kings 23:24; Ezek. 21:21; Zech. 10:2). When Samuel condemned Saul's disobedience, he likened teraphim to the sin of divination (1 Sam. 15:23). The Ephraimite Micah's shrine included an ephod and teraphim (Judg. 17:5; 18:14–31). Hosea also linked teraphim with the ephod (Hos. 3:4) in the list of cultic and national icons of which Israel would be deprived.

Tertius–Tertius addresses the Roman Christians directly in Rom. 16:22 as Paul's amanuensis, the one who "wrote down this letter." He is Paul's only named amanuensis. Tertius's Latin name and first-person greeting to the church at Rome suggest that he was one of their number.

Tertullus–A lawyer brought by Ananias and some of the elders to Caesarea to present their case against Paul before the Roman governor Felix (Acts 24:1–8). Tertullus's consistent use of "we" language may indicate that he too was a Jew, although it may reflect his professional technique as the Jews' advocate. In his speech, Tertullus begins by flattering Felix and then goes on to portray Paul as a troublemaker, "stirring up riots among the Jews all over the world" (24:5). Being a public nuisance, a disturber of the peace, and a leader of the sect of the Nazarenes were all serious charges in Roman law. However, Paul's subsequent defense proves these charges to be false (24:10–21).

Tetrarch–The ruler of a fourth part of a realm. At the death of Herod the Great in 4 BC, his kingdom was divided and bequeathed to his three sons. Archelaus, assigned half of the realm (Judea, Idumea, and Samaria), assumed the title of ethnarch. His brothers Herod Antipas and Philip were tetrarchs of Galilee-Perea and Trachonitis/Gaulanitis-Iturea respectively (see Matt. 2:22; Luke 3:1). Herod Agrippa I (Acts 25:13), by the imperial grant of Emperor Claudius, reestablished the kingdom of the Jews in AD 41, thereby terminating tetrarchy in ancient Palestine.

Thaddaeus–One of the twelve apostles (Matt. 10:3; Mark 3:18). Thaddaeus was also called "Judas son of James" (Luke 6:16; Acts 1:13) or "Judas (not Judas Iscariot)," whose only recorded words appear in John 14:22.

Thebes–This town is now modern Luxor in Egypt, about three hundred miles south of Cairo. Second only to Memphis in importance and size, it first emerged as significant around 2000 BC. Known as "the City" and "the city of Amon" (an Egyptian deity), it was sacked by the Assyrians in 663 BC (cf. Nah. 3:8, 10), and further judgment was predicted (Jer. 46:25–26; Ezek. 30:14–16).

Theophilus–The person to whom Luke dedicated both his Gospel and the book of Acts (Luke 1:3; Acts 1:1). The name means "friend of God" or "beloved by God" and was common in the Greco-Roman world. Some have claimed that the name is a symbolic reference to a generic Christian reader, but it is more likely that Luke was addressing his works to a specific individual known to him. The use of the title "most excellent Theophilus" could indicate that he was of high social standing, or it may simply be a greeting that Luke used to indicate respect or admiration.

Thessalonians, First Letter to the–In 1 Thessalonians the apostle Paul writes to the church shortly after his first visit there to commend it for its faith and faithfulness to the Lord and to note its good testimony through the regions of Macedonia, Achaia, and everywhere else. He instructs it as to certain issues in the Christian life, the future of the believers in the assembly who have already died, and the relation of these believers to Christ's coming as they continue to quietly work and wait for him.

Greeting and thanksgiving (1:1–10). As Paul opens the letter, he greets the church and notes his thanksgiving to God for their work and their endurance in the things of Christ (1:2–5). Paul notes that they themselves are now an example to the other churches (1:6–10).

Defense of apostolic actions (2:1–16). Paul notes his apostolic disposition toward the Thessalonians as one of humility as he has taught them the gospel (2:1–12). Paul and his missionary companions do not seek to please human beings, and they do not do what they do for greed, but in fact they work night and day for a living. They have treated the Thessalonians well, insisting that they live in a manner reflective of the kingdom. After accepting the gospel as the word of God (2:13), the Thessalonians have experienced persecution from those who opposed the gospel. These opponents will incur God's wrath (2:14–16).

Separation from the Thessalonians and sending of Timothy (2:17–3:13). In this section, Paul insists that even though he has desired to see the Thessalonians, he has been persistently hindered by Satan (2:17–20). Because of this prolonged absence, Paul had been forced to send Timothy as a messenger. Paul has done this because he had urgently desired to know their spiritual state (3:1–5). When Timothy came back with the report about the faithfulness of the Thessalonians, Paul had rejoiced and given thanks (3:6–10). Paul notes that their longing to see him has been a joyful thing to him, and he is glad to know of their disposition toward him. Paul concludes as he prays for their increased love and holiness (3:11–13).

Holy living and continued work (4:1–12). Paul notes that the Thessalonians have been living ethically, but that he wants to remind them to do so more and more. They are to live their lives in sanctification and honor instead of sexual immorality (4:1–8). They should love one another and continue to live in the quietness and peace of regular work (4:9–12). Though the Lord will soon come, this is no reason to abandon work. Paul instructs them to continue working hard so that they will not be in need as they watch and wait for Christ (a problem continuing into 2 Thessalonians [3:10–11]).

The Lord's return gives the Thessalonians hope (4:13–5:11). In order to correct another misunderstanding about the Lord's coming, Paul turns to the issue of the believer's future hope. Some of the church members had been confused about the destiny of the believers now deceased. Paul instructs them that at the coming of the Lord those who have died will be raised to meet the Lord with the living (4:13–18). This should be a matter of comfort to the believers. As to the time of Christ's coming, Paul notes that it will be sudden and unknown (5:1–2). The unbelievers will be unaware as sudden destruction comes upon them (5:3). But believers, who are sensitive to the life of Christ and his coming, should not be caught off guard when he comes. This expectation should have an impact on the way they live now (5:4–9). In any event, whether the believers are still alive or are deceased in Christ, both will come together in him at his coming (5:10).

Closing comments (5:12–28). In the last section, Paul gives final ethical instructions to the church. The church should highly esteem those in leadership because they are working hard. In a final word about prayer, thanksgiving, and the Holy Spirit's work in the believer, Paul concludes that the believers should shun every form of evil. He instructs that the letter be read to all the believers.

THESSALONIANS, SECOND LETTER TO THE–Paul's second letter to the Thessalonians addresses a church troubled by an overly realized eschatology. Whereas at the time of the first letter the Thessalonians were expecting the imminent return of Christ (1 Thess. 5:6), by the time of the second letter some believed that Christ had already come (2 Thess. 2:2). Because of this, some were being drawn from their work into idleness (2 Thess. 3:6). Paul's purpose, then, was to correct their eschatology, restore them to their tasks, and rebuild their confidence in Christ. He does this both by emphasizing Jesus Christ as Lord (the letter is uniquely consistent in the NT in applying the title "Lord" [Gk. *kyrios*] to Jesus) and by describing two apocalyptic events that must happen before the coming of the Lord Jesus Christ: the great apostasy and the appearance of the man of lawlessness (2 Thess. 2:3). Scholars have noted that Paul most often refers to Jesus as Lord in hortatory and eschatological passages. Indeed, though brief, 2 Thessalonians emphasizes exhortation and eschatology.

THESSALONICA–Founded in 315 BC, the city of Thessalonica is located on the eastern coast of Macedonia, on the western shore of the Aegean Sea. The city was well situated for trade, both as a port for seagoing trade vessels along the Aegean and for land trade along the Via Egnatia. The city is approximately 77 miles from Philippi, also on the Via Egnatia, and 320 miles from Athens in the south of Greece. No doubt the apostle Paul traveled from Asia Minor to Philippi to reach several major cities on this route, going through Amphipolis and Apollonia to come to Thessalonica, where the Via Egnatia then turns westward.

Paul had not been well received by many in the city of Philippi, and after being escorted out of town there, he made his way to Thessalonica (Acts 17:1). As was his custom, he went to the synagogue of the Jews. Paul planted a church here after preaching only a few weeks. Though it is not certain from the account in Acts 17 just how long Paul spent in Thessalonica, the text leaves the impression that his time there was short, cut off due to opposition.

After Paul was ill treated in Thessalonica, he went to Berea. According to Luke, the Jews in Berea were more noble than those in Thessalonica because they were willing to search the Scriptures and test what Paul was saying to them (Acts 17:11). In fact, the Jewish leaders in Thessalonica were so upset by the message of Paul that they followed Paul and company to Berea to stir up trouble there (17:13).

Because his visit had been cut short, Paul was concerned about the spiritual condition of the church. After sending Timothy to check on their welfare, he was elated to find this church walking faithfully.

The two final references in the NT to Thessalonica note that Paul was sent a gift from those in the church of Philippi when he was in Thessalonica (Phil. 4:16), and when Demas abandoned Paul, Demas then went to Thessalonica (2 Tim. 4:10).

THEUDAS–A political agitator, quite likely a messianic pretender, mentioned by the Pharisee Gamaliel in Acts 5:36. At some time prior to AD 6 Theudas gathered a group of four hundred men, but soon he was killed and his followers were dispersed. This may have occurred in the aftermath of Herod the Great's death in 4 BC. The Jewish historian Josephus also mentions a magician named "Theudas," who led a band of followers to the Jordan River sometime in AD 44–46 (*Ant.* 20.97–99). He and many of his supporters were killed by the Romans.

Thomas–One of Jesus' original twelve apostles (Matt. 10:3; Mark 3:18; Luke 6:15), referred to as "Didymus," meaning "twin" (John 11:16; 20:24; 21:2). The infamous title of "Doubting Thomas" comes from his refusal to believe in Jesus' resurrection. Thomas said, "Unless I see the nail marks in his hands and put my finger where the nails were, and put my hand into his side, I will not believe" (John 20:25). A week later the risen Jesus again appeared to the apostles, including Thomas. Thomas's response was "My Lord and my God!" (John 20:28). Despite his previous disbelief in Jesus' resurrection, Thomas was present with the other apostles in the upper room (Acts 1:13).

Three Taverns–The last stop on Paul's recorded trip to Rome (Acts 28:15). Three Taverns lay on the Mediterranean coast of Italy, about twenty-five miles southeast of Rome. Roman Christians traveled down to Three Taverns when they learned of Paul's presence nearby.

Thyatira–*See* Asia Minor, Cities of.

Tiberias–A city founded on the western coast of the Sea of Galilee in AD 20 by Herod Antipas to replace Sepphoris as the new capital of Galilee. It was the administrative center of one of the five toparchies in Galilee. The city was named after the Roman emperor Tiberius, the successor of Augustus. The Gospel of John mentions Tiberias only in passing, noting that people from Tiberias traveled in boats to search for Jesus (John 6:23; cf. references to the Sea of Galilee as the "Sea of Tiberias" in John 6:1; 21:1). Herod built the city on top of a gravesite, rendering it unclean, and he had to compel people to settle there. He included non-Jews, poor people, and former slaves as part of its inhabitants.

Tiberius Caesar–*See* Rome, Roman Empire.

Tibni–The son of Ginath. After the death of King Zimri of Israel, Israel split into two factions, the stronger one supporting Omri for the throne of Israel, the other supporting Tibni (r. 882–878 BC). After four years of struggle, the rivalry ended with Tibni's death (1 Kings 16:21–22).

Tidal–The king of Goyim, one of four kingdoms that raided Canaan during the time of Abraham (Gen. 14:1, 9). After they plundered the region and kidnapped Lot, Abraham successfully defeated them and regained what they had taken. His name has been connected with the name of four Hittite kings (Tudhaliya).

Tiglath-pileser III–The founder of the Neo-Assyrian Empire (r. 744–727 BC), Tiglath-pileser (in the Bible, also known as "Pul"; a variant spelling is Tiglath-pilneser) annexed conquered territories and started the practice of deporting populations to minimize national sentiments of resistance. He took tribute from Menahem (2 Kings 15:19–20), captured the Transjordan and other tribes of Israel (1 Chron. 5:26; 2 Kings 15:29), and conquered Babylon. King Ahaz of Judah appealed to him for help and paid him tribute.

Tigris River–*See* Rivers and Waterways.

Timaeus–The father of the blind beggar Bartimaeus, whom Jesus healed at Jericho (Mark 10:46).

Timon–One of the seven men chosen to help with food distribution in the Jerusalem church (Acts 6:1–6). Tradition suggests that he was among the seventy disciples whom Jesus sent out (cf. Luke 10:1), a bishop of Bostra in Arabia, and a martyr at Basrah.

Timothy–*See* Timothy, First Letter to; Timothy, Second Letter to.

Timothy, First Letter to–First Timothy, along with 2 Timothy and Titus, is known as one of the apostle Paul's Pastoral Epistles. These letters have earned this designation because they were addressed to pastors and deal with particular problems that they were facing in their respective churches. This letter was addressed to Timothy, whom Paul affectionately called "my son," most likely because the apostle had led him to faith in Christ (1:18; cf. 1:2). At Paul's urging, Timothy took on the role of providing leadership to the church in Ephesus (1:3), which had been infiltrated by false teachers (1:3–4). Paul wrote this letter to Timothy, instructing him to rebuke the false teachers in the church and to fight the good fight of faith (1:18). The apostle concisely summarized the major theme of this letter by saying, "I am writing you these instructions so that . . . you will know how people ought to conduct themselves in God's household, which is the church of the living God, the pillar and foundation of the truth" (3:14–15).

T

Timothy, Second Letter to–Paul's second letter to Timothy is one of his three Pastoral Epistles (together with 1 Timothy and Titus). In this letter the apostle reminds Timothy of his call to ministry, encourages him to endure suffering for the sake of the gospel, exhorts him to pursue personal godliness, warns him of false teachers and evil persons, and urges him to give himself completely to the ministry of the word. In short, Paul exhorts his protégé to fulfill his ministry. The overall message of the book can be summed up in Paul's call for Timothy to be a "good soldier of Christ Jesus" (2:3) who fights the "good fight" of faith (4:7). In the benediction, Paul's use of the plural "Grace be with *you* all" indicates that the apostle's words are directed not only to Timothy but also to the whole church (4:22).

Tirhakah–The Egyptian pharaoh (r. 690–664 BC) who aided King Hezekiah's campaign in Judah against the Assyrian king Sennacherib (2 Kings 19:9; Isa. 37:9). His title "king of Cush" reveals his Nubian (Sudanese) roots.

Tithe–An offering of a tenth of the whole. Abram gives Melchizedek a tenth (Gen. 14:20; Heb. 7:2–9), and Jacob promises God a tenth (Gen. 28:22). These occasions reflect a practice already established in patriarchal times.

Under Moses, Israel is to give God a tithe of all its crops, flocks, and herds (Lev. 27:30–32). These tithes are received by the Levites for their sustenance; they in turn tithe from all that they have received (Num. 18:25–32). Deuteronomy specifies a yearly tithe eaten by the worshipers and every three years a storehouse tithe to provide for the Levites and for aliens, the fatherless, and widows (Deut. 14:22–29). Hezekiah (2 Chron. 31:5–8) and, later, Nehemiah (Neh. 10:37–38; 12:44–47; 13:10–13) reestablish this system. Malachi warns against slackness in tithing (Mal. 3:8–10).

Amos uses irony to underline that tithing cannot replace righteousness (Amos 4:4). Similarly, Jesus condemns scribes and Pharisees for neglecting justice, mercy, and faithfulness while tithing meticulously; instead, they should practice all of these (Matt. 23:23; cf. Luke 11:42; 18:11–12).

Titus–*See* Titus, Letter to.

Titus, Caesar–*See* Rome, Roman Empire.

Titus, Letter to–The Letter to Titus, along with 1–2 Timothy, is among the Pastoral Epistles. These three letters from the apostle Paul are his instructions to the young pastors Timothy and Titus.

Paul's greeting and self-identification are more expansive here than in any of his letters except Romans. He emphasizes that his apostleship and ministry lead to godly living, based on the knowledge of truth (1:1–2). Paul has been entrusted to preach by God; he now reinvests that trust in Titus and reminds Titus that his primary job is to establish leadership in the churches of Crete.

Paul lays out guidelines for elders, which focus on ethical living, evidence of leadership qualities, and a vigorous faith that may encourage others (1:6–9). These characteristics are important because the leaders will be required to stand up to many in the church who are rebellious, ruinous, and in need of rebuke (1:10).

The rebellious people on Crete probably are Judaizers, teaching against Paul's instruction and enriching themselves in the process. They are to be rebuked, so as to bring them back into correct doctrine (1:13–14). However, after two rebukes, continuing offenders should be ignored; they are apostate (3:10–11).

The remedy for the false teaching is sound doctrine and holy living, so that the opposition has no valid criticism. Titus must set an example for all with his integrity, seriousness, and soundness of speech (2:7–8). This is made possible by the grace of God, which enables people to live "self-controlled, upright and godly lives in this present age" (2:12). We have been redeemed from wickedness and purified to be a people of God's very own (2:14).

Titus must take complete charge of the church, allowing no one to marginalize him or limit his authority (2:15). In fact, the church needs to submit to all levels of authority in peace and humility (3:1–2). Paul reminds Titus that all were once as rebellious and divisive as the opposition; it is only the kindness and love of God that save and cleanse, changing the rebellious into heirs of eternal life (3:3–7).

Putting emphasis on these thoughts will keep the church focused on godly living, while arguing about minor points will be divisive and worthless. People who do the latter should be marginalized and rejected (3:8–11). This is a closing inclusio from Paul's mention of the knowledge of truth leading to godly living (1:1).

Paul concludes with practical communications to Titus. Zenas and Apollos are likely the ones who brought the letter, and Paul encourages Titus and his church to assist them as a lesson to the church and a blessing for the travelers.

Tobiah–An Ammonite, perhaps governor, who resisted Nehemiah's efforts to rebuild Jerusalem's walls (Neh. 2:10, 19; 6). He and his associates Sanballat and Geshem appealed to the Persian king but ultimately were unsuccessful. Even later, Nehemiah deposed a priest, Eliashib, who was renting rooms at the temple to Tobiah (13:4, 7). Many believe that the Tobiah family mentioned in the Lachish ostraca and even later extrabiblical sources are people connected with his family.

Topheth–Topheth, whose name is associated with the Hebrew word for "spit," was located in the Valley of Ben Hinnom to the immediate southwest of Jerusalem. At times, it served as the city dump, where trash was burned. In the NT period, the valley was known as Gehenna, which was associated with hell. Josiah had destroyed this place because it was the location of the false worship of the foreign god Molek (2 Kings 23:10–11), but the idolatrous worship site must have been rebuilt. In the time of Jeremiah, some Israelites performed child sacrifice in this location, so the prophet announced judgment against them (Jer. 7:30–34; 19:6–15).

Torah–The Hebrew word *torah* most broadly means "teaching" or "instruction." In the OT, *torah* most commonly refers to the collection of teachings divinely revealed to Moses by God. This collection of teachings preserved in the Pentateuch became authoritative and binding, not only for the community of Hebrews wandering in the Sinai Desert, but also for each successive generation with whom the covenant with Yahweh was renewed (Exod. 24; Deut. 4:5–14, 44).

Tower of Babel–A tower whose construction was begun in a town on the plain of Shinar (Gen. 11:1–9), although it is never actually called the "tower of Babel" in the Bible. The name "Babel" (Gen. 11:9) is likely a pun involving the Akkadian word for "gate of god" and the Hebrew word for "confuse." Some scholars believe that "Babel" alludes to the city of Babylon. Most ancient structures described as towers would have been ziggurats, which are terraced pyramids with steps. Ziggurats were designed to be places where the gods could access land, much like a staircase. Interestingly, the builders' plan in Gen. 11:1–9 actually worked, since God did come down into the city; however, they did not anticipate the consequences of their actions. Some commentators have suggested that this story is an etiology explaining the beginning of languages.

Traconitis, Trachonitis–One of the five Roman provinces northeast of the Sea of Galilee, which was the northeastern extent of the kingdom of Herod the Great. The name "Traconitis" refers to the "rough, rocky" topography of this extremely desolate region. It was deeded to Herod the Great on the condition that he control the local bandits. Following Herod's death in 4 BC, Traconitis was passed on to Herod Philip (Luke 3:1), brother of Herod Antipas. It later became a part of the Roman province of Syria.

Transfiguration–The event in which Jesus' inward, hidden glory became visible for his inner circle of disciples (Peter, James, John) to see. The episode is recorded in Matt. 16:28–17:8; Mark 9:1–8; Luke 9:27–36 and is alluded to in 2 Pet. 1:16–21. The Gospel episode may be summarized as follows: Immediately after Peter confessed that Jesus was the Christ, Jesus predicted that some of his disciples would not see death until they tasted of the kingdom of God. Some six days later (Luke rounds it off to eight days [Luke 9:28]), Jesus took Peter, James, and John to a mountaintop (traditionally identified as Mount Tabor, though Mount Hermon may be more likely since it was close to Caesarea Philippi, the place of Peter's confession). There, suddenly, the inward, hidden glory of Jesus shone through his body, and he was seen conversing with Moses and Elijah. Peter wanted his companions to build booths, temporary shelters, to prolong the visit of the three heavenly personages: Moses, the representative of the law; Elijah, the representative of the prophets; and Jesus, the Messiah. But God the Father mildly rebuked Peter, announcing that Jesus is his beloved Son; he is the preeminent one, the one who should be heard.

Second Peter 1:16–21 simply says that Peter was an eyewitness of the transfiguration, and that the divine voice that he heard proclaiming Jesus to be the Son of God is the same voice speaking through him in his letter confirming that the second coming of Christ will truly happen.

T

Treasure, Treasury–Treasure was stored in the Jerusalem temple and palace (Josh. 6:24) and was collected from the spoils of war (Josh. 6:19), from offerings (2 Kings 12:4; Mark 12:41), and from royal gifts (2 Kings 12:18; 1 Chron. 29:3). The temple treasury contained gold, silver, other metals, and precious stones (1 Chron. 29:8). Treasuries also housed written records (Ezra 6:1). Treasure was stored in the small rooms that surrounded the sanctuary (1 Chron. 28:12; see also Jer. 38:11) and was guarded by Levites (1 Chron. 9:26). Several treasurers are named (1 Chron. 9:26; 26:20, 22; 2 Chron. 25:24). The Ethiopian eunuch who met Philip was a treasurer in the court of the Kandake (Acts 8:27). The treasury funded repairs to the temple (2 Kings 12:7; Ezra 7:20).

Invading kings frequently raided the temple treasury, including Shishak of Egypt (1 Kings 14:26), Jehoash of Israel (2 Kings 14:14), and finally Nebuchadnezzar of Babylon (2 Kings 24:13; Dan. 1:2), as foretold by Jeremiah (Jer. 15:13). On other occasions, the kings of Judah drew money from the treasury to make tribute payments to foreign rulers (1 Kings 15:18; 2 Kings 12:18; 16:8; 18:15). "Treasury" can also refer to a private account (Prov. 8:21).

Jesus taught that his followers should store up their treasures in heaven and not on earth (Matt. 6:19–21). Earthly treasures will be destroyed over time or perhaps even stolen. In this vein, he urged the rich young ruler to sell his possessions so he might have "treasure in heaven" (Matt. 19:21).

Tree of Life–In Gen. 2:9 the tree of life is at the very center of the lush landscape of the garden of Eden. In Gen. 3:22–24 the man and the woman are exiled from the garden as a consequence of their disobedience, but more specifically they are barred from the immortality granted by eating the fruit of the tree.

In the book of Proverbs the tree of life is a symbol of that which brings joy in life: wisdom (3:18), righteousness (11:30), "a longing fulfilled" (13:12), "a soothing tongue" (15:4). In Revelation the tree represents the reversal of the consequences of humankind's disobedience in the garden. Eternal life is now again offered to those who persevere in Christ (Rev. 2:7; 22:14). And in Rev. 22:2 the tree of life is part of the scenery of the new Jerusalem. Its branches span over the river of the water of life, and its leaves are imbued with healing for the nations (cf. Ezek. 47:12). *See also* Tree of the Knowledge of Good and Evil.

Tree of the Knowledge of Good and Evil–In Gen. 2–3 the tree of the knowledge of good and evil and the tree of life are the centerpiece of the verdant landscape of the garden of Eden. Before the formation of the woman, the man is explicitly commanded not to eat of the fruit of the tree of the knowledge of good and evil, for the ensuing result would be death (2:16–17). Thus, the tree of knowledge is contrasted with the tree of life, whose fruit is imbued with immortality (3:22). Under the influence of the serpent's persuasion, the woman describes the fruit of the tree as "desirable for gaining wisdom," and the effect of eating the fruit upon the man and the woman was that "the eyes of both of them were opened, and they realized they were naked" (3:6–7). The "knowledge of good and evil" represented by the fruit of this tree is a wisdom of humankind's own fashioning, a law independent of the revealed will of God in the commandment not to eat of the fruit. The consequence of eating the fruit is shame and banishment, not only from the garden itself, but also from the eternal life provided by the tree of life. *See also* Tree of Life.

Tribune–A high-ranking Roman military officer. Translated "commander" in the NIV, the Greek word *chiliarchos* designates an officer (Lat. *tribunus*) in charge of a cohort, which ideally consisted of six hundred soldiers, including over a hundred cavalry (Mark 6:21; John 18:12; Acts 21:31–33, 37; 22:24, 26–29; 23:10, 15, 17–19, 22; 24:22; 25:23; Rev. 6:15; 19:18). A legion consisted of ten cohorts and typically had four to six tribunes. At the arrest of Jesus (John 18:12), it is likely that only a small detachment from a cohort was present.

Tribute–In the ancient biblical world, tribute was a payment made by one state to another, which was a mark of subjugation. The state required to pay the tribute (the vassal) often was a conquered people. The payment could consist of precious metals, currency, commodities, animals, and even human beings. Tribute allowed the sovereign state (the suzerain) to increase residual capital and gain large amounts of valuable materials, at the same time impoverishing and severely weakening the subjugated state (making future rebellions unlikely). Its administration was straightforward: every year the vassal was required to bring tribute to the suzerain. If such a payment was not made, it was a tacit sign of rebellion, and the suzerain sent a military force to punish the rebels.

At times, Israelite kings had occasions to impose tribute on other nations (e.g., 2 Sam. 8:2, 6; 1 Kings 4:21; 2 Chron. 17:11; cf. Ezra 4:20). However, in most instances described in the Bible, Israel appears to be on the other side of the tributary arrangement and makes monetary payments to foreign nations. Some of these instances are clear examples of Israel paying regular tribute payments to their overlord (e.g., Judg. 3:15; 2 Kings 23:33; Ezra 4:13), while others refer to bribes paid to foreign nations in order to secure military assistance against another enemy (1 Kings 15:18; 2 Kings 16:8) or settlement payments made to an attacker in exchange for its withdrawal (2 Kings 12:18; 18:15–16). On other occasions, the wealth of Israel is taken by foreign monarchs as spoils of war rather than as regular tribute (e.g., 1 Kings 14:26; 2 Kings 24:13–14). However, in nearly all these circumstances such payments resulted in Israel being required to give regular tributary payments thereafter to the foreign monarch.

Trinity–The biblical writers proclaim that only one God exists, yet they also refer to three persons as "God." The Father, the Son, and the Holy Spirit are all God. Furthermore, these three persons relate to one another as self-conscious individuals. Jesus prays to the Father (John 17). The Father speaks from heaven concerning the Son (Matt. 3:17; Luke 3:22). Jesus vows to send the Spirit as "Advocate" after his ascension, and he will do what Jesus himself did while he was among us (John 16:7–8).

Triumphal Entry–The occasion on which Jesus entered Jerusalem during a Passover celebration shortly before his arrest and crucifixion (Matt. 21:1–11; Mark 11:1–11; Luke 19:28–40; John 12:12–19).

The mode of Jesus' arrival in Jerusalem represented a deeply symbolic action meant to evoke images of a messianic or kingly figure for Israel. Jesus, by entering in the manner in which he did, was providing a messianic demonstration; he was, in effect, claiming to be Israel's long-awaited Messiah. Zechariah 9:9–17 is an important OT passage that functions as background to this issue. This prophetic text speaks of Israel's king coming to his people "lowly and riding on a donkey" (9:9). This connotation would have been foremost in the minds of those present during the entry of Jesus into the royal city who were proclaiming their loyalty to him. Jesus was acting out and thereby fulfilling the prophetic promises of Zechariah, for which the people of Israel had long waited. The words of Ps. 118:26 are echoed in the cries of the jubilant crowd that hailed Jesus as the arriving Messiah of Israel, as their reference to Jesus as "Son of David" reflects an understanding of him as a messianic figure (Matt. 21:9; Mark 11:9–10; Luke 19:38; John 12:13). In all four Gospels the triumphal entry of Jesus into the holy city of Jerusalem reinforces the image of him as the Messiah.

Troas–*See* Asia Minor, Cities of.

Trogyllium–A settlement on the like-named peninsula of Asia Minor that extends westward toward the island of Samos. The Western text of Acts 20:15 suggests that, at the end of his third missionary campaign, Paul's ship stopped at Trogyllium before continuing to Miletus.

Trophimus–Trophimus is mentioned three times in the NT as an associate of Paul (Acts 20:4; 21:29; 2 Tim. 4:20). In Acts, Luke identifies him as a Gentile Christian from Ephesus who accompanied Paul in delivering the collection to Jerusalem. Paul was falsely accused of bringing a Gentile into the temple because he had been seen with Trophimus in Jerusalem. In 2 Tim. 4:20 Paul says that he left Trophimus sick in Miletus. Since Paul did not pass by Miletus on the way to his Roman imprisonment, this must either be another Trophimus or evidence for a second Roman imprisonment.

Tryphena and Tryphosa–Two women whom Paul asks the Romans to greet on his behalf, noting their hard work in the Lord (Rom. 16:12 [NRSV, ESV, NASB: "Tryphaena"]). Tryphena and Tryphosa are two of several female Christians named in Rom. 16, including Phoebe (v. 1), Priscilla (v. 3),

Mary (v. 6), Persis (v. 12), Julia (v. 15), and possibly Junia(s) (v. 7). Both "Tryphena" and "Tryphosa" appear in Roman inscriptions related to the household of Caesar.

Tubal–The fifth of the seven sons of Japheth (Gen. 10:2; 1 Chron. 1:5). Listed in the Table of Nations, he probably is the ancestor of a people in Asia Minor, perhaps Cilicia. Tubal traded slaves and bronze vessels with Tyre (Ezek. 27:13).

Tubal-Cain–A descendant of Cain through Lamech and Zillah, he is attributed with the invention of metallurgy (Gen. 4:22). By his other wife, Adah, Lamech also fathered Jabal, the father of nomadism and animal husbandry, and Jubal, the father of musicians (Gen. 4:20–21).

Tychicus–An Asian Christian and trusted friend of Paul, Tychicus occasionally accompanied Paul on his missionary voyages and was frequently sent by Paul to represent him and to deliver his letters to the churches (Acts 20:4; Eph. 6:21; Col. 4:7; 2 Tim. 4:12; Titus 3:12). Paul must have thought very highly of Tychicus, trusting him to minister to the churches and referring to him as "dear brother and faithful servant in the Lord" and "dear brother, a faithful minister and fellow servant in the Lord" (Eph. 6:21; Col. 4:7). Tychicus was likely with Paul while the apostle was imprisoned in Rome (Col. 4:7).

Tyrannus–Tyrannus is mentioned in Acts 19:9, where his name is associated with a lecture hall in which Paul held daily discussions in Ephesus after his withdrawal from the synagogue. He was probably a Christian or a sympathizer who owned a lecture hall made available to Paul.

Tyre and Sidon–Two ancient city-states of the Phoenicians that have a long and well-documented history predating many of the events in the Bible. Genesis 10:15 notes that Sidon was a son of Canaan, likely hinting at the importance of this city for the Canaanites. Several times in the Bible the term "Sidon" or "Sidonians" serves as an alternate name for the Phoenicians or Canaanites and usually refers to the southern part of this northern neighbor. There was much social and political interaction between Sidon and Tyre and the kingdoms of Israel and Judah, including Solomon's marriage to several women from Sidon (1 Kings 11:1) and the Omride dynasty's treaties and intermarriage with the Phoenicians (16:31). For much of the tenth through seventh centuries BC, Israel and the Phoenicians were close economic allies, with Israel providing materials for trade, and the cities of Sidon and Tyre offering the transport of those goods in their famed ships. Like Israel, Sidon and Tyre suffered under the expansions of the Assyrians and the Babylonians. Both Sidon and Tyre often were recipients of the OT prophets' ire. Tyre especially was subject to many prophetic denouncements of which Ezekiel's is an archetype (Ezek. 26:1–28:19). Ezekiel prophesied the total destruction of the city. Both cities had special cultic centers that advocated various versions of Baal worship and attempted to propagate their religion, as demonstrated by the actions of Jezebel, the wife of King Ahab and daughter of the king of Sidon.

Tyre and Sidon continued to be significant cities under Roman rule during the NT period. Jesus went to these two locations and condemned Jewish cities by saying that even the pagan Tyre and Sidon would have repented if they had witnessed miracles he had performed around them (Matt. 11:20–23). Paul also traveled to Tyre, staying there for seven days during a missionary journey (Acts 21:3–4).

Tyropoeon–The valley in central Jerusalem that separates the eastern hill of original Jerusalem and the Temple Mount from the higher western hill to which Jerusalem expanded during the Israelite monarchy. At the time of the NT, priests living on the western hill crossed to the Temple Mount by means of a bridge constructed by Herod the Great. "Tyropoeon" does not appear in Scripture, but it was used by the Jewish historian Josephus. The term may mean "cheesemakers," perhaps for commercial activity that took place there. Today the valley is largely filled in by debris from the numerous destructions of the city.

U

Ucal–*See* Ukal.

Ukal–"Ukal" is found only in Prov. 30:1: "This man says to Ithiel, to Ithiel and to Ukal" (NET; see NIV mg.). Although many translations (NET, NASB, NKJV, KJV) treat "Ukal" (also spelled "Ucal") as a personal name, it may be a form of the verb "to be able," as in the NIV: "I am weary, God, but I can prevail" (see also NRSV).

Ulai–A river or canal near the Persian capital of Susa where Daniel witnessed the revelation of the ram and the goat (Dan. 8:2, 16).

Unleavened Bread–Any type of bread made without a leavening agent to make it rise. It developed symbolic value after the exodus (Exod. 12:17–20). Leaven became a symbol of sin and was removed from homes during feasts as a physical reminder of the need to remove sin from one's life. Unleavened bread was also the only acceptable form of bread to be offered as a sacrifice or placed in the tabernacle (Exod. 25:30; Lev. 6:17). *See also* Leaven.

Uphaz–A region well known for its gold (Dan. 10:5 [KJV, NRSV, NASB]; Jer. 10:9), though its location remains uncertain. Some scholars believe that "Uphaz" is a misspelling of "Ophir," a famous gold-bearing region. *See also* Ophir.

Upper Gate–One of the gates of the temple in Jerusalem. The KJV calls it the High Gate. It apparently was also called the Upper Gate of Benjamin (Jer. 20:2). Its location is uncertain, but it apparently faced north (Ezek. 9:2). Second Chronicles 27:3 and 2 Kings 15:35 identify it with a gate of the temple that Jotham rebuilt, but 2 Chronicles 23:20 suggests it (or a similarly named gate) led into the king's palace.

Upper Room–A room on an upper story or roof of a building. King Ahaziah's fall through the lattice of an upper room caused his death (2 Kings 1:2). Jesus instructed his disciples to prepare their final meal together in an upper room (Mark 14:15; Luke 22:12). Tradition holds that the disciples met to pray in this room after Jesus' ascension (Acts 1:13). Widows grieved over Dorcas in an upper room until Peter's prayer restored her life (Acts 9:39). Paul revived Eutychus, who had died after dozing off and falling from an upper room to the ground (Acts 20:8–12).

Ur–An ancient Sumerian city that can be identified with modern Tell Muqayyar near the Euphrates River in modern-day Iraq.

The four biblical references to Ur mention it as the place of origin of Abraham's family (Gen. 11:28, 31; 15:7; Neh. 9:7). Genesis 11:31–12:9 describes Abraham's journey from "Ur of the Chaldeans" northwest to Harran and then south into Canaan. The name "Ur of the Chaldeans" for the city at the time of Abraham (Middle Bronze Age [2000–1550 BC]) is most likely an anachronism, since the Chaldeans did not arise as a recognizable group until the ninth century BC.

Urbanus–A prominent Christian in Rome. He was a coworker with Paul and the Christians in Rome in the work of Christ (Rom. 16:9). Some have claimed that Urbanus was a freed slave, since "Urbanus" was a common slave name. This is debated, however, and the epigraphic evidence for Urbanus as a slave name is not conclusive.

Uriah–**(1)** The ill-fated husband of Bathsheba, with whom David had an illicit affair. His designation as "the Hittite" implies an ethnic tie to the Anatolian Hittite Empire, in modern-day Turkey. David conspired with his military leader Joab to have Uriah murdered in order to cover up the scandal of a child conceived from David's unchecked lust for Bathsheba (2 Sam. 11; 1 Chron. 11:41). **(2)** A priest of Judah, the southern kingdom of Israel, during the reign of Ahaz, he built a new altar in the temple in accordance with the sketch and plan of a foreign altar that Ahaz had seen in Damascus (2 Kings 16:10–16). This is likely the same Uriah referred to in Isa. 8:2–4 as one of two reliable witnesses Isaiah uses to testify to a prophetic oracle written on a tablet. **(3)** The son of Shemaiah from Kiriath Jearim, he joined Jeremiah in prophesying against the city of Jerusalem and the land of Judah during the reign of Jehoiakim. He was persecuted, captured, and put to death by Jehoiakim, and his body was thrown in the burial place of common people (Jer. 26:20–23).

Urim and Thummim–Objects used in the OT for determining the will of God. "Urim" traditionally is taken to mean "light," while "Thummim" is generally connected with a word for "perfect."

The size and shape of these objects is unknown. They may have been two disks, each with a shiny side and a dull side. They belonged in the breastpiece of the high priestly garments (Lev. 8:8), and presumably they were drawn out by the priest or thrown down in a particular way in response to a question posed (Exod. 28:30; Num. 27:21) and could give a yes or no answer.

Uruk–The Sumerian city Uruk (modern Warka; rendered "Erech" in Hebrew) is located on a subsidiary branch of the Euphrates River, forty miles northwest of Ur. It is mentioned in Gen. 10:10 as one of the cities founded by Nimrod in the country of Shinar (Mesopotamia). Information about this city comes from excavations of this site conducted during the mid-twentieth century and comments about the city in Sumerian and Akkadian literature. It was founded around 4000 BC, in the Ubaid period (5500–4000 BC), and continuously inhabited until the end of the Parthian Empire (AD 224). Prominent rulers include the legendary Gilgamesh, from the Sumerian flood story, and Sargon of Akkad (2300–2230 BC), whose birth legend mirrors that of Moses. The city's most prominent temple was Eanna ("house of heaven"), dedicated to Anu, the sky god, and Inanna/Ishtar, the chief goddess of the pantheon.

Uz–**(1)** The homeland of Job (Job 1:1), its location is uncertain. According to Lam. 4:21, the land of Uz is equivalent to Edomite territory (probably also Jer. 25:20). The geographical designations of Job's companions (particularly Eliphaz the Temanite) suggest a setting in Transjordan rather than northern Mesopotamia (Aram). **(2)** The oldest of the four sons of Aram and a grandson of Shem, he appears in the genealogy of the Arameans (Gen. 10:23; 1 Chron. 1:17). **(3)** The son of Abraham's brother Nahor and Milkah, also associated with Arameans (Gen. 22:21).

Uzzah–This name is a shortened form of "Uzziah." **(1)** The son of Abinadab and brother of Ahio. The brothers were guiding the cart on which the ark of the covenant was being transported to Jerusalem. Uzzah touched the ark and was stricken by God (2 Sam. 6:1–11; 1 Chron. 13:7–11). Here, "Uzzah" might be a nickname for the Eleazar of 1 Sam. 7:1. **(2)** The son of Shimei, a Merarite Levite (1 Chron. 6:29).

Uzziah–Also known as Azariah, he was the king of Judah from approximately 783 to 742 BC. The account of his rule is in 2 Kings 14:21–22; 15:1–7; 2 Chron. 26:1–23. He likely ruled as coregent with his father, Amaziah, starting in 792 BC, before he was sole ruler. He became king at the age of sixteen, when his father was assassinated. Much of his reign overlapped with that of Jeroboam II of Israel, and both kingdoms prospered economically during this time.

Uzziah was a relatively faithful king. He was also successful, maintaining a robust building program and achieving victory over the Philistines. His reign and life turned in a negative direction, however, when he pridefully presumed to offer incense in a holy area of the temple. Such actions were permitted only for the priests. The priests tried to stop him, but he continued, and so God caused him to become leprous for the rest of his life and thus excluded from the temple. Thereafter, his son Jotham discharged the kingly duties. When Uzziah died, he was buried with his fathers, but at some distance because of his condition (2 Chron. 26:23).

Although their messages were directed to the northern kingdom, the superscriptions to the books of Amos and Hosea indicate that these two prophets ministered during Uzziah's reign (Hos. 1:1; Amos 1:1). Isaiah was called to be a prophet in the year Uzziah died (Isa. 1:1; 6:1), and Zech. 14:5 records an earthquake that took place during his rule.

V

Vashti–The Persian queen of King Xerxes I (r. 485–464 BC) and the precursor to Queen Esther (Esther 1). During an extravagant banquet, King Xerxes became intoxicated and sent for Queen Vashti in order to put her on display to his guests. Queen Vashti refused and remained at the women's banquet that she was hosting. This not only elicited the king's fury but also alarmed the royal advisers, who worried that all women in the kingdom would follow Vashti's lead and refuse to obey their husbands. This led to the banishment of Vashti and ultimately the installment of Esther as the new queen.

Veil–In the harsh desert of the Middle East, a veil is useful protection from the sun and windblown sand. While Hebrew women tend to appear without veils (Gen. 12:14; 24:16; 29:10; 1 Sam. 1:12), dressing in veils in public may have been considered appropriate for women of certain status (Song 4:1, 3; 5:7; 6:7), so that forced removal becomes an act of shaming (Isa. 3:18–19; 47:2; Ezek. 13:21).

However, in the Bible, veils also serve as more than protection from the elements. Rebekah puts on a veil in deference before encountering her future husband, Isaac (Gen. 24:65). Tamar veiled herself in order to deceive Judah, her father-in-law, into sleeping with her (Gen. 38:14–19). And judgment is said to await the women who "make veils of various lengths for their heads in order to ensnare people" (Ezek. 13:18, 21).

Perhaps the most celebrated of veils in the Bible is the veil (*masweh*) worn by Moses over his face in order to keep its glow, caused by his encounter with God, from affecting the people (Exod. 34:33, 35). A veil also hung at the entrance of the tabernacle (Exod. 26:36, 37), while another significant veil hung in the tabernacle and the temple, separating the holy place from the most holy place (2 Chron. 3:14), into which the high priest entered but once a year (on Yom Kippur) for the atonement of sin (Exod. 30:10; Heb. 9:3). This veil was torn in two when Jesus died (Matt. 27:51; Mark 15:38; Luke 23:45), symbolizing open access into the presence of God (Heb. 10:20).

God is figuratively described as being veiled by clouds that keep us from his sight (Job 22:14), while divine judgment can be characterized as the "veil over their hearts" (Lam. 3:65).

In the NT, Paul requires women to veil their heads, particularly in worship, while veiling of the head by men is considered inappropriate (1 Cor. 11:6–7; cf. Isa. 3:17–18). He also compares Moses' veiled and fading glory to the surpassing and unfading glory of the ministry of the Spirit (2 Cor. 3:7–14) and says of the spiritually blind that "a veil covers their hearts," blinding them to God's grace that comes through Christ (3:15). The gospel is veiled to those that are perishing (4:3); however, this veil is removed by the Spirit when one turns to Christ (3:16–18).

Venomous Serpent–When the Israelites grumbled in the wilderness, God sent "venomous [lit., 'burning'; Heb. *serapim*] snakes" that bit the people (Num. 21:4–9; cf. KJV: "fiery serpents"). In response to Moses' prayer on their behalf, God commanded Moses to make a *sarap* and put it on a pole; the people who looked at it would live. Moses made a bronze serpent. Because the people worshiped the bronze serpent, Hezekiah destroyed it (2 Kings 18:4). Jesus likened the bronze serpent lifted up in the wilderness to the Son of Man being lifted up (John 3:14). From a human perspective, both a serpent and a crucified messiah were unlikely objects of faith.

Vinegar–In the Bible, vinegar is wine that during the fermentation process has become acidic and soured. It is mentioned only five times in the OT. In Num. 6:3 Nazirites are prohibited from drinking wine or wine vinegar. In Ruth 2:14 vinegar is mentioned as a condiment for dipping bread. Other references, however, point out vinegar's undesirable qualities (Prov. 10:26; 25:20). In Ps. 69:21 the psalmist complains that his enemies gave him vinegar for his thirst, evidently undiluted, therefore making the gesture cruel and mocking.

All four references to vinegar in the NT are in the Gospel accounts of the crucifixion (Matt. 27:48; Mark 15:36; Luke 23:36; John 19:29). Matthew and Mark narrate that at an early point in the crucifixion the soldiers had tried to give Jesus wine to drink, but he refused it. Most commentators believe that Jesus refused this drink because of its sedative properties. All four Gospels indicate that at some point later during the crucifixion, they gave Jesus wine vinegar to drink, which this time he accepted. The Gospel narrators almost certainly want the reader to see here a fulfillment of Ps. 69:21.

Virgin Birth–The traditional designation "virgin birth" refers to the supernatural conception of Jesus Christ by the Holy Spirit, apart from sexual relations. Technically, one should speak of a "virginal conception," since Jesus was virginally conceived but was born normally. The virgin "birth" is considered by some theologians to be the means by which the two natures of Jesus Christ are preserved: his humanity stems from the fact that he was born of the virgin Mary, while his deity proceeds from the reality that God was his father and he was conceived by the Holy Spirit. The later Apostles' Creed formulates the matter this way: Jesus Christ "was conceived by the Holy Spirit and born of the Virgin Mary." Here, two aspects of the virgin birth are discussed: the virgin birth and Isa. 7:14, and the virgin birth in the NT.

Isaiah 7:14 reads, "The virgin shall conceive and bear a son, and shall call his name Immanuel" (ESV). Two key issues are involved in Isaiah's prophecy. First, should the Hebrew word *'almah* be translated as "virgin" or as "young woman"? While the Hebrew term does not necessarily mean a virgin, but only a young woman of marriageable age, the Greek term *parthenos* used in the LXX of Isa. 7:14 and quoted in Matt. 1:23 has stronger connotations of virginity. Second, when was Isa. 7:14 fulfilled? Most likely the OT text was partially fulfilled in Isaiah's day (with reference to King Ahaz's unnamed son or to Isaiah's son Maher-Shalal-Hash-Baz [Isa. 8:1]) but found its ultimate fulfillment in Jesus, as Matt. 1:23 points out.

The infancy narratives recorded in Matt. 1–2 and in Luke 1–2 provide the story line for Jesus' virginal conception: (1) Mary was a virgin engaged to Joseph (Matt. 1:18; Luke 1:27, 34; 2:5); (2) she was found to be pregnant while still engaged to Joseph, a conception produced by the Holy Spirit (Matt. 1:18, 20; Luke 1:35; cf. Matt. 1:18–25; Luke 1:34); (3) only after Jesus was born did Mary and Joseph have sexual relations (Matt. 1:24–25). Even though there is nothing in these narratives like the hypostatic union formulated in the later church creeds, it is clear that Matthew and Luke in some way associate Jesus' deity and humanity with the virginal conception. Other NT texts are considered by some as possible references to the virgin birth. John 1:14 states that "the Word became flesh," which certainly highlights Jesus' two natures—deity and humanity—but does not thereby explicitly mention the virgin birth. Paul does something similar in Rom. 1:3 ("[God's] Son, who as to his earthly life was a descendant of David"), Gal. 4:4 ("God sent his Son, born of a woman"), and Phil. 2:6–11 (Jesus existed in the form of God but took on human likeness). Beyond these passages, there is little else regarding the virgin birth stated or alluded to in the NT.

Vision–A divine communication in the form of visual imagery, usually accompanied by words, and often using symbols that require explanation and spur reflection about God's otherwise imperceptible presence and activity. Presumably, the recipient "sees" the vision as an event of inward perception, often within a dream during sleep or in a divinely induced state of ecstasy (Gen. 15; Dan. 7:1; 10:1–9; 2 Cor. 12:1–4). Characteristically, visions entail conversation with God or an angelic representative, often following a question-and-answer format (Dan. 7:15–28; Zech. 1:8–15, 18–21). The visionary is actually in the scene as direct observer and active participant (Dan. 8:1–2).

Prophetic visions are meant to be retold. For example, imagery is accompanied by the authentication of divine commissioning (Isa. 6; Ezek. 1:1–3:15; Rev. 10), leading to announcement of judgment (Jer. 1:4–19). This close conjunction of image and word (1 Sam. 3:21) is reinforced by statements about a prophet "seeing" God's word (e.g., Mic. 1:1 ESV, NRSV, NASB) and about prophetic books as collections of visions (2 Chron. 32:32; Nah. 1:1). Vision reports join oracles and other forms of prophetic speech as essential features of these works. Visions contribute to the community's spiritual well-being (Prov. 29:18; Ezek. 7:26), but not always (Lam. 2:14; Ezek. 13; Zech. 13:4; Col. 2:18).

Visions drive the narrative surrounding Jesus' birth (Matt. 1:18–2:23; Luke 1:1–2:20). The baptism of Jesus includes a visionary element, the Holy Spirit's anointing of Jesus for his ministry, accompanied by the Father's word (Matt. 3:16–17; Mark 1:10–11; Luke 3:22; John 1:32–33). Jesus' transfiguration is comparable (Matt. 17:1–9; Mark 9:2–10; Luke 9:28–36). Visions mark key transition points in the narrative of Acts (e.g., chaps. 9–11). The book of Revelation opens with a vision of the Son of Man (1:9–20) and is structured around three vision cycles of judgment interspersed with visions of heaven meant to bolster the readers' faithfulness.

Vows–Binding promises made to God while awaiting God's help (Gen. 28:20; Num. 21:2; 1 Sam. 1:11). When God's answer comes, worshipers fulfill their vows by performing what they have promised (1 Sam. 1:21; Acts 21:23–24).

Mosaic regulations address how and by whom vows are to be implemented (e.g., Lev. 7:16; 22:17–25; 23:38; 27:2–11; Num. 30; Deut. 12:5–28), including the "Nazirite vow" of radical separation to God (Num. 6:1–21; cf. Judg. 13:2–5; Acts 18:18). Lament psalms connect vows with the outcry to God and portray their fulfillment in thank offerings that respond to God's deliverance (Pss. 50:14–15; 56:12–13; 66:13–15; cf. Job 22:27; Jon. 2:9). Since vows are intended to distinguish God's faithful worshipers (e.g., Ps. 116:14, 17–18), Scripture condemns rash or unfulfilled vows (Num. 30:2; Deut. 23:21–23; Prov. 20:25; Eccles. 5:5–6; cf. Judg. 11:30–39). Some vows are made insincerely (2 Sam. 15:7–8; Prov. 7:14) or to idols (Jer. 44:25).

W

Wadi–A ravine, gorge, valley, or streambed, sometimes steep, in an arid region that is dry except during rainy season, when it becomes susceptible to torrential, life-threatening flash flooding. Job compares his fickle friends to a wadi (Job 6:15–20; NIV: "intermittent streams").

Wadi of Egypt–*See* Rivers and Waterways.

Wall, Dividing–Within the temple infrastructure stood a wall of one and a half meters. This temple balustrade separated the court of the Gentiles from the inner courts and the sanctuary in the Jerusalem temple. Because the wall is a powerful symbol of the separation of Gentiles from Jews, the NT declaration that this wall has been broken down is rhetorically significant (Eph. 2:14; cf. 1 Macc. 9:54). Christ has (symbolically) broken down this dividing wall through his death. Jews and Gentiles now stand as one as they approach God.

Washerman's Field–The road to the Washerman's Field (NIV: "Launderer's Field" in Isa. 7:3; 36:2) locates where Ahaz was inspecting Jerusalem's water supply in preparation for an attack by Syria and Israel (Isa. 7:3), and where the Assyrian commander stood (2 Kings 18:17; Isa. 36:2). Jerusalem was supplied by a series of pools connected by channels. The launderer's occupation of cleaning cloth required much water (cf. Mal. 3:2). The field was located outside the city, at its southern end.

Watch–A chronological division of the night. The term is derived from soldiers or others guarding, or "watching," something during specified portions of the night. In the OT, there apparently were three watches or divisions in the night. Gideon and his men struck the Midianites at the beginning of the "middle watch" (Judg. 7:19). The Roman system had four divisions or watches in the night, and the Gospels report Jesus walking on the lake during the "fourth watch" (Matt. 14:25; Mark 6:48 ESV, NASB, NKJV). The term can also be used to refer to the guard placed on duty to guard something (Neh. 4:9).

Watchman–The watchman was stationed on the city wall or in a watchtower. He was to identify potential enemies approaching the city and alert the city's inhabitants by blowing a trumpet (Jer. 6:17; Amos 3:6). It was the duty of some watchmen to inform the king of any suspicious person approaching the city wall (2 Sam. 18:24–27). Just as the watchman warned of potential danger so that people could prepare themselves, so the prophet was to warn of impending judgment on the unrighteous (Ezek. 33:1–11).

Watchtower–Military watchtowers could be part of city battlements (Isa. 21:8) or more-isolated lookouts (2 Chron. 20:24 NRSV). Vineyards also had watchtowers (Isa. 5:2; Matt. 21:33; Mark 12:1).

Water–Water is mentioned extensively in the Bible due to its prevalence in creation and its association with life and purity. The cosmic waters of Gen. 1 are held back by the sky (Gen. 1:6–7; cf. Pss. 104:6, 13; 148:4). God is enthroned on these waters in his cosmic temple (Pss. 29:10; 104:3, 13; cf. Gen. 1:2; Ps. 78:69; Isa. 66:1). These same waters were released in the time of Noah (Gen. 7:10–12; Ps. 104:7–9).

Water is also an agent of life and fertility and is therefore associated with the presence of God. Both God himself and his temple are described as the source of life-giving water (Jer. 2:13; 17:13; Joel 3:18; cf. Isa. 12:2–3). Ezekiel envisions this water flowing from beneath the temple and streaming down into the Dead Sea, where it brings life and fecundity (Ezek. 47:1–12; cf. Zech. 14:8). The book of Revelation, employing the same image, describes "the river of the water of life, as clear as crystal, flowing from the throne of God and of the Lamb" (22:1). This imagery is also illustrated in archaeological remains associated with temples. Cisterns are attested beneath the Dome of the Rock (presumably the location of the Jerusalem temple) and beneath the Judahite temple at Arad. Other temples, such as the Israelite high place at Tel Dan, are located close to freshwater springs. The Gihon spring in the City of David may also be associated with the Jerusalem temple (Ps. 46:4; cf. Gen. 2:13).

This OT imagery forms the background for Jesus' teaching regarding eternal life in the writings of the apostle John. Jesus claims to be the source of living water, and he offers it freely to everyone who thirsts (John 4:10–15; 7:37; Rev. 21:6; 22:17; cf. Rev. 7:17). This water, which produces "a spring of water welling up to eternal life" (John 4:14), is the work of the Holy Spirit in the believer (John 7:38–39).

Water is also described in the Bible as an agent of cleansing. It is extensively employed in purification rituals in the OT. In the NT, the ritual of water baptism signifies the purity and new life of the believer (Matt. 3:11, 16; Mark 1:8–10; Luke 3:16; John 1:26, 31–33; 3:23; Acts 1:5; 8:36–39; 10:47; 11:16; 1 Pet. 3:20–21; cf. Eph. 5:26; Heb. 10:22).

Finally, the NT also reveals Jesus as the Lord of water. He walks on water (Matt. 14:28–29; John 6:19), turns water into wine (John 2:7–9; 4:46), and controls water creatures (Matt. 17:27; John 21:6). Most important, Jesus commands "the winds and the water, and they obey him" (Luke 8:25; cf. Ps. 29:3).

Web–Thread arranged on a loom for weaving (Judg. 16:13–14 [NIV: "fabric"]). Also, the silken netting spun by a spider as a snare is used as a negative metaphor for flimsiness and/or evil entrapment (Job 8:14–15; Isa. 59:5–6). More generally, "web" refers to an entangling mesh or net (Job 18:8).

Weights and Measures–The metrological systems employed in biblical times span the same concepts as our own modern-day systems: weight, linear distance, and volume or capacity. However, the systems of weights and measurements employed during the span of biblical times were not nearly as accurate or uniform as the modern units employed today.

Weights

Weights in biblical times were carried in a bag or a satchel (Deut. 25:13; Prov. 16:11; Mic. 6:11) and were stones, usually carved into various animal shapes for easy identification. Their side or flat bottom was inscribed with the associated weight and unit of measurement. Thousands of historical artifacts, which differ by significant amounts, have been discovered by archaeologists and thus have greatly complicated the work of determining accurate modern-day equivalents.

Beka. Approximately ⅕ ounce, or 5.6 grams. Equivalent to 10 gerahs or ½ the sanctuary shekel (Exod. 38:26). Used to measure metals and goods such as gold (Gen. 24:22).

Gerah. 1/50 ounce, or 0.56 grams. Equivalent to 1/10 beka, 1/20 shekel (Exod. 30:13; Lev. 27:25).

Mina. Approximately 1¼ pounds, or 0.56 kilograms. Equivalent to 50 shekels. Used to weigh gold (1 Kings 10:17; Ezra 2:69), silver (Neh. 7:71–72), and other goods. The prophet Ezekiel redefined the proper weight: "The shekel is to consist of twenty gerahs. Twenty shekels plus twenty-five shekels plus fifteen shekels equal one mina" (Ezek. 45:12). Before this redefinition, there were arguably 50 shekels per mina. In Jesus' parable of the servants, he describes the master entrusting to his three servants varying amounts—10 minas, 5 minas, 1 mina—implying a monetary value (Luke 19:11–24), probably of either silver or gold. One *mina* was equivalent to approximately three months' wages for a laborer.

Pim. Approximately ⅓ ounce, or 9.3 grams. Equivalent to ⅔ shekel. Referenced only once in the Scriptures (1 Sam. 13:21).

Shekel. Approximately ⅖ ounce, or 11 grams. Equivalent to approximately 2 bekas. The shekel is the basic unit of weight measurement in Israelite history, though its actual weight varied significantly at different historical points. Examples include the "royal shekel" (2 Sam. 14:26), the "common shekel" (2 Kings 7:1), and the "sanctuary shekel," which was equivalent to 20 gerahs (e.g., Exod. 30:13; Lev. 27:25; Num. 3:47). Because it was used to weigh out silver or gold, the shekel also functioned as a common monetary unit in the NT world.

Talent. Approximately 75 pounds, or 34 kilograms. Equivalent to approximately 60 minas. Various metals were weighed using talents: gold (Exod. 25:39; 37:24; 1 Chron. 20:2), silver (Exod. 38:27; 1 Kings 20:39; 2 Kings 5:22), and bronze (Exod. 38:29). This probably is derived from the weight of a load that a man could carry.

Litra. Approximately 12 ounces, or 340 grams. A Roman measure of weight. Used only twice in the NT (John 12:3; 19:39). The precursor to the modern British pound.

Linear Measurements

Linear measurements were based upon readily available natural measurements such as the distance between the elbow and the hand or between the thumb and the little finger. While convenient, this method of measurement gave rise to significant inconsistencies.

Cubit. Approximately 18 inches, or 45.7 centimeters. Equivalent to 6 handbreadths. The standard biblical measure of linear distance, as the shekel is the standard measurement of weight. The distance from the elbow to the outstretched fingertip. Used to describe height, width, length (Exod. 25:10), distance (John 21:8), and depth (Gen. 7:20). Use of the cubit is ancient. For simple and approximate conversion into modern units, divide the number of cubits in half for meters, then multiply the number of meters by 3 to arrive at feet.

1 cubit = 2 spans = 6 handbreadths = 24 fingerbreadths

Day's journey. An approximate measure of distance equivalent to about 20–25 miles, or 32–40 kilometers. Several passages reference a single or multiple days' journey as a description of the distance traveled or the distance between two points: "a day's journey" (Num. 11:31; 1 Kings 19:4), "a three-day journey" (Gen. 30:36; Exod. 3:18; 8:27; Jon. 3:3), "seven days" (Gen. 31:23), and "eleven days" (Deut. 1:2). After visiting Jerusalem for Passover, Jesus' parents journeyed for a day (Luke 2:44) before realizing that he was not with them.

Fingerbreadth. The width of the finger, or ¼ of a handbreadth, approximately ¾ inch, or 1.9 centimeters. The fingerbreadth was the beginning building block of the biblical metrological system for linear measurements. Used only once in the Scriptures, to describe the bronze pillars (Jer. 52:21).

Handbreadth. Approximately 3 inches, or 7.6 centimeters. Equivalent to ⅙ cubit, or four fingerbreadths. Probably the width at the base of the four fingers. A short measure of length, thus compared to a human's brief life (Ps. 39:5). Also the width of the rim on the bread table (Exod. 25:25) and the thickness of the bronze Sea (1 Kings 7:26).

Milion. Translated "mile" in Matt. 5:41. Greek transliteration of Roman measurement *mille passuum*, "a thousand paces."

Orguia. Approximately 5 feet 11 inches, or 1.8 meters. Also translated as "fathom." A Greek unit of measurement. Probably the distance between outstretched fingertip to fingertip. Used to measure the depth of water (Acts 27:28).

Reed/rod. Approximately 108 inches, or 274 centimeters. This is also a general term for a measuring device rather than a specific linear distance (Ezek. 40:3, 5; 42:16–19; Rev. 11:1; 21:15).

Sabbath day's journey. Approximately ¾ mile, or 1.2 kilometers (Acts 1:12). About 2,000 cubits.

Stadion. Approximately 607 feet, or 185 meters. Equivalent to 100 orguiai. Used in the measurement of large distances (Matt. 14:24; Luke 24:13; John 6:19; 11:18; Rev. 14:20; 21:16).

Span. Approximately 9 inches, or 22.8 centimeters. Equivalent to three handbreadths, and ½ cubit. The distance from outstretched thumb tip to little-finger tip. The length and width of the priest's breastpiece (Exod. 28:16).

Land Area

Seed. The size of a piece of land could also be measured on the basis of how much seed was required to plant that field (Lev. 27:16; 1 Kings 18:32).

Yoke. Fields and lands were measured using logical, available means. In biblical times, this meant the amount of land a pair of yoked animals could plow in one day (1 Sam. 14:14; Isa. 5:10).

Capacity

Cab. Approximately ½ gallon, or 1.9 liters. Equivalent to 1 omer. Mentioned only once in the Scriptures, during the siege of Samaria (2 Kings 6:25).

Choinix. Approximately ¼ gallon, or 0.9 liters. A Greek measurement, mentioned only once in Scripture (Rev. 6:6).

Cor. Approximately 6 bushels (48.4 gallons, or 183 liters). Equal to the homer, and to 10 ephahs. Used for measuring dry volumes, particularly of flour and grains (1 Kings 4:22; 5:11; 2 Chron. 2:10; 27:5; Ezra 7:22). In the LXX, cor is also a measure of liquid volume, particularly oil (1 Kings 5:11; 2 Chron. 2:10; Ezra 45:14).

Ephah. Approximately 3/5 bushel (6 gallons, or 22.7 liters). Equivalent to 10 omers, or 1/10 homer. Used for measuring flour and grains (e.g., Exod. 29:40; Lev. 6:20). Isaiah prophesied a day of reduced agricultural yield, when a homer of seed would produce only an ephah of grain (Isa. 5:10). The ephah was equal in size to the bath (Ezek. 45:11), which typically was used for liquid measurements.

W

Homer. Approximately 6 bushels (48.4 gallons, or 183 liters). Equivalent to 1 cor, or 10 ephahs. Used for measuring dry volumes, particularly of various grains (Lev. 27:16; Isa. 5:10; Ezek. 45:11, 13–14; Hos. 3:2). This is probably a natural measure of the load that a donkey can carry, in the range of 90 kilograms. There may have existed a direct link between capacity and monetary value, given Lev. 27:16: "fifty shekels of silver to a homer of barley seed." A logical deduction of capacity and cost based on known equivalences might look something like this:

> 1 homer = 1 mina; 1 ephah = 5 shekels; 1 omer = 1 beka

Koros. Approximately 10 bushels (95 gallons, or 360 liters). A Greek measure of grain (Luke 16:7).

Omer. Approximately 2 quarts, or 1.9 liters. Equivalent to 1/10 ephah, 1/100 homer (Ezek. 45:11). Used by Israel in the measurement and collection of manna in the wilderness (Exod. 16:16–36) and thus roughly equivalent to a person's daily food ration.

Saton. Approximately 7 quarts, or 6.6 liters. Equivalent to 1 seah. The measurement of flour in Jesus' parable of the kingdom of heaven (Matt. 13:33; Luke 13:21).

Seah. Approximately 7 quarts, or 6.6 liters. Equivalent to 1/3 ephah, or 1 saton. Used to measure flour, grain, seed, and other various dry goods (e.g., 2 Kings 7:1; 1 Sam. 25:18).

Liquid Volume

Bath. Approximately 6 gallons, or 22.7 liters. Equivalent to 1 ephah, which typically was used for measurements of dry capacity. Used in the measurement of water (1 Kings 7:26), oil (1 Kings 5:11), and wine (2 Chron. 2:10; Isa. 5:10).

Batos. Approximately 8 gallons, or 30.3 liters. A Greek transliteration of the Hebrew word *bath* (see above). A measure of oil (Luke 16:6).

Hin. Approximately 4 quarts (1 gallon, or 3.8 liters). Equivalent to 1/6 bath and 12 logs. Used in the measurement of water (Ezek. 4:11), oil (Ezek. 46:5), and wine (Num. 28:14).

Log. Approximately 1/3 quart, or 0.3 liter. Equivalent to 1/72 bath and 1/12 hin. Mentioned five times in Scripture, specifically used to measure oil (Lev. 14:10–24).

Metretes. Approximately 10 gallons, or 37.8 liters. Used in the measurement of water at the wedding feast (John 2:6).

WELL–Unlike a spring, a well allows access to subterranean water through a shaft that has been dug into the ground. Wells typically were deep and lined with stone or baked brick for stability, often capped with heavy stone to prevent exploitation. In an arid environment, wells were invaluable to the community. Here, livestock were watered and conversations were held (Gen. 24:10–27; 29:1–14; John 4:6–8). Figuratively, the well is used of a lover (Song 4:15), an adulteress (Prov. 23:27), and a city (Jer. 6:7). Wells commonly were named (Gen. 21:25–31 [Beersheba, "well of an oath"]) and often fought over (Gen. 21:25–30; 26:18).

Three kinds of "well encounters" can be seen in Scripture: (1) human being with deity (Gen. 16:7–14), (2) clan with clan (26:20), and (3) man with woman (29:1–14). The latter became highly developed as a betrothal-type scene that included standard elements: stranger's arrival (= otherness), meeting (= bond), paternal announcement (= hospitality), and domestic invitation (= acceptance) (see Rebekah [Gen. 24]; Jacob and Rachel [Gen. 29:1–14]; Moses and Zipporah [Exod. 2:15–22]).

Jesus' encounter with the Samaritan woman (John 4:1–42) draws on multiple aspects of a well encounter: divine (Jesus) with human (the woman), Jew and Samaritan, a traveler, foreign (i.e., hostile) land, refreshment, announcement, invitation, and so on. However, now Jacob's well (4:6) hosts Jesus' presentation of himself as the groom whom she has been seeking (4:26). The patriarch's well becomes a symbol of salvation, just as water becomes a metaphor for transformation (4:14–15). What could have been another "well of nationality" conflict (John 4:9,

Biblical Weights and Measures and Their Modern Equivalents

Hebrew/Greek	Biblical Equivalent	US Equivalent	Metric Equivalent
Weights			
Beka	10 gerahs; ½ shekel	⅕ ounce	5.6 grams
Gerah	1/10 beka; 1/20 shekel	1/50 ounce	.56 grams
Mina	50 shekels	1¼ pounds	.56 kilograms
Pim	⅔ shekel	⅓ ounce	9.3 grams
Shekel	2 bekas; 20 gerahs	⅖ ounce	11 grams
Talent	60 minas	75 pounds	34 kilograms
Litra		12 ounces	340 grams
Linear Measurements			
Cubit	6 handbreadths	18 inches	45.7 centimeters
Day's Journey		20–25 miles	32–40 kilometers
Fingerbreadth	¼ handbreadth	¾ inch	1.9 centimeters
Handbreadth	⅙ cubit	3 inches	7.6 centimeters
Milion		1 mile	1.6 kilometers
Orguia	1/100 stadion	5 feet 11 inches	1.8 meters
Reed/Rod		108 inches	274 centimeters
Sabbath Day's Journey	2,000 cubits	¾ mile	1.2 kilometers
Stadion	100 orguiai	607 feet	185 meters
Span	3 handbreadths	9 inches	22.8 centimeters
Capacity			
Cab	1 omer	½ gallon	1.9 liters
Choinix		¼ gallon	.9 liters
Cor	1 homer; 10 ephahs	6 bushels; 48.4 gallons	183 liters
Ephah	10 omers; 1/10 homer	⅗ bushel; 6 gallons	22.7 liters
Homer	1 cor; 10 ephahs	6 bushels; 48.4 gallons	183 liters
Koros		10 bushels; 95 gallons	360 liters
Omer	1/10 ephah; 1/100 homer	2 quarts	1.9 liters
Saton	1 seah	7 quarts	6.6 liters
Seah	⅓ ephah; 1 saton	7 quarts	6.6 liters
Liquid Volume			
Bath	1 ephah	6 gallons	22.7 liters
Batos		8 gallons	30.3 liters
Hin	⅙ bath; 12 logs	4 quarts; 1 gallon	3.8 liters
Log	1/72 bath; 1/12 hin	⅓ quart	.3 liters
Metretes		10 gallons	37.8 liters

11–12 [cf. Gen. 26:20: "Esek = argument"]) was elevated to a "living water" conversion (John 4:10, 13–15 [cf. Gen. 16:14: "Beer Lahai Roi = well of the Living One who sees me"]). Her plea "Come, see a man" (John 4:29) echoes an earlier "outcast," Hagar, who exclaimed, "I have now seen the One who sees me" (Gen. 16:13).

Wheat–Wheat was a major crop in Palestine throughout biblical times and was the most important crop during the patriarchal times (Gen. 30:14). Wheat is a winter crop that was sown by hand in November or December; it was ready for harvest in May and was commemorated by the Festival of Weeks. Between the time of the late monarchy and the time of the NT, wheat was not only a food source but also a source of export income (Amos 8:5). Wheat can be eaten in a variety of ways and was often used, ground into fine flour, as an offering at the tabernacle and temple (Lev. 2:1). In the NT, wheat is used to symbolize the good produce of the kingdom of God (Matt. 13:24–31; cf. 3:12).

Wheel–There is no mention of wheels in the NT, while four different types of wheels are described in the OT. They include a potter's wheel, a chariot wheel, a wheel used for processing grain, and the wheel referred to in Ezekiel's theophany. The potter's wheel was a simple device for creating pottery that was symmetrical and strong. Jeremiah observed a potter working with a pottery wheel (Jer. 18:3). Chariot wheels may have been invented by the Sumerians and were a common part of warfare during most of the OT. These wheels were either a solid wheel made of two or three planks of wood held together with wooden pegs or the more common wheel-and-spoke assembly. The spoke assembly was favored as iron and other metal technology was developed (Exod. 14:25). This sort of wheel also functioned in the temple to hold the lavers (1 Kings 7:30–33). Wheels also were used to crush grain in order to separate the husk from the harvested grain, to grind grain into flour, and to extract oil from olives (Isa. 28:28). There is much speculation about the specifications of the phantasmagorical wheels in Ezekiel's visions, which include the enigmatic description of a wheel intersecting a wheel (Ezek. 1:15–16). It is clear from this description that the wheels are intended to guide a vehicle that can go in any direction instantly, but nothing else is known about them.

Whirlwind–Elijah the prophet, at the end of his earthly career, was taken up alive into heaven in a whirlwind (2 Kings 2:11). The Hebrew word there behind "whirlwind" (*se'arah*) also describes the atmospheric phenomenon of Ezek. 1:4, the "windstorm"—the early impression the prophet had of the flying chariot cherubim, above which God was enthroned. Thus, God communicates in a special way to these two prophets in the whirlwind/windstorm; in both cases, this encounter initiated a climactic event in their prophetic ministries: Elijah's ended, and Ezekiel's began. The same Hebrew word is used when God speaks to Job: "Then the Lord answered Job out of the whirlwind [*se'arah*]" (Job 38:1; 40:6 NRSV [NIV: "storm"]). God appears at times in wind and storm (e.g., Ps. 77:18; Isa. 66:15; Jer. 23:19; Nah. 1:3).

Wilderness–A broad designation for certain regions in Israel, typically rocky, although also plains, with little rainfall. These areas generally are uninhabited, and most often "wilderness" refers to specific regions surrounding inhabited Israel. A fair amount of Scripture's focus with respect to the wilderness concerns Israel's forty-year period of wandering in the wilderness after the exodus (*see also* Wilderness Wandering).

More specifically, the geographical locations designated "wilderness" fall into four basic categories: the Negev (south), Transjordan (east), Judean (eastern slope of Judean mountains), and Sinai (southwest).

The Negev makes up a fair amount of Israel's southern kingdom, Judah. It is very rocky and also includes plateaus and wadis, which are dry riverbeds that can bloom after rains. Its most important city is Beersheba (see Gen. 21:14, 22–34), which often designates Israel's southernmost border, as in the expression "from Dan to Beersheba" (e.g., 2 Sam. 17:11).

Transjordan pertains to the area east of the Jordan River, the area through which the Israelites had to pass before crossing the Jordan on their way from Mount Sinai to Canaan. (Israel was denied direct passage to Canaan by the Edomites and Amorites [see Num. 20:14–21; 21:21–26].) Even though this region lay outside the promised land of Canaan, it was settled by the tribes of Reuben, Gad, and the half-tribe of Manasseh after they had fulfilled God's command to fight alongside the other tribes in conquering Canaan (Num. 32:1–42; Josh. 13:8; 22:1–34).

The Judean Desert is located on the eastern slopes of the Judean mountains, toward the Dead Sea. David fled there for refuge from Saul (1 Sam. 21–23). It was also in this area that Jesus was tempted (Luke 4:1–13).

The Sinai Desert is a large peninsula, with the modern-day Gulf of Suez to the west and the Gulf of Aqaba to the east. In the ancient Near Eastern world, both bodies of water often were referred to as the "Red Sea," which is the larger sea to the south. In addition to the region traditionally believed to contain the location of Mount Sinai (its exact location is unknown), the Sinai Desert is further subdivided into other areas known to readers of the OT: Desert of Zin (northeast, contains Kadesh Barnea), Desert of Shur (northwest, near Egypt), Desert of Paran (central).

Wilderness is commonly mentioned in the Bible, and although it certainly can have neutral connotations (i.e., simply describing a location), the uninhabited places often entail both positive (e.g., as a place of solitude) and negative (e.g., as a place of wrath) connotations, both in their actual geological properties and as metaphors. The very rugged and uninhabited nature of the wilderness easily lent itself to being a place of death (e.g., Deut. 8:15; Ps. 107:4–5; Jer. 2:6). It was also a place associated with Israel's rebellions and struggles with other nations. Upon leaving Egypt, Israel spent forty years wandering the wilderness before entering Canaan, encountering numerous military conflicts along the way. This forty-year period was occasioned by a mass rebellion (Num. 14), hence casting a necessarily dark cloud over that entire period, and no doubt firming up subsequent negative connotations of "wilderness." Similarly, "wilderness" connotes notions of exile from Israel, as seen in the ritual of the scapegoat (lit., "goat of removal" [see Lev. 16]). On the Day of Atonement, one goat was sacrificed to atone for the people's sin, and another was sent off, likewise to atone for sin. The scapegoat was released into the desert, where it would encounter certain death, either by succumbing to the climate or through wild animals.

On the other hand, it is precisely in this uninhabited land that God also showed his faithfulness to his people, despite their prolonged punishment. He miraculously supplied bread (manna) and meat (quail) (Exod. 16; Num. 11), as well as water (Exod. 15:22–27; 17:1–7; Num. 20:1–13; 21:16–20). God's care for Israel is amply summarized in Deut. 1:30–31: "The LORD your God, who is going before you, will fight for you, as he did for you in Egypt, before your very eyes, and in the wilderness. There you saw how the LORD your God carried you, as a father carries his son, all the way you went until you reached this place."

The harsh realities of the wilderness also made it an ideal place to seek sanctuary and protection. David fled from Saul to the wilderness, the Desert of Ziph (1 Sam. 23:14; 26:2–3; cf. Ps. 55:7). Similarly, Jeremiah sought a retreat in the desert from sinful Israel (Jer. 9:2).

Related somewhat to this last point is Jesus' own attitude toward the wilderness. It was there that he retreated when he could no longer move about publicly (John 11:54). John the Baptist came from the wilderness announcing Jesus' ministry (Matt. 3:1–3; Mark 1:2–4; Luke 3:2–6; John 1:23; cf. Isa. 40:3–5). It was also in the desert that Jesus went to be tempted but also overcame that temptation.

WILDERNESS WANDERING–In the biblical account of the exodus, Israel's departure from Egypt begins in Exod. 12:37. The original intention was for the Israelites to go to Mount Sinai to receive the law and instructions for the tabernacle and then to proceed to Canaan. But Israel's trip was not to be quite that simple. Because of the Israelites' disobedience in the desert, they were condemned to a forty-year period of wilderness wandering, enough time for those twenty years of age or older during the rebellion to die in the wilderness (see Num. 14, which describes what is actually the final rebellion in a series of grumbling incidents that go back to Exod. 15:22–27).

Technically, the wilderness period began immediately after the crossing of the Red Sea. The Israelites passed through the Desert of Shur, the Desert of Sin, Rephidim, and then Sinai itself. These locations, however, were only stations on the way to Sinai, and so they do not pertain to the specific forty-year period of punishment, which begins in Num. 14. Their wandering period would not be officially over until they crossed the Jordan River and entered Canaan (Josh. 3:17).

WILL OF GOD–The accomplishment of God's purposes. This was most clearly expressed by Jesus' prayer, "Not my will, but yours be done" (Luke 22:42). Jesus stipulated in the Gospel of John that he was pursuing not his own will but that of God (5:19, 30; 6:38). God's will is revealed in creation (Rev. 4:11), Scripture (2 Pet. 1:20–21), his standards (Ezra 10:11; Rom. 12:1–2; 1 Thess. 4:3), his calling (1 Cor. 1:1), and his purpose (Isa. 46:10).

WINE–An alcoholic beverage made primarily by fermenting grapes, wine was valued as both a pleasurable and a functional drink (Ps. 104:15; 1 Tim. 5:23) and therefore a staple of ceremonial practice and social gatherings (Exod. 29:40; John 2:1–3). For this reason, wine is a symbol of God's blessing (Gen. 27:28; John 2:11), particularly for his covenant people (Isa. 25:6; 55:1; 1 Cor. 11:25). Yet the Bible also warns against the abuse of alcohol, which can lead to drunkenness and debauchery (Prov. 9:4–5; Eph. 5:18). Such abuse becomes a symbol of God's curse for disobedience (Hos. 4:11; 9:2; Matt. 27:48–49).

Winepress–A mechanical device that extracts juice from grapes for use in making wine. Winepresses in ancient Israel were hewn from bedrock to form a flat surface for treading. They consisted of a pair of square or circular vats arranged at different levels and connected by a channel. The vat in which the grapes were trodden (*gat*) was higher and larger than its deeper counterpart (*yeqeb*) into which the juice flowed from the press.

The vintage season was a joyous occasion accompanied by celebrating, feasting, shouting, and rejoicing as family members trod the grapes. Thus, the imagery of a winepress overflowing with new wine often stands for divine blessing (Prov. 3:10; Joel 2:24), and the lack of new wine from a winepress is a picture of divine judgment (Job 24:11; Jer. 48:33; cf. Isa. 16:10). As a metaphor based upon the treading of the grapes in the vats, the winepress connotes divine destruction and judgment. In Joel 3:13 the image of God's mighty army trampling the enemy is couched in the language of a vintner treading the grapes. The abundant flow from the presses is then compared to the greatness of the wickedness of the nations. Isaiah 63:3 likens a judging God to a lonely treader of a winepress, and the juice from the press to blood. This is best understood against the background that normally treading in vintage is communal work. The lonely treader conveys the idea that God is the only judge of the nations. The metaphor of the winepress for judgment is used climactically in Rev. 14:19–20; 19:15, where the winepress is identified with divine wrath and the juice with bloodshed. In Sir. 33:17, however, the winepress is used as a positive metaphor connoting the learning of Torah.

The winepress and wine occur in various places in the book of Judges, yet in each there is a literary twist. Gideon was introduced as threshing wheat in a winepress to hide it from the Midianites (6:11). Zeeb, the Midianite general, was killed at the winepress of Zeeb (7:25). Gideon calmed the anger of the Ephraimites by reference to Abiezrite wine (8:2). A vintage festival marked the beginning of the end for Abimelek (9:27). Finally, the kidnap of the women of Shiloh occurred during a vintage festival (21:20–22).

Wisdom, Wise–In the OT, wisdom is a characteristic of someone who attains a high degree of knowledge, technical skill, and experience in a particular domain. It refers to the ability that certain individuals have to use good judgment in running the affairs of state (Joseph in Gen. 41:33; David in 2 Sam. 14:20; Solomon in 1 Kings 3:9, 12, 28). It can also refer to the navigational skills that sailors use in maneuvering a ship through difficult waters (Ps. 107:27). Furthermore, wisdom includes the particular skills of an artisan (Exod. 31:6; 35:35; 1 Chron. 22:15–16). In all these cases, wisdom involves the expertise that a person acquires to accomplish a particular task. In these instances "wisdom" is an ethically neutral term, or at least that dimension is not emphasized. The wise are those who have mastered a certain skill set in their field of expertise.

The uniqueness of the OT wisdom literature (Job, Proverbs, Ecclesiastes, etc.) is that it highlights the moral dimension of wisdom. Here "wisdom" refers to developing expertise in negotiating the complexities of life and managing those complexities in a morally responsible way that honors God and benefits both the community and the individual. Although it is difficult to pin down a concise definition, one can gain a better understanding of wisdom by investigating two important dimensions: wisdom as a worldview, and the traits of a person who is considered to be wise.

Who is wise? First, the wise are those involved in a lifelong process of character development. They manifest the virtues of righteousness, justice, and equity (Prov. 1:3; 2:9). The embodiment of these virtues culminates in the description of the woman of noble character at the conclusion of Proverbs (31:10–31). She exhibits self-control, patience, care, diligence, discipline, humility, generosity, honesty, and fear of the Lord (cf. James 3:13–18). She is the epitome of wisdom in its maturity and the model that all should emulate.

Second, the wise know the value of words and how to use them. They know when to speak, what to say, and how to say it (Job 29:21–22; Prov. 15:23; 25:11; Eccles. 3:7; 12:9–10). Wisdom and the wise place a premium on the power of words.

Third, the wise place great importance on relationships and on interaction with others. The wise person is the one who is open to the give-and-take of relationships (Prov. 27:5–6, 17, 19). Such a person develops the humility necessary to receive correction and criticism from others. Hearing criticism and changing wrong behavior are integral to wisdom (3:1–11). The wise appreciate insightful criticism because it helps them live life more productively (15:12). Wisdom is, ultimately, relational.

Fourth, the wise person develops the art of discernment (Prov. 1:2, 4–6). The sage is equipped with the ability to think critically. The very quality of wisdom itself invites the reforming and rethinking of ideas. Sages are not interested in pat answers (26:4–5). Proverbs 16:1–9 throws a wrench in the conventional cogs of wisdom, claiming that although humans make their plans, God has the final say. Both Job and Ecclesiastes go head to head with conventional beliefs, probing more deeply into the complexities of life and the relationship between human and divine. No easy answers exist here. In contrast, fools do not use their mental faculties. They view wisdom as a commodity, a matter of learning some techniques, accepting certain beliefs, and memorizing a few proverbs (17:16). The wise, however, know that wisdom involves the art of critical thinking and interacting with others.

Fifth, and most fundamental, the wise person takes a God-centered focus toward life. Wisdom literature affirms, "The fear of the LORD is the beginning of wisdom" (Prov. 9:10; cf. Prov. 1:7; Job 28:28; Eccles. 12:13). That this is the beginning step in the process of gaining wisdom means that one who misses this step can proceed no further along the path to wisdom. The fear of the Lord is to wisdom as the letters of the alphabet are to forming words. The wise gain wisdom by being in relationship with the Lord (Prov. 3:5–8). The fear of the Lord is the beginning as well as the culmination of wisdom.

Wisdom is a highly prized quality, superior to might and power (Prov. 25:15; Eccles. 9:13–16), and one must diligently seek it (Prov. 2:1–5). Yet in the end, wisdom is a gift that only God can give (Prov. 2:6–8; 1 Kings 3:9).

WITNESS–The English term "witness" occurs in both Testaments numerous times, with a wide range of meanings. One common meaning relates to someone who gives legal testimony and to the legitimacy of that testimony (Num. 35:30; Deut. 17:6; 19:15–16, 18; Prov. 12:17; Isa. 8:16, 20). Throughout the NT the term occurs primarily in the context of someone bearing witness—especially God—or testifying to something (Rom. 1:9; 2 Cor. 1:23; Phil. 1:8; 1 Thess. 2:5, 10), though it also has a forensic dimension in regard to one who establishes legal testimony (e.g., Acts 6:13; 7:58; 2 Cor. 13:1; 1 Tim. 5:19; Heb. 10:28).

Central to the concept of witness is the truthfulness of the witness. This was a vital component of the OT concept of witness. Thus, in legal proceedings a lone witness was insufficient to establish testimony against anyone (Deut. 17:6). This principle carries over into the NT (cf. Matt. 18:16; 2 Cor. 13:1). Such truthfulness was so significant that the ninth commandment expressly forbids bearing false witness (Exod. 20:16; Deut. 5:20; cf. Prov. 19:5, 9).

Truth-telling was not something that the people of Israel were called to merely among themselves. They were to be God's witnesses to the nations (Isa. 43:10; 44:8). As witnesses of God's existence and holiness, they were called to be separate from the nations (Exod. 19:6) and to be a light to them (Isa. 49:6). Tragically, Israel failed in this responsibility and was deemed "blind" (Isa. 42:19).

The NT continues the concept that the people of God are to be God's witnesses. John the Baptist is commissioned "to testify concerning that light" (John 1:7). It is in this context that Jesus later declares himself to be "the light of the world" (John 8:12; 9:5). Jesus himself is the exemplar of a "faithful witness" (Rev. 1:5). And his followers, whom he has designated as "the light of the world" (Matt. 5:14), are then called to bear witness to the ends of the earth (Acts 1:8).

"Witness" is also employed in terms of a legal testimony regarding what one has seen. That the disciples were intent on establishing such legal testimony is evident in their stipulation that the person to replace Judas Iscariot be someone from among those who had been with Jesus from the beginning of his ministry to his ascension, so that "one of these must become a witness with us of his resurrection" (Acts 1:22). This forensic aspect of witness appears in the close of the Gospel of John: "This is the disciple who testifies to these things and who wrote them down. We know that his testimony is true" (21:24). Paul demonstrates this forensic concern for witnesses when he references Peter, the Twelve, some five hundred others, and himself as among those who have witnessed the resurrection (1 Cor. 15:3–8).

Throughout Revelation there resides a direct link between Christians bearing witness and suffering, and perhaps dying, as a consequence of this witness. This is evident in the mention of Antipas, who was martyred, and is then designated as "my faithful witness" (Rev. 2:13). Also, the two unnamed witnesses in 11:1–12, who explicitly function as witnesses, are the subject of attack and are eventually murdered. Their murder occurs only after they have finished "their testimony" (11:7).

It is this association of persecution and martyrdom that likely leads to the second-century employment of "martyr" as a designation for those who bear witness to Christ to the point of death.

Woman–In the Bible, woman is first encountered along with man in Gen. 1:26–28. God created "man" in the plural, male and female, and commanded them to reproduce and to fill the earth and subdue it. Being created male and female is set in parallel to being created in the image of God. In the ancient Near East, perhaps the king would be thought of as the image of God. But in Genesis, not only is the first man the image of God, but the first woman participates in the image as well. This is all but unthinkable in the ancient world, and it suggests an unparalleled dignity and worth in womankind.

Genesis records that the human race fell through the instrumentality of a man, a woman, and the serpent. The serpent approached the woman, not the man. The woman was convinced by the serpent and ate the forbidden fruit. She gave some to her husband, who also ate it without saying a word. Thus, the woman can be blamed in part for the fall of the race. Adam was condemned because he "listened to [his] wife" (Gen. 3:17). Her judgment, for heeding the serpent, was pain in childbirth and a desire for her husband, who would rule over her (Gen. 3:16). The exact parameters of this judgment are unclear, but it appears that her desire will be for his position of leadership and will be perpetually frustrated.

Often in the Bible, women are motivated by their desire to have children. Rachel demanded of Jacob, "Give me children, or I'll die!" (Gen. 30:1). She saw herself in competition with her sister, Leah, in this respect (30:8). The "fruit of the womb" is a reward, and like arrows, the blessed man's quiver is full of them (Ps. 127:1–5). Note also the beatitude of Ps. 128:3: "Your wife will be like a fruitful vine within your house; your children will be like olive shoots around your table."

In Genesis, the reproductive capability of slave girls is at the disposal of their owners. Thus, Rachel and Leah's maidservants became surrogate mothers for a number of their sons (Gen. 30:3–10). Sarah also became frustrated at her inability to conceive, so she gave Hagar to Abraham. The result was great familial turmoil, finally resulting in the banishment of both Hagar and Ishmael, whom she bore to Abraham.

In the beginning, God joined one man and one woman together as husband and wife. But soon this idea was corrupted, and Lamech, a man from Cain's lineage, is credited with the first polygamous marriage (Gen. 4:19). Although the patriarchs (such as Jacob) did have more than one wife, the household discontent and strife are what is highlighted in those stories, such as with Hagar. In the NT, an elder is to be, literally, a "one-woman man" (1 Tim. 3:2; ESV, KJV: "the husband of one wife"), meaning monogamous.

The Torah contains significant legislation regarding women. The daughters of Zelophehad argued that their father died without sons, so in Canaan they were disinherited. God agreed and decreed that in Israel daughters would inherit land in the absence of sons. Only if there were no children at all would the land pass to other kin (Num. 27:1–11).

When a man made a vow, he must fulfill it, but a young woman's vow was subject to her father. If he remained silent, the vow stood, but if he expressed disapproval, then she was freed from it. If she was married, her husband governed her vows, but if she was divorced, then there was no responsible male over her, and her vow was treated as a man's (Num. 30:1–16).

Sexual intercourse was also regulated in the law of Moses, insofar as the act rendered both parties ritually impure (Lev. 15:18). Both must bathe and were unclean until evening. A woman's menstrual discharge also made her unclean for a week. Everything she sat or lay upon was unclean, as was anyone who touched these things. She must wash and offer sacrifice to become clean again (15:18–31).

If a man discovered on his wedding night that his bride was not a virgin, he could accuse her publicly. If her parents provided evidence that she had in fact been a virgin, then the man was severely punished for lying and not allowed to divorce her (otherwise, it was simply a matter of writing a letter to divorce her [Deut. 24:1]). If her virginity could not be proved, she was to be put to death by stoning (Deut. 22:13–21).

In the case of a rape of a betrothed virgin, if it occurred in the city, both the rapist and the victim were stoned, since apparently she had failed to cry out for help and thus, the law assumed, consented to sexual intercourse. If she was raped in the countryside, only the man was killed. But if he raped a woman who was not spoken for, his punishment was that he must marry her without possibility of divorce (Deut. 22:23–29).

Numbers 5:11–31 treats cases where a husband was suspicious that his wife had been unfaithful—that is, a matter of covenantal jealousy. The unprovable was left to God to punish.

In the Bible, women sometimes are afforded dignity beyond what is expected in an ancient Near Eastern provenance. Hagar is the only woman in all ancient Near Eastern literature who gave a name to a deity (Gen. 16:13). In Judg. 4:4, Deborah "judged" Israel (despite the NIV's "leading," the underlying Hebrew verb indicates "judging," as in the NRSV). Even as judge, however, she did not lead the army against the enemy general Sisera; Barak did so. But Barak was unwilling to undertake this mission unless Deborah went with him (4:8). Thus, God ensured that the prestige of killing Sisera went to a woman, Jael (4:9, 21). Another prominent woman was Huldah, to whom the priests turned for guidance when the law was rediscovered (2 Kings 22:14).

Many biblical stories feature heroines. Mighty Pharaoh was undermined by two midwives in his attempt to destroy Israel (Exod. 1:15–21). Ruth the Moabite woman gave her name to the book that recounts her trek from Moab to Israel, including her famous oath of loyalty (Ruth 1:16–17). Esther too was a courageous woman whose book bears her name. Heroines are especially prominent in the Gospels, and the women there have the distinction of being the first to witness the risen Lord. Luke's birth narrative is largely organized around Mary. Priscilla (with her husband) taught and helped to shape the early church (Acts 18:26). Paul lists many women in Rom. 16, calling them "deaconess," "fellow worker," and possibly even "apostle."

Scripture also at times portrays various women as being temptations to men. Eve handed the fruit to Adam (Gen. 3:6). In the wilderness Israel worshiped Moabite gods in conjunction with sexual activity (Num. 25:1–9). Later, Israelites intermarried with Canaanite women, directly leading to worship of their idols (Judg. 3:6). Bathsheba was a temptation to David, and this began a series of events that marred his career as a man after God's own heart. Solomon loved many foreign women, who turned him to worship their gods. After the exile, the Israelites were admonished by Nehemiah to put away their foreign wives lest history repeat itself (Neh. 13:26).

Women and marriage are used in the Bible as images for spiritual things. Paul writes that marital love mirrors the church's relationship with Christ (Eph. 5:32–33). A man should love his wife as Christ loved the church. Revelation portrays the climax to human history in the figure of two women: the bride of Christ, adorned with righteous deeds for her husband (19:7–8), and the whore Babylon, drunk on the blood of the saints (17:5–6). The consummation of the age is when one is judged and the other enters her eternal marital bliss.

The book of Proverbs also separates humankind into two groups, symbolized by two women. Along the path of life, the youth hears the voices of Woman Folly (9:13–18) and of Woman Wisdom (1:20–33) calling out to him. Folly is incarnated in the flesh-and-blood temptation of the immoral woman (7:6–27), whereas Woman Wisdom has her counterpart at the end of the book in the detailed description of the woman of virtue (31:10–31). There, the woman who fears God is set as a prize far above earthly wealth—the highest blessing of the wise.

Paul uses two women from sacred history to help explain his gospel of law versus grace. Hagar the slave woman represents the Mosaic covenant given at Sinai, and the earthly Jerusalem—that is, a mind-set of slavery that futilely attempts to earn God's favor by works of the law. Sarah was the free woman, and her son was the promised son, who represents the heavenly Jerusalem, the new covenant, and freedom from the requirements of the law (Gal. 4:21–31). Again, two women symbolize two paths and two peoples—one being slaves, the other being God's free people.

Wonders–*See* Miracles; Sign.

Word–"Word" is used in the Bible to refer to the speech of God in oral, written, or incarnate form. In each of these uses, God desires to make himself known to his people. The communication of God is always personal and relational, whether he speaks to call things into existence (Gen. 1) or to address an individual directly (Gen. 2:16–17; Exod. 3:14). The prophets and the apostles received the word of God (Deut. 18:14–22; John 16:13), some of which was proclaimed but not recorded. The greatest revelation in this regard is the person of Jesus Christ, who is called the "Word" of God (John 1:1, 14).

The psalmist declared God's word to be an eternal object of hope and trust that gives light and direction (Ps. 119), and Jesus declared the word to be truth (John 17:17). The word is particularized and intimately connected with God himself by means of the key phrases "your word," "the word of God," "the word of the Lord," "word about Christ," and "the word of Christ" (Rom. 10:17; Col. 3:16). Our understanding of the word is informed by a variety of terms and contexts in the canon of Scripture, a collection of which is found in Ps. 119.

The theme of the word in Ps. 119 is continued and clarified in the NT, accentuating the intimate connection between the word of God and God himself. The "Word" of God is the eternal Lord Jesus Christ (John 1:1; 1 John 1:1–4), who took on flesh and blood so that we might see the glory of the eternal God. The sovereign glory of Christ as the Word of God is depicted in the vision of John in Rev. 19:13. As the Word of God, Jesus Christ ultimately gives us our lives (John 1:4; 6:33; 10:10), sustains our lives (John 5:24; 6:51, 54; 8:51), and ultimately renders a just judgment regarding our lives (John 5:30; 8:16, 26; 9:39; cf. Matt. 25:31–33; Heb. 4:12).

WORKS–The Bible has much to say about works, and an understanding of the topic is important because works play a role in most religions. In the most generic sense, "works" refers to the products or activities of human moral agents in the context of religious discussion. God's works are frequently mentioned in Scripture, and they are always good. His works include creation (Gen. 2:2–3; Isa. 40:28; 42:5), sustenance of the earth (Ps. 104; Heb. 1:3), and redemption (Exod. 6:6; Ps. 111:9; Rom. 8:23). Human works, therefore, should be in alignment with God's works, though obviously of a different sort. Works in the Bible usually reflect a moral polarity: good or evil, righteous or unrighteous, just or unjust. The context of the passage often determines the moral character of the works (e.g., Isa. 3:10–11; 2 Cor. 11:15).

Important questions follow from the existence of works and their moral quality. Do good works merit God's favor or please him? Can good works save at the time of God's judgment? When people asked Jesus, "What must we do to do the works God requires?" he answered, "The work of God is this: to believe in the one he has sent" (John 6:28–29). Without faith it is impossible to please God (Heb. 11:6). The people from the OT commended in Heb. 11 did their works in the precondition of faith. Explicitly in the NT and often implicitly in the OT, faith is the condition for truly good works. God elects out of his mercy, not out of human works (Rom. 9:12, 16; Titus 3:5; cf. Rom. 11:2). Works not done in faith, even if considered "good" by human standards, are not commendable to God, since all humankind is under sin (Rom. 3:9) and no person is righteous or does good (Rom. 3:10–18; cf. Isa. 64:6). Works cannot save; salvation is a gift to be received by faith (Eph. 2:8–9; 2 Tim. 1:9; cf. Rom. 4:2–6). Even works of the Mosaic law are not salvific (Rom. 3:20, 27–28; Gal. 2:16; 3:2; 5:4). Good works follow from faith (2 Cor. 9:8; Eph. 2:10; 1 Thess. 1:3; James 2:18, 22; cf. Acts 26:20). The works of those who have faith will be judged, but this judgment appears to be related to rewards, not salvation (Matt. 16:27; Rom. 2:6; 2 Cor. 5:10; cf. Rom. 14:10; 1 Cor. 3:13–15).

WORSHIP–Worship of God is a critical dimension of both Testaments. One might argue that it is the very goal for which Israel and the church were formed.

The living God is the sole object of worship. He delights in the satisfying joy that his children find in him. The nature of worship is not about servant entertainment or passive observation; it is an active acknowledgment of God's worth in a variety of humble ways.

A genuine selfless focus on the person and work of God brings about a humble response that affects one's posture, generates works of service, and stirs up a healthy attitude of fear and respect. Knowledge of God is the foundational element in worship. God is worshiped for who he is and what he does. He is the Eternal One (Ps. 90:1; 1 Tim. 1:17), unique in every way (Isa. 44:8); he is God alone (Deut. 6:4). He is distinguished by his self-existence, the self-reliant quality of his life (Exod. 3:14; Deut. 32:30). The psalmist calls God's people to shout joyfully to their good, loving, eternal, and faithful Creator (Ps. 100).

God is worshiped as the Creator of all life. This magnificent creative work of God, declared in the opening of Genesis, is a critical focus in worship (Ps. 95:6; Rom. 1:25; Rev. 4:11). Along with this is the companion declaration that God is the redeemer. The redemptive work of God is celebrated in the Song of Moses (Exod. 15:1–18) and in the Song of the Redeemed (Rev. 14:3).

Worship is also associated with the royal aspects of God's character. It was the desire of the magi to find Jesus the king and worship him (Matt. 2:1–2). The final scenes of history will be characterized by humble submission to and worship of the King of kings (1 Tim. 6:15; Rev. 17:14; 19:16; cf. Rev. 15:3–4). The psalms often draw the reader's attention to God's royal character as a basis for worship (Pss. 45:11; 98:6).

Finally, God is worshiped as the Lord of his covenant relationship with the nation of Israel. This covenant theme and metaphor summarize the varied aspects of God's character and his relationship with Israel. The God who brought Israel into a covenant relationship is to be sincerely and exclusively worshiped (2 Kings 17:35, 38; cf. Deut. 31:20). These confessional statements about the character of God are a glorious weight that moves believers to prostrate themselves, to have an attitude of awe and respect, and to obediently serve.

Wrath–The words "wrath" and "anger" are used in Bible translations for a variety of Hebrew and Greek words that refer to the disposition of someone (including God) toward persons (including oneself [Gen. 45:5]) or situations considered to be seriously displeasing. There may be degrees of anger (Zech. 1:15), and it may be accompanied by other sentiments such as distress (Gen. 45:5), hatred (Job 16:9), jealousy (Rom. 10:19), grief (Mark 3:5), and vengeance (Mic. 5:15).

Anger may be a proper response to sin or a sin-distorted world, as seen in, for example, Moses' reaction to the golden calf (Exod. 32:19). Paul envisages an anger that does not necessarily involve sin (Eph. 4:26). Jesus is said to display anger at the willful stubbornness of his contemporaries (Mark 3:5), and his response to the mourning for Lazarus (John 11:33) might be rendered as "outrage," an anger directed not so much at the mourners as at the ugliness of death, the consequence of sin, and with thoughts, perhaps, of his own impending death necessitated by this fallen world.

On the other hand, a display of anger may be the result of distorted perceptions or values (Gen. 4:5–6). A tendency to anger in oneself needs to be kept in check (James 1:19) and in others needs to be handled prudently (Prov. 15:1). Unchecked, anger may lead to violence and murder (Gen. 49:6). In several NT lists anger is associated with such other sinful behavior as quarreling, jealousy, selfishness, slander, malice, gossip, conceit, strife, idolatry, sorcery, and bitterness (2 Cor. 12:20; Gal. 5:20; Eph. 4:31; Col. 3:8).

In Ps. 76:10 NLT (cf. ESV, NASB, NRSV) God is said to cause human anger to bring him praise (but see NIV, NET, where it is God's wrath against human beings that brings him praise). Perhaps an instance of this is seen in Rom. 13:4–5, where the wrath of the civil authority serves to maintain justice under God.

Wrath of God–Despite tendencies to downplay the reality of God's anger (God is classically described as "without passions"), if we are to do justice to both Testaments, we must allow the language of Scripture to stand, where God often is said to be angry with individuals or nations, including Israel. Although God is changeless (Mal. 3:6), he interacts in a personal way with a time-bound world. The Bible writers intend us to understand that there is something in God's anger to which human anger is analogous, though God's anger is not identical to ours (Hos. 11:9). God's anger is not an automatic response; he can restrain it (Ps. 78:38). God is said to be characteristically slow to become angry; that is, his anger is a deliberate response (Exod. 34:6, a text with numerous echoes) and may also be short-lived (Ps. 30:5; Mic. 7:18).

God's anger against Israel in the wilderness is noteworthy (Heb. 3:10, 17). The apostasy with the golden calf (Exod. 32:10–12), the complaining (Num. 11:1, 33), and the failure to enter the promised land following the report of the spies (Num. 32:10–11) all provoke God to anger. Failure to heed God's word (Zech. 7:12) or that of his prophets (2 Chron. 36:16), neglect of his worship (2 Chron. 29:6–8), and intermarriage with idolaters (Ezra 9:14) are behaviors that incur the wrath of God.

God's anger is directed against individuals, particularly for failures of leadership, as with Moses (Exod. 4:14; Deut. 1:37) and Solomon (1 Kings 11:9–11). God's anger often is directed against the Israelite and Judean kings, not just those who committed idolatry (2 Chron. 25:15), but even those who are faithful in most respects, for their failure to remove the idolatrous high places (2 Kings 23:19).

Picking up on the warning that God's anger will be directed against those who do not pay homage to God's appointed king (Ps. 2:5, 12), Jesus declares that disobedience to God's Son brings upon one the wrath of God (John 3:36), which evidently is not incompatible with his love for the world (3:16). According to Rom. 4:15, God's wrath is a consequence of the law; that is, the law, giving concrete expression to the character of God, brings culpability for transgression. God's wrath is revealed against all forms of ungodliness and its tendency to suppress the truth (Rom. 1:18). Those who demonstrate their disobedience to God or his truth will be subjected to his anger (Rom. 2:8; Eph. 5:6; Col. 3:6).

The judgment that follows as a consequence of God's anger being aroused takes the form of the withholding of God's covenant favor (Ps. 95:11; Isa. 54:8) or the implementation of his covenant curses (Deut. 29:27), specifically through drought (Deut. 11:17), plague (Ps. 78:50), the sword (Ps. 78:62), and deliverance into the hands of enemies (2 Kings 13:3), leading to exile (2 Chron. 6:36). God's anger can be depicted in various forms of cosmic upheaval or the undoing of creation (2 Sam. 22:8–16; Ps. 18:7; Jer. 4:26). God's anger is beyond human ability to endure (Ps. 76:7), such that hiding in Sheol is considered preferable (Job 14:13).

God's wrath becomes particularly associated with a coming day of wrath at the end of the age, when God's justice will be powerfully displayed (Dan. 8:19; Zeph. 2:3; Luke 21:23; Rom. 2:5; Rev. 6:17).

The NT brings to fulfillment these forms of mediation in presenting the ultimate remedy for God's wrath in the person and work of Jesus Christ (Rom. 5:9; 1 Thess. 1:10; 5:9). The use of "propitiation" language (Rom. 3:25; Heb. 2:17; 1 John 2:2), though its significance is disputed, is classically understood in terms of the need for God's wrath to be satisfied. In that case, it is specifically the cross of Christ that ultimately deals with God's righteous anger against sinners.

X

Xerxes–The king of Persia from 486 to 465 BC. He inherited the throne from his father, Darius; his son Artaxerxes was king during the time of Ezra and Nehemiah. In the Bible Xerxes is called "Ahasuerus" (though the NIV and some other versions use "Xerxes"), a Hebrew equivalent (*'akhasherosh*) of his Persian name. Esther (Hadassah) was wed to Xerxes in 479 BC and became queen (Esther 2:17), and thus she was in a position to save the Jewish nation from the annihilation plotted by Haman (Esther 4:12–17). Additionally, the "enemies of Judah and Benjamin" (Ezra 4:1) wrote a letter to Xerxes when the Jews began rebuilding God's temple in Jerusalem.

Y

Yahweh–*See* Lord.

Year of Jubilee–*See* Festivals.

Yeast–*See* Leaven.

YHWH–*See* Lord.

Yoke–A wooden crosspiece fastened to the neck and shoulders of one or, more often, two animals (e.g., 1 Sam. 6:7) to facilitate labor. Yokes were also used by individuals to balance a load suspended from the shoulders (Num. 4:10, 12; 13:23). As such, the yoke also functioned as a symbol of subjection (Gen. 27:40; Lev. 26:13; Deut. 28:48; Jer. 27:2–7; Gal. 5:1; 1 Tim. 6:1), sometimes of joint labor (2 Cor. 6:14; Phil. 4:3), and is closely associated with pairs of animals (Luke 14:19; 1 Sam. 11:7). *See also* Weights and Measures.

Z

Zacchaeus–A wealthy tax collector in Jericho who, being short in height, climbed a Sycamore tree to see Jesus as he was walking by (Luke 19:1–10). A Jew—Jesus calls him a "son of Abraham"—his position as "chief tax collector" (*architelōnēs*) suggests that he had several others working for him. Since tax collectors were hated by their fellow Jews, Zacchaeus's senior position would have made him especially despised. Jesus initiated the contact with Zacchaeus, and he responded by bringing Jesus to his home. After time with Jesus, Zacchaeus responded in faith, giving money to the poor and making restitution to those whom he had cheated.

Zadok–The son of Ahitub, and a descendant of Aaron (1 Chron. 6:1–15, 53), he was a priest during the time of David and became high priest during the time of Solomon. Initially, Zadok is mentioned alongside the high priest Abiathar (2 Sam. 8:17). Both men served as spies for David when Absalom, the king's son, took Jerusalem during a civil war. The priests' sons, Ahimaaz and Jonathan, were runners reporting to David. Toward the end of David's life, Abiathar supported Adonijah's bid for the kingship, so when Solomon became king, he was removed from the high priesthood.

Zadok anointed Solomon as king and became the sole high priest, fulfilling a prophetic word uttered against the house of Eli years before (1 Kings 2:35; cf. 1 Sam. 2:27–36). In his vision of a future temple, Ezekiel often references the priestly line of Zadok (Ezek. 40:46; 43:19; 44:15; 48:11).

Zalmunna–A Midianite king who, along with Zebah, was captured by Gideon and later executed to avenge the killing of his brothers (Judg. 8:18–21). Their deaths became symbolic of God's judgment on Israel's enemies (Ps. 83:11).

Zealots–*See* Jewish Parties.

Zebah–He and another Midianite king, Zalmunna, were killed by Gideon in retaliation for their execution of his brothers (Judg. 8:18–21). The Midianites were known for camel raids into Israel during harvesttime to ravage the land and impoverish the Israelites (Judg. 6:1–6). The psalmist names Zebah and Zalmunna among God's enemies (Ps. 83:1–11). Israel's victory over Midian under Gideon was a direct result of Israel's crying out to God, and the circumstances of the battle strategy were such that God received the glory for the victory. Upon the defeat of Midian, Gideon pursued the two kings and executed them.

Zebedee–The father of the disciples James and John, he was a Galilean fisherman by trade (Mark 1:16–20; Matt. 4:18–22). Zebedee's sons worked with him in the fishing business, and he seems to have possessed some wealth, as indicated by his ownership of a boat and the use of hired servants (Mark 1:20). His wife's name appears to have been Salome (cf. Mark 15:40; 16:1; Matt. 27:56).

Zeboyim–**(1)** A city in the Valley of Siddim that was attacked and plundered along with Sodom and Gomorrah. Shemeber ruled over it when Abraham rescued the five cities on the plain from Kedorlaomer (Gen. 14:2, 8). Although Zeboyim is always mentioned along with Admah, its exact location is unknown, though it must be within the Valley of Siddim around the area of the Dead Sea. The account of Zeboyim is also recorded in Deut. 29, and reference is made to its destruction in Hos. 11:8. Zeboyim is not to be confused with the Zeboim mentioned in Neh. 11:34. **(2)** The Valley of Zeboyim, which is a valley facing the desert, was raided by the Philistines while Saul and Jonathan were staying in Gibeah (1 Sam. 13:18). This would place it near Gibeah and Mikmash. The exact valley referenced is unknown.

Zebulun–*See* Zebulun, Tribe of.

Zebulun, Tribe of–Descended from the tenth son of Jacob, Zebulun, this tribe did not drive out the Canaanites but instead subjected them to forced labor (Judg. 1:30). During the wilderness journey this tribe was one of the foremost in marching order, along with the tribes of Judah and Issachar. It responded to Gideon's summoning (Judg. 6:35) and also helped to enthrone David in Hebron (1 Chron. 12:33). It was later dispossessed by the Assyrians under Tiglath-pileser III (744–727 BC). Matthew 4:13–16 points to Jesus' ministry in the regions of Zebulun and Naphtali in Galilee as the fulfillment of Isa. 9:1–2.

Zebulunite–A title of Elon, one of the minor judges, who was from the land of Zebulun. He led Israel for ten years (Judg. 12:11).

Zechariah–**(1)** A king of Israel, the son of Jeroboam II (2 Kings 14:29). His reign was cut short at six months due to his assassination by Shallum (15:8–12). **(2)** *See* Zechariah, Book of.

Zechariah, Book of–The tenth and longest book of the twelve Minor Prophets. Zechariah's prophecy is one of the most intriguing in the OT, beginning with eight chapters of night visions and ending with six additional chapters of oracles. The second part of the book is quite obscure and apparently more randomly presented than the first part.

The night visions of chapters 1–8 fit in with their historical setting. The people and their leaders had been discouraged by internal economic concerns and pressures from external forces that did not want them to flourish. Zechariah spoke of divine visions that expressed God's intention to protect the people and to lead them to a new level of prosperity. Accordingly, the people should complete the construction of the temple, whose foundation had been laid (4:1–14). The visions also address the need for continual purification from the type of sin that led to the exile in the first place (3:1–10; 5:1–11).

Chapters 9–14 culminate in a vision of God's ultimate victory over those who continue to resist his will. This section includes oracles against foreign nations (9:1–8) as well as a vision of a new king in Zion (9:9–13). Chapter 14, the final chapter, describes a final battle in which God will come as a warrior to save his people and judge their enemies.

Zedekiah–The last king of Judah. Named "Mattaniah" at birth, he was the youngest son of Josiah and Hamutal (2 Kings 24:18; Jer. 1:3). Zedekiah was renamed when Nebuchadnezzar placed him on the throne and made him swear a covenant before God (2 Chron. 36:13). He was twenty-one years old when he was given the throne, after Nebuchadnezzar deposed his nephew Jehoiachin. He ruled nine years, and then he rebelled against Nebuchadnezzar, and war ensued for two years. He also refused to follow the rule of the prophet Jeremiah (2 Chron. 36:12). He was considered "evil in the eyes of the Lord," along with all the ruling parties of priests and officials during his reign.

Zeeb–*See* Oreb and Zeeb.

Zelophehad–The son of Hepher, he was the leader of a Manassite family that was left without male heirs (Num. 26:33; 1 Chron. 7:15). Upon his death in the wilderness, his five daughters approached Moses and asked that they might inherit their father's allotment (Num. 27:1–4). Moses brought their case before God, who granted their request and then amended the law to include the right of female inheritance (Num. 27:5–11). Later, it was also mandated that they marry within the tribe so that the tribal land did not go outside the tribe of Manasseh (Num. 36; cf. Josh. 17).

Zenas–A disciple in the early church who traveled with Apollos (Titus 3:13). Paul used "the lawyer" as a title for him, thus indicating that he was a Jewish scribe who continued to use the title after conversion. Paul urged Titus to supply Zenas and Apollos for their journey.

Zephaniah–The priest second in rank to the high priest during the fall of Jerusalem (2 Kings 25:18). He was operative during the days of the prophet Jeremiah, and as a member of the "patriotic" party he openly opposed Jeremiah. He and Pashhur were sent by

King Zedekiah to ask Jeremiah about the fate of Judah, which was under attack from King Nebuchadnezzar of Babylon (Jer. 21:1–2). Upon hearing from Jeremiah the bad news of long-term foreign occupation, Zephaniah read to him a letter from Shemaiah, asking why Jeremiah had not been reprimanded and punished (Jer. 29:24–29). Zephaniah eventually was taken by Nebuzaradan to Nebuchadnezzar at Riblah, where he was executed (Jer. 52:27). **(2)** *See* Zephaniah, Book of.

Zephaniah, Book of–The book of Zephaniah is the ninth of the twelve Minor Prophets. This short book moves dramatically from divine anger to divine compassion. Zephaniah is one of the more overlooked prophets, ministering during the same period of crisis as the well-known prophet Jeremiah.

As with Amos (5:18–20; 8:3–13), Joel, Isaiah (2:6–22), and other prophets, Zephaniah speaks of a coming day of the Lord (1:14). This will be a day of judgment, when those who have rejected and disobeyed God will receive the punishment due them. Zephaniah points out that God will bring his retributive judgment against the nations (2:14–15) as well as his own people (1:14–2:3). The book thus emphasizes the sinfulness of the people (1:7–13; 3:3–5) as well as God's sovereignty to carry out his punishment.

However, Zephaniah also speaks of God's mercy. God will restore a remnant. The remnant is those people who survive the judgment. They are purified and will be the basis of a new people of God (2:3; 3:13, 19–20).

Zerah–The Cushite leader of Egypt who attempted to conquer Judah under the reign of Asa. Asa and his army defeated Zerah in the Valley of Zephathah, and the men of Judah took a large amount of plunder. Zerah is possibly one of the Osorkons known to have ruled Egypt (2 Chron. 14:9).

Zeresh–The wife of Haman, she encouraged him to conspire against Mordecai (Esther 5:9–14; 6:12–14).

Zerubbabel–A Jewish leader immediately after the exile who in 539/538 BC or soon after led Jewish exiles back from Babylon to Jerusalem (Ezra 2:1–6:22; Haggai; Zech. 4:1–14).

Cyrus the Great defeated Babylon in 539 BC and then issued a decree allowing Babylon's vassals to return to their homelands and rebuild their temples (2 Chron. 36:22–23; Ezra 1:1–4). Zerubbabel led the first contingent to Jerusalem and then headed up the effort to rebuild the temple to Yahweh in Jerusalem. Zerubbabel saw to the immediate construction of the altar, which allowed sacrificial ritual to resume. However, after running into opposition from the Samaritans, the rebuilding of the temple proper was delayed. God sent Haggai and Zechariah to revitalize the effort, and in 515 BC the second temple finally was completed.

Zerubbabel was the Persian-appointed governor of Judah (Hag. 1:1). He was a descendant of Shealtiel. Sometimes the text implies he is Shealtiel's son, though 1 Chron. 3:19 says that he is the son of Shealtiel's brother Pedaiah, another of Jehoiachin's sons. Whatever the precise connection, there is no doubt that Zerubbabel was a Davidic descendant. The prophets Zechariah and Haggai both speak of Zerubbabel in messianic terms (Haggai; Zech. 4:1–14). Eventually, he simply disappears from the historical record. Some speculate that the Persians removed him because of the high expectation that surrounded him as a son of David. However, he was the governor of Judah, not the ultimate Messiah. A greater one, one of his descendants (Matt. 1:12–13; Luke 3:27), would be the true Messiah—Jesus Christ.

Zeus–The king of the Greek pantheon. When Barnabas and Paul were in Lystra, Paul healed a man who was born unable to walk. When the people saw it, they were confused and thought that Barnabas was the incarnation of Zeus, and Paul of the god Hermes, one of Zeus's many offspring. The priest of Zeus in Lystra, joined by a crowd, even wanted to offer sacrifices to the two men. Upon hearing of their intentions, Paul and Barnabas tore their clothes in dismay and stopped the crowd from proceeding (Acts 14:8–18).

Ziba–A servant in Saul's house who played a role in the court history of David recorded in 2 Sam. 9:2–12; 16:1–3; 19:17–29. David sought to show kindness to Saul's house, and Ziba informed him of a crippled son of Jonathan, Mephibosheth. By David's command, Ziba was charged with providing for Mephibosheth. Later, as David was fleeing for his life from Absalom, Ziba arrived with provisions. Ziba wrongly told him that Mephibosheth stayed behind to regain Saul's throne. David then gave all of Mephibosheth's

Z

property to Ziba. After David returned victorious, Mephibosheth said that he unwillingly stayed behind because he was crippled. So David commanded that half of Mephibosheth's property be given back to him; however, Mephibosheth told David to let Ziba keep it all, as David's return was sufficient reward.

Ziggurat–An important architectural form in the ancient Near East, the ziggurat was a stepped structure made of mud-brick and built on a raised platform. Similar to a pyramid, except with a platform at the top, the ziggurat was thought to span heaven and earth and as such was used as an artificial mountain for the worship of deities. Many believe that the tower of Babel was a ziggurat (Gen. 11:1–9).

Ziklag–A town in the Negev of Judah, originally given to the tribe of Simeon during the settlement of Canaan (Josh. 15:31; 19:5). This town subsequently was taken by the Philistines, only later to come into focus as the town given to David by Achish king of Gath (1 Sam. 27:6). David and his six hundred men stayed at Ziklag for a year and four months. During this time, David and his men joined Achish in battle against Saul. While David and his men were out with Achish, Ziklag was overrun, plundered, and burned by marauding Amalekites (1 Sam. 30:1). David quickly caught the Amalekites and saved Ziklag's inhabitants. Ziklag is also the location where David received the news of Saul's death (2 Sam. 1:1–4). Ziklag is said to have been resettled under Nehemiah after the Babylonian captivity (Neh. 11:28). Current archaeology has proposed several possible excavations of Ziklag, but none has been shown conclusively to be the biblical Ziklag.

Zillah–One of the two wives of Lamech, a descendant of Cain, she bore a son, Tubal-Cain, and a daughter, Naamah (Gen. 4:19, 22).

Zilpah–The maidservant of Leah, she was given to Jacob to provide children (Gen. 30:9–12). Zilpah was initially given to Leah by her father, Laban (Gen. 29:24). Zilpah gave birth to Gad and Asher (Gen. 35:26).

Zimri–A military officer of King Elah of Israel, he killed the king and usurped the throne. In doing so, he fulfilled the prophecy of Jehu against Baasha, the father of Elah. Zimri reigned for only seven days before he committed suicide in the face of another military coup led by Omri (1 Kings 16:8–20).

Zin, Desert of–A region in the extreme southeast of the land of Judah, forming a boundary between the land of Israel and that of Edom (Num. 34:3; Josh. 15:1, 3). This desert or wilderness is the same as the Desert of Kadesh (Num. 33:36; Ps. 29:8). There is also a town of Zin located in this wilderness, which most likely is the origin of the name (Num. 34:4). The Israelite spies started from Zin and traveled northward to scout the promised land (Num. 13:21). The region is also the location of the waters of Meribah Kadesh, where Moses disobeyed God and struck the rock for water (Num. 27:14; Deut. 32:51). It is also the place where Miriam died (Num. 20:1). It is not to be confused with the Desert of Sin.

Zion–Jerusalem was held by the Jebusites, who mocked David's forces. But David captured the city, which from then on bore the title "City of David," also called "fortress of Zion" (2 Sam. 5:5–9). David made it his capital. Later, Solomon built the temple there, making it also the religious center of the nation (1 Kings 8:1–14). "Zion" (of uncertain meaning) sometimes is a designation for the city of Jerusalem. It is said to have towers, ramparts, and citadels (Ps. 48:12–13), and Jeremiah prophesied its razing (Jer. 26:18). But it is also a designation for the mountain on which the city is built (Isa. 24:23; Zech. 8:3).

Since the God of Israel has a special relationship with Israel and its king, God's purposes for the world often are couched in terms of Mount Zion. God set his king on Mount Zion (Ps. 2:6). The psalmist praises God, who has established Zion "forever" (Ps. 48:1–8). It is there that God is said to reign (Isa. 24:23). Nevertheless, the king on David's throne and the inhabitants of Zion can be censured by God and found wanting (Amos 6:1). In fact, it is precisely because God identifies with the city that the people bear particular responsibility to represent his character. Thus, the time came when Zion was indeed "plowed like a field" (Mic. 3:12). Lamentations mourns Zion's destruction numerous times. After God's people spent a period of time in exile, God brought them back to Zion (Ps. 126). Although the ancient city was again destroyed by the Romans, Zion has become in the NT a symbol of the present heavenly dwelling place of God, entered into by faith (Heb. 12:22), and the future destiny of the saints (Rev. 14:1).

Zipporah–The daughter of Reuel (Jethro), the Midianite priest for whom Moses worked. She became the wife of Moses, bearing him two sons, Gershom and Eliezer. Zipporah quarreled with Moses over the necessity of circumcision, calling Moses a "bridegroom of blood" (Exod. 4:25). She was sent back to Midian before Moses returned to Egypt, but later she stayed with the migrating Israelites on their way to the promised land (18:2–5). There is much speculation around whether Zipporah was the Cushite woman who was the source of Miriam and Aaron's opposition to Moses (see Num. 12:1).

Zobah–A city of the monarchical period of Israel, first mentioned as an antagonist to Saul (1 Sam. 14:47) and then to David (2 Sam. 8:3, 5, 12). The Ammonites hired mercenaries from this city to try to defeat David in a two-front war (2 Sam. 10:6, 8 [KJV: "Zoba"]). The city, situated north of Damascus in Syria, was one of the leading cities in the Syrian Empire.

Zophar–The third of Job's three friends who sit with him while he is in misery (Job 2:11). He is known to have the harsher, more philosophical stance in terms of theology, as he takes a very abrasive realist position in regard to Job's situation. He blames Job for being too anthropocentric in his theological position. Zophar speaks in Job 11; 20; and possibly 27:13–23. He is said to be a Naamathite, which probably places his origin east of the Jordan River.